The Origin
of
Paul's Gospel

by
SEYOON KIM

WILLIAM B. EERDMANS PUBLISHING COMPANY
Grand Rapids, Michigan

To the Memory of My Parents

© Seyoon Kim / J. C. B. Mohr (Paul Siebeck) Tübingen 1981
First published 1981 by J. C. B. Mohr (Paul Siebeck) Tübingen as vol. 4 in the second series of *Wissenschaftliche Untersuchungen zum Neuen Testament*.
This American edition published 1982 through special arrangement with J. C. B. Mohr (Paul Siebeck), Federal Republic of Germany.

Library of Congress Cataloging in Publication Data

Kim, Seyoon.
  The origin of Paul's gospel.

  Revision of thesis (Ph.D.) — University of Manchester, 1977.
  Bibliography: p. 336
  Includes indexes.
  1. Bible.   N.T.   Epistles of Paul — Theology.   2. Paul,
the Apostle, Saint.   I. Title.
BS2651.K55   1982   227'.06   82-5121
ISBN 0-8028-1933-8   AACR2

Foreword

The message of the New Testament knows no boundaries, for it addresses all peoples. For that reason, the scholarly task involving this unique document cannot be limited to a few peoples and cultures, since the truth it contains has universal validity and is indivisible. It is therefore most welcome that today the scholarly interpretation of the New Testament no longer remains the exclusive right of theologians from Western Europe and North America, but is becoming — in the full sense of the word — an ecumenical task.

In this context, it is perhaps symbolic that the message of the crucified and risen Christ was first proclaimed in a country that was already in antiquity, as it still is sometimes today, regarded as part of Asia, a country situated in close proximity to the border between Asia and the African continent. The first Gentile Christian, even before the Roman centurion Cornelius, was an African, the Minister of Queen Candace of what was then Ethiopia, the kingdom of Meroë on the Upper Course of the Nile, who as a newly baptized convert "went on his way rejoicing" (Acts 8:39, RSV), back, that is, to his native country of Ethiopia. A few verses later there follows Luke's account of the call of Saul/Paul near the Syrian metropolis of Damascus, where presumably the new convert made his first missionary efforts in "Arabia" (Gal. 1:17). That event, which shook the history of the world, forms the starting point of the present work by the young Korean New Testament scholar Dr. Seyoon Kim, and it also marks the beginning of that universal, worldwide mission whose task is still not completed today. The events that Luke and Paul have recorded took place many years before the gospel penetrated Europe or gained a foothold in Greece and Rome. If then, after almost two thousand years, the scholarly interpretation of the New Testament steps beyond the long too restrictive traditional bounds of the old European culture, this only fulfills what from the beginning was the deepest intention of the early Christian message, which Paul describes in Romans 10:18 using the words of Psalm 19:14:

> Their voice has gone out to all the earth,
> and their words to the ends of the world.

With this study, written under the direction of Dr. F. F. Bruce, Dr. Kim earned the degree of Doctor of Philosophy at Victoria University in Manchester, England. His theme is the christological center of Paul's gospel, which, according to the apostle's own testimony, was revealed to him by means of the Christophany near Damascus. In this penetrating, detailed work, which is a remarkable achievement by the young Korean theologian on linguistic grounds alone, Dr. Kim tries to make the Christology of the apostle understood as the fruit of his call from the risen and glorified Lord himself. He has not only incorporated the essential recent literature regarding this hotly debated issue in biblical research but has also consulted those contemporary Jewish and Hellenistic sources capable of illuminating the religious and historical background of the Pauline conception. The work supplies the reader with abundant information about the lively discussion in this area of biblical research, while it also shows the author's own standpoint, which is thoroughly critical of the prevailing notions in German scholarship. Totally independent of any single critical position, Dr. Kim comes to terms primarily with the previous interpretations of the call of the apostle to the Gentiles and his Christology and does not introduce new sources of religious history or present fundamentally new perspectives. That he proceeds in this way, however, is due to his special circumstance: he was forced to acquaint himself with an unfamiliar realm of scholarship couched in several languages new to him. To that end he sought to formulate, within a bewildering area of research, his own point of view, which he grounded historically and theologically in his sources; in this regard, Dr. Kim has succeeded in an entirely convincing manner!

We must emphasize, finally, that as an interpreter of the New Testament Dr. Kim understands his scholarship to be in the service of the church. Thus, this valuable contribution to the theological and historical understanding of the christological center of Paul's theology, coming from a young Third World exegete, deserves our special interest.

Martin Hengel

Preface

This book is a revised version of my Ph. D. thesis submitted to the University of Manchester in August 1977. On the whole I do not yet feel any need to revise the work substantially, so that the revision work was limited mainly to stylistic improvement. But at a couple of places I feel I could have developed my theses more thoroughly and convincingly. They are the sections dealing with the question of 'the Son of Man' (pp.239–252) and the question why faith is the means of justification (pp.297–307). I hope to take these matters up in future researches, but at present I have to be content with adding a few lines to the original version of my work for a greater clarity. Back in Asia, where the library facilities are still very inadequate, I have found it practically impossible to consult the literature that has appeared since the completion of my thesis at Manchester. I humbly beg readers for understanding about this.

Now it is a pleasant duty to thank all those who helped me during the years of my research for this thesis. I would like especially to thank Prof. F.F. Bruce who supervised my work throughout with great patience and unfailing helpfulness. His encouragement and guidance were most valuable. I am indebted also to Rev. S.S. Smalley who gave generously of his time in the initial stage of my work. For almost three semesters Prof. Otto Betz acted as my *Doktorvater* in Tübingen with unfailing kindness. Even after I returned to England, he kept an interest in my work so that he read all but the last chapter of this thesis and gave me encouragement and helpful criticisms. Prof. M. Hengel and Prof. P. Stuhlmacher also made available to me several sessions for discussion on various aspects of my thesis. Prof. P. Beyerhaus' personal friendship and encouragement were also of great value. Prof. E.E. Ellis both in Tübingen and later on in Cambridge gave generously of his time in reading my thesis and discussing with me some aspects of it.

The personnel at the University Libraries of Manchester, Tübingen and Cambridge, at John Rylands Library, Manchester, at the Library of the Evangelisch-theologische Fakultät, Tübingen, and at the Tyndale Library, Cambridge, are to be thanked for their ready help with literature.

I am grateful to Professors M. Hengel, J. Jeremias and O. Michel for their acceptance of this work for publication in the series of WUNT 2. Prof.

Hengel has given me some helpful editorial suggestions and voluntarily contributed the *Vorwort* to this book, and for the help and the honour he has rendered I am especially grateful.

I would also like to thank Herrn Georg Siebeck (jun.) for his friendly correspondence and ready help. Mr. S.C. Leong of Sam Boyd Enterprise, Singapore who typeset this book and the printers in Tübingen are also to be thanked for their dedicated labour.

This research could not have been carried out without the generous financial assistance of the following institutions: Fong Shien Trust, Overseas Missionary Fellowship, Albrecht-Bengel-Haus (Tübingen), and Clifton Theological Fund (Bristol). I owe further to Albrecht-Bengel-Haus for their generous provision of the *Druckkostenzuschuß*. I can hardly thank all these institutions adequately.

Among many friends who have helped me with the production of the book, I would especially mention Prof. O. Betz and Dr. H. Lichtenberger for careful proofreading, Miss Mildred Young for thorough checking of my Greek accents, and Misses Songhee Hong and Unsoon Kwon for compiling the indices. Their sacrificial labour has spared me many errors, and I would like to record my sincere gratitude to them.

Finally, I record affectionately the debt of love that I owe to Mr. & Mrs. David H. Adeney who took care of me as my spiritual parents during the years of my sojourn abroad.

Seoul, May 1979 – January 1980   Seyoon Kim.

Contents

Abbreviations

I. Reference Works

Bauer-Arndt-Gingrich	W.F.Arndt & F.W.Gingrich, *A Greek-English Lexicon of the New Testament and Other Early Christian Literature* (E.T. & ed. of W.Bauer's *Griechisch-Deutsches Wörterbuch*) (Chicago, [4]1952)
B-D	F.Blass & A.Debrunner, *A Greek Grammar of the New Testament and other Early Christian Literature*, tr. & ed. R.W.Funk (Chicago, 1961)
BDB	F.Brown, S.R.Driver, & C.A.Briggs, *A Hebrew and English Lexicon of the Old Testament* (London, 1953)
Beginnings	*The Beginnings of Christianity*, ed. F.H.Foakes-Jackson & K.Lake, 5 vols., (London, 1920–1933)
Begriffslexikon	*Theologisches Begriffslexikon zum Neuen Testament*, ed. L.Coenen, E.Beyreuther & H.Bientenhard, 3 vols. (Wuppertal, 1967–1971)
Liddell-Scott	H.G.Liddell & R.Scott, *A Greek-English Lexicon*, 9th ed. H.S.Jones & R.McKenzie (Oxford, 1968)
Moore i, ii, iii	G.F.Moore, *Judaism in the First Centuries of the Christian Era*, 3 vols. (Cambridge, Mass. 1927–1930)
Moulton i, ii, iii	*A Grammar of the New Testament Greek, I. Prolegomena* by J.H.Moulton (Edinburgh, [3]1908); *II. Accidence and Word-Formation* by J.H.Moulton & W.F.Howard (1929); *III. Syntax* by N.Turner (1963)
RGG[2]	*Religion in Geschichte und Gegenwart*, 2nd ed. H.Gunkel & L.Zscharnack, 5 vols. (Tübingen, 1927–1932)
RGG[3]	*Religion in Geschichte und Gegenwart*, 3rd ed. K.Galling, 6 vols. with Register (Tübingen, 1957–1965)
Str.-Bill.	H.Strack & P.Billerbeck, *Kommentar zum Neuen Testament aus Talmud und Midrasch*, 6 vols., (München, 1922–1961)
TDNT	*Theological Dictionary of the New Testament*, E.T. by G.W. Bromiley, 9 vols. (Grand Rapids, 1964–1974), of *ThWb: Theologisches Wörterbuch zum Neuen Testament*, ed. G.Kittel & G.Friedrich (Stuttgart, 1933–1979)
ThHAT	*Theologisches Handwörterbuch zum Alten Testament*, ed. E.Jenni & C.Westermann, 2 vols. (München, 1971, 1976)

ThWAT	*Theologisches Wörterbuch zum Alten Testament*, ed. J.Botterweck & H.Ringgren, I, II – (Stuttgart, 1973 –)
W.Baumgartner,	*Hebräisches und Aramäisches Lexikon zum Alten Testament*, I, II (Leiden, 1967, 1974)
J.Jastrow,	*A Dictionary of the Targumim, the Talmuds, and the Midrashic Literature* (New York, 1926)
L.Köhler & W.Baumgartner,	*Lexicon in Veteris Testamenti Libros* (Leiden, 1953)
S.Krauss,	*Griechische und lateinische Lehnwörter im Talmud, Midrasch und Targum*, 2 vols. (reprint: Hildesheim, 1964)
I.Levy,	*Neuhebräisches und chaldäisches Wörterbuch über die Talmudim und Midraschim*, 4 vols., (Leipzig, 1876–1889)
C.F.D.Moule,	*An Idiom-Book of New Testament Greek* (Cambridge, ^{2}1968)

II. *Periodicals and Serials*

As listed in *Journal of Biblical Literature* 95 (1976), pp.339–344, except:

BNTC	Black's New Testament Commentaries
EvTh	*Evangelische Theologie*
ExpT	*Expository Times*
NCB	New Century Bible
NLC	New London Commentary on the New Testament (= NICNT)
StTh	*Studia Theologica*
TED	Translations of Early Documents
ThLZ	*Theologische Literaturzeitung*
ThZ	*Theologische Zeitschrift*
TynB	*Tyndale Bulletin*
ZThK	*Zeitschrift für Theologie und Kirche*

III. *Others*

AnBib 17 (1963)	*Studiorum Paulinorum Congressus internationalis Catholicus, 1961*, Vol. I, An Bib 17 (1963)
EVB i, ii	E.Käsemann, *Exegetische Versuche und Besinnungen*, i (Göttingen, ^{5}1967); ii (^{2}1965)
E.T.	English Translation
FS	Festschrift

Introduction

What is the origin of Paul's gospel?

In his preface to the second edition of his epoch-making work *The Epistle to the Romans,* K. Barth raises some fundamental questions of Scriptural exegesis, which are still of great relevance today. In the course of his confrontation with the exegesis current in his day, Barth launches a scathing attack upon the exegetes:

> Taking Jülicher's work as typical of much modern exegesis, we observe how closely he keeps to the mere deciphering of words as though they were runes. But, when all is done, they still remain largely unintelligible. How quick he is, without any real struggling with the raw material of the Epistle, to dismiss this or that difficult passage as simply a peculiar doctrine or opinion of Paul! How quick he is to treat a matter as explained, when it is said to belong to the religious thought, feeling, experience, conscience, or conviction, – of Paul! And, when this does not at once fit, is manifestly impossible, how easily he leaps, like some bold William Tell, right out of the Pauline boat, and rescues himself by attributing what Paul has said, to his 'personality', to the experience on the road to Damascus (an episode which seems capable of providing at any moment an explanation of every impossibility), to later Judaism, to Hellenism, or, in fact, to any exegetical semi-divinity of the ancient world![1]

In many ways much of today's exegesis continues the kind of work that is attacked by Barth. Just as in Barth's day, so today also many interpreters of Paul rest content with drawing out alleged parallels between Paul's theology and the thoughts of the ancient Mediterranean world. When they have analysed Paul's theology and suitably assigned its various elements to this or that background of Paul, 'to later Judaism, to Hellenism, or . . . to any exegetical semi-divinity of the ancient world', they presume to have *explained* the origin of Paul's gospel and the gospel itself. But are they right? Have they explained what is the ground of Paul's belief and proclamation; what is the factor or factors that shaped Paul's gospel so that it might become what it is; and, ultimately, what is Paul's gospel?

One does not immediately know how Barth would have judged the sort of

---

[1]K. Barth, *The Epistle to the Romans* (E.T. Oxford, 1933, 1968), pp. 7f.

question that we are setting for our enquiry in this thesis, namely the origin of Paul's gospel, which will of necessity involve much historical as well as exegetical work on the Pauline epistles. However, we are convinced that when we have answered the question after listening carefully to Paul's own testimony, we shall be able to understand much better the theological truths that Paul expounds in his letters — which surely is Barth's concern and should be the concern of every sincere Scriptural exegete.

Paul's testimony is that he received his gospel 'through the revelation of Jesus Christ' (Gal 1.12). His gospel is not a 'human' gospel, for he did not receive it from man, nor was taught it (Gal 1.11), but received it when on the road to Damascus God 'was pleased to reveal his Son to me, in order that I might preach him as the content of the gospel among the Gentiles'. Having thus received the gospel and the apostolic commission, 'I did not confer with flesh and blood, nor did I go up to Jerusalem . . . but went away into Arabia . . . ' (Gal 1.16f.).

In some ways it is paradoxical that quoting himself the two clauses of Gal 1.17 at the head of his afore-mentioned preface Barth condemns the tendency of the exegetes of his day to attribute some elements of Paul's theology to his Damascus experience. But even with a slight acquaintance with the tendency of the exegetes at the turn of the century to make the Damascus event 'capable of providing at any moment an explanation of every impossibility' by means of psychologizing and romanticizing we can well understand the sharp criticism of Barth and readily agree with it.

When in the following pages we enquire of the Damascus event, we do so not because we would like to continue the work already condemned by Barth and others, but because we feel obliged to take Paul's own testimony seriously. So in the study that follows we strictly exclude a psychological and romanticizing method and concentrate on listening to Paul's own testimony with a strictly historico-philological method, but at all times with the theological alertness that is required of a Scriptural exegete.

Chapter I Preliminary Considerations

It is often said that while the author of the Book of Acts repeats the account of Paul's conversion and call three times at length (9.1–19; 22.3–16; 26.4–18) Paul himself mentions it only in a few places and all too briefly[1]. This is said to be due to Paul's deep reserve about his experience[2]. For this reason, says G. Bornkamm, Paul's experience on the road to Damascus should not be placed at the centre of his life and thought[3].

1) It is generally recognized that these few places, at which Paul mentions his experience of conversion to Christ and call to apostleship, are 1 Cor 9.1; 15.8–10; Gal 1.13–17; and Phil 3.4–11. Now it cannot be so lightly said that these are only a few places if it is taken into account that these passages represent about half of the churches to which Paul wrote a letter. But these are not the only places; there are many more places in his letters, including those which are not mentioned above, in which he refers or alludes in varying degrees of explicitness to his experience on the road to Damascus.

2) Rom 10.2–4 is recognised by many interpreters[4] as one such passage. It has been noted that what Paul says of Israel in Rom 10.2–10 corresponds

---

[1] U.Wilckens, 'Die Bekehrung des Paulus als religionsgeschichtliches Problem', *Rechtfertigung als Freiheit: Paulus Studien* (1974), p.11: 'nur an wenigen Stellen . . . und auch dort nur in aller Kürze – gleichsam im Vorübergehen –'. Similarly but more negatively G.Lohfink, *Paulus vor Damaskus* (1966), p.21: 'an ganz wenigen Stellen, in aller Kürze'. Still more negatively G.Bornkamm, *Paulus* (1969), p.39: 'überraschend selten'. Cf. also G.Bornkamm 'Paulus', *RGG*[3] v, c. 169.

[2] G.Lohfink, *op.cit.*, p.21.

[3] *G.Bornkamm, Paulus*, p.39.

[4] F.F.Bruce, *Romans*, An Introduction and Commentary (1969), pp.200f.; O.Michel, *Der Brief an die Römer*, ([13]1966), pp.253f.; U.Wilckens, 'Bekehrung', p.14: 'Was heißt bei Paulus: "Aus Werken des Gesetzes wird kein Mensch gerecht"?', *Rechtfertigung als Freiheit*, pp.98–104; W.Grundmann, 'Paulus, aus dem Volke Israel, Apostel der Völker', *Nov T* 4(1960), pp.268f.; P.Stuhlmacher, "Das Ende des Gesetzes", *ZThK* 67(1970), pp.30ff.; E.Käsemann, 'Paulus und Israel', *EVB* ii, p.195; H.G.Wood, 'The Conversion of St. Paul: Its Nature, Antecedents and Consequences', *NTS* 1(1954/55), p.279; cf. Bornkamm, *Paulus*, p.40.

with his autobiographical statements especially in Phil 3.4ff[1]. He understands the tragedy of Israel in the light of his conversion experience. Just as Paul was zealous for God before the Damascus experience, Israel also has a zeal for him. However, it is an unenlightened zeal. For while God through Christ has put an end to the law as a way of obtaining righteousness, Israel is still zealous for the law; while God grants *his* righteousness to everyone who has faith, Israel seeks *its own* righteousness on the basis of the works of the law. But in the Christophany on the road to Damascus Paul received the knowledge of Christ as the end of the law. So he surrendered all his righteousness based on the law to receive God's righteousness which comes from faith in Christ. But Israel at present remains still in the state in which Paul was before his conversion.

3) Many scholars have also recognized in 1Cor 9.16–17 Paul's allusion to his call to apostleship on the road to Damascus[2]. Paul, who in Phil 3.12

---

[1]Wilckens, 'Was heißt bei Paulus.', pp.102ff.; E.Käsemann, *op.cit.*, p.195; Stuhlmacher, *op.cit.*, pp.30ff.; F.F.Bruce, *op.cit.*, pp.200ff.; cf. also Grundmann, *op.cit.*, pp.268f.

[2]A.Robertson & A.Plummer, *The First Epistle of St.Paul to the Corinthians* ([3]1929), p.189; H.Lietzmann & W.G.Kümmel, *An die Korinther I/II* ([5]1969), p.43; A.Schlatter *Paulus der Bote Jesu* ([3]1969), p.276; H.Conzelmann, *Der erste Korintherbrief* ([11]1969), p.186, n.26; F.W.Grosheide, *Commentary on the First Epistle to the Corinthians*, (1972), p.209; C.K.Barrett, *A Commentary on the First Epistle to the Corinthians* (1968), p.209; F.F.Bruce, *1 & 2 Corinthians* (1971), p.86; J.Munck, *Paul and the Salvation of Mankind* (1959), pp.22f; L.Cerfaux, 'La vocation de S.Paul', *Euntes Docete* (1961), pp.8f.; J.Reumann, 'Oἰκονομία–Terms in Paul in Comparison with Lucan *Heilsgeschichte*', *NTS* 13(1966/67), pp.158f.; H.Kasting, *Die Anfänge der urchristlichen Mission* (1969), p.56; J.Dupont, 'The Conversion of Paul and Its Influence on His Understanding of Salvation by Faith', *Apostolic History and the Gospel*, F.F.Bruce FS (1970), p.192. Cf. E.Käsemann, 'Eine paulinische Variation des "amor fati" ', *EVB* ii, pp.233f. Käsemann appears to reject the interpretation that ἀνάγκη γάρ μοι ἐπίκειται alludes to the forceful call of Paul the persecutor to apostleship, which came to him in an irresistable way. But when Käsemann says, ' "ἀνάγκη liegt auf mir" sagt man vom Schicksal, das einen ergreift, nicht von Gefühlen, die uns beseelen, oder von einer Pflicht, der wir zu genügen haben', his differentiation of 'Schicksal', 'Gefühl' and 'Pflicht' seems in this case unnecessary. And his next statement, 'Die Erinnerung an Damaskus aber taugt als Illustration, jedoch nicht zur Interpretation, weil Paulus nicht einen Rückblick auf vergangenes Geschehen und dessen Auswirkungen wirft, sondern von der Gegenwart seines Dienstes spricht', is difficult to understand. When Paul says, 'ἀνάγκη γάρ μοι ἐπίκειται', certainly he refers to his present service, but his present service which was determined by the forceful commission of the past. The perfect πεπίστευμαι in v.17 expresses precisely this, i.e., that ἀνάγκη is laid upon or presses upon (cf. Robertson-Plummer, *1Cor.*, p.189) Paul because he has been entrusted with an οἰκονομία.

says he was 'seized' ($\kappa \alpha \tau \epsilon \lambda \dot{\eta} \mu \phi \theta \eta \nu$)[1] by Christ, says here similarly that he has been entrusted with a commission so that necessity or divine constraint ($\dot{\alpha} \nu \dot{\alpha} \gamma \kappa \eta$)[2] presses upon him to preach the gospel. Paul 'was conscripted into the service of Christ on the Damascus road'[3], so that he is now under compulsion to preach the gospel.

4) 2Cor 3.4–4.6 is the next passage that shows allusions to Paul's experience of the Christophany on his way to Damascus. Many scholars have seen in 4.6 an allusion to it[4]. H. Windisch, who thinks the view worthy of consideration, raises, however, three points for caution[5]: a) Paul here describes no 'individual but a typical experience' [6]; b) He describes 'no vision, but a purely internal seeing'; and c) 'The words can also be understood without a view to an experience as it is described in Acts 9'. The first point depends on who is the subject in 4.1–6. If the subject 'we' is $\dot{\eta} \mu \epsilon \hat{\iota} \varsigma$ $\pi \dot{\alpha} \nu \tau \epsilon \varsigma$ of 3.18, then it can be said that Paul here gives a typical conversion experience of a Christian. But the subject of 4.1–6 must be different from $\dot{\eta} \mu \epsilon \hat{\iota} \varsigma$ $\pi \dot{\alpha} \nu \tau \epsilon \varsigma$ of 3.18. For, first, the $\dot{\eta} \mu \epsilon \hat{\iota} \varsigma$ $\pi \dot{\alpha} \nu \tau \epsilon \varsigma$, all the Christians, who are contrasted with the Jews in the Synagogue, cannot be said to have $\tau \dot{\eta} \nu$ $\delta \iota \alpha \kappa o \nu \dot{\iota} \alpha \nu$ $\tau \alpha \dot{\upsilon} \tau \eta \nu$ (4.1), i.e. the apostolic ministry of the new covenant (cf.3.6); and, secondly, it is clear from 4.5 that Paul distinguishes 'ourselves' ($\dot{\epsilon} \alpha \upsilon \tau o \dot{\upsilon} \varsigma$) from the Corinthian Christians. So the subject 'we' of 4.1–6 must, as in 3.1–6, be limited to Paul and his co-workers, especially to Paul alone[7]. Windisch recognises the change of subject between 3.18 and 4.1, but thinks that in 4.6

---

[1] Cf. Bauer-Arndt-Gingrich, s.v.

[2] Cf. Bauer-Arndt-Gingrich, s.v.; W.Grundmann, $\dot{\alpha} \nu \dot{\alpha} \gamma \kappa \eta$, *TDNT* i, p.346; E. Käsemann, "amor fati", pp.233f.

[3] Bruce, *Cor.*, p.86.

[4] A.Plummer, *The Second Epistle of St. Paul to the Corinthians* ([5]1948) p.92; R.V.G. Tasker, *2 Corinthians* (1958), pp.71f.; P.Hughes, *Commentary on the Second Epistle to the Corinthians* (1971), pp.133f.; Bruce, *Cor.*, p.196; C.K.Barrett, *The Second Epistle to the Corinthians* (1973), p.134; M.Dibelius & W.G.Kümmel, *Paulus* (1964), p.55; W.G.Kümmel, 'Römer 7 und die Bekehrung des Paulus', *Römer 7 und das Bild des Menschen im NT* (1974), pp.146f.; *Die Theologie des NT* ([2]1972), p.198; R.Bultmann, 'Ursprung und Sinn der Typologie als Hermeneutischer Methode', *Exegetica* (1967), p.374; O.Kuss, *Paulus* (1971), p.283; Stuhlmacher, "Ende", p.25; Cerfaux, *op. cit.*, p.8; H. – J. Schoeps, *Paul* (1961), p.54.

[5] H.Windisch, *Der zweite Korintherbrief* ([9]1970), p.140.

[6] Cf. Schlatter, *Der Bote.*, p.530.

[7] So Plummer, *2Cor.*, pp.110,120 (but cf. p.121); Strachan, *2Cor.*, p.92. See further K.Dick, *Der schriftstellerische Plural bei Paulus* (1900), pp.95ff., who maintains that 'we' in 2Cor 3–6 is a literary plural for Paul himself. Cf. Bruce, *Cor.*, p.194; Barrett, *2Cor.*, p.134. Paul frequently involves his co-workers when he makes assertions primarily

'we' is once again widened as in 3.18[1]. But there is no reason to think so. The ὅτι – clause in v.6 provides the reason why Paul preaches not himself but Christ Jesus as Lord (v.5)[2]. In this context it is difficult to think that the 'we' in v.5 refers to Paul (and his co-workers) and 'our' in v.6 refers to Christians in general. However, if Windisch is right in taking ἡμῶν in v.6 as referring to all Christians, all the apostles or at least Paul's co-workers, as many commentators think, it must be understood that in v.6 Paul is describing a typical conversion experience by means of his own[3]. The second point of Windisch refers to Paul's expression ὁ θεός . . . , ὃς ἔλαμψεν <u>ἐν ταῖς καρδί-</u><u>αις ἡμῶν</u> . . . . This is reminiscent of Paul's report of the Christophany on the road to Damascus in Gal 1.16: . . . ἀποκαλύψαι τὸν υἱὸν αὐτοῦ ἐν ἐμοί . . . . There seems to be no more serious debate whether the Damascus event was a purely subjective, internal experience or an objective event, and it seems widely accepted that not only the author of Acts but also Paul himself lets his readers understand it to be an objective appearance of the risen Christ (1Cor 15.8). From this the phrase ἐν ἐμοί in Gal 1.16 has often been taken to stand for the simple dative[4]. But H. Schlier observes that ἀποκαλύπτειν normally takes the simple dative and appears nowhere else with ἐν (cf. 1Cor 2.10; Eph 3.5; 1Pet 1.12). So he suggests that 'with ἐν ἐμοί the intensity of the unveiling of the Son is expressed, an unveiling

---

about himself (see Strachan, *2Cor.*, p.xxxv), so that he may be doing the same here. It is not probable that 'we' here means 'we apostles' because Paul is not contrasting 'the apostles' with another group in the Church but defending himself and his gospel against the charges of his opponents who, especially if they are the same ones as those in 2Cor 10–13, may have claimed apostolic status for themselves (cf. 2Cor 11.5,13). However, it is not necessary to conclude from this that Paul claims such an experience as described in 2Cor 4.6 and such a commission as described in 2Cor 4.1–6 only for himself and denies them to other apostles whom he recognised as genuine apostles of the new covenant (cf. Gal 2; 1Cor 4; 15). He sees his Christian existence as typical and often uses his Damascus experience to describe conversion of others (*infra* pp.231, 288ff.; cf. Stuhlmacher, 'καινὴ κτίσις', pp.27f.), so that what is said primarily about his own Damascus experience in 2Cor 4.6 can apply to all other Christians.

[1] Windisch, *2.Kor.*, p.131.

[2] See Plummer, *2Cor.*, p.119 and Windisch, *2.Kor.*, p.138 for not taking v.5 as a parenthesis. But both recognize close connection between vs. 4 & 6. It may thus provide also the ultimate reason why Paul's gospel is not veiled, but, on the contrary, issues illumination (v.4).

[3] So Kümmel, *Theologie*, p.198; cf. Bruce, *Cor.*, p.196.

[4] B–D, § 220.1; cf. C.F.D.Moule, *An Idiom-Book of NT Greek* (1968), p.76; A.Oepke, *Der Brief des Paulus an die Galater* ([2]1957), p.33.

which penetrated into the innermost part of the apostle's life'[1]. A somewhat similar interpretation seems possible also in 2Cor 4.6. The Christophany on the Damascus road was an objective vision of the risen Lord. This affected Paul to the innermost part of his life, creating the conviction in the seat of his understanding, thought, feeling and will[2] that what appeared to him was Christ, revealed by God in glory. This fact seems to be expressed by the phrase ἐν ταῖς καρδίαις ἡμῶν[3]. If this is so, Paul is not here describing 'a purely internal seeing' (whatever it may be) but God's objective disclosure of the risen Christ which 'touched' the heart (in its Biblical sense!) of Paul[4]. As to Windisch's third point, it will be shown in the following that the words of 2Cor 4.6 can be better understood if it is supposed that they refer to the Damascus event.

The aorist ἔλαμψεν refers back to a definite point of time in the past, the moment of the Damascus event. God, the Creator, shone in Paul's heart on the road to Damascus πρὸς φωτισμὸν τῆς γνώσεως τῆς δόξης τοῦ θεοῦ ἐν προσώπῳ Χριστοῦ. Nowhere else in his letters does Paul mention explicitly light or glory in connection with the Christophany on the Damascus road. But that the risen Christ must have appeared to Paul as clothed in glory can be deduced from his other testimonies. For he claims that the risen Christ appeared to him (1Cor 15.8; also 9.1). He characterizes the body of resurrection as that of glory (1Cor 15.43)[5] and explicitly calls the body of the Lord Jesus Christ 'the body of glory' (Phil 3.21)[6]. In the Bible δόξα normally means 'divine and heavenly radiance' or the 'divine mode of being'

---

[1]H.Schlier, *Der Brief an die Galater* ([14]1971), p.55; cf. F.Mussner, *Der Galaterbrief* (1974), pp.86f.

[2]Cf. Baumgärtel and Behm, καρδία, *TDNT* iii, pp.606–613.

[3]Schlier, *Gal.*, p.55, refers also to Phil 3.12. Paul may be expressing the same fact by κατελήμφθην ὑπὸ Χριστοῦ Ἰησοῦ there.

[4]This interpretation fits in well with Plummer's observation that Paul here gives both a subjective and an objective element in his conversion experience: ὃς ἔλαμψεν ἐν ταῖς καρδίαις ἡμῶν describes the former, and ἡ δόξα τοῦ θεοῦ ἐν προσώπῳ Χριστοῦ the latter (Plummer, *2Cor.*, p.122; cf. also Dibelius-Kümmel, *Paulus*, p.55).

[5]Cf. 2 Bar. 50.1–51.10; M.Thrall, 'The Origin of Pauline Christology', *Apostolic History and the Gospel*, Bruce FS, p.309.

[6]These verses make it clear that Paul is not just reproducing a Jewish idea, such as that in 2 Bar. 50.1–51.10, that the resurrection body will be gradually transformed into glory. 2 Bar. conceives of a hiatus between resurrection and transformation. The hiatus is said to be necessary for the identification of the resurrected by the living. But Paul does not seem to conceive of such a hiatus. Cf. W.D.Davies, *Paul and Rabbinic Judaism* ([3]1970), pp.305ff. for a comparison between Paul's conception of the risen body and

made visible as radiance[1]. So the risen Christ must have appeared to Paul accompanied by the radiance of light which was perceived by him as the divine glory. Now this is precisely what the three accounts of the Damascus event in Acts relate: in his encounter with the risen Christ Paul suddenly saw the heavenly light shining round him (Acts 9.3; 22.6; 26.13). Thus the motifs of light and glory in 2Cor 4.6 point to the Damascus event[2]. It is significant that Paul fixes the divine glory 'in the face of Christ'. By this he may be contrasting the permanent and unveiled glory in the face of Christ with the fading and veiled glory in the face of Moses (3.7ff.)[3]. But more certainly he is thinking of the radiant face of Christ which he saw on the Damascus road (cf. 1Cor 9.1)[4]. It is probable that this experience led him to make a contrast between the ministry of the old covenant and that of the new in the present passage.

Paul compares God's shining light to him on the Damascus road with his creation of the light. Bultmann sees here the equation *Endzeit = Urzeit*,[5] but thinks that here the parallelism is not between creation and Paul's conversion, but between creation and the apostolic office. For the emphasis lies upon the statement of purpose: πρὸς φωτισμὸν κτλ[6]. But the parallelism between creation and Paul's conversion intended by the construction of the sentence:

ὁ θεὸς ὁ εἰπών, 'Εκ σκότους φῶς λάμψει,

ὃς ἔλαμψεν ἐν ταῖς καρδίαις ἡμῶν πρὸς φωτισμὸν κτλ.

is unmistakable[7]. Moreover, along with Paul's actual experience of the light on the Damascus road, the traditional idea of conversion as transference from darkness into light[8] may have led Paul to cite Gen 1.3 here[9]. God, who

---

that of the Rabbis. Paul's conception of the risen body both as a 'spiritual body' (over against the Rabbinic crude physical conception) and as the 'body of glory' may be a modification of the Rabbinic conception in the light of his experience of the risen Christ, who appeared to him as a spiritual reality in the radiance of glory on the Damascus road.

[1]G.von Rad & G.Kittel, δόξα, *TDNT* ii, pp.233–252.

[2]Cf. Acts 22.11; Schoeps, *Paul*, p.54.

[3]So Windisch, *2.Kor.*, p.140; Schlatter, *Der Bote*, p.530.

[4]So Plummer, *2Cor*, p.121; Bruce, *Cor.*, p.196.

[5]Cf. also Windisch, *2.Kor.*, p.139.

[6]Bultmann, 'Ursprung', pp.374f.; cf.also Barrett, *2Cor.*, p.135.

[7]Cf.Windisch, *2.Kor.*, p.139; Hughes, *2Cor.*, p.132.

[8]Cf.Acts 26.18; Rom 2.19; Eph 5.8; 1Th 5.4f.; 1Pet 2.9. For the evidence drawn from Jewish and Hellenistic material, see Windisch, *2.Kor.*, p.139; also H.Conzelmann, φῶς, *TDNT* ix, pp. 325f., 332.

[9]Cf. Windisch, *2.Kor.*, p.139. Paul cites Gen 1.3 not literally but according to sense.

created light over the primeval chaos, shed light into the darkness of Paul's heart. So Paul's conversion was an act of God's new creation (cf. 2Cor 5.17). However, God's shedding light in Paul's heart was not for its own sake, but it was for Paul to disseminate the light (πρὸς φωτισμὸν κτλ). Paul, who has experienced the light of the new creation at his conversion, is to convey it to others through his proclamation. His apostolic office is an instrument through which God shines light to others. In their experiencing the light through Paul's proclamation, i.e., in their conversion, the new creation takes place in respect of them. So Paul's apostolic office is an instrument of God's new creation activity. To that extent, there is also a parallelism, if secondarily, between Paul's proclamation and God's creation.

It is difficult to understand precisely the phrase πρὸς φωτισμὸν τῆς γνώσεως τῆς δόξης τοῦ θεοῦ. τῆς γνώσεως could be a subjective genitive (the knowledge of God's glory illuminates)[1], an objective gen. (the knowledge of God's glory is illuminated)[2], or an appositional gen. (illumination consists in the knowledge of God's glory)[3]. However, the parallelism between this phrase and the phrase in v.4 τὸν φωτισμὸν τοῦ εὐαγγελίου τῆς δόξης τοῦ Χριστοῦ[4] makes it more probable that it is to be taken as a subj. gen. God shone in Paul's heart 'with a view to (πρός)[5] illumination with the knowledge of God's glory'. The implied object of φωτισμὸν may be ἡμᾶς[6]: God shone in Paul's heart to illuminate him with the knowledge of God's glory in the face of Christ[7]. Through God's revelation on the Damascus road Paul came

---

His wording may have been influenced by such OT texts as 2Sam 22.29; Job 37.15; Ps 18.28; 112.4; Isa 9.2. He may have emphasized ἐκ σκότους in order to make the parallelism of creation and his conversion clearer (cf. Plummer, *2Cor.*, p.120).

[1]Plummer, *2Cor.*, p.121; Windisch, *2.Kor.*, p.140; Bruce, *Cor.*, p.196; apparently also NEB.

[2]Lietzmann-Kümmel, *Kor.*, p.115; cf. also H.D.Wendland, *Die Briefe an die Korinther* (¹²1968), p.187.

[3]Barrett, *2Cor.*, p.134.

[4]Plummer, *2Cor.*, pp.120f.; cf. also Windisch, *2.Kor.*, p.139f. Lietzmann-Kümmel, *Kor.*, p.115, sees the sense of. φωτισμός changed from an active sense in v.4 ('the gospel illuminates') to a passive sense in v.6 ('the γνῶσις is illuminated by the light of God which shines in our hearts'). This view is bound up with Lietzmann's taking τῆς γνώσεως as an obj. gen. But it seems unnecessary to see such a change in the sense of φωτισμός.

[5]Plummer, *2Cor.*, p.121; Barrett, *2Cor.*, p.134.

[6]Cf. Lietzmann-Kümmel, *Kor.*, p.115; RSV.

[7]This amounts almost to the same meaning which Lietzmann-Kümmel, *Kor.*, p.115, makes out of the verse, taking τῆς γνώσεως as an obj. gen; 'die γνῶσις wird vom Licht Gottes, das in unsere Herzen strahlt, erleuchtet, . . . so daß, mir leuchtend aufging die Erkenntnis der δόξα, die ich auf Christi Antlitz (. . .) strahlen sehe'. 'God's glory

to know Christ exalted and glorified by God. It is instructive to compare this
verse with Phil 3.4–11, where also Paul describes his conversion experience
as a process of knowing Christ[1]. However, probably the implied object of
φωτισμόν is not primarily ἡμᾶς but 'men' or 'hearers' in general: God shone
in Paul's heart 'with a view to illuminating men with the knowledge of the
glory of God'[2]. For v.6 would suit the context better if it describes not just
Paul's conversion but his commission as well, as in the context Paul is concerned with establishing the rightness of his apostolic ministry. God revealed
Christ to Paul so that he might proclaim him (cf. Gal 1.16). There is no
doubt, however, that here Paul is interpreting the Damascus event in terms
both of conversion and call. God revealed Christ to Paul, so that he might
first know him and then illuminate others with this knowledge. This knowledge of the glorified Christ constitutes the gospel of Paul and so Paul preaches
Christ Jesus as the exalted Lord (4.3–5). This is exactly the same thought as
that in Gal 1.11–16, where Paul implies that the Son of God[3] revealed by God
to him is the gospel that he received by revelation. Paul is commissioned to
illuminate men with the gospel, the knowledge of the Christ exalted and glorified. There is probably an echo of the call of the עבד יהוה in Isa 42.6f. and
49.6: the Servant is called by Yahweh εἰς φῶς ἐθνῶν and 'to open the eyes
that are blind'. It seems that in the present passage Paul is describing his
apostolic commission in terms of that of the Servant of Yahweh. This is
highly probable since elsewhere (Gal 1.15) also he describes his call in terms
of that of the Servant[4]. This may also explain his description of the unbelievers as blind to the light of the gospel in v.4. He is conscious of having
been commissioned 'to open the eyes of the blind' (Isa 42.7) with the gospel.

---

in the face of Christ' is 'the glory of Christ'. For God, to whom glory essentially belongs, has bestowed his glory upon Christ, so that it may shine in his face. In other
words, God has glorified Christ, so that Christ now has glory. The variation from τῆς
δόξης τοῦ Χριστοῦ to τῆς δόξης τοῦ θεοῦ ἐν προσώπῳ Χριστοῦ is caused by Paul's
reference to God, the creator of the light and author of the event described in this verse,
to whom glory essentially belongs (cf. Windisch, *2. Kor.*, p.140). It would be awkward
if 'the glory of Christ' instead of 'the glory of God' stood here, as if Christ had himself
an inherent, not bestowed, glory.

[1] Cf. Stuhlmacher, "Ende", p.31.

[2] Plummer, *2Cor.*, p.121; so also Bruce, *Cor.*, p.196; Barrett, *2Cor.*, p.134.

[3] Just like κύριος, the title 'Son of God' implies the exaltation of Jesus – cf. Rom
1.3f., where interestingly both titles are found side by side in the definition of the gospel;
also 2Cor 1.19.

[4] Munck, *Paul*, pp.24ff; T.Holtz, 'Zum Selbstverständnis des Apostels Paulus', *ThLZ*
91(1966), 324ff.; J.Blank, *Paulus und Jesus*(1968), pp.224ff.;Cerfaux, 'La vocation de
Saint Paul', pp.12ff.; H.Windisch, *Paulus und Christus*(1934), p.137.

Some, however, persist in their unbelief. This proves not that he has exercised his apostolic commission untruthfully or that his gospel is 'veiled', but rather that their minds have been blinded and kept in blindness[1] by Satan, so that they may not see the light of the gospel. If it is correct to see an echo of the call of the Ebed here, the parallelism between this passage and Acts 26. 16—18 is remarkable[2].

Thus it is clear that in 2Cor 4.3—6 Paul alludes to his experience of conversion and call on the Damascus road. But the allusion to the Damascus event is not limited to the four verses. It is in fact already made in 4.1. The aorist ἠλεήθημεν of the verse points to a definite moment in the past in which Paul received the ἔλεος (cf. 1Tim 1.12f.). It was of God's ἔλεος that Paul, the persecutor, was called into the ministry on the Damascus road[3]. 'This ministry' refers to the ministry of the new covenant, of which Paul was qualified to be a minister (3.6)[4]. Like ἠλεήθημεν in 4.1, the aorist ἱκάνωσεν in 3.6 also refers to Paul's call on the Damascus road[5]. Since he persecuted the Church of God, Paul knows that he is 'not fit (ἱκανός) to be called an apostle' (1Cor 15.9; 2Cor 3.5). Nevertheless God has qualified him to be a minister of the new covenant.

Some scholars have seen also in 2Cor 3.16 an allusion to Paul's conversion experience[6]. In the verse Paul refers to Ex 34.34a:

ἡνίκα δ'ἂν εἰσεπορεύετο Μωυσῆς ἔναντι κυρίου λαλεῖν αὐτῷ,
περιῃρεῖτο τὸ κάλυμμα ἕως τοῦ ἐκπορεύεσθαι,

but with a few variations[7] : a) In 2Cor 3.16 the subject is lacking; b) εἰσεπορεύετο. . . ἔναντι κυρίου λαλεῖν αὐτῷ of Ex 34.34 is replaced by ἐπιστρέψῃ πρὸς κύριον; and c) the imperfect περιῃρεῖτο is changed into

---

[1]This gloss seems called for in the context. For all would be blind without the illumination of the knowledge of the exalted Christ. But while some among them receive the illumination by faith, others persist in their unbelief and so are kept in blindness.

[2]Cf. Plummer, *2Cor.*, p.121.

[3]Barrett, *2Cor.*, p.127; Plummer, *2Cor.*, p.110: cf. 1Tim 1.13, 16; also 1Cor 7.25. In view of his activities as a persecutor of the Church, Paul regularly underlines that his call to apostleship is purely of God's grace — e.g. 1Cor 15.9f.; Rom 1.5; 15.15f. There is a parallelism between the ἐλάβομεν χάριν καὶ ἀποστολὴν in Rom 1.5 and ἔχοντες τὴν διακονίαν ταύτην,καθὼς ἠλεήθημεν here(χάρις and ἔλεος being synonymous, and ἀποστολή and διακονία being likewise synonymous).

[4]Windisch, *2.Kor.*, p.131; Bruce, *Cor.*, p.190; Hughes, *2Cor.*, p.121.

[5]Plummer, *2Cor.*, p.85; Windisch, *2.Kor.*, p.109; Blank, *Paulus*, p.191.

[6]Plummer, *2Cor.*, p.102; Hughes, *2Cor.*, p.112; W.C. van Unnik, ' "With Unveiled Face" (2Cor III.12—18)', *Sparsa Collecta*(1973), p.206.

[7]Cf. Windisch, *2.Kor.*, p.123.

the present $\pi\epsilon\rho\iota\alpha\iota\rho\epsilon\hat{\iota}\tau\alpha\iota$ as $\epsilon\hat{\iota}\sigma\epsilon\pi o\rho\epsilon\acute{u}\epsilon\tau o$ into $\hat{\epsilon}\pi\iota\sigma\tau\rho\acute{\epsilon}\psi\eta$, and d) the phrase $\H{\epsilon}\omega\varsigma$ $\tau o\hat{u}$ $\hat{\epsilon}\kappa\pi o\rho\epsilon\acute{u}\epsilon\sigma\theta\alpha\iota$ is removed. These changes indicate, first, that Paul is drawing out a general principle from the particular episode of Moses in Ex 34[1], and secondly that the principle drawn out is of conversion[2]. To this day when the Torah is read in the Synagogue[3] a veil lies upon the hearts of the Israelites, so that they are not able 'to realise the transitory character of the Mosaic order and to recognize the unfading glory of the gospel dispensation'[4]. 'But when a man[5] turns to the Lord[6] the veil is taken

---

[1]Cf. Bruce, *Cor*, p.193. Failing to understand this, I.Hermann, *Kyrios und Pneuma* (1961), p.38, regards v.16 not as a citation of Ex 34.34 but as 'a free play with a well-known idea from the OT', 'a completely new statement . . . which remains in the sphere of the idea of the OT *Vorlage* only through free association of words'. Against this J.D. G.Dunn is correct in classifying v.16 in the category of a Christian *pesher* ('2 Corinthians III.17 – "The Lord is the Spirit" ', *JTS* 21(1970), pp.314ff.).

[2]See esp. the second change $\hat{\epsilon}\pi\iota\sigma\tau\rho\acute{\epsilon}\phi\epsilon\iota\nu$, which is almost a *term. techn.* for conversion in the LXX and the NT when it is not used for spatial turning. Cf. Bertram, $\hat{\epsilon}\pi\iota\sigma\tau\rho\acute{\epsilon}\phi\omega$, *TDNT* vii, pp.722–29; Windisch, *2.Kor.*, p.123; Hughes, *2Cor.*, p.114; Lietzmann-Kümmel, *Kor.*, p.200; Barrett, *2Cor.*, p.122.

[3]Cf. Acts 15.21.

[4]Bruce, *Cor.*, p.192; so similarly also Plummer, *2Cor.*, p.101; Windisch, *2.Kor.*, p.122; Hughes, *2Cor.*, p.111; van Unnik, *op. cit.*, p.205. See the last named, pp.202ff., for an illuminating analysis of the passage (2Cor 3.13–16).

[5]The unexpressed subject of $\hat{\epsilon}\pi\iota\sigma\tau\rho\acute{\epsilon}\psi\eta$ seems most likely to be $\tau\iota\varsigma$: 'anyone in the Synagogue', 'any who hears the Law read' (Plummer, *2Cor.*, p.101; cf. also van Unnik, *op. cit.*, p.207; Barrett, *2Cor.*, p.122; Hughes, *2Cor.* p.113; Hermann, *Kyrios*, p.38).

[6]In view of the parallelism between this verse and v.14c the $\kappa\acute{u}\rho\iota o\varsigma$ here is to be taken as Christ. As he does frequently elsewhere, Paul here transfers to Christ the title $\kappa\acute{u}\rho\iota o\varsigma$ which in the OT belongs to Yahweh (see F.F.Bruce, "Jesus is Lord", *Soli Deo Gloria*, W.C.Robinson FS(1968), pp.23–36). In our present passage Paul is no longer thinking of Moses but of the Jews in the Synagogue. They have no need to turn to Yahweh. So Plummer, *2Cor.*, p.102; Barrett, *2Cor.*, p.112; Wendland, *Kor.*, p.183; Hermann, *Kyrios*, pp.39ff. Against this generally accepted view, recent attempts by Dunn (*op. cit.*) and his teacher C.F.D. Moule ('2Cor 3.18b, $\kappa\alpha\theta\acute{\alpha}\pi\epsilon\rho$ $\hat{\alpha}\pi\grave{o}$ $\kappa\upsilon\rho\acute{\iota}o\upsilon$ $\pi\nu\epsilon\acute{u}\mu\alpha\tau o\varsigma$', *NT und Geschichte*, Cullmann FS, pp.231–37) to see the $\kappa\acute{u}\rho\iota o\varsigma$ in 2Cor 3.16–18 as referring not to Christ but to Yahweh are not convincing. In spite of his recognition of the changes that Paul introduces in his citation of Ex 34.34, Moule fails to understand that Paul is here drawing out a general principle from the particular episode of Moses in Ex 34. Thus Moule tries to read v.16 as though it were standing in Ex 34 and referring to Moses. But Paul is speaking of the Jew's turning to the Lord *now* ($\hat{\epsilon}\pi\iota\sigma\tau\rho\acute{\epsilon}\psi\eta$– $\pi\epsilon\rho\iota\alpha\iota\rho\epsilon\hat{\iota}\tau\alpha\iota$!). While emphasizing that the decisive factor in such a discussion as this is the context, Dunn (and also Moule) nevertheless totally fail to give any weight to the parallel statement in v.14. Their arguments from Paul's use of $\kappa\acute{u}\rho\iota o\varsigma$ are nullified by their own citations of three or more 'exceptions' each time. At any rate, they were already met adequately and rejected by Hermann, *Kyrios*, pp.40f. Moule and

away'[1] (2Cor 3.16), so that he 'sees the glory of the Lord and reflects[2] it with unveiled face' (2Cor 3.18). When Paul so contrasts the state of the Jews in the Synagogue with the state of the converted to Christ, he must be speaking out of his own experience. When he saw thè glory of the Lord on the road to Damascus (3.18; cf. 4.6) he realised that his understanding of the Torah had been wrong. The encounter with Christ was like removing a veil from his mind that had hindered his true understanding of the Torah and acceptance of the gospel[3].

5) Commentators have seen also in 2Cor 5.16 an allusion to Paul's conversion[4]. ὥστε in v.16 indicates that v.16 is a consequence of the foregoing. So ἀπὸ τοῦ νῦν may refer to the time since Paul arrived at the judgement (the aorist part. κρίναντας) concerning the significance of Christ's death as expressed in vs. 14f., i.e., the time since his conversion[5]. Or it may refer to the eschatological situation brought about by the death and resurrection of Christ (vs.14f.)[6]. But since this objective turning-point from the old aeon to the new is made real in an individual's life at the moment of his conversion,

---

Dunn notice neither that Paul usually speaks about the Christian's transformation into the image of Christ rather than of God (Rom 8.29; 1Cor 15.49; cf. also Phil 3.21; Gal 4.19, one apparent exception being the disputed Col 3.9) nor that the language of 2Cor 3.16–18 together with that of 2Cor 4.4–6 is to be seen in the light of the Damascus Christophany. On this last point, *infra* pp.229–239.

[1] περιαιρεῖται is taken by most commentators as passive. The agent of the removing is 'the Lord'. But Barrett, *2Cor.*, p.122, takes it to be middle and its subject 'the Lord'.

[2] κατοπτριζόμενοι may be rendered either 'beholding as in a mirror' or 'reflecting as a mirror'. Commentators are evenly divided on this. The correct rendering seems to depend on the understanding of the context. If ἡμεῖς δὲ πάντες in v.18 is contrasted with Moses in v.13, then the latter is obviously the meaning. If however it is contrasted with the Jews, the former is meant. It is difficult to decide which contrast is intended. It may be that Paul intends both contrasts. For the appropriateness of the word here, *infra* p.232. Cf. Windisch, *2.Kor.*, p.127; also Plummer, *2Cor.*, pp.104f.

[3] For an antithetical typology between the Sinai Theophany to Moses (Ex 33–34) and the Damascus Christophany to Paul that we perceive underlying 2Cor 3.1–4.6, *infra* the excursus on pp.233–239.

[4] Windisch, *2.Kor.*, p.184f.; Lietzmann-Kümmel, *Kor.*, p.127; Plummer, *2Cor.*, p.177; Hughes, *2Cor.*, p.197; Bruce, *Cor.*, p.208; Stuhlmacher, 'Erwägungen zum ontologischen Charakter der καινὴ κτίσις bei Paulus', *EvTh* 27(1967), pp.4f. Cf. G.Friedrich, 'Die Gegner des Paulus im 2.Korintherbrief', *Abraham unser Vater*, O.Michel FS, eds. O.Betz, *et al.*(1963), p.214.

[5] Plummer, *2Cor.*, p.176; Hughes, *2Cor.*, p.197; Barrett, *2Cor.*, p.170; cf. also Moffatt translation; NEB.

[6] Lietzmann-Kümmel, *Kor.*, p.205; Bultmann, 'Exegetische Probleme des zweiten Korintherbriefes', *Exegetica*, p.310.

the ἀπὸ τοῦ νῦν of v.16 still refers also to the time since Paul's conversion[1]. κατὰ σάρκα is to be taken with the verbs (οἴδαμεν and ἐγνώκαμεν)[2] rather than with the objects (οὐδένα and Χριστόν)[3]. For Paul could hardly mean that since his conversion he knows 'no one in so far as he is of fleshly nature' or 'who lives still in flesh'[4]. Paul means rather that since his conversion he knows no one in a fleshly way, according to worldly standards[5].

V.16b is a special application of this principle[6]. Among the various interpretations of this statement[7] the best seems to be that 'to know Christ in a fleshly way' means to know him or judge him according to the conception of the Messiah which was current at that time[8]. Many commentators feel that there is a polemical note in the statement, but they define the exact nature of the polemic differently according to their various interpretations of the statement[9]. Paul may be directing his polemic against his Jewish opponents who used particular features of the historical Jesus in order to protect their own views and claims[10]. Probably the opponents judged Christ from Jewish viewpoints and categories[11], and while boasting of their relation to him (cf.

---

[1]Lietzmann-Kümmel, *Kor.*, p.205; Stuhlmacher, 'καινὴ κτίσις', p.5. Windisch, *2.Kor.*, p.184, takes ἀπὸ τοῦ νῦν without further ado as referring to conversion. Similarly also Wendland, *Kor.*, p.202.

[2]Schlatter, *Der Bote*, p.559; Wendland, *Kor;.* p.202; Burce, *Cor.*, p.208; Barrett, *2Cor.* pp.170f.; O.Michel, ' "Erkennen dem Fleisch nach" *2.Kor.* 5, 16)', *EvTh* 14(1954), p.23; C.F.D.Moule, 'Jesus in NT Kerygma', *Verborum Veritas*, G.Stählin FS, ed. O. Böcher u. K.Haacker(1970), pp.17f.

[3]Plummer, *2Cor.*, p.176; Lietzmann-Kümmel, *Kor.*, p.125; cf. Windisch, *2.Kor.*, p.185, who thinks it impossible to differentiate between the two.

[4]Windisch, *2.Kor.*, p.185; cf. Wendland, *Kor.*, p.203; Moule, *op.cit.*, p.18.

[5]Cf. Wendland, *Kor.*, p.202; Bruce, *Cor.*, p.208; NEB; RSV.

[6]Windisch, *2.Kor.*, pp.184f.

[7]For the various interpretations, see Windisch, *2.Kor.*, pp.186ff.; also Plummer, *2Cor.*, pp.177f.; E.Güttgemanns, *Der leidende Apostel und sein Herr*(1966), pp.284ff., who attacks strongly the view that Paul is here rejecting a knowledge of the historical Jesus, but whose view that 2Cor 5.16 is a Gnostic gloss(following W.Schmithals, *Die Gnosis in Korinth*(³1969), pp.286ff.) is hardly tenable.

[8]Cf. O.Michel, *op.cit.*, p.26; Barrett, *2Cor.*, p.171; F.F.Bruce, *Paul and Jesus*(1974), pp.22–25.

[9]See Plummer, *2Cor.*, p.177; Windisch, *2.Kor.*, p.188; Schlatter, *Der Bote*, pp.563f.; Lietzmann-Kümmel, *Kor.*, p.125; Wendland, *Kor.*, p.203; Strachan, *2Cor.*, p.110; Michel, *op.cit.*, pp.26f.; Güttgemanns, *op.cit.*, pp.282–304.

[10]Michel, *op.cit.*, p.26.

[11]E.g., as the Jewish national Messiah. Cf. *ibid.*, pp.26f.; Schlatter, *Der Bote*, pp. 561, 563. From the Jewish point of view the crucified Messiah is, of course, a contra-

v.12), they perhaps insinuated that Paul had hated him and persecuted his followers[1]. This may explain why in the present passage Paul rejects judging Christ in a fleshly way on the one hand and emphasizes at the same time the idea of reconciliation on the other. At first, Paul concedes that, like his opponents[2], he judged Christ according to the Jewish conceptions of Messiah, and became, unlike them, a persecutor of the adherents of Christ, because he thought that they were blasphemously proclaiming Jesus of Nazareth as the Messiah, the man who as the pretender to Messiahship was helplessly condemned and crucified under God's curse[3]. This was a fleshly judgement, however. Now that he came to perceive the significance of Jesus' death, he no longer entertains such a fleshly judgement of Christ.

ὥστε in v.17 introduces a statement parallel to v.16 as a consequence of Christ's dying for all so that the living may live for him (vs.14f.)[4]. At the same time, however, v.17 seems to be building upon v.16[5]. The new creation has taken place in the death and resurrection of Christ, in which all have participated (vs.14f.). But ' it is when a person comes to be *in Christ*, that is,

---

diction in terms (cf. Gal 3.13f.), a scandal (1Cor 1.23). But convinced of Jesus' resurrection and therefore of God's exaltation of him, the Jewish Christian opponents may have seen Jesus as the Davidic national Messiah. Cf. Acts 15.16–18 (on this passage, see Bruce, *NT History,* p.269; *This is That* (1968), p.79); Rom 1.3f. (on this passage *infra* pp.109ff.). This is suggested by the contrast between knowing someone κατὰ σάρκα and being καινὴ κτίσις in Christ. Rom 2.25–29; 4.1ff.; 9.3ff.; 1Cor 10.18; Gal 4.21ff. make it clear that Paul looks upon the Jews and their claims in terms of the 'flesh' over against the divine promise and the Spirit. In Gal 6.12–16 Paul invalidates the Jewish glorying in the circumcision in the flesh, i.e., in being part of the covenant people, Israel, by pointing to a 'new creation', the true 'Israel of God' made up of the believing Jews and Gentiles (cf. also Gal 3.26–29). So, it is probable that as in Gal 6.12–16 so also in 2Cor 5.16f. Paul is invalidating the Jewish nationalistic claims with regard to the Messiah by asserting that what matters is God's καινὴ κτίσις in Christ which transcends the old *heilsgeschichtliche* division between Israel and the Gentiles. In view of the καινὴ κτίσις in Christ, Israel and their claims can only be designated as κατὰ σάρκα.

[1] Cf. Friedrich, 'Gegner', p.214. But Friedrich's doubt about Paul's persecution of Stephen and his friends in Jerusalem cannot be based on Gal 1.22. *Infra* pp.48f. So his conjecture that the account of Paul's persecution of Stephen and the 'Hellenists' may have arisen from the later estrangement between the 'Hellenists' and Paul, is unconvincing.

[2] Cf. Michel, *op. cit.*, pp.26f.

[3] Plummer, *2Cor.*, p.177; Schlatter, *Der Bote*, p.562; Michel, *op.cit.*, p.26.

[4] Plummer, *2Cor.*, p.179; Schlatter, *Der Bote*, p.564; Lietzmann-Kümmel, *Kor.*, p.126; Michel, *op.cit.*, p.23; Stuhlmacher, 'καινὴ κτίσις', p.5.

[5] Windisch, *2.Kor.*, p.189; Plummer, *2Cor.*, p.179; Michel, *op.cit.*, p.27; cf. Bultmann, 'Exegetische Probleme', *Exegetica*, p.310.

on his conversion, that in respect of him the new creation ... takes place'[1].
Paul gained this theological insight in his experience on the road to Damascus.
That on the Damascus road God's act of new creation took place in respect of
him, he already implied in 2Cor 4.6. There he said that God, who let light
shine at the first creation, shone in his heart driving darkness out of him.
Although in the present verse, 2Cor 5.17, Paul speaks of 'being in Christ'
as being a new creation gnomically in general terms ($\tau\iota\varsigma$), he thinks primarily
of his own case. This is clear from the context: v.17 is a part of Paul's apologetic polemic, and he speaks mainly of himself both before and after the
verse[2]. 'Being $\dot{\epsilon}\nu$ X$\rho\iota\sigma\tau\tilde{\omega}$' begins with baptism[3], in which one dies and rises
with Christ (cf.vs.14f.)[4] and becomes incorporated into the Body of Christ,
the Last Adam[5]. But Paul uses the same word-group $\kappa\alpha\lambda\epsilon\hat{\iota}\nu$ for his apostolic
call and for the call of an individual to be a Christian through baptism[6],
thus indicating that his Damascus call was the call to be $\dot{\epsilon}\nu$ X$\rho\iota\sigma\tau\tilde{\omega}$ as well as
to be an apostle of Christ. At the Damascus call Paul was crucified to the
(old) world through the cross of Christ and the (old) world to him (Gal 6.14),
so that he can say, 'I have been crucified with Christ; it is no longer I who live,
but Christ who lives in me . . . ' (Gal 2.20). Thus at the Damascus call Paul
became a $\kappa\alpha\iota\nu\dot{\eta}$ $\kappa\tau\dot{\iota}\sigma\iota\varsigma$ $\dot{\epsilon}\nu$ X$\rho\iota\sigma\tau\tilde{\omega}$[7].

---

[1]Barrett, *2Cor.*, p.174.

[2]The first person plural in vs. 11–20 should be taken throughout as referring to Paul
(and secondarily his colleagues). So Plummer, *2Cor.*, p.182; cf. also Schlatter, *Der Bote*,
pp.565ff. Güttgemanns, *Apostel*, pp.313f. Some see $\dot{\eta}\mu\hat{\alpha}\varsigma$ in v.18 as referring to all
Christians and $\dot{\eta}\mu\hat{\iota}\nu$ (similarly also $\dot{\epsilon}\nu$ $\dot{\eta}\mu\hat{\iota}\nu$ in v.19) to Paul and his colleagues (e.g.,
Barrett, *2Cor.*, p.175; cf. also Windisch, *2.Kor.*, pp.193f.; Bultmann, 'Exegetische
Probleme', p.309). But, then as Barrett (*loc. cit.*) recognises, the change from 'us Chris-
tians' to 'us ministers' within a verse is 'abrupt and difficult'. Taking $\dot{\eta}\mu\hat{\alpha}\varsigma$ in v.18 to
refer to Paul (and his colleagues), of course, does not mean that Paul is saying God re-
conciled only him (and his colleagues) to himself through Christ. The universal scope of
God's work of reconciliation is expressed in the immediately following verse (v.19).
The reason why Paul singles himself out as having been reconciled by God to himself,
can be well understood in the context. See the immediately following. See further
p.5 (n.7) above.

[3]Cf. Bultmann, 'Exegetische Probleme', p.310(n.23); F.Neugebauer, *In Christus*
(1960), p.112(n.63a); Stuhlmacher, '$\kappa\alpha\iota\nu\dot{\eta}$ $\kappa\tau\dot{\iota}\sigma\iota\varsigma$', p.28.

[4]Cf. R.C.Tannehill, *Dying and Rising with Christ* (1967), p.66, who finds v.14 to be a
variant formulation of the motif of dying with Christ; cf. also Lietzmann-Kümmel,
Kor., p.126; Windisch, *2.Kor.*, p.189.

[5]Cf. Lietzmann-Kümmel, *Kor.*, p.205; Wendland, *Kor.*, p.181; Windisch, *2.Kor.*,
p.189; Tannehill, *op.cit.*, p.69.

[6]See Stuhlmacher, '$\kappa\alpha\iota\nu\dot{\eta}$ $\kappa\tau\dot{\iota}\sigma\iota\varsigma$', pp.27ff.; A.Satake, 'Apostolat und Gnade bei
Paulus', *NTS* 15(1968/69), pp.96ff. *Infra* pp.288ff. for the significance of this.

[7]$\kappa\alpha\iota\nu\dot{\eta}$ $\kappa\tau\dot{\iota}\sigma\iota\varsigma$ is in Paul a cosmological, *heilsgeschichtlicher*, collective term for 'new

If Paul's reference to Christ's representative death (vs. 14f.) and the ἐν Χριστῷ formula thus provide us with a ground for the inference that here Paul is thinking of the Damascus call as God's act of new creation in respect of him, in 2Cor 5.18ff. he clearly explains that indeed God's act of new creation took place in respect of him on the Damascus road. It is clear from the opening words of 2Cor 5.18ff. that Paul is explaining how he was made a καινή κτίσις, since τὰ δὲ πάντα refers to the fundamental changes that he has been talking about in vs. 16f. Paul says that he was made a καινή κτίσις by God, who reconciled him to himself. At this point Paul may have in mind the Rabbinic idea which compares forgiveness and atonement for sin on the New Year's Day or on the Day of Atonement with a new creation (בריאה חדשה)[1]. Paul's concept of καινή κτίσις, being eschatological, in that it designates the new being in the new aeon inaugurated by Christ[2], cannot simply be identified with the Rabbinic concept, which is largely a pictorial expression for changes in the religio-ethical sphere[3]. However, this difference between the Rabbinic concept of בריאה חדשה and the Pauline concept of καινή κτίσις is only a natural consequence of Paul's belief that the forgiveness and atonement in Jesus Christ is the eschatological consummation of that which had to be repeated in Judaism[4]. If the forgiveness and atonement on the Day of Atonement or any other day effected renewal which could be described

---

creation' (Gal 6.15; cf. 2Cor 5.17b) (cf. Stuhlmacher, 'καινή κτίσις', p.20). But in 2Cor 5.17 the anthropological, individual dimension ('new creature') is also implied, if it does not come to the fore (note the individualising τις). So Tannehill, *op.cit.*, p.68; Bauer-Arndt-Gingrich, s.v.1 b.

[1]Cf. Str.–Bill. ii, pp.421f.; iii, p.519; Moore i, pp.334f.; E.Sjöberg, 'Wiedergeburt und Neuschöpfung im palästinischen Judentum', *StTh* 3 (1950/51) pp.45ff. Sometimes forgiveness in general without any connection with the New Year's Day or the Day of Atonement is compared with a new creation: e.g., Lev.R.30.3 (to Lev 23.40); Midr. Ps. 18.6 (Str.–Bill. iii, p.519). See Sjöberg, *op.cit.*, pp.58f., 67f.

[2]Cf. Stuhlmacher, 'καινή κτίσις', pp.20ff.

[3]Cf. Sjöberg, *op.cit.*, pp.62ff.: Stuhlmacher, 'καινή κτίσις', p.22.

[4]Cf. Midr. Ps.102.3(216a) in Str.–Bill. ii, p.422. For this reason the Qumran idea of cleansing and renewal at the entry into the eschatological community of the new covenant as a new creation, to which passages like 1QH 3. 19–22 and 11.10–14(cf. also 1QS 11.13f.) seem to allude, may offer a closer parallel to Paul's concept here than the Rabbinic idea does (cf. Stuhlmacher, 'καινή κτίσις', pp.12ff., 16,20; Sjöberg, 'Neuschöpfung in den Toten-Meer-Rollen', *St Th* 9(1956), pp.130ff.). However, it must be pointed out that in the above noted passages from Qumran the word 'new creation' itself does not appear.

Stuhlmacher, 'Zur neueren Exegese von Röm 3,24–26', *Jesus und Paulus*, Kümmel FS, pp.315ff., argues that in Rom 3.24ff. Paul accepts the pre-Pauline interpretation of

pictorially as a new creation, the forgiveness and atonement in Jesus Christ effects the eschatological and therefore real, new creation. Now the motif of reconciliation in 2Cor 5.18 clearly refers to the Damascus event[1]. Up to that moment Paul was acting as an enemy of the adherents of Christ, therefore of Christ and ultimately of God. But by grace God forgave him and reconciled him to himself (cf. Rom 5.10). That the Damascus event meant for Paul God's forgiveness as well as his call to the apostolic service, Paul expresses repeatedly by recalling his past persecution of the Church and by using the word χάρις for the call, as we have seen above. It is also suggested by the fact that Paul interprets his experience of God's call at the Christophany in the light of the call of Isaiah at the Theophany (Isa 6)[2], in which Isaiah is forgiven and atoned for (כפר) in a cultic setting which is reminiscent of that of the Day of Atonement (cf. Isa 6.6f. (also v.4b) with Lev 16.12f.).

Thus Paul was made a καινὴ κτίσις through God's reconciliation of him to himself on the Damascus road. With this Paul replies to his opponents who boast of their relation to Christ, estimating him in Jewish categories, and insinuate that Paul hated him. Paul, who had estimated Jesus in a fleshly way and persecuted his followers, has now become a new creature in Christ. All old value-judgements and relations have ceased to matter; they have chang-

---

the atoning work of Christ as the eschatological antitype to the atonement on the Day of Atonement in Judaism. He thinks that Paul's idea of the reconciled man as καινὴ κτίσις (2Cor 5.17) also suggests this. Whether in Rom 3.24ff. Paul thinks of Christ's atoning work as the antitype to the atonement on the Day of Atonement, depends on the question whether ἱλαστήριον there refers to כפרת or simply has the general sense of 'a means of propitiation'. Over against E.Lohse, *Märtyrer und Gottesknecht* (²1963), pp.149ff., Stuhlmacher argues for the former. But he seems not to be aware of the arguments for the latter advanced by L.Morris, 'The Meaning of 'ΙΛΑΣΤΗΡΙΟΝ in Romans III.25', *NTS* 2(1955/56), pp.33ff. However we interpret Rom 3.24ff., there is no doubt that there as elsewhere (e.g., Rom 4.25–5.11; 2Cor 5.19) Paul sets forth the atonement in Christ as final. When Paul speaks of his becoming καινὴ κτίσις through God's reconciliation through Christ in 2Cor 5.17ff., he need not have had the forgiveness and atonement specifically *on the Day of Atonement* in mind. For, as noted above (in n.1, p.17) and also suggested by 1QH 3.19–22; 11.10–14, in Judaism forgiveness and atonement without any connection with the cultic ceremonies on the Day of Atonement was also compared with a new creation.

[1]Cf. Schlatter, *Der Bote*, pp.565ff., emphasizes that in the present passage 2Cor 5.16ff. Paul has his own experience in mind.

[2]*Infra* pp.91ff. 2Cor 5.17b seems to allude to the contrast of 'the former things' – 'new things' in Isa 42.9; 43.18f.; 48.6 (cf. also 65.17; 66.22). See Stuhlmacher, 'καινὴ κτίσις', pp.10ff. for the view that Deutero-Isa. is the source of the apocalyptic concept of καινὴ κτίσις. Is Paul thinking of the call of Isaiah together with his in 2Cor 5.16ff.?

ed[1]. This has been brought about by God's reconciling him to himself. So there is no point of talking about Paul's past as an enemy of Christ and God any longer. God's reconciliation of Paul to himself is already an act of pure grace, but there is still more: God has not only reconciled Paul to himself but has also given him the ministry of reconciliation and entrusted to him the message of reconciliation[2]. This is the climax of Paul's apologetical polemic[3].

In the NT only Paul uses καταλλάσσειν/καταλλαγή of the relation between God and man. Even outside the NT the religious use of the term is rare. In Hellenistic Judaism, where it is used, though infrequently, and in Rabbinic Judaism, where its Hebrew or Aramaic equivalents (רִצָּה / רְצִי and פַּיִּס / פַּיִּס) are used, it means invariably God being appeased or reconciled to

---

[1]Cf. Barrett, *2Cor.*, pp.174f.; Foester, κτίζω, κτλ, *TDNT* iii, p.1034.

[2]καὶ θέμενος ἐν ἡμῖν in v.19 is not to be taken as parallel with μὴ λογιζόμενος αὐτοῖς , both subordinated to ἦν . . . καταλλάσσων. For a) the change in the tense ·speaks against the construction (Büchsel, καταλλάσσω, *TDNT* i, p.257); b) it is difficult to force the sense of a pluperfect upon ἦν θέμενος (Barrett, *2Cor.*, p.178); and more fundamentally c) it is not easy to see how Paul's ministry of preaching can be put on par with Christ's death and resurrection as constituting together God's work of reconciliation. 'Die Predigt gehört selbst mit zum Heilsgeschehen' (Bultmann, 'Jesus und Paulus', *Exegetica*, p.228; cf. also p.312), only in so far as it is the means through which individuals are made aware of God's objective work of reconciliation and appropriate it. It is wrong, therefore, to blur the distinction between God's objective work of reconciliation in Christ and the preaching as Bultmann does (cf. also Barrett, *2Cor.*, p.178). So Büchsel, *op.cit.*, suggests taking θέμενος as an instance of a participle continuing a construction begun with a finite verb (cf. B–D, §468.1). May it be that καὶ θέμενος ἐν ἡμῖν is to be taken as parallel with δόντος ἡμῶν in v.18? If so, ὡς ὅτι... τὰ παραπτώματα αὐτῶν of v.19ab would be a parenthesis, describing the ground of the διακονία τῆς καταλλαγῆς. For ὡς ὅτι see B–D, §396; Moulton i, p.212; and commentaries by Plummer (p.183), Windisch(p.191) and Barrett(pp.176f.). According to Schlatter, *Der Bote*, p.566, Paul begins the sentence of v.19 with ὡς because he compares his own experience with what God has done for the world. However, since the particle alone does not adequately express the relation between the two as the latter is the ground of the former, he adds ὅτι to ὡς. If this is correct, it supports the view that ὡς ὅτι... τὰ παραπτώματα αὐτῶν is a parenthesis.

The nom. θέμενος instead of the gen. θεμένου may appear here under the influence of the endings – ος either of λογιζόμενος, δόντος and καταλλάξαντος or of θεός of v.19 (F.F.Bruce tells me that the latter is more likely).

[3]Cf. Plummer, *2Cor.*, p.182. Failing to see this context, Barrett, *2Cor.*, p.175, speaks of Paul returning 'to deal more.directly with the theme of the apostolic ministry entrusted to him' from v.18 onwards, and Lietzmann-Kümmel, *Kor.*, p.126, say that there is no 'erkennbarer Gedankenfortschritt und klarer Zusammenhang' in vs. 18f. See further Güttgemanns, *Apostel*, pp.312ff., for the perplexities of various commentators in their unsuccessful explanation of the connection between vs. 18ff. and the foregoing. But Güttgemanns' own explanation of the connection is hardly plausible.

man by man's prayer, confession or sacrifice[1]. But for Paul it is not God who is reconciled to man, but man who is reconciled to God. Certainly the idea that Christ's death was an atoning sacrifice and that it was God who provided it as the means of atonement, was pre-Pauline (1Cor 11.25ff.; 15.3; cf. also Rom 3.24ff.)[2]. So the material was already there for the Pauline doctrine of reconciliation. However, it may well be that it was Paul who for the first time in *Religionsgeschichte* used the theologumenon καταλλάσσειν/καταλλαγή in the significant sense of God's reconciling rebellious mankind to himself; and he did so out of his own experience on the Damascus road, where he was reconciled to God while he was acting as his enemy (cf. Rom 5.10)[3].

6)   Eph 3.1–13 is the next passage, where Paul speaks of his call[4]. This

---

[1]Cf. Büchsel *op. cit.*, p.254; H. Vorländer, 'Versöhnung', *Theologisches Begriffslexikon zum NT* ii/2(1971), pp.1309ff.; Str.-Bill. iii, pp.519f.; L.Morris, *The Apostolic Preaching of the Cross*(31965), pp.215ff.

[2]It is widely recognized that Rom 3.25 is a pre-Pauline quotation. See Bultmann, *Theology of the NT* i (1965), p.46; E.Käsemann, 'Zum Verständnis von Röm 3,24–26', *ZNW* 43(1950/51), pp.150ff.; *An die Römer* (²1974), pp.88f.; Lohse, *Märtyrer*, pp. 149ff.; Stuhlmacher, 'Zur neueren Exegese von Röm 3,24–26', pp.315ff. Against this view, see C.E.B.Cranfield, *The Epistle to the Romans* i (1975), pp.200f. (n.1).

[3]This view contradicts E.Käsemann's view that the 'reconciliation' motif stems from the doxology of the Hellenistic community and 2Cor 5.19–21 is 'ein vorpaulinisches Hymnenstück"' ('Erwägungen zum Stichwort "Versöhnungslehre im NT" ', *Zeit und Geschichte*, Bultmann FS, ed. E.Dinkler(1964), pp.48–50) and also P.Stuhlmacher's view which, while rejecting Käsemann's view on the whole, still takes v.19ab as 'ein (hellenistisches) Zitat' (*Gerechtigkeit Gottes bei Paulus*(²1966), pp.77f.). Stuhlmacher's reasons for taking the other verses as Pauline are sound enough. But his acceptance of Käsemann's arguments for taking v.19ab as a quotation seems unfortunate: a) it is not certain whether ὡς ὅτι is an *Einleitungsformel*(see the literature cited in n.2 on p.19; Stuhlmacher himself says that ὡς ὅτι in 2Cor 11.21 is not one); b) the presence of participles does not necessarily show a liturgical style(cf.v.18); c) Paul uses the plural παραπτώματα also in Rom 5.16; and d) the idea of the universal reconciliation of v.19 fits in well with that of our reconciliation in v.18, the former being the basis of the latter (cf. Windisch, *2.Kor.*, p.191). God's objective work of reconciling the world in Christ is the basis of an individual's reconciliation to God, i.e., an individual's reconciliation takes place when he appropriates to himself the reconciliation that God has wrought for the whole world. So on the basis of God's work of reconciliation of the world(v.19), Paul appeals to individuals to be reconciled to God(v.20). Cf. Kasting, *Anfänge.*, p.141; Lohse, *Märtyrer*, pp.159ff.; Büchsel, *op.cit.*, pp.256f. On the other hand, v.19ab shows positively two uniquely Pauline elements καταλλάσσειν and λογίζεσθαι (cf. Heidland, λογίζομαι *TDNT* iv, pp.286–292). Cf. Kasting, *Anfänge*, p.141(n.49) for a criticism of Käsemann's view.

[4]See W.G.Kümmel, *Introduction to the NT*(²1977), pp.357–363, for a summary of the arguments against Pauline authorship of Eph., and M.Barth, *Ephesians*(1974), pp.

section is an excursus in which Paul explains how he was made a servant of Christ for the Gentiles. He assumes that the readers have heard of his apostolic commission and the gospel that he received by revelation (εἴ γε ἠκούσατε ... vs.2f.). While this general sense of vs.2f. is unmistakable, the exact meaning of οἰκονομία in v.2 is confusingly disputed. C.L. Mitton argues that, while in Col 1.25 it means Paul's 'assignment', in Eph 3.2 it has the sense of 'God's planned economy' or 'strategy'[1]. This alleged difference in the sense of οἰκονομία between Col. and Eph. provides him with one of the arguments for the conclusion that Eph. is non-Pauline[2]. Others think that οἰκονομία in Eph 3.2 means Paul's apostolic office as in Col 1.25, although in Eph 1.10 & 3.9 it means God's plan of salvation[3]. J. Reumann argues, however, that in Col 1.25 it means primarily God's plan or administration and secondarily Paul's apostolic office[4]. He argues that οἰκονομία is similarly used for God's 'administration' in Eph 1.9; 3.2,9, and that in Eph 3.2,9 as in Col 1.25 there is also implied the role in the divine administration given to Paul as an apostle, to make it known[5]. H. Schlier thinks that οἰκονομία in all three verses of Eph. means the divine 'Heilsveranstaltung'; not the divine 'Heilsplan' but the

---

3–50; and A.van Roon, *The Authenticity of Ephesians*(1974) for the latest defences of Pauline authorship.

[1] C.L.Mitton, *The Epistle to the Ephesians*(1951), pp.92ff.; cf. also E.Lohse, *Die Briefe an die Kolosser und an Philemon*([14]1968), p.117; H.Merklein, *Das kirchliche Amt nach dem Epheserbrief*(1973), p.174.

[2] Mitton, *op.cit.*, p.245; also Kümmel, *Introduction*, p.360.

[3] O.Michel, οἰκονομία, *TDNT* v, p.152; M.Dibelius & H.Greeven, *An die Kolosser, Epheser, An Philemon*([3]1953), p.73; J.Roloff, *Apostolat – Verkündigung – Kirche*(1965), p.113.

[4] J.Reumann, 'οἰκονομία-Terms', p.163. Reumann's three reasons for the view that οἰκονομία in Col 1.25 has 'the nuance of God's plan or administration' are: a) In Hellenistic world the phrase οἰκονομία τοῦ θεοῦ denoted God's administration of the universe; b) the subjective gen. τοῦ θεοῦ; and c) the preposition κατά 'implies a plan, rather than an office'. E.Lohmeyer, *Die Briefe an die Philipper, an die Kolosser und an Philemon* ([13]1964), p.80, also argues on the basis of the preposition κατά that it means 'Ratschluß Gottes', 'Heilsplan Gottes' rather than 'Amt'. But Reumann seems to concede that the participial phrase τὴν δοθεῖσάν μοι demands also a sense of 'office' here, if only secondarily, and accepts Masson's rendering of the verse: 'according to plan of God, the execution of which has been conferred upon me in that which concerns you' (*L'Epître de Saint Paul aux Colossiens*(1950), pp.111f.). Cf. also J.T.Sanders, 'Hymnic Elements in Eph. 1–3', *ZNW* 56(1965), pp.230f.; C.F.D.Moule, *The Epistles of Paul the Apostle to the Colossians and to Philemon*(1957), p.80; even Michel, *op.cit.*, p.153, concedes that in Col 1.25 & Eph 3.2 'there is room for doubt whether οἰκονομία denotes office or the divine plan of salvation: the two are closely linked in the Prison Letters'.

[5] Reumann, *op.cit.*, p.164f.

'execution of the divine arrangement'[1]. Interpreting χάρις in Eph 3.2 as the grace of the apostolic office (as in Rom 1.5; 12.3; 15.15; 1Cor 3.10; Gal 2.9)[2] and the genitive τῆς χάριτος as *gen. obj.*[3] or *explic.*, Schlier explains Eph 3.2 to mean: 'The Gentile Christians, to whom Paul writes, have heard of the divine undertaking which concerns the grace that was given to Paul together with apostleship. This divine undertaking consists in giving this grace to Paul and Paul's passing it on'[4].

As in Rom 12.3; 15.15; 1 Cor 3.10; Gal 2.9 so in Eph 3.2,7 & 8 the formula χάρις + the aorist passive form of δίδωμι + μοι indicates God's call of Paul to apostleship. This call has two sides: the revelation of the gospel and the commission to proclaim it (cf. Gal 1.15f.). Eph 3.3–6 explains the former and Eph 3.7ff. the latter.

ὅτι in v.3 introduces an explanation of v.2[5]. The divine οἰκονομία of calling Paul to apostleship took place in the revelation of the mystery to Paul. The mystery is the mystery τοῦ Χριστοῦ (v.4). This mystery is further defined in v.6[6]: 'that the Gentiles are fellow-heirs, members of the same body, and partakers of the promise in Jesus Christ through the gospel'. C.L. Mitton has argued that μυστήριον in Eph 3 has an entirely different sense from that in Col 1.26f.[7] But he overlooks a) that just as in Col 1.27 so in Eph 3.4 also μυστήριον is equated with Christ (if τοῦ Χριστοῦ in v.4 is a gen. of apposition)[8] or at least it concerns Christ (if τοῦ Χριστοῦ in v.4 is a *gen. obj.*)[9]; and b) that in Col 1.27 μυστήριον is not simply Christ or 'the indwelling of Christ in his people, whether Jews or Gentiles'[10] but 'the Christ

---

[1] H.Schlier. *Der Brief an die Epheser*([7]1971), p.148.   Similarly M.Barth, *Eph.,* pp.86ff., 328f.

[2] *Infra* pp. 25f., 288ff.

[3] Also T.K.Abbott, *The Epistles to the Ephesians and to the Colossians*(1897), p.79; M.Barth, *Eph.,* p.328

[4] Schlier, *Eph.,* p.148. With this interpretation Schlier agrees with Reumann in seeing in Eph 3.2 both God's administration and Paul's role within it. Cf. also M.Barth, *Eph.,* pp.358f.

[5] Abbott, *Eph.,* p.79; Schlier, *Eph.,* p.148.

[6] The infinitive εἶναι is epexegetical.   So Abbott, *Eph.,* p.83; Schlier, *Eph.,* p.151; cf. also M.Barth, *Eph.,* p.336.

[7] C.L.Mitton, *Epistle,* p.89; cf. also Kümmel, *Introduction,* pp.359f.

[8] Schlier, *Eph.,* p.149; M.Barth, *Eph.,* p.331. Mitton, *Epistle,* p.89, takes (τὸ μυστή-ριον) τοῦ Χριστοῦ in Col. 4.3 as gen. of apposition. But without considering the same phrase in Eph 3.4 he concludes on the basis of Eph 3.6 & 1.9 that whereas in Col μυστήριον is equated with Christ, in Eph. it is not.

[9] Abbott, *op.cit.,* p.80.

[10] E.F.Scott, *The Epistles of Paul to the Colossians, to Philemon and to the Ephesians*

preached among the *nations*[1]. The μυστήριον is not simply 'the eschatological redemptive act of God in Christ'[2] but that saving act that includes the Gentiles among the recipients of its benefits[3]. Thus both in Col 1.26f. and in Eph 3.4,6 μυστήριον has the Christological and *heilsgeschichtliche* or ecclesiological aspects[4]; the difference in the use of the word in the two epistles is one of emphasis: while in Col 1.26 the former is emphasized, in Eph 3 the latter comes to the fore[5].

H. Merklein shows that the μυστήριον in Eph 3 stands for the εὐαγγέλιον in Gal 1.12,15f.[6] As Paul says in Gal 1.12 that he received the gospel δι᾽ ἀποκαλύψεως Ἰησοῦ Χριστοῦ, so he says in Eph 3.3 that the μυστήριον was made known to him κατὰ ἀποκάλυψιν[7]. Just as in Gal 1.12,15f. the content of the gospel is Jesus Christ, so in Eph 3.4 the content of the mystery is Christ[8]. But the further definition of the μυστήριον in Eph 3.6 shifts its emphasis to the *heilsgeschichtliche* and ecclesiological nature. However, there is no contradiction but a logical connection between the Christological 'gospel' in Gal 1.12,15f. and the ecclesiological 'mystery' in Eph 3.6[9]. For Gal 1.15f. says that God revealed his Son to Paul so that Paul might proclaim him as the content of the gospel among the Gentiles. This means that the inclusion of the Gentiles among the beneficiaries of God's saving act in Christ was part of the content of God's revelation of Christ or at least its integral

---

[9]1958), p.34. Mitton, *Epistle*, p.98, quotes Scott with approval.

[1]E.Lohse, *Kol.*, p.121(emphasis by me). The problem whether ἐν ὑμῖν should be rendered 'within you' or 'among you' does not affect the point here being made. But the latter seems to be the better rendering. See Lohse, *Kol.*, pp.121f.

[2]Kümmel, *Introduction*, p.359.

[3]Cf. E.Schweizer, 'The Church as the Missionary Body of Christ', *Neotestamentica* (1963), p.327: 'The preaching of the gospel to the world, Christ among the Gentiles, is . . . the mystery hidden for ages, now revealed. It is the eschatological fulfilment of God's plan of salvation(1.26f.)'.

[4]Cf. Moule, *Col.*, p.82f.; F.F.Bruce, *The Epistle to the Colossians*(1957), pp.218f.; M.Barth, *Eph.*, p.331; Merklein, *op.cit.*, p.209.

[5]Cf. Bruce, *Col.*, pp.218f.; Merklein, *op.cit.*, p.209; G.Bornkamm, μυστήριον *TDNT* iv, p.820.

[6]Merklein *op.cit.*, pp.193−209, esp. 208f.; cf. also Dibelius-Greeven, *Eph.*, p.74.

[7]Merklein, *op.cit.*, pp.196−199, observes, however, the difference of accent between Gal 1.12, 15f. and Eph 3 reflected in their different formulations.

[8]Merklein does not make this point.

[9]*Ibid.*, p.208. Against K.M.Fischer, *Tendenz und Absicht des Epheserbriefes*(1973), p.99.

consequence[1]. Eph 3.6 emphasizes this part as the content of the mystery revealed[2]. Merklein thinks that with the term μυστήριον and its definition in terms of 'Christ who is proclaimed among the Gentiles' Col 1.26f acted as 'catalyst' for the ecclesiological interpretation in Eph 3.6 of the revelation of Christ in Gal 1[3]. Though the metaphor 'catalyst' seems unfortunate, it seems correct to see a line of development from Gal 1 to Eph 3 in the shifting of emphasis from the Christological to the ecclesiological definition of the revelation – the line that passes through Col 1.26f.[4]

The divine οἰκονομία consisted not only in revealing the gospel, the mystery, to Paul, but also in making him a servant of the gospel (v.7)[5]. The statement that Paul became a servant of the gospel is reminiscent of Rom 1.1 where he interprets the significance of his call to apostleship in terms of the commission to preach the gospel[6]. Paul's self-description ἐμοὶ τῷ ἐλαχιστοτέρῳ πάντων ἁγίων in v.8 is reminiscent of ὁ ἐλάχιστος τῶν ἀποστόλων in 1 Cor 15.9 and alludes to his past as a persecutor of the Church of Christ before his call[7]. God's call of Paul to apostleship was for the Gentiles

---

[1]L.Cerfaux, *The Church in the Theology of St. Paul*(1959), p.176.

[2]Merklein, *op.cit.*, p.208: 'Der Inhalt des Mysteriums Eph 3, 6 ist die ekklesiologische Interpretation der Offenbarung Jesu Christi in ihrer heilsgeschichtlichen Konsequenz. Indem der Verfasser die heilsgeschichtlichen Konsequenzen der ἀποκάλυψις Jesu Christi(Gal. 1) zum Gegenstand der ἀποκάλυψις selber macht, bekommt sein Mysterium ekklesiologischen Inhalt'.

[3]*Ibid.*, pp.208f.

[4]There may be another line of development from Gal 1 through Col 1.25ff. to Eph 3: Gal 1 speaks of the gospel – Col 1.25ff. speaks of the gospel and mystery and identifies them – Eph 3 speaks only of the mystery (in the place of the gospel in Gal 1). In Eph 3.1–13 Paul emphasizes that the mystery of the Gentiles' sharing in God's salvation in Christ was revealed to him and the grace of the apostolic office for the Gentiles was given to him. This accords well with other Pauline passages like Gal 1 & 2. But a problem arises because Paul says also that the mystery was revealed τοῖς ἁγίοις ἀποστόλοις αὐτοῦ καὶ προφήταις ἐν πνεύματι. Could Paul, who had many troubles to get his εὐαγγέλιον τῆς ἀκροβυστίας accepted by the other apostles(Gal 1–2), say that it was revealed to 'the apostles and prophets' as a body? In view of Paul's emphasis that it is he who received the gospel by revelation, it may be that in v.5 Paul is pointing to the later acceptance of his gospel by the apostles (cf. Abbott, *Eph.*, pp.82f.).

[5]V.7 takes up v.2 and begins to explain the other side of the event of Paul's call to apostleship, namely the actual commission to proclaim the gospel.

[6]Cf. Lohse, *Kol.*, pp.110f.

[7]The intensification of self-degradation in Eph 3.8 in comparison with 1Cor 15.9 is often seen as betraying the deutero-Pauline tendency to paint the pre-conversion Paul darker and darker(cf. 1Tim 1.15). So Fischer, *op.cit.*, pp.95ff. But cf. Abbott, *Eph.*, p.86; Schlier, *Eph.*, p.152; M.Barth, *Eph.*, p.340.

(v.3): it was for Paul to preach the gospel to the Gentiles (v.8), so that through his preaching they might share in the salvation in Christ (v.6f.); and thus Paul was commissioned to bring to light the divine administration of the mystery (v.9)[1].

Finally, it may be added that the aorist forms of δίδωμι in connection with the χάρις given to Paul (vs.2,7,8) and the ἐγνωρίσθη in v.3 fix the revelation of the mystery and the call upon the Damascus event.

7) In the course of the exegesis of Eph 3.1—13 the parallel passage Col 1.23c—29 has constantly been drawn into discussion[2]. This indicates that in Col 1.23c—29 too, Paul speaks of his apostolic commission[3]. First of all, as in Eph 3.7, he says that he became a servant of the gospel (v.23c). As such he became also a servant of the Church (v.25). This he became 'according to the plan of God, the execution of which was conferred upon'[4] him for the Gentiles. The purpose of God's commissioning Paul was that he should 'carry out to the full the preaching of the gospel'[5]. The word of God, i.e., the gospel, is identified with the μυστήριον, and the μυστήριον in turn with Χριστός ἐν ὑμῖν. The significance of this has been already observed above in connection with Eph 3. It is Christ whom Paul proclaims to all men (v.28; cf. Gal 1.16).

8) There is a series of the aorist forms of the verbs that refer to the call of Paul to apostleship on the Damascus road. It has already been noted that in Rom 12.3; 15.15; 1 Cor 3.10; Gal 2.9; Eph 3.2,7,8 Paul uses the formula[6] χάρις + the aorist passive form of the verb δίδωμι + μοι to indicate God's apostolic commission of him on the Damascus road. As in Eph 3 so in Rom 15.15f. he expands the formula to explain the purpose of the grace of his apostolic commission: 'that I should be a minister of Jesus Christ to the Gentiles, discharging the priestly ministry of the gospel of God, so that the offering of the Gentiles may be acceptable, consecrated by the Holy Spirit'. A variation of the formula appears in Rom 1.5. Here also the verb (λαμβάνω) is in the aorist form,[7] indicating a definite point of time when Paul received

---

[1] Accepting the reading that omits πάντας after φωτίσαι (ℵ*, A, 1739, etc.).

[2] See Merklein, *op.cit.*, pp.159f. for a comparison between Col 1.23—27 and Eph 3.1—7.

[3] Lohse, *Kol.*, p.111, gives the passage Col 1.24—2.5 the heading 'Amt und Auftrag des Apostels'.

[4] *Supra* p.21, n.4.

[5] Abbott, *Eph.*, p.233.

[6] Cf. O.Michel, *Römer*, pp.296, 364; Käsemann, *Römer*, pp.317, 374.

[7] The plural ἐλάβομεν is, as often in Paul's letters, a literary plural. So Michel, *Römer*, p.40; Käsemann, *Römer*, p.11.

the apostolic commission[1]. Here by adding ἀποστολή to χάρις thus forming a hendiadys[2] Paul clearly indicates that the χάρις means the χάρις of apostleship. A statement about the purpose of Paul's apostolic commission follows here also: to bring about the obedience that consists in faith[3] among all the Gentiles for the sake of the name of Jesus Christ. The fact that Paul uses χάρις to denote his apostleship indicates that he perceived the call to apostleship as an act of God's pure grace for him, the persecutor of the Church (cf. 1Cor 15.10)[4]. The same thought appears in the two passages that have already been observed: ἔχοντες τὴν διακονίαν ταύτην, καθὼς ἠλεήθημεν . . . (2Cor 4.1)[5]; and (ἀλλ᾿ ἡ ἱκανότης ἡμῶν ἐκ τοῦ θεοῦ), ὃς καὶ ἱκάνωσεν ἡμᾶς διακόνους καινῆς διαθήκης . . . (2Cor 3.6). And as observed above it lies also behind 2Cor 5.18: τὰ δὲ πάντα ἐκ τοῦ θεοῦ τοῦ καταλλάξαντος ἡμᾶς ἑαυτῷ διὰ Χριστοῦ καὶ δόντος ἡμῖν τὴν διακονίαν τῆς καταλλαγῆς. (See also καὶ θέμενος ἐν ἡμῖν τὸν λόγον τῆς καταλλαγῆς in v.19).

Challenged by the Corinthians, Paul reminds them of the apostolic authority that the Lord gave him (2Cor 10.8; 13.10). Here again he uses the aorist ἔδωκεν indicating his apostolic commission on the Damascus road[6]. The purpose of God's commissioning him with the apostolic authority was for the building up of the Church and not for its pulling down. Another instance of the aorist form of δίδωμι used for Paul's apostolic commission is, as already observed, Col 1.25, where it is used with οἰκονομία as the object. Paul says that Christ sent him (or commissioned him as an apostle – ἀπέστειλεν) to preach the gospel (1Cor 1.17). Again, an aorist verb appears in Gal 2.8 in the context in which Paul defends the legitimacy of his apostleship: 'God who worked (ἐνεργήσας) for Peter to make him an apostle to the circumci-

---

[1]Cf. Michel. *Römer*, p.40.

[2]B–D, §442. 16; Bruce, *Romans,* p.74; Käsemann, *Römer*, p.12; cf. also Michel, *Römer*, pp.40f.

[3]Taking πίστεως as appositional. So Bultmann, *Theology* i, p.314; J.Murray, *The Epistle to the Romans*(1970), p.13; Käsemann, *Römer*, p.12. But cf. Michel, *Römer*, p.41; Bruce, *Romans*, p.74.

[4]*Infra* pp.288ff. for a discussion of the significance of this fact.

[5]Cf. 1Tim 1.12f., 16; and also 1Cor 7.25. A comparison of 2Cor 4.1 with 1Cor 7.25 is helpful in clarifying the force of the aorist tense. Whereas in 1Cor 7.25 through the perfect ἠλεημένος Paul is concerned to bring out the present effect, i.e., his trustworthiness (πιστὸς εἶναι), of his receiving the Lord's mercy on the road to Damascus (cf. Robertson & Plummer, *1Cor*, p.151), in 2Cor 4.1 through the aorist ἠλεήθημεν he emphasizes the event itself of his receiving the Lord's mercy for the ministry of the new covenant at a definite point of time – i.e., the event on the Damascus road.

[6]Cf. Plummer, *2Cor*, p.281.

zed, also worked (ἐνήργησεν) for me to make me an apostle to the Gentiles'[1]. This is a parenthetical remark giving the ground for the statement πεπίστευμαι τὸ εὐαγγέλιον τῆς ἀκροβυστίας καθὼς Πέτρος τῆς περιτομῆς in Gal 2.7 only, and not for the entire verse 7[2]. Whereas ἐνήργησεν in v.8 and δοθεῖσαν in v.9 fix the attention on the Damascus event, the perfect πεπίστευμαι in v.7 brings to the fore the continuing effect of the event: Paul has the gospel as the result of God's entrusting him with it on the Damascus road (cf. 1Cor 9.17). However, in 1Th 2.4 the moment of God's entrusting Paul with the gospel becomes the centre of attention (cf. 1Tim 1.11; Tit 1.3).

9) Finally, the opening verses of Rom.; 1 & 2 Cor.; Gal.; Eph.; and Col. may be added here as alluding to God's call of Paul to apostleship on the Damascus road. Paul introduces himself as 'called to be an apostle' (Rom 1.1; 1Cor 1.1) and 'set apart for the gospel of God' (Rom 1.1)[3] 'through the will of God' (2Cor 1.1; Eph 1.1; Col 1.1). In Paul's becoming an apostle a human will or mediation is excluded. This is emphasized in Gal 1.1 antithetically, and it seems that the narration of his call and career thereafter in

---

[1]Cf. NEB: 'For God whose action made Peter an apostle to the Jews, also made me an apostle to the Gentiles'. Commentators usually interpret the verse as if Paul were arguing here for the legitimacy of his apostleship on the basis of the success of his missionary work which shows that in it God was at work. So, e.g., Mussner, *Gal.*, p.116; Schlier, *Gal.*, p.78. Cf. RSV for an extremely loose rendering of the verse on the basis of this interpretation. But this interpretation fails to observe the force of the preposition εἰς before ἀποστολήν. It expresses purpose or goal (Bauer-Arndt-Gingrich, p.264), so that εἰς ἀποστολήν means ' "for or unto the creation of", i.e., "so as to make him an apostle" ' (E.Burton, *The Epistle to the Galatians* (1921), p.94). It is strange that Burton, who correctly interprets the phrase εἰς ἀποστολήν, adopts the view under question after considering the alternative (*ibid.*, pp.93f.). Does Paul mean here that God was at work in his ministry to make him an apostle? Did the success of his missionary work make him an apostle? The aorists (ἐνεργήσας & ἐνήργησεν) are better understood as referring to God's work that resulted in the apostolic commissions of Peter and Paul or directly to God's work of commissioning them rather than to God's work in their missionary activities so far (against Mussner, *Gal.*, p.117). God's work for Peter and Paul (Πέτρῳ and ἐμοί are *dat. commodi*) need not be 'the inner experience' of them (cf. Burton, *Gal.*, pp.93f.); in Paul's case it would be God's revelation of Christ on the Damascus road.

[2]Cf. Burton, *Gal.*, p.93. Commentators seem often misled on this point, and this leads them to interpret Gal 2.8 as they do. Again Mussner, *Gal.*, p.117, provides the best example of this mistake. Cf. also Schlier, *Gal.*, p.77.

[3]Does ἀφωρισμένος refer to God's setting Paul apart before his birth or 'to the effectual dedication that occurred in the actual call to apostleship and (indicate) what is entailed in the call' (Murray, *Romans*, p.3)? A comparison with Gal 1.15 seems to point to the former. So Michel, *Römer*, pp.35f.; Bruce, *Romans*, p.71; Käsemann, *Römer*, p.4. But unlike Gal 1.15 Rom 1.1 has ἀφωρισμένος after κλητός. This seems to suggest the latter. So K.L.Schmidt, κλητός, *TDNT* iii, p.494; Kasting, *Anfänge*, p.56.

Gal 1.11ff. is a demonstration of the statement made in Gal 1.1.

These observations show that the references to Paul's conversion and call on the Damascus road abound in his letters. Certainly they are brief and are often in the nature of allusion bringing out the consequences of the event, rather than being an explicit narration of the event itself. This differentiates Paul from the author of the Book of Acts. But this gives no ground for the assertion that Paul shows deep reserve about his Damascus experience[1] or that it should not be placed at the centre of his life and thought[2]. The reason why Paul does not narrate it in his letters as Acts does is to be found elsewhere. It is for this reason, that whereas Luke was writing history, Paul was writing letters to the churches which had already heard of it. The word ἠκούσατε in Gal 1.13 (cf. also Eph 3.2) suggests that the Galatian Christians already knew the details concerning Paul's pre-conversion past. That they came to know them and also to know of the Christophany on the Damascus road through Paul's own report rather than indirectly through hear-say or tradition[3] is suggested by 1Cor 15.3–8, where Paul includes the Christophany to him together with the other resurrection appearances in the gospel that he delivered to the Corinthians[4]. Even if τὸ εὐαγγέλιον ὃ εὐηγγελι-σάμην ὑμῖν (1Cor 15.1) is to be limited to 1Cor 15.3b–5, there is no doubt that in his preaching Paul attached to 'the gospel' the reports of the resurrection appearances (vs. 6–7) including the Christophany to himself (v.8) as evidence of Christ's resurrection. This was inevitable. For when Paul preached that Jesus was raised from the dead he must have depicted the evidence of the resurrection in detail as far as he could, including his encounter with the

---

[1]*Contra* Lohfink, *Paulus vor Damaskus*, p.21.

[2]*Contra* Bornkamm, *Paulus*, p.39.

[3]Cf. Burton, *Gal.*, p.44; Schlier, *Gal.*, p.49; Roloff, *Apostolat*, p.42.

[4]Cf. Lietzmann-Kümmel, *Kor.*, p.77; B.Gerhardsson, *Memory and Manuscript* (1961), pp.299f., sees 1Cor 15.3–8 set out as 'a series of *simanim*'. סימן is the Rabbinic term for a title or heading which summarises a piece of teaching or tradition in a key-word or catch-word. It was used as a technique of memory (*ibid.*, pp.143ff., 153ff.). On 1Cor 15.3–8 Gerhardsson says: 'each individual part is a short, heading-like designation for some passage of the tradition about Christ' (p.299). J.Roloff, *Apostolat*, p.48, accepts this view. P.Stuhlmacher, *Das paulinische Evangelium* i (1968), pp.266–276, esp. pp.274f., similarly thinks that 1Cor 15.3–7 is a 'credo that concludes a catechetical lesson' and that as such it 'speaks in a highly abbreviated form of God's saving work in Christ which has become history', i.e., it is 'a summary of historical news'. The early Church knew to which concrete historical realities the abbreviations referred. Stuhlmacher thinks further that Paul expanded the tradition to include the Christophany to him: 'Denn für die Gemeinden, in denen sein apostolisches Wort Autorität besaß, ist die Geschichte Gottes mit dem Apostel Paulus eben Teil der Geschehnisse, die es als konstitutiv zur Kenntnis zu nehmen galt'. (p.275).

risen Jesus, in order to convince his hearers of the truth of Jesus' resurrection — the truth which was hitherto unheard of by his hearers and not easily believable to them. If B. Gerhardsson and P. Stuhlmacher are right, as it seems they are, in thinking that each part of 1Cor 15.3–8 stands for a tradition that was unfolded in catechetical lessons, the tradition represented by v.8 must have been of the same kind as that of three reports of the Damascus event in Acts (9.1–19; 22.3–16; 26.4–18), including Paul's pre-conversion past, the circumstances of the Christophany, the Christophany itself and its consequences[1]. Having thus made his churches acquainted with the Damascus event as an integral part of his gospel, in his letters Paul needed only to refer to it briefly whenever he felt it necessary to remind them of it. Against this background must be understood not only the brief *siman*-like reference to it in 1Cor 15.8 and the reference in Gal 1.13–17, which are both explicitly prefaced as being a reminder (1Cor 15.2; Gal 1.13 (ἠκούσατε); cf. also Eph 3.2), but also the question οὐχὶ Ἰησοῦν τὸν κύριον ἡμῶν ἑώρακα; in 1Cor 9.1. Seen against this background the question appears to be a rhetorical one which presupposes the Corinthians' knowledge of the Christophany to Paul and therefore their affirmative answer. Paul needed to remind his churches of the Damascus event, however, not for its own sake, but in order to re-affirm the divine origin and therefore the authenticity of his gospel and apostleship. Hence in his letters he did not recount the event in detail, but only referred to it in connection with his gospel and apostleship[2].

10) The fact that the Damascus event formed part of Paul's preaching and catechetical tradition explains not only the stereotype form in which Paul's conversion and call is referred to in his letters, but also the preservation of the tradition in other writings: 1Tim 1.11–14[3]; Acts 9.1–19; 22.3–16; 26.4–18[4]. Against the earlier attempts to see different traditions behind the

---

[1]*Infra* pp. 91ff., 223ff.

[2]The rather lengthy descriptions of Paul's past in Judaism in Gal 1.13f. and Phil 3.4ff. do not contradict this statement. In Gal 1.13f. it was called for by the situation in which a demonstration was necessary that Paul could not possibly have received his gospel from man before he received it by the revelation of Christ. Similarly in Phil 3.4ff. Paul mentioned his privileges and achievements in Judaism not because the Philippians needed anew to be informed of them but because his confrontation with the Judaizers required him to mention them in order to show that their way was mistaken.

[3]That is, if 1Tim. is not Pauline but deutero-Pauline. Two recent authors rather convincingly argue for the Pauline authorship of the Pastoral Letters: B.Reicke, 'Chronologie der Pastoralbriefe', *ThLZ* 101 (1976), 81–94; J.A.T. Robinson, *Redating the NT* (1976), pp.67–84.

[4]Stuhlmacher, *Evangelium*, pp.73, 275.

three accounts of the Damascus event in Acts[1], nowadays most scholars agree that they are based on one tradition[2]. Except for the episode of Ananias, they agree with one another on the whole, and the variations are of little significance as they are limited to the area of expression[3]. On essential points they agree also with Paul's own accounts in his letters[4]: a) Paul persecuted the Church; b) the change took place in or before Damascus; c) Christ appeared to him; d) he appeared in the light as the exalted Lord; and e) he commissioned Paul to be the apostle to the Gentiles[5]. Besides, Acts 26. 16–18 and 9.15–16 show allusions to the same passages of the call of the Ebed Yahweh and the prophet Jeremiah as those to which Paul alludes in his accounts in his letters[6]. In Acts 26.4–18 Luke may have left the Ananias episode out either because he felt it to be irrelevant for the occasion or because giving the gist of what Paul actually said before King Agrippa he remembered that Paul did not include it in his speech. If the former was the case, Luke may not have been of very different opinion from Paul in estimating the role of Ananias in Paul's conversion and call[7]. In spite of the modern tendency to give little historical value to the speeches in Acts, the latter possibility is not excluded. At any rate, the similarities between the accounts

---

[1]E.g., E.Hirsch, 'Die drei Berichte der Apostelgeschichte über die Bekehrung des Paulus', *ZNW* 28(1929), pp.305–312 and K.Lake, 'The Conversion of Paul and the Events immediately following it', *The Beginnings of Christianity* v, ed. F.J.Foakes-Jackson & K.Lake (1933), pp.188–191.

[2]Haenchen, *Die Apostelgeschichte* ([15]1968), p.276; G.Stählin, *Die Apostelgeschichte* ([10]1962) pp.309f.; H.Conzelmann, *Die Apostelgeschichte* ([2]1972), pp.66; Lohfink, *op. cit.*, pp.29f.; S.G.Wilson, *The Gentiles and the Gentile Mission in Luke-Acts* (1973), p.161; Ch.Burchard, *Der dreizehnte Zeuge* (1970), pp.120f. (but in pp.125, 128f. he seems to contradict himself when he unsuccessfully tries to distinguish between one 'überlieferte Geschichte von Paulus Bekehrung' and another 'überlieferte Auffassung von Paulus Berufung' (p.129) and assigns Acts 9.1–18 to the former and Acts 26.12–18 to the latter).

[3]Cf. Wilson, *op. cit.*, p.161.

[4]J.Jeremias, *Der Schlüssel zur Theologie des Apostels Paulus* (1971), p.21; Lohfink, *op. cit.*, p.18.

[5]The problem of whether Luke thought of Paul as an apostle cannot be discussed here. See Roloff, *Apostolat*, pp.199ff., 232ff.

[6]See Munck, *Paul*, pp.24–33 together with our comment on 2Cor 4.6 in pp.10f. above.

[7]The fact that Luke was able to narrate Paul's conversion and call without mentioning Ananias shows that for him Ananias was only a dispensable mouthpiece of the Lord. This militates against G.Klein's view that Luke introduces Ananias as the mediator of Paul's call through whom Luke subordinates Paul to the ecclesiastical tradition and the Twelve (*Die Zwölf Apostel* (1961), pp.144ff.; cf. also Conzelmann, *Apg*, p.67; for sound criticisms of Klein's view see Wilson, *op.cit.*, pp.163ff. and Roloff, *Apostolat*,

in Acts themselves, and between them and those in Paul's letters, lead us to think that all three accounts in Acts go back to Paul[1]. So they can be used along with Paul's accounts in his letters as sources for a discussion of Paul's call.

Many of Paul's references and allusions to his conversion and call on the Damascus road (1Cor 9.1; 15.5–10; Gal 1.13–17; Phil 3.4–11; 2 Cor 3.4–4.6; 5.16–21; cf. also Acts 22.3–16; 26.4–18) stand in the polemical context of defending his gospel and apostleship. However, not only these but also the rest of his allusions to the Damascus event make it clear that his gospel and apostleship are grounded solely in the Christophany on the Damascus road and that he understands himself solely in the light of it. The Damascus event is the basis both of his theology and his existence as an apostle[2]. This is the reason why Paul, who otherwise comes to speak of his life reluctantly under provocation (e.g., 2Cor 11 & 12), makes an exception when he constantly refers to the event[3]. This, however, is to be further substantiated in the following pages through an investigation as to how Paul interprets the event.

---

pp.200, 205f.). Paul does not mention Ananias at all. It is just possible that Paul's protest that he is an apostle 'οὐκ ἀπ' ἀνθρώπων οὐδὲ δι' ἀνθρώπου' (Gal 1.1; cf. also 1.11f.) was provoked by the Judaizers' perversion of the significance of Ananias. But it is not very probable, for in Gal 1 & 2 Paul seems to be arguing for his independence from Jerusalem but not from the church in Damascus (cf. Munck, *Paul*, pp.18f.; Haenchen, *Apg.*, p.277; Wilson, *op.cit.*, p.162). At any rate, in view of the categorical denial of a role 'of a human agency in his apostolic commission, it seems clear that for Paul Ananias' role was not substantial. It is probable, however, that Ananias healed the blinded Paul and baptised him and also helped him in his meditation upon and interpretation of the Christophany (cf. Munck, *Paul*, pp.17f.; Roloff, *Apostolat*, pp.205f.). In Acts 9 & 22 Luke may give an impression of exaggerating this role of Ananias – perhaps unintentionally (cf. ch.26 and the comment at the beginning of this note. Roloff, *Apostolat*, pp.205f., sees here, probably correctly, no exaggeration of the significance of Ananias. What Ananias does for Paul is a 'Minimalprogramm' for Paul to be admitted to the Church). Paul's silence on this role of Ananias in Gal 1 is understandable because in asserting his independence from a human agency for his apostolic commission he would not have found it helpful to mention it or bring it anew to the attention of his readers (if, as argued above, the Damascus event, including Ananias episode, was known to them). For no matter how little significance he himself attached to it, his opponents could exploit it in their argument against him.

[1]So Munck, *Paul*, p.29: 'It is the apostle himself who shaped the story of his conversion and call as the churches were to hear it'; cf. also Schoeps, *Paul*, p.54.

[2]Cf. Jeremias, *Schlüssel.*, pp.20–27; Blank, *Paulus.* p.184; O.Kuss, *Paulus*, p.285; Kasting, *Anfänge*, p.56.

[3]Cf. G.Eichholz, 'Prolegomena zu einer Theologie des Paulus im Umriß', *Tradition und Interpretation* (1965), p.175 (but cf. his *Die Theologie des Paulus im Umriß* (1972), p.29); Stuhlmacher, *Evangelium*, p.73.

Chapter II Paul The Persecutor

1 Paul before His Conversion

Before investigating Paul's interpretation of the Damascus event, it is necessary, for its background, to describe his life and thought before the conversion and call.

Among the fundamental data about Paul's life belongs his own testimony that he was an Israelite (Rom 11.1; 2Cor 11.22; Phil 3.5) and was from the tribe of Benjamin (Rom 11.1; Phil 3.5). With the latter statement fits well the tradition in Acts (13.9) that besides his Roman name 'Paul' he had also the Jewish name 'Saul', the name borne by the greatest figure in the history of the tribe, namely the first king of Israel.

In Acts Paul is reported to have said that he was born in Tarsus (Acts 22.3). Tarsus was the capital city of the Roman province Cilicia. It lay on the border between Orient and Occident and was a centre of communication and trade. Thus in this Hellenistic city the Greek and the Oriental peoples and cultures met and mixed. About the time of Paul's birth, which was probably at the beginning of our era, Tarsus was a significant centre of learning devoted to philosophy, rhetoric and general education[1]. So some scholars have attributed to this Tarsus background of Paul the Hellenistic elements in Paul's letters: not only his good knowledge of Greek and preference for the Septuagint over the Hebrew Bible, but also his use of the imagery drawn from the mystery-cult and the emperor-cult, of the Hellenistic rhetoric, especially the Cynic-Stoic diatribe, and of some popular Stoic concepts like conscience, nature, freedom, duty, etc[2].

It is, however, unlikely that Paul had a formal education in Greek philosophy and rhetoric. For beyond such popular elements of the Hellenistic culture as those mentioned above he does not show the kind of deep influence by Greek philosophy that we see in his contemporary, Philo of Alexandria. Therefore it is usually proposed that the above mentioned Hellenistic

---

[1] Strabo, *Geographica* xiv. 5, 13, 673.

[2] R.Bultmann, 'Paulus', *RGG*² iv, 1020; G.Bornkamm, 'Paulus', *RGG*³ v, 168; Dibelius-Kümmel, *Paulus*, pp.28f.; cf. Jeremias, *Schlüssel*, pp.8f.

elements were mostly mediated by the *diaspora* Judaism which assimilated Hellenism to some degree[1]. If Paul grew up in Tarsus, he would have been taken regularly to the synagogue there by his parents. In the synagogue, which acted also as a school[2], he may have learned, besides the Septuagint, the Hellenistic cultural elements, although his parents were careful in bringing him up in a strict line of Judaism (cf. Phil 3.5; Acts 23.6).

However, on the basis of Acts 22.3, W.C. van Unnik has shown it to be probable that though Paul was born in Tarsus he actually grew up in Jerusalem[3]. There Paul is reported to have said to the hostile crowd in Jerusalem: 'I am a Jew, born at Tarsus in Cilicia, but brought up in this city (= Jerusalem), educated at the feet of Gamaliel according to the strict manner of the law of our fathers'[4]. According to this report Paul spent his childhood in his parents' house ($\dot{\alpha}\nu\alpha\tau\epsilon\theta\rho\alpha\mu\mu\acute{\epsilon}\nu o\varsigma$) at Jerusalem and the ensuing school years ($\pi\epsilon\pi\alpha\iota\delta\epsilon\upsilon\mu\acute{\epsilon}\nu o\varsigma$) at the feet of Gamaliel. This report presupposes that Paul's family moved to Jerusalem when he was still a child or even a baby (cf. Acts 26.4f.)[5].

Referring to Gal 1.22, however, R. Bultmann denies the trustworthiness of the report that Paul studied under Gamaliel in Jerusalem[6]. But Bultmann's inference from Gal 1.22 that Paul had never stayed long in Jerusalem before his conversion, is illegitimate. For it is unrealistic to assume that in the city of 55,000 inhabitants[7] people would know all the pupils of the rabbis, and moreover it is 'the churches of Judaea' that are said in the verse not to have known Paul by face[8]. That Paul must have spent at least the years of his education in Jerusalem is suggested by his own testimony that he was a Pharisee who made great progress in Judaism (Gal 1.13f.; Phil 3.5f.). For, as M. Hengel says, 'a study of the law such as Paul describes in Gal 1.13f. and Phil 3.5f. was — precisely for the "diaspora" Pharisee — possible only in

---

[1]*Ibid.*, pp.10f.; Bornkamm, *Paulus*, pp.34f.

[2]Str.-Bill. ii, pp.150, 662; iv, p.121: Moore i, p.314; W.Schrage, $\sigma\upsilon\nu\alpha\gamma\omega\gamma\acute{\eta}$, *TDNT* vii, pp.824f.

[3]W.C. van Unnik, 'Tarsus or Jerusalem. The City of Paul's Youth', *Sparsa Collecta*, pp.259-320.

[4]This is the punctuation of the Nestle Greek text and the BFBS Greek text. See van Unnik, *op.cit.*, pp.272ff. for an argument for this punctuation.

[5]*Ibid.*, pp.296–299.

[6]Bultmann, 'Paulus', 1020f.; H.Conzelmann, *Geschichte des Urchristentums* (1971), p.65; Haenchen, *Apg.*, p.554, citing Bultmann, *op.cit.*

[7]Jeremias, *Jerusalem in the Time of Jesus* ([3]1976), pp.83f.

[8]van Unnik, *op.cit.*, p.301; H.Hübner, 'Gal 3.10 und die Herkunft des Paulus', *KD* 19(1973), p.228.

Jerusalem'[1], and, as G. Bornkamm observes, 'the sources available to us show Pharisaism as a Palestine movement and Jerusalem as its centre; about a *diaspora*-Pharisaism we know almost nothing'[2]. It seems somewhat incongruous to say this and at the same time to reject Luke's report that Paul's teacher was Gamaliel with the inadequate argument that the report betrays Luke's tendency to evaluate Pharisaism highly and to portray Paul as an orthodox Jew even after his conversion[3]. There is no inherent reason why Gamaliel the elder could not have been Paul's teacher[4].

But if it is almost certain that Paul received his education in Jerusalem, was he then also brought up there? The information in Acts (23.16), that Paul had a nephew in Jerusalem, may lend weight to this view[5]. However, can Paul's own testimony that he is a Ἑβραῖος (2Cor 11.22; Phil 3.5) shed some light upon the question?

The latest research by M. Hengel confirms the view that the 'Hellenists' of Acts 6.1 were the Jews in Palestine who spoke Greek as their mother-tongue[6] and the 'Hebrews' were the Jews in Palestine who spoke Aramaic (or Hebrew) as their mother-tongue[7]. Many of the 'Hellenists' were the Greek-

---

[1]M.Hengel, 'Die Ursprünge der christlichen Mission', *NTS* 18(1971/72), p.24; cf. also his 'Zwischen Jesus und Paulus. Die "Hellenisten", die "Sieben" und Stephanus (Apg 6, 1–15; 7, 54–8, 3)', *ZThK* 72(1975), pp.172f.

[2]Bornkamm, 'Paulus', 168.

[3]Bornkamm, *Paulus*, p.35; cf. his 'Paulus', 168; Haenchen, *Apg.*, p.554.

[4]Cf. J.Klausner, *From Jesus to Paul* (1946), p.310, who identifies Paul with the unnamed pupil of Gamaliel mentioned in b. Shab. 30b, who is said to have 'manifested impudence in matters of learning'. Cf. Bruce, *NT History*, p.225.

[5]Cf. Bornkamm, 'Paulus', 168, who does not think that the report about Paul's relatives in Jerusalem was invented by Luke. Similarly Burchard, *Zeuge*, p.32, thinks, 'Nothing speaks against its historicity'. Burchard judges further that though the present formulation in Acts 22.3 is Lucan, the tradition about Paul's upbringing and education in Jerusalem (cf. also Acts 26.4f.; 23.6) is pre-Lucan. He adds that, over against this, for Paul's upbringing and education in Tarsus we have no tradition, and appeals to stop 'so kindliche Argumente' as attributing some Hellenistic elements in Paul's letters to his Tarsus background (*ibid.*, p.35). To be fair, however, it must be pointed out that Burchard is open to the historicity of the pre-Lucan tradition but does not firmly decide for it (*ibid.*, pp.34f.).

[6]Hengel, 'Zwischen Jesus und Paulus', pp.157–169; cf. Bauer-Arndt-Gingrich, Ἑλληνιστής; H.Windisch,Ἑλληνιστής, *TDNT* ii, pp.511f.; H.J.Cadbury, 'The Hellenists', *Beginnings* v, pp.59–74; M.Simon, *St. Stephen and the Hellenists*(1958), pp.9ff.; C.F.D.Moule, 'Once More, Who Were the Hellenists?' *ExpT* 70(1958/59), 100–102; Haenchen, *Apg.*, pp.213ff.; J.N.Sevenster, *Do You Know Greek?* (1968), pp.31ff.; Bruce, *NT History*, pp.206ff.; O.Cullmann, *The Johannine Circle* (1976), pp.41f.

[7]Hengel, *op.cit.*, pp.169–171; cf. Bauer-Arndt-Gingrich, Ἑβραῖος; Str.-Bill. ii,

speaking *diaspora* who moved to live in Palestine[1]. And the 'Hebrews' were native to Palestine or at least closely bound to it in a special way[2]. In the *diaspora* 'the Hebrews' was the designation of the Jews who came from Palestine and organized themselves into a separate synagogue from the native Greek-speaking Jews[3]. By this designation, together with the Palestinian origin of the newly immigrant Jews, their Aramaic language and Palestinian culture must have been indicated[4]. When these 'Hebrews' in the *diaspora* ceased to be Ἐβραῖοι is not certain[5].

Against this background, Paul's claim to be Ἐβραῖος ἐξ Ἐβραίων (Phil 3.5) need mean nothing beyond that coming from the family which had a close connection with Palestine or even had only recently immigrated into the *diaspora*[6] he maintained the Aramaic language and the Palestinian custom even in the Greek-speaking environment[7]. So, Phil 3.5 is no help for solving the question of Paul's upbringing in Jerusalem. What about then 2Cor 11.22? Here the polemical question form: 'Are they Hebrews?', 'Are they Israelites?' and 'Are they Abraham's seed?', and Paul's reply 'κἀγώ' to each of

---

p.444; K.G.Kuhn & G.Gutbrod, Ἐβραῖος, *TDNT* iii, pp.359–69, 372–75, 389–91; and the literature cited in the note immediately preceding.

[1] See Bruce, *NT History,* pp.206ff. for evidence that apart from the *diaspora* who moved to Palestine there were also native 'Hellenists' in Palestine.

[2] Cf. Hengel, *op.cit.,* p.169.

[3] See Hengel, *op.cit.,* 178f.; Gutbrod, *op.cit.,* p.374f.; H.J.Leon, *The Jews of Ancient Rome* (1960), pp.147ff., 154ff.; Lietzmann-Kümmel, *Kor.,* p.150; Windisch, *2.Kor.,* pp. 350f.; Bruce, *Cor.,* p.240.

[4] This is so in the use of Ἐβραῖος by Philo and Josephus. See Gutbrod, *op.cit.,* pp.373f.; Hengel, *op.cit.,* pp.170f.

[5] The fact that the inscriptions of the synagogues of 'Hebrews' found in Rome (and also the one found in Corinth) were all written in Greek (with the exception of one bilingual Greek-Aramaic inscription), suggests that even after the 'Hebrews' gave up Aramaic and began to speak Greek they still maintained the designation. Cf. Hengel, *op.cit.,* p.179.

[6] According to Jerome Paul's family was brought from Gischala in Galilee to Tarsus as prisoners of war when Paul was an adolescent (*De viris illustribus,* 5). This information as a whole is hardly trustworthy. For if it is true that Paul received his Rabbinic training in Jerusalem the adolescent Paul must have found himself in a Rabbinic school in Jerusalem as according to Pirqe Aboth 5.21 it seems a pupil started his education in a Rabbinic school when he was 15. However, it may suggest that Paul's family were recent immigrants in Tarsus.

[7] So E.Lohmeyer, *Die Briefe an die Philipper, an die Kolosser und an Philemon* ([13]1964), p.130; M.Dibelius, *An die Thessalonicher I/II. An die Philipper* ([3]1937), pp.67f.; G.Friedrich, *Der Brief an die Philipper,* NTD 8(1962), p.117; F.W.Beare, *A Commentary on the Epistle to the Philippians,* (1958), p.107.

these questions, as well as the context (2Cor 11.21b), clearly indicate that Paul's opponents in Corinth boasted specifically of the designations[1], and so Paul feels obliged to counter their boasting by saying that in respect of his origin he is not inferior to them at all. Therefore the identity of his opponents in Corinth who boasted of being Ἑβραῖοι would indicate the sense in which Paul also claims himself to be Ἑβραῖος. If they were Christians drawn originally· from the synagogue of the 'Hebrews' in the *diaspora*[2], Paul's claim to be Ἑβραῖος may mean nothing more than that he was like them from a family which had its root in Palestine and spoke Aramaic. But if they were Jewish Christians native to Palestine[3] Paul's claim must probably mean more than that. For in order to match their boasting a relation with Palestine which is closer than that is required of him.

The kind of relation that Acts 22.3 envisages between Paul and Jerusalem might perhaps meet the requirement[4]. Yet a third possibility may be contemplated: Paul's opponents were 'Hellenists' in Jerusalem who, however, had lived there for a long time and spoke Aramaic as well as Greek, so that when they came out again into the *diaspora* world they could claim to be 'Hebrews', indicating thereby especially that they came from Palestine and spoke Aramaic[5]. Then with a perfect conscience Paul could counter their boasting with

---

[1]D.Georgi, *Die Gegner des Paulus im 2. Korintherbrief* (1964), pp.51–82. It is highly improbable that the three designations are mere synonyms used for the concept 'full Jew' (Gutbrod, Ἑβραῖος *TDNT* iii, p.390; Plummer, *2Cor.*, p.319; against Lietzmann-Kümmel, *Kor.*, p.150; G.Friedrich, 'Gegner', p.182; cf. also Barrett, *2Cor.*, pp.293f.).

[2]Georgi, *Gegner*, p.58, infers from the designation of the 'Hebrews' that Paul's opponents stemmed from the families who had not been *diaspora* for generations but who lived until recently in Palestine. He thinks that perhaps the opponents were even born and brought up in Palestine. But he locates them in the spiritual world of Hellenistic Judaism, which, he believes, used boasting to be 'Hebrews', 'Israelites' and 'Abraham's seed' as part of the propaganda in the mission and apologetic (pp.51–82).

[3]Kümmel in Lietzmann-Kümmel, *Kor.*, p.211; Barrett, *2Cor.*, pp.30, 294 (though it is not clear how Barrett can think on the one hand that 'Hebrew' means simply Jew (p.293) and accept on the other hand Kümmel's argument on the basis of the word 'Hebrew' that Paul's opponents were Palestinian Jews (p.294)); E.Käsemann, 'Die Legitimität des Apostels. Eine Untersuchung zu II. Korinther. 10–13' *ZNW* 41(1942), pp.36, 46; Barrett, 'Paul's Opponents in II Corinthians', *NTS* 17(1970/71), pp.251ff.; E.E.Ellis, 'Paul and his Opponents', *Prophecy and Hermeneutic* (1977), pp.103ff.

[4]It is true that the claim of Paul's opponents to be Ἑβραῖοι itself is drawn as an evidence for the Palestinian Jewish provenance of Paul's opponents in 2Cor. However, since most of those advocating the Palestinian Jewish provenance see some other pieces of evidence for it, it is not a circular argument to say that the reference to Ἑβραῖος in 2Cor 11.22 may point to Paul's close relationship with Jerusalem.

[5]Friedrich, 'Gegner', pp.181–215, suggests that the opponents were the Hellenistic Jewish Christians of Stephen's party, i.e., the 'Hellenists' of Acts 6.1. His delineation of

the same claim, that he is likewise a 'Hebrew'[1]. This possibility also presupposes, however, Paul's close relation with Jerusalem such as that which Acts 22.3 envisages.

Paul's good command of Greek, preference of the Septuagint over the Hebrew Bible, and display of some popular Hellenistic elements are not real objections to the view of Paul's early upbringing in Jerusalem. J.N. Sevenster has shown that Greek was widely used in Palestine even before A.D. 70 not only among the educated or Hellenized but also among the ordinary people[2]. So even the 'Hebrews', or at least some of them, could easily have spoken Greek as their secondary language[3]. If Paul, as Acts lets one presume (6.9; 7.58; 9.29)[4], belonged to the synagogue of the Hellenists in Jerusalem (Acts

---

the similarities in characteristics of the 'Hellenists' in Acts and Paul's opponents in 2Cor. is on the whole impressive. For a critique, however, see Barrett, 'Paul's Opponents in II Cor.', pp.235f. M.Hengel, 'Zwischen Jesus und Paulus', p.186 (n.125), thinks that in 2Cor. 'Paul is confronted with emissaries of a Jewish-Christian-Hellenistic mission (of Cephas-mission?)' and that Friedrich has 'correctly circumscribed the "milieu" of this Greek-speaking, Jewish-Christian-Palestine emissaries, even if we can determine their exact origin only hypothetically'. Cf. also Hengel, 'Ursprünge', p.28. It seems that Hengel hesitates to identify outright, as Friedrich does, Paul's opponents in 2Cor. with the 'Hellenists' of Acts. Presumably this reservation of Hengel's stems from the fact that the opponents called themselves 'Hebrews'. Friedrich avoids this difficulty by saying that the term 'Hebrew' is used differently in Acts and in 2Cor. and in 2Cor. it means simply 'Jew' (*op. cit.*, pp.197f.), which is unsatisfactory. However, may not our suggestion here advanced, by explaining the term 'Hebrew' in 2Cor 11 more satisfactorily than Friedrich, remove the ground of Hengel's hesitation to identify Paul's opponents in 2Cor. with the scattered missionaries of Stephen's party with whom Paul at first worked together and then later parted company (cf. Hengel, 'Ursprünge', p.28)? Even if Paul's opponents (ψευδαπόστολοι) in Corinth are to be thought of as emissaries of the 'pillars' of Jerusalem (ὑπερλίαν ἀπόστολοι) (so Käsemann, *op. cit.*, pp.41ff.; Barrett, 'Paul's Opponents', pp.242f., 252f.), which is questionable since it seems both ψευδαπόστολοι and ὑπερλίαν ἀπόστολοι designate the one and the same group of Paul's opponents in Corinth (so most commentators; Bultmann, 'Exegetische Probleme des zweiten Korintherbriefes', *Exegetica*, pp.319f.; Ellis, *op. cit.*, p.101), there is little difficulty in imagining that the former Jerusalem 'Hellenists' acted as emissaries of the 'pillars', especially of Peter, because the earlier conflict between them (Acts 6.1ff.) would not have lasted so long and especially because Peter himself seems to have joined the mission of the 'Hellenists' later (Gal 2.11).

[1] Cf. I.H.Marshall, 'Palestinian and Hellenistic Christianity: some critical comments', *NTS* 19 (1972/73), p.278.

[2] J.N.Sevenster, *Do You Know Greek?*, see esp. his conclusions in pp.176–91.

[3] Moule, *op. cit.*, pp.100ff.; Hengel, 'Zwischen Jesus und Paulus', p.172.

[4] Cf. Bruce, *The Book of the Acts*, (1970), p.133.; van Unnik, 'Tarsus or Jerusalem', p.299; Blank, *Paulus*, p.246.

6.9)[1], his good use of Greek and the Septuagint would be only natural. Moreover, it seems that sometimes the pupils of Rabbis were instructed also in Greek culture[2]. So Paul may have obtained the rudiments of Greek learning in Gamaliel's school[3]. Some of the Hellenistic influences in Paul's letters may also be traced to his acquaintance with the Hellenistic world later during his some 14 years residence in Syria and Cilicia after his conversion (Gal 1.21; 2.1) and also during his missionary journeys.[4] His preference of the Septuagint over the Hebrew Bible was due, besides his close acquaintance with it in the Hellenists' synagogue in Jerusalem, partly also to his dealing with the Greek-speaking Christians in his mission. But his occasional deviations from the Septuagint in favour of the original text show that he knew Hebrew and the Hebrew Bible well[5]. Indeed, van Unnik has emphasized that Paul's mother-tongue was Aramaic rather than Greek[6]. It may be that he was equally proficient in Greek and Aramaic and that he sometimes thought in Aramaic.

The real possibility of Paul's upbringing and education in Jerusalem weakens the basis of the view that his Tarsus background was an important factor for his becoming a missionary to the Gentiles later. His birth in Tarsus and his Roman citizenship (Acts 16.37; 22.25–28), which presupposes a relatively high social status, may have given him an awareness of the Empire, the larger world outside Judaism[7]. His return to Tarsus later (Acts 9.32; 11.25; Gal 1.21) shows that his connection with the city, whose citizen he was (Acts 21.39), was more than a nominal one[8]. At the time of Jesus and

---

[1]The question whether in the verse Luke has one synagogue, two or five in view, need not be discussed here.

[2]b,Sotah 49b. Josephus is an example of a Rabbinically trained Jew who was conversant with Greek learning (although he says in *Ant.* xx. 264 that he made an exceptional effort to master Greek). Cf. Hengel, 'Zwischen Jesus und Paulus', p.171.

[3]Bruce, *NT History*, p.125.

[4]*Ibid.*, pp.224, 233; van Unnik, *op. cit.*, pp.305f.

[5]See E.E.Ellis, *Paul's Use of the Old Testament* (1957), pp.12ff.; cf. Jeremias, *Schlüssel*, p.12.

[6]van Unnik, *op. cit.*, pp.304f., and see also his articles in the same volume, *Sparsa Collecta*: 'Aramaisms in Paul'; 'Reisepläne und Amen-Sagen. Zusammenhang und Gedankenfolge im 2.Korintherbrief i, 15–24'; and ' "With Unveiled Face". The Exegesis of 2 Corinthians iii, 12ff.'.

[7]W.D.Davies, 'The Apostolic Age and the Life of Paul', *Peake's Commentary on the Bible*, ed. H.H.Rowley & M.Black (1967), p.873.

[8]B.Rigaux, *Saint Paul, Les Epîtres aux Thessaloniciens* (1956), p.5, cited by van Unnik, 'Tarsus or Jerusalem', p.300 (n.2), who comments however that this fact does not affect his view of Paul's upbringing in Jerusalem.

Paul Jewish missionary propaganda seems to have reached its peak, and *diaspora* Judaism was the main bearer of it[1]. Hence, if Paul grew up in Tarsus, he would have gained early an awareness of the problem of winning Gentiles for Judaism. Nevertheless, it is certainly an exaggeration to say, as G. Bornkamm does[2], that 'the young Paul was predestined already as a Jew to become a Gentile-missionary' by his origin from Tarsus and his alleged education at the *diaspora* synagogue in the city[3].

On the basis of Gal 5.11 a number of scholars have suggested that Paul was a Jewish missionary before his conversion[4]. The verse runs: Ἐγὼ δέ, ἀδελφοί, εἰ περιτομὴν ἔτι[5] κηρύσσω, τί ἔτι διώκομαι; ἄρα κατήργηται τὸ σκάνδαλον τοῦ σταυροῦ. In this verse Paul seems to have in mind the Jewish Christian agitators who, in order to persuade the Galatian Christians to be circumcised, misinterpreted Paul's attitude to circumcision such as that expressed in 1Cor 7.18f.; Gal 5.6; 6.15, and, pointing to the case of Timothy's circumcision (Acts 16.3), said that Paul still advised circumcision when it suited his purpose[6]. The ἔτι in the protasis should mean 'still as in my pre-Christian days' because it is impossible to imagine that there was ever a time after Paul's conversion in which he preached circumcision. This means that he here implies that he had preached circumcision before his conversion. This may seem to confirm the view that Paul was a Jewish missionary.

But the fact of the matter is that in the Judaism of Paul's day there was no 'missionary' in the sense of one who is sent out by a religious community to propagate its faith. The traditions, whether the Rabbinic sayings about proselytes or the Hellenistic Jewish propaganda literature, contain little that would remotely indicate there was a conscious *sending* of missionaries out to

---

[1]According to Hengel, 'Ursprünge', p.23, 'eine Darstellung der jüdischen Mission wäre ein dringendes Desiderat'. In the following literature there are summaries, though fragmentary and inadequate, of the Jewish missionary activities: E.Schürer, *Geschichte des jüdischen Volkes im Zeitalter Jesu Christi* iii (1890), pp.162ff., 553ff.; *Beginnings* i, pp.164ff.; Str. -Bill. i, pp.924ff.; Moore i, pp.323ff.; K.G.Kuhn, προσήλυτος, *TDNT* vi, pp.730ff.; J.Jeremias, *Jesus' Promise to the Nations* (1958), pp.11ff.; Schoeps, *Paul*, pp.220ff.; F.Hahn, *Das Verständnis der Mission im NT* (1963), pp.15ff.; Georgi, *Gegner*, pp.83–187; Bornkamm, *Paulus*, pp.29ff.; Kasting, *Anfänge*, pp.11ff.

[2]Bornkamm, *Paulus*, p.33.

[3]Cf. W.D.Davies, *op. cit.*, p.873.

[4]E.Barnikol, *Die vorchristliche und frühchristliche Zeit des Paulus* (1929); pp.18ff.; Bultmann, 'Paulus', 1021; Bornkamm, *Paulus*, p.35; Hübner, 'Herkunft', p.222; cf. also M.Hengel, 'Ursprünge', p.23.

[5]The ἔτι should be read as original in spite of its absence in D*, G, and old Latin texts.

[6]Cf. Burton, *Gal.*, p.286; Schlier, *Gal.*, p.239.

win Gentiles for Judaism[1]. Rather, even the Judaism that was relatively open
to the Gentiles seems to have been mostly content with receiving Gentiles as
proselytes or 'God-fearers' who came to it on their own initiative[2]. Or, at
most, there were individual Jews who recruited to Judaism Gentiles who
came into contact with them in the course of their ordinary life[3]. The scribes
and Pharisees who are said to have traversed 'sea and land to make a single
proselyte' (Mt 23.15), are perhaps to be thought of in terms of such individuals, who, to be sure, must often have been so zealous as to undertake a
long journey if they saw the possibility of making a proselyte. If they were
to be thought of as (professional) missionaries deliberately sent out by their
Gemeinde, Mt 23.15 would be the only evidence for the existence of such
missionaries in Judaism. However, the fact that there is no title or designation
for a missionary in Judaism seems to argue against such an assumption[4].

Therefore, if Gal 5.11 implies that Paul 'preached'[5] circumcision in his
pre-Christian days, it does not mean that he did so as a Jewish *missionary*.
Probably his Jewish 'missionary' activities in which he advocated circumcision
are to be thought of as private, occasional proselytizing activities rather than
a regular, professional missionary enterprise[6].

---

[1]Moore i, p.324; Jeremias, *Promise*, pp.16f.; Munck, *Paul*, pp.264ff.; Hahn, *Mission*,
pp.16, 18; Wilson, *Gentiles*, pp.2f.; Kasting, *Anfänge*, p.20. The universalism of some
sections of Judaism has always been centripetal rather than centrifugal. It is not clear
whether the Hellenistic Jewish propaganda literature itself was written with the heathen
readers or the Jewish readers in mind. That is, it is not clear whether it aimed at winning
the pagans over to Judaism or protecting the Jews from pagan influence by denouncing
the stupidity of idolatry and other pagan ways and extolling Judaism (cf. Schürer,
Geschichte iii, pp.162ff.; Jeremias, *Promise*, pp.12ff.; Munck, *Paul*, pp.267ff.; Kasting,
Anfänge, pp.18f.).

[2]Cf. Str.-Bill. i, pp.925ff., for the Jewish insistence that Gentiles should take initiative in becoming proselytes.

[3]Cf. K.H.Rengstorf, ἀπόστολος, *TDNT* i, p.418; Wilson, *Gentiles*, p.2. Ananias the
merchant and Eleazer the strict Jew (a Pharisee?) from Galilee who, according to Josephus, *Ant.* xx. 34–48, made Izates the king of Adiabene a proselyte, would serve as
examples of such individuals. Probably they are not to be thought of as wandering missionaries in the model of the wandering preachers of Hellenistic popular philosophy (cf.
Georgi, *Gegner* pp.100ff.; against Georgi, see Kasting, *Anfänge*, p.20)

[4]O. Betz (orally). Cf. Rengstorf, *op.cit.*, p.418: שׁלִיחַ and its cognate words were
never linked with the 'missionary' activities of Judaism; also A.Oepke, 'Probleme der
vorchristlichen Zeit des Paulus', *Das Paulusbild in der neueren deutschen Forschung*, ed.
K.H.Rengstorf (1964), p.427.

[5]The περιτομὴν κηρύσσειν seems to be a Pauline formulation in analogy to his often
used phrase Χριστὸν κηρύσσειν (1Cor 1.23; 2Cor 4.5; Phil 1.15). Cf. Schlier, *Gal.*,
p.239; Oepke, *Gal.*, p.124.

[6]Cf. Rengstorf, *op. cit.*, p.418; Oepke, *Gal.*, p.124; Schlier, *Gal.*, p.238.

Paul makes clear his theological position before his conversion when he says of himself: 'according to the law a Pharisee' (Phil 3.5; cf. Acts 26.5). According to Acts 23.6 his parents were also Pharisees. For Paul the Pharisee the Torah was the decisive factor in his life, being the only and assured means of obtaining righteousness. So he was exceedingly zealous in learning and observing both the written and oral Torah and advanced in this far beyond his colleagues (Gal 1.14f.). Indeed, he could say, he was 'blameless according to the criterion of the righteousness that rests on the law' (Phil 3.6). This testimony of Paul about himself should be respected; it should not be claimed that he was unacquainted with Rabbinic Judaism of Palestine and knew only *diaspora* Judaism that was contaminated by Hellenism[1], or that his conception of the law was not Rabbinic but apocalyptic[2]. Paul certainly was an 'apocalyptic theologian'[3], but he was that as a Pharisee. For 'apocalyptic was by no means alien to Pharisaic Judaism' in Paul's day[4].

K. Haacker has attempted to define Paul's pre-Christian theological position more precisely from his association of 'zeal' with his persecution of the

---

[1]C.G.Montefiore, *Judaism and St. Paul* (1914), pp.93ff.; Schoeps, *Paul*, pp.213ff. Cf. also Klausner, *From Jesus to Paul*, p.312. Against this, see W.D.Davies, *Paul and Rabbinic Judaism* ([2]1955), pp.1ff.; W.G.Kümmel, 'Jesus und Paulus', *Heilsgeschehen und Geschichte* (1965), pp.449f.; cf. also O.Betz, 'Paulus als Pharisäer nach dem Gesetz: Phil. 3, 5–6 als Beitrag zur Frage des frühen Pharisäismus', *Treue zur Thora*, G. Harder FS, ed. P.v.d. Osten-Sacken (1977), pp.54–64.

[2]Following D.Rössler, *Gesetz und Geschichte* (1962), Wilckens, 'Bekehrung', pp. 20ff., distinguishes between the Rabbinic and the apocalyptic conception of the law: according to the former, the law was a bundle of God's commandments which should be obeyed; but according to the latter, the law was a unity and had the *heilsgeschichtliche* function of providing the proof of the election of Israel in this aeon. Wilckens maintains that only the supposition that Paul had this apocalyptic conception of the law explains Paul's insight into the *heilsgeschichtliche* turning from the law to Christ (Rom 10.4) which he gained at his conversion. But Rössler has been criticised by many, especially for his arbitrary selection of sources to arrive at the conclusion. See, e.g., Kümmel, *op. cit.*, p.450; A.Nissen, 'Tora und Geschichte im Spätjudentum', *NovT* 9(1967), pp.241–77; H.D.Betz, 'Apokalyptik in der Theologie der Pannenberg-Gruppe', *ZThK* 65(1968), pp.260ff. It is now generally recognised that the two conceptions that are distinguished by Rössler, one as Rabbinic and the other as apocalyptic, are found both in the Rabbinic and the apocalyptic literature, i.e., there is an essential agreement in the conception of the law between them.

[3]Wilckens, 'Bekehrung', p.24; Kümmel, *op. cit.*, p.450; cf. E.Käsemann, 'Zum Thema der urchristlichen Apokalyptik', *EVB* ii, pp.125ff.

[4]W.D.Davies, *Paul*, pp.9ff. (quotation from p.10); also his 'Apocalyptic and Pharisaism', *Christian Origins and Judaism* (1972), pp.19–30; D.S.Russell, *The Method and Message of Jewish Apocalyptic* (1964), pp.25ff.

Church (Gal 1.14; Phil 3.5; cf. also Acts 22.3f.)[1]. From the parallelism in Phil 3.5f.:

κατὰ νόμον Φαρισαῖος,
κατὰ ζῆλος διώκων τὴν ἐκκλησίαν

Haacker infers that 'zeal' here signifies not merely a psychological state but a theological category: 'Just as the law for Paul *qua* Pharisee was the norm which governed everything, so was zeal for Paul *qua* persecutor the norm which obliged him to persecute, the determining motive'[2]. Paul's testimony about his pre-Christian days to the Jerusalem mob seeking to kill him, '(I was) a zealot for God as you all are today' (Acts 22.3), indicates, according to Haacker, that the word 'zeal' is a concept for violent religious intolerance such as that which Paul displayed before his conversion and to which now he himself is subjected[3]. Having shown this, Haacker connects the pre-conversion Paul with the spiritual tradition of the Maccabees and the Zealots.

The Maccabean uprising started when out of zeal for the law Mattathias killed an Israelite apostate who offered sacrifice to idols in obedience to the command of Antiochus Epiphanes (1Macc 2.23ff.). In this act Mattathias is compared with Phinehas, who by slaying an apostate Israelite out of his zeal for God became the prototype of the 'zealot' (Num 25.1–18; Ps 106.31; Sir 45.23; 1Macc 2.26, 54; 4Macc 18.12)[4]. The Maccabees were in some sense the precursors of the Zealots[5]; and they shared, among other things, the prototype Phinehas and his zeal, and the primary religious motive of their struggles, which were directed first against the apostate Israelites and then against the oppressive heathen powers[6]. The goal of their zeal for God and the law was 'to recover the purity of Israel, her faith and Temple through spontaneous punishment of the trespassers of the law'[7]. The killing of apostates was apparently thought to have the effect of atoning sacrifice for

---

[1]K.Haacker, 'Die Berufung des Verfolgers und die Rechtfertigung des Gottlosen', *Theol. Beiträge* 6 (1975), pp.5ff.

[2]*Ibid.*, p.8. At this point Haacker refers to E.Lohmeyer, *Phil.*, p.130.

[3]Haacker, 'Berufung', p.8.

[4]Cf. W.R.Farmer, *Maccabees, Zealots and Josephus* (1956), pp.177f.; M.Hengel, *Die Zeloten* (1961), pp.69f.; Bruce, *NT History*, pp.88f.; Dupont, 'The Conversion of Paul', p.184.

[5]Farmer; *Maccabees, passim;* Hengel, *Zeloten*, pp.176ff.

[6]*Ibid.*; Haacker, 'Berufung', p.9.

[7]Hengel, *Zeloten*, p.70.

God's wrath upon Israel for apostasy[1]. The Rabbinic interpretation of Num 25.13 draws a parallel between killing apostates and offering sacrifice: ' . . . if a man sheds the blood of the wicked it is as though he had offered a sacrifice'[2]. According to Haacker, Jn 16.2 gives evidence that the Christians could be included among the 'wicked' thus to be killed: 'The time is coming when everyone who kills you will think that he is offering a sacrifice to God'[3]. From all this, Haacker concludes that Paul's persecution of the Christians out of zeal for the law shows that he belonged to this spiritual tradition[4]: not that Paul belonged to a zealotic organization[5]; but rather that he belonged to the radical wing of the Pharisaic movement, perhaps the school of Shammai[6].

If this is so, there is no ground for the presumption that before his conversion, following the tradition of Hillel[7], Paul must have been rather open to mission to the Gentiles, if he himself was not actually engaged in it[8]. On the

---

[1]Sifre Num. 131. Cf. Hengel, *Zeloten*, p.161f., 164,; Haacker, 'Berufung', p.9; Farmer, *Maccabees*, p.178.

[2]Num. R. 21.3. Cf. Hengel, *Zeloten*, p.164; Haacker, 'Berufung', p.10.

[3]*Ibid.*; cf. Str.-Bill. ii, p.565.

[4]Haacker, 'Berufung', p.10; cf. Farmer, *Maccabees,* pp.178f., who makes a very similar suggestion.

[5]Cf. Hengel, *Zeloten*, p.184; Bruce, *NT History*, p.89.

[6]Haacker, 'Berufung', p.10. When in his article 'Paulus als Hillelit' in *Neotestamentica et Semitica*, Studies in Honour of M. Black (1969), pp.88–94, J.Jeremias attempted to prove that Paul was a Hillelite from his theological characteristics and method of exegesis, he was in fact seeking to provide a firm ground to the widely held belief arising out of Acts 22.3 that Paul sat at Gamaliel's feet. But this view has been challenged by K. Haacker, 'War Paulus Hillelit?', *Das Institutum Judaicum der Universität Tübingen 1971–72*, pp.106–120; and Hübner, 'Herkunft', pp.215–231. The former questions closely the validity of each point that Jeremias has raised to prove that Paul was a Hillelite. From an examination of the theological background underlying Gal 3.10 (and also 5.3) the latter comes to the conclusion that Paul was on the contrary a Shammaite. And both question the traditional view that Gamaliel the elder was a Hillelite. Haacker supports himself with J.Neusner's study on Gamaliel I in his *The Rabbinic Traditions about the Pharisees before 70*, Part I (1971), pp.341–76, which sees little evidence for linking Gamaliel I with the school of Hillel but finds on the contrary Gamaliel standing nearer to Shammai than to Hillel.

[7]b.Shab. 31a contrasts between the attitudes of Shammai and Hillel to the Gentiles. The latter is said to have won three proselytes through his liberal attitude to proselytism and through his gentleness to the Gentiles in contrast to the former's strictness and un-friendliness. In this connection Pirqe Aboth 1.12 is also often cited: 'Hillel used to say: Be thou the disciples of Aaron, loving peace and pursuing peace, (Be thou) one who loveth (one's fellow-) creatures and bringeth them nigh to the Torah'. Cf. Moore i, pp.341f.

[8]Cf. Hengel, 'Ursprünge', p.23.

contrary, it may be presumed that he was rather hostile to the Gentiles and had little interest in winning them for Judaism[1].

2 Paul the Persecutor

It was, therefore, as a 'zealot' for the law and the ancestral traditions that Paul persecuted the Church (1Cor 15.9; Gal 1.13f.; Phil 3.6; Acts 9.1ff; 22.3ff.; 26.9ff.). The foregoing description of Paul's radical Pharisaic theological position makes it easy to understand why Paul persecuted the Christians: namely because he saw them as apostates of the law. This leads to Luke's account of Stephen's martyrdom (Acts 6–7). According to Acts 6.11, 13f. Stephen is accused by the Jews of the Hellenist synagogue(s) in Jerusalem of blaspheming the Temple and the law. There are good grounds for holding that this is not a Lucan invention but reflects the Jewish charge of the Hellenist Jewish Christians' criticism of the Temple and the law[2]. The Hellenist Jewish Christians who experienced the Pentecostal outpouring of the Holy Spirit as the gift of the last days took over Jesus' eschatological and critical interpretation of the Mosaic law and the Temple[3]. Some have suggest-

---

[1]Hübner, 'Herkunft', pp.222f., thinks that before his conversion Paul was a Shammaite missionary among the Gentiles. As he argues, the ideas in Gal 3.10, 22; 5.3, behind which there seems to lie the Rabbinic tradition that a proselyte is obliged with his circumcision to keep the whole law, i.e., all the individual commandments of the law without exception (see the references in Moore i, p.331), suggest that in the matters of proselytism the Pharisee Paul represented the strict view of Shammai (cf. b.Shab. 31a) rather than the liberal view of Hillel, who summarised the entire Torah in a single sentence, the negative formulation of the 'golden rule', for a would-be proselyte (b.Shab. 31a). But it has been already denied above that one can picture on the basis of Gal 5.11 the pre-conversion Paul as a Jewish missionary. The linking of Paul with the school of Shammai seems to strengthen this denial. Moore i, p.341, presents R.Eliezer ben Hyrcanus (c. 90A.D.) as 'a true heir of Shammai's spirit' in his attitude to the Gentiles and proselytes with his alleged sayings such as that there is a bad streak in proselytes (Mekilta Ex. 22.20) or that the 'enemy' in Ex 23.4 refers to a proselyte who has relapsed into his old ways (Mekilta Ex 23.4). Even if R.Eliezer's attitude cannot be looked upon as typical of the school of Shammai before the fall of Jerusalem (cf. Str.-Bill i, pp.924ff. for the increasingly negative attitude to proselytism after A.D.70), it, together with the attitude of Shammai, seems to suggest at least that the Shammaites were not very enthusiastic about proselytes. In spite of the bad opinion about proselytes, could a Shammaite have been a missionary to make proselytes? This consideration of Paul as a Shammaite seems only to strengthen the interpretation of Gal 5.11 offered above, namely that it does not envisage the pre-conversion Paul as a (regular) missionary; it points at most to Paul's having been engaged in private, occasional proselytizing activities. As a Shammaite he would take little initiative on his part to proselytize Gentiles. However, if he met a would-be proselyte, he would lay the stringent condition before him that he should not only be circumcised but also with the circumcision take upon himself the obligation to keep the whole law (cf. Gal 3.10; 5.3).

[2]Cf. Hengel, 'Ursprünge', p.26.

[3]See Hengel, 'Zwischen Jesus und Paulus', pp.191ff., where he shows the Spirit-

ed that the Hellenists thought the Mosaic law was completely abrogated by the Christ-event, and that they founded the law-free Gentile mission[1]. But the criticism of the law by the Hellenists does not seem to have been so advanced. M. Hengel is probably right in contending that the Hellenists saw only the Temple cult and the ritual part of the law as abrogated, while still keeping the Decalogue and the ethical side of the law[2]. Luke's joining of the Temple *and* the law as the objects of Stephen's criticism may support this view[3]. But Hengel's other observation seems to be of more weight: the charge that Stephen preached 'Jesus of Nazareth . . . will change the customs that Moses delivered to us' (Acts 6.14), suggests that Stephen thought of Jesus more as a new law-giver than as 'the end of the law' (Rom 10.4)[4]. Carrying on the criticism of the Temple by Jesus (Mk 11.15–18 & par.; 14.58 & par.) and reinforced by their conviction that the death of Jesus was an atonement offered once for all 'for our sins' (1Cor 15.3), the Hellenists saw the Temple cult as not only superfluous but positively objectionable. Together with the cultic law they must have attacked also the casuistic commandments for ritual purification, since Jesus taught that what matters is not the external observances of such commandments but the pure heart (Mk 7.1–23 & par.). While criticising the externalism of the cultic and ritual law, they must have emphasized the true obedience of the heart to God's will which was revealed anew by the Messiah Jesus, especially the commandment of love (Mk 12.28–34 & par.). It may well be, as Hengel suggests[4], that the Hellenists correctly understood Jesus' setting himself over against Moses and his substitution of the new, radically internalized ethical commandments for the Mosaic law, which are implied, for example, in the antithesis: 'You have heard that it was said to the men of old . . . But I say to you . . .' (Mt 5.21ff.) and that they

---

inspired eschatological enthusiasm of the Hellenists as the basis of their criticism of the law and the Temple, and also outlines the line of their criticism; also his 'Ursprünge', pp.29ff. Cf. also W.Manson, *The Epistle to the Hebrews* (1951), pp.25–46. For the charismatic nature of Stephen's party, see also Friedrich, 'Gegner', pp.199ff.

[1] F.Hahn, *Der urchristliche Gottesdienst* (1970), pp.50f.; W.Schrage, ' "Ekklesia" und "Synagoge" ', *ZThK* 60 (1963), pp.196ff.; W.Schmithals, *Paulus und Jakobus*, (1963), p.20.

[2] Hengel, 'Ursprünge', pp.27ff.; 'Zwischen Jesus und Paulus', pp.191ff. In both places Hengel argues for the legitimacy of differentiating the ritual law and the ethical law, against F.Hahn, who thinks there is no basis in the NT for such a differentiation (*op. cit.*, p.50). Cf. also P. Stuhlmacher, *Evangelium*, pp.251f.

[3] Hengel, 'Ursprünge', p.27.

[4] Hengel, 'Zwischen Jesus und Paulus', p.191.

[5] Hengel, 'Ursprünge', pp.28f.; 'Zwischen Jesus und Paulus', pp.191f. (esp. n. 137), 195f.

saw Jesus as the new law-giver and his teaching as the new Torah of the messianic age, inaugurated by his death and resurrection and confirmed by the experience of the Spirit[1].

Now Paul, the 'zealot' for the Mosaic law and the ancestral tradition, could hardly bear such an attack upon the law and the Temple cult, two of the three pillars upon which according to Pirqe Aboth 1.2 the world rests (the last being good works). So Paul persecuted the Christians who by such an attack proved themseves to be apostates in his eyes. Paul's joining of his persecution of the Church with his zeal for the law (Gal 1.13; Phil 3.5f.; Acts 22.3f.) certainly shows that the Christians' criticism of the law was the main reason for his persecution. But it does not seem to have been the only reason. The Christian proclamation of the crucified Jesus of Nazareth as the Messiah seems also to have been an offence that provoked his wrath.

In Gal 3.13, in order to show that Christ bore the curse of the law on our behalf, the curse that falls upon all who do not keep the whole law, Paul quotes Dt 21.23: 'Cursed is everyone who is hanged on a tree' (LXX). The original text envisages hanging the corpse of a criminal stoned to death until the sunset. But 4QpNah. 3–4, I.7f. and the Temple Scroll of Qumran 64.6–13 show that already in the pre-Christian period Dt 21.23 was applied to crucifixion and that the crucified was regarded as accursed by God[2]. So the Jews must have looked upon the crucified Jesus as accursed by God. To them the Christian proclamation of the crucified Jesus as the Messiah was a contradiction in terms. The Jewish sentiment about the crucified Jesus is well represented by Trypho when he, pointing to Dt 21.23, rejects the messiahship of Jesus[3]. The allusions to Dt 21.23 in Acts 5.30; 10.39; 13.29; 1Pet 2.24 suggest that from the beginning the Christians encountered Jewish opposition based upon Dt 21.23 to their proclamation of Jesus as the Messiah. The Christians would hardly have applied Dt 21.23 to Jesus on their own initiative. Rather, they must have taken it from their Jewish opponents, and turned it into a weapon of counter-attack. For God, by raising Jesus from the dead, vindicated him and at the same time condemned the Jews who delivered his

---

[1] For Jesus' attitude to the law of Moses, see R.Banks, *Jesus and the Law in the Synoptic Gospels* (1975).

[2] See Y.Yadin, 'Pesher Nahum (4Q pNahum) Reconsidered', *IEJ* 21(1971), pp. 1–12; G.Jeremias, *Der Lehrer der Gerechtigkeit* (1963), pp.133ff.; M.Hengel, 'Mors turpissima crucis', *Rechtfertigung*, E.Käsemann FS, ed. J.Friedrich *et al.* (1976), pp.176ff.; M.Wilcox, ' "Upon the Tree" – Deut. 21:22–23', *JBL* 96(1977), pp.85–99.

[3] Justin Martyr, *Dial.*, 39.7; 89.1–90.1; cf. also the Gospel of Nichodemus, 16.7. See E.Fascher, *Jesaja 53 in christlicher und jüdischer Sicht* (1958), pp.22f., for a discussion of both places.

Messiah to be crucified at the hands of the Gentiles[1].

Apart from Gal 3.13, 1Cor 1.23 and Gal 5.11 prove that Paul himself found the cross a scandal. Paul must have judged the Christian proclamation of the crucified Jesus as the Messiah to be a blasphemy against God[2]. For in his view God could not possibly have made him the Messiah whom he had cursed. To claim that Jesus was the Messiah was to attribute self-contradiction to God. So Paul, the 'zealot' for God's honour, was compelled to persecute the Christians. Dt 21.23 must have been a catch-phrase of Paul when he went about persecuting the Christians[3].

Now it has been repeatedly asserted that the Christian proclamation of the crucified Jesus as the Messiah was not a reason for the Jewish persecution, even though it certainly presented to the Jews a stumbling-block[4]. R. Akiba's proclamation of Bar Kochba as the Messiah in A.D. 132 is often cited to show that there were many Messiah-pretenders and their adherents in Judaism who were not persecuted for their wrong claims[5]. But the critics seem often to forget that there is no real parallel between proclaiming the Messiahship of Jesus and that of Bar Kochba. The latter was a national hero who seemed to be about to deliver Israel from the Romans. But the former was one who was crucified under the pronouncement of God's curse by the law (Dt 21.23). Thus to proclaim the crucified Jesus as the Messiah was positively a blasphemy against God and a transgression of the law; and, moreover, it was also a strong reproach to the Jews for their guilt of delivering the Messiah to the Romans for crucifixion (Acts 5.30f.; 10.39f.; 13.29f.). To this provocation the answer of Paul the 'zealot' could only be persecution.

However, the two offences, the criticism of the law and the proclamation of the crucified Jesus as the Messiah, belonged together: the Christians criticised the law in the name of Jesus the Messiah. Their criticism of the law was based not only on the example and teaching of Jesus but also on the

---

[1]Cf. B.Lindars, *NT Apologetic* (1961), pp.232–237; Bruce, *NT History*, p.228. Wrenching Dt 21.23 from the Jewish opponents, the early Christians developed from it soteriological insights into the death of Christ (*infra* pp.274ff.).

[2]Bruce, *NT History*, p.228; J.Jeremias, *Der Opfertod Jesu Christi* (1963), p.13.

[3]P.Feine, *Das gesetzesfreie Evangelium des Paulus* (1899), p.18, is acknowledged as having first recognized this. See G.Jeremias, *op.cit.*, pp.133ff.; J.Jeremias, *op.cit.*, pp.14f.; Bruce, *NT History*, p.228; J.Blank, *Paulus*, p.245; Stuhlmacher, "Ende", p.29; Ph.H.Menoud, 'Revelation and Tradition', *Interpretation* 7 (1953), p.133; W.G. Kümmel, *Die Theologie des NT* (1972), pp.133f.

[4]Bultmann, 'Paulus', 1021; Bornkamm, 'Paulus', 169; *Paulus*, p.38; W.Schrage, ' "Ekklesia" und "Synagoge" ', pp.197f.; J.Dupont, 'The Conversion of Paul', pp.187ff.; Kasting, *Anfänge*, p.54.

[5]Bornkamm, *Paulus*, p.38; Schrage, *op. cit.*, p.198.

saving significance of his cross and resurrection. So Paul was confronted with the alternative: either the law or the crucified Christ[1].

These considerations suggest that it was the Hellenist Jewish Christians in Jerusalem who bore the brunt of Paul's persecution. For it was they who were critical of the Temple-cult and the law while it seems that the 'Hebrew' Christians were tolerably conforming to the traditions. To be sure, the 'Hebrew' Christians must have also proclaimed the crucified Jesus as the Messiah and relaxed, though not to the same degree as their 'Hellenist' brethren, the chain of the law under the influence of Jesus at least during the early years before James took over the leadership from Peter in Jerusalem[2]. If the ἡμᾶς in the quoted saying, 'He who once persecuted *us* is now preaching the faith which he formerly tried to destroy' (Gal 1.23), includes 'the churches in Judaea' (Gal 1.22)[3], as it seems it does, then the 'Hebrew' Christians did not escape Paul's persecution completely unscathed[4]. Nevertheless, because of their more conservative attitude to the law they seem to have suffered far less than their 'Hellenist' brethren and were able to stay on in

---

[1]Bultmann, 'Paulus', 1021; Bornkamm, 'Paulus', 169. Thus the alternative – the law or Christ – was presented to Paul by the Hellenist Jewish Christians' criticism of the law in the name of the crucified Christ, rather than by his apocalyptic conception of the law (against Wilckens, 'Bekehrung', pp.16ff.). Cf. Stuhlmacher, "Ende", p.29; Schrage, *op.cit.*, p.198.

[2]Hengel, 'Zwischen Jesus und Paulus', p.199, suggests that there was this change of leadership in Jerusalem between the persecution of Agrippa I and the apostolic council (i.e., between 44 and 48/49 A.D.) (cf. Acts 12.17 & see the comments of Haenchen *Apg.,* p.335 and Stählin, *Apg.*, pp.169f.; Gal 2.9) and that with the change the Jerusalem church became stricter in observing the law. A similar suggestion was made already by T.W. Manson, *Studies in the Gospels and Epistles* (1962), pp.195ff.; O.Cullmann, *Petrus: Jünger – Apostel – Märtyrer* ([2]1960), pp.46f.; Πέτρος, *TDNT* vi, pp.109f.

[3]So Oepke, *Gal.*, p.38; Mussner, *Gal.*, p.99; W.G.Kümmel, 'Römer 7 und die Bekehrung des Paulus', *Römer 7 und das Bild des Menschen im NT* (1974), p.152; Ch. Burchard, *Zeuge*, p.50; cf. also Schlier, *Gal.*, p.63.

[4]Some have argued that Gal 1.22 excludes any possibility of Paul's persecution activity in Jerusalem or Judaea (Haenchen, *Apg.*, p.248; Stählin, *Apg.,* p.118; Bornkamm, *Paulus*, p.38). So Damascus and the surrounding region is suggested as the place of Paul's persecution activity (Haenchen, *Apg.*, p.249; Bornkamm, 'Paulus', 169; Conzelmann, *Geschichte des Urchristentums*, p.65; Stuhlmacher, *Evangelium*, p.74). But Gal 1.22 can hardly mean, as the critics assume, that Paul was literally unknown to any member of the churches in Judaea (which, as generally recognized, include the church in Jerusalem). This seems already contradicted by Gal 1.18f., where Paul says he went to Jerusalem to visit Peter and stayed with him for a fortnight. During his stay in Jerusalem he saw only Peter and James 'among the apostles', perhaps other apostles being away. So Paul is already known personally at least to two members of the church in Jerusalem. And can it be imagined that he saw no other *Christians* there, no matter

Jerusalem while the latter were driven out[1]. So it was the 'Hellenist' Christians who were the main target of Paul's campaign. M. Hengel has well written: 'Paul's confession that he not only "persecuted beyond measure" but, still further, "destroyed" the church of God (ἐπόρθουν αὐτήν. Gal 1.13; cf. 1.23 and Acts 9.21)[2], fits best with the driving out of Stephen's party. Here was "destroyed" a concrete church'[3].

These expressions in Gal 1.13 already point to the use of force in his persecution. Further, his mention of 'zeal' in connection with his persecution activity (Gal 1.14; Phil 3.6; cf. Acts 22.3) suggests that after the examples of Phinehas, Mattathias and the like he violently persecuted Christians — the apostates in his eyes[4]. Calling down curses upon the crucified Jesus on the basis of Dt 21.23 (cf. 1Tim 1.13), he attacked anyone who called upon the name of Jesus as the Messiah or the Lord, and forced him to blaspheme,

---

how private or even how secret the visit might have been? It seems more natural to interpret Gal 1.22 as meaning that Paul was personally unknown to the *churches* in Judaea (as a whole), yes, the churches in *Judaea*, although he was known personally to some members of the church in Jerusalem (cf. Burton, *Gal.*, p.60; Schlier, *Gal.*, p.63). This leads us to think that even if Paul persecuted the Christians in Jerusalem and therefore was known to some of them he could still say after a decade and half what he says in Gal 1.22. Even if the Lucan description of Paul's searching house to house for Christians (Acts 8.3) is true, it would hardly be the case that he persecuted *all* the Christians in this manner. The number of Christians who were directly attacked by Paul may not have been great (cf. Oepke, *Gal.*, p.39; Mussner, *Gal.*, p.99). Blank, *Paulus*, p.246, and Hengel, 'Zwischen Jesus und Paulus', pp.196f., have made efforts to affirm Paul's persecution activity in Jerusalem by insisting that he persecuted only the 'Hellenist' Christians, who had scarcely anything to do with the 'Hebrew' Christians, and therefore that he was unknown to the latter. But it is probably more sensible historically to modify the thesis: the target of Paul's persecution having been mainly the 'Hellenist' Christians, there may not have been many among the 'Hebrew' Christians who were directly affected by Paul's campaign, so that Paul could say what he says in Gal 1.22 (and also 1.23).

[1]It may be, as Hengel supposes ('Zwischen Jesus und Paulus', p.199), that the 'Hebrew' Christians had to accommodate their views with the pressures of the Jewish population around them for a stricter observance of the law in order to survive in Judaea, while the 'Hellenist' Christians, having the way back to the *diaspora* open, could afford to be less accommodating. The result of the 'Hebrew' Christians' accommodation was their 're-Judaizing' over against the attitude and message of Jesus (Stählin, *Apg.*, p.117).

[2]The word πορθεῖν occurs only in these three places in the NT.

[3]Hengel, 'Zwischen Jesus and Paulus', p.172; cf. also Bruce, *NT History*, p.215. See Burchard, *Zeuge*, pp.26–31 (esp. n.23) for the grounds supporting the view that Paul participated in the persecution of Stephen. Cf. also Bruce, *op.cit.*, p.226; Blank, *Paulus*, p.245.

[4]K.Haacker, 'Berufung', pp.8ff.; Dupont, 'The Conversion of Paul', pp.183ff.

probably, to call Jesus accursed (Acts 26.9–11)[1]. It seems probable that the formula 'Cursed is Jesus' (1Cor 12.3) was already what Paul forced his victims to pronounce[2]. Anyone who refused to do this he would hand over to punishment, perhaps of the kind which he himself was later to experience at the hands of the Jews for the sake of the name of Jesus Christ (2Cor 11.24f.)[3]. When the Hellenist Jewish Christians of Jerusalem were scattered by the persecution he pursued them to Damascus – there, however, to come to the most critical moment of his life.

---

[1]G.Jeremias, *Lehrer*, p.135; J.Jeremias, *Opfertod*, p.14; Bruce, *The Book of the Acts*, p.490.

[2]G.Jeremias, *loc. cit.*; J.Jeremias, *loc. cit.* See J.D.M.Derrett, 'Cursing Jesus (1Cor xii. 3): The Jews as Religious "Persecutors" ', *NTS* 21(1975), pp.544–54, for the view that the formula ΑΝΑΘΕΜΑ ΙΗΣΟΥΣ stems from the context of the Jewish persecution of the Christians. Cf. also A.Schlatter, *Der Bote*, pp.332ff.

[3]The scourging in the synagogue could sometimes result in death. See Hengel, 'Zwischen Jesus und Paulus', p.189 (n. 133).

Chapter III   The Damascus Event

1 'Preparations'?

Paul's persecution of the Church presupposes that before his conversion he knew at least part of the Hellenist Jewish Christian kerygma: that Jesus is the Messiah; that he was crucified, but was raised by God from the dead and exalted to be the 'Lord'; and that through him the law of Moses was fundamentally devalued as the way of salvation and part of it completely abrogated. Without the presupposition of this knowledge Paul's persecuting activity cannot be explained. Whether this knowledge can be regarded as a 'preparation' for his conversion is a semantic question[1]. However, it certainly cannot be regarded as having persuaded Paul and thus led to his conversion[2].

However, there have been many attempts to elucidate the psychological preparation for Paul's conversion[3]. Sometimes it is presumed that the constancy of the Christians under persecution must have made a deep impression upon the persecutor Paul and that his fanatic persecution was the expression of his repressed inner doubt about Judaism. Some have been led to see a psychological preparation in the proverb: 'It is hard for you to kick against the goads' (Acts 26.14) and in the conflict of the man under the law described in Rom 7. But the proverb in Acts 26.14 can, and probably should (cf. Acts 26.9), be understood as meaning simply that it is pointless to resist divinity, without any implication that Paul's conscience was pricked when he persecuted Christians in order to resist being persuaded by the rightness of their

---

[1]Cf. Blank, *Paulus*, pp.247f.; Kasting, *Anfänge*, p.55; Bornkamm, *Paulus*, pp.45f.; Stuhlmacher, "Ende", pp.28f.; Kuss, *Paulus*, p.286.

[2]*Contra* R.Bultmann, *Theology* i, p.187:   Paul was won for the Christian faith through the kerygma of the Hellenistic Church. Cf. Blank, *Paulus*, p.248: 'Sie (the above mentioned points of the kerygma known to Paul) erklären, wie Paulus zum Verfolger der Ekklesia Gottes wurde. Wie er zum Apostel des Gekreuzigten wurde, erklären sie nicht mehr und können sie nicht erklären. Das ist . . . sowohl historisch wie psychologisch *unableitbar*' (emphasis by B.).

[3]Kümmel, *Römer 7*, pp.154ff. and the literature cited there.

message[1]. And W.G. Kümmel has shown that it is impossible to interpret Rom 7 autobiographically[2]. Through a careful exegesis he comes to the conclusion that the first person singular in Rom 7.7−25 is not autobiographical but rhetorical or stylistic[3], and that here Paul describes the non-Christian, i.e., the man under the law, as needing redemption, from the Christian standpoint[4]. But while Kümmel contents himself with the conclusion that the 'I' of Rom 7 is everyman and Rom 7 is not a description of a definite experience but a 'general, more or less theoretical description of the thought that the law of sin must lead to man's death and that the man under the law therefore does not come out of the state of impotency'[5], E. Käsemann argues more concretely that in Rom 7.9−11 the subject is Adam, who incorporates mankind in himself, so that his experience with the law is described in the verses as the prototype of man's experience with the law[6], and that in Rom 7.14ff. the subject is 'the man in the shadow of Adam'[7]. Käsemann also emphasizes that Paul describes the situation of Adam and the Adamitic man under the law from his Christian standpoint[8].

This true observation, usually made against the attempts to interpret Rom 7 autobiographically and psychologically, is, however, not to be understood as meaning that there is in Rom 7 no reflection whatsoever of Paul's

---

[1]Cf. *ibid.,* pp.155ff.; Munck, *Paul,* pp.20ff.; Haenchen, *Apg.,* p.611.

[2]Kümmel, *Römer 7,* esp. pp.74ff.

[3]*Ibid.,* pp.87ff., 118−126.

[4]*Ibid.,* pp.118, 132ff. This view is nowadays widely accepted among the continental authors. E.g., Bultmann, 'Römer 7 und die Anthropologie des Paulus', *Exegetica,* pp. 198ff.; G.Bornkamm, 'Sünde, Gesetz und Tod', *Das Ende des Gesetzes* (1958), pp.53ff.; P. Althaus, *Der Brief an die Römer* ([10]1966), pp.74ff.; S.Lyonnet, *Les étapes du mystère du salut selon l'épître aux Romains* (1969), pp.113ff.; U.Luz, *Das Geschichtsverständnis des Paulus* (1968), pp.158ff.; E.Käsemann, *Römer,* p.183; R.Schnackenburg, 'Römer 7 im Zusammenhang des Römerbriefes', *Jesus und Paulus,* W.G.Kümmel FS, ed. E.E.Ellis & E.Grässer (1975), pp.283ff. It goes without saying that these authors still differ from one another considerably in their understanding of the details of Rom 7. Cf. J.D.G.Dunn, 'Rom.7, 14−25 in the Theology of Paul', *ThZ* 31 (1975), pp.257−273, who ably defends the classical view that in Rom 7 Paul describes the *Christian* experience.

[5]Kümmel, *Römer 7,* p.132.

[6]Käsemann, *Römer,* p.186; also Lyonnet, *op. cit.,* pp.113ff.; Schnackenburg, *op. cit.,* pp.293f. See Kümmel, *Römer 7,* pp.85ff., for earlier authors who interpreted Rom 7.7−13 similarly in terms of Adam and the 'corporate personality'. Cf. Bornkamm, *op. cit.,* pp.58f.; Luz, *op. cit.,* pp.166f.; C.H.Dodd, *The Epistle of Paul to the Romans* (1970), pp.123ff.

[7]Käsemann, *Römer,* p.190; Schnackenburg, *op. cit.,* p.295.

[8]Käsemann, *Römer,* p.183 *et passim.*

real experience in his Pharisaic past[1]. To be sure, no pious Jew, and certainly not the zealous and successful Pharisee Paul, could say that the law is a spur to sin[2]. But it is hardly conceivable that Paul was unaware of the very human experience that prohibition tends to awaken desire to do what is forbidden. Despite the deep consciousness of sin and pessimism about fulfilling the law that 4 Ezra (7.65ff., 116ff.; 8.35; 9.36, etc.) shows, it is difficult to believe that the zealous and successful Pharisee Paul thought so radically that being 'sold under sin' (Rom 7.14) it was impossible for him to obtain righteousness by the law. But again it is scarcely conceivable that he did not have the very human experience of the inner conflict between the will to do good and the actual act of evil, and that he never had any doubt about his ability to keep the law and was never troubled by it[3]. To deny to Paul these human, all too human, experiences is to make him twice divine. For it would imply that Paul was a super-human being who was exempted from such experiences as are common to man, and yet that without having suffered them, he could still describe them as vividly as he does in Rom 7[4]. Furthermore, it is to rob Paul's statements about the freedom in Christ from the law of their empirical reality. For he who has had no experience of the bondage of the law (of sin) cannot know freedom from it, either. It is probably not wrong to read the Thanksgiving Hymns of Qumran (esp. 1QH 1.21ff.; 3.23ff.; 4.29ff.) and the song at the end of 1QS (9.26–11.22, esp. 11.9ff.) as suggesting that it was possible for the rigorous Jews, who could claim perfect righteousness for themselves (especially over against the less rigorous ones), as Paul says he did during his Pharisaic days (Phil 3.6), sometimes to doubt about their ability to keep the law perfectly[5]. So O. Kuss has rightly protested against the interpretations of Rom 7 that would not allow any

---

[1]It must be admitted, however, this is the impression that one often gets from the unqualified statements brandished against the autobiographical and psychological interpretations of Rom 7.

[2]But cf. j.Yoma vi. 41, 43d, and the comment on it in *A Rabbinic Anthology*, ed. C.G.Montefiore and H.Loewe (1938), p.302.

[3]Cf. Kümmel, *Römer 7*, pp.115ff. One can deny this only if with Bultmann ('Römer 7', pp.201ff.) one holds the unlikely view that the θέλεω in Rom 7.14ff. is not the willing of an individual subject but the 'transsubjektive Tendenz der menschlichen Existenz überhaupt'. For criticisms of Bultmann's view, see G.Schrenk, θέλω, *TDNT* iii, pp.50ff.; P.Althaus, *Paulus und Luther über den Menschen* ([4]1963), pp.469ff.; O.Kuss, *Der Römerbrief* ([2]1963), pp.469ff.

[4]Cf. Dunn, *op. cit.*, pp.260f.

[5]Cf. W.Bousset and H.Greßmann, *Die Religion des Judentums* ([4]1966), pp. 388–392, 402–409; G.H.Box, '4 Ezra', *Apoc. & Pseud.* ii, ed. Charles, pp.555ff.; Davies, *Paul*, pp.11, 13; Betz, 'Paulus als Pharisäer', p.58.

possibility of seeing Paul's own experiences under the law reflected in the chapter[1]. Rom 7.7–25 is certainly not meant to be a description of Paul's past in Judaism; it is rather a description of the *objective* existence of the Adamitic man under the law as seen *from the Christian viewpoint*. As such it contains elements that cannot be easily fitted into Paul's life, and some of the common human experiences and especially the doubt about man's ability to keep the law are radicalized. The insight into the total helplessness of the Adamitic man under the law could have come to Paul, the zealous and successful Pharisee, only after his conversion. However, in the description of this man, especially in that of his common human experiences with the law, Paul uses his own experiences under the law as raw-material[2]. He cannot do otherwise.

We must now ask whether the admission of some of Paul's experiences in Judaism as reflected in Rom 7 has made the conclusion inevitable that the chapter shows a preparation for Paul's conversion. This is so according to O. Kuss[3]. He argues that Paul's positive assessment of his Pharisaic past in Phil 3.5f. and Gal 1.14 does not stand in the way of his conclusion because in both places it is determined by the need for Paul to counter the claims of his Jewish opponents and to say that he also has had the privileges of which they boast. Thus in these passages Paul has no need to say otherwise than he actually does, without necessarily being untrue[4]. There is undoubtedly some force in this argument. But B. Rigaux is surely right in saying that O. Kuss' argument is not entirely valid since there is no evidence that Paul related his experiences of the inner conflict and the doubt about his ability to keep the law to his conversion[5]. The picture of the pre-conversion Paul in Gal 1.14 and Phil 3.5f. suggests rather that Paul found such common experiences no real problem and was rather satisfied with his achievement in Judaism. It suggests that Paul was a man who would, if found in such conflicts and doubts, (to quote from Käsemann's characterization of the pious man in Qumran), 'bind the helmet for the further fight in the sign of the Torah only tighter'[6], but would not doubt the fundamental belief that by keeping the law man can obtain righteousness. So it is difficult to see the

---

[1] O.Kuss, *Römer*, pp.479f.

[2] Cf. *ibid.*; H.Ridderbos, *Paulus: ein Entwurf seiner Theologie* (1970), p.99; further Michel, *Römer*, pp.170f.; Dodd, *Romans*, pp.105f.; Barrett, *The Epistle to the Romans* (1957), p.152; Bruce, *Romans*, pp.148f.; P.Althaus, *Paulus und Luther*, pp.40f.

[3] Kuss, *Römer*, pp.479f.

[4] *Ibid.*, p.480.

[5] B.Rigaux, *The Letters of St.Paul* (1968), pp.50f.

[6] Käsemann, *Römer*, p.193.

reminiscences of Paul's experiences under the law in Rom 7 as a preparation, let alone a psychological pre-conditioning, for Paul's conversion, if by preparation is meant in this context that Paul's doubt about the law made him ready or readier to accept the Christian gospel without the law.

2 The Vision of the Risen Christ

Paul's conversion took place through an encounter with the risen Christ when he was on the road to Damascus in pursuit of the Christians driven out of Jerusalem. He describes the event as a Christophany to him. Christ appeared (ὤφθη) to him (1Cor 15.8; cf. Acts 9.17; 26.16) and so he saw (ἑώρακα) Christ (1Cor 9.1)[1]. Paul considers this Christophany to be of the same kind as the appearances of the risen Christ to his disciples, and therefore he reckons himself among the witnesses to Christ's resurrection (1Cor 15.5—11)[2]. The Christophany was in other words an ἀποκάλυψις Ἰησοῦ Χριστοῦ (Gal 1.12)[3]: it was God's revelation of his Son, the exalted Christ (cf.

---

[1]According to W.Michaelis, ὁράω, *TDNT* v, pp.315—367 (esp. 355—360), when the word ὤφθη is used as a *term. techn.* for the resurrection appearances, the primary emphasis lies not on seeing as a sensual or mental perception but on revelation in word. Similarly W.Marxsen, *The Resurrection of Jesus of Nazareth* (1970), pp. 98—111, maintains that on the Damascus road Paul did not *see* the risen Jesus Christ but rather received a revelation (in the sense of 'uncovering') of the truth about Jesus. But his attempt to explain away Paul's language in 1Cor 9.1; 15.8 is so plainly arbitrary for any unbiased exegete that we do not have to repudiate it in detail here. However, against his wrong interpretation of the concept ἀποκάλυψις / ἀποκαλύπτειν in Gal 1.11, 16, *infra* pp.71ff. In his investigation of the use of the word ὤφθη in the LXX, Judaism and the NT, K.H. Rengstorf stresses, against Michaelis, that the ὤφθη in the report of the resurrection appearances should be understood 'in the specific sense of becoming visible, therefore in the sense of perception with the eyes' (*Die Auferstehung Jesu* ([4]1960), pp. 48—62, 117—127, quotation from p.119). J.Lindblom, *Gesichte und Offenbarungen* (1968), pp.88ff., emphasizes that the word ὤφθη always implies, even where not clearly indicated, a seeing, whether in dream, in vision, or with the physical eyes. Various questions concerning the nature of the Damascus Christophany are carefully discussed by J.D.G.Dunn, *Jesus and the Spirit* (1975), pp.97—109 (esp. 104—109), who affirms that the Damascus revelation of Christ involved a 'visionary perception' on the part of Paul (p.106). But Dunn is mistaken in his contention that Paul 'is unable to affirm more than the bare *that* of the experience — "I saw Jesus" — . . . ' (p.108, emphasis by D.) and therefore Paul does not describe his experience (p.107) (*supra* Ch. I; *infra* pp.71ff., 223ff.)

[2]This is shown not only by Paul's inserting the Christophany on the Damascus road in the traditional list of the resurrection appearances but also by his use of ὤφθη, the *term. techn.* for the resurrection appearances, for the Damascus Christophany just as for the other resurrection appearances.

[3]In view of Gal 1.16 Ἰησοῦ Χριστοῦ seems to be a *gen. obj.* (So Burton, *Gal.*, pp. 41ff.; Stuhlmacher, *Evangelium*, p.71; Mussner, *Gal.*, p.68). But since in the immediate

Rom 1.4) , to Paul (Gal 1.16). Paul's use of the word ἀποκάλυψις for the Christophany suggests that it was a proleptic realization or an anticipation of the parousia and that Christ was revealed to Paul in the form in which he will come at the End-time[1]. As a resurrection appearance and proleptic parousia, the ἀποκάλυψις Ἰησοῦ Χριστοῦ on the Damascus road was a unique event in Paul's life and therefore was different in kind from the later charismatic ἀποκάλυψις κυρίου (2Cor 12.1)[2]. As the risen and exalted one, Christ appeared to Paul accompanied by the radiance of glory (2Cor 4.6; Acts 9.3; 22.6; 26.13).

This objective, external event had a soul-stirring effect on the very centre of Paul's being (2Cor 4.6; Gal 1.16). It was for Paul an experience of an inner illumination (2Cor 4.6) and of receiving God's judgement upon his righteousness attained by the law. Thus it was a moment of decision to give up his own righteousness in order to obtain the knowledge of the risen and exalted Christ and God's righteousness attained by faith in him (Phil 3.7–9). It was the moment when Paul was transferred from his false judgement of Jesus (2Cor 5.16; Gal 3.13) to the true knowledge of him as God's exalted Messiah, as God's Son, and as the Lord (2Cor 5.16; Gal 1.16; Phil 3.8). Thus it brought about a complete change in Paul's life: the enemy of Christ became his servant. Indeed, he was made a new creature in Christ (2Cor 5.17).

3 The Apostolic Commission

However, the Damascus experience was not just a matter of Paul's private conversion. As frequently observed, in fact, Paul speaks of it in terms of an apostolic commission rather than a conversion. The risen Christ appeared to him, so that, though unworthy to be called an apostle because of his persecution of the Church, Paul was made an apostle (1Cor 15.8ff.; also 9.1).

---

context of vs. 11–12 the phrase Ἰησοῦ Χριστοῦ stands as antithesis to παρὰ ἀνθρώπου and ἐδιδάχθην it may be a *gen. subj.* (So Oepke, *Gal.*, p.29). Some take it both as *gen. obj.* and *subj.* (Schlier, *Gal.*, p.47; Blank, *Paulus*, p.213). If it is a *gen. subj.* the object of ἀποκαλύψεως is, of course, τὸ εὐαγγέλιον. Since, however, Paul usually defines the gospel Christologically (Rom 1.3f.; 1Cor 15.3–5) as he will immediately do here also (Gal 1.16), even if the phrase Ἰησοῦ Χριστοῦ is taken as *gen. subj.*, the content of the ἀποκάλυψις by Jesus Christ is still Jesus Christ himself. Thus the phrase ἀποκάλυψις Ἰησοῦ Χριστοῦ means the self-revelation of Jesus Christ.

[1]The phrase ἀποκάλυψις Ἰησοῦ Χριστοῦ in the NT refers properly to the parousia (1Cor 1.7; 2Th 1.7; 1Pet 1.7, 13). Cf. A.Oepke, καλύπτω, *TDNT* iii, p.583; Schlier, *Gal.*, pp.47, 55; Cerfaux, 'La vocation de S.Paul', 17f.; Stuhlmacher, *Evangelium*, p.71; Dupont, 'The Conversion of Paul', p.192.

[2]H.Grass, *Ostergeschehen und Osterberichte* ([2]1962), pp.229ff.; Lindblom, *Gesichte*, pp.110f.; especially Dunn, *Jesus*, pp.98–103.

Whether Paul *heard* this commission from Christ on the Damascus road (Acts 26.11–18), Paul does not say in his letters. Nevertheless, the possibility is not excluded[1]. In fact, there are two factors that speak for it: first, that the OT and Judaism seem to know no epiphany without revelation by word[2]; and second, that Paul reckons the Christophany to him to be of the same kind as the other resurrection appearances, which are described always as accompanied by the word of Jesus' testimony to himself and/or of his commissioning his apostles (Mt 28.9–10 & par.; 28.16–20; (Mk 16.14–18); Lk 24.13–35, 36–43; Jn 20.19–29; 21.1–23; Acts 1.3–9)[3]. At any rate, Paul considers the Christophany on the Damascus road in terms of the resurrection appearance in which the commissioning of the apostles by the risen Lord took place (Mt 28.16–20; (Mk 16.14–18); Lk 24.36–43; Jn 20.19–23; 21.15–19; Acts 1.8)[4].

The same thought of the apostolic call governs Paul's description of the Christophany on the Damascus road in Gal 1.16: God 'was pleased to reveal his Son to me, so that I might preach him (as the gospel) ($\dot{i}\nu a$ $\dot{\epsilon}\dot{\nu}a\gamma\gamma\epsilon\lambda\dot{i}\zeta\omega\mu a\iota$ $a\dot{\upsilon}\tau\dot{o}\nu$)[5] among the Gentiles'. From this it is clear that for Paul the Christophany on the Damascus road constituted both his gospel (see also Gal 1.12) and his apostolic commission for the Gentile mission. To this, as observed above, Paul constantly appeals: he 'was entrusted with the gospel' (1Th 2.4), 'the gospel of uncircumcision' (Gal 2.7), 'was set apart for the gospel of God' (Rom 1.1), through Jesus Christ the Lord 'received grace and apostleship to bring about the obedience of faith among all the Gentiles for the sake of his name' (Rom 1.5), was given the grace by God to be a minister for the Gen-

---

[1]Kümmel, *Römer* 7, p.159.

[2]See Michaelis, *op. cit.*, pp.329–340; G.Kittel, $\dot{a}\kappa o\dot{\upsilon}\omega$, *TDNT* i, pp.217ff.

[3]Cf. Rengstorf, *op. cit.*, pp.124f.; Michaelis, *op. cit.*, p.356. O.Betz holds the view that Paul only saw the risen Christ enthroned at the right hand of God in heaven and the Scriptures Jer 1.4–10; Isa 49.1–6 and especially Isa 6.1–13 provided him with the key to the interpretation of the Christophany as his call to apostleship for the Gentiles ('Die Vision des Paulus im Tempel. Apg. 22,17–21 als Beitrag zur Deutung des Damaskuserlebnisses', *Verborum Veritas*, G.Stählin FS, ed. O.Böcher and K.Haacker (1970), pp. 117ff.). Certainly Paul interprets the Christophany and his call therein in the light of the texts from Isa. and Jer. (*infra*, pp.91ff.). But this does not necessarily preclude Paul's hearing the commissioning words from Christ who appeared to him. Having heard Christ's call in the Christophany, Paul would naturally have turned to the Scriptures and meditated upon the texts of the prophetic calls in order to see the significance of his call in the light of them. The question of how the heavenly voice is to be imagined is of the same nature as the question of how the resurrected body of Christ is to be imagined.

[4]Cf. Roloff, *Apostolat*, pp.52f.; Dunn, *Jesus*, pp.110–114.

[5]Cf. Burton, *Gal.*, p.53; Schlier, *Gal.*, p.56.

tiles in the priestly service of the gospel (Rom 15.15f.), was commissioned by Christ as an apostle to preach the gospel (1Cor 1.17), etc.[1]

However, it has often been questioned whether Paul's call to the Gentile mission really coincided with the Christophany on the Damascus road[2]. Some suppose that for some years after his conversion Paul was active as an evangelist among the Jews but through the failure of the Jewish mission and his subsequent experience of the successful Gentile mission in Antioch he came to the conviction that God wanted him to turn to the Gentiles. They think that Paul then received from God a definite call to the Gentile mission, the tradition of which is reflected in Acts 22.17–21[3].

From this view P. Gaechter explains Paul's joining the Christophany and the apostolic commission in Gal 1.16; 1Cor 15.9f. and Acts 26.16b–18 to be the result of a telescoping the historical development: that is to say, having arrived at the conviction around 46–48 A.D. that his task was a mission to the Gentiles Paul realized in retrospect that on the Damascus road Christ commissioned him for the Gentile mission, and so joined the Christophany with his call to it[4]. Similarly some think that the ἵνα-clause in Gal 1.16, which explains the purpose of God's revelation of his Son to Paul as having been that Paul should preach him among the Gentiles, reflects Paul's understanding of the purpose of the Christophany at the time of the writing of Gal. but nothing about the time of his call to the Gentile mission[5].

These interpretations, however, hardly do justice to the polemical context

---

[1] *Supra*, pp.25ff.; cf. Kasting, *Anfänge*, pp.56f.

[2] R.Liechtenhan, *Die urchristliche Mission* (1946), pp.78ff.; A.Fridrichsen, 'The Apostle and his Message', pp.13, 23; E.P.Blair, 'Paul's Call to the Gentile Mission', *Biblical Research* 10 (1965), pp.19–33; Oepke, *Gal.*, p.33; W.D.Davies, 'The Apostolic Age and the Life of Paul', *Peake's Comm.*, p.874.; cf. Rigaux, *Letters*, pp.61f. P.Gaechter, *Petrus und seine Zeit* (1958), pp.408–15, goes so far as to say that there was no call of Paul by God on the Damascus road, let alone a call to the Gentile mission. According to Gaechter, in the Damascus event one has to reckon not with God's call of Paul but with Paul's subjective element, that is, that having found his devotion to the law completely mistaken he realized that he should devote himself completely to Christ and began to see himself as being in the service of Christ. Fortunately for this view Gaechter stands alone. So no separate treatment of this view will be given. It will, however, be implicitly dealt with under the more significant question whether Paul's call to the Gentile mission coincided with the Christophany on the Damascus road.

[3] Fridrichsen, *loc. cit.*; Blair, *loc. cit.*; Liechtenhan, *loc. cit.*; Gaechter, *loc. cit.*

[4] Gaechter, *Petrus*, pp.413f.

[5] Blair, 'Paul's call', p.23; Oepke, *Gal.* p.33; Liechtenhan, *op. cit.*, p.78; Jeremias, *Schlüssel*, p.26; cf. also H.Frh. von Campenhausen, 'Der urchristliche Apostelbegriff', *StTh* 1 (1948), p112.

of Gal 1.16. In Gal 1 & 2, against the challenges of his Judaistic opponents, Paul defends the legitimacy of his gospel and apostleship, and therefore of his law-free Gentile mission, by showing their divine origin (Gal 1.1, 11f.). Hence he refers to the Christophany on the Damascus road as the source of both his gospel and apostleship, which are inseparably bound together. In this context, unless he had been conscious of his call to the Gentile mission from the beginning, he could scarcely have so confidently or so unguardedly said that the Christophany had the purpose of commissioning him specifically for the Gentile mission. For, if he had come to realize the purpose only after some years of missionary work among the Jews, Paul's testimony with the specific reference to the Gentiles in Gal 1.16 would have received an easy repudiation from his opponents: 'If you had been called by God on the Damascus road to the law-free Gentile mission, as you now claim, why did you betray no such call so long after your conversion? And why did you instead go about among the Jews until some years ago?'[1] According to the theory that Paul came later on to realize the purpose of the Christophany as his call to the Gentile mission, Paul would reply to this question by some such words as: 'Well, at that time I was not conscious of the call, but later I realised that the Christophany was God's call for me to go and preach the gospel among the Gentiles'. But then this would rob much of the credibility of Paul's argument for the divine origin of his apostleship, if not destroy it completely. For his opponents would then say: 'So you were not really called at the Christophany. You merely interpreted your experience on the Damascus road to have been God's call — and only later at that! Does not this prove that you are in fact a self-made "apostle"?' Considering such a polemical context, therefore, Gal 1.16 should be interpreted exactly as saying that Paul received his call to the Gentile mission at the Christophany on the Damascus road.

For this view speaks also the fact that having set out to prove the divine origin of his *gospel* by referring to the revelation of Jesus Christ on the Damascus road (Gal 1.11f.) Paul concludes not with a statement just to the effect that the Son of God revealed to him was the gospel which he received,

---

[1]To make the point here presented it need not be presupposed that Paul's opponents or the Galatian Christians knew much about his activities in the years immediately following the Damascus event. It is sufficient to take into account the polemical context in which it would be required of Paul to be as exact as possible about his statements, lest he should somehow give his opponents an opportunity to attack on the basis of the inexactness of his statements. And it is sufficient to take into consideration the psychological inhibition that would have lain upon Paul in making such a claim as in Gal 1.16, had he not really been conscious of his call to the Gentile mission from the beginning.

but rather with one that goes beyond this to indicate his call at the same time. The clause ἵνα <u>εὐαγγελίζωμαι αὐτόν</u> (τὸν υἱὸν αὐτοῦ) ἐν τοῖς ἔθνεσιν with the striking expression underlined is a remarkable compression of the two thoughts: one, that the revealed Son of God is the content of the gospel; and the other, that Paul was called to preach this gospel among the Gentiles. Although the challenge against his gospel and apostleship which the larger context of Gal 1 & 2 presupposes demands that Paul should see and defend them as an inseparable unity, strictly speaking, the immediate context (from Gal 1.11 onwards) requires only the former. But Paul goes on to include the latter. Indeed, it is the latter that comes to the fore. Taking the whole sentence of Gal 1.15f. in view, it may even be said that Paul sees his receiving the gospel as a necessary part of his receiving the apostolic commission. This shows not only how inseparably Paul's gospel and apostleship are bound together, but also how both are together inseparably rooted in the Christophany on the Damascus road[1]. From this it is impossible to say that Paul received his gospel at the Christophany on the Damascus road and then later realized that the Christophany had also the purpose of commissioning him for the Gentile mission[2]. If he received the gospel through the revelation of Jesus Christ on the Damascus road, as he says he did (Gal 1.11), then he received his call to the Gentile mission also there and then.

The fact that Paul interprets his call in Gal 1.15f. (cf. also Acts 26.16–18; 9.15) in the light of the calls of the prophets (Isa 49.1–6; Jer 1.5, etc.)[3] does not argue against the view that Paul received his call on the Damascus road[4]. For while it is hardly believable that through meditations upon the texts of the prophetic calls in the OT Paul came to the conviction about his call, it is only natural to think that having received the call at the Christophany on the Damascus road he meditated upon these texts in order to see the significance of his call in the light of them.

To say that Paul received his call to the Gentile mission at the Christophany on the Damascus road is, however, to deny neither that there was a process of development in his consciousness toward an ever growing conviction about the call and about its magnitude, nor that his conception of a world-wide mission took time, perhaps more than a decade, for its full devel-

---

[1]Cf. O.Haas, *Paulus der Missionar* (1971), p.16.

[2]Cf. Blair, 'Paul's Call', pp.28f., 32f.

[3]*Infra* pp.91ff.

[4]*Contra* Gaechter, *Petrus*, pp.409f.

opment[1]. It would be totally unrealistic, however, to argue that if he had received a clear call from God to the Gentile mission at his conversion, Paul should have plunged into a world-wide Gentile mission immediately. When he received the commission Paul had no precedent, no model, in reference to which he could think of the ways and means of discharging it. In these circumstances it was only natural for him to turn to synagogues which were familiar to him as the places where the word of God was proclaimed and where he expected to find many Gentiles, the 'God-fearers'. So the fact that during the years immediately after his conversion he seems to have preached in synagogues (Acts 9.19–22) does not argue against the view here advocated[2]. In fact, even during the full swing of his world-wide mission Paul seems to have regularly begun his preaching in the synagogue wherever he went (Acts 13.5–14; 14.1; 17.1f., 10, 17; 18.4, 19; 19.8). This description of Acts reflects neither purely the Lucan *heilsgeschichtliche* scheme nor Paul's lack of conviction about his call to the Gentile mission, but simply the historical reality[3]. For that Paul preached to the Jews as well as to the Gentiles during his later world-wide missionary work is suggested not just by Luke but also by Paul himself (1Cor 9.20ff., 32f.; 2Cor 11.24; 1Th 2.15f.). For Paul the pioneer missionary the network of the synagogues in the *diaspora* was an institution that could be properly described only as God's providential preparation for his missionary work. For it provided Paul the travelling Jew with a temporary lodging and mediated job[4]. It provided Paul the travelling preacher also with an opportunity to preach his gospel, as it seems to have been customary for the ruler of the synagogue to invite someone suitable in the congregation to give a 'word of exhortation' after the reading of the lessons

---

[1]Cf. Hengel, 'Ursprünge', pp.18–23; Burchard, *Zeuge*, p.164 (n.12); Roloff, *Apostolat*, p.56. Note at this stage especially the necessary distinction that Roloff makes between the *concept* 'apostle' and the matter that is described by it. When it is advocated here that on the Damascus road Paul received his apostolic commission for the Gentile mission, it does not mean, of course, that Paul received then the *name* 'apostle'! It only means that Paul was called and sent to preach the gospel to the Gentiles. This fact Paul later interpreted as his *apostolic* commission using the given concept 'apostle'.

[2]*Contra* Gaechter, *Petrus*, pp.411f.; Blair, 'Paul's Call', pp.23f.

[3]W.Schrage, συναγωγή, κτλ, *TDNT* vii, p.835; G.Bornkamm, 'The Missionary Stance of Paul in 1Corinthians 9 and in Acts', *Studies in Luke-Acts*, P.Schubert FS, ed. L.E.Keck & J.L. Martyn (1968), p.200; Bruce, *NT History*, p.261; I.H.Marshall, *Luke: Historian and Theologian* (1970), pp.184f.; Stuhlmacher, *Evangelium*, p.99; Hengel, 'Ursprünge', p.21. *Contra* W.Schmithals, *Paulus und Jakobus*, pp.46ff.; Kasting, *Anfänge* p.57.

[4]Hengel, 'Die Synagogeninschrift von Stobi', *ZNW* 57(1966), 170ff.; Schrage, *op. cit.*, p.826.

at worship (cf. Acts 13.14ff.)[1]. Still more important, it provided Paul the Christian missionary with a well prepared audience, namely the 'God-fearers' — the Gentiles who adhered to Judaism to a certain extent without actually taking upon themselves the whole law and being incorporated through circumcision as proselytes in the Jewish community[2] — among whom he apparently found greatest success and whom he used as bridgehead into the Gentile world (Acts 13.16; 14.1; 17.4, 12, 27; 18.4; 19.8ff.)[3]. So for Paul the synagogue was the obvious starting-point for his missionary work wherever he went. Moreover, Paul as the Gentiles' apostle to the end never lost interest in the salvation of Israel because of her *heilsgeschichtlichen* privilege (cf. Rom 1.16; 9.1ff.; 11.13f.).

If Paul's preaching to the Jews in synagogues in the years immediately after the Damascus event does not argue against the view that Paul received his call to the Gentile mission at the Christophany on the Damascus road, there is some evidence for his missionary work beyond synagogues in those years which tends to confirm the view here advocated. First to be considered in this connection is the fact that it was the 'Hellenist' Jewish Christians whom Paul persecuted and then after his conversion he joined himself in Damascus (Acts 9.19b–22). Now these 'Hellenist' Jewish Christians driven out of Jerusalem were the very ones who had taken the first step of overcoming the Jewish particularism and started preaching to non-Jews (Acts 8.4ff., 26ff., 40; 11.20ff.). In these circumstances Paul's call to the Gentile mission was, though certainly a *novum,* not completely a *novum*[4]. Accord-

---

[1]Moore i, p.305; Bruce, *NT History*, p.137; cf. also Str.-Bill. iv, pp.171ff.

[2]Against this traditional understanding of φοβούμενος or σεβόμενος τὸν θεόν, or in short θεοσεβής (See e.g., Moore i, pp.325f.; K.G.Kuhn, προσήλυτος, *TDNT* vi, pp. 731f., 743f.) lately Kasting, *Anfänge*, p.27, has taken the view, as did K.Lake, *Beginnings* v, pp.84ff. before him, that they are not technical terms reserved only for the group of such Gentiles as described above, but general terms of honour for both pious Jews and Gentiles. However, see H.Bellen, 'Συναγωγὴ τῶν 'Ιουδαίων καὶ θεοσεβῶν: Die Aussage einer Bospranischen Freilassungsinschrift (CIRB 71) zum Problem der "Gottesfürchtigen" ', *Jahrbuch für Antike und Christentum* 8/9 (1965/55), pp.171–76; and K. Romaniuk, 'Die "Gottesfürchtigen" im NT', *Aegyptus* 44 (1964), pp.66–91, who argue for the traditional view. Even if the terms are not *term. techn.* for such Gentiles as described above, it is 'the fact that the words are applied at least most often to this class in Acts'; 'these passages (i.e., the passages in Acts that contain the terms) show that φοβούμενοι τὸν θεόν and σεβόμενοι τὸν θεόν were used as appropriate phrases to describe those who though non-Jews believed in the monotheistic God of the Jews and possibly attended the synagogue' (Lake, *op. cit.*, pp.87f.).

[3]See Bruce, *NT History*, p.261.

[4]Hengel writes about the Gentile mission of the 'Hellenists': 'Zunächst ging es den Hellenisten vermutlich nicht um eine offene, großzügige "Heidenmission", sondern um

ing to Paul's testimony in Gal 1.17 immediately after the vision on the
Damascus road he left for Arabia, that is, the Nabataean kingdom. The
purpose and duration of his stay there cannot be ascertained with certainty.
However, the fact that Paul had to flee from the ethnarch of the Nabataean
king Aretas in Damascus (2Cor 11.23; cf. Acts 9.24f.) may suggest that he
had been engaged in missionary work in 'Arabia' and so incurred the hostility
of the Nabataean authorities[1]; After his return from Arabia to Damascus, it
may be presumed that Paul did evangelistic work in the synagogue among the
God-fearers as well as among the Jews along with the 'Hellenist' Jewish
Christians in the city (Acts 9.19b–25). His stay in Damascus was terminated
with the flight from the Nabataean ethnarch. After the 14 day visit with
Peter in Jerusalem he went to the region of Syria and Cilicia (Gal 1.21; Acts
9.30). It was 2–3 years after his conversion (Gal 1.18)[2]. And in the region
he worked for some 13 years until his second visit to Jerusalem (Gal 2.1)[3].
That he was actively engaged in missionary work during those years is suggested by the news that the churches in Judaea are said to have kept on hearing:
'He who once persecuted us is now preaching the faith he once tried to
destroy' (Gal 1.23)[4]. Some time during this period (about 45 A.D.?) Barna-

---

die gleichberechtigte Einholung der Samaritaner und "gottesfürchtigen" Heiden, der
Außenstehenden und Entrechteten in das zu konstituierende neue Gottesvolk. Wirk-
liche Heidenmission im vollen Sinne mag dann erst in Antiochien eingesetzt haben (Apg.
xi, 19ff.)' ('Ursprünge', p.30). Cf. F.Hahn, *Mission*, pp.48–50, who judges the Gentile
mission of the 'Hellenists' more positively; Kasting, *Anfänge*, pp.103ff. Hengel thinks
that it was of decisive importance for Paul that he should have encountered these
'Hellenist' Christians who were themselves on the point of taking the step from the
Jewish mission to the Gentile mission (*op. cit.*, p.24). Cf. also Stuhlmacher, *Evangelium*,
p.74.

[1] K.Lake, 'The Conversion of Paul', *Beginnings* v, pp. 192–94; Haenchen, *Apg.*, p.67;
Bruce, *NT History*, p.230; Conzelmann, *Apg.*, p.67; Bornkamm, *Paulus*, pp.48f. For
the problem associated with Paul's flight from the Nabataean ethnarch in Damascus,
see Lake, *op. cit.*, pp.193f.; H.Windisch, *2.Kor.*, pp.363ff.; Dibelius-Kümmel, *Paulus*,
p.45. Without a reference to the incident of Paul's flight from the Nabataean ethnarch
in Damascus, the following authors infer from the context of Paul's statements in Gal
1.15–24 that Paul started his missionary work in 'Arabia': Dibelius-Kümmel, *Paulus*,
pp.45, 63; Schlier, *Gal.*, p.58; Stuhlmacher, *Evangelium*, p.84; Kasting, *Anfänge*, p.56;
Ch. Burchard, *Zeuge*, p.126.

[2] Taking μετὰ τρία ἔτη in Gal 1.18 to be reckoned from Paul's conversion (with
the majority of commentators) rather than from his return to Damascus from Arabia (so
Mussner, *Gal.*, p.93).

[3] Taking διὰ δεκατεσσάρων ἐτῶν in Gal 2.1 to be reckoned from Paul's first Jerusalem visit (Gal 1.18) – so the majority of commentators.

[4] Gaechter, *Petrus*, p.412 and Blair, 'Paul's Call', p.24, infer from Gal 1.23f. that in
Syria and Cilicia Paul did his missionary work among the Jews. They think that if he

bas, who went to Antioch to investigate the Gentile mission there and approved of it, turned to Paul in Tarsus for help in the expanding work and brought him to Antioch (Acts 11.22–26). This seems to suggest that Paul 'had already gained some kind of reputation in work connected with the Gentiles'[1]. If so, even before coming to Antioch Paul was actively engaged in the Gentile mission[2]. Thus there is some evidence for the view that sooner rather than later Paul began preaching to the Gentiles (even if partly to the Gentiles in synagogues), and this supports the interpretation of Paul's testimony in Gal 1.16 here offered, namely that Paul received his call to the Gentile mission at the Christophany on the Damascus road.

This seems also to be essentially what Luke conveys in his three accounts of the Damascus event. From Acts 9.15; 22.25; and 26.16ff. two points are clear: 1) at the Christophany on the Damascus road Paul was called to witness to what he had seen in the self-revelation of Christ[3]. (So according to Acts 9.20 Paul begins his preaching immediately in Damascus and its content is that Jesus is 'the Son of God' − cf. Gal 1.16). 2) Paul was sent to the Gentiles, even if not to them exclusively. Thus Luke agrees with Paul in so far as he also understands the Damascus event in terms of Paul's receiving his message and call for missionary work among the Gentiles. However, Luke differs from Paul in reporting that at the Christophany on the Damascus road Paul was sent not only to the Gentiles but also to the Jews (Acts 9.15), indeed, 'to all men' (Acts 22.15). The phrase $υἱῶν$ $τε$ $'Ισραήλ$ in Acts 9.15 may be Lucan addition to the tradition which had only $τῶν$ $ἐθνῶν$ $τε$ $καὶ$ $βασιλέων$, before whom Paul was commissioned to carry the name of Christ[4]. And in Acts 22.15 Luke may have described the recipients of Paul's witness in the general terms 'all men' in view of the episode of the vision in

---

had preached the gospel to the Gentiles the Jewish Christians in Jerusalem would not have 'glorified God' for it. But this is not a correct inference because it presupposes in those early years an unproved tension between Paul and Jerusalem of the kind that later existed between Paul and the Judaizers in Galatia. See Burton, *Gal.*, p.65: 'the strenuous opposition to the offering of the gospel to the Gentiles apart from the law had not yet developed in the churches of Judaea . . . See especially (Gal) 2.4 with its distinct implication that the opponents of Paul's liberalism were a recent and pernicious addition to the Jerusalem church'.

[1]Davies, 'The Apostolic Age and the Life of Paul', *Peake's Comm.*, p.874.

[2]*Contra* Blair, 'Paul's Call', pp.26ff.

[3]In view of Acts 26.1ff. it is not necessary to think that Luke conceives of Paul's call to be indirect, mediated through Ananias, as Acts 9.15f. and 22.15, taken alone, might suggest. *Supra* pp. 30f.

[4]The position of $υἱῶν$ $τε$ $'Ισραήλ$ after $τῶν$ $ἐθνῶν$ $τε$ $καὶ$ $βασιλέων$ seems to suggest this. So Burchard, *Zeuge*, p.123.

the Temple that he was about to narrate (Acts 22.17–21)[1]. He seems to suppose that the vision took place during Paul's first visit to Jerusalem (Acts 9.26–30). In the vision, against Paul's wish to stay in Jerusalem and to bear witness there, the Lord commands him: 'Depart; for I will send you far away to the Gentiles' (Acts 22.21). With this episode attached immediately next to his description of Paul's call on the Damascus road, Luke seems to be saying that the call on the Damascus road was for Paul to witness for Christ generally 'to all men' (Acts 22.15) and that the sending of Paul specifically to the Gentiles took place later in the Temple in Jerusalem. But then this understanding of Paul's sending stands apparently in conflict with Luke's description of the Damascus event in Acts 26.16ff., where it is said that the call and sending of Paul to the Gentiles took place at the Christophany on the Damascus road[2]. It is hardly possible, however, to go further into the whole question of Luke's view of Paul's sending here[3]. For the present purpose it is enough to ascertain two points: 1) that Luke agrees with Paul in seeing that at the Damascus Christophany Paul received his message and call for missionary work among the Gentiles (even if not exclusively among them as far as Luke is concerned)[4]; and 2) that the vision in the Temple (Acts 22.17–21), behind which there may be tradition[5], does not, at any rate, seem to have been of decisive importance for Paul, for he never mentions it in his letters.

So it is to be concluded that at the Christophany on the Damascus road Paul received his call to the Gentile mission as well as his gospel[6]. Only this

---

[1]Haenchen, *Apg.*, p.556.

[2]In view of the purpose of Paul's sending, which is described in Acts 26.18, and also of the connection (ἐξ) ἀποστέλλεω with ἔθνη in Acts 22.21; 28.28, the relative sentence εἰς οὓς ἐγὼ ἀποστέλλω σε is probably to be taken as referring to ἐκ τῶν ἐθνῶν alone. So Haenchen, *Apg.*, p.612; Burchard, *op. cit.*, p.113. But Stählin, *Apg.*, p.309 and Conzelmann, *Apg.*, p.149 take it to refer both to λαός and ἔθνη, that is, the Jews and the Gentiles. The latter possibility is suggested by Paul's testimony that in obedience to the call of the Lord he preached in Jerusalem and Judaea as well as in the Gentile world (Acts 26.19f.). So Burchard (*loc. cit.*) wonders whether this incongruity within Acts 26.17–20 is not due to Luke's working with a tradition.

[3]We refer just to the following authors, although we are by no means in complete agreement with them: Burchard, *op. cit.*, esp. pp.166–68; J.Jervell, 'Paul: The Teacher of Israel', *Luke and the People of God* (1972), pp.158ff.; O.Betz, 'Die Vision des Paulus', pp.113–123.

[4]Cf. Stählin, *Apg.*, pp.310f.

[5]Cf. Conzelmann, *Apg.*, p.135; Burchard, *Zeuge*, pp.163ff.; Blair, 'Paul's Call', pp.19ff.; but cf. also Betz, 'Vision', pp.115ff.

[6]This view is shared by, e.g., Dibelius-Kümmel, *Paulus*, pp.46, 61; Wilckens, 'Bekehrung,' pp.12ff.; Stuhlmacher, *Evangelium*, p.82; Blank, *Paulus*, p.230; Kasting, *Anfange;* p.57; Betz, 'Vision', p.117; Hengel, 'Ursprünge', 22f.; Haas, *Paulus der Missionar,*

fact can adequately explain the element of compulsion that there is in Paul's apostolic call: Paul felt that he was 'seized' by Christ (Phil 3.2) and put under a fateful divine constraint to preach the gospel (1Cor 9.16f.). While Paul was acting as an enemy, Christ arrested him, turned him into his bond-slave (Rom 1.1; Gal 1.10; Phil 1.1), and charged him with a commission to preach the gospel, so that from then on he could no longer break himself free from Jesus Christ his Lord and from the necessity (ἀνάγκη) to preach the gospel. And this call was for Paul to preach the gospel specifically to the Gentiles. So Paul is 'under obligation both to Greeks and to barbarians' (Rom 1.14).

---

pp.16ff.; Hahn, *Mission,* pp.82f.; Dunn, *Jesus,* pp.110–114. By saying that the Christophany on the Damascus road 'contained the germ of a vocation that was to be revealed later', Rigaux, *Letters,* p.62, tries to steer the middle course between the view that Paul received his call to the Gentile mission at the Damascus Christophany and the opposing view that he became the Gentile apostle gradually and through another vision later. But what is meant by 'germ' here?

Chapter IV Paul's Gospel: A. The Revelation

1 The Revelation of the Gospel

Paul received his gospel 'through a revelation of Jesus Christ' (Gal 1.12, 16) on the road to Damascus. This Paul asserts against the allegation of his Judaizing opponents in Galatia that he received the gospel from the Jerusalem apostles but then perverted it into a 'human'[1] gospel by cutting away from it the requirements of the Torah and circumcision in order to suit man's wishes and tastes (Gal 1.10–12)[2]. Paul denies the allegation categorically by using a *term. techn.* παραλαμβάνευ (קבל) for receiving a tradition and another term, διδάσκευ, which also seems to point to the Rabbinic practice of learn-

---

[1]κατὰ ἄνθρωπον in Gal 1.11 seems to express the general idea of 'human' over against 'divine' in describing the quality of Paul's gospel (Burton, *Gal.*, pp.37f.; Schlier, *Gal.*, p.44).

[2]It would be to go too far afield if it were attempted here to describe the whole course of the debate about Paul's opponents in Galatia. However, at least some different opinions concerning the criticisms of the opponents that Paul is countering in Gal 1 & 2 must be indicated here. In view of the fact that the opponents of Paul in Galatia apparently pressed the Galatian Christians to the observance of the law (Gal 2.16; 3.2, 21b; 4.21; 5.4) and especially circumcision (5.2; 6.12f.) for salvation, they have traditionally been identified as the Judaising Jewish Christians probably from Jerusalem. And in view of Paul's sustained apology for his apostleship and gospel as independent of the Jerusalem authorities, it has been thought that the Judaisers denied their legitimacy by suggesting that Paul was dependent on the commission and tradition of the Jerusalem authorities (cf. Kümmel, *Introduction*, pp.298ff.). However, W.Schmithals sees the 'decisive' weakness of this traditional view in the logical contradiction: 'Es (ist) undenkbar, daß die Jerusalemer Apostel in Galatien Paulus vorwerfen, er sei von ihnen selbst oder, falls es nur Vertreter der Jerusalemer Autoritäten sind, er sei wie sie selbst von den Aposteln in Jerusalem abhängig. Damit kann man zwar seine Autorität als Apostel herabsetzen, aber gerade nicht sein Evangelium verwerfen. Vielmehr wäre solche Behauptung, so sehr sie Paulus als Apostel degradierte, gerade eine Belobigung seines Evangeliums' (*Paulus und die Gnostiker* (1965), p.16. So already J.H.Ropes, *The Singular Problem of the Epistle to the Galatians* (1929), pp.20f.). Schmithals' own view is: the opponents were Jewish Christian Gnostics (*op. cit.*, p.41) who criticised that Paul received his apostolic commission and gospel from men, namely the Jerusalem apostles, whereas a genuine apostle must, so argued the Gnostic opponents according to Schmithals, receive them directly

ing a tradition³, when he solemnly announces:

γνωρίζω γὰρ ὑμῖν, ἀδελφοί, τὸ εὐαγγέλιον τὸ εὐαγγελισθὲν ὑπ'
ἐμοῦ ὅτι οὐκ ἔστιν κατὰ ἄνθρωπον· οὐδὲ γὰρ ἐγὼ παρὰ ἀνθρώπου
παρέλαβον αὐτὸ οὔτε ἐδιδάχθην, ἀλλὰ δι' ἀποκαλύψεως Ἰησοῦ Χριστοῦ.

But this raises immediately the question how to square it with what Paul
says equally solemnly in 1Cor 15.1–11, using the same formula: γνωρίζω
δὲ ὑμῖν, ἀδελφοί, τὸ εὐαγγέλιον ὃ εὐηγγελισάμην ὑμῖν, ὃ καὶ παρελά-

---

from God or Christ (*op. cit.*, pp.18ff.). But this view has been found untenable by
Kümmel, *Introduction*, pp. 299ff., and R.McL. Wilson, 'Gnostics – in Galatia?', *StEv* 4
(1968), pp.358–367. D.Georgi thinks that the opponents criticised not Paul's dependence upon Jerusalem but on the contrary his neglect of the tradition (of Jerusalem?)
(*Die Geschichte der Kollekte des Paulus für Jerusalem* (1965), p.36 (n.113)). Georgi has
found two followers: one, D.Lührmann, who believes that the opponents criticised Paul
for lacking a tradition that could legitimize his gospel – the Jerusalem tradition that was
grounded upon the 'revelation' of the law to Moses on Mt. Sinai (*Das Offenbarungsverständnis bei Paulus und in paulinischen Gemeinden* (1965), pp.71ff.); and the other,
P.Stuhlmacher, who, likewise developing Georgi's thesis, says: 'Die Gegner haben Paulus
den Vorwurf gemacht, er sei nichts als ein Gemeinde-Apostel der Antiochener, also
Sprecher eines illegitimen (weil die Tora abrogierenden) Evangeliums' (*Evangelium*, p.67).
But then these three writers can hardly explain satisfactorily why Paul has to argue for
his independence of Jerusalem in Gal 1 & 2. If Paul had been criticised for the reasons
that they postulate, he would have defended himself better by saying what he says in
1Cor 15.1–11 than Gal 1.11f.! It seems that our view stated above is the least problematic as it adequately takes into account Paul's need to demonstrate his independence
from Jerusalem for his gospel and apostleship, while avoiding the weakness of the traditional view that Schmithals has pointed out (cf. Burton, *Gal.*, pp.liv f.; R.Bring,
Commentary on Galatians (1961), p.6; J.Jeremias, 'Chiasmus in den Paulusbriefen',
Abba (1960), pp.285f.). It seems that in the minds of the opponents Paul's apostleship
and gospel were questionable not so much because he had received them from the
Jerusalem apostles (ἀπ' ἀνθρώπων 1.1; παρὰ ἀνθρώπου 1.12) as because he, so they
believed, perverted the gospel into a human gospel that accords with the human wishes
and tastes (κατὰ ἄνθρωπον) by not requiring the Gentiles to observe the law and circumcision. For while Paul's eagerness in Gal. to demonstrate his independence from Jerusalem
for his gospel and apostleship clearly suggests that he was accused of having received them
from the Jerusalem apostles there is no suggestion that on account of his dependence
upon Jerusalem the legitimacy of his apostleship and gospel was questioned. In this
connection two facts are to be noted. Firstly, in Gal. Paul does not conduct the kind of
apologetic for his apostleship that he does in the Corinthian letters (1Cor 9.1f.;
15.9–11; 2Cor 3.1ff.; 10–13): in Gal. his defence of the legitimacy of his apostleship
is only a subsidiary concern. Secondly, Paul concentrates rather on the defence of his
gospel, in which he is eager to demonstrate the Jerusalem apostles' approval of it (Gal
2.2, 7f.) as much as his not having received it from them. However, Paul felt it necessary
to make his independence from Jerusalem absolutely clear not only because the allegation was untrue and degrading to his gospel and apostleship but more because he had to
demolish the very basis of the real charge that he perverted the gospel of Jerusalem.

βετε . . . Is there 'an absolute contradiction'[1] between the two statements? Is it impossible to resolve the tension between them?[2]

Among the various solutions the best one seems to be the one that starts from making a distinction between the essence and the form (or the formal expression)[3] of the gospel and which sees Paul as referring to the former in Gal 1.12 and to the latter in 1Cor 15.1ff[4]. Basic to the divergent opinions within this approach is the supposition that through the 'revelation of Jesus Christ' on the Damascus road Paul came to realize the truth of the Christian proclamation that the crucified Jesus is the risen and exalted Lord and that the tradition of 1Cor 15.3ff. is a formal expression of this essence of the gospel. Paul says that he received his gospel through a 'revelation of Jesus Christ' because he was convinced of the truth of the gospel, namely Christ as God's saving event, not through man's preaching but only through God's revelation of his Son to him. In the words of K. Wegenast,

> The gospel in the sense of the text (Gal 1f.) is the crucified, dead and risen Jesus Christ who is revealed by God as Son, who is the only possibility to attain salvation. The gospel is therefore no formula or tradition, even if it can make use of certain

---

So Paul is saying in Gal 1.10−12: 'The charge that I have turned the original divine gospel of Jerusalem into a human thing (κατὰ ἄνθρωπον) by accommodating it to man's wishes, is absolutely groundless. For (γάρ v.12) already its presupposition is wrong: contrary to the allegation of the Judaisers I have not (they may have, but certainly I have not − for οὐδὲ γὰρ ἐγώ in v.12 see Oepke, *Gal.*, p.29) received my gospel from any man (παρὰ ἀνθρώπου) but directly through the revelation of Jesus Christ!' (cf. Bornkamm, *Paulus*, p.42). Having stated this thesis, Paul goes on to prove it, first by demonstrating his independence from Jerusalem and then the truth of his gospel which even the Jerusalem 'pillars' recognized.

[3] Blank, *Paulus*, p.212.

[1] J.T.Sanders, 'Paul's Autobiographical Statements in Galatians 1−2', *JBL* 85(1966), p.337, an essay marked by extreme arbitrariness.

[2] So E.Dinkler, 'Tradition im Urchristentum', *RGG*³ vi, 971.

[3] 'Essence' and 'form' are certainly not Pauline terms, and so to introduce such categories in order to explain Paul's conception of the gospel may seem illegitimate. However, from a comparison of other passages such as Rom 1.3f. and 4.24f. on the one hand and Rom 1.16f. and 1Cor 1.18ff. on the other, it seems possible to suppose that Paul defines the gospel in two different ways which we can today best represent in our conception by employing 'essence' for one and 'form' for the other. Cf. W.Baird, 'What is the Kerygma?', *JBL* 76(1957), pp.190f.

[4] Cf. Schlier, *Gal.*, p.48; P.H.Menoud, 'Revelation and Tradition', *Interpretation* 7 (1953), pp.137ff.; W.Baird, 'What is the Kerygma?', pp.190f.; K.Wegenast, *Das Verständnis der Tradition bei Paulus und in den Deuteropaulinen* (1962), pp.68f.; J.Roloff, *Apostolat*, pp.84ff. For other suggestions, see O.Cullmann, *Die Tradition als exegetisches, historisches und theologisches Problem* (1954), p.20; A.Fridrichsen, 'The Apostle and His Message', pp.8ff.

kerygmatic traditions (so, e.g., Gal 1.4), but the salvation that is proclaimed in Jesus, the proclaimed Christ (cf. 1.16 ἵνα εὐαγγελίζωμαι αὐτόν). The gospel is therefore, according to Paul's opinion, prior to every tradition.[1]

But this gospel must be proclaimed in the words of the apostle and therefore become a concrete message. Since God's saving work in Christ took place in history, that is, in the life, death and resurrection of Jesus Christ, the gospel can be unfolded only through the narration of the historical facts about Jesus Christ which are interpreted as God's saving event[2]. But the historical facts about Jesus Christ are the object of tradition. The tradition in 1Cor 15.3ff. is such a tradition that unfolds the gospel. It is, in fact, a normative one[3]. Paul received from others and transmitted to others the tradition as his gospel because it thus brings his gospel to expression[4]. It is not necessary to go further into the complex question of a more precise definition of the relationship between the gospel as revelation (Gal 1.12ff.) and the gospel as tradition (1Cor 15.1ff.), on which there is a great divergence of opinions[5]. For the present purpose it is enough to see the mutually complementary character of Paul's statements in Gal 1.12 and 1Cor 15.1ff. as shown above and to note: in the Galatian passage Paul asserts that he received his gospel not from man but directly 'through a revelation of Jesus Christ' because here he is concerned with the origin and essence of his gospel, while in 1Cor 15.1ff. he reproduces the early Christian tradition as the gospel that he preached to the Corinthians because there he is concerned to remind them of the terms (*Wortlaut*) in which he actually preached the gospel to them (τίνι λόγῳ εὐηγγελισάμην ὑμῖν), and to emphasize the resurrection of Christ as being the common preaching of all the apostles (1Cor 15.11).

---

[1] Wegenast, *op. cit.*, p.44.

[2] Cf. Menoud, *op. cit.*, pp.137ff.; Baird, *op. cit.*, p.91; esp. Roloff, *Apostolat*, pp.87ff.

[3] The normative character of the tradition is implied in Paul's language in 1Cor 15.1f., 11. But the fact that he considers it normative for the preaching of the gospel does not mean that he considers it word for word juristically sacrosanct and that his gospel is bound to it, as his expansion of the tradition (1Cor 15.3b–5) transmitted to him with a series of statements about Christ's resurrection appearances, including the one to himself, shows (1Cor 15.6–8). Cf. Roloff, *Apostolat*, p.86; Wegenast, *op. cit.*, p.69; Stuhlmacher, *Evangelium*, pp.70f.

[4] Schlier, *Gal.*, p.48; Baird, *op. cit.*, pp.190f.; Wegenast, *op. cit.*, pp.68f.; Roloff, *Apostolat*, pp.86, 88.

[5] See the debate among H.Schlier, 'Kerygma und Sophia', *Die Zeit der Kirche* (⁵1972), pp.206–232, esp. 214–217; Wegenast, *op. cit.*, pp.42ff.; Roloff, *op. cit.*, pp.84–90. A good survey of the debate is found in J.H.Schütz, *Paul and the Anatomy of Apostolic Authority* (1975), pp.54ff.

When Paul says that he received his gospel δι᾿ ἀποκαλύψεως Ἰησοῦ Χριστοῦ(Gal 1.12), that is, through God's revealing (ἀποκαλύπτεω) his Son to him (Gal 1.16), he seems to be using ἀποκαλύπτεω / ἀποκάλυψις as an apocalyptic *term. techn.*[1] This is confirmed by Eph 3.3, in which Paul, referring to the Damascus event, says ὅτι κατὰ ἀποκάλυψιν ἐγνωρίσθη μοι τὸ μυστήριον, thus joining ἀποκάλυψις with μυστήριον, which is its complementary word in the apocalyptic language (cf. also Col 1.25f.)[2]. It is further confirmed by Paul's testimony of having seen the δόξα of God in the face of Christ who was revealed to him on the Damascus road (2Cor 4.6; cf. also 3.18), as the revelation of the δόξα of God (יהוה כבוד) was part of the eschatological expectation in the prophetic, apocalyptic and Rabbinic writings[3]. Thus it is clear that Paul applies the apocalyptic language and thought-forms to describe his experience on the Damascus road.

D. Lührmann has summarized the conception of revelation in the apocalyptic writings in two points:

> In the apocalyptic literature revelation is an eschatological act of God which brings in the new aeon, but is at the same time also the anticipatory disclosure of the eschatological revelation in (the interpretation of)[4] dreams and visions, which should strengthen the hope for the eschatological act of God and the obedience to the law[5].

Against this background, then, how are Paul's statements in Gal 1.12,

---

[1]Cf. Oepke, καλύπτω, κτλ, *TDNT* iii, pp.578f.; Lührmann, *Offenbarungsverständnis*, pp.74f.; Stuhlmacher, *Evangelium*, p.76; Jeremias, *Schlüssel*, p.21; Bornkamm, *Paulus*, p.44; U.Wilckens, 'Der Ursprung der Überlieferung der Erscheinung des Auferstandenen', *Dogma und Denkstrukturen*, E.Schlink FS, ed. W.Joest u. W.Pannenberg (1963), pp.84ff.

[2]E.g., Dan 2.19, 22, 28, 30, 47; 1En 16.3; 30.3; 61.5; 106.19; 4Ezra 10.38; 2Bar 48.3. Cf. Bornkamm, μυστήριον, *TDNT* iv, pp.815f.; Lührmann, *op. cit.*, pp.98ff.

[3]G.v.Rad & G.Kittel, δόξα, *TDNT* ii, pp.245ff.; W.Pannenberg, 'Dogmatische Thesen zur Lehre von der Offenbarung', *Offenbarung als Geschichte*, ed. W.Pannenberg (²1963), p.93.

[4]At this point Lührmann's view should be corrected, based, as it is, upon a wrong interpretation of 2Bar 76.1 that apocalyptists' visions and dreams of heavenly realities themselves are not revelations but only their interpretations are revelations (*op. cit.*, pp.40, 75, 100f.). A comparison of 2Bar 56.1 with 76.1 shows,contrary to Lührmann's view, that their visions and dreams of heavenly realities as well as their interpretations are revelations (cf. also Dan 2.28). So Paul's synonymous use of vision and revelation in 2Cor 12.1 (ὀπτασίαι καὶ ἀποκαλύψεις κυρίου) is not his innovation but stands in line with the apocalyptic understanding of revelation (cf. also Rev 1.1. *Contra* Lührmann, *op. cit.*, p.40). See Stuhlmacher, *Evangelium*, pp.76f. (n.3).

[5]Lührmann, *op. cit.*, p.104; similarly U.Wilckens, *loc. cit.*. For a very different conception of revelation in the Qumran sect, however, see O.Betz, *Offenbarung und Schriftforschung in der Qumransekte* (1960), *passim*; Lührmann, *op. cit.*, pp.84ff.

16 to be understood? The first point to consider is that what Paul describes
as God's revelation of Jesus Christ in Gal 1.12, 16 is Christ's resurrection appearance to him (1Cor 9.1; 15.8ff.)[1]. Through God's disclosure of the risen
Christ Paul realized that the Christian proclamation of the Messiahship
of Jesus and of his resurrection was true. Since both the revelation of the
Messiah and resurrection from the dead were expected in Judaism to be
God's eschatological act signalling the end of this aeon and the beginning
of the new, Paul was convinced that the *eschaton* had broken in with God's
saving act in Jesus Christ. So Paul could say, 'When the time had fully come,
God sent forth his Son . . . ' (Gal 4.4). In the old aeon the wrath of God was
the ruling factor, 'but now the righteousness of God has been revealed apart
from the law' through God's redemptive work in Christ (Rom 3.21ff.). So
Paul says, 'Behold, now is the acceptable time; behold, now is the day of
salvation' (2Cor 6.2).

But this eschatological time of salvation is not yet fully realized. 'The
present evil aeon' (Gal 1.4) still continues; the 'god of this age' is still active

---

[1]G.Bornkamm and D.Lührmann deny that by the 'revelation of Jesus Christ' Paul
here refers to the vision of the risen Christ on the Damascus road. According to Lührmann, the 'revelation of Jesus Christ' here means neither an anticipatory disclosure in
vision of the eschatological revelation nor the Christ-event itself, but rather 'eine auf den
Menschen bezogene Interpretation dieses Geschehens (i.e., Christusgeschehens) als den
Menschen angehend durch ein neu einsetzendes Handeln Gottes'(*op. cit.*, pp.73–81,
107, *et passim*. Quotation from p.79). According to Bornkamm, however, the 'revelation of Jesus Christ' in Gal 1.12, 16 is 'ein objektives, weltenwendendes Geschehen,
das durch Gottes souveränes Handeln eine neue Weltzeit heraufgeführt hat und im
Evangelium verkündet wird' (*Paulus*, p.44; similarly already in his 'Paulus', *RGG*[3]
v, 169; again more elaborately in his 'Revelation of Christ to Paul on the Damascus
Road and Paul's Doctrine of Justification and Reconciliation. A Study in Galatians 1',
Reconciliation and Hope, L.L. Morris FS, ed. R.Banks (1974), pp.91ff.). If for Lührmann the 'revelation of Jesus Christ' to Paul means God's informing him of the significance of the Christ-event for him, for Bornkamm it seems to mean the Christ-event
itself. But both do not seem to understand the relation between the Christ-event and the
Damascus revelation quite correctly. For a critique of Lührmann's view, see Stuhlmacher, *Evangelium*, p.81. Bornkamm's view, if we have understood it correctly, can
hardly be maintained without further qualification: it stumbles on $\dot{\epsilon}\nu$ $\dot{\epsilon}\mu o\acute{\iota}$ in Gal 1.16.
Fundamentally, their denial that by the 'revelation of Jesus Christ' Paul means Christ's
resurrection appearance, seems to be at fault. Probably K.Kertelge has expressed the
relation between the Christ-event and the Damascus revelation correctly: the revelation
of Jesus Christ as God's Son to Paul in Gal 1.12, 16 is 'die auf seine Beruf bezogene
Verlängerung der *einen* in Christus vorweggenommenen eschatologischen Selbstmitteilung
Gottes' ('Apokalypsis Jesou Christou (Gal 1, 12)', *Neues Testament und Kirche*, R.
Schnackenburg FS, ed. J.Gnilka (1974), p.275).

(2Cor 4.4; cf. also 1Cor 2.6, 8; Gal 4.9; Col 2.20); and Christ's lordship is not yet universally confessed (1Cor 15.24f.). 'Christ has been raised from the dead', but he is only 'the firstfruits of those who have fallen asleep' (1Cor 15.20) and the general resurrection does not yet take place. We, the Christians, who already have the eschatological gift of the Spirit as the firstfruits of our salvation, groan, 'as we wait for adoption as sons, the redemption of our bodies' (Rom 8.23). So we wait for the ἀποκάλυψις of Christ (1Cor 1.7; 2Th 1.7; cf. also Col 3.4), his parousia (1Cor 15.23; 1Th 2.19; 3.13; 4.15; 5.23; 2Th 2.1, 8f.; cf. also Phil 3.20). The revelation of Christ will bring in the last judgement (Rom 2.5; 14.10; 1Cor 3.13; 2Cor 5.10) and the consummation of our salvation (Rom 8.18ff.; 1Cor 15.5ff.; Phil 3.20f.).

This means that Christ's first coming and the salvation that he has already brought in are the provisionary realization of his final revelation and of our final salvation. Paul learned this through the ἀποκάλυψις Ἰησοῦ Χριστοῦ on the Damascus road. For it confirmed on the one hand the Christian proclamation that the Messiah had come in the person of Jesus while on the other hand it pointed to the final revelation of Jesus Christ as the Judge and Saviour, which is already prepared in heaven and will take place at the *eschaton*.

In so far as Paul describes his vision of the risen Christ exalted at the right hand of God in heaven as the ἀποκάλυψις Ἰησοῦ Χριστοῦ, he indicates that his vision, like those in Jewish apocalyptic writings, was of the heavenly reality that will be revealed at the end of time and so it was an anticipation or prolepsis of the eschatological ἀποκάλυψις of Jesus Christ[1]. But it was at the same time fundamentally different from the visions described in Jewish apocalyptic writings, in that for Paul it was not a vision of an exclusively future event but a vision of the one who had already come to earth and who will also come to earth again at the end of time. This has made Paul's gospel fundamentally different from the apocalyptists' message. While the latter directs its attention exclusively to the future salvation that is to be revealed at the *eschaton*, the former proclaims the salvation that has already been realized in the Messiah Jesus, although it still envisages the *consummation* of that salvation at the *eschaton*. Thus, because Jesus was revealed on the Damascus road as the Messiah who has already come as well as the Messiah who will come at the *eschaton*, Paul's gospel that proclaims God's saving act in Jesus Christ bursts the apocalyptic schema in which the revelation to a seer through

---

[1] So Schlier, *Gal.*, pp.47, 55; Stuhlmacher, *Evangelium*, pp.71, 76–82; cf. also Wilckens, *op. cit.*, p.86; *contra* Lührmann, *op. cit.*, pp.107f., *et passim*.

a vision is *merely* a prolepsis of the eschatological revelation[1]. However, in so far as the Damascus revelation of Jesus Christ shares the characteristic of an apocalyptic revelation through a vision, in that it is a prolepsis of the final revelation, the parousia, at the *eschaton*, the salvation proclaimed by Paul's gospel has the character of being a prolepsis of the final salvation at the *eschaton*. Thus, from Paul's Damascus experience of the revelation of Jesus as the Messiah who has already come and as the one who will come at the *eschaton*, there results the characteristic of his gospel that proclaims salvation as a present reality and yet expects its consummation at the *eschaton*[2].

2 The 'Mystery'

The Spirit builds the bridge between the present and the final salvation. For he is the ἀπαρχή and ἀρραβών of our final salvation (Rom 8. 23; 2Cor 1.22; 5.5; Eph 2.14). Until the ἀποκάλυψις of Jesus Christ at the parousia, however, the gospel that proclaims the proleptic revelation of Jesus Christ, like the revelations given to Jewish apocalyptists, remains a μυστήριον[3]. For

---

[1]We are much indebted to Stuhlmacher in this section. However, at this point a criticism is due: namely, that he does not seem to see the difference between the revelations described in Jewish apocalyptic writings and the Damascus revelation (cf. *Evangelium*, pp.76ff.).

[2]Cf. Stuhlmacher, 'Gegenwart und Zukunft in der paulinischen Eschatologie', *ZThK* 64(1967), p.429: 'Paulus beschreibt jenen Berufungsvorgang in 1.Kor. 9, 16f. sowohl wie in Gal. 1, 12–17 mit alttestamentlich autorisierten, apokalyptischen Begriffen. Diese Darstellungsweise ist wichtig, weil sie zu erkennen gibt, *daß die uns beschäftigende Spannung zwischen Heilsgegenwart und Zukunft des Heils dem Apostel schon im Ursprung seiner Sendung begegnet'* (emphasis by St.). It is not clear, however, how Stuhlmacher can derive this conclusion when he sees Paul completely within the apocalyptic schema without emphasizing at the same time the difference between Paul and apocalypticism as we have done here. Only at the end of his article does Stuhlmacher refer to the difference: 'Daß der Apostel nicht mehr alles Heil aus der Zukunft erwartet wie die eschatologische Prophetie . . . , ist Folge seiner Begegnung mit dem Christus und sicheres Kennzeichen dafür, daß sich bei ihm eine Umschichtung des Denkens vollzogen hat' (p.449, n.56).

[3]Cf. Bornkamm's definition of the apocalyptic concept of mystery: 'The mysteries are God's counsels destined finally to be disclosed. They are final events and states which are already truly existent in heaven and may be seen there, and which will in the last days emerge from their concealment and become manifest events' (μυστήριον, *TDNT* iv, p.816). See further, R.E.Brown, 'The Semitic Background of the NT *Mysterion*', *Biblica* 39 (1958), esp. pp.434–448 and *Biblica* 40 (1959), pp.70ff.; O.Betz, *Offenbarung*, pp.83ff.; J.Coppens, ' "Mystery" in the Theology of Saint Paul and its Parallels at Qumran', *Paul and Qumran*, ed. J.Murphy-O'Connor (1968), pp.132ff. For a special affinity of the use of the concept mystery in Eph. and in the Qumran literature, see K.G.Kuhn, 'Der Epheserbrief im Lichte der Qumrantexte', *NTS* 7 (1960/61), p.336.;

the content of the gospel, the salvation-occurrence in Christ and the consummation of that salvation at the parousia, though visible to the enlightened, the believers, is still invisible to the blind, those who have no faith, in this aeon (2Cor 4.3f.). Only at the final revelation of Jesus Christ, that is, at the parousia, will it be visible to all, free of the dialectic of concealment and revelation[1].

So Paul applies the concept of mystery to the gospel and to Christ, the content of the gospel. This is clear, first of all, in 1Cor 1.18–2.16. Instead of saying that he came to Corinth proclaiming the gospel of Christ, Paul can say that he came to Corinth 'proclaiming the mystery of God' (1Cor 2.1)[2]. Jesus Christ the crucified is 'the mystery of God' (1Cor 1.23; 2.2) or 'God's wisdom ἐν μυστηρίῳ' (2.7)[3]. In this passage Paul is concerned to oppose the error of the Corinthian 'pneumatics' who, having 'been made rich' in the spiritual gifts of words and knowledge (1Cor 1.5), turn these gifts into the human or worldly wisdom of this aeon by boasting of them and engaging in divisive arguments with one another to show off their superior knowledge and wisdom[4]. In view of this error Paul reminds them that they are in fact no

---

also J.Coppens, *op. cit.*, pp.151f.; F.Mussner, 'Contributions made by Qumran to the Understanding of the Epistle to the Ephesians', *Paul and Qumran*, pp.99f.

[1]See Stuhlmacher, *Evangelium*, pp.77ff., for the inherent dialectic of concealment and revelation in the apocalyptic phenomenon of proleptic revelation. Cf. also Bornkamm, μυστήριον, *TDNT* iv, pp.820f.

[2]Reading τὸ μυστήριον τοῦ θεοῦ instead of τὸ μαρτύριον τοῦ θεοῦ. 'From an exegetical point of view the reading μαρτύριον τοῦ θεοῦ, though well supported (B D G P, etc.), is inferior to μυστήριον, which has more limited but early support in p46 ℵ* A C etc. The reading μαρτύριον seems to be a recollection of 1.6, whereas μυστήριον here prepares for its usage in v.7' (B.M.Metzger, *A Textual Commentary on the Greek NT* (1971), p.545). So also J.Weiss, *Der erste Korintherbrief* (⁹1910), pp.45f.; Lietzmann-Kümmel, *Kor.*, p.11; Bornkamm, *op. cit.*, p.818 (n. 141).

[3]It seems better to take ἐν μυστηρίῳ with θεοῦ σοφίαν rather than with λαλοῦμεν. For, as U.Wilckens (*Weisheit und Torheit* (1959), p.64. n.1) says, μυστήριον always indicates in the LXX, apocalyptic literature and the NT a content rather than a form. Moreover, the following τὴν ἀποκεκρυμμένην as an explanatory gloss seems to be decisively in favour of connecting ἐν μυστηρίῳ with θεοῦ σοφίαν rather than with λαλοῦμεν (so Barrett, *1Cor.*, p.70). J.Weiss, *1.Kor.*, pp.54f., however, takes the phrase with the verb, referring to 1Cor 14.6 as a parallel to the construction λαλεῖν ἐν μυστηρίῳ here. But he admits that the resulting phrase '(to speak God's wisdom) in the form of a mystery' 'goes easily over into the nuance: "as a mystery" '.

[4]Against the anachronistic attempts to see the Corinthian situation underlying 1Cor. in the light of Gnosticism, of which we know at the earliest from the sources of 2nd c.A.D. (e.g., Wilckens, *Weisheit*; also his σοφία, *TDNT* vii, p.519), E.E.Ellis, ' "Wisdom" and "Knowledge" in 1Corinthians', *TynB* 25 (1974), pp.82–98, has rather convincingly shown that the phenomena of wisdom and knowledge in 1Cor. are to be explained

real pneumatics, as their jealousy and strife show (1Cor 3.1ff.). And against their mistaken notion of wisdom Paul holds out 'Christ crucified' as the real wisdom, the wisdom of God (1Cor 1.24, 30). Now 'Christ crucified' is according to the worldly standard no wisdom but simply a folly (1Cor 1.21, 23). He is known as the wisdom of God only to those who are called (1Cor 1.24, 30). This is so because he is God's wisdom ἐν μυστηρίῳ, the hidden wisdom (1Cor 2.7). 'Christ crucified' is God's wisdom ἐν μυστηρίῳ because he embodies 'God's wise plan of redeeming the world through a crucified

---

against the background of the OT and Jewish apocalypticism, where wisdom is a charismatic gift granted to prophets or apocalyptists. Ellis shows, first of all, the connection between wisdom and prophecy, between wise men and prophets in the OT, and then how the traits of prophet and those of wisdom teacher are merged in the apocalyptic seer. He finds the similarities between the *maskilim* in Qumran and the pneumatics in 1Cor. especially striking: 'the *maskilim* at Qumran are recipients and transmitters of divine mysteries, possessors of wisdom, interpreters of knowledge, guides to a mature life, and discerners of spirits. As such they not only reflect their kinship with the earlier prophets but also bear a striking resemblance to the pneumatics in the Pauline community' (p.95). So, according to Ellis, the Corinthian Christians who claim to be wise are those who having received the spiritual gifts of inspired words and knowledge, act as prophets. The problem with them, however, is: 'having "been made rich" in Christ's gifts of words and knowledge, they "boast as though the gifts were their own attainment. Having been endowed in order to "build" God's temple, they are instead destroying it by their boasting, envy, strife, and dissension. In consequence, their cherished wisdom, in a subtle transformation that even they have not discovered, has become mere cleverness, a manifestation of human words rather than of divine power. And, apparently, they have failed to distinguish the resulting "wisdom of this age" from "the wisdom from above" (cf. Jas 3.13–15, 17)' (E.E.Ellis, "Christ Crucified", *Reconciliation and Hope*, Morris FS, pp.74f.). This seems to be a much more sensible explanation of the Corinthian situation than, e.g., U.Wilckens' hypothesis that the Corinthian pneumatics represent a Gnostic sophia-Christology which holds Christ as the pre-existent wisdom of God who has been exalted to be κύριος τῆς δόξης through descent and ascent in the pattern of the presumed Gnostic redeemer myth and which therefore has no room for the cross (*Weisheit*, esp. pp.205ff.; *TDNT* vii, pp.509ff.). Against this hypothesis two arguments are in order: first, there is no *religionsgeschichtliche* basis for such a developed myth in the first c.A.D. Even if the personified wisdom in the pre-Christian Jewish wisdom literature were to be understood as reflecting not just a figure of speech or tendency to hypostatization of a divine attribute but a myth (Wilckens, *Weisheit*, pp. 160ff.; *TDNT* vii, pp.507ff.), the myth is very far from the later Gnostic redeemer myth *(infra*, pp.162ff.). Secondly, there is little justification for Wilckens' procedure to read out of what Paul says in 1Cor 1f. the Corinthian sophia-Christology and then say that Paul partly accepts it and partly corrects it. 'Andeutungen (und nicht mehr als das!) einer Sophia-Christologie finden sich *gerade nicht im Munde der Gegner des Paulus, sondern in seinem eigenen Mund*: 1, 24 u.30; 2,6ff. (vgl. noch 10,1ff.), an jenen Stellen also, wo Paulus seine eigene Auffassung vorträgt, die er der korinthischen gegenüberstellt' (K.Niederwimmer, 'Erkennen und Lieben', *KD* 11 (1965), p.79. Emphasis by N.). See further two more objections of Niederwimmer to Wilckens' hypothesis;

Messiah'[1], 'which God foreordained for our glory before the course of ages began' (1Cor 2.7), and salvation 'which God prepared for those who love him' (1Cor 2.9)[2]. This wisdom of God was completely hidden both to the spiritual forces that dominate this aeon and to men (1Cor 2.7–9). But now God has revealed it to Paul and his colleagues[3] through the Spirit, so that they speak this wisdom ἐν μυστηρίῳ among the mature (1Cor 2.6), the real pneumatics who, having received the Spirit of God, are able to discern the wisdom of God in the crucified Christ (cf. 1Cor 2.10–3.1)[4]. So Paul and his

---

and also criticism by H.Köster in his review of Wilckens' book in *Gnomon* 33 (1961) pp.590–595; by R.McL.Wilson, 'How Gnostic were the Corinthians?', *NTS* 19 (1972/ 73), pp.72f.; and by R.Scroggs, 'Paul: ΣΟΦΟΣ and ΠΝΕΤΜΑΤΙΚΟΣ', *NTS* 14 (1967/ 68), pp.33ff. If Ellis seems to have successfully explained the problem of wisdom in Corinth, R.Scroggs seems to have succeeded in showing that the background of Paul's exposition on God's wisdom in 1Cor 2.6–16 is the Jewish apocalyptic-wisdom tradition, as there are many parallels in terms and ideas between them. Cf. R.G.Hamerton-Kelly, *Pre-Existence, Wisdom, and the Son of Man* (1973), pp.112ff., who similarly sees the Jewish appocalyptic tradition represented by 1En. as the background of Paul's thought here but unconvincingly attempts to show that the Corinthian trouble-makers in 1Cor 1–4 represent the Hellenistic mysticism of Philo's kind.

[1]Barrett, *1Cor.*, p.68.

[2]This is an attempt to do justice to two fluctuating senses in which Paul seems to designate 'Christ crucified' as God's wisdom – God's plan of salvation (*Heilsplan*) and salvation itself (*Heilsgut*) as the eschatological blessing brought about through God's plan of salvation. Cf. Barrett, *1Cor.*, p.68; also Conzelmann, *1.Kor.*, pp.80, 82.

[3]ἡμεῖς / ἡμῖν in vs. 10ff. should be taken as referring primarily to Paul (and his colleagues), though they may perhaps be capable of being extended secondarily to include other 'pneumatics' besides Paul and his colleagues. For they refer primarily to the subject of v.6. So J.Lindblom, *Gesichte und Offenbarungen*, pp.154f.; R.Scroggs, *op. cit.*, pp.50, 53.

[4]The context makes it clear that Paul distinguishes between τὸ μυστήριον τοῦ θεοῦ which he preached to the Corinthians (2.1; 3.1f.) and θεοῦ σοφίαν ἐν μυστηρίῳ which he speaks only among the mature (2.6f.) and therefore could not speak among the Corinthians because of their immaturity (3.1f.). From this R.Scroggs (*op. cit.*, pp.35, 37, 54f.) maintains a rigid distinction between Paul's kerygma and sophia, the former being, according to him, 'Christ crucified' and the latter 'an esoteric wisdom teaching' (p. 35; cf. H.Conzelmann, 'Paulus und die Weisheit', *NTS* 12 (1965/66), pp.238ff.) which Paul insists he has but does not disclose. But such an essential distinction is ruled out by Paul's identification of God's wisdom with Christ who is the content of his kerygma (1.24, 30). Scroggs' repeated assertion that while insisting on his possession of wisdom Paul does not disclose it (p.37, *et passim*), can be made only when 1Cor 2.6ff. is unjustifiably disjointed from the foregoing (1Cor 1.18–2.5) as is done by Scroggs, or when the readers are expected to forget what Paul has just said (esp. 1.24, 30). In view of Paul's identification of Christ with God's wisdom, θεοῦ σοφία ἐν μυστηρίῳ cannot be therefore, in terms of its content, an esoteric doctrine besides 'Christ crucified', the mystery of God. So it must be thought of as an unfolding or an explanation in detail

fellow apostles are οἰκονόμοι μυστηρίων [1] θεοῦ (1Cor 4.1).

The aorist ἀπεκάλυψεν in 1Cor 2.10 leads us to ask when God revealed his hidden wisdom to Paul. Three considerations suggest that here Paul is alluding to the ἀποκάλυψις of Jesus Christ to him on the Damascus road. First, historically it was the ἀποκάλυψις Ἰησοῦ Χριστοῦ on the Damascus road that made Paul, the Pharisee, see in the 'Christ crucified' no longer a σκάνδαλον (1Cor 1.23; Gal 3.13) but instead the wisdom of God ἐν μυστηρίῳ. Paul's reference in 1Cor 2.10 to the mediating agency of the Spirit for the revelation of God's wisdom ἐν μυστηρίῳ may seem to suggest that he has in mind here one of the later charismatic revelations mentioned in 2Cor 12.1ff. rather than the Damascus revelation, in connection with which he never refers to the mediating agency of the Spirit (except in Eph 3.5 which is reminiscent of 1Cor 2.10). But in view of Paul's clear testimony elsewhere that at the Damascus revelation he received his gospel and apostolic call to preach the gospel among the Gentiles (Gal 1.12, 15f.; cf. also 2Cor 4.6) it is scarcely possible to imagine that he came to realise God's wise plan of salvation embodied in Christ not at the Damascus revelation but at another revelation some time after it. At the later 'visions and revelations of the Lord' (2Cor 12.1ff.) Paul may have been led to learn more deeply about God's wise counsel embodied in the crucified Christ. But the decisive revelation of it came to him on the Damascus road. Although Paul does not refer

---

of the wonder of God's plan of salvation contained in 'Christ crucified' (So Robertson-Plummer, *1Cor.*, pp.38f.; Bruce, *Cor.*, p.38; Bornkamm, *TDNT* iv, p.819; Niederwimmer, *op. cit.*, p.86). There is no need to see, with Wilckens (*Weisheit*, pp.52, 85) and Conzelmann (*1.Kor.*, p.81), a contradiction here between 1Cor 2.6ff. and 1.18–2.5 (see Niederwimmer, *op. cit.*, pp.86f.).

[1]Whereas in the apocalyptic and Qumran writings mostly the plural form of the word (רז / סוד /μυστήριον) appears, Paul always uses the singular μυστήριον except in three places (1Cor 4.1; 13.2; 14.2). In Eph 5.32 the singular μυστήριον refers to the allegorical meaning of Gen 2.24. In 1Cor 15.51 and 2Th 2.7 Paul refers with the singular μυστήριον to specific eschatological events of bodily metamorphosis of the living at the parousia and of 'lawlessness'. The plural μυστήρια in 1Cor 13.2 seems to mean similarly such specific eschatological events that are concealed in the divine plan and proleptically revealed to prophets under the inspiration of the Spirit. The 'mysteries' that are spoken by a tongue-speaker (1Cor 14.2) may mean the same, though in this case they remain unintelligible. In applying the word 'mystery' to Christ, the gospel or God's plan of salvation that Christ embodies, Paul always uses the singular (1Cor 2.1; Eph 1.9; 3.3f., 9; 6.19; Col 1.26f.; 2.2; 4.3; Rom 11.25; 16.25; cf. also 1Tim 3.9, 16). So, with the plural μυστήρια in 1Cor 4.1, does Paul refer not just to the Christ-mystery but to the plural number of God's eschatological counsels revealed to the apostles? Or does it reflect an early stage of Paul's thought in which the Christ-mystery was not yet terminologically fixed as τὸ μυστήριον. Cf. R.E.Brown, 'The Semitic Background', *Biblica* 39, p.440.

to the mediating role of the Spirit for the Damascus revelation elsewhere, we are to think that he presupposes it when he describes his Damascus experience as God's call of him analogous to the calls of the prophets of the OT[1] and as God's revelation (Gal 1.12, 16). For in the OT and Judaism the prophetic and apocalyptic revelations are regularly attributed to the mediating agency of the Spirit[2]. Paul's emphasis on the mediating agency of the Spirit here can be well understood in the light of his need to show the Corinthian 'pneumatics' what really is the wisdom imparted through the Spirit.

Secondly, Paul's calling 'Christ crucified' κύριος τῆς δόξης (1Cor 2.8) is reminiscent of his descriptions of the risen Christ who appeared to him, in other passages in which he alludes to his Damascus experience (1Cor 9.1; 2Cor 3.18; 4.4–6; cf. also Gal 1.16)[3]. As parallels to some terms and motifs in 1Cor 2.6–16 are found in various Jewish apocalyptic-wisdom literature[4], the title 'the Lord of glory' also appears frequently in 1Enoch (22.14; 25.3, 7; 27.3, 4; 63.2; 75.3). It is rather striking that in 1En. 63 the title appears within the motif that at the end the rulers of this age are to be punished for their failure to believe and glorify 'the Lord of glory and the Lord of wisdom' (v. 2), and this may be regarded as a rough parallel to the motif of 1Cor 2.6ff.[5]. Since the title seems to appear only in 1Enoch and in 1Cor 2.8 (cf. Jas 2.1), it is possible that Paul took it over from 1Enoch or the Jewish apocalyptic tradition represented by 1Enoch. However, tracing the title to the apocalyptic tradition does not in itself explain what has caused Paul to apply to Jesus the title which is ascribed to God in 1Enoch. Certainly the parallelism of the terms and motifs in 1En. 63 and 1Cor 2.6ff. is not close enough to allow any suggestion that in unfolding his thought here in dependence upon 1En. 63 Paul took over the title from it. It seems that the question can be explained best in the light of Paul's Damascus experience. As we

---

[1] *Infra.* pp.91ff.

[2] See, e.g., Gen 41.38; Num 24.2; 2Sam 23.2; 1Ki 22.24; Isa 61.1; Ezek 2.2; 8.3; 11.5; Zech 7.12; Sir. 48.12f., 24; 1En. 91.1; Test. Levi 2.3; 4Ezra 14.22; 1QH 12.11ff.; cf. also 1QS 9.18. Ezek 2.2 is particularly striking as the heavenly vision and the Spirit are brought together in the prophet's call. Cf. also Rev 1.10. See F.Baumgärtel & E.Sjöberg, πνεῦμα, *TDNT* vi, pp.362f., 381f. On the Qumran sect's understanding of the Spirit as the mediating agency of revelation, see Betz, *Offenbarung.*, pp.119ff. For the Rabbinic understanding of נבואה רוח see Str.-Bill. ii, pp.127ff. For the relation between the Damascus revelation (Gal 1.12ff.) and 'the visions and revelations of the Lord' (2Cor 12.1), see Stuhlmacher, *Evangelium*, pp.77ff. (n.1).

[3] This was already recognized by P.Feine, *Theologie des NT* ([3]1919), p.320. *Infra* pp.193f., 228.

[4] See Scroggs, *op. cit.*, pp.37ff.

[5] Cf. *ibid.*, p.46.

have observed above[1], Paul perceived the brilliant light accompanying the
exalted Jesus Christ in his revelation to him on the Damascus road as God's
glory and therefore the exalted Jesus as the Lord invested with God's glory
(2Cor 3.18; 4.4–6; Acts 9.4ff.; 22.6, 11; 26.13). So when he alludes to
the revelation of the exalted Christ to him on the Damascus road he speaks
of 'the glory of Christ' (2Cor 4.4) or 'the glory of the Lord' (2Cor 3.18) and
characterises the body of the exalted Jesus as 'the body of glory' (Phil 3.21).
The title 'the Lord of glory' for the crucified, risen and exalted Jesus Christ
therefore fits best in this context. Had he previously known the title in
1Enoch or the Jewish apocalyptic tradition represented by 1Enoch, he might
have thought that it appropriately described the exalted Jesus Christ revealed
to him. However, there is no compelling reason why Paul could not have
coined it himself, independent of 1Enoch, in the light of his Damascus
experience[2].

---

[1] *Supra* p.7; *infra* pp.229ff.

[2] 1Cor 2.8 is one of the two Pauline passages (the other being Gal 6.14) where the
title κύριος appears directly in connection with the cross. It is striking, since Paul
usually uses the title Χριστός in connection with the cross (1Cor 1.17, 23; 2.2; 2Cor
13.3f.; Gal 3.1; 6.12; Phil 3.18) while reserving the title κύριος for the motifs of the
exaltation of Jesus, of his present lordship over the universe and the Church, of the
Church's confession of his lordship, and of his parousia. In Gal 6.14, against the agitators in Galatia who would glory in the flesh and in their success scored on the flesh of
the circumcised Galatians, Paul says that his glory is only ἐν τῷ σταυρῷ τοῦ κυρίου
ἡμῶν Ἰησοῦ Χριστοῦ. The Judaisers would well understand, though they may not
practise, the injunction, ὁ καυχώμενος ἐν κυρίῳ καυχάσθω (Jer 9.23), cited by Paul
elsewhere against those who boast in the things of the world (1Cor 1.31; 2Cor 10.17).
Here, however, Paul radicalizes the antithesis between the ground of the Christian boasting and that of the worldly boasting by making not simply the Lord but specifically 'the
cross of the Lord' the sole object of the Christian boasting. For the cross is to the man
of the world a scandal (1Cor 1.23; Gal 5.11) and a cause for persecution (Gal 5.11;
6.12). By joining the cross with the title κύριος Paul heightens still further the scanda-
lous character of the cross for the man of the world and at the same time explains most
effectively why the cross is the ground of boasting for the Christian. The cross is the
ground of boasting for the Christian because it is the cross of the *Lord*, that is, of him
who was not defeated on the cross, as is supposed by the man of the world, but who has
triumphed over the world and its rulers precisely on that cross (cf. 1Cor 2.6ff.), as
acknowledged by the man of faith. The Christian has done away with the world through
the cross and has become καινὴ κτίσις, so that to him a reversal of values has taken
place: the cross that is regarded as an absurdity and a scandal in the world, is to him the
ground of glory, and the flesh that is the ground of glory in the world, is to him the
ground of shame. This radical reversal of values is most effectively expressed in the
confession that the crucified one is the Lord. The same pattern of thought appears in
1Cor 2.8. He whom the rulers of this aeon crucified is none other than 'the Lord of
glory'. The cross which is a sign of defeat and shame, foolishness and scandal for those
who are perishing in the world, is a sign of triumph and boasting, wisdom and glory for

Thirdly, the present passage, 1Cor 2.6–10 (together with 2.1; 4.1), is very similar to Col 1.23c–29 and Eph 3.1–13, both passages, as observed above[1], dealing with Paul's call at which God's mystery was revealed to him. The three passages show at least three common charcteristics. One is what N.A. Dahl calls 'Revelation-Schema': the mystery which existed from eternity in concealment is now revealed[2]. The second is the fact that the recipients

---

those who are called. Just as in Gal 6.14 by joining the title κύριος with the cross Paul expresses the absolute antithesis between the ground of the worldly boasting and that of the Christian boasting, so here in 1Cor 2.8 also by joining the title κύριος with the cross he expresses the absolute antithesis between the wisdom of the world and that of God and the radical hiddenness of God's wisdom to the world (Cf. Lührmann, *Offenbarungs-verständnis*, p.137). A similar pattern of thought is also discernable in Phil 3.17–21. Although in this passage the title κύριος is not directly connected with the cross, there is the same antithesis between those who live as 'enemies of the *cross* of Christ', pre-occupied with the earthly things and glorying in the flesh (cf. 3.3f.), and the Christians who live under the sign of the cross (by implication -- cf. 3.10f.) and yet as citizens of heaven, waiting for 'a Saviour, namely the *Lord* Jesus Christ'. So here also the σταυρός-κύριος paradox hovers at least in the background. It is probable that here when Paul speaks of the Christians waiting for 'a Saviour, namely the Lord Jesus Christ' from heaven, he is remembering the proleptic parousia of the Lord Jesus Christ to him on the Damascus road, from which he learned that the risen and exalted Lord Jesus Christ is to be revealed from heaven at the end (*supra*, pp.72f.). Paul's calling the body of the exalted Jesus as 'the body of glory' supports this (*infra*, p.228.). And the context seems to confirm it. Since the present passage, Phil 3.18–21, is in fact a concluding summary of the foregoing (3.2–16. So Gnilka, *Der Philipperbrief* (1968), p.203), in which Paul has countered the Judaisers' boasting in the flesh by drawing a radical contrast between his pre-Damascus Pharisaic existence and his post-Damascus Christian existence, it is likely that in the present passage he writes still in conscious memory of his Damascus experience. All three passages set forth the contrast between worldly and Christian existence and make it clear with the σταυρός-κύριος paradox that the fundamental point of the contrast is their attitudes to the cross. For the man of the world the cross is foolishness and a scandal so that he is hostile to it; and this man was typified by Paul the Pharisee who persecuted the Church because of the scandal of the cross. But for the Christian the cross is God's wisdom and the ground of glorying; and the Christian is now typified by Paul the Christian apostle. The conversion from the former to the latter occurred to Paul when God revealed to him that the crucified one is the Lord of glory. With this we are back at the first point that we made above.

[1] *Supra* pp.20–25.

[2] N.A.Dahl, 'Formgeschichtliche Beobachtungen zur Christusverkündigung in der Gemeindepredigt', *Neutestamentliche Studien für R.Bultmann*, ed. W.Eltester ([2]1957), pp.4f. Cf. also Rom 16.25f. A variation of the schema which lacks the concepts 'mystery' and 'hidden' appears in the Pastoral Epistles and the non-Pauline writings: 2Tim 1.9–11; Tit 1.2f.; 1Pet 1.19–21 (cf. 1.10–12); 1Jn 1.1–3. Lührmann, *Offen-barungsverständnis*, pp.133ff., thinks that Paul quotes it from his Corinthian Gnostic opponents and at the same time corrects it. Against this view, however, Conzelmann,

of the revelation of the mystery are first Paul and his colleagues[1] and then Christians who receive the revelation of the mystery through their preaching[2]. The third common point is that the mystery designates Christ and God's plan of salvation that Christ embodies. However, there is a shift of emphasis in defining the mystery from 1Cor 2.1ff. through Col 1.24ff. to Eph 3.1ff. In 1Cor 2 the mystery of God, or God's wisdom ἐν μυστηρίῳ, implies simply Christ or God's plan of salvation embodied in Christ. But in Col 1.24ff. the mystery is defined more specifically as Χριστὸς ἐν ὑμῖν, the Christ who is preached among the Gentiles, and therefore it denotes God's plan of salvation that makes the Gentiles participants in salvation. This thought is made still more explicit in Eph 3, where 'the mystery of Christ' (v. 4) is that 'the Gentiles are fellow heirs, members of the same body, and fellow partakers in the promise in Christ Jesus through the gospel' (v. 6). But these are not essential differences: we have to do here not with three different mysteries but one mystery, Christ.

At the ἀποκάλυψις of Jesus Christ on the Damascus road, Paul perceived Christ as God's mystery, that is, the embodiment of God's plan of salvation which God determined from eternity and which is now revealed. In Col 1.23c–29 and Eph 3.1–13 Paul emphasizes as the mystery God's plan of salvation that includes the Gentiles among the recipients of the salvation in Christ. In doing so, however, he makes only more explicit what he has already implied in Gal 1.16 by saying that the purpose of God's revealing his Son to him was for him, Paul, to preach the Son of God among the Gentiles.

If God's will to call the Gentiles to participate now in the salvation in Christ through the proclamation of the gospel was revealed to Paul on the

---

1.Kor., p.75, points out that outside the range of Paul's influence the schema itself does not appear, except as isolated motifs. Conzelmann thinks that it developed within the Pauline school and that in 1Cor 2.6ff. we have it *in statu nascendi*. He contends that it contains no Gnostic motifs (*contra* Lührmann, *loc. cit.*) but the motifs of the Hellenistic σωτήρ - ἐπιφάνεια -religiosity. But there is no trace of the Hellenistic σωτήρ - ἐπιφάνεια-religiosity in 1Cor 2.6ff.; Col 1.24ff.; Eph 3.1ff.; Rom 16.25f.

[1] In Eph 3.5 the recipients are formally named as God's 'holy apostles and prophets'.

[2] In Col 1.24ff. it is not explicitly said that Paul received the revelation of the mystery as in 1Cor 2.10 and Eph 3.3, and so the Colossian passage may seem to give the impression that the mystery was revealed (ἐφανερώθη) to God's saints directly (v.26). But the context clearly implies that in the preaching of Paul (and his colleagues) the mystery is revealed to believers (so Lührmann, *op. cit.*, pp.117f.; Lohse, *Kol.*, pp.120ff). On the other hand, there is little ground for Lührmann's attempt to see a difference between what he considers the deutero-Pauline Eph 3 and Col 1 on the one hand and the Paul of the 'genuine' letters on the other in their understanding of the apostolic office as a medium of revelation to believers (*op. cit.*, p.122; cf. also pp.93–97).

Damascus road as part of God's plan of salvation, was then the μυστήριον mentioned in Rom 11.25f. also revealed at the time of the ἀποκάλυψις of Jesus Christ? In Rom 11 Paul repeatedly says that the unbelief of Israel has led to the Gentiles' obtaining salvation (vs. 11, 12, 15, 28–30): it is because Israel have rejected the gospel that it is now preached to the Gentiles (cf. Acts 13.46; 18.6; 22.18ff.; 28.28). In this actual missionary situation, however, Paul recognizes God's plan of salvation at work. Behind Israel's hardening against the gospel there is God's purpose to bring the Gentiles first to salvation and then, at the conclusion of the Gentile mission, to save all Israel. In Rom 11.25f., wary of the possible complacency and boasting of the Gentile Christians over against unbelieving Israel, Paul solemnly lets them know the mystery: ὅτι πώρωσις ἀπὸ μέρους τῷ Ἰσραὴλ γέγονεν ἄχρι οὗ τὸ πλήρωμα τῶν ἐθνῶν εἰσέλθῃ, καὶ οὕτως πᾶς Ἰσραὴλ σωθήσεται, καθὼς γέγραπται, Ἥξει ἐκ Σιὼν ὁ ῥυόμενος,, κτλ.

Before answering the question whether this mystery was revealed to Paul on the Damascus road, we must understand its content precisely. The majority of the commentators give to καὶ οὕτως a temporal sense, 'and then'[1]. But since οὕτως is not preceded here by a temporal dependent clause, a participial phrase or a genitive absolute[2], the temporal rendering does not seem to be correct[3]. So it has been suggested that the οὕτως should be taken as correlative with the following καθὼς and rendered, 'in the following way ... as'[4]. This is certainly possible. If this is so, however, the mixed quotation of Isa 59.20f. and 27.9 introduced here by the regular citation formula, καθὼς γέγραπται, has primarily the function not of providing a Scriptural proof for the statement, 'all Israel will be saved', but of foretelling the *way* in which all Israel will be saved. But this seems to involve a leap in thought. Since from Rom 11.11 onwards and especially in the present paragraph of Rom 11.25ff. Paul is concerned to assert that Israel's fall is not final, he might have been expected, first of all, to assert clearly that Israel will be saved, thus drawing the positive consequence from the preceding statement, 'partial hardening has come upon Israel until the fullness of the Gentiles come in', before jumping

---

[1]E.g., Michel, *Römer*, p.278; Althaus, *Römer*, p.107; Barrett, *Romans*, p.223; latest Käsemann, *Römer*, p.300.

[2]See Liddell-Scott, s.v., 1, 7.

[3]Luz, *Geschichtsverständnis*, p.293; P.Stuhlmacher, 'Zur Interpretation von Römer 11, 25–32', *Probleme biblischer Theologie*, G.v.Rad FS, ed. H.W.Wolff (1971), pp.559f.; cf. also Leenhardt, *Romans*, pp.293f.

[4]Bauer-Arndt-Gingrich, s.v., 2; C.Müller,, *Gottes Gerechtigkeit und Gottes Volk* (1964), p.43; C.Plag, *Israels Wege zum Heil* (1969), p.37 (n.148); Stuhlmacher, 'Interpretation', p.560.

to describe the way in which Israel will be saved[1]. In other words, taking οὕτως together with καθώς as a correlative particle shifts concern from Israel's fate as such to the way of Israel's salvation, and this shift is abrupt. Were there no other way to interpret the οὕτως here, this solution might be adopted, notwithstanding the logical flaw.

But there is a possibility of interpreting the οὕτως precisely so as to avoid this problem. It is to take it as inferential and render it 'so' or 'therefore'[2]. Then the καὶ οὕτως introduces an inference from the foregoing ὅτι-clause[3]. If this interpretation is correct, then the μυστήριον is, strictly speaking, limited to the ὅτι-clause, namely, 'partial hardening has come upon Israel until the full number of the Gentiles come in', the next statement, 'all Israel will be saved', being an inference from the fact that the partial hardening of Israel is limited to a definite time span. However, with the conjunction καὶ Paul connects the mystery proper and the inference from it very closely together[4], so that in his mind the inference seems to form a part of the mystery. On this showing, καθώς γέγραπται introduces, as usual, a Scriptural proof for the truth of the foregoing statement, namely 'all Israel will be saved', thus emphasizing it quite in harmony with the general tendency of the context which from v.11 on has moved toward this climax. So we

---

[1]*Contra* Luz, *Geschichtsverständnis*, p.294, who does not take the οὕτως as correlative to καθώς and yet thinks that Paul's concern here is about 'die Art und Weise der Bekehrung Israels'. It is far-fetched to read out of the οὕτως Paul's idea that 'Israel wird auf unerwartete paradoxe Weise gerettet'.

[2]Cf. Liddell-Scott, s.v., II; Bauer-Arndt-Gingrich, s.v., 1b.

[3]So D.Zeller, *Juden und Heiden in der Mission des Paulus* (1973), p.251; cf. also Murray, *Romans* ii, p.96. Michel, *Römer*, p.280, also considers this interpretation before opting for the temporal interpretation.

[4]When it is inferentially used, οὕτως usually stands at the beginning of a sentence (e.g., Rom 1.15; 6.11). However, a preceding καὶ does not seem to affect its meaning, except that the inference led by καὶ οὕτως is more closely connected with what precedes (cf. Rom 5.12. See Cranfield, *Romans*, p.272 (n.5)). The position of οὕτως in Rom 11.26 seems to be an additional argument for taking it as inferential rather than correlative with καθώς . For if the latter is meant, οὕτως would be more properly placed either immediately before or after the verb σωθήσεται (cf. Phil 3.17; Lk 24.24). Against this Rom 15.20f may be cited, where οὕτως stands at the head of the sentence and is explained by καθὼς γέγραπται which introduces a Scriptural citation at the end to explain Paul's missionary principle. But there the position of οὕτως is easily explained in terms of emphasis. For there Paul's concern is to enunciate the principle of his missionary method. If the position of οὕτως in Rom 11.26 is explained similarly in terms of emphasis, as though Paul were not just stating but emphasizing that Israel will be saved in the way as foretold by Isaiah (59.20f. and 27.9), then the abruptness in the logical sequence that we have noted above will be all the more serious.

would suggest that the μυστήριον consists in two parts: 'partial hardening has come upon Israel until the full number of the Gentiles come in'; and 'all Israel will be saved'[1]. If this is correct, by introducing the mystery Paul lays stress rather on the fact of Israel's eventual salvation than on the temporal sequence of it, although he quite clearly has in view also a temporal sequence: 1) the partial hardening of Israel, 2) the entry of the full number of the Gentiles, and 3) the salvation of all Israel[2].

Was this divine plan of salvation revealed to Paul at the Damascus Christophany? This question will be answered negatively by anyone who thinks with R. Bultmann that the mystery sprang from Paul's 'speculative fantasy'[3]. To be sure, Paul does not expressly appeal to a revelation here. However, by applying the term μυστήριον to the divine plan of salvation he implies that it is not something that he has obtained through speculation but that it is a revelation of God. Indeed he imparts the μυστήριον here precisely in order to prevent the Gentile Christian readers from indulging in their own cleverness, and the condemnation of indulgence in one's own cleverness and conceit must have applied to Paul himself as well[4]. That by the μυστήριον Paul means not a human speculation but a divine revelation, is confirmed by the concluding doxology in Rom 11.33−36, with which Paul crowns his unfolding of the divine *Heilsgeschichte* in Rom 9−11 and especially his disclosure and unfolding of the mystery in Rom 11.25ff. by making a humble confession that a human being can neither fathom the depth of God's riches, wisdom and knowledge nor grasp the wonder of his judgements and ways which the mystery represents[5]. The rhetorical question that Paul asks in the

---

[1]If οὔτως is to be taken as correlative with καθώς, then the two parts of the mystery will be: 1) 'Partial hardening has come upon Israel until the full number of the Gentiles come in'; and 2) 'All Israel will be saved in this way, namely as Isaiah has prophesied (59.20f.; 27.9) . . . '. Some who take καὶ οὔτως as temporal particles analyse the mystery in three parts: 1) a partial hardening has come upon Israel; 2) this state will last until the full number of the Gentiles come in; and 3) when this will have taken place, all Israel will be saved (Zahn, *Römer*, p.253; Michel, *Römer*, p.280).

[2]Luz, *Geschichtsverständnis*, p.293; Zeller, *Juden*, p.251.

[3]R.Bultmann, *Theology* ii, p.132. Similarly Scroggs, *op. cit.*,: 'a particular eschatological speculation' (p.46); 'a fragment of his (Paul's) wisdom teaching' (p.53). Against Bultmann, see Käsemann, *Römer*, p.299 and also Luz, *Geschichtsverständnis*, p.293.

[4]Cf. Luz, *Geschichtsverständnis*, pp.292f.; Käsemann, *Römer*, p.299.

[5]Against the misunderstanding that in the doxology Paul confesses that God and his ways are fundamentally unknowable, so that what he has just unfolded as a mystery is itself only an attempt to fathom God's ways in history which cannot claim absolute validity (Delling, ἀνεξερεύνητος, *TDNT* i, p.357; cf. also Conzelmann, *Outline*, p.252;

doxology, τίς . . . ἔγνω νοῦν κυρίου; (Rom 11.34a), he asks also in 1Cor 2.16 and answers there that he has the νοῦν Χριστοῦ, by which he probably intends to say that he has God's wisdom, namely the knowledge of God's plan of salvation revealed through the Spirit as well as the Spirit that he has received (1Cor 2.12)[1]. This is the concluding remark to his assertion in 1Cor 2.6–16 that through the Spirit God has revealed to him (and his colleagues) his hidden wisdom, i.e., his wise plan of salvation which was completely hidden both to the spiritual forces and to men. So while the doxology in Rom 11.33ff. completely negates the possibility of man's fathoming God's counsel and way for himself, it does not negate the possibility of man's knowing them through God's own revelation. Rather, it intensifies the revelation character of any knowledge of God's counsel and way. Therefore the mystery of Rom 11.25f. cannot be a mere human speculation; it is rather the νοῦς κυρίου that has been revealed to Paul through the Spirit[2].

Paul could have received the revelation of the mystery either through one of the 'visions and revelations' that he experienced (2Cor 12.1ff.) in much the

---

Luz, *Geschichtsverständnis*, pp.299f.), Käsemann, *Römer*, pp.306f., rightly points out that if that were so, that would contradict the entire Pauline kerygma. Käsemann's exposition of the doxology, drawing parallels from 1Cor 1–2, is very instructive.

[1]The Hebrew text of Isa 40.13 has רוח, which the LXX renders by νοῦς (only here; in all other places רוח is rendered by πνεῦμα). Since Paul quotes Isa 40.13 at the end of this discussion on the mediatory role of the Spirit in God's revelation of his wisdom, it is probable that he knew the original Hebrew text (so Scroggs, *op. cit.*, pp.53f.). If this is so, it would be expected of him to quote in 1Cor 2.16 the Isaianic question according to the Hebrew text and answer ἡμεῖς δὲ πνεῦμα Χριστοῦ ἔχομεν (cf. 1Cor 7.40). But why does he follow the LXX here instead? Some commentators think that the νοῦς here means the same as πνεῦμα (Conzelmann, *1.Kor.*, p.87; Käsemann, *Römer*, p.307); but Scroggs, *op. cit.*, p.54 (n.1) and J.Behm, νοῦς, κτλ, *TDNT* iv, p.959 argue against the simple identification. The meaning of the νοῦς κυρίου in the quotation seems to be quite straightforward: the thought, decree or plan of the Lord (Bauer-Arndt-Gingrich, s.v., 4; Behm, *TDNT* iv, p.959; cf. Bultmann, *Theology* i, p.211). Paul's use of the verb ἔχειν rather than γινώσκειν in his assertion, ἡμεῖς δὲ νοῦν Χριστοῦ ἔχομεν, seems to provide the answer to the question why Paul follows the LXX here: apparently he wants to express here both thoughts at once that he has the Spirit of God and that therefore he knows God's wisdom, i.e., his *Heilsplan*, revealed through the Spirit. This would be a fitting, though cramped, conclusion to his exposition of God's wisdom in 1Cor 2.6–16, in which he asserts that he has received the Spirit of God and the true wisdom, i.e., God's wisdom, that only the Spirit can reveal.

[2]Hence it is against the mind of Paul here to say merely that the mystery is derived from Paul's interpretation of Israel's present obduracy in the light of the divine election of Israel (*contra* Bornkamm, μυστήριον, *TDNT* iv, pp.822f.; also F.Leenhardt, *Romans*, p.292).

same way as the Jewish apocalyptists did[1], or in other charismatic inspira-
tions, as did the Christian prophets and tongue-speakers (1Cor 13.2; 14.2;
Eph 3.5)[2], or through an interpretation of the Scriptures (cf. Eph 5.32) in
consciousness of the Spirit's inspiration as did the Teacher of Righteousness in
Qumran (1QpHab 7.4f.)[3]. In the absence of Paul's clear statement as to
when and how the mystery was revealed to him, many have sought to bring
light to these questions by analysing the content of the mystery and drawing possible parallels to its elements from the OT, Judaism and the primitive
Christian tradition. We must, however, first dismiss the view that Paul
obtained the mystery from Isa 59.20f. and 27.9, which he quotes in Rom
11.26f.[4] For while the quoted Scriptures do provide a proof to the latter
part of the mystery that all Israel will be saved, they do not contain the
motifs of the other part, the mystery proper.

C. Müller suggests that in Rom 11.25f. Paul spiritualises and remoulds the
tradition about the eschatological surrender of Jerusalem or Israel to the
Gentiles for a limited period of time before the eventual restitution of Israel
(Dan 9.24–27; Zech 12.3LXX (cf. 14.1–11); Test. Zeb. 9; Test. Benj. 10;
Ass. Moses 12; 4Ezra 5.23ff.; 9.26–10.58; Lk 21.24; Rev 11)[5]. But this
can hardly be the case since the mystery in Rom 11.25f. speaks neither of
Israel's surrender to the Gentiles nor of the punishment of the Gentiles at the
eventual restitution of Israel[6].

---

[1]See Bornkamm, *TDNT* iv, pp.815f. See D.S.Russell, *The Method and Message of
Jewish Apocalyptic* (1964), pp.164ff., for the view that behind the Jewish apocalytists'
descriptions of their visions and revelations there lie some authentic experiences of
ecstasy (or ecstatic revelation).

[2]For the nature of prophet and prophecy in the NT, see G.Friedrich, προφήτης,
TDNT vi, pp.828ff., esp. 848–856; J.Lindblom, *Gesichte und Offenbarungen*, pp.
162ff.; E.E.Ellis, 'The Role of the Christian Prophet in Acts', *Apostolic History and the
Gospel*, pp.55ff.; D.Hill, 'Prophecy and Prophets in the Revelation of St.John', *NTS* 18
(1971/72), pp.401–418; 'On the Evidence for the Creative Role of Christian Prophets',
NTS 20 (1974), pp.262–294. Here we do not intend to say that Paul's 'visions and
revelations' (2Cor 12.1ff.) could not have been in fact the same as some of the experiences that the Christian prophets and tongue-speakers had in rapture at times.

[3]See O.Betz, *Offenbarung*, esp. pp.82–88; Lührmann, *Offenbarungsverständnis*,
pp.84ff.; P.Benoit, 'Qumran and the NT', *Paul and Qumran*, pp.22f.; cf. also Luz,
Geschichtsverständnis, p.288 (n.96).

[4]A.Pallis, *To the Romans* (1920), p.131.

[5]C.Müller, *Gottes Gerechtigkeit*, pp.38ff.; similarly also P.Borgen, 'From Paul to
Luke', *CBQ* 31 (1969), 172ff.

[6]Luz, *Geschichtsverständnis*, pp.81 (n.22), 289; Zeller, *Juden*, p.250; Plag, *Israels
Wege*, p.56 (n.233); cf. also Käsemann, *Römer*, pp.299f.

Some[1] have attempted to elucidate the mystery in terms of the tradition of the Gentiles' eschatological pilgrimage to Zion which foresees the day when Zion will be lifted up, God's glory or the Messiah will appear there, Israel will be restored, and all the nations will stream toward Zion with their gifts to worship Yahweh and serve the Messiah (and Israel)[2]. To support this view C. Plag argues that with the absolute use of εἰσέρχεσθαι in Rom 11.25 Paul has in view not the Gentiles' entry into the Kingdom of God as the majority of commentators think[3], but their coming to Zion[4]. But, as Plag himself recognises, the word εἰσέρχεσθαι never appears in the passages where the eschatological pilgrimage of the Gentiles is spoken of. And his objection to the usual interpretation of the word is not valid. For while it is true that the majority of the absolute uses of εἰσέρχεσθαι in the Synoptic Gospels can be easily supplied with the reference-point from the context, Lk 11.52 (par. Mt 23.13) clearly uses the word technically as an abbreviation for εἰσέρχεσθαι εἰς τὴν βασιλείαν τοῦ θεοῦ (cf. also Mt 7.13; par. Lk 13.24)[5]. D. Zeller also objects to the usual interpretation, claiming that it fits ill in the missionary context to give such a *'jenseitige'* meaning to εἰσέρχεσθαι[6]. But again while it is true that the majority of the sayings concerning entry into the Kingdom of God have a futuristic eschatological sense, Lk 11.52 and its Matthean parallel (Mt 23.13) clearly envisage entry into the Kingdom of God as a present process[7]. So it is possible to regard εἰσέρχεσθαι as a missionary term for accepting the Christian faith and entering now into the sphere of

---

[1] Plag, *Israels Wege*, pp.43ff., 56ff.; Stuhlmacher, 'Interpretation', pp.560f.; Käsemann, *Römer*, p.299; also E.Käsemann, 'Paulus und der Frühkatholizismus', *EVB* ii, p.244.

[2] It is impossible to list here all the places where the idea of the Gentiles' eschatological pilgrimage appears in its many variant forms. See Str.-Bill. iii, pp.144ff.; J.Jeremias, *Jesus' Promise*, pp.57ff.

[3] E.g., Sanday-Headlam, *Romans*, p.335; Michel, *Römer*, p.280; Murray, *Romans* ii, p.93; Käsemann, *Römer*, p.300; H.Windisch, 'Die Sprüche von Eingehen in das Reich Gottes', *ZNW* 27 (1928), pp.171f.; Luz, *Geschichtsverständnis*, pp.288f. (n.98).

[4] Plag, *Israels Wege*, pp.43f., inspired by L.Baeck, 'The Faith of Paul', *JJS* 3 (1952), p.108; approved by Stuhlmacher, 'Interpretation', pp.560f. (n.29).

[5] Cf. T.W.Manson, *The Sayings of Jesus* (1949), p.103; C.H.Dodd, *The Parables of the Kingdom*, Fontana Ed. (1969), p.108; J.Jeremias, *The Parables of Jesus* ([3]1976), pp.55, 58.

[6] Zeller, *Juden*, p.254.

[7] W.Grundmann, *Das Evangelium nach Matthäus* (1972), p.490; G.E.Ladd, *Jesus and the Kingdom* (1966), pp.192ff., interprets more passages (Mt 11.11f. & par Lk 16.16; Mt 21.31; Mk 12.34) in this sense. Jeremias, *Parables*, p.125 (n.46), following Windisch, *op. cit.*, pp.163ff., thinks that all sayings about entry into the Kingdom of God are

God's kingship which is proleptically realized in the present and awaits its consummation in the future.

The real problem with the attempt to see behind the mystery of Rom 11.25f. the tradition of the Gentiles' eschatological pilgrimage to Zion is, however, that whereas the tradition always has the exaltation of Zion and the epiphany of God or the Messiah there as the preconditions of the Gentiles' pilgrimage, and conceives of the restitution of Israel as preceding it, the mystery of Rom 11.25f. says nothing about the exaltation of Zion[1] and con-

---

futuristic; so also W.G.Kümmel, *Promise and Fulfilment* (1966), pp.52f. But Jeremias and Kümmel do not discuss Lk 11. 52 and Mt 23.13 in this connection.

[1] Is it possible to recognise the motif of the exaltation of Zion and the epiphany of the Messiah in the Scriptural quotation (Isa 59.20f. + 27.9) in Rom 11.26, as Stuhlmacher, 'Interpretation', p.563, suggests? (The ῥυόμενος in the quotation refers to Christ as in 1Th 1.10. Cf. b.Sanh. 98a, where Isa 59.20 is messianically interpreted). Before answering the question, there is another question that should be cleared up first, namely, whether with the quotation Paul refers to the first or the second coming of Christ. For the reference to the parousia the following two points may be observed from the quotation itself: 1) the future ἥξει; and 2) the title ὁ ῥυόμενος which usually means the deliverer from the eschatological woe (Luz, *Geschichtsverständnis*, p.294). But the future form of ἥξει stands already in Isa 59.20 (Luz, *loc. cit.*) and the future form of a verb in a prophecy is retained when it is cited to prove the fulfilment of the prophecy that has already taken place (e.g., Rom 15.12) (Zeller, *Juden*, p.261). And for Paul ὁ ῥυόμενος, the Messiah, has already come! (Zeller, *Juden*, p.26; Sanday-Headlam, *Romans*, p.336). Against the reference to the parousia Luz (*Geschichtsverständnis*, pp.294f.) advances the following arguments: 1) 'the parousia is never an object of Scriptural proof in Paul'; 2) 'the saving work of "the deliverer", namely the removal of sin and establishment of the covenant, lets (us) think, without further ado, of the grace which has already been given through the coming of Jesus'; 3) 'that in his parousia Christ will come out of Zion, is a singular and – in view of 1Th 4.15ff. –striking statement. So, if the statement "out of Zion" is to be interpreted at all, and appears here not simply as a reminiscence of the places like Ps 14.7; 53.7, it is rather to think of the first coming of the Messiah'; 4) for Paul the alternative is not 'Christ's coming in the world' or 'parousia': Christ's past act of salvation effects also the future deliverance from the judgement; and 5) Isa 59.20f. was messianically interpreted in Judaism, so that an exclusive reference of the quotation to the parousia is difficult. To these arguments the following answers may be made: 1) Paul does use the Scriptural citations sometimes to describe the parousia (2Th 2.8–10) and the themes associated with it such as the final overthrow of death (1Cor 15.54ff.) and the last judgement (Rom 14.11) (cf. E.E.Ellis, *Paul's Use*, p.116); 2) when Paul replaces the LXX ἕνεκεν Σιών of Isa 59.20 by ἐκ Σιών in Rom 11.26 he may be thinking of Christ's second coming from the heavenly Jerusalem (cf. Gal 4.26; 1Th 1.10; Phil 3.20f.) (cf. Michel, *Römer*, p.281; Stuhlmacher, 'Interpretation', p.561; Käsemann, *Römer*, p.301); and 3) for Paul the Messiah has come and yet he is to come again! Hence it is possible for him to apply a messianic prophecy to the parousia as well as to the first coming of Christ. Zeller's additional argument against the reference to the parousia, namely that it contradicts

ceives of Israel's salvation as taking place only after that of the Gentiles[1]. So
E. Käsemann and P. Stuhlmacher speak of Paul's remoulding and Christianis-
ing the motifs of the Gentiles' eschatological pilgrimage here and reversing the
order of salvation between Israel and the Gentiles[2]. However, in this situation it is very doubtful whether we are justified to speak, with Stuhlmacher,
of 'the fulfilment of the OT-Jewish hope of the Gentiles' pilgrimage to Zion
and the eschatological glorification of Israel'[3]. According to Käsemann, the
mystery provides 'a particularly instructive example of forceful remoulding
of Jewish-Jewish-Christian tradition which is turned completely into its
opposite'[4], and 'the remoulding characterises him (sc. Paul) as a prophet . . .
who passes on the revelation that has been imparted to him . . .'[5]. But even
if somehow we are to trace the tradition of Israel's restitution and the Gentiles' eschatological pilgrimage to Zion behind the mystery, we still have to

---

Paul's conviction expressed, for example, in 1Cor 1.23 that man – whether Gentile or
Jew – is confronted by the crucified Lord for $\dot{\alpha}\pi o\lambda\acute{u}\tau\rho\omega\sigma\iota\varsigma$ and not by the redeemer
who comes in glory (*Juden*, p.260), carries little weight. For even at the parousia Israel
will receive their $\dot{\alpha}\pi o\lambda\acute{u}\tau\rho\omega\sigma\iota\varsigma$ only on the basis of Christ's work on the cross and only
through their faith in him. Paul would hardly have thought otherwise (cf. Stuhlmacher,
'Interpretation', p.562, against Plag, *Israels Wege*, esp. pp.37, 55ff.).

Thus, as far as the content of the quotation is concerned, it can, though it need not,
refer to the parousia. Whether it indeed does or not, should be decided therefore from
the context. If $\kappa\alpha\grave{\iota}$ $o\breve{\upsilon}\tau\omega\varsigma$ is to be taken as correlative with $\kappa\alpha\theta\acute{\omega}\varsigma$, then, of course,
with the quotation Paul refers to the parousia (so Stuhlmacher, 'Interpretation', esp. pp.
560ff.; cf. Käsemann, *Römer*, p.301). But if our interpretation of $\kappa\alpha\grave{\iota}$ $o\breve{\upsilon}\tau\omega\varsigma$ is correct,
Paul may, but need not, refer to the parousia. Since Paul is concerned here primarily not
about the time or the way of Israel's salvation but rather about its certainty, he seeks to
provide with the quotation a basis for that certainty. So here whether he has in view the
first or the second coming of Christ, is a secondary, if not irrelevant, question, although
in view of Rom 11.15 it may be presumed that if asked when the prophecy of Isa
59.20f. and 27.9 is to be realized Paul would answer: 'at the parousia of Christ'.

If this interpretation is correct, then we must conclude that the mystery of Rom
11.25f. says nothing of the exaltation of Zion. Even if the $\kappa\alpha\grave{\iota}$ $o\breve{\upsilon}\tau\omega\varsigma$ is to be taken
with $\kappa\alpha\theta\acute{\omega}\varsigma$ and therefore the quotation to refer to the parousia, in which case we may
see the motif of the epiphany of the Messiah in Zion and the restitution of Israel, the
difficulty remains because these are envisaged to take place *after* the Gentiles will have
come in.

[1]Cf. Zeller, *Juden*, p.255.

[2]Käsemann, *Römer*, p.299f.; Stuhlmacher, 'Interpretation', pp.560f. See also
Käsemann, 'Frühkatholizismus', p.244.

[3]Stuhlmacher, 'Interpretation', p.561. But against Stuhlmacher says Zeller, *Juden*,
p.255: 'Weder strömen die Heiden zum Sion, noch wird Israel verherrlicht'.

[4]Käsemann, *Römer*, p.299.

[5]*Ibid.*, p.300.

explain how Paul was able to remould it so 'forcefully' (*gewaltsam*) and call it a 'mystery', an eschatological truth made known by God's revelation, unless we are prepared simply to say that Paul's experience of Israel's rejection of the gospel in the mission field led him to speculate on the *Heilsgeschichte* and obtain the mystery from the tradition of Gentiles' eschatological pilgrimage to Zion – a thought, however, which we have found incompatible with Paul's use of the term μυστήριον and the doxology in Rom 11.33ff.

Some scholars see yet another tradition in connection with the mystery of Rom 11.25f., namely the isolated logion of Mk 13.10 (par. Mt 24.14) that the gospel must first be preached to all the Gentiles before the end[1]. It is impossible to discuss here the complex problem of the authenticity of the logion, as it involves the whole question of Jesus' eschatology as well as that of the history of the primitive Church[2]. Stuhlmacher argues that the logion is a Markan creation and tradition-historically later than the mystery of Rom 11.25ff.[3] If this is so, of course, it cannot help us to ascertain how and when Paul obtained the mystery. Even if it is a genuine dominical saying, which is not impossible, and was known to Paul, we cannot say that Paul derived his mystery directly from it, any more than that he derived it directly from the tradition of the Gentiles' eschatological pilgrimage to Zion. For it contains neither the idea of the hardening of Israel nor Israel's eventual salvation. At most it can be said that the tradition in Mk 13.10 could have been one of the elements which Paul might have utilized in some way to obtain the mystery. Here we are back at the question that we raised at the end of the preceding paragraph.

It seems that it is best to understand the μυστήριον in the light of Isa 6. It is widely recognized that in Gal 1.15f. Paul describes his call to the Gentile apostleship with the words taken from the narrative of the call of the Ebed Yahweh in Isa 49.1–6, thus indicating that he saw his apostolic call in the

---

[1]O.Cullmann, 'Der eschatologische Charakter des Missionsauftrags und des apostolischen Selbstbewußtseins bei Paulus', *Vorträge und Aufsätze 1925–1962* (1966), p.328; Stuhlmacher, 'Interpretation', pp.565f.; Käsemann, *Römer*, p.300; cf. Luz, *Geschichtsverständnis*, p.289. Zahn, *Römer*, pp.522f., believes that the basis of the mystery is the prophetic words of Jesus concerning the hardening of Israel (Mt 12. 38–45; 13.11–16; 23.29–36; Jn 9.39–41; (12.37–43)), the conversion of the Gentiles during the interim period until his return (Mt 22.7ff.; 24.14) and finally the conversion of Israel also (Mt 23.39 & par. Lk 13.35).

[2]See the comprehensive discussion by S.G.Wilson, *Gentiles*, pp.18–28; further Kümmel, *Promise*, pp.85f.; Hahn, *Mission*, pp.70ff. Against these who deny the authenticity of the logion, see G.R.Beasley-Murray, *A Commentary on Mark Thirteen* (1957), pp.44f.; cf. Jeremis, *Promise*, pp.22f.

[3]Stuhlmacher, 'Interpretation', pp.565f.

light of the call of the Ebed[1]. However, one of the most famous call narratives in the OT, namely Isa 6, has not received as much attention in connection with Paul's call as it deserves. As far as we know, O. Betz has been the only one who has attempted to show that Paul interprets his Damascus experience in the light of Isa 6[2].

Now W.Zimmerli[3] has analysed the 'Form- und Traditionsgeschichte der prophetischen Berufungserzählung' and delineated two types of call narratives in the OT. One is the type represented by the call narrative of Jeremiah (1.4–10): it does not contain a visionary element or at least subordinates it to the motif of receiving the word of Yahweh. This type is further characterized by a very close personal encounter between Yahweh and the one called, in which the latter shows hesitation and objection which Yahweh overcomes by giving his personal word of assurance and granting a sign. To this type belongs also the narrative of the call of Moses (Ex 3.1–22; 4.1–17; 6.2–12; 7.1–7)[4]. The other type is represented by the call narrative of Isaiah (6). In this type the prophetic commission of the word takes place in a vision of the heavenly throne. To this type belongs also the call narrative of Ezekiel (1.1–3.15)[5]. Zimmerli finds these two types reflected in the narratives of Paul's call: the latter type in Luke's narratives of Paul's call in Acts 9.3ff.; 22.6ff.; 26.12ff. and the former type in Paul's own narrative in Gal 1.15ff.[6]. However, as we have seen above, the word ἀποκαλύπτειν/ἀπο-

---

[1]See e.g., Munck, *Paul*, pp.24ff.; L.Cerfaux, 'La vocation de saint Paul', *Euntes Docete* (1961), pp.13ff.; T.Holtz, 'Selbstverständnis des Apostels Paulus', *ThLZ* 91 (1966), 324ff.

[2]O.Betz, 'Die Vision des Paulus im Tempel von Jerusalem', *Verborum Veritas*, pp. 118ff.

[3]W.Zimmerli, *Ezechiel* (1969), pp.16–21; cf. also H.Wildberger, *Jesaja* (1972), pp.234ff.

[4]Cf. also the call of Gideon (Judg 6.11–18) and that of Saul (1Sam 9.21).

[5]Cf. also the commission of Micaiah, the son of Imlah (1Ki 22.19–22), which is a close parallel to the call narrative of Isaiah (6), though it may not be a report of his call in the strict sense. See Zimmerli, *Ezechiel*, pp.18f.

[6]*Ibid.*, pp.20f.; also Wildberger, *Jesaja*, p.236. In his recent essay 'Formgeschichtliche Bemerkungen zur Darstellung des Damaskusgeschehens in der Apostelgeschichte', *ZNW* 67 (1976), pp.20–28, O.H.Steck questions Zimmerli's classification of the vision of Isa 6 as a form of *Berufungsbericht*. The vision of Isa 6 represents, according to Steck, rather a separate *Gattung* for the 'Vergabe eines außergewöhnlichen Auftrags in der Thronversammlung' (p.26). Steck denies further a *formgeschichtliche* link between the Lucan narratives of the Damascus event and both *Gattungen*. Nevertheless, Steck concedes: 'Daß den Act-Berichten vielleicht in Aufnahme von Überlieferungsvorgaben auch an der Entsprechung zwischen der Beauftragung des Paulus durch Christus und

κάλυψις which Paul uses to describe his call in Gal 1.12, 16, as well as his testimonies elsewhere (1Cor 9.1; 2Cor 4.6), suggests that he had a vision of Christophany at the Damascus call. So when Paul narrated his Damascus call to his churches as part of his proclamation of the gospel of the risen Christ[1] he must have done it in the pattern of the Lucan narratives and therefore of the Isaianic narrative[2]. Therefore it is possible that Paul narrated his experience at the Damascus call in the pattern of the Isaianic narrative while, seeing the typological correspondence between his call and the call of the Ebed, he interpreted its significance in the light of the call of the Ebed in Isa 49.1–6. More precisely it is submitted here that Paul saw his Damascus call in the light of both Isa 49.1–6 and Isa 6. Since for Paul the unity of the Book of

---

der Berufung der Propheten gelegen sein dürfte, zeigen Einzelzüge wie die Bezugnahmen in 26.17f. . . .' (p.27). Furthermore, Steck's distinctions between the *Gattung* of *Berufungsbericht* and the *Gattung* of extraordinary commission and between these *Gattungen* and the reports of the Damascus event in Acts seem to be far too rigid. At any rate, Steck's criticisms of Zimmerli's view do not affect in any substantial way our argument here that Paul saw his Damascus call in the light of Isa 6 and 49.1–6.

[1]*Supra*, pp.28ff.

[2]J.Roloff, *Apostolat*, pp.43f., observes that 'Paul never calls himself prophet', thus forbidding a simple identification of his apostleship with the prophetic office of the OT. This is due to Paul's consciousness that his apostolic function belongs to a stage of the *Heilsgeschichte* fundamentally different from that of the OT prophets, in that it is to preach the gospel of the exalted Jesus Christ which the latter prophesied (cf. Rom 1.2). However, there is a *tertium comparationis* between Paul and the OT prophets, and it is God's call and sending for the ministry of a messenger. So Roloff speaks of 'a typological correspondence' between them. However, it is strange that having correctly ascertained this fact Roloff goes on to say: 'Darum nimmt Paulus auch keinen direkten Bezug auf die Berufungserlebnisse der Propheten. Es fehlt in Gal 1.15f. jede Anspielung auf ein Sendewort, wie es in den alttestamentlichen Berufungsberichten zentral ist (z.B. Am 7,14f.; Jes 6, 9f.; Jer 1,7f.; Hes 2,3ff.), im Unterschied übrigens zu der Schilderung der Paulusberufung in Apg 9,15, die deutlich auf Jer 1,10 (LXX) anspielt' (p.44). We have already noted (above pp.28ff.) that it is wrong to see a contrast on this point between Paul's reports of the Damascus event and those of Luke. Roloff's remark that Paul does not allude to a word of sending, is incredible in the face of Paul's words like οὐ γὰρ ἀπέστειλέν με Χριστὸς βαπτίζειν ἀλλὰ εὐαγγελίζεσθαι (1Cor 1.17), not to mention his insistence that he is an ἀπόστολος, behind which ultimately lies the concept of שלח/שליח (cf. Isa 6.8f.; Jer 1.7; Ezek 2.3; etc. See K.H.Rengstorf, ἀποστέλλω, κτλ, *TDNT* i, pp.400ff.; cf. also Roloff, *Apostolat*, pp.10ff., 36). Does not the ἵνα-clause in Gal 1.16 already imply a *Sendewort*? Precisely because there is a typological correspondence in the motif of call and sending for the service of a messenger between Paul's apostolic office and the office of the OT prophets, should we not rather expect Paul to narrate his call and sending in the pattern in which the prophetic calls and sendings used to be narrated? And does not Paul's allusion to the call of the Ebed in Gal 1.15f. confirm this?

Isaiah was no matter of dispute as it is for the modern critics, and both Isa 6 and 49.1–6 deal with God's call of his servant, Paul would have found no difficulty in combining them both to shed light on his Damascus experience.

To support this thesis we would, first of all, show the parallel motifs between Paul's reports of his Damascus call and the call narrative of Isaiah 6. First, both Isaiah and Paul saw the κύριος (Isa 6.1 // 1Cor 9.1) in glory (Isa 6.1 // 2Cor 4.6). Of course, Isaiah saw Yahweh as the κύριος while Paul saw the risen and exalted Christ as the κύριος. But this difference is not real because, as is well known, Paul regularly transfers the OT title κύριος from God to Christ (e.g., Rom 10.13; 2Cor 3.16ff.; Phil 2.9ff.!). Indeed, according to Jn 12.41, Isaiah saw the glory of Jesus and spoke about him[1]. The second parallel is the fact that both Isaiah and Paul received forgiveness and atonement at their call (Isa 6.7// 2Cor 5.16ff.; 1Cor 15.8ff.; etc.)[2]. Thirdly, just as Isaiah was 'sent' (שלח / ἀποστέλλειν. Isa 6.8) at the Theophany, so was Paul 'sent' (ἀποστέλλειν/ἀπόστολος. 1Cor 1.17; 9.1; Rom 1.1; etc) at the Christophany[3]. The fourth parallel, which is the most important in our present context, is: just as Isaiah describes that in the vision he was let into the council at the throne of God and heard God's counsels (Isa 6.8ff.), so Paul also implies with the concepts ἀποκαλύπτειν/ἀποκάλυψις (Gal 1.12, 16; Eph 3.3) and μυστήριον (1Cor 2.1, 6ff.; Col 1.26ff.; Eph 3.4ff.) that he received the gospel and God's counsel from the enthroned Christ in vision[4].

---

[1] According to the Targum, Isaiah 'saw the glory of the Lord sitting upon a throne . . .' (J.F.Stenning ed. and tr., *The Targum of Isaiah* (1953), p.20). Cf. O.Betz, 'Vision', p.118.

[2] Cf. *ibid.*, pp.118f.

[3] Betz sees in Paul's questions in 1Cor 9.1 (οὐκ εἰμὶ ἀπόστολος; οὐχὶ Ἰησοῦν τὸν κύριον ἡμῶν ἑόρακα;) more than just the early Christian view that having seen the risen Christ is a pre-requisite for genuine apostleship (cf. 1Cor 15.5ff.; Acts 1.22): 'Die Frage 1.Kor 9,1 (ist) an Jes 6 orientiert und erhält von dorther ihre beweisende Kraft . . . . Vision und Berufung zum Apostel sind deshalb bedeutungsgleich, weil auch Jesaja von seiner Berufung sagen konnte: "Ich habe den Herrn gesehen (εἶδον τὸν κύριον, Jes 6, 1), dem er auf seine Frage nach einem Boten antwortete: "Siehe hier bin ich! Sende mich!" (ἀπόστειλόν με. Jes 6, 8).' (*ibid.*, p.118).

[4] At this point it may be worthwhile to cite from Wildberger, *Jesaja*, p.236: 'Er (Jesaja) ist aber gleich den himmlischen Wesen in den Kronrat Gottes hineingenommen. Daraus ergibt sich eine andere Konzeption der Prophetie als beim ersten Typus (i.e., Jeremiah's type). Der Prophet fungiert als *göttlicher Bote*. Als solcher war er mit dabei in der himmlischen *Ratsversammlung*, "denn der Herr Jahwe unternimmt nichts, er habe denn seinen Ratschluß (סוד) seinen Knechten, den Propheten enthüllt", Am 3, 7. Auch nach Jeremia, dem diese Vorstellung trotz seines traditionsgeschichtlich anders verwurzelten Berufungsberichtes keineswegs fremd war, ist der Prophet als solcher dadurch legitimiert, daß er in Jahwes Ratsversammlung (wiederum סוד) gestanden (עמד),

In view of these parallels it is difficult to believe that Paul would not have seen his Damascus experience in the light of the call narrative of Isaiah and narrated it in the pattern of Isa 6. We cannot say for sure whether Paul's knowledge of Isa 6 guided him already in his experience on the Damascus road or whether, having had an experience on the Damascus road parallel to that of Isaiah, he later found the pattern of Isa 6 useful to illustrate his experience for his hearers. What is important for us is the fact that Paul sees his Damascus experience in the light of Isa 6 as well as Isa 49. 1–6.

Now, one fundamental fact about Paul's Damascus call is that he was called to preach the gospel to the Gentiles. Being a Jew through and through, Paul must have been shocked at this call. For no theology known to him at that time envisaged the possibility of the Gentiles' obtaining salvation before the Jews, if they were to obtain it at all. But in spite of this theological preconception and psychological prejudice against the Gentiles Paul was convinced from the beginning of his apostolic career that he had been called to be the Gentiles' apostle[1]. For this conviction he must have had from the beginning an understanding about God's will for the Jews such as that which the mystery of Rom 11.25f. reveals. This understanding he obtained when he saw in Isa 6 and 49.1–6 the pre-figuration of his Damascus call. Or, shall we say, he *heard* the mystery of Rom 11.25f. together with God's call to the Gentile apostleship on the Damascus road and later found in Isa 6 and 49. 1–6 their confirmation? At any rate, the combination of Isa 6 and 49.1–6 explains Paul's Gentile apostleship and the mystery of Rom 11.25f. very clearly.

First of all, in the divine counsel that Isaiah received in his inaugural vision, namely the divine will for hardening the heart of Israel, Paul saw the divine will for the obduracy of Israel which he talks about in the mystery of Rom 11.25f.[2] An objection may be raised against this view from the fact that whereas Isaiah was commissioned to harden the heart of Israel through his proclamation (Isa 6.10 MT) Paul is not conscious of God's commission for him to harden the Jews by his preaching of the gospel, although this is in fact precisely what happens in his mission field. But this raises no real difficulty here if it is realized that in the LXX the divine imperative for Isaiah to harden the heart of Israel is turned into an indicative statement about the

---

in das dortige Geschehen Einblick gewonnen (ראה) und das Wort gehört hat, 23, 18.22' (emphasis by W.). סוד, just like רז, is equivalent to μυστήριον. See also R.N.Why-bray, *The Heavenly Counsellor in Isaiah xl 13–14* (1971), esp. pp.39–53.

[1] *Supra* pp.58ff., against the view that Paul turned to the Gentiles only later in his apostolic career after disappointing experiences with the mission to the Jews.

[2] Cf. Betz., 'Vision', p.119.

obduracy of Israel. In the NT the LXX version is generally quoted to prove the fulfillment of Isaiah's prophecy about the obduracy of Israel in their refusal to accept the gospel (Mt 13.14f. & par. Mk 4.12; Lk 8.10; Acts 28.26f.). Jn 12.40 introduces Isaiah as saying that God has blinded and hardened the Jews. The mystery of Rom 11.25f. stands close to Jn 12.40 with its implication that it is the divine will that partial hardening has come and will remain upon Israel until the full number of the Gentiles come in. In so far as Rom 11.25f., like Jn 12.40, knows that the hardening of Israel has originated from the divine will, it retains the sense of the Hebrew text. However, just like Jn 12.40, the mystery in Rom 11.25f. also speaks of Israel's obduracy in an indicative statement, thus following the LXX version. In view of Paul's overwhelming preference for the LXX over the Hebrew Bible in his Scriptural citation[1] it is not at all difficult to think that Paul read the LXX version of Isa 6 and found in the indicative statement there the divine will for the obduracy of Israel.

Secondly, the $\check{\alpha}\chi\rho\iota$ $o\check{\upsilon}$ of Rom 11.25 corresponds formally with Isaiah's question, 'How long ($\check{\epsilon}\omega\varsigma$ $\pi\acute{o}\tau\epsilon$), O Lord?', and the divine answer, 'Until ($\check{\epsilon}\omega\varsigma$ $\check{\alpha}\nu$) . . . ' (Isa 6.11)[2]. The question, 'How long (עד-מתי), O Lord?', appears often as a cry of lamentation over Israel's fate in the OT (e.g., Ps 74.10; 79.5; 90.13; 94.3; etc.)[3]. But sometimes it appears in the context of a vision in which the plan of God is revealed (Isa 6.11; Dan 8.13; 12.6; Zech 1.12; cf. also Rev 6.10f.)[4]. Sometimes without the question there appear in the apocalyptic literature statements about God's schedule concerning Israel's fate containing 'until ($\check{\epsilon}\omega\varsigma$ or $\check{\alpha}\chi\rho\iota$ $o\check{\upsilon}$) . . . ' (e.g., Dan 9.25ff.; Tobit 14.4–7; Test. Levi 16.5; Test. Jud. 22.5; 23.5; Test. Naph. 4.5; Test. As. 7.2f.; Lk 21.24)[5]. However, it is not in this 'eschatological epoch formula' (as P. Borgen calls it)[6] in general, but specifically in Isa 6.11 that Paul found a parallel to the revelation which he received in the Christophany concerning the limitation of Israel's hardening to a definite period of time.

Paul's call to the Gentile apostleship is logically connected with the hardening of Israel. God has hardened Israel, as it were, in order to create room for a Gentile mission in time (Rom 11.11f., 15, 28ff.). Since Israel is

---

[1] See the statistics in Ellis, *Paul's Use*, pp.12ff.

[2] For the synonymous nature of $\check{\epsilon}\omega\varsigma$ and $\check{\alpha}\chi\rho\iota\varsigma$ ($o\check{\upsilon}$), see B–D, § 383.1–2; Moulton iii, pp.110f.

[3] Cf. E.Jenni, מתי, *ThHAT* i, 933–936.

[4] Cf. Zeller, *Juden*, pp.249f.

[5] Cf. *ibid.*; Müller, *Gottes Gerechtigkeit*, pp.38ff.

[6] P.Borgen, 'From Paul to Luke', p.172.

hardened and while she remains so, Paul is to proclaim the gospel to the Gentiles and thus be a light to them 'that my (God's) salvation may reach to the end of the earth' (Isa 49.6).

But once the Gentile mission is complete and the full number of the Gentiles have entered the Kingdom of God the obduracy of Israel will be terminated and therefore all Israel will be saved. In inferring this hope of Israel's eventual salvation from the fact that Israel's hardening is limited to a definite time span, Paul may have been helped by the word of hope at the end of Isa 6.13 ('The holy seed is its stump') which the MT has while the LXX does not (except in *L, C, O*)[1]. The Targum expands it still further in a midrashic form: 'like a terebinth and like an oak, which appear to be dried up when their leaves fall, though they still retain their moisture to preserve a seed from them: so the exiles of Israel shall be gathered together, and shall return to their land; for a holy seed is their plant'[2]. Or Paul may have been helped by Isa 49.5–6a, in which the Lord commissions the Servant to gather together and restore Israel as well as to be a light to the nations. Since the mystery of Rom 11.25f. implies that Paul understood his apostleship to be crucial for the salvation of the Jews as well as for the Gentiles, as his Gentile mission would bring in the full number of the Gentiles, thus creating the condition for Israel's salvation (cf. also Rom 11.13f.; 15.19), Isa 49.5f. seems to have played some part in Paul's confident inference of the hope of Israel's eventual salvation at the conclusion of the Gentile mission.

Thus Paul's Gentile apostleship, his view of his Gentile apostleship as having a crucial importance for the salvation of Israel, and the details of the mystery of Rom 11.25f. which are closely connected with the former two, are neatly explained in the combined light of Isa 6 and 49.1–6[3]. Seeing thus the importance of Isa 6 for Paul's apostolic call, we now realize that Luke was not entirely mistaken when he reported Paul as saying that the Jews rejected the gospel because of their obduracy, just as the Holy Spirit prophesied through Isaiah, and that therefore the gospel of salvation has been sent to the Gentiles (Acts 28.25ff.)[4].

The fact that the key-word in the mystery of Rom 11.25f., πώρωσις, does not actually appear in Isa 6, cannot be an objection to the view that Paul obtained the mystery through reflection on the Damascus experience in the

---

[1]Cf. Betz, 'Vision', p.119 (n.15).

[2]Translation by Stenning, *op. cit.*, p.22.

[3]Betz, 'Vision', p.119 (n.15), wonders whether Paul's imagery of the olive tree in Rom 11.16b–24 itself was not inspired by Isa 6.13.

[4]Cf. *ibid.*, p.119.

light of Isa 6. For just as in Rom 11.7 so here also Paul seems to be using the word to sum up the content of Isa 6.10 about the fat heart, hindered ears and closed eyes of Israel. Nor is it an adequate objection to this view that Paul quotes Dt 29.3, Isa 29.10 and Ps 69.23f. rather than Isa 6.10 to prove the hardening of Israel in Rom 11.8ff. For in the abundance of references to Israel's obduracy there is no reason why Paul should always stick to the one passage which first proved to him Israel's obduracy. In Rom 11.8f., citing from the Torah (Dt 29.3), the Prophets (Isa 29.10) and the Writings (Ps 69.23f.) quite in Rabbinic manner[1], Paul would like to prove clearly that the whole Scripture speaks of Israel's obduracy. Finally, it may be urged that in view of 1Th 2.14ff., in which Paul says 'God's wrath has come upon them (the Jews) $\epsilon\iota\varsigma$ $\tau\epsilon\lambda o\varsigma$'[2], the mystery of Rom 11.25f., with its hope for their eventual salvation represents a change that took place later in Paul's view on Israel's fate[3]. But 1Th 2.14ff. is probably 'an unreflected, traditional statement'[4], made in the face of the fanatic opposition of the Jews to the Church and to Paul's Gentile mission (cf. Acts 17.1–9; also Mt 23.29–38; par. Lk 11. 46–52). That such language was possible, is shown by Isa 6.11–13 (LXX), which leaves no room for hope for Israel's salvation. Nevertheless Isaiah held out a hope for the remnant (Isa 4.3ff.; 8.18; 10.20f.; etc.). In the same way, knowing from the beginning that Israel would be eventually saved, Paul could have said on the spur of the moment 'Israel is finished!' So even the comparison with 1Th 2.14ff. does not affect our conclusion that Paul received the mystery of Rom 11.25f. at his Damascus call and under-

---

[1] Cf. Michel, *Römer*, p.269.

[2] Does $\epsilon\iota\varsigma$ $\tau\epsilon\lambda o\varsigma$ mean 'in the end, finally', 'to the end, until the end', 'forever', or 'decisively, completely' (cf. Bauer-Arndt-Gingrich, s.v., 1, d, γ)? Besides commentaries, see also E.Bammel, 'Judenverfolgung und Naherwartung', *ZThK* 56 (1959), pp. 308f.; Hahn, *Mission*, pp.105f. (n.3); Luz, *Geschichtsverständnis*, p.290. If $\epsilon\iota\varsigma$ $\tau\epsilon\lambda o\varsigma$ means here 'to the end, till the end', 1Th 2.16c, with its implication that the Jews are under the wrath of God 'until the end' and therefore that at the end the wrath of God will be removed from them, fits in very well with the mystery of Rom 11.25f. (so Hahn, *Mission*, p.106 (n.3)).

[3] Cf. E.Bammel, *op. cit.*, pp.313f.; A.Schweitzer, *The Mysticism of Paul the Apostle* ([2]1956), p.185; E.Best, *The First and Second Epistle to the Thessalonians* (1972), p.122.

[4] Luz, *Geschichtsverständnis*, pp.290f.; similarly, Hahn, *Mission*, p.105 (n.3); O.Michel, 'Fragen zu 1Thessalonicher 2, 14–16: Antijüdische Polemik bei Paulus', *Antijudaismus im NT?* ed. W.Eckert *et al.* (1967), pp.58f.; E.Best, *op. cit.*, pp.121f. For recent restatements of the view that 1Th 2.13–16 is a late anti-Jewish interpolation, see B.A.Pearson, '1Thessalonians 2: 13–16: a Deutero-Pauline Interpolation', *HTR* 64 (1971), pp.79–94; H.Boers, 'The Form critical Study of Paul's Letters. 1 Thessalonians as a Case Study', *NTS* 22 (1976), pp.140ff., esp. 151f.

stood it in the light of Isa 6 and 49.1–6.

To *sum up* briefly the results of the investigation in this section: at the Christophany on the Damascus road Paul received the revelation of the gospel, the good news concerning the salvation in Christ which has been realised in the death and resurrection of Jesus Christ and awaits its consummation at his parousia, and, together with it or as part of it, the revelation of the mystery, namely God's plan of salvation embodied in Christ both for the Jews and the Gentiles.

In the following chapters we propose to examine the content of this gospel more closely[1].

---

[1] Originally we planned to devote a chapter to an investigation of Paul's apostolic self-understanding, his conception of the *Heilsgeschichte*, and his understanding of the role of his Gentile mission in the *Heilsgeschichte*. That chapter would have completed our description of Paul the apostle and his theology in the light of the Damascus Christophany. But for reasons of time and space we have to drop it here and postpone it to another opportunity.

Chapter V Paul's Gospel: B. Christology

1 Introduction

The gospel that he received on the Damascus road Paul defines, first of all, Christologically: it is Jesus Christ, the Son of God (Gal 1.12, 16), 'the glory of Christ, who is the image of God' (2Cor 4.4), or 'the unsearchable riches of Christ' (Eph 3.8). So the object of his apostolic preaching ($\epsilon \dot{v} a \gamma \gamma \epsilon \lambda i \zeta \epsilon \sigma \theta a \iota /$ $\kappa \eta \rho \dot{v} \sigma \sigma \epsilon \omega$)[1] is Jesus Christ, the crucified (1Cor 1.23) and risen (1Cor 15.12), he as the Lord (2Cor 4.5) and as the Son of God (Gal 1.16; 2Cor 2.19). That by the gospel Paul understands primarily God's saving act in Christ is further made clear in his Christological definitions of the gospel in Rom 1.2–4 and 1Cor 15.3–5. But why is Jesus Christ, the crucified and risen, the gospel? It is because he embodies God's saving act for man and the world, that is, because through the death and resurrection of Jesus Christ God has brought in the promised salvation of the Messianic age. So the gospel can be defined soteriologically as well as Christologically (Rom 1.16). In fact, in Paul Christology and soteriology are not two separate doctrines but one, the former being the ground of the latter and the latter the anthropological and cosmological application of the former (e.g., Christ's death $\dot{v} \pi \dot{\epsilon} \rho$ $\tau \hat{\omega} \nu$ $\dot{a} \mu a \rho \tau \iota \hat{\omega} \nu$ $\dot{\eta} \mu \hat{\omega} \nu$ in 1Cor 15.3)[2]. However, for the sake of convenience, Christology and soteriology may at first be separated to provide two different perspectives to the gospel of Paul.

---

[1] For the synonymous nature of the two words in the NT, see G.Friedrich, $\epsilon \dot{v} a \gamma \gamma \epsilon \lambda$ $i \zeta o \mu a \iota$, $\kappa \tau \lambda$, *TDNT* ii, p.718; *idem*, $\kappa \eta \rho \dot{v} \sigma \sigma \omega$, $\kappa \tau \lambda$, *TDNT* iii, p.711.

[2] See E.Käsemann, 'Zur paulinischen Anthropologie', *Paulinische Perspektiven* (^{2}1972), pp.9–60, esp. 26ff., for the primacy of Christology over against anthropology and soteriology in the Pauline theology; also P.Stuhlmacher, "Ende", pp.14–39; Cullmann, *Christology*, pp.1ff.; Ridderbos, *Paulus*, pp.39ff.; Blank, *Paulus*, pp.301f.; against Bultmann, *Theology* i, p.191, who spoils his valuable insights into the connection between Paul's theology and anthropology and between his Christology and soteriology by setting a wrong priority in Paul's thought, namely by making anthropology the centre of Paul's theology and consequently reducing Paul's entire thought to 'his doctrine of man' conceived as an individual with little or no connection with the world in which he exists in solidarity with the rest of mankind. With this view of Paul's theology corresponds

Now, in spite of Paul's claim to have received his gospel at the Damascus revelation (Gal 1.12, 15f.) and of his repeated appeals to it whenever his gospel and apostleship are challenged (1Cor 9.1; 15.3–11; 2Cor 4.1–6; 5.16–21; Gal 1.11–16; Phil 3.3–14), R. Bultmann warns against the attempt to derive Paul's theology from his Damascus experience, designating it an 'Irrweg'[1]. But it is strange that to this Bultmann should immediately add what seems to undermine his warning: 'The question about the material content of (Paul's) conversion is . . . a question about his theology itself'[2]. For, as P. Stuhlmacher points out[3], precisely this shows that what Paul experienced at the Damascus revelation is constitutive of his theology. G. Bornkamm observes correctly that Paul's statements about his call 'are completely interwoven into the unfolding of his gospel'[4]. But Bornkamm draws the following strange conclusion from this: 'Paul's own witness about his call in Gal 1 as well as in Phil 3 shows how the understanding of his conversion and sending is completely determined by the content of his preaching and theology and not by an arbitrary claim to have received a *revelatio specialissima* (special revelation – *sic!*)'[5]. This conclusion is mistaken in two ways. First, it is plain in Gal 1.12, 15f. that Paul does claim to have received a special revelation of Jesus Christ and obtained his gospel through it[6]. Secondly, it is more in line with Paul's own testimony to say that 'the content of his preaching and theology' is determined by his 'understanding of his conversion and sending'

Bultmann's interpretation of the significance of Paul's conversion experience primarily in terms of his resolve to surrender his former self-understanding and in terms of his obtaining a new self-understanding ('Paulus', *RGG*[2] iv, 1022f.; *Theology* i, p.188). It is true that the Damascus experience involved God's judgement upon Paul's Pharisaic self-understanding and consequently his surrender of it and obtaining a new self-understanding (Phil 3.3ff.). However, this was the *consequence* of his knowledge of Christ, of his encounter with the crucified and risen Christ (Phil 3.7ff.) (see esp. Blank, *Paulus*, p.231; also Stuhlmacher, *op. cit.*, p.22). The content of his gospel is therefore primarily not a doctrine concerning 'a new self-understanding' or 'authentic existence' but Jesus Christ who leads man to a new self-understanding.

[1]Bultmann, 'Paulus', 1027; cf. also Bornkamm, *Paulus*, pp.39, 44f. For earlier attempts to derive various aspects of Paul's theology from the Damascus event and oppositions to them, see E.Pfaff, *Die Bekehrung des Hl.Paulus in der Exegese des 20. Jahrhunderts* (1942), pp.161ff.

[2]Bultmann, 'Paulus', 1027.

[3]Stuhlmacher, "Ende", p.20 (n.15).

[4]Bornkamm, *Paulus*, p.39.

[5]*Ibid.*, pp.44f.; cf. also Bultmann, 'Paulus', 1027.

[6]*Supra* p.72, n.1 for Bornkamm's wrong interpretation of the concept ἀποκαλύπτειν/ἀποκάλυψις in Gal 1.12, 16 which leads him to deny this.

than to say the reverse. For it is inconceivable that 'the content of his preaching and theology' which Paul had previously had, led him to interpret his Damascus experience in line with it. In fact, the essential and constitutive character of the Damascus experience for Paul's theology is widely recognised by recent interpreters[1], who approach Paul's theology historically, even without the aid of the dubious psychological approach that some earlier writers used in order to derive Paul's theology from his Damascus experience. This has been demonstrated especially clearly by P. Stuhlmacher in his various writings[2].

To assert that Paul's theology is to be derived from his Damascus experience, is not, however, to say that Paul at once obtained explicitly at the Damascus revelation his whole theology as seen in his letters. It says only that the main lines of his theology have their origin in the fundamental event. To express it in the words of O. Kuss, it says that 'in the fundamental event as in a germ the entire later development of the Apostle was contained' and that the mature theology witnessed to by his letters represents the results of Paul's interpretations, thinking to the end, and drawing consequences of what happened on the Damascus road[3]. Again one has to agree with O. Kuss that it is difficult to know exactly how many of Paul's theological insights — beyond the fundamental realization that Jesus of Nazareth is the Christ and he is God's saving act — were explicitly available to him from the beginning and how much of his theology is only the consequence drawn later from the fundamental realizations[4].

However, the primitive Christian kerygma which his persecution of the Church indicates he had known before the Damascus event and which was

---

[1]E.g., O.Michel, 'Die Entstehung der paulinischen Christologie', *ZNW* 28 (1929), pp.324ff.; Dibelius-Kümmel, *Paulus*, pp.42ff.; Wilckens, 'Bekehrung', p.12; Bruce, *NT History*, pp.228f.; Blank, *Paulus*, pp.184ff.; Dupont, 'The Conversion of Paul', pp.176–194; Kümmel, *Theologie*, pp.133f.; Haacker, 'Berufung', pp.1–19; Jeremias, *Schlüssel*, pp.20ff. T.W.Manson, *On Paul and John* ([2]1967), p.12, says: 'In so far as we understand and appreciate what that event (i.e., his conversion) meant to him we may understand the central thing in his theology'. Cf. also J.D.G.Dunn, *Jesus and the Spirit* (1975), pp.4,110ff. For earlier authors, see Pfaff, *op. cit.*

[2]'καινὴ κτίσις', pp.27f.; 'Erwägungen zum Problem von Gegenwart und Zukunft in der paulinischen Eschatologie', pp.428ff.; *Evangelium*, pp.69ff.; 'Christliche Verantwortung bei Paulus und seinen Schülern', *EvTh* 28 (1968), pp.165ff.; above all, ' "Das Ende des Gesetzes": über Ursprung und Ansatz der paulinischen Theologie', *ZThK* 67 (1970), pp.15–39; recently again, 'Achtzehn Thesen zur paulinischen Kreuzestheologie', *Rechtfertigung*, Käsemann FS, pp.511ff.

[3]Kuss, *Paulus*, pp.286f.

[4]*Ibid.*

confirmed to be true by the Christophany, his swift response to the call to preach the gospel to the Gentiles, and the nature of the elements of his theology which have their origin in the Damascus event, all help us at least approximately to circumscribe the extent to which Paul formulated his theology very soon after the Damascus event. At latest by the time of the Apostolic Council or on the eve of his first world-wide missionary journey Paul must have drawn all the necessary consequences from the Damascus event to obtain the main lines of his theology. M. Hengel observes that from his earliest letter to his last Paul shows no essential development of his Christology and that he presupposes his Christological titles, formulae and views as known to the churches to which he writes letters, thus indicating that they go back to his missionary preaching that founded those churches. From this Hengel concludes that 'the Pauline Christology was there fully developed in all essential lines already toward the end of the 40's before the beginning of the great missionary journeys into the West'[1]. Exactly the same can be said for Paul's soteriology with its doctrine of justification by grace through faith apart from works of the law at its centre. For Paul says that some 15–16 years after his conversion and call he went to Jerusalem (c.A.D. 48) and laid before the 'pillars' 'the gospel which I preach among the Gentiles ' (Gal 2.1ff.) – the gospel of justification through faith alone which is disputed in Galatia – suggesting that already by the time of his missionary work in Syria and Cilicia his doctrine of justification was clearly formulated as part of his gospel[2]. In the exposition of Paul's theology below it will be seen that it is more sensible to suppose that Paul had clearly formulated the main lines of his theology very soon after the Damascus revelation than to posit a rather slow development in Paul's interpretation of it, although they were constantly deepened and sharpened – so, developed – in the light of his missionary situations and especially of the controversies with his opponents.

Again, to assert that Paul's theology originated from his Damascus experience, is not to say that up to that moment Paul's mind was theologically

---

[1] M.Hengel, 'Christologie und neutestamentliche Chronologie: zu einer Aporie in der Geschichte des Urchristentums', *Neues Testament und Geschichte*, Cullmann FS (1972), p.45. C.K.Barrett, *From First Adam to Last* (1962), p.3, goes even further: ' . . . we *know* how Paul understood him (sc. Jesus) in the forties, fifties, and sixties of the first century – and, we may add, in the thirties too, for there is no indication whatever that Paul radically changed his views of Jesus between his conversion and the beginning of his letter-writing; rather the contrary' (emphasis by B.).

[2] If the '14 years' in Gal 2.1 should be dated from the Damascus call and the visit that Paul mentions in Gal 2.1ff. is to be identified with the famine-relief visit mentioned in Acts 11.27ff., then the *terminus ad quem* for the formulation of Paul's soteriology is a couple of years earlier (c. 46 A.D.).

a *tabula rasa*[1] or that he derived all his theology from his Damascus experience without the interpretative categories and concepts provided by the
messianic beliefs, the conception of the law, and other ideas and concepts in
Judaism, by the primitive Christian kerygma, and perhaps also by the ideas
and concepts that he met later in his mission field. As a pupil of a Rabbi
and as a zealous Pharisee who originated from the Hellenistic *diaspora,* Paul
had certainly been well aware of the major theological currents in Judaism —
apocalyptic and Rabbinic, Palestinian and Hellenistic, if these distinctions are
historically meaningful at all. And as a persecutor of the Church he had
known at least the content of its proclamation, if not Jesus himself and his
proclamation. But these in themselves did not make Paul a Christian and
produce his theology[2]. The relationship between Paul's background and the
Damascus experience in their bearing upon his theology may be indicated in
a diagram as:

So, the background provided Paul with certain categories and concepts with
which he could interpret the Damascus experience and produce his theology.
To look at it from the standpoint of his Christian theology, the elements of
his background remained suspended in need of the catalyst of the Damascus
revelation for solution into his theology[3]. So, the Damascus experience has
the fundamental character for Paul's theology. Therefore, in order to understand Paul's theology adequately, one has to see how Paul derives the main
lines of his theology from that experience as he interprets it in the light of his
background.

2 *Christ, Lord, Son of God*

Now in those passages which we have argued above[4] as referring or alluding
to the Damascus event, there appear the Christological titles Christ (2Cor
4.4–6; 5.16ff.; Gal 1.12; Eph 3.1–13; Phil 3.3ff.; Col 1.27), Lord (1Cor
9.1; 2Cor 3.16–18; 4.5; 10.8; 13.10; Phil 3.8), and Son of God (Gal 1.16;
cf. Acts 9.20). Does this mean that at the Damascus revelation Paul perceived

---

[1]Cf. Blank, *Paulus*, p.184.

[2]*Ibid.* Bultmann is surely incorrect when he says that Paul was won to the Christian
faith by the kerygma of the Hellenistic Church (*Theology* i, p.187).

[3]Cf. Dunn, *Jesus*, p.4, who makes a similar point with reference to Paul's 'religious
experience' in general rather than specifically to his Damascus experience.

[4]*Supra* Ch. 1.

Jesus as the Christ, the Lord and the Son of God? Since these titles are universally recognized as pre-Pauline, it is very probable that before his conversion Paul knew that the Christians were attributing these titles to the crucified Jesus of Nazareth and was therefore provoked to persecute them. For he thought that they were blasphemously proclaiming Jesus of Nazareth, the man crucified under the pronouncement of God's curse by the law (Dt 21.23; Gal 3.13), as the Messiah, the Lord, and the Son of God. But then at the Damascus Christophany Paul realized that Jesus of Nazareth was not dead but alive, not cursed but exalted by God, and therefore that the Christian proclamation of him was correct. So he adopted these titles to interpret the crucified and risen Jesus of Nazareth who appeared to him.

But at the time of Paul's conversion (c. 32–34A.D.), what did the early Christians mean when they proclaimed Jesus of Nazareth as the Messiah, the Lord and the Son of God? This question leads us to the tumultuous sea of present NT scholarship concerning the development of NT Christology[1]. Obviously it is impossible to survey the various hypotheses put forward about it and reach a criticial conclusion here. So we would simply present the thesis of M. Hengel, who has paid special attention to this question[2], and see how Paul adopted the titles and the ideas associated with them as his experience of the Damascus Christophany confirmed them and how he advanced the Christological development of the early Church in the light of the Damascus experience.

In his masterly essay, Hengel states: 'The real problem of the origin of the early Christian Christology is above all the first 4 or 5 years which are "pre-Pauline" in its proper sense'[3]. Then he outlines the course of the

---

[1]Out of the vast amount of literature in this area the following may be noted: W. Bousset, *Kyrios Christos* ([2]1921); Bultmann, *Theology* i, part I; Cullmann, *Christology;* V.Taylor, *The Names of Jesus* (1953); *idem, The Person of Christ* (1958); F.Hahn, *Christologische Hoheitstitel* ([3]1974); W.Kramer, *Christ, Lord, Son of God* (1966), part one; R.H.Fuller, *The Foundations of NT Christology* (1974); W.Thüsing, *Erhöhungsvorstellung und Parusieerwartung in der ältesten nachösterlichen Christologie* (1969); R.N.Longenecker, *The Christology of Early Jewish Christianity* (1970); I.H. Marshall, *The Origins of NT Christology* (1976); C.F.D.Moule, *Origin of Christology* (1977). The last two books appeared too late to be used for our present study.

[2]Hengel, 'Christologie und neutestamentliche Chronologie', *Neues Testament und Geschichte*, pp.43–67.

[3]*Ibid.*, p.63. This conclusion is drawn from a sober consideration of the problem of 'space and time' in the development of the NT Christology and a critical examination of the prevalent attempts to explain the development of the NT Christology before Paul in terms of a two-Church scheme (the Palestine Jewish Church – the Hellenistic Church) (e.g., Bousset, *op. cit.*; Bultmann, *op. cit.*) and of a three-Church scheme (the Palestine Jewish Church – the Hellenistic Jewish Church – the Hellenistic Gentile Church) (e.g.,

Christological development during the period, starting from Jesus' work and proclamation through the various stages of the primitive Church's Christological reflections spurred on by the events of the resurrection, the giving of the Spirit, and the missionary commission, and by the need to provide Scriptural proofs for Jesus' messiahship and the saving significance of his death. In this outline Hengel shows how these events and needs led the primitive Church to recognise and affirm Jesus as the exalted and enthroned Son of Man who is the coming Judge; as the Messiah, the Son of David, who is the Redeemer and Ruler of God's people; as the Servant of God who wrought atonement through his suffering; as the Lord, and as the Son of God. Then Hengel concludes:

> Apparently the fundamentals of the so-called 'pre-Pauline' Christology – with the exception of the pre-existence Christology and the idea of the sending of the Son – were laid by the time of the conversion of Paul. *The 'dynamic-creative impulse' of the fundamental event that grounded the Church laid thus within a very short time the Christological foundation that is predominant in the NT.* In some ways the last appearance of the Risen One to the diaspora Pharisee from Tarsus concluded the first period of the early Church – a period decisive for the entire future development. A new epoch of Christological development dawned which then came to its proper unfolding and brought rich fruits ca. 14–16 years later in the Pauline 'world mission' after the Apostolic Council[1].

If Hengel's thesis holds, it is easy to see how Paul could perceive Jesus of Nazareth who appeared to him on the Damascus road as the Christ, the Lord and the Son of God. The Damascus Christophany was Paul's Easter, so that the primitive Church's Christological conceptions developed out of their Easter experience were confirmed to be true for him at that moment. So he accepted not only the Christian confession of the crucified Jesus of Nazareth

---

Hahn, *op. cit.*,; Kramer, *op. cit.*; cf. also Fuller, *op. cit.*). See also I.H.Marshall, 'Palestine and Hellenistic Christianity: Some Critical Comments', *NTS* 19 (1972/73), pp. 271–287, which, though essentially independent of Hengel's article, supplements it well, sometimes with different material and evidence: also his *Origins*, pp.32–42.

[1] Hengel, 'Christologie', pp.64–67 (emphasis by H.). It goes without saying that there are some important points in Hengel's outline about which we have some reservation. On the whole we would see Jesus' messianic self-consciousness not just in his self-designation as 'the Son of Man' but also his addressing God *'abba'* and his self-designation as 'the Son' (Mt 11.27 par. Lk 10.22; Mk 12.6 par. Mt 21.37, Lk 20.13; Mk 13.32). Cf. Jeremias, *Abba*, pp.1–67; I.H.Marshall, 'The Divine Sonship of Jesus', *Interpretation* 21 (1967), pp.91ff.; Dunn, *Jesus*, pp.21–40. And we would see at least the germs of the various Christological ideas represented by the titles Messiah, Son of David, Servant of God, Lord (*mar*), etc. already in Jesus' proclamation rather than attributing them exclusively to the post-Easter Church. However, our present concern is with the stage of Christological development at the time of Paul's conversion and not with the course of it from Jesus up to that point.

as the Messiah, the Lord and the Son of God but also the ideas contained in the confessions. This means, however, not that Paul now simply transferred all the diverse messianic conceptions in Judaism to Jesus since he saw that Jesus of Nazareth, crucified as a messianic pretender, had been vindicated and therefore confirmed by God as the Messiah, but rather that his messianic beliefs and conceptions were now determined by what Jesus showed himself to be[1]. This is the reason why Paul connects the title 'Christ' closely with the proper name 'Jesus', making the earliest Christian confession 'Jesus (is) Christ (Messiah)' more or less a proper name, 'Jesus Christ'. And this is the reason why Paul's Christology expressed through the titles Christ, Lord and Son of God means something else and something much more than the Messiah for the Jews, although the messiahship of Jesus is fundamental to his Christology and the rest of his theology[2].

Whereas he had previously seen Jesus of Nazareth as cursed by God, Paul

---

[1]See F.F.Bruce, *Paul and Jesus* (1974), pp.25f., who, arguing against W.Wrede, puts the matter well: 'The truth of the matter, in fact, is exactly the other way round. Once the glorified Jesus appeared in him, and he learned that Jesus is Lord, it was no longer a question of adapting Jesus to his previous conception of the Christ: "the Christ", says Paul in other words, "is not the figure I formerly imagined Him to be; the true Christ is the crucified Jesus, risen from the dead and glorified. As for the Christ of my former 'worldly' imagination, henceforth, I know *that* Christ no more" . . . Of course, if Jesus was the Christ, Paul's whole attitude to Jesus, as well as his conception of the Messiah, was revolutionized'.

[2]N.A.Dahl, 'Die Messianität Jesu bei Paulus', *Studia Paulina*, J.de Zwaan FS (1953), pp.83–95. See esp. pp.86f., where after surveying Paul's use of Χριστός in order to discover whether it is used as the title for 'Messiah' Dahl says: 'Die Sache liegt deutlich so, daß der Christus-Name seinen Inhalt bekommt durch das, was Jesus Christus ist, nicht durch einen im voraus bestehenden Messiasbegriff. Eine *interpretatio christiana* ist restlos durchgeführt. Jedoch behält der Christus-Name eine gewisse Eigenart gegenüber dem eigentlichen Eigennamen "Jesus". Der Name "Christus" ist mehr inhaltlich gefüllt und bringt mehr das Wesen und die Bedeutsamkeit Jesu zum Ausdruck. Dabei ist aber zwischen "Person" und "Amt" nicht zu unterscheiden. Alles was Jesus ist und wirkt, das ist und wirkt er als der Christus. Der Christus-Name ist bei Paulus kein von der Person und dem Werk Jesu Christi ablösbarer Titel. Unter diesen Umständen ist es nur natürlich, daß man im Einzelnen nicht klar unterscheiden kann zwischen Aussagen, wo der Christus-Name nur als Eigenname gebraucht ist und anderen, wo die appellative Bedeutung noch mitklingt. Wirklich relevant ist eigentlich nur die Frage, inwiefern und in welcher Weise die Messianität Jesu in der gesamten Christusverkündigung des Paulus zum Ausdruck kommt'. With this Dahl goes on to demonstrate that the messiahship of Jesus is fundamental to Paul's entire Christology, soteriology, eschatology and ecclesiology. Cf. Hengel, 'Christologie', p.57. This seems to be more satisfactory than Kramer's view that 'Christ' is used in Paul's letters as a mere proper name although we may assume that Paul himself had 'some latent awareness' of the original meaning of it (*Christ*, pp.64f.).

now came to believe with the Christians that he was indeed the Messiah who vicariously bore the curse of the law for us on the cross (Gal 3.13; Rom 8.3; 2Cor 5.21) and that his death was God's atoning sacrifice for us (Rom 3.21ff.; 2Cor 5.19ff.). Paul firmly connects the title 'Christ' with what W. Kramer calls the 'pistis-formula', namely the statement that sets out the death on the cross and resurrection of Jesus Christ as the saving events and therefore as the content of faith and preaching (e.g., Rom 5.6ff.; 6.3f., 8f.; 7.4; 8.34; 14.9; 1Cor 1.23; 8.11; 15.3, 12ff.; Gal 3.1; 6.12; Phil 3.8ff., etc.). In this Paul seems to follow a practice already established (cf. 1Cor 15.3ff.)[1]. However, does this reflect also Paul's previous opposition to the crucified Messiah (cf. Gal 3.13; 6.12; 1Cor 1.23) and subsequent realization that the crucified Messiah is indeed the saving event of God?

At any rate, if he had previously looked upon the Christian confession 'Jesus is the Lord' as a blasphemy against the God of Sinai, now he came to believe that Jesus of Nazareth was indeed the Lord of his Church and of the whole universe. For he saw him exalted by God and enthroned at his right hand in fulfilment of Ps 110.1 (cf. 1Cor 15.25; Phil 2.9f.), having a spiritual mode of being in glory (2Cor 3.17f.) and being ready to return for judgement and redemption[2], so that he was compelled to address him *'κύριε'*(Acts 9.5; 22.8; 26.15)[3].   So he came to believe that now salvation depends on confessing 'Jesus is Lord' and believing that 'God raised him from the dead' (Rom 10.9), and the Christians' prayer *'maranatha'* became his prayer (1Cor 16.22).   However, Paul's experience of the risen and exalted Jesus as the Lord had a unique personal dimension beyond the dimensions of the cultic acclamation in worship and of the confessional formula.   For on the Damascus road the risen and exalted Jesus as the Lord of his Church and of the universe arrested him with his overwhelming power (Phil 3.12) and made him his apostle (1Cor 9.1–27),   that is, his bond-slave (δοῦλος: Rom 1.1; 2Cor 4.5;

---

[1]Cf. Kramer, *Christ*, pp.19–64, 133ff.; G.Bornkamm, 'Taufe und neues Leben bei Paulus', *Das Ende des Gesetzes* (1966), p.40.

[2]*Supra* pp.56, 73 for the view that the Damascus ἀποκάλυψις of Jesus Christ was a proleptic realization of the parousia for Paul.

[3]*'κύριε'* seems to be *formgeschichtlich* an address for the figure at an angelophany or a theophany.   See, e.g., Dan 10.16; 4Ezra; 5; 6; 7; 3Bar 3; 4; 5; 6; Philo, *Somn.* i. 157; Acts 10.4, 14; Rev 7.14 (?).   Hengel, 'Christologie', pp.57f. (n.40), suggests the possibility that the absolute ὁ κύριος could have developed from this way of addressing the heavenly figure at an epiphany: when the disciples saw the risen Christ at the Easter as the exalted 'Son of Man' and 'Messiah – God's Son', they could have addressed him *'mari'* (κύριε), which, being consistent with their address *'mari'* for the earthly Jesus but meaning now more than this, could have developed into the absolute ὁ κύριος. Cf. M. Werner, *Die Entstehung des christlichen Dogmas* (²1954), pp.308ff.

Gal 1.10; Phil 1.1)[1]. This thought Paul expresses in Phil 3.8, where he speaks of his conversion and call as 'the surpassing worth of knowing Christ Jesus my Lord', the only occasion where Paul uses the expression '*my* Lord'[2].

Finally, the vision of Jesus enthroned at God's right hand confirmed to him that Jesus of Nazareth is indeed the Messiah, the Son of David in his physical descent, exalted and enthroned to be the Son of God through (or from the time of) the resurrection according to the Holy Spirit in fulfilment of God's promise in 2Sam 7.12–14 (cf. also Ps 2.7), as the Christians confessed (Rom 1.3f.)[3]. Just as '*κύριε*' was the proper address for the heavenly

---

[1]Cf. Blank, *Paulus*, p.205.

[2]Cf. Jeremias, *Schlüssel*, p.21; also Manson, *On Paul and John,* pp.13f.

[3]On the pre-Pauline confession in Rom 1.3f., which must go back to the earliest Jewish Christianity in Jerusalem, see, besides commentaries, recent literature by E. Schweizer, 'Röm. 1,3f. und der Gegensatz von Fleisch und Geist vor und bei Paulus', *Neotestamentica* (1963), pp.180ff.; H.Schlier, 'Zu Röm 1,3f.', *Neues Testament und Geschichte*, Cullmann FS, pp.207ff.; Blank, *Paulus*, pp.250ff.; Hengel, *Der Sohn Gottes* (1975), pp.93ff.

O.Betz, *What Do We Know about Jesus?* (1968), pp.94ff. (also 87ff.), emphasizes that behind the confession there stands Nathan's oracle in 2Sam 7.12–14 which was the source of Israel's hope for the Davidic Messiah in the OT and in post-Biblical Judaism, including Qumran (4QFlor.). (For an account of the development of this tradition, see D.C.Duling, 'The Promises to David and Their Entrance into Christianity – Nailing Down a Likely Hypothesis', *NTS* 19 (1974), pp.55–77.) God's promise to David through Nathan runs: '. . . I will raise up (והקימתי /καὶ ἀναστήσω) your offspring (זרע / σπέρμα) after you, who shall come forth from your body, and I will establish his kingdom . . . I will be his father, and he shall be my son'. Betz finds that in the confession of Rom 1.3f. Jesus' resurrection or God's 'raising' him is interpreted also as God's exalting or enthroning him to be the messianic king according to Nathan's prophecy as both the idea of God's resurrecting the dead and that of his enthroning the messianic king were expressed by the same Hebrew verb הקים (see also Duling, *op. cit.*, pp.70f.). This is almost certainly correct since the same oracle is used in Acts 13.33–37 exactly for the same purpose of confirming the messiahship of Jesus who was raised by God (see D.Goldsmith, 'Acts 13.33–37: A *Pesher* on II Samuel 7', *JBL* 87 (1968), pp.321ff.; also J.W.Doeve, *Jewish Hermeneutics in the Synoptic Gospels and Acts* (1954), pp.172ff.). So, in Jesus of Nazareth who was 'raised' by God at Easter, the disciples saw the Son of David 'raised up', i.e., exalted and enthroned by God to be the messianic king, the Son of God, according to his promise to David through Nathan. It seems highly arbitrary for Duling (*op. cit.*) to insist that both the original confession and Paul in Rom 1.2–4 affirm only Jesus' descent from David and divine Sonship on the basis of the tradition of 2Sam 7.12ff. without actually affirming him to be 'the Son of David'; that the ascription of the title to Jesus took place 'no earlier than the latter half of the first c.' (p.68); and that outside the Synoptic Gospels Jesus is associated only 'with the non-titular, metaphorical materials of the promise tradition, materials which occur largely, in *contrast* to the title Son of David' (p.71, emphasis by D.) – i.e., Jesus is understood only in terms of those texts of the promise tradition that have

figure at a theophany or an angelophany, 'son of God' or 'one like a son of
God' may have been a common designation for the heavenly figure at an

---

metaphors like 'seed of David., 'branch of David', etc. (pp.68, 71, 75, *passim*). Quite apart
from the clear implication of Rom 1.2–4 (and Acts 13.33–37), Duling's demonstration
that various texts of 'the promise tradition' (i.e., of 2Sam 7.12ff.) are later conflated
within the OT and Judaism (pp.62ff.) and his (reluctant) recognition that there was a
titular use of 'Son of David' in pre-Christian Judaism (pp.68f.), would make the thesis
a curious one. To be sure, 'Son of David' as a title plays little role in Paul. But this is
to be explained probably rather in terms of his desire to avoid the politico-nationalistic
understanding of Jesus' Messiahship.

Now it is evident that 4QFlor. 1.1–13 is a *pesher* on 2Sam 7.10–14 conflated with
other supporting texts (Ex 15.17f.; Am 9.11. See W.R.Lane, 'A New Commentary
Structure in 4QFlorilegium', *JBL* 78 (1959), pp.343ff.). In 1.11 the future son of
David whom God will raise as his son is identified as 'the shoot of David' (צמח דויד),
thus indicating that here the Nathan oracle is blended with its related messianic oracles
(Jer 23.5f.; 33.15f.; Zech 6.12f.; cf. also Isa 4.2; Zech 3.8. Cf. Duling, *op. cit.*, pp.
64ff., who also shows a similar conflation in 4QPB). Does a similar tradition of exegesis
stand behind Philo's exegesis of Zech 6.12 in *Conf. Ling.* 62f? There Philo identifies the
'man' ἀνατολή (following the LXX=MT צמח) with ὁ ἀσώματος ἐκεῖνος, 'who differs
not a whit from the divine εἰκών' (i.e., the Logos), the πρεσβύτατος υἱός, whom the
Father of all raised up (ἀνέτειλε), and elsewhere calls πρωτόγονος; and indeed the Son
thus begotten followed the ways of his Father and shaped the different kinds, looking
to the archetypal pattern which that Father supplied'. First to note here is 1) the fact
that the concept ἀνατέλλειν (צמח) is both closely related to ἀνιστάναι (קום) and very
important in 'the promise tradition' that carries on the oracle of 2Sam 7.12ff., as Duling
demonstrates (*op. cit.*, pp.61, 67f., 75ff.; cf. also H.Schlier, *TDNT* i, pp.351–353, who
says that ἀνατολή became a name for the Messiah in the synagogue. Cf. Lk 1.78). Then,
2) note how Philo, like 4QFlor., brings the titles ἀνατολή (= צמח) and the son (of God)
together and identifies them with each other. While in Zech 6.12 the verb ἀνατέλλειν
stands as intransitive, Philo uses it here as transitive. This he may be doing under the
influence of such texts as 2Sam 7.12–14; Jer 23.5f.; etc. which contain the idea of
God's (active) 'raising' the son of David (= of God) or the shoot of David. If so, 3) this,
together with Philo's identification of the ἀνατολή with the son (of God), may indicate
that Philo was acquainted with a tradition such as that witnessed to by 4QFlor. which
conflates various oracles on the Davidic Messiah. 4) This would be made more credible if
in saying, '(God) calls him elsewhere πρωτόγονος' (*Conf. Ling.* 63) Philo refers to Ps
89.28, where God promises to make the son of David 'the first-born' (MT בכור/LXX Ps
88.28 πρωτότοκος), another passage that derives from or is closely related to 2Sam
7.12ff. (on Philo's avoidance of πρωτότοκος in favour of πρωτόγονος in designating the
Logos, see K.L.Schmidt, *TDNT* vi, p.875). If it is correct to see in *Conf. Ling.* 62f.
various messianic texts conflated, the text would confirm what Duling (*op. cit.*, p.67)
calls 'the tendency toward cumulative conflation' of various texts of the messianic
promises in the later OT and Jewish texts. There are, to be sure, obvious differences:
Philo identifies ἀνατολή with the Logos while 4QFlor. צמח with the Davidic Messiah,
and correspondingly Philo uses the aorist (ἀνέτειλε) while 4QFlor. the future (והקי-
מתי). But is not Philo, who has no real eschatology, in fact, here turning the messianic
tradition into a Platonic and Stoic Logos doctrine? Cf. A.J.M.Wedderburn, 'Philo's

epiphany[1]. If an angel could be called 'son of God', how much more should the exalted Davidic Messiah who appeared as sitting on the throne of God be given that title?[2]

Now, the pre-Pauline confession cited in Rom 1.3f. taken in itself does not imply the pre-existence of the Son of God[3]. Some have suggested, however, that by his introduction of the confession as 'concerning his (sc. God's) Son' (Rom 1.3) and closing it with the appositional 'Jesus Christ our Lord' Paul shows his own understanding of the gospel as concerning the pre-existent Son of God who was incarnate in the seed of David as the messianic king and then installed as the Son of God, that is, the universal Lord, through the resurrection[4].

This is very likely because the pre-existence of the Son of God is an essential element in Paul's Son-Christology (cf. e.g, Rom 8.3; Gal 4.4; Col 1.13ff.). In the above mentioned essay M. Hengel suggested that it could well have been Paul who introduced for the first time in the early Church the ideas of the pre-existence and sending of the Son of God and of his mediatory role in creation by applying the characteristics of Wisdom to the exalted Jesus[5]. However, three years later, in his monograph on the Son of God, he withdraws this thesis and speaks of Paul taking over two formulations — the sending of the pre-existent Son into the world and the giving-up of the Son in

---

"Heavenly Man" ', *NovT* 15 (1973), pp.316ff.

If it be judged that *Conf. Ling.* 62f. witnesses to Philo's acquaintance with the exegetical tradition of the messianic promise such as that exhibited by 4QFlor., i.e., if there is an original connection between the two exegeses, then we may find it easy to understand why Paul appears to be standing, as it were, between them, holding on the one hand the messianic Son-Christology and on the other the Son- and εἰκών-Christology some of whose motifs find their parallels in Philo's *Conf. Ling.* 62f., 146, etc. This consideration also confirms the basic Jewish background of the Pauline (and the NT) Son-Christology. *Infra* pp.256ff., 315ff.

[1]Cf. Hengel, *Sohn*, pp.36, 57 (n.48). *Infra* pp.215f.

[2]Cf. *ibid.*, p.57 (n.48).

[3]Schlier, 'Zu Röm. 1, 3f.', p.213, conjectures that the original form of the confession transmitted to Paul ran as: Jesus Christus aus dem Samen Davids
                    bestellt zum Sohn Gottes
                    aus der Auferstehung der Toten.
Cf. Fuller, *Christology*, p.165.

[4]Stuhlmacher, 'Theologische Probleme des Römerbriefpräskripts', *EvTh* 27 (1967), pp.382f.; Käsemann, *Römer*, p.11; Cranfield, *Romans*, p.58; Hengel, *Sohn*, pp.94f.; Schweizer, πνεῦμα, κτλ, *TDNT* vi, p.417. Against this, however, Blank, *Paulus*, p.255. If ἐν δυνάμει is a Pauline insertion and ὁ υἱὸς θεοῦ ἐν δυνάμει means Jesus as the exalted Lord, then this is even clearer.

[5]Hengel, 'Christologie', pp.62f., 66.

death — from 'der vor- oder exakter nebenpaulinischen Gemeinde (vermutlich in Syrien)'[1]. The reasons for this change of view Hengel does not explicitly state anywhere, except alluding to two factors that seem to have weighed in favour of the later position: one, that Paul already connects the title 'Son of God' with the Damascus event[2]; and the other, that the above mentioned statements about the Son of God are firmly built formulae which appear also in non-Pauline texts (e.g., Jn 3.17; 1Jn 4.9, 10, 14; Jn 3.16)[3].

However, these two factors are not sufficient to establish the pre-Pauline character of the ideas contained in the formulae. For, to begin with, Paul's mentioning 'the Son of God' as the object of the Damascus revelation does not prove that before that event the fully developed Son-Christology was already available. It in no way deters one from thinking that at the time of Paul's call the Son-Christology of the primitive Church could have been only at the stage of the confession cited in Rom 1.3f. For through his seeing the exalted and enthroned Jesus Paul could have received the confirmation of the veracity of the confession on the one hand *and* other factors that led him to deepen the primitive Son-Christology and affirm the Son's pre-existence and sending into the world on the other, so that the Son-Christology became an essential part of his testimony to the Damascus experience. It is true that Hengel's second factor is the sole reason for many authors' conclusion that the statements about the sending and giving-up of the Son are pre-Pauline formulae and the idea of the pre-existence of the Son implied therein is therefore pre-Pauline[4]. But here we must bring in the earlier Hengel to argue against the later Hengel. Earlier, complaining rightly about W. Kramer's procedure of taking everything that smacks of a formula or formal structure as pre-Pauline[5], Hengel wrote: 'The problem that the Paul of the letters possesses a 16- to 18-year "christliche Vorgeschichte" in which in certain cases he himself participated in this "pre-Pauline" development, scarcely

---

[1] Hengel, *Sohn*, pp.23ff., 104ff.

[2] *Ibid.*, pp.23f.

[3] *Ibid.*, p.26.

[4] Kramer, *Christ*, pp.111ff.; Hahn, *Hoheitstitel*, pp.315ff.; E.Schweizer, 'Zum religionsgeschichtlichen Hintergrund der "Sendungsformel" Gal.4,4f., Röm.8,3f., Jn 3,16f., 1Jn. 4,9' *ZNW* 57 (1966), pp.199–210; *idem,* υἱός, *TDNT* viii, pp.374ff.; Mussner, *Gal.*, pp.271ff. Käsemann, *Römer*, p.206, characteristically goes so far as to declare: 'the Christologically applied motif of the sending of the pre-existent Son is typically Johannine . . . but is in Paul unusual'. But as we hope to show, this is quite mistaken. Against this, Blank, *Paulus*, pp.262f., insists that Gal 4.4 is a completely Pauline construction. K.Wengst, *Christologische Formeln und Lieder des Urchristentums* (1972), p.59 (n.22), denies even the existence of a 'sending' formula.

[5] Kramer, *Christ*, part I, esp. p.15, where he sets forth this procedure.

comes to the author's (sc. Kramer's) consciousness'[1]. Indeed Hengel specifically warned against the prevalent tendency of present NT scholarship
exemplified by Kramer in these terms: 'The proof that individual Christological and soteriological formulations appear also in a — always later —
non-Pauline context, is not sufficient to identify them *eo ipso* as "pre-Pauline",
i.e., originally strange material to the Apostle'[2]. Then Hengel considered the
question: to what extent did Paul himself participate in the Christological
development of the young missionary church in Syria and Cilicia before he
launched his mission into the West?[3] That Paul must have exerted a considerable, if not the dominant, theological influence in that development
between his conversion (c. 32—34 A.D.) and his world-wide mission (c. 49
A.D.), is suggested by his former Pharisaic and Rabbinic training, by his call
to the Gentile mission, and by the fact that he together with Barnabas represented the Antioch church and negotiated for the recognition of the law-free
Gentile mission at the Apostolic Council in Jerusalem[4]. Now, these sober
considerations seem to undermine completely the sole ground put forward for
the view that the formulae of sending and giving-up of the Son are pre-Pauline.
However, they also do not prove in themselves that the formulae and the
ideas contained therein are then Pauline. They just nullify the validity of the
ground often suggested for the view that the formulae are pre-Pauline. Thus
they leave wide open the question of the authorship of the formulae and the
origin of the ideas contained therein.

In this situation there are four possibilities that can be contemplated:
1) the formulae are 'pre-Pauline' in the strict sense that they were developed
before Paul's Damascus experience; 2) they are *nebenpaulinisches* material
which was developed by others and then taken over by Paul during his collab-
oration with them in Syria and Cilicia; 3) they are the result of a joint development by Paul and his co-workers; or 4) they are entirely from Paul. The
second possibility seems to be the later Hengel's view[5]. But for the first two
possibilities there is simply no positive evidence, as we have seen above. So, it
is worth considering whether in fact they are not a Pauline contribution to

---

[1] Hengel, 'Christologie', pp.53f.

[2] *Ibid.*, p.46. Cf. H.Frh. v. Campenhausen, 'Das Bekenntnis im Urchristentum',
ZNW 63 (1972), p.231 (n.124), who critizes some scholars' excessive eagerness to label
every sentence that is written in an elevated style as 'formula' in spite of the warnings
by Dibelius, 'Zur Formgeschichte des NT (außerhalb der Evangelien)', *Theol. Rundschau*
3 (1931), pp.225f. and N.A.Dahl, 'Christusverkündigung', p.3.

[3] Hengel, 'Christologie', p.46.

[4] *Ibid.*, p.62f.

[5] Hengel, *Sohn*, pp.24, 105.

the early Christian Christology, as Hengel originally suggested. Taking them as a Pauline contribution would not necessarily rule out completely the share of other Christians in the course of their development, but it would mean that Paul took a leading or decisive role in this. It is our thesis that the ideas of the pre-existence, mediatorship in creation, and sending and giving-up of the Son of God are a Pauline contribution and they are grounded ultimately in Paul's Damascus experience.

To substantiate this thesis we again avail ourselves of Hengel's masterly depiction of the development of the Son-Christology in the NT. For we are convinced that our own thesis is confirmed by his, i.e., that the ideas of pre-existence, mediatorship in creation and sending of the Son in the NT are the necessary consequences of the early Christian conviction that Jesus Christ has taken the place of the Torah-Hokmah[1]. Hengel arrives at this conclusion through a compact but careful examination of the *religionsgeschichtlichen* material of both Hellenism and the OT/Judaism. His examination of the alleged Hellenistic parallels – the mystery-cults, θεῖος ἀνήρ, the Gnostic redeemer myth, and others – reveals very clearly the hollowness of the repeated claims that these formed the background of the NT Christology in general and of the NT Son-Christology in particular[2]. Having examined the OT/Jewish use of the designation 'son of God' and the ideas of pre-existence, mediatorship in creation, and 'sending' into the world, Hengel concludes that here we have 'essential building material which was used by the primitive Church in its Christological conception'[3]. After persuasively explaining the rise of the pre-Pauline confession in Rom 1.3f.[4], Hengel asks how the step was taken from the confession of the exaltation of Jesus to divine Sonship (the Messiah *designatus*), to the ideas of his pre-existence, mediatorship in creation and sending into the world[5]. Hengel's answer is that this development came about chiefly through the early Church's transference to Jesus of the characteristics of the hypostatized and personified divine Wisdom developed in Jewish wisdom literature[6]. Now this suggestion itself is not new at all. It was already made by H. Windisch[7] in 1914 and since then has been repeated-

---

[1]*Ibid.*, pp.104ff.; also 'Christologie', pp.62f.

[2]Hengel, *Sohn*, esp. pp.39–67, against e.g., Bultmann, *Glauben und Verstehen* i, pp. 253f.; *G.u.V.* ii, p.251; *Theology* i, pp.121ff.; Conzelmann, *Outline*, pp.78ff.; Hahn, *Hoheitstitel*, pp.292ff., 209ff. (also 120ff.); cf. also Fuller, *Christology*, pp.203ff.

[3]Hengel, *Sohn*, pp.35–39, 67–89 (quotation from p.90).

[4]*Ibid.*, pp.93–104.

[5]*Ibid.*, pp.104f.

[6]*Ibid.*, pp.106–120; also 'Christologie', pp.62f.

[7]H.Windisch, 'Die göttliche Weisheit der Juden und die paulinische Christologie',

ly confirmed[1].

That this is correct, can be demonstrated by a glance at the Jewish wisdom literature. As is well known, already Prov 8.22—31 introduces Wisdom as a hypostatized and personified being created before the universe and existing closely at God's side:

> The Lord created me the beginning of his works,
> before all else that he made, long ago.
> Alone, I was fashioned in times long past,
> at the beginning, long before earth itself.
> When there was yet no ocean I was born,
> No springs brimming with water.
> Before the mountains were settled in their place,
> long before the hills I was born,
> when as yet he had made neither land nor lake
> nor the first clod of earth.
> When he set the heavens in their place I was there,
> when he girdled the ocean with the horizon,
> when he fixed the canopy of clouds overhead
> and set the springs of ocean firm in their place,
> when he prescribed its limits for the sea
> and knit together earth's foundations.
> Then I was at his side each day,
> his darling and delight,
> playing in his presence continually,
> playing on the earth, when he had finished it,
> while my delight was in mankind (NEB).

Here there is not only the idea of Wisdom's pre-existence (i.e., existence before the creation of the universe) clearly expressed but also the idea of her mediatory role in creation is at least implied (cf. also Prov 3.19; Job 28. 23—27). The same thoughts of Wisdom's pre-existence and mediatory role appear in Sir. 24.3ff., in which Wisdom praises herself alluding to the creation account of Gen 1:

> I am the word which was spoken by the Most High;
> it was I who covered the earth like a mist.
> My dwelling-place was in high heaven;
> my throne was in a pillar of cloud.

Neutestamentliche Studien, G.Heinrici FS (1914), pp.220—234. To be precise, it should be noted that while Windisch explains Paul's ideas of Christ's pre-existence and mediatorship in creation in the light of Wisdom he does not deal with the idea of the sending of the Son into the world in this connection.

[1] C.F.Burney, 'Christ as the APXH of Creation', *JTS* 27 (1926), pp.160ff.; W.D. Davies, *Paul and Rabbinic Judaism* ([3]1970), pp.147ff.; A.Richardson, *Introduction to the Theology of the NT* ([4]1969), pp.155ff.; E.Schweizer,'Zur Herkunft der Präexistenz-

Alone I made a circuit of the sky
and traversed the depth of the abyss.
The waves of the sea, the whole earth,
every people and nation were under my sway.
Among them all I looked for a home:
in whose territory was I to settle?
Then the Creator of the universe laid command upon me;
My Creator decreed where I should dwell.
He said, 'Make your home in Jacob;
find your heritage in Israel'.
Before time began he created me,
and I shall remain for ever.
In the sacred tent I ministered in his presence,
and so I came to be established in Zion.
Thus he settled me in the city he loved
and gave me authority in Jerusalem.
I took root among the people whom the Lord had honoured
by choosing them to be his special possession (Sir. 24.3–12) (NEB).

(cf. also Sir. 1.4ff.; 42.21).

The same ideas appear again in Wis. 9.1f., 9, in which Solomon prays: 'God of our father, merciful Lord, who hast made all things by thy word, and in thy wisdom hast fashioned man . . . And with thee is wisdom, who is familiar with thy works and was present at the making of the world by thee . . . ' (cf. also 7.21) (NEB).

In the absence of other really valid *religionsgeschichtlichen* background, the above mentioned passages already seem to prove that the ideas of the hypostatized Wisdom's pre-existence and mediatorship in creation formed the background of Paul's or the early Church's conception of Christ as pre-existent and as the mediator of creation. However, there are yet three more pieces of evidence that Paul indeed transferred the characteristics of the divine Wisdom to Jesus Christ. The first of these is 1Cor 10.1–4, in which Paul says that 'the spiritual rock' which accompanied the Israelites in the wilderness was Christ. This is to be compared with Philo's interpretation of Dt 8.15, in which he identifies 'the rock of flint' with the divine Wisdom[1]. A similar thought appears in the Wisdom of Solomon, where Wisdom is said to have guided the Israelites on the Exodus and appears as the medium through which God supplied them with 'water out of the flinty rock' (Wis. 10.17f.; 11.4). So it is very probable that in 1Cor 10.1–4 Paul is thinking of Christ

---

vorstellung bei Paulus', *Neotestamentica*, pp.105ff.; 'Aufnahme und Korrektur jüdischer Sophiatheologie im NT', *ibid.,* pp.110ff.; 'Zum religionsgeschichtlichen Hintergrund der "Sendungsformel" ', *ZNW* 57 (1966); Hamerton-Kelly, *Pre-existence*, pp. 103ff.; cf. also Fuller, *Christology*, pp.212, 216.

[1]Philo, *Leg. Alleg.* ii. 86; *Quod Det. Pot.* 115ff.

as the divine Wisdom[1]. Another passage often considered in this connection is Rom 10.6f. There Paul says that, in order to obtain righteousness which comes from faith, we need not go up to heaven nor go down into the deep to bring Christ down or up since he is near to us in the word of the apostolic preaching. This he says through a midrash upon Dt 30.12–14. From the fact that Bar. 3.29ff. takes the Deuteronomic passage to refer to Wisdom as the object searched for, some suppose that in Rom 10.6f. also Paul is probably thinking of Christ as Wisdom[2]. Secondly, Paul's reference to Christ as the εἰκών τοῦ θεοῦ (2Cor 4.4; Col 1.15; cf. also Phil 2.7) clearly suggests that he conceives of Christ in terms of Wisdom (cf. Wis. 7.25f.). About this more will be said later[3]. Finally, we have Paul's explicit identification of Christ as Wisdom: 'But to those who are called, both Jews and Greeks, Christ the power of God and the wisdom of God' (1Cor 1.24); '... Christ Jesus, who became for you wisdom from God, righteousness, sanctification and redemption . . . ' (1Cor 1.30; cf. also Col 2.3). Thus it is clear that Paul has a Wisdom-Christology[4] and that his ideas of Christ's pre-existence and mediatorship in creation are a result of his transferring the characteristics of the divine Wisdom to Christ.

The idea of God's sending his pre-existent Son is also to be seen against the background of Jewish Wisdom speculation[5]. Already the OT knows the idea of God's sending his prophets, his word, his spirit, or his angel. In Mal 4.5 God promises to send the prophet Elijah at the end-time. The Sibylline Oracles speaks of God's sending the messianic king (Sib.III.286, 652; V.108, 256, 414f.)[6]. These ideas appear also in the NT (sending of prophets: Mt 23.34; Lk 11.49; 13.34; of angels: Mt 11.10; Mk 1.2; Lk 1.19, 26; 7.27; Acts 22.6). In Acts 3.20 Peter calls upon the Jews to repent and turn to God 'so that the Lord may grant you a time of recovery and send the Messiah whom he has already appointed for you, namely Jesus'. But these passages

---

[1]Windisch, *op. cit.*, p.223; Davies, *Paul*, pp.152f.; Schweizer, *Neotestamentica*, pp.106f.; Hengel, *Sohn*, p.114.

[2]Windisch, *op.cit.*, p.224; Schweizer, *Neotestamentica*, p.107; Käsemann, *Römer*, p.227; cf. the unjustified objection by Davies, *Paul*, pp.153f. *Infra* pp.129f.

[3]*Infra* pp.258ff.

[4]But it is to go too far when H.Conzelmann speaks of a 'school of Paul' 'wo man "Weisheit" methodisch betreibt bzw. Theologie als Weisheitsschulung treibt' ('Paulus und die Weisheit', *NTS* 12 (1965/66), p.233).

[5]See Schweizer, "Sendungsformel", pp.199ff. for an examination of the Greek Hellenistic material that fails to provide an analogy to the NT formula of the sending of the pre-existent Son. Cf. also Hengel, *Sohn*, pp.39ff.

[6]See Hengel, *Sohn*, p.112.

where the sending of prophets, Elijah or the messianic king is spoken of lack the idea of their pre-existence and so 'sending' contains only the idea of 'commission'[1]. Jesus' consciousness of having been sent by God is expressed very often in the Synoptic Gospels (Mt 15.24; Lk 4.18, 43; Mk 9.37 & par.; Mt 10.40; Lk 9.48; 10.16) as well as in the Gospel of John. The most striking of these passages is the parable of the Wicked Husbandmen (Mk 12.1–11; par. Mt 21.33–44; Lk 20.9–18), where Jesus speaks of God's sending his servants, the prophets, and his Son, Jesus himself. However, here as elsewhere in the Synoptic Gospels where the title 'Son' appears, the idea of the pre-existence of the Son does not appear (at least not explicitly), since the sending of the Son is analogous to the sending of the servants, the prophets[2].

However, analogous to the OT idea of God's sending his word, spirit or angels, there is in the Jewish wisdom literature the idea of God's sending the pre-existent Wisdom (Wis. 9.10–17) as well as the idea of Wisdom's descent from heaven to earth (Sir. 24)[3]. So E. Schweizer suggests that the formula of God's sending of his pre-existent Son in the NT is rooted in the Jewish wisdom speculation[4]. He notes especially two points of contact between Gal 4.4–6 and Wis. 9.10–17: the connection of the sending of the Son with that of the Spirit in Gal 4.4–6 finds a parallel in the double sending of Wisdom and Spirit in Wis. 9.17; and the verb $\dot{\epsilon}\xi\alpha\pi\sigma\sigma\tau\dot{\epsilon}\lambda\lambda\epsilon\iota\nu$ used by Paul only in Gal 4.4 appears also in Wis. 9.10[5]. However, these parallels are not close enough or substantial enough for us to suppose that Paul was consciously dependent upon Wis. 9.10–17[6]. Nevertheless, since it is clear that Paul thought of Christ's pre-existence and mediatorship in creation in terms of

---

[1]Cf. Rengstorf, $\dot{\alpha}\pi\sigma\sigma\tau\dot{\epsilon}\lambda\lambda\omega$, $\kappa\tau\lambda$., *TDNT* i, pp.400ff.

[2]Hahn, *Hoheitstitel*, pp.315f.; Schweizer, "Sendungsformel", pp.207, 210: 'Eine Präexistenzchristologie mag hier (sc. in Mk 12.1–9) noch nachklingen, aber jedenfalls in einer völlig unreflektierten, wahrscheinlich nicht einmal bewußt gemachten Art' (p.210). Cf. however, Hamerton-Kelly, *Pre-existence*, p.100f.

[3]Some of the predicates of Wisdom in wisdom literature are applied to the Logos by Philo. E.g., Philo designates the Logos as God's 'first-born' ($\dot{o}$ $\pi\rho\omega\tau\dot{o}\gamma\sigma\nu\sigma\varsigma$, *Somn.* i.215; *Conf. Ling.* 146), identifies the angel sent by God in Ex 23.20 with the divine Logos, 'the first born Son of God' (*Quaest. Ex.* ii.13; *Agric.* 51), and calls it God's 'chief messenger' ($\dot{\alpha}\rho\chi\dot{\alpha}\gamma\gamma\epsilon\lambda\sigma\varsigma$, *Rer.Div.Her.* 205).

[4]Schweizer, "Sendungsformel", p.207; also Hengel, *Sohn*, p.112.

[5]Schweizer, "Sendungsformel", p.207.

[6]On the question whether Paul knew and used Wisdom of Solomon, see E.Grafe, 'Das Verhältnis der paulinischen Schriften zur Sapientia Salomonis', *Theologische Abhandlungen*, C.v.Weizsäcker FS (1892), pp.251ff.; Sanday-Headlam, *Romans*, pp.51 ff.; Ellis, *Paul's Use*, pp.77ff.; K.Romaniuk, 'Le Livre de la Sagesse dans le NT', *NTS* 14 (1967/68), pp.503–513.

Wisdom's, it is natural to think that he thought of God's sending his Son into the world also in terms of his sending Wisdom into the world. Once Jesus Christ, like Wisdom in Jewish speculation, is conceived of as having existed in heaven from the beginning, his appearance on earth — again like Wisdom — is naturally regarded as God's sending him or his descent from heaven[1].

Now it is to be noted that the ideas of Jesus' pre-existence and mediatorship in creation appear with the titles 'Christ' (1Cor 8.6; 10.4; 2Cor 8.9; Phil 2.6)[2] and 'Lord' (1Cor 8.6; 2Cor 8.9) as well as 'Son' (Col 1.13ff.). Thus the ideas of Jesus' pre-existence and mediatorship in creation are not bound up exclusively with the title 'Son'. This is natural because the predicates of Wisdom, when applied to Jesus, do not demand the title 'Son'. However, the 'sending' formula is invariably associated with the title 'Son' (Rom 8.3; Gal 4.4; cf. also Rom 1.3; Jn 3.17; 1Jn 4.9, 10, 14). This is probably because this title implies, beyond the ideas of Jesus' pre-existence and mediatorship in creation, his close relationship with God, in fact, his belonging together with him and his origin from the Godhead[3]. Furthermore, in accordance with the Semitic conception of representation in which the son, when he is sent, is, as the heir, specially authorized by the father to be his plenipotentiary, the 'sending' formula with the title 'Son' probably seeks to express also the idea that Jesus is the specially authorized agent of God (cf. Mk 12.1–11 & par.)[4]. The 'giving-up' formula also appears with the title 'Son of God' not only because it is perhaps modelled after the Akedah,

---

[1]Otherwise C.H.Talbert, 'The Myth of a Descending-Ascending Redeemer in Mediterranean Antiquity', *NTS* 22 (1976), pp.418–440. He strings together Graeco-Roman materials containing a myth of a descending and ascending divine figure and OT/Jewish materials concerning Wisdom and angelic figures descending for the purpose of delivering individuals or nations. Then, having abstracted the NT kerygma in terms of 'a pattern of pre-existence – descent (redemptive activity) – ascent (redemptive activity) – parousia' (p.435, *et passim*), Talbert concludes that Paul, John, the author of Heb., and Christians in 2nd and 3rd century all independently from one another(!), drew on the Hellenistic Jewish myth of a descending-ascending redeemer (Wisdom – Logos – Angel – High Priest all identified with one another) and applied it to Christ. But this hardly explains *why* and *how* the Christians began to confess Jesus of Nazareth as the pre-existent Son who was sent by God into the world, wrought salvation through his death and resurrection, ascended into heaven until his return.

[2]In these passages (except 1Cor 10.4) the title 'Christ' is inseparably linked with the name 'Jesus', so that it may not have a titular significance for the Messiah, but be a proper name. See above p.107, n.2.

[3]So Schweizer, υἱός, *TDNT* viii, p.375; also Hengel, *Sohn*, pp.23, 99ff.; Blank, *Paulus*, pp.283f., 300f.

[4]I owe this point to O.Betz's private communication. For the Jewish conceptions of sending and representation, see K.H.Rengstorf, ἀπόστολος, *TDNT* i, pp.414–420.

Abraham's offering his son Isaac (Gen 22.12, 16)[1], but probably also because with it the formula seeks to express the magnitude of God's love for lost mankind (Rom 8.32; Gal 2.20; cf. also Jn 3.16; 1Jn 4.10; Rom 5.10)[2]. So, although the idea of God's sending his Son in the NT is conceived of in analogy to the idea of his 'sending' Wisdom in Jewish wisdom literature, the title 'Son of God' is chosen for the 'sending' formula. For the only other title that would express the above ideas equally (or nearly equally!) well, and with which Wisdom is in fact designated by Philo, namely 'daughter of God' (*Fuga* 50ff.; *Virt.* 62; *Quaest. Gen.* iv. 97; cf. Prov 8.30; Wis. 8.3), is completely unsuited for Jesus, a male (!)[3].

At last we are in a position to ask what then led Paul and the early Church to conceive of Christ in the light of the personified divine Wisdom and transfer to him its predicates. According to H. Windisch, already in Judaism the figure of the Messiah had become merged with that of Wisdom[4]. He derives this conclusion from two observations. First, he finds some passages in 1En. approximating 'Son of Man' to Wisdom: like Wisdom 'Son of Man' is pre-existent and hidden to the world (48.2, 6); Wisdom dwells in 'Son of Man' (49.3); like Wisdom (92.1) 'Son of Man' has the ability to judge the hidden

---

[1]On this see G.Vermes, *Scripture and Tradition in Judaism* (1961), pp.218ff.; N.A. Dahl, 'The Atonement – an Adequate Reward for the Akedah? (Ro 8:32)', *Neotestamentica et Semitica*, Black FS, pp.15–29; Wilcox, "Upon the Tree", pp.94ff. But cf. also Blank, *Paulus*, pp.294–298, who points out that Gen 22 is echoed only in Rom 8.32a: ' . . . who did not spare his own Son.' (p.298); likewise Käsemann, *Römer*, p.237.

[2]Where the idea of *God's* great love is not the primary concern, the 'giving-up' formula is also associated with other titles: Rom 4.25; Eph 5.2, 25. Cf. Kramer, *Christ*, pp.118f., whose view that in these passages the original title 'Son of God' was replaced by 'Lord' or 'Christ' thus reflecting a later stage in which there was 'no longer any awareness that a particular title has its proper setting in a particular complex of traditional material' (p.18), is, however, to be rejected. In Gal 2.20, it is no longer God who 'gave up' his Son but the Son of God who gave up himself for 'me'. But here again the concern is love – the love of Christ which is nothing other than the love of God. That is why Paul immediately adds: οὐκ ἀθετῶ τὴν χάριν τοῦ θεοῦ (Gal 2.21).

[3]Cf. M.E.Thrall, 'The Origin of Pauline Christology', *Apostolic History and the Gospel*, Bruce FS, p.311, who overlooks this point. Windisch explains the reason why Paul does not apply the *title* Σοφία to Christ in this way: 'Paulus wird Scheu getragen haben, den κύριος mit einem weiblichen Prädikate auszustatten. Der Messias Jesus, der Sohn Gottes, war die Persönlichkeit, die sich ihm offenbart hatte. Ihm eignete er die bedeutsamen Züge der Weisheit zu; anders ausgedrückt: der Sohn Gottes verdrängte in seinem Bewußtsein die Weisheit, indem er ihre Charakteristika aufsog' (*op. cit.*, p.227). Because of the same shyness, according to Windisch (p.230), John also avoided using the title Σοφία for Christ and chose instead the male gender Λόγος in the Prologue.

[4]Windisch, *op. cit.*, pp.227ff.

things (49.4); and like 'Son of Man' Wisdom is also unknown to the world and dwells among the angels (42). Secondly, Windisch thinks that the LXX translators rendered Mic 5.1 and Ps 110 (109 LXX).3 with the purpose of approximating the Messiah to the figure of Wisdom. According to Windisch, the clause in Mic 5.2 (καὶ αἱ ἔξοδοι αὐτοῦ ἀπ' ἀρχῆς ἐξ ἡμερῶν αἰῶνος) with its idea of the pre-existent Messiah, is reminiscent of Prov 8.22f. (κύριος ἔκτισέν με ἀρχὴν ὁδῶν αὐτοῦ ... πρὸ τοῦ αἰῶνος ἐθεμελίωσέν με ἐν ἀρχῇ) and still more of Sir. 24.9 (πρὸ τοῦ αἰῶνος ἀπ' ἀρχῆς ἔκτισέν με). Still more striking is, according to Windisch, Ps 110 (109 LXX).3 (ἐκ γαστρὸς πρὸ ἐωσφόρου [ἐξ]εγέννησά σε), where the idea of the 'birth' of the Messiah before the creation of the world has its analogy only in the origin of Wisdom (cf. Prov 8.24f.; Sir. 24.3). A comparison of Ps 110.1 with Wis. 9.4, 10 shows, according to Windisch, how the LXX translators could identify Wisdom with the Messiah: 'Both persons are thought of as God's companions at the throne. He who could think of only one person as enthroned beside God, to him the two had to merge into one'[1]. So Windisch suggests that Paul was led by Ps 110.3 (LXX) to read Ps 110.1 in the light of Prov 8 and so took over the Jewish identification of the Messiah with Wisdom.

However, W. D. Davies finds none of these arguments advanced by Windisch convincing. Davies finds that the comparison of Mic 5.2 (LXX) with Prov 8.22 and Sir. 24.9 and of Ps 110.3 (LXX) with Prov 8.24f. and Sir. 24.3 fall far short of proving the LXX translators' identification of the Messiah with Wisdom[2]. Had the merging of the figures of the Messiah and Wisdom really taken place in Judaism, we should find also the other predicates of Wisdom beside that of pre-existence, namely the role in creation and in history, transferred to the Messiah in Jewish sources. But this is not the case[3]. Certainly Sir. 24.8–12 moves in the direction of connecting the figure

---

[1]*Ibid.*, p.229.

[2]Davies, *Paul*, pp.160ff.

[3]Cf. *ibid.*, p.162, where Davies appeals to W.L.Knox, *St. Paul and the Church of the Gentiles* (1939), pp.112f., in order to show that the pre-existence of a person or an object – e.g., the Torah, Moses, the Temple, the Messiah – in itself had no particular significance for Rabbinic Judaism. Cf. Bousset-Greßmann, *Die Religion des Judentums*, pp.262ff.; Moore ii, p.344. Only some later Rabbinic traditions connect the Messiah with creation: R.Simeon b.Lakish (middle of 3rd c.A.D.) identifies 'the Spirit of God' in Gen 1.2 with 'the spirit of the Messiah' (Gen. R.2.4; Lev.R.14.1; cf. Pes.R.33.6); and Pes.R.36.1 identifies the light of Gen 1.4 with 'the light of the Messiah'. The latter tradition does not seem to go back earlier than 7th c.A.D. And both traditions have the Messiah's pre-existence and his eschatological role for Israel in view rather than the Messiah's role in creation or in history. This is clear especially in Pes.R.33.6. On these Rabbinic passages see Hengel, *Sohn*, pp.110f.

of Wisdom with that of the Messiah, as it speaks of Wisdom's descending from heaven to dwell upon Zion, the place where according to the prophetic promise the throne of the Messiah would stand[1]. But even here there is not yet an explicit identification of the Messiah with Wisdom[2]. What then of Windisch's first point? Since Windisch, there have been others who, pointing to the similarities between the statements about 'Son of Man' and those about Wisdom in Dan., 1En., etc., also suggest that 'Son of Man' may be 'an apocalypticized and mythological Wisdom'[3]. However, while it is true that some predicates of Wisdom are applied to 'Son of Man' in 1En. 48.1–7; 49.2–4, so that we may speak of the figure of 'Son of Man' as *approximating* the figure of Wisdom, we do not find here their identification. C. Colpe writes: 'Jewish wisdom speculation . . . belongs in part at least . . . to the same tradition as the idea of the Son of Man. But where there is a connection wisdom manifests the Son of Man (Eth. En. 48.7) or the Son of Man has wisdom . . . This inter-relationship of the two makes it most unlikely that the Son of Man is another version of wisdom . . . Again, there are in detail considerable differences between the Son of Man concept and the wisdom myth

---

[1] Cf. Hengel, *Judentum und Hellenismus* (^{2}1973), pp.284ff.; *Sohn*, p.79.

[2] Cf. H.Gese, 'Natus ex virgine', *Probleme biblischer Theologie*, G.v.Rad FS, p.87: 'Die in der späteren Weisheitstheologie hypostasierte Weisheit, die als in der Urzeit geschaffenes Kind Gottes vorgestellt werden mußte (Spr. 8, 22ff.), hat als Repräsentant der Ordnung Jahwes eine mit dem Zionskönig vergleichbare Funktion. Ihre Identität mit der Jahweoffenbarung an Israel führt zu der Vorstellung, daß sie als präexistenter göttlicher Logos (Sir. 24,3ff.) wie die Lade nur auf dem Zion die מנוחה, die bleibende Wohnung finden kann (V.7ff.) . . . *So verbindet sich die Weisheitstheologie mit dem Zionmessianismus in der Wurzel, und diese Verbindung ist in jenen verhältnismäßig frühen* υἱὸς θεοῦ *-Stellen des NTs vorausgesetzt, die von der Sendung des Sohnes sprechen (Gal.4,4f.; Röm.8,3f.; Joh.3,16f.; 1Joh.4,7) . . . Die sapientiale Interpretation der Zionstheologie führt zur Präexistenzvorstellung des* υἱὸς θεοῦ, und in neuem Licht mußte die Überlieferung erscheinen, die in der Davidzeit die Urzeit sah und wie Mi.5,1 daher den protologischen Ursprung des eschatologischen Messias lehrte' (my emphasis). It will be shown below that the connection of Wisdom with the Torah in Sir.24 is an essential presupposition for the NT ideas of the pre-existence and sending of the Son of God. But if Gese means that the connection of Wisdom with the Messiah in wisdom theology was the presupposition for those NT ideas, against him we would point out that the confession cited in Rom 1.3f., in spite of its motif of the Davidic Messiah (the Son of David – the Son of God), does not contain the ideas of the pre-existence and sending of the υἱὸς θεοῦ. W.Manson, *The Epistle to the Hebrews*, p.95, points out that in wisdom literature there is no place for the Messiah and so concludes that the identification of Wisdom with Christ first occurred within the Church.

[3] Muilenburg, 'The Son of Man in Dan. and the Eth.Apoc. of Enoch', *JBL* 79 (1960), pp.197–209 (quotation from p.209); similarly, F.Christ, *Jesus Sophia* (1970), pp.69f.; cf. also E.Larsson, *Christus als Vorbild* (1962), pp.131f.

of Eth. En. 42'[1]. So, in so far as some predicates of Wisdom are applied to 'Son of Man' in the Similitudes of 1En., we may see an analogy here to the NT application of the predicates of Wisdom to Jesus[2]. However, it is probably truer to say that in 1En. 'Son of Man' represents Wisdom than that they are identified[3]. Therefore, we cannot suppose that from this background the conception of Jesus as the Son of Man led the early Church to see him as having taken the place of the divine Wisdom.

We must now consider whether Jesus himself had already identified himself with the divine Wisdom. For this question the following five passages in the Synoptic Gospels are often discussed: Mt 11.16–19 (par. Lk 7. 31–35); Mt 11.25–27 (par. Lk 10.21f.); Mt 11.28–30; Mt 23.34–36 (par. Lk 11. 49–51); and Mt 23.37–39 (par. Lk 13.34f.). Obviously it is impossible to analyse these passages here, and so again we have to rely upon the results of the investigations carried out by others. Through a thorough examination of the redactional processes of these passages F. Christ comes to the conclusion that not only Matthew and Luke but already Q[4], in fact, the tradition even before Q, identified Jesus with Wisdom, and leaves open the possibility that Jesus himself understood himself as Wisdom[5]. However, an equally thorough examination of the material by M. J. Suggs results in the conclusion that in Q Jesus appears as a representative, in fact, the greatest representative and the final prophet or envoy of Wisdom. Only in Matthew is Jesus identified with Wisdom and so with the Torah (which had already been identified with Wisdom in Judaism)[6]. Scholarly opinions seem to be largely in favour of the latter's judgement[7]. In spite of Suggs' implied denial[8] Q may faithfully

---

[1]C.Colpe, ὁ υἱὸς τοῦ ἀνθρώπου, *TDNT* viii, pp.411f.; similarly also Davies, *Paul*, pp.159f.

[2]Cf. Hengel, *Sohn*, p.117.

[3]*Infra* pp. 245f. for a more precise definition of the relationship between Wisdom and the figure 'like a son of man'.

[4]So also Wilckens, σοφία, *TDNT* vii, p.515; D.R.Catchpole, 'Tradition History', *NT Interpretation*, ed. I.H.Marshall (1977), pp.169f.

[5]F.Christ, *Jesus Sophia*, pp.61ff. (*passim*, summary in pp.153f.).

[6]M.J.Suggs, *Wisdom, Christology and Law in Matthew's Gospel* (1970), *passim*.

[7]See, e.g., J.M.Robinson, 'LOGOI SOPHŌN: on the Gattung of Q', *Trajectories through Early Christianity* by J.M.Robinson and H.Koester (1971), pp.112f.; H.Koester, 'The Structure of Early Christian Beliefs', *ibid.*, p.221; Hamerton-Kelly, *Pre-existence*, pp.35f., 46, 83, 96f.; R.Banks, *Jesus and the Law in the Synoptic Tradition* (1975), pp.259f. (n.2); cf. also Davies, *Paul*, pp.155ff. However, R.Banks objects to Suggs' view that Matthew *identifies* Jesus with Wisdom and the Torah and sees him as 'Wisdom incarnate' and 'the embodiment of the Torah' (Suggs, *op. cit.*, pp.118, 130, etc.): 'This

represent the historical Jesus' own understanding, i.e., that he, as the Son of Man (Mt 11.16–19; par. Lk 7.31–35)[1] and the Son (of God) (Mt 11.25–27; par. Lk 10.21f.)[2], is the greatest and final representative of Wisdom. Furthermore, it is probable that Jesus' proclamation and teaching bore the traits of wisdom teaching, so that in the primitive Church his sayings were collected as λόγοι σοφοῦ in Q just as sayings of the wise were collected in Judaism[3]. But how did it happen that a representative of Wisdom was 'identified'[4] with Wisdom herself? Hengel suggests that just as some predicates of Wisdom were transferred to the Son of Man in the Similitudes of 1En., they were similarly transferred to Jesus when he was seen to be the representative of Wisdom[5]. But 'Son of Man' in 1En. falls short of providing a real analogy to the 'identification' of Jesus with Wisdom in the NT, since in 1En. there is no real 'identification' between 'Son of Man' and Wisdom, as we have seen above. So Hengel is right in saying that in Jesus' own teaching we have a *preparation* for the later 'identification' of Jesus with Wisdom[6], but we have to look elsewhere for the decisive cause for the 'identification'.

---

cannot really be sustained. Certainly Jesus' teaching stands in the place the Torah stood but it is inadequate to describe it in terms of his being Torah-incarnate. Given Suggs' demonstration of Matthew's desire to set Jesus in the place of Wisdom, it may be more pertinent to speak of Jesus' subsuming the role assigned to Wisdom within his unique person rather than of the "identification" or "equation" of the two' (*op. cit.*, p.259 (n.2); cf. pp.229ff.). On this question the formulation of F.Christ is more adequate: 'Indem Jesus an die Stelle der Sophia tritt, gewinnt die Weisheit einen neuen Sinn. Das Verhältnis der alten zur neuen Weisheit bietet sich als kompliziertes Ineinander von Kontinuität und Diskontinuität dar. Jesus *ist* die Weisheit. Gleichzeitig ist der Bezug aber auch antithetisch. Als die wahre Weisheit und das wahre Gesetz "erfüllt", ja ersetzt Jesus die alttestamentlich-jüdische Sophia' (*op. cit.*, p.153). See also D.E.H.Whiteley, *The Theology of St.Paul* (1963) pp.111f.

[8]Suggs, *Wisdom*, esp. pp.18, 33f.

[1]Cf. *ibid.*, pp.48ff.; F.Christ, *Jesus Sophia*, pp.69ff.; Hamerton-Kelly, *Pre-existence*, pp.96ff.

[2]Cf. Suggs, *Wisdom*, pp.91ff.; F.Christ, *Jesus Sophia*, pp.87ff.; also K.Berger, 'Zum Problem der Messianität Jesu', *ZThK* 71 (1974), pp.17ff.; Taylor, *Names*, pp.60ff.; J.Jeremias, *Abba*, pp.47ff.

[3]J.M.Robinson, *op. cit.*, esp. pp.112f.; Koester, *op. cit.*, pp.220f.; Hengel, *Sohn*, pp.116f.

[4]With the inverted commas we wish to indicate that we use the word 'identify/identification' in this connection in the sense defined by R.Banks and F.Christ – see p.123f., n.7 above.

[5]Hengel, *Sohn*, p.117.

[6]*Ibid.*, pp.116f. Cf. also F.F.Bruce, *This is That* (1968), pp.16f.

Hengel unfolds the process of the early Church's transference of the predicates of Wisdom to Jesus as a logical consequence of the confession that Jesus is exalted and enthroned as the Son of Man and the Son of God through the resurrection[1]. For, according to Hengel, this confession immediately raised the question how Jesus is then related to other mediatory beings like angels and Wisdom-Torah on the one hand and to other means of salvation in Judaism like the Temple sacrifice and the Torah on the other. Furthermore, corresponding to the well-known schema *Endzeit = Urzeit* (cf. Barn. 6.13), the early Church's consciousness that the eschatological messianic age had broken in, raised also a protological interest, i.e., an interest in Jesus' role in the beginning of creation. Hengel also observes that the idea of pre-existence was a favourite means of expressing the saving significance of certain phenomena in Judaism. Hence the eschatological redeemer (Mic 5.1; Ps 110.3), 'Son of Man' (1En. 48.6; 62.7) and his name (1En. 48.3; cf. 69.26), and the name of the Messiah[2] were all supposed to have existed before the creation. All these factors were at work, according to Hengel, when the idea of Jesus' pre-existence was introduced into the Christology of the early Church. With the idea of the pre-existence of Jesus there arose as a logical consequence the idea of the sending of the pre-existent Jesus as the Son of God from heaven into the world, i.e., the incarnation. Hengel writes:

> After the introduction of the idea of pre-existence it was natural that the exalted Son of God also attracted to himself the functions of Jewish Wisdom as a mediator in creation and salvation. Even the pre-existent Wisdom, which was connected with God in a unique way, could no longer be regarded as an independent entity over against the risen and exalted One and superior to him. Rather, all the functions of Wisdom were transferred to him, for 'in him are hid all the treasures of wisdom and knowledge' (Col 2.3). Only in this way was the *unsurpassibility and finality of God's revelation* in Jesus of Nazareth expressed in a final, conclusive way[3].

And Hengel goes on:

> If, however, the Son of God entered into the all-embracing function of Wisdom as mediator, then the function of the Torah, which was identified with Wisdom, was also completely shattered. For the Jews the Torah had an authoritative, ontologically based function in the ordering of the world and in salvation. Paul, the former Pharisee and scribe, drew the ultimate radical consequences here. If others before him pondered as to what changes were brought about in the Torah through the interpretation of the true will of God in the message of the Messiah Jesus, his characteristic statement 'Christ is the end of the law to every believer for righteousness' (Rom 10.4) expresses in a fundamental way, against the claim of the Torah, the

---

[1] Hengel, *Sohn*, pp.105ff.

[2] See Str.-Bill. ii, pp.333ff.

[3] Hengel, *Sohn*, p.113 (emphasis by H.).

unique soteriological function of the crucified and risen One as the all embracing, final, eschatological revelation of God. Not just Moses, but the Christ of God alone mediates salvation[1].

Now, as we have seen and shall see in more detail later[2], Paul obtained the insight that Christ was the end of the law in his Damascus experience. For it was Jesus of Nazareth crucified under the pronouncement of God's curse by the law (Dt 21.23) who was revealed to him as the exalted and enthroned Son of God. If Hengel's description of the Christological development is correct, the all-embracing mediatorial function of Wisdom must have been transferred to Jesus at least by the time of Paul's conversion, that is, within two to four years after the resurrection of Jesus. Hengel himself seems hesitant to think that at such an early date the primitive Church had thought through the consequences of the resurrection, had transferred the predicates of Wisdom to Jesus, and had produced the formulae of the sending and the giving-up of the pre-existent Son of God. So he emphasizes that it is more exact to say that these developments occurred in the *nebenpaulinischen* Church (in Syria) rather than in the pre-Pauline Church[3]. If, however, they occurred in the *nebenpaulinischen* Church, what part did Paul as a trained theologian play in this process? Since Paul obtained the insight that Christ was the end of the law at the Damascus revelation and therefore was forced from then on to reflect upon Christ's relationship to Wisdom, is it not likely that Paul's theological contribution was decisive in that process?

That this was indeed so, may be confirmed by another consideration. Hengel's description of the factors at work in the process in which pre-existence came to be predicated of Jesus Christ, may be broadly correct. However, his suggestion that the primitive Church thought of Jesus Christ first in terms of Wisdom and transferred the all-embracing functions of Wisdom to him *before* it was led to reflect upon his relationship to the Torah, seems to be a confusion of the order in the thinking of the early Church. Jesus attacked the contemporary expositions of the Torah, and claimed himself to be the fulfilment of the Torah (Mt 5.17f.; 11.13; par. Lk 16.16)[4], a teaching which constantly brought him into conflict with the contemporary exponents of the Torah. Also, by his crucifixion he was pronounced by the Torah to have been cursed by God. And the Christian 'Hellenists' were driven out of Jerusalem because they were critical of the Temple-cult and the

---

[1]*Ibid.*, p.115ff.

[2]*Supra* pp.3f.; *infra* pp.274, 307f.

[3]Hengel, *Sohn*, p.24.

[4]Banks, *op. cit.*, esp. pp.234f.

contemporary expositions of the Torah[1]. Therefore, it is almost certain that the early Church was forced to reflect upon the relationship of the exalted Christ to the Torah before anything else. So it is likely that the early Church first thought of Jesus Christ taking the place of the Torah as the means of salvation and only consequently was led to think of him in terms of Wisdom. If this is so, Paul's conversion was the decisive landmark in this process. For, as Hengel himself writes, if the pre-Pauline Church (esp. the 'Hellenists') 'pondered as to what changes were brought about in the Torah through the interpretation of the true will of God in the message of the Messiah Jesus', it was Paul who made the decisive declaration: 'Christ is the end of the law, that every one who has faith may be justified' (Rom 10.4)[2]. And he did so out of his Damascus experience.

When Jesus of Nazareth crucified under the pronouncement of the curse of God by the Torah was revealed to Paul as the exalted and enthroned Messiah, that is, as God's Son (Rom 1.3f.; cf. 2Sam 7.12–14), he realized that his devotion to the Torah had led him to sin against the Messiah and his people and ultimately against God himself. He knew then that Christ had brought the Torah to an end as the embodiment of the divine will and as the means of salvation, that Christ himself superseded it as the true mediator of God's revelation and salvation. This led Paul to reflect upon Christ's relationship with Wisdom. If the Torah was formerly thought of as the embodiment of the divine Wisdom and was indeed identified with her (Sir. 24.23; Bar. 3.37f.; 4Macc. 1.17; 7.21–23; 8.7), it is now Christ who has revealed himself (instead of the Torah) to be the true revelation of God, that is, the true embodiment of the divine Wisdom, indeed Wisdom herself. Thus Paul 'identified' Christ with Wisdom and transferred to him the predicates of Wisdom — pre-existence and mediatorship in creation which were in Rabbinic Judaism transferred to the Torah[3]. If this view is correct, it is easy to suppose that also in the development of the formulae of God's sending his

---

[1] *Supra* pp.44ff.

[2] Hengel, *Sohn*, p.115; cf. also his two articles, 'Die Ursprünge der christlichen Mission', *NTS* 18 (1971/72), pp.27ff.; 'Zwischen Jesus und Paulus. Die "Hellenisten", die "Sieben" und Stephanus (Apg. 6,1–15; 7,54–8,3)', *ZThK* 72 (1975), pp.191f., 195f.; *supra* pp.44ff.

[3] E.g., Gen.R.1.4; b.Pes.54a; b.Ned.39b; b.Shab.88b-89a; Sifre Dt 11.10; Pirqe Aboth 3.23. See Moore i, p.526; Davies, *Paul*, pp.170f. Our argument here may be compared with Davies' view that Paul identifies Christ with Wisdom because Paul thinks of Christ as the New Torah (*ibid.*, pp.141–176). However, his view that Paul thinks of Christ as the New Torah has often been found to be problematic. See criticisms by F. Feuillet, *Le Christ Sagesse de Dieu* (1966), pp.191ff.; Thrall, *op. cit.,* pp.310f.; cf. also Banks, *op. cit.*, pp.233ff.; Hengel, *Sohn*, p.107 (n.123).

pre-existent Son into the world and giving him up, Paul's contribution was dominant.

That at the Damascus revelation Paul realized that Christ had superseded the Torah and is therefore the true Wisdom, can be clearly seen in 2Cor 3.4–4.6, the passage which we have seen as based upon Paul's Damascus experience[1]. In this passage Paul contrasts the ministry of Moses in the old covenant of the Torah with that of his in the new covenant of the gospel of Christ. The former was of the letter that kills, but the latter is of the Spirit that gives life. The former was accompanied by glory, but the latter by much greater glory. The former was transient and its glory fading, but the latter abides and abides in glory. So, while Moses put a veil upon his face, so that the Israelites might not see the end of the old covenant of the Torah that was being abolished, Paul exercises his ministry of the new covenant with great confidence and freedom. 'Furthermore, the minds of Israelites were hardened' (3.14). This state of the Mosaic covenant and the Israelites has not changed. For 'to this day the same veil remains whenever the old covenant is read (in the synagogue)' (3.14) and a veil lies upon the Israelites' hearts whenever the Torah is read. But when a man turns to the Lord, the risen Christ, the veil is taken away, and he receives the freedom that the Spirit gives. Paul realized this truth and received the ministry of the new covenant of Christ's gospel when he saw the surpassing light of the glory of God in the face of Christ who appeared to him while he was treading the road to Damascus in blind obedience to the Torah. If the Torah as God's revelation had fomerly been supposed by him to be light and to give man light (cf. Ps 19.8; 119.130; Prov 6.23; 2Bar. 17f.; Wis. 18.4; Sifre Num. 6.25., etc.)[2], Paul now saw the perfect revelation of God in the person of Christ which is the true divine light, the creation light (esp. 2Cor 4.6)[3]. This Corinthians passage indicates not only that at the Damascus revelation Paul realized that Christ had superseded the Torah but also that at the same time he perceived Christ as the true Wisdom. This is made clear not only by the light motif here, as Wisdom as the medium of the divine revelation was also regarded as light (Wis. 7.10, 25–30), but above all by Paul's identification of Christ as the εἰκὼν τοῦ θεοῦ (4.4). It will be seen in the next chapter that with that desig-

---

[1] *Supra* pp.5ff.; *infra* pp.229ff.

[2] Cf. Conzelmann, φῶς, κτλ, *TDNT* ix, pp.322ff.

[3] Cf. W.L.Knox, *St.Paul and the Church of the Gentiles*, p.133: 'The original light created by God in the beginning had been equated not with the Torah, the mere reflection of the light which had been vouchsafed to Moses, but with the true knowledge of God revealed in the person of Jesus who . . . was Himself that primal light'. Cf. also Davies, *Paul*, pp.148f.

nation Paul seeks to describe Christ who appeared to him in the divine glory on the Damascus road and that that concept, together with Paul's realization that Christ superseded the Torah as the divine revelation, led him to 'identify' Christ with the divine Wisdom. For, according to Wis. 7.26, Wisdom is 'the brightness that streams from everlasting light, the flawless mirror of the active power of God and the image of his goodness'.

Rom 10.1–13 has the same thought as in 2Cor 3.4–4.6. Similarly to what he does in the latter, in the former Paul contrasts the Jewish way of seeking righteousness with the way of obtaining righteousness that is now opened up in Christ. The former is through the observance of the Mosaic law while the latter is through faith. In the Romans passage Paul acknowledges that the Jews have zeal for God and therefore seek righteousness diligently. However, just as in the Corinthians passage he says that the Mosaic covenant is covered with a veil and also the Israelites' minds are made dull, so that they are not able to understand the transitory nature of the ministry of the letter and condemnation in the old covenant and accept the ministry of the Spirit and righteousness in the new, so here in the Romans passage he says that their zeal is not enlightened (οὐ κατ᾽ ἐπίγνωσιν) and they misunderstand (ἀγνοοῦν- τες) the righteousness of God. Just as in the Corinthians passage he implies that the Mosaic covenant has been terminated by Christ and replaced by the new covenant in Christ, so in Rom 10.4 he says that Christ is the end of the law for the sake of giving righteousness through faith. Just as in the Corin- thians passage he says that by turning to the Lord, the exalted Christ, we can obtain the true revelation and salvation of God, so in the Romans passage he says that by confessing 'Jesus is Lord' and believing that God raised him from the dead we obtain righteousness and salvation. Just as in the Corinthians passage he says that God's true revelation and salvation is granted to believers (cf. 2Cor 4.4) in the apostolic proclamation of the gospel, i.e., the proclama- tion of Jesus Christ as the Lord (2Cor 4.5), so in the Romans passage he says that God's righteousness that is obtained through faith is granted to believers in the word of the apostolic proclamation. We may go on drawing more parallels between the two passages[1]. But those already drawn are sufficient to demonstrate the similarity of structure and ideas in the two passages.

It is then no surprise to discover that just as in the Corinthians passage so also in the Romans passage Paul presents Christ as the end of the Torah and therefore as the true divine Wisdom and that just as in the Corinthians passage

---

[1]Käsemann, *Römer*, pp.272, 274f., draws out another parallel: the contrast be- tween Μωϋσῆς . . . γράφει . . . and ἡ . . . ἐκ πίστεως δικαιοσύνη . . . λέγει in Rom 10.5f. finds its parallel in the contrast between γράμμα and πνεῦμα in 2Cor 3.6ff. So similarly also Stuhlmacher, *Gerechtigkeit*, pp.93f.; cf. also Michel, *Römer*, p.256.

so also in the Romans passage he does so on the basis of the Damascus revelation. As we have already suggested, Paul's midrash upon Dt 30.12ff. in Rom
10.6ff should probably be seen *traditionsgeschichtlich* in the light of Bar.
3.29ff.[1]. In Bar. 3.29ff. 'the commandment (מצוה/ ἐντολή) of Dt 30.11ff. is
replaced with wisdom (ἐπιστήμη or φρόνησις which seems to be used interchangeably with σοφία − see esp. Bar. 3.12, 23) as the object searched for.
However, from Bar. 3.9; 4.1 it is clear that wisdom in Bar. 3.29ff. refers to
none other than the Torah (ἡ βίβλος τῶν προσταγμάτων, ὁ νόμος, ἐντολαὶ
ζωῆς) which is totally unknown to the Gentiles but revealed exclusively to
Israel. Now in his midrash in Rom 10.6ff. Paul replaces the Torah-Wisdom of
Dt 30.12ff and Bar. 3.29ff. with Christ as the object searched for. This is
completely understandable because, as we have already seen, for Paul Christ
has superseded the Torah and is therefore the true embodiment of the divine
Wisdom[2]. So Paul's midrash is completely in line with his dictum in Rom
10.4: 'Christ is the end of the law for righteousness to everyone who believes'.
In fact, the midrash which is set forth to contrast the way of obtaining the
righteousness based on faith with the Mosaic way of obtaining the righteousness based on the law (v.5), is an unfolding of the dictum which is likewise set
over against the Jews' futile attempt to establish their own righteousness
(v.3). Being ignorant of God's righteousness and therefore failing to submit to it, the Jews seek to establish their own righteousness − the righteousness that is based on the law. They seek to do this by keeping the law according to Moses' direction − an impossible, therefore futile attempt. However, 'the righteousness that is based on faith', which, personified, stands
over against Moses, so that in dependence upon 2Cor 3.4ff. it could be ren-

---

[1]Käsemann, *Römer*, pp.276f., not uncharacteristically presumes: 'Jewish meditation
on Dt 30.11f. was apparently anti-Jewishly applied by Jewish Christianity in the confrontation of Church and Synagogue and reached Paul in this form' (p.277). But the evidence that Käsemann presents for the view that, prior to Paul, Dt 30.11ff. was already
used by Christians in this manner, is dubious: the motif of 'Erniedrigung und Erhöhung',
the combination of terms ἀναβαίνειν and καταβαίνειν (cf. Jn 1.51; 3.13), and the antithesis of Christ's journey into hades and heaven (cf. 1Pet 3.19; Eph 4.8), Käsemann
finds non-Pauline. But the first two are already in Dt 30.12ff.! And the last point (N.B.
Christ's *journey* into hades or heaven is not explicit in Rom 10.6f.) is a natural consequence of seeing Christ, who was after all on earth as Jesus of Nazareth, as the object
searched for by man on earth in two extreme spheres of the universe in the place of the
Torah-Wisdom of Dt 30.11ff. and Bar. 3.29ff.! So, there is no reason why Paul could
not have directly used Dt 30.11ff. and Bar. 3.29ff. or the tradition represented by the
latter. For Rabbinic exegesis of and allusions to Dt 30.11ff., see Str.-Bill. iii, pp.278ff.

[2]So, Paul's replacing the Torah-Wisdom of Dt 30.11ff. and Bar.3.29ff. with Christ
and seeing the words of Dt 30.12ff. as referring in fact to Christ is not a 'purely fanciful'
interpretation of Scripture as Dodd, *Romans*, p.177 declares. Cf. also M.Black, 'The
Christological Use of the OT in the NT', *NTS* 18 (1971/72), p.9.

dered as 'the ministry of the Spirit and righteousness' or 'the ministry of faith-righteousness'[1], says that to obtain righteousness we need not make impossible efforts but only to respond to the apostolic preaching by confessing 'Jesus is Lord' and believing that God raised him from the dead. For Christ, who has superseded the Torah and is therefore the true Wisdom and the true embodiment of righteousness, is present in the word of the apostolic preaching. But where and when did Paul initially obtain this insight? It was on the Damascus road when in his blind zeal (ζῆλος) for God and for the Torah and in zealous pursuit of his own righteousness (compare Rom 10.2f. with Phil 3. 6ff.) he was opposing the Christian proclamation of Jesus Christ as the Lord.

Thus, it has become clear that Paul's 'identification' of Christ with the divine Wisdom was based upon the Damascus revelation. So it is now made very probable that it was Paul who initiated in the early Church the 'identification' of Christ with Wisdom, transferring her predicates to Christ. We would still further strengthen our argument by observing the rationale of Paul's statement that the content of the gospel which he received at the Damascus revelation to preach among the Gentiles was the Son of God (Gal 1. 15f.). Why is the Son of God the content of the gospel? This question is best answered by an examination of the 'sending' formula. Paul says in Rom 8.3f. and Gal 4.4f.: When the fullness of time came, that is, when the time for fulfilment of all divine promises of salvation came, God sent forth his pre-existent Son to be born of a woman as a Jew under the law and to bear the curse of the law on our behalf and in our stead, thus bringing the law to an end which, though originally given as a means of salvation, in fact proved to be a bondage and a means of condemnation (cf. Rom 7.7–25; Gal 3.23ff.). In sending his Son in this way God's purpose was to redeem us from sin and the law and grant us his sonship. This is a paraphrase of Rom 8.3f. and Gal 4.4f. We will examine the passages more closely in the last chapter. What has already become clear from this paraphrase, however, is that for Paul, first, the sending of the Son of God was the fulfilment of the divine promises of salvation and, secondly, the Son of God has superseded the law as the means of salvation. This is the reason why Paul can abbreviate his gospel — the gospel which announces that God's eschatological salvation is obtained by faith in Jesus Christ without works of the law — simply with 'the Son of God'[2]. Now, as we have said repeatedly, on the Damascus road Paul obtained the revelation that Christ has superseded the law as the means of obtaining righteousness. This revelation is one and the same as the revelation of the Son of God.

---

[1]Cf. Käsemann, *Römer*, p.272 and Stuhlmacher, *Gerechtigkeit*, pp.93f.

[2]Cf. Bornkamm, 'The Revelation of Christ', pp.97f.

This is why in Gal., where he is called upon to prove the divine authenticity of his law-free gospel, Paul points simply to the Damascus revelation of the Son of God (Gal 1.15f.; cf. also Acts 9.20). This is why the content of his preaching in Corinth was 'the Son of God', in whom all the promises of God have found their 'yes' (2Cor 1.18ff.).

Finally, from this we are to understand also the famous double definitions of the gospel in Rom 1.2ff., 16f. First, using the early Christian confession Paul defines the 'gospel of God' as 'concerning the Son of God'. While in Gal 4.4 he only implies it, here in Rom 1.2 he explicitly declares that this gospel concerning the Son of God was the fulfilment of God's promises made through his prophets in the Holy Scriptures (cf. 2Cor 1.18ff.). Then he unfolds the gospel as 'concerning the Son of God, who was born of the seed of David according to the flesh and installed as the Son of God in power according to the Spirit of Holiness through his resurrection from the dead' (Rom 1. 3f.). Whereas the pre-Pauline confession cited in vs. 3–4 does not contain an idea of the pre-existence of the Davidic Messiah installed as God's Son[1], the Pauline text with περὶ τοῦ υἱοῦ αὐτοῦ as the preface conveys the idea of the incarnation of God's pre-existent Son in the house of David just as the sending formula in Gal 4.4 does (compare περὶ τοῦ υἱοῦ αὐτοῦ(sc. τοῦ θεοῦ) τοῦ γενομένου ἐκ σπέρματος Δαυὶδ κατὰ σάρκα . . . of Rom 1.3 with ἐξαπέστει-λεν ὁ θεὸς τὸν υἱὸν αὐτοῦ, γενόμενον ἐκ γυναικός . . . of Gal 4.4). Thus, for Paul the Davidic Messiah who has through his resurrection been installed as the sovereign Son of God is none other than the pre-existent Son who was sent by God into the world to redeem us from sin and the law. Then Paul defines the gospel again in Rom 1.16f. as 'the power of God for salvation to everyone who believes, to the Jew first and also to the Greek. For in it the righteousness of God is revealed from faith to faith . . . '. If the Torah was formerly supposed to be the means of salvation[2], it is now the gospel that is the power of God for salvation; if righteousness was formerly supposed to be obtained by the observance of the law, the righteousness of God is now revealed in the gospel and obtained by faith. Since we have seen that for Paul the Son of God is the content of the gospel because he as the fulfilment of God's promises has wrought salvation through his incarnation, death and resurrection, and so superseded the law as the means of salvation, that is, as the means of obtaining righteousness, we can now understand how the two definitions of the gospel in Rom 1.2–4 and 16f. mean one and the same thing, though one

---

[1] *Supra* p.111.

[2] Cf. Mek. Ex.15.13; 18.1; b.Pes.148a, in which the Torah seems to be attributed with the divine power of salvation. See W.Grundmann, δύναμις, *TDNT* ii pp.297, 309; cf. also Käsemann, *Römer*, p.19.

is defined Christologically while the other soteriologically. The gospel is God's saving power for every believer because it concerns what God has wrought through sending his Son and because in its proclamation God's grace of declaring and making the sinner righteous, that is, creating him anew, is revealed[1]. Thus, for Paul the 'Son of God' means, when used in definition of the gospel, the one who has brought the law to an end, redeemed the believer from sin and the law, and therefore superseded the law as the means of salvation[2].

---

[1]That the two definitions of the gospel in Rom 1 are closely related to each other, the Christological definition being the foundation of the soteriological and the latter the interpretation of the former, is often noted by those who refuse to be content just with subscribing to the prevalent view that Paul cites the old confession as the gospel in the beginning of his letter to a church not founded by him in order to show that he stands on the common foundation of the faith with them: cf. Bornkamm, *Paulus*, pp.128f., 249ff.; Stuhlmacher, 'Römerbriefpräskript', pp.384f.; "Ende", pp.25ff.; also Käsemann, *Römer*, p.21. However, these authors have not made it clear that the two definitions mean the same because for Paul the title *Son of God*, when used as a definition of the gospel, carries the meaning that we have indicated here.

[2]The salvation through the Son of God, i.e., justification, is already appropriated through faith, but its consummation will take place at the end. Hence, in 1Th 1.10, where he alludes to his missionary preaching of the gospel in Thessalonica (cf. τὸ εὐαγγέλιον ἡμῶν in 1Th 1.5; τὸ εὐαγγέλιον (τοῦ θεοῦ) in 2.2ff. Cf. E.Best, *Thess.*, pp.85ff.; U.Wilckens, *Die Missionsreden der Apostelgeschichte* ([3]1974), pp.81ff.; Stuhlmacher, *Evangelium*, p.259), Paul says that the Thessalonian Christians 'wait for his (sc. God's) Son from heaven, whom he raised from the dead, Jesus, who will deliver us *from the wrath to come*'. It is widely recognised that the schema of the conversion preaching in 1Th 1.9f. has its *traditionsgeschichtliche* root in the monotheistic missionary preaching of the Hellenistic Jewish Synagogue (see, e.g., Bultmann, *Theology*, i, pp.74, 79f.; Bornkamm, 'Glaube und Vernunft bei Paulus', *Studien zu Antike und Urchristentum* (1970), p.125; Stuhlmacher, *Evangelium*, pp.260f.). However, as Stuhlmacher, *Evangelium*, pp.261f. points out, there are three essential differences between the Christian missionary preaching reflected in 1Th 1.9f. and that of the Synagogue: 1) the expectation of an imminent end in 1Th 1.10; 2) the messianic motif in 1Th 1.10; and 3) the fact that whereas in the missionary preaching of the Synagogue monotheism is essentially tied to the Torah, especially to the first commandment in which the entire Torah is supposed to be contained, in 1Th 1.9f. there is no reference to the Torah. 'Der Ton liegt in 1Th.1,9f. statt auf der Tora auf der Christologie und dem durch Christus (ohne Beschneidung und Gesetz) eröffneten Zugang zu Gott' (Stuhlmacher, *Evangelium*, p.262). From this Stuhlmacher infers that in 1Th 1.9f. we may have a form of the missionary preaching of the 'Hellenists' of Acts 6 (p.262). It is indeed widely presumed that in 1Th 1.9f. Paul reproduces a pre-Pauline Hellenistic Christian missionary preaching (Dibelius, *An die Thessalonicher*, ([3]1937), pp.6f.; Bultmann, *loc. cit.*; Bornkamm, *loc. cit.*; Wilckens, *loc. cit.*; Best, *Thess.*, pp.85ff.). It is certainly possible that the 'Hellenists' and other Hellenistic Jewish Christian missionaries used a similar content and schema in their missionary preaching as that in 1Th 1.9f. (cf. Acts 14.15ff.; Heb 6.1f.). But is there any concrete evidence that before Paul already they connected their preach-

Other titles ('Christ' or 'Lord') could have been used for Jesus who by superseding the Torah has become the content of the gospel (cf. Rom 10.4ff.; 1Cor 1.17–30). For, as we have seen, Wisdom-Christology is associated with these titles as well as the title 'Son of God', to express Jesus' pre-existence and mediatorship in creation. But the title 'Son of God' is invariably used as the definition of the gospel because it is the best suited to designate the exalted

---

ing with the title *Son of God* in the manner Paul does in 1Th 1.10? For this there seems to be no evidence. In Acts 14.15ff.; Heb 6.1f. the title 'Son of God' does not appear. It is striking that in 1Th 1.10 the title 'Son' appears in connection with the parousia instead of 'Lord' which is usually connected with the parousia in Paul (see Kramer, *Christ*, pp.173ff.). So Kramer declares: 'The connection of the title *Son of God* with the statement about the parousia is a secondary one, but nonetheless very early, i.e., Pre-Pauline' (p.126). But Kramer provides no valid evidence for the view that the connection was already made before Paul. For, first, it is not convincing to take the statements in 1Th 1.9f. as a fixed pre-Pauline formula reproduced by Paul without modification and then conclude that since the formula is pre-Pauline all the elements therein are also pre-Pauline. This is a common assumption with regard to 1Th 1.9f. (see the literature cited above). But it is commonplace that even when Paul cites a fixed formula he modifies it, expands it and inserts into it his interpretative glosses (e.g., Rom 1.2ff.; 3.23ff.; 1Cor 15.3–8). Why could he not then have done the same in 1Th 1.9f. (if he cites a pre-Pauline 'formula' here at all)? And why could he not himself have connected the title 'Son' with the parousia? Secondly, Kramer says that the conception of Jesus as Redeemer in a purely eschatological sense as in 1Th 1.10 is 'not in keeping with the general trend of Paul's theology' (p.124). (Cf. also a similar argument by Wilckens, *op. cit.*, p.82; also G.Friedrich, 'Ein Tauflied hellenistischer Judenchristen', *ThZ* 21 (1965), p.506). But this is quite mistaken. Is it not one of Paul's concerns in 1Th. to correct the Thessalonians' deviations which have apparently resulted from their misunderstanding of Paul's preaching there of the imminent futuristic eschatology? And does not Paul speak of the redemption sometimes as a present reality (e.g., 2Cor 6.2; Rom 3.21; 5.11; Gal 4.4) and other times as a future hope (e.g., Rom 13.11; 2Cor 4.14; Phil 4.5)? Should we expect Paul to make in every sentence a statement about 'realized eschatology' balancing 'futuristic eschatology'? E.Schweizer, υἱός, *TDNT* viii, pp.370, 382f., suggests that in 1Th 1.10 Paul substitutes the 'Son of God' for 'Son of Man' which stood in the original apocalyptic saying (so already G.Friedrich, *op. cit.*, pp.512ff.). This is possible because the title 'Son of Man' appears often in connection with the parousia and the last judgement in the Synoptic Gospels. No matter whether Paul replaced the original 'the Son of Man' with the 'Son' (of God) in 1Th 1.10 or constructed the entire verse himself, we can well understand the rationale of his connecting the title 'Son of God' here with the parousia in the light of our observations up to now as to what the title, when used in connection with his εὐαγγέλιον, means for him. For it is at the parousia that the believers will be delivered 'from the wrath to come', i.e., completely justified (*infra* pp.226, 252 for another reason why the title 'Son of God' is apt here). Thus our understanding of the meaning of the 'Son' (of God) in 1Th 1.10 confirms Stuhlmacher's observation that 1Th 1.9f. replaces the Torah in the Hellenistic Jewish missionary preaching with Christology, and enables us to understand why and how this was done. However, while Stuhlmacher regards 1Th 1.10 as a pre-Pauline Hellenistic-Jewish Christian statement, we are inclined to think that in its present form it is a genuine Pauline construction

one who by superseding the Torah has proved himself to be the true divine Wisdom, the one who stood in an intimate relationship with God from the beginning, acted as his agent in creation and was sent forth into the world to redeem us from sin and the law[1]. In the 'identification' of Jesus with Wisdom which was made because Jesus on the cross superseded the Torah and which then led logically to the conception of Jesus as the Son of God and as a divine being, there is laid bare the root of the paradox: the crucified One is the Son of God[2].

If all these arguments are correct, it has become clear that Paul's Wisdom-Christology is rooted in the Damascus revelation and it is made very likely that it was therefore Paul who initiated the 'identification' of Jesus with the divine Wisdom in the early Church as early as the first half of the 30's[3]. If Paul knew the Wisdom sayings of Jesus, then he must have found them as

---

or at least that the title 'Son' (of God) in it is a Pauline insertion (*infra* pp.226, 252). So, like Gal 1.16 and Rom 1.2ff., 1Th 1.10 also shows that the title 'Son of God' is the content of Paul's gospel (note εὐαγγέλιον in 1Th 1.5; 2.2ff.) because it signifies Jesus' supersession of the Torah as the means of obtaining righteousness (though in this case it is seen in the futuristic eschatological terms).

[1] Against Kramer's judgement that 'in Paul's view both the title *Son of God* and the ideas associated with it are of relatively minor importance' (*Christ*, p.189), Hengel, *Sohn*, p.23, points out that Paul usually uses the title at the climax of his theological assertions in order to express the intimate relationship of Jesus Christ with God and his function as the mediator of salvation between God and men. Similarly also Blank, *Paulus*, p.283; already Bousset, *Kyrios Christos*, p.151, cited by Hengel, *Sohn*, p.23. In spite of his observation that Paul uses the title 'Son of God' as a definition or abbreviation of his gospel and missionary preaching (*Sohn*, pp.20ff.), Hengel fails to make it clear that Paul does so because the title expresses best and most comprehensively the one who has superseded the Torah and proved to be the divine Wisdom. Nevertheless, see Hengel, *Sohn*, p.29, for a good explanation of the reason why the title, despite its centrality, appears much less frequently in Paul than κύριος which has in many respects a meaning similar to it.

[2] Cf. Hengel, *Sohn*, p.119. Barrett, *Adam*, p.71, makes the following sage remark, though without elaboration: 'He (sc. Paul) was perhaps the first, though certainly not the last, theologian to encounter the paradox of the person of one who is confessed as both truly human and truly divine'.

[3] If the above arguments have been correct, they contradict the view that Paul 'identified' Christ with Wisdom in response to the Corinthian opponents' misconception of Jesus Christ as one of Wisdom's envoys or Wisdom teachers (Suggs, *Wisdom*, pp.60f.), not to mention U.Wilckens' thesis that the Corinthian opponents first identified Christ with Wisdom and developed Sophia-Christology in the pattern of the Gnostic redeemer myth which is, according to Wilckens, already found in the Jewish Gnostic Sophia myth, and that in 1Cor 1–2 Paul makes use of this while correcting it at the same time (*Weisheit*, esp. pp.205ff.; σοφία, *TDNT* vii, esp. pp.519ff.). Paul knew that Christ has superseded the Torah from the Damascus revelation and so 'identified' Christ with Wisdom himself from the very beginning! It may well be that the Corinthians misunderstood the spirit-

confirming his belief that Jesus who taught and acted on earth as the final representative of Wisdom had revealed himself to be the embodiment of Wisdom itself through his crucifixion and resurrection. When the crucified Jesus of Nazareth appeared to him exalted and enthroned at God's right hand, Paul realized that he was the Messiah, the Lord and the Son of God – this, not only in the sense of the Davidic Messiah who was confessed by the Christians then as having been installed as God's Son through his resurrection but more profoundly in the sense of the being who stood in an intimate relationship with God from the beginning, acted as his agent in creation and was sent forth by God into the world to redeem us from sin and the law. For the revelation of the crucified Jesus of Nazareth as enthroned at God's right hand proved to Paul that through the cross he has superseded the Torah as the medium of the divine revelation and salvation and therefore that he is the one who had formerly been described as Wisdom. *So, the Son of God who was revealed to Paul on the Damascus road is the content of his gospel (Gal 1.15f.; Rom 1.2ff.; 2Cor 1.19f.; 1Th 1.10; Acts 9.20)!*

---

ual gifts of words and knowledge given to them as signs of their wisdom (*supra* pp.75f.) and the apostles and even Christ as bringers of wisdom or wisdom teachers (cf. Suggs, *Wisdom*, pp.60f.; Koester, *op. cit.*, pp.222f.; on similarity between Q and 1Cor 1–2 in regards to wisdom see, besides Suggs, *Wisdom*, pp.82ff., also J.M.Robinson, 'Kerygma as Hermeneutical Language Event', *Trajectories*, pp.42f.). But Paul's correction of their misunderstandings is not based on an impromptu Sophia-Christology but on one that has been an essential element in his Christology from the beginning. In the light of our arguments above, we can now appreciate better the paradox of the crucified Christ as the Wisdom of God that Paul so emphatically proclaims against the Corinthians' boasting of their wisdom and therefore misunderstanding of the nature of wisdom (1Cor 1.24, 30): only as the crucified, hence as the scandal to the Jews and a folly to the Gentiles, is Christ the Wisdom of God, the saving power of God. For precisely on that cross Christ abolished the Torah and proved himself to be the true revelation of God and the true means of salvation, 'the Wisdom from God, righteousness and sanctification and redemption . . . ' (1Cor 1.30).

It is true that 'the stream of the tradition of this Wisdom-Christology that affirms the pre-existence of Jesus is surely broader than the letters of Paul let (us) presume' (Hengel, *Sohn*, p.114). For this we need only to have a glance at the Logos-Christology of the Johannine Prologue and at Heb 1 (cf. also Rev 3.14). And we have already observed briefly the developing Wisdom-Christology in the Synoptic Gospels. However, when we judge that Paul initiated the 'identification' of Jesus with the pre-existent, personified divine Wisdom in the early Church, we do so because we have seen that his Damascus experience forced him to do so and to do so at once. This was an early date in the early Church. Now the Wisdom-Christology developed by Paul could have entered into the common stream of the early Christian tradition in Syria and been drawn by the First Evangelist, the Fourth Evangelist and the author of the Letter to the Hebrews, or they could have developed Wisdom-Christology directly from Jesus' Wisdom teaching and independently of Paul and of each other. Although we are inclined to the former alternative, we cannot stop here to prove this.

Chapter VI Paul's Gospel: B. Christology

3 Christ the Εἰκὼν τοῦ θεοῦ

1) The Texts

It is significant that Paul speaks of Christ as the εἰκὼν τοῦ θεοῦ in the passage where he alludes to the Damascus Christophany (2Cor 3.16–4.6)[1]. That concept, as we shall see later in detail, involves here both Paul's Adam-Christology (cf. Gen 1.27) and Wisdom-Christology (cf. Wis 7.26)[2]. So it seems worthwhile to ask whether Paul perceived Christ to be the εἰκὼν τοῦ θεοῦ at the Damascus revelation and whether his Adam-Christology as well as Wisdom-Christology is rooted in it.

It is also significant that the designation of Christ as the εἰκὼν τοῦ θεοῦ (2Cor 4.4; Col 1.15; cf. also the virtually synonymous μορφὴ θεοῦ in Phil 2.6[3]) and the motif of Christians being conformed or transformed to the image of Christ explicitly appear only in Pauline letters in the NT. In Rom 8.29 Paul speaks of God having 'foreordained (his elect) to be conformed to the image of his Son' (προώρισεν συμμόρφους τῆς εἰκόνος του υἱοῦ αὐτοῦ). In 2Cor 3.18 Paul says similarly: ἡμεῖς δὲ πάντες ἀνακεκαλυμμένῳ προσώπῳ τὴν δόξαν κυρίου κατοπτριζόμενοι τὴν αὐτὴν εἰκόνα μεταμορφούμεθα ἀπὸ δόξης εἰς δόξαν. In 1Cor 15.49 Paul says that just as we have borne the image of the fallen Adam, the man of dust, so we shall bear the image of the Last Adam, the heavenly man (καθὼς ἐφορέσαμεν τὴν εἰκόνα τοῦ χοϊκοῦ, φορέσομεν καὶ τὴν εἰκόνα τοῦ ἐπουρανίου) (cf. 1Cor 15.52). A similar thought is expressed in Col 3.9f.: ἀπεκδυσάμενοι τὸν παλαιὸν ἄνθρωπον σὺν ταῖς πράξεσιν αὐτοῦ, καὶ ἐνδυσάμενοι τὸν νέον τὸν ἀνακαινούμενον εἰς ἐπίγνωσιν κατ' εἰκόνα τοῦ κτίσαντος αὐτόν (cf. Eph 4.24). Again similarly Paul says in Phil 3.21 that we the citizens of heaven are

---

[1] *Supra* Ch. 1, 4).

[2] Cf. Windisch, *2.Kor.*, p.137; Plummer, *2Cor.*, pp.106, 118; Lietzmann-Kümmel, *Kor.*, p.201; Barrett, *2Cor.*, pp.125, 132f.

[3] See R.P.Martin, *Carmen Christi: Phil. ii.5–11* (1967), pp.99–133, esp. 107–120. *Infra* pp.195ff.

waiting for the Lord Jesus Christ, ὃς μετασχηματίσει τὸ σῶμα τῆς ταπεινώσεως ἡμῶν σύμμορφον τῷ σώματι τῆς δόξης αὐτοῦ, κατὰ τὴν ἐνέργειαν τοῦ δύνασθαι αὐτὸν καὶ ὑποτάξαι αὐτῷ τὰ πάντα. Lamenting over
his backsliding converts in Galatia Paul says: τέκνα μου, οὓς πάλιν ὠδίνω
μέχρις οὗ μορφωθῇ Χριστὸς ἐν ὑμῖν (Gal 4.19). He exhorts the Roman
Christians: μὴ συνσχηματίζεσθε τῷ αἰῶνι τούτῳ, ἀλλὰ μεταμορφοῦσθε
τῇ ἀνακαινώσει... (Rom 12.2). He recounts the resolution that he made at
the Damascus Christophany and has been carrying ever since as his principle:
To know Christ and the power of his resurrection and sharing in his suffering,
συμμορφιζόμενος τῷ θανάτῳ αὐτοῦ (Phil 3.10; cf. Rom 6.5). Finally, as
will be shown later, Paul's concept of the Christian as καινὴ κτίσις (2Cor
5.17; Gal 6.15) also belongs to this motif of the Christian's transformation
into the image of Christ, the Last Adam.

Now it is true that when the piece of a hymn in Heb 1.3[1] designates the
Son of God, the final and perfect bearer of the divine revelation, as ἀπαύγασμα
τῆς δόξης καὶ χαρακτὴρ τῆς ὑποστάσεως αὐτοῦ (sc. θεοῦ) it displays a
Wisdom-Christology similar to that which provides one of the two grounds
(the other being Adam-Christology) for Paul's conception of Christ as the
εἰκὼν τοῦ θεοῦ (especially compare Heb 1.2f. with Col 1.13ff.). For it is
reminiscent of Wis 7.26 where Wisdom is said to be 'radiance (ἀπαύγασμα)
of eternal light, the flawless mirror (ἔσοπτρον) of the active power of God
and the image (εἰκών) of his goodness'[2]. Furthermore, both predicates,
'radiance' (ἀπαύγασμα) of God's glory and 'impress' or 'an exact representation'[3] (χαρακτήρ) of God's nature (ὑπόστασις), are similar to or even
synonymous with the concept of εἰκών (τοῦ θεοῦ)[4].

Still further, Jesus as the Son is in Heb. related to the Christians as the
sons in terms of the eldest (cf. πρωτότοκος in Heb 1.6) to his brothers (Heb
2.5ff.), and this is very similar to Paul's thought in Rom 8.29 (cf. also Gal
4.4ff.). In Heb. this relationship can be defined in terms of a twofold solidarity. On the one hand, the Christians are the sons (of God) and brothers

---

[1] For the view that a hymn is cited here see Bornkamm, 'Das Bekenntnis im Hebräerbrief', *Studien zu Antike und Urchristentum*, Ges. Aufsätze ii (1959), pp.188ff.;
R.Deichgräber, *Gotteshymnus und Christushymnus in der frühen Christenheit* (1967),
pp.137ff.; most recently O.Hofius, *Der Christushymnus Phil 2, 6–11* (1976), pp.80ff.

[2] Cf. Philo, *Op. Mundi* 146; *Quod Det. Pot.* 83; *Plant.* 18.

[3] Bauer-Arndt-Gingrich, s.v.

[4] Cf. G.Kittel, ἀπαύγασμα, *TDNT* i, p.508; U.Wilckens, χαρακτήρ, *TDNT* ix, pp.
421f.; F.–W. Eltester, *Eikon im NT* (1958), pp.149ff.; O.Michel, *Der Brief an die
Hebräer* ([12]1966), p.98; F.F.Bruce, *The Epistle to the Hebrews* ([3]1971), p.6; E.Käse-
mann, *Das wandernde Gottesvolk* ([4]1961), pp.61ff.

of Jesus because they share the salvation, sanctification, perfection (τελείωσις) and glorification pioneered by Christ, the Son (2.10f.; cf. 5.9; 6.20; 10.14; 12.2). On the other hand, Christ and the Christians are brothers because the former partook of the same 'flesh and blood' as the latter (2.11ff.). In this connection it may be observed that the idea of the pre-existent Son's incarnation in order to deliver us from the bondage of the devil and his power of death (2.14ff.) and to lead us to the divine sonship (2.10f.) is essentially the same as that which Paul expresses through his sending-formula in Rom 8.3f. and Gal 4.4ff. Now the solidarity between Christ, the Son, and the Christians, the sons, in terms of brothers is in Paul closely related to his idea of the Christians' συμμόρφωσις to the image of Christ (Rom 8.29). Finally, there is to be discerned in Heb 1–2 (esp. 2.5–18) an Adam- or Son-of-Man-Christology similar to that which probably forms a background of Phil 2.6–11 and Paul's εἰκών-Christology. In Heb 2.6–9, where Ps 8.4–6 is applied to the *erniedrigte* and then *erhöhte* Christ, we may see a conception of Christ as the second Adam who has recovered the glory and dominion that God originally gave to Adam (Gen 1.26, 28)[1]. All these show how close the conception of Christ as the εἰκών τοῦ θεοῦ in the sense of the Second Adam (cf. Gen 1.26) and the conception of the Christian's μεταμόρφωσις into or συμμόρφωσις to the image of Christ lie to the author of Heb.

Yet he never designates Christ as the εἰκών τοῦ θεοῦ in the sense of the Second Adam (except, of course, in the sense of Wisdom in 1.3) and he has no idea of the sons' μεταμόρφωσις into or συμμόρφωσις to the image of Christ, the Son. Especially in 2.10 when he says that God has begun to bring many sons to glory by making the pioneer of their salvation perfect through suffering[2] the conception of the Christian's συμμόρφωσις to the image of Christ, the one who has recovered the glory and dominion that Adam lost (2.6–9), lies within his arm's reach. Yet he stops short of it, and instead emphasizes the solidarity of the Son with the sons in his incarnation. So when he speaks of the likeness between the two, he lays emphasis rather on the Son's incarnation into the likeness of the sons (2.14ff.). He does so because it is vitally important for his conception of Christ as the perfect High

---

[1] Bruce, *Hebrews*, pp.34ff.; Michel, *Hebräer*, pp.138, 159. Käsemann, *Gottesvolk*, pp.61ff. finds the Gnostic redeemer myth behind the Son-Christology in Heb. However, against Käsemann, see Michel, *Hebräer*, pp.64ff., 143ff., *et passim*, and also below p.146, n.3. For the often observed similarities in the structure and ideas between Heb 1–2 and the hymn in Phil 2.6–11, see E.Lohmeyer, *Kyrios Jesus* ([2]1961), pp.77ff.; Käsemann, *Gottesvolk*, pp.61ff.; most recently Hofius, *loc. cit.*

[2] For this understanding of v.10 see Michel, *Hebräer*, p.147: 'Gott hat viele Söhne zur Herrlichkeit zu führen begonnen (ingressiver Aorist), indem Er den Herzog der Seligkeit durch Leiden vollendete'.

Priest: Christ, the Son, 'had to be made like (ὁμοιωθῆναι) his brethren in every respect, so that he might become a merciful and faithful high priest in the service of God, to make expiation for the sins of the people' (2.17; cf. 4.14ff.; 5.5ff.). This shows that the conception of Christ as the εἰκών τοῦ θεοῦ is not essentially his theologoumenon[1].

What has been said of Heb. applies to the Johannine literature also. John never uses the word εἰκών. But when he speaks of Christ as the pre-existent Λόγος who was the medium of creation and as the only Son (μονογενὴς παρὰ πατρός or ὁ ὢν εἰς τὸν κόλπον τοῦ πατρός) who, becoming incarnate, has revealed the invisible God to men (Jn 1.1–18), it is clear that here is a thought that Paul expresses by designating Christ as the εἰκών τοῦ θεοῦ (τοῦ ἀοράτου) (Col 1.15; 2Cor 4.4). Because Christ is the revealer of God, he who has seen him has seen God (Jn 12.45; 14.9). So this Johannine conception of Christ as the revealer of God corresponds to the Pauline conception of Christ as the εἰκών τοῦ θεοῦ in terms of Wisdom-Christology. However, when John says that we as the children of God 'shall be like him (ὅμοιοι αὐτῷ ἐσόμεθα)[2] when he appears, for we shall see him as he is' (1Jn 3.2), he shows also a thought that corresponds to Paul's anthropological conception of Christ as the εἰκών τοῦ θεοῦ and to his idea of the Christian's συμμόρφωσις to the image of Christ (cf. 2Cor 3.18; 1Cor 15.52; Phil 3.21). Thus it is clear that materially there is in John the conception of Christ as the εἰκών of God[3]. Therefore it is significant that John nevertheless never uses the term εἰκών, especially in view of the fact that his designation of Christ as the λόγος would have brought him to the term so easily since λόγος

---

[1]Cf. Michel, *Hebräer*, p.70, who observes that, although the hymn in Heb 1.3 is set as a program for the entire letter, the first two members of the hymn (i.e., ὃς ὢν ἀπαύγασμα τῆς δόξης καὶ χαρακτὴρ τῆς ὑποστάσεως αὐτοῦ, φέρων τε τὰ πάντα τῷ ῥήματι τῆς δυνάμεως αὐτοῦ) are not expounded in the letter, while the last two members are. This may indicate that Wisdom-Christology is not an essential motif of Heb., either, except that it fulfils a vital function of providing the pre-supposition of the pre-existence and superiority of Christ, the Son. Michel (p.135) further observes: 'Man hat überall das Empfinden, daß eine reiche Kenntnis der Evangelientradition (einschließlich des Joh) vorliegt, daß entscheidende paulinische Argumente sich durchgesetzt haben und ganz selbstverständlich weitergegeben werden. Sie brauchen nicht mehr durchgekämpft zu werden'. If so, all the similarities that we have ascertained above between Paul and Heb. cannot lead us to the conclusion that Paul obtained the εἰκών-motif from Heb. or the tradition embedded in Heb. The reverse must have been the case. Cf. T.W.Manson, 'The Problem of the Epistle to the Hebrews', *BJRL* 32 (1949), pp.1–7; H.W.Montefiore, *The Epistle to the Hebrews* (1964), pp.9–28.

[2]Here the reference is to Christ rather than to God.

[3]So R.Bultmann, *Das Evangelium des Johannes* ([19]1968), p.56; L.H.Brockington, 'The Septuagintal Background to the NT use of Δόξα', *Studies in the Gospels*, Essays in

and εἰκών belonged to the same conceptual world[1]. It is not clear why John avoids the term[2]. However, if one thing is clear, it is that the conception of Christ as the εἰκών τοῦ θεοῦ is not essentially John's theologoumenon, just as it is not one of the author of Heb.

So, the recognition that there are in John and Heb. the ideas that are similar to Paul's Εἰκών-Christology and anthropology, does not alter the fact that the conception of Christ as the εἰκών τοῦ θεοῦ both in the revelatory and anthropological sense is a distinctive Pauline theologoumenon. However, many of the passages cited above which contain the conception of Christ as the εἰκών τοῦ θεοῦ and the motif of the Christian's transformation into that image, are claimed to be in fact pre-Pauline by many recent authors.

First, J. Jervell believes that while in 2Cor 3.1–17 Paul argues Rabbinically, in 2Cor 3.18 he uses the Hellenistic terminology of transformation through beholding God. Jervell finds this a problem and proposes to solve it by recognizing that Paul here counters a Rabbinic interpretation of the divine image with his own, at first purely Rabbinically in 2Cor 3.1–17 and then in terms of the concepts and ideas which originated from the Hellenistic Church in 2Cor 3.18–4.6[3]. But Jervell gives no convincing reason why the terminology of transformation through beholding God could not have been borrowed by Paul himself rather than the Hellenistic Church from the Hellen-

---

Memory of R.H.Lightfoot, ed. D.E.Nineham (1955), p.8; Eltester, *Eikon*, p.151; Jervell, *Imago*, p.191; P.Schwanz, *Imago Dei* (1970), pp.59ff. However, Schwanz goes too far when he tries to connect many diverse motifs in John directly with the conception of Christ as the εἰκών of God.

[1]Philo designates λόγος as εἰκών τοῦ θεοῦ: *Conf. Ling.* 97, 147; *Fuga* 101; *Somn.* i. 239; ii.45, etc.

[2]Eltester, *Eikon*, p.152, presumes that John avoids the term because it is 'too much cosmologically loaded' (following Bultmann, *Johannes*, p.56). But this is hardly correct. Is not λόγος also or perhaps even more cosmologically loaded? And does not in fact John refer to the cosmological role of Christ as the λόγος in 1.1–3? (Cf. Schwanz, *Imago Dei*, p.206, n.300). According to Schwanz (p.84): '... indem Johannes gnostische Begrifflichkeit übernimmt, zugleich aber Entscheidendes wie den Eikon-Begriff und die dualistischen anthropologischen Formeln wegläßt, überhaupt aber die übernommene Begrifflichkeit am Christusgeschehen orientiert, wird das christliche Verständnis herausgestellt, in gnostischer Form und doch gegen den gnostischen Inhalt'. But this explanation is, to say the least, a muddle. If John uses 'gnostische Begrifflichkeit' but avoids 'Gnostic' terms like εἰκών or dualistic anthropological formula, how can it be said that he expresses the Christian understanding 'in gnostischer Form und doch gegen den gnostischen Inhalt'? Is not the reverse true? Schwanz's presupposition that the εἰκών concept as used in the NT is Gnostic is already problematic.

[3]J.Jervell, *Imago*, pp.173f.

istic environment, if it is borrowed from the latter at all[1]. Observing the concept φωτισμός (2Cor 4.4, 6) and the idea of καινὴ κτίσις (v.6), which belong to the context of baptism, the clause ὅς ἐστιν εἰκὼν τοῦ θεοῦ, which he claims to be a confession in a baptismal hymn (cf. Col 1.15), the genitive constructions (vs. 4, 6), which he suggests have a liturgical style, and finally the idea of seeing God or the glory of Christ, which he suggests belongs to a cultic context, Jervell argues that 2Cor 4.4–6, though not a hymn, is nevertheless reminiscent of a baptismal hymn. Then from the fact that words such as λάμπω, αὐγάζω, φωτισμός and κατοπτρίζομαι, appear only here in Paul, Jervell concludes that in 2Cor 4.4–6 (and 3.18?) Paul uses baptismal ideas of the Hellenistic Church[2].

It is probably correct to see some of the language in 2Cor 3.16–18; 4.4–6 as reminiscent of baptism. But this does not mean that Paul is here quoting from a baptismal hymn or liturgy of the (pre-Pauline) Hellenistic Church. Paul describes his Damascus conversion and call with the language that he otherwise applies to the baptism of the Christians[3]. The concepts and ideas above can adequately be explained in terms of Paul's Damascus experience as we have already shown[4]. So it is just as much possible to argue that Paul describes baptism in terms of his Damascus experience as to argue that Paul describes his Damascus experience in terms of the baptismal language that obtained in the pre-Pauline Church. The argument from the rare words is useless. For there is no evidence that those words were common or uniquely significant in the Hellenistic Church[5]. The genitive constructions in vs. 4 and

---

[1]The similarity of language between Paul and the Hellenistic mystery religions concerning the idea of transformation through beholding God, is often pointed out (see J. Behm, μορφή, *TDNT* iv, pp.757f.; Lietzmann-Kümmel, *Kor.*, pp.114f.; Windisch, *2.Kor.*, p.128). But among the passages often cited such as Herm. iv. 11ab; x.6; xiii.3; Apuleius, *Metamorphoses*, xi.23f. only Herm. x.6 seems to be able to provide a loose parallel to the language of 2Cor 3.18. Even so, the essential differences in content between Paul's idea and that of the Hellenistic mysticism are well noted by Behm, *op. cit.*, pp.758f. See also Kümmel, *Theologie*, pp.198f.; Jervell, *Imago*, p.173.

[2]Jervell, *Imago*, pp.196f., 209.

[3]Cf. Satake, 'Apostolat', pp.96ff.; Stuhlmacher, 'καινὴ κτίσις', pp.27ff.

[4]*Supra* Ch.1, 4).

[5]The only possible exception is φωτισμός. φωτισμός is, like αὐγάζω and κατοπτρίζομαι, a *hapax legomenon* not only in Paul but in the entire NT. However, φῶς is an important theological term especially in Jn and φωτίζω appears in the metaphorical sense of spiritual and intellectual illumination (Eph 1.18; 3.9; 1Tim 1.10; Heb 6.4; 10.32: in the last two places it may have been used for baptism – cf. Michel, *Hebräer*, p.241; Bruce, *Hebrews*, p.120; Conzelmann, φῶς, κτλ., *TDNT* ix, p.355) as well as in the literal sense. φωτισμός as a technical term appears in Justin Martyr (*Apol.* I. 61.12;

6, which are in both cases lengthened through a reference to the glory of Christ or God, can easily be explained in the light of the contrast that Paul makes in 2Cor 3.7–4.6, between the Mosaic dispensation of fading glory and the dispensation of the gospel of Christ which has abiding glory, without recourse to a liturgy. Jervell suggests that the clause ὅς ἐστιν εἰκὼν τοῦ θεοῦ in 2Cor 4.4 is a confessional formula which has its *Sitz im Leben* in the (pre-Pauline) Hellenistic Church's baptismal liturgy[1]. Whether Jervell is justified in speaking of a confessional *formula* on the basis of the relative sentences in 2Cor 4.4, Col 1.15 (ὅς ἐστιν εἰκὼν τοῦ θεοῦ τοῦ ἀοράτου) and Phil 2.6 (ὅς ἐν μορφῇ θεοῦ ὑπάρχων) (cf. Heb. 1.3), does not concern us at this stage. What concerns us at present is whether the above passages are in fact pre-Pauline. For the view that ὅς ἐστιν εἰκὼν τοῦ θεοῦ in 2Cor 4.4 is a pre-Pauline confessional formula, Jervell has not provided any substantial reason, except that it is similar to Col 1.15 and Phil 2.6. His two other reasons are hardly compelling. First, he says that Paul uses the concept εἰκὼν τοῦ θεοῦ without a further explanation and that this indicates that the concept or confession is well known in the Corinthian church[2]. But in 2Cor 3.7–4.6 where Paul speaks so much about seeing God and his glory (see esp. 3.18: 'beholding the glory of the Lord with unveiled face as in a mirror we are changed into that image from glory to glory . . . '), it can hardly be said that Paul introduces the concept of Christ as the εἰκὼν τοῦ θεοῦ abruptly. If the concept was already known in Corinth, is it not at least as likely that it was through Paul's preaching there as that it was through the preaching of others? In fact, if the conception of Christ as the εἰκὼν τοῦ θεοῦ is rooted in the Damascus Christophany, as we believe, it is easy to suppose that in giving an account of his Damascus experience as part of his preaching[3] he already introduced the concept to the Corinthians during his missionary work in Corinth. Secondly, Jervell argues that while in the Hellenistic Church the idea of εἰκὼν is used for the pre-existent one and in cosmology (Col 1.15; Heb 1.3; Jn 1.1) Paul uses it for the risen one (2Cor 4.4; Rom 8.29; 1Cor 15.45ff.). It is true that in the majority of cases Paul uses the concept εἰκὼν for the risen Christ, but this does not mean that for Paul Christ *became* εἰκὼν

Dial. 122.5) for the first time. But φῶς and its cognates are so common in religious language that there is no reason why Paul could not have used φωτισμός here on his own initiative. The word would have suggested itself so naturally in the context of speaking about the Damascus Christophany which was accompanied by light (cf. Acts 9.3; 22.6, 11; 26.13) and resulted in his spiritual and intellectual illumination.

[1] Jervell, *Imago*, pp.198, 209, 214.

[2] *Ibid.*, pp.209, 214.

[3] *Supra*, pp.28f.

τοῦ θεοῦ for the first time at his resurrection. For Paul Christ *became manifest* at the resurrection as what he always *was, is* and *will be* – in protology and in eschatology. This can be best illustrated by Son-Christology which is closely related to Εἰκών-Christology. The Son, to whose image the Christians are predestined to be conformed (Rom 8.29)[1], is none other than the preexistent Son who was sent by God into the world in a human form and proved to be God's Son through his death and resurrection (Rom 8.3; Gal 4.4; Rom 1.2–4). In Col 1.15 Εἰκών-Christology is essentially Wisdom-Christology while in Rom 8.29; 1Cor 15.45ff. Εἰκών-Christology is Adam-Christology. The former is oriented to Christ's functions in creation and revelation while the latter is oriented to his functions in eschatology as the Last Adam. In 2Cor 3.18–4.6 we find them fused together: here Christ as the εἰκών τοῦ θεοῦ has both functions of revelation (4.4ff.) and of the *Vorbild* as the Last Adam (3.18). This shows how natural it was for Paul to use the concept εἰκών for both functions. Moreover, if Col 1.15 is Pauline, of course, Jervell's argument falls to the ground. So the question whether the conception of Christ as the εἰκών τοῦ θεοῦ is pre-pauline or uniquely Pauline, depends solely on the determination whether Col 1.15–20 (and Phil 2.6–11) is pre-Pauline or Pauline. All other arguments of Jervell for the view that in 2Cor 3.18–4.6 Paul borrows the εἰκών conception from the (pre-Pauline) Hellenistic Church, do not carry any weight.

As the great majority of recent writers think that the hymnic passage in Col 1.15–20 is a non-Pauline hymn[2], it takes nowadays considerable courage as well as critical independence to stand with the minority of writers who still take it as Pauline[3]. There are two main arguments against Pauline authorship of the hymn. One is that some words in this passage are said to be non-

---

[1]It is not clear whether the Son in Rom 8.29 refers to the risen Christ (as Jervell, *Imago*, p.209, says) or the pre-existent Christ. Perhaps this distinction is artificial and foreign to Paul.

[2]See, e.g., E.Käsemann, 'Eine urchristliche Taufliturgie', *EVB* i, pp.34–51; E. Schweizer, 'Die Kirche als Leib Christi in den paulinischen Antilegomena', *Neotestamentica*, pp.293ff.; Jervell, *Imago*, pp.209ff.; Deichgräber, *Christushymnus*, pp.152f.; Lohse, *Kol.*, pp.77ff. See further the history of exegesis with bibliography in H.J.Gabathuler, *Jesus Christus. Haupt der Kirche–Haupt der Welt* (1965).

[3]E.Lohmeyer, *Die Briefe an die Philipper, an die Kolosser und an Philemon* ([8]1930), pp.41ff.; E.Percy, 'Zu den Problemen des Kolosser- und Epheser-briefes', *ZNW* 43 (1950/51), pp.183ff.; M.Dibelius, *An die Kolosser, Epheser, an Philemon*, neubearbeitet v. H.Greeven ([3]1953), pp.10f.; C.Maurer, 'Die Begründung der Herrschaft Christi über die Mächte nach Col 1,15–20'; *Wissenschaft und Dienst* NF 4 (1955), pp.79ff.; C.F.D.Moule, *Col.*, pp.60ff.; A.Feuillet, *Le Christ, Sagesse de Dieu*, pp.246ff. Most recently again Kümmel, *Introduction*, pp.342f. Cf. also N.Kehl, *Der Christushymnus im Kolosserbrief* (1967), pp.163f.

Pauline[1]. The Christological predicate εἰκὼν τοῦ θεοῦ (v.15) appears only in a formula-like sentence in 2Cor 4.4. ὁρατός (v.16) is a *hapax legomenon* in the NT while ἀόρατος (v.15f.) is rare (Rom 1.20; 1Tim 1.17; Heb 11.27) and appears never in opposition to ὁρατός. θρόνοι (v.16) appears only here in Paul and κυριότης (v.16) only once more (Eph 1.21). The intransitive συνεστηκέναι (v.17) appears only here in Paul. In Christological context Paul uses ἀπαρχή (1Cor 15.20) but never ἀρχή (v.18). πρωτεύειν and εἰρηνοποιεῖν are *hapax legomena* in the NT. κατοικεῖν (v.19) appears only in Col 2.9 and Eph 3.17 besides here in Paul while ἀποκαταλλάσσειν only in Eph 2.16. Paul mentions the blood of Christ (v.20) only in the passages where he adopts traditional Christian expressions (Rom 3.25; 5.9; 1Cor 10.16; 11.25, 27; cf. also Eph 1.7; 2.13). The connection αἷμα τοῦ σταυροῦ αὐτοῦ (v.20) is without parallel. But these observations are hardly a convincing argument against the Pauline authorship of the hymn. First of all, what does the fact that the Christological predicate εἰκὼν τοῦ θεοῦ appears only in a formula-like sentence in 2Cor 4.4 prove? That Paul in 2Cor 4.4 cites a confession from a hymn like Col 1.15−20? Why could not Paul have composed the confession that Jesus Christ is the εἰκὼν τοῦ θεοῦ and used it both in 2Cor 4.4 and Col 1.15?[2] What does the observation of the rare words − ὁρατός, ἀόρατος, θρόνοι, κυριότης, συνεστηκέναι, κατοικεῖν, πρωτεύειν and εἰρηνοποιεῖν − prove? Is there any reason why Paul was incapable of using these words as the subject matter demanded?[3] Why are ὁρατός and ἀόρατος to be judged as strange vocabulary for one who uses precisely ἀόρατος for the invisible nature of God in Rom 1.20? It is worth remembering that the derivatives of the stem καταλλαγ- appear only in Paul in the NT[4]. Is it not possible to suppose that in a passage in which the supremacy of Christ is emphasized and the first creation and the new creation are paralleled ἀρχή rather than ἀπαρχή is used precisely in order to designate Christ as the beginning of the new creation and indicate his resurrection as initiating the new creation? It is not certain whether all the Pauline passages mentioning the blood of Christ are pre-Pauline in origin (esp. Rom 5.9). At any rate, does not the fact that Paul uses the theologoumenon in the decisive argument for his doctrine of justification in

---

[1] Lohse, *Kol.*, pp.78f.; Deichgräber, *Christushymnus*, pp.152f.

[2] Deichgräber's argument that εἰκὼν τοῦ θεοῦ is a predicate of Wisdom and therefore not only pre-Pauline but pre-Christian, is meaningless. Nobody denies that it is a predicate of Wisdom and that it appears also in Gen 1.27. The question is: who applied it to Christ for the first time − Paul or somebody else before him? The same applies to Deichgräber's argument concerning the title πρωτότοκος.

[3] So Moule, *Col.*, pp.61f.

[4] Percy, 'Zu den Problemen', p.186.

Rom 3.25 prove that Paul has made it very much his own even if it was originally what he took over from others? Just as in Rom 5.1–11, so also here the motif of reconciliation and peace seems to lead Paul to emphasize the blood of Christ, for it is the means of atonement (Rom 3.25).

The second argument against Pauline authorship of the hymn is based on the detection of a redactional hand upon the original hymn, which critics claim to be able to reconstruct by considering rhythm, parallelism and strophic arrangement[1]. But there are a multitude of different reconstructions of the original hymn[2]. By reconstructing the original hymn, critics claim that the author of Col. took it over and reworked it. Now, if, as most of the critics who deny Pauline authorship of the hymn believe, the letter to the Colossians is deutero-Pauline, the hymn also may not be *pre-Pauline*. For if it originated in the Hellenistic Jewish or the Hellenistic Church contemporary with Paul, if not after Paul,[3] then the hymn could bear testimony to Wisdom-Christology as a whole and Εἰκών-Christology in particular, in the shaping of which Paul could have exerted a decisive influence in the early Church. However, since we believe that Paul is the author of Col., if the critics' theories of redaction of the hymn are right, we are obliged to treat the original hymn as

---

[1]Deichgräber, *Christushymnus*, p.152.

[2]See, e.g., Käsemann, 'Taufliturgie', pp.36f.; J.M.Robinson, 'A Formal Analysis of Colossians 1.15–20', *JBL* 76 (1957), pp.270ff.; E.Bammel, 'Versuch zu Col 1.15–20', *ZNW* 52 (1961), pp.88ff.; Schweizer, *Neotestamentica*, pp.294ff.; Gabathuler, *op. cit.*, pp.125ff.; Deichgräber, *op. cit.*, pp.146ff.

[3]Jervell, *Imago*, p.209, and Deichgräber, *op. cit.*, p.154: the (pre-Pauline) Hellenistic Church. Lohse, *Kol.*, pp.84f.: the hymn was known in the church in Asia Minor. Schweizer, *Neotestamentica*, p.313: 'Behind Col 1.15–20 we see a Christian group which tries to formulate in a hymn the Pauline and the common Christian preaching as answer to those problems (i.e., the problems of the men of the Hellenistic world) in strong dependence upon this (i.e., Hellenistic) language.' Gabathuler, *op. cit.*, p.141, believes that the hymn belonged to the tradition of the Hellenistic Church 'vor und neben Paulus'. However, he believes also that 'the word about the body of Christ . . . goes back to Pauline influence, though cosmologically misunderstood and "re-paulinised" (*repaulinisiert*) by the author of Col. through the gen. epexeg.' (p.141.n.809) – a tortuous reconstruction! Käsemann's view that the hymn was originally a pre-Christian Gnostic hymn about the metaphysical drama of the *Urmensch*-redeemer ('Taufliturgie', pp.39f.) has found little support. Now that Käsemann himself recognizes that in order to reconstruct the *Urmensch*-redeemer mythology reference was made 'fast durchweg auf nachchristliches, widersprüchliches Material' and that 'die Debatte ist im Augenblick religionsgeschichtlich durch zwei negative Ergebnisse gekennzeichnet: Der Mythos vom "erlösten Erlöser" bildet nicht das Zentrum einer vor- und außer-christlichen Gnosis . . . ' (*Römer*, p.134), may it be assumed that Käsemann has now withdrawn his view on the Colossian hymn together with his theses in his other earlier works, including 'Kritische Analyse von Phil. 2, 5–11', *EVB* i, pp.51–95?

pre-Pauline. But are they correct? The very multiplicity of reconstructions seems to prove the veracity of W.G. Kümmel's fundamental criticism: 'The assumption is not yet proved that a hymn constructed according to a strict scheme has been used and that accordingly every fragment of a sentence beyond the scheme must stem from the author of Col.'[1] Any attempt to reconstruct the original hymn on the basis of supposed rhythm, parallelism, scheme or even theological motif is bound to be subjective and may result in imposing an alien structure upon a hymn[2]. Is it beyond the stretch of imagination to think that Paul is using here a hymn which he earlier composed with interpretative glosses here and there in view of the situation of his readers, or expressing in an exalted hymnic style his beliefs about Christ in view of the situation of his readers and making use of some of their language?

It requires no less courage and critical independence to advocate Pauline authorship of the hymn in Phil 2.6–11 than the one in Col 1.15–20. For a vast majority of the recent writers take the pre-Pauline character of the hymn as an assured fact while only a few are still not overwhelmed by the arguments against Pauline authorship[3]. R.P. Martin has set out the various arguments – language, style, theology, etc. – against Pauline authorship and the answers to them in defence of Pauline authorship[4]. Martin's assessment of the arguments for and against Pauline authorship is that they are finely balanced: 'Both positions are arguable and neither is absolutely certain'[5]. So he proposes to postpone judgement upon authorship until the completion of his exegesis of the text. Then, without any new argument, he comes out against Pauline authorship[6]. We cannot, therefore, help but agree with a reviewer when he says: 'I fail to see how the results of Martin's exegesis tip the very finely poised balance against Paul'[7].

Since the argument from language is never conclusive, we will confine ourselves to the theological argument, which J. Gnilka designates as 'the most

---

[1] Kümmel, *Introduction*, p.343.

[2] Moule, *Col.,* 61; cf. also Deichgräber, *Christushymnus*, p.150; Lohse, *Kol.*, p.82.

[3] Some of those who hold to Pauline authorship are listed in Deichgräber, *Christushymnus*, p.120 (n.2) and in R.P.Martin, *Carmen Christi*, pp.55ff. Recently again Kümmel, *Introduction*, p.335: 'Nothing compels the conclusion that Paul himself could not have formulated this hymn on the basis of' traditional material.

[4] Martin, *Carmen Christi*, pp.45–61.

[5] *Ibid.*, p.61.

[6] *Ibid.*, pp.287ff.

[7] I.H.Marshall, 'The Christ-Hymn in Philippians 2:5–11. A Review Article', *TynB* 19 (1968), p.120.

decisive'[1]. Deleting θανάτου δὲ σταυροῦ in Phil 2.8 as a Pauline gloss, many scholars argue that the hymn lacks the ideas characteristic of Paul's soteriology, namely the cross and the resurrection, which are replaced by the scheme of *Erniedrigung und Erhöhung,* and Christ's redeeming work on the cross ὑπὲρ ἡμῶν[2]. But on the assumption that θανάτου δὲ σταυροῦ is indeed a Pauline gloss, it should be argued, as Martin does: 'When Paul adds his own phrase even that phrase contains no distinctly Pauline doctrine; and all that Schweizer has said about the absence of a personal interest in the redeeming work of Christ is not altered even when the Apostle does add his own contribution. Does not this expose the weakness of the whole approach which makes the absence of certain ideas a determining criterion in matters of authorship?'[3] That this is indeed the case, is shown by the fact that in Rom 10.6ff., where Paul speaks of the saving event, the content of the kerygma, which is the object of faith and confession, there is no explicit mention of the cross or Christ's death ὑπὲρ ἡμῶν[4]. The question is whether we should expect Paul to express his soteriology − that many-sided soteriology! − *in toto* whenever he comes to speak of the saving event[5]. However, recently O. Hofius[6] has rather convincingly argued on the grounds of form and content against what has become a *communis opinio* among the critics who deny Pauline authorship of the hymn, namely, that the phrase θανάτου δὲ σταυροῦ is a Pauline gloss and that with it Paul qualifies Jesus' death as the saving event and so builds a bridge from the incarnation−exaltation scheme of the hymn to his cross−resurrection scheme[7]. If the phrase θανάτου δὲ σταυροῦ belongs originally to the hymn, then 'the most decisive' argument

---

[1] J.Gnilka, *Der Philipperbrief* (1968), p.132.

[2] See esp. E.Schweizer, *Erniedrigung und Erhöhung* (1955), pp.111ff.

[3] Martin, *Carmen Christi*, pp.58f.

[4] Cf. Marshall, *op. cit.,* p.120. For the similarities between Phil 2.8ff. and Rom 10.4−11 see J.Munck, *Christ and Israel* (1967), pp.88f. *Supra* p.130, n.1 against Käsemann's view that in Rom 10.6ff. Paul is making use of a Jewish-Christian tradition (*Römer,* pp.176f.).

[5] Martin, *Carmen Christi*, p.56, puts it well: 'If the section was originally composed as a hymn, or confession of faith, in tribute to the Church's Lord, the employment of exceptional words and constructions might well be expected. Presumably the author had a certain picture in mind of the subject in whose praise and honour the hymn would be written. It would be unnatural to ask that every truth about Him and His work should be included in one short tribute. The author would have to be selective of his ideas, and this one fact may go far to explain the omission of those features which we find in the undoubtedly Pauline works'.

[6] O.Hofius, *Christushymnus*, p.317.

[7] E.Käsemann, 'Kritische Analyse', p.82; Gnilka, *Phil.,* pp.124, 132f.

against Pauline authorship of the hymn, namely that it does not contain
the characteristic Pauline soteriology of the cross, falls down. For although
in the hymn the phrase refers rather to the shameful character of Jesus'
death as the climax of his *Erniedrigung* than to its substitutionary character as the saving event, the latter may be at least implicit[1] (or so those critics
who take the phrase as a Pauline glosss believe). Another observation also
may bear on the question of authorship: some of the ideas and vocabulary
of the hymn are woven into the whole letter of Phil.[2],and the thought of
the hymn as a whole seems to have parallel in Paul's other letters, especially
Rom 14–15[3]. In view of this 'it may be asked whether it is more likely that
in his use of the ideas in the hymn Paul is drawing on his own or on somebody else's inspiration'[4].

The application of the *formgeschichtliche* method to the Pauline corpus
for a generation has been fruitful in demonstrating that Paul takes over much
traditional material from his Christian predecessors, often in the form of
confession, kerygmatic formula, liturgy or catechetical tradition and, therefore, that Paul was not a lone genius but stood in continuity as well as dis-
continuity with his predecessors and contemporaries within the early Church.
However, the search for pre-Pauline formulae seems to have gone too far[5],
and, if it progresses at the present rate, one wonders whether before long all
the sentences written in exalted language and style in the Pauline corpus will
not be declared pre-Pauline or at least non-Pauline, just as some critics in 19th
c. managed to declare that all the letters of the Pauline corpus were non-
Pauline[6]. How weak a basis critics sometimes provide to claim this or

---

[1]Hofius, *op. cit.*, p.17. Cf. 1Cor 1.18ff., where the cross refers to both the saving and
shameful character of Jesus' death – cf. Martin, *Carmen Christi*, pp.49f. (n.4). Despite
his view that the phrase θανάτου δὲ σταυροῦ is an integral part of the hymn, Hofius,
op. cit., p.1, holds that the hymn is pre-Pauline. M.Dibelius, who before him argued on
the basis of form and content against the view that the phrase was Paul's gloss, however,
held to Pauline authorship of the hymn (*Phil.*, pp.73, 81).

[2]See the table and accompanying comments in Martin, *Carmen Christi*, pp.58f. (n.2);
cf. also L.Cerfaux, *Christ in the Theology of St.Paul* (1959), p.376; N.Flanagan, 'A
Note on Philippians iii. 20–21', *CBQ* 18 (1956), pp.8f.

[3]See Marshall, *op. cit.*, pp.118ff.

[4]*Ibid.*, p.120.

[5]Cf. H.Frh.v. Campenhausen, 'Das Bekenntnis im Urchristentum', *ZNW* 63 (1972),
p.231 (n.124).

[6]The twin brother to the search for pre-Pauline formulae in Paul is the search for
what we may call the passages of 'take-over-and-correct', that is, the search for concepts,
formulae or large passages in Paul's letters which are alleged to be what Paul takes over
from his opponents and partly corrects. We do not wish to deny that these searches are

that passage in Paul's letters as pre- or non-Pauline we have shown in the foregoing part of this book (not only in the present context). As we come to examine the claim that Phil. 3.20f. is a pre-Pauline hymn, we would refer to two authors who in our mind best demonstrate the arbitrariness and far-fetchedness involved in some of the attempts to find pre-Pauline material: E. Güttgemanns and J. Becker[1]. But for the unnecessary demand of Güttgemanns[2] we would not feel obliged to waste time in examining their arbitrary arguments.

Following E. Lohmeyer's hint[3], Güttgemanns and Becker begin by asserting that the passage is a 6 line hymn. According to Becker (pp. 18, 26), who curiously arranges the six lines not in Greek original but in German, the hymn runs as follows (in Greek) (p.18):

1a τὸ πολίτευμα ἡμῶν ἐν οὐρανοῖς ὑπάρχει,
 b ἐξ οὗ καὶ σωτῆρα ἀπεκδεχόμεθα κύριον Ἰησοῦν Χριστόν,
2a ὃς μετασχηματίσει τὸ σῶμα τῆς ταπεινώσεως ἡμῶν,
 b σύμμορφον τῷ σώματι τῆς δόξης αὐτοῦ,
3a κατὰ τὴν ἐνέργειαν τοῦ δύνασθαι αὐτόν,
 b καὶ ὑποτάξαι αὐτῷ τὰ πάντα.

But can we here really speak of a hymn composed in *parallelismus membrorum*[4]? They

---

in principle valid methods of Biblical research or even that sometimes they have been fruitful. We object only to the application of wrong criteria in these searches and to the excessive zeal which leads critics to declare this or that passage non-Pauline all too lightly with little sound basis. The excessive zeal is perhaps only too natural in an atmosphere in which the dominant impression seems to be: the more of Pauline passages one is able to declare pre-Pauline, the more critical (=the better) exegete one is. It would be a long study to assemble and examine all the Pauline passages which have been claimed to be pre- or non-Pauline through these methods. And if we set aside all those passages there may be left very little of Paul. There must be, in the language of v. Campenhausen (*ibid.*), a Hercules who, taking heed to the plea of M.Hengel ('Christologie und neutestamentliche Chronologie', *NT und Geschichte*, Cullmann FS (1972), pp.43ff.) and others, can burn off the formula-hungry (or pre-Pauline material hungry) Hydra of her ever increasing heads. Otherwise, before long Paul may be portrayed as nothing more than, to use another picture, the archetype of a modern salesman, who went about in the *oecumene* selling the ready-made goods produced by the 'Hellenistic-Jewish' and 'Hellenistic' theologians in their factories back in Syria and was also engaged occasionally in take-over bids for the goods of his rivals.

[1]Güttgemanns, *Der leidende Apostel*, pp.240–247; Becker, 'Erwägungen zu Phil. 3,20–21', *ThZ* 27(1971), pp.16–29; also G.Strecker, 'Redaktion und Tradition im Christushymnus Phil.2,6–11', *ZNW* 55(1964), pp.75ff., who follows Güttgemanns.

[2]'Jede von dieser These abweichende Exegese muß für die gemachten Beobachtungen eine zureichende Begründung abgeben' (*op. cit.*, p.141, n.1).

[3]Lohmeyer, *Phil.*, pp.156f.

[4]According to Güttgemanns, 'Das entscheidende Argument für den hymnischen

claim that the relative pronouns (ἐξ οὖ and ὅς) indicate the passage as having a hymnic' relative style (Gütt. pp.242f.; Becker pp.26f.). But does mere presence of relatives make a passage a hymn? Then Rom 1.5–6; 1Cor 1.7–9; 4.5; 2Cor 13.3; Phil 3.7ff. and host of other passages must also be hymns! They claim that originally the hymn started τὸ πολίτευμα ἡμῶν ἐν οὐρανοῖς ὑπάρχει, from which Paul brings ἡμῶν forward to the head in order to build an emphatic antithesis to vs. 18f. But, as J. Gnilka observes, 'a hymn which starts with the words τὸ πολίτευμα ἡμῶν ἐν οὐρανοῖς ὑπάρχει would appear . . . remarkable enough'[1]. Becker attempts to draw the hymn in 2Tim 2.11–13 as a parallel to the present passage (pp.26f.). But a mere glance upon the form of 2Tim 2.11–13 reveals this attempt as far-fetched. Then Güttgemanns appeals to the apparent contacts between 3.20f. and 2.6–11[2]:

μορφή	(2.6, 7)	–	σύμμορφον	(3.21)
ὑπάρχων	(2.6)	–	ὑπάρχει	(3.20)
σχῆμα	(2.7)	–	μετασχηματίσει	(3.21)
πᾶν γόνυ κάμψῃ κτλ	(2.10)	–	τοῦ δύνασθαι αὐτὸν καὶ	
			ὑποτάξαι αὐτῷ τὰ πάντα	(3.21)
κύριος Ἰησοῦς Χριστός	(2.11)	–	... κύριον Ἰησοῦν Χριστόν	(3.20)

These parallels (at least the 1st, 3rd and 4th) show that both passages stem from the same milieu of language and thought (Gütt. p.241). But this does not mean, as Güttge-

---

Charakter dieser Verse ist . . . die stark kolometrisch gegliederte Struktur vor allem in V.21, in dem die meisten hellenistisch geprägten Worte vorkommen, und der vor allem gegen Ende sehr stark an liturgisch geprägte Wendungen der Deuteropaulinen erinnert. Natürlich *kann* diese gehobene Sprache auch das Produkt des Paulus sein. Aber nach allen Analogien, die wir kennen, kommt man zu der entgegengesetzten Vermutung' (*op. cit.,* pp. 243. Emphasis by G.). This is Güttgemanns' typical way of argumentation, which begs questions at every point. Can the above 6 lines be called 'die stark kolometrisch gegliederte Struktur'? For an examination of vocabulary see below. But, for the moment, is the observation that v.21 has the 'hellenistisch geprägten Worte', relevant to the question of hymnic character of the passage? To show that the phrase κατὰ τὴν ἐνέργειαν κτλ. in v.21 is reminiscent of 'liturgically formulated expressions of the deutero-Paulines', he cites the κατά-phrases in Eph 1.5b, 7b, 9b, 11, 19b; 3.7; 4.16; Col 1.11, 29. But why does he not cite also Rom 2.16; 9.11; 11.5; 12.6; 1Cor 3.10; 2Cor 13.10; Gal 1.4; Phil 4.19, etc.? Are all these places hymns? 'Nach allen Analogien, die wir kennen . . . ' – which analogies?

[1]Gnilka, *Phil.*, p.209. No amount of polemic by Becker (*op. cit.*, p.26) against Gnilka makes his case really convincing. It is beyond our comprehension how Güttgemanns (*op. cit.*, p.243) can argue that the alleged displacement of ἡμῶν 'confirms *per analogiam* the supposition of a hymn'. This argument *presupposes* that Phil 3.20f. is a hymn and that its first line originally started τὸ πολίτευμα ἡμῶν κτλ. But that Phil 3.20f. is a hymn is at the moment in need of proof!

[2]Güttgemanns, *op. cit.*, pp.241f. Already Flanagan, *op. cit.*(p.149, n.2). Becker, *op. cit.*, pp.16f., believes that there is a parallel in structure between Phil 3.17–4.1 and 2.1–2.12 and from this infers that in analogy to Phil 2.6ff. from the point of view of structure Phil 3.20f. provides a good space for a traditional piece of Christological content. Unfortunately we can only designate this as a piece of wishful thinking!

manns supposes, that Phil 3.20f. is a pre-Pauline hymn. Even if Phil 2.6–11 is pre-Pauline, Phil 3.20f. could have been composed by Paul making use of traditional formula-like materials, as Gnilka argues[1]. However, we believe that precisely because of the parallels Phil 3.20f. can be used for the view that Phil 2.6–11 is Pauline as we have shown in the foregoing paragraph.

To buttress their view that Phil 3.20f. is pre-Pauline, Güttgemanns and Becker go on arguing from vocabulary. πολίτευμα is a *hapax legomenon* in the NT. But what reason is there why Paul, who knows the idea of a heavenly Jerusalem (Gal 4.24ff.; cf. also 2Cor 5.1ff.; Phil 1.21ff.; Heb 11.13ff.; 13.14), could not have used the word on his own initiative? For Becker, the plural formulation ἐν οὐρανοῖς is un-Pauline. But his painful attempt to explain away the occurrences of the plural οὐρανοί in 2Cor 5.1; 1Th 1.10 (cf. also 2Cor 12.2), not to mention the passages in Eph. and Col., is simply astounding. At least 2Cor 5.1 is not generally claimed to be non-Pauline[2]. Becker argues that while ὑπάρχειν in Paul is used only to describe earthly circumstances, here in Phil 3.20 and 2.6 it is used for being in heaven (p.20). But ὑπάρχειν is a verb equivalent to εἶναι, and only the following prepositional phrase determines whether it describes circumstances in heaven or on earth. Was Paul so earth-bound that he was incapable of describing circumstances in heaven using the neutral verb ὑπάρχειν as the subject-matter demanded (Phil 3.14, 19!)?[3] The title σωτήρ appears in Paul only here (except in Eph 5.23) while it is frequent in the Pastorals and in non-Pauline writings. But is the title to be thought so strange for one who uses the concept σῶσαι/σωτηρία so often? As Gnilka points out[4], Phil 3.20 has a close parallel in 1Th 1.10 in terms of content: ἀναμένειν τὸν υἱὸν αὐτοῦ ἐκ τῶν οὐρανῶν... Ἰησοῦν τὸν ῥυόμενον ἡμᾶς ἐκ τῆς ὀργῆς τῆς ἐρχομένης. So, as in 1Th 1.10, in Phil 3.20 Paul may be formulating the hope for the eschatological redeemer from heaven using traditional language. Against this explanation[5], Becker polemicizes by saying: 'The Christ-hymn in Phil 2.6–11 stands, e.g., at the end under the influence of a formulated cry of acclamation which was taken from tradition. Yet 2.6–11 is a pre-Pauline hymn, not merely a passage (*Abschnitt*) which reworks various traditional material' (p.20). But this argument is far less compelling than Gnilka's. For the hymnic character of Phil 2.6–11 is not determined by the traditional formula at the end of the hymn. Would Becker then regard, e.g., 1Cor 12.3 as a hymn, since it contains not only the traditional confession κύριος Ἰησοῦς but is also built in chiasmus which is neater than the alleged *parallelismus membrorum* in Phil 3.20f.? It is beyond our comprehension why Paul's use of σωτήρ here should be judged as indicating that Paul is here citing a *pre*-Pauline hymn when vocabulary statistics show clearly that the use of the title σωτήρ in the NT is rather late[6]. According to Becker, κύριος Ἰησοῦς Χριστός

---

[1] Gnilka, *Phil.*, p.209; Luz, *Geschichtsverständnis*, p.312; Lohmeyer, *Phil.*, pp.156f.

[2] Except, of course, by Becker, *op. cit.*, p.19: 'In 2.Kor. 5,1ff. ist mit aufgegriffenem Vorstellungsmaterial zu rechnen, das auf die paulinische Formulierungen Einfluß nahm'.

[3] Cf. Gnilka, *Phil.*, p.209.

[4] *Ibid.*, p.207.

[5] Cf. *Ibid.*

[6] Cf. the strange logic of Güttgemanns: 'Dieses Schrifttum (i.e., die Deuteropaulinen und andere Briefe, in denen der Titel σωτήρ vorkommt) ist zum größen Teil *viel später* als die Paulus-Briefe entstanden, bringt *also stärker das vor- und nebenpaulinische*

without ἡμῶν/ὑμῶν inserted in Phil 3.20 is yet another piece of evidence that the passage is a pre-Pauline hymn (pp.21f.). According to him, κύριος Ἰησοῦς (Χριστός) without ἡμῶν/ὑμῶν inserted is a sign of liturgical language: so, e.g., in Rom 10.9; 1Cor 12.3; Phil 2.11; 1Cor 8.6. In the salutation at the beginning of his letters Paul uses only κύριος Ἰησοῦς Χριστός without ἡμῶν. Becker explains this as due to the fact that after πατὴρ ἡμῶν καί . . . another ἡμῶν would disturb the style. Then he observes that in the benediction at the end of his letters Paul uses κύριος Ἰησοῦς Χριστός again without ἡμῶν (1Cor 16.23; 2Cor 13.13; Phil 4.23; Phlm 25). According to Becker, this shows again that the plain κύριος Ἰησοῦς Χριστός is liturgical. But he quietly drops Gal 6.18 out of sight, where Ἡ χάρις τοῦ κυρίου ἡμῶν Ἰησοῦ Χριστοῦ appears[1]. Moreover it is not clear why the benediction at the end of a letter is liturgical while that at the beginning, where according to Becker ἡμῶν is omitted only on stylistic ground, is not. Still further, the plain κύριος Ἰησοῦς (Χριστός) appears in Rom 13.14; 14.14; 2Cor 4.14; 11.13; 1Th 4.1, 2; Philm 5, where one can hardly speak of a liturgy or even a formula. Does Becker think that he can get away with the kind of explanation such as: 'Dabei mag offenbleiben, ob der Apostel an allen diesen Stellen unbeeinflußt von Tradition formuliert' (p.21)? Of course, the confession κύριος Ἰησοῦς Χριστός and the titles in it are what Paul took over from his predecessors, and the use of the full titles with or without ἡμῶν[2] echoes often a liturgical style. But a survey of Paul's use of κύριος (ἡμῶν) Ἰησοῦς Χριστός clearly reveals that he uses the formula 'in places where he is writing in an elevated style'[3]. The presence of the formula in Phil 3.20 proves only that Paul is here writing in an elevated style making use of the pre-Pauline Christological titles which he has made so much his own[4]. If Becker wants to see it as a sign that Phil 3.20f. is a pre-Pauline hymn, we would again urge him that he had better claim 1Cor 12.3 to be a pre-Pauline hymn. Does the fact that the rare word ταπείνωσις occurs only once here in Paul (only 3 more times in the NT: Lk 1.18; Acts 8.23; Jas 1.10), indicate that Phil 3.20f. is pre-Pauline? (Becker, p.22). Words deriving from the same stem occur frequently in Paul. Becker argues that whereas Paul uses those words for 'one possible mode of earthly human existence', only in Phil 2.8 and 3.21 is the word used more fundamentally indicating the background of the idea of the slavery of human existence which stands in contrast to the heavenly possibility (p.22). But this difference is contrived and presumed. For the word-group is in itself neutral, so that it can be used in contrasting the humble to the haughty (Rom 12.16; 2Cor 10.1; Phil 2.3), the weak and downcast to the powerful and haughty in this world (2Cor 7.6; 11.7; Phil 4.12), and the lowly existence on earth to the glorious existence in heaven (Phil 2.8; 3.21). Is there any reason why Paul could not make the third contrast using the word-group as the subject-matter demanded (cf. 2Cor 5.1ff.)? When

---

hellenistische Christentum zu Wort' (*op. cit.*, pp.241f. Emphasis by me).

[1] ἡμῶν is omitted only by ℵ, P, *69, 1739, pc.*

[2] Kramer, *Christ, Lord, Son of God*, pp.91, 154, concludes that the presence or absence of ἡμῶν makes no difference in substance.

[3] *Ibid.*, p.216.

[4] So Gnilka's comment upon Güttgemann's attempt to read significance out of the parallels, κύριος Ἰησοῦς Χριστός and ὑπάρχειν in Phil 2.6–11 and 3.20f., is fully justified: 'Die Parallelen des ὑπάρχειν und des Kyrios Jesus Christus (besagten) überhaupt nichts' (*Phil.*, p.209).

Güttgemanns (pp.245f.) and Becker (p.22) argue that whereas Paul speaks of τὸ σῶμα τῆς ἁμαρτίας (Rom 6.6) and τὸ σῶμα τοῦ θανάτου τούτο (Rom 7.24) as the body from which the Christian is already redeemed, τὸ σῶμα τῆς ταπεινώσεως in Phil 3.21 refers to the Christian's existence in a "heilslosen Zustand" with a hope only for the future transformation, one wonders whether they know the characteristic tension between 'already' and 'not yet' in Pauline eschatology. Does not Paul also designate the Christian existence as τὰ θνητὰ σώματα ὑμῶν (Rom 8.11; cf. also 6.12; 2Cor 4.11) and say 'we ourselves who have the firstfruits of the Spirit groan inwardly as we wait for adoption as sons, τὴν ἀπολύτρωσιν τοῦ σώματος ἡμῶν ' (Rom 8.23)? (*pace* Becker, p.22). Does he not say that our present σῶμα ψυχικόν will be changed into the σῶμα πνευματικόν at the general resurrection (1Cor 15.35–54)? τὸ σῶμα τῆς ταπεινώσεως in Phil 3.21 describes the Christian existence no more or no less '*heilslos*' than τὰ θνητὰ σώματα ὑμῶν (Rom 8.11) whose ἀπολύτρωσις we still wait for (Rom 8.23). What is there so remarkable in the ˙phrase τὸ σῶμα τῆς ταπεινώσεως in Phil 3.21 that Paul could not have formulated it in contrast to the glorious body of Christ in heaven, especially in view of the fact that it is precisely Paul who characterizes the resurrection body with glory (1Cor 15.42f.)? Becker argues that the concept σῶμα in Phil 3.21 comes near to the meaning 'form' (*Gestalt*) which man *has* rather than *is*, as in 1Cor 15.44, where, appealing to Bultmann, he argues that Paul uses the concept σῶμα under the influence of his opponents' arguments in a way not characteristic of him (pp.22f). But this is another manifestation of his presumption. We simply cannot see what difference there is between the σῶμα concept, e.g., in Rom 8.11, 23 and that in Phil 3.21, as in both places we can speak of both our *having* and *being* σῶμα. According to Becker, whereas μορφή and its derivatives are used in Paul for a process that affects the earthly Christian existence, in Phil 3.21 σύμμορφος speaks of the eschatological event of becoming like Christ (p.23). Since Rom 8.29, which is similar to Phil 3.21, is also disputed and will be discussed below, we would not use it for an argument against Becker. But here again Becker constructs an arbitrary distinction between the present eschatology and the futuristic eschatology as though they were entirely different, mutually unrelated systems of two entirely different advocates. 2Cor 3.18 shows that the process of transformation into the image of Christ is an eschatological process that is ἀπὸ δόξης εἰς δόξαν, i.e., that leads up to the consummation in the future. Does not 1Cor 15.49 also speak of our bearing 'the image of the heavenly man', which is materially the same as the transformation of our body into the glorious body of Christ in Phil 3.21, in terms of the futuristic eschatology? Becker should not forget (or rather should be aware of) the salient fact that συμμόρφωσις or μεταμόρφωσις terminology occurs only in Paul in the NT. For Becker even the word ἐνέργεια poses a problem (p.23). But quite apart from the fact that the word occurs only in Pauline corpus (Eph 1.19; 3.7; 4.16; Phil 3.21; Col 1.29; 2.12; 2Th 2.9, 31) in the NT and that the words deriving from the same stem (ἐνεργεῖν/ἐνέργημα/ἐνεργήκ) occur frequently in Paul, what is so remarkable about Paul's using such a harmless word?! Finally (!), Becker argues that the phrase ὑποτάξαι αὐτῷ τὰ πάντα in Phil 3.21 as in 1Cor 15.24–28 goes back to the tradition which used Ps 8.6 Christologically (pp.23f). This is correct. But this no more proves that Phil 3.20f. is a pre-Pauline hymn than that 1Cor 15.25–28 is one. Becker concludes his study of vocabulary as follows: 'Die auf so kurzem Raum beobachtete Fülle sprachlicher Auffälligkeiten, hinter denen sehr oft noch dazu theologisch-sachliche Differenzen zur paulinischen Theologie standen, stützt die These, daßi Phil 3.20f. auf Tradition beruht' (p.25). But our examination reveals that only a couple of expressions – κύριος 'Ιησοῦς Χριστός; ὑποτάξαι τὰ πάντα (and just possibly also the idea of waiting for the Saviour from heaven) – seem to be traditional. However, as we shall see in more detail later, the idea in the ὅς-clause of Phil 3.21 is uniquely Pauline. So Becker's conclusion, at which he arrives through such arbitrary arguments, can hardly be sustained.

When Güttgemanns (pp.244ff.) and Becker (p.28) claim to find more theological differences between the passage and Paul, we again witness the extent to which'exegetes' can become arbitrary. According to Güttgemanns, there are three differences. First, in contrast to Paul's statements elsewhere the raising of the Christians is here attributed to Christ. But Güttgemanns himself adds: 'In bezug auf 1.Kor. 15,44ff. muß das (i.e., the alleged difference) jedoch etwas eingeschränkt werden . . . ' (p.244, n.26). It should not only be 'eingeschränkt' but completely withdrawn. We may set aside the fact that Phil 3.21, strictly speaking, does not refer to the *resurrection* of the Christians as such but their transformation at the parousia, in which Christ is the active agent, and that the thought of Christ being the agent in transforming the Christians into his image is already present in 2Cor 3.18. Even if we concede that Phil 3.21 speaks of Christ as the agent of Christians' resurrection, the idea should not be judged as strange to Paul at all. For already in 1Cor 15.45 Paul designates Christ, the Last Adam, πνεῦμα ζωοποιοῦν. The second difference Güttgemanns alleges is: 'The verses do not differentiate, as Paul does elsewhere, between the fate of the living and the dead Christians at the time of the parousia; they think only of the former. They use here for the process of resurrection the expressions which stem from the Hellenistic mystery-religions, whereas Paul elsewhere uses ἀλλάττεσθαι in reference to the living'. But surely Gnilka points out correctly the arbitrariness of this sort of argument: 'Die dem Soter zugesprochene Verwandlung = Umschaffung wird man im Blick des Paulus auf die Lebenden, d.h., bis zur Parusie Übrigbleibenden, beschränken müssen, so daß es nicht zutrifft, wenn man sagt, Paulus (in Phil 3.21) differenziere nicht zwischen Verwandlung und Auferweckung, vielmehr ist ihm letztere im konkreten Zusammenhang nicht erwähnenswert' (*Phil.*, p.209). μετασχηματίζειν or συμμόρφωσις, whether originally from mystery language or not, is an important concept in Paul. Ἀλλάττεσθαι (1Cor 15.51) is a general concept of the eschatological change whose specific concept is μεταμορφοῦσθαι into the image of Christ. In view of what has just been said the third difference which Güttgemanns alleges proves untenable: 'Phil 3,20f. scheinen im Unterschied zur sonstigen Auffassung des Paulus die Auferweckung nicht als eine völlige Neuschöpfung, sondern als eine Umschaffung der alten Leiblichkeit aufzufassen, womit sie sich ebenfalls stärker an die Theologie der hellenistischen Gemeinde anlehnen'. Does not Paul in 1Cor 15.51ff. speak of the resurrection body as a *changed* (ἀλλάττεσθαι) body? For Paul it is assumed, as we shall see later, that the resurrection body = the body conformed to that of Christ = new creation. So Güttgemanns' assertion is doubly untenable and demonstrates his presumption when he demands that others provide 'Begründung' for his absurd 'Beobachtung'. Further, his appeal to 'the theology of the Hellenistic Church' at this point is an appeal to a ghost! We turn now to examine some other quite implausible claims by Becker (p.28). According to him, since Paul demands that the Church, in contrast to 'the enemies of the cross' whose minds are set on the earthly things, should imitate him who 'presses on toward the goal for the prize of the upward call of God in Christ Jesus' (Phil 3.14), v.20 would have been enough for Paul's purpose here in the context. 'Was in v.21 folgt, ist weder vom Gedankengang her erwartet noch gefordert'. Against this arbitrary argument we would simply say that v.21 is necessary to bring out the concrete blessing implied in v.20, upon which the suffering Christians on earth can set their hope over against 'the enemies of the cross'. Becker argues that in contrast to Phil 3.2–15 which is characterized by Paul's *theologia crucis* and his existential attitude in the tension between *Heilsgegenwart* and *Heilszukunft*, Phil 3.20f. has neither *theologia crucis* nor the dialectic between the present and the future. There is no mention of the righteousness of

God. The cross and the resurrection of Christ are neither mentioned nor alluded to. Rather there is only a futuristic soteriology which is developed from the idea of exaltation as in 1Th 1.10b. So, as 1Th 1.10b, Phil 3.20f. should be declared pre-Pauline. We have reproduced Becker's last argument in length, just to show in closing how arbitrary the method of his entire argumentation is. For the last argument can only be put forward by one who *presupposes* that Phil 3.20f. is a pre-Pauline hymn cited by Paul here and which therefore originally had nothing to do with the preceding verses. But that Phil 3.20f. is a self-contained pre-Pauline hymn − that must first be *proved*! If Phil 3.20f. is read in the context without that presupposition, it fits the context well and exhibits the typical Pauline theology: the present dialectic of the Christian existence between the firstfruits of salvation already obtained and the still continuing suffering finally giving way to the eschatological consummation of salvation (cf., e.g., Rom 8; 2Cor 4.7−5.5). We would urge Becker to take two verses each time from Paul's letters throughout and see how often he can find there all or even one of the marks of Paul's theology that he enumerates: the cross and the resurrection of Christ, the righteousness of God, *theologia crucis*, the dialectic between the present and the future . . . . And we would ask him whether he would take, e.g., Rom 12.1f.; 13.11−14; 1Cor 13.11−13; 15.53f. . . . as pre-Pauline because they unfortunately fail to contain above points. When Güttgemanns (p.245) and Becker (pp.25, 28) speak of the theological differences, even tension, between Paul and Phil 3.20f. in order to claim the latter as a pre-Pauline hymn, they follow the standard practice of modern critics who look for pre-Pauline formulae in Paul. But they never seem to ask themselves the most obvious question: Why at all does Paul cite the allegedly pre-Pauline formulae which are so evidently different from his own theology? Was Paul too stupid to see the differences which the modern critics (who are often determined to be more Pauline than Paul himself, to be sure) can so easily find for him?

Thus the arguments of Güttgemanns and Becker from the form, language and ideas of Phil 3.20f. for the view that the passage is pre-Pauline and a pre-Pauline hymn, are completely without foundation. The passage is Paul's own composition[1].

Finally, Rom 8.29 is also claimed by some critics as pre-Pauline[2]. The arguments on the grounds of language, style and content for the view that Rom 8.29f. is pre-Pauline are by no means certain. The argument from the words, προγωώσκειν, προορίζειν, πρωτότοκος and δοξάζειν (in the sense of Rom 8.30), are indecisive. For these are rare in the entire NT. The very fact that Paul uses προγωώσκειν and προορίζειν elsewhere (Rom 11.2; 1Cor 2.7;

---

[1]So Luz, *Geschichtsverständnis*, p.312; Gnilka, *Phil.*, pp.208ff., whose presumption that Paul took over the idea of transformation of man from the preaching of his opponents in order to correct it, is, however, baseless. See now also R.H. Gundry, *Sôma in Biblical Theology* (1976), pp.178−82.

[2]Jervell, *Imago*, p.272; K.Grayston, 'The Doctrine of Election in Romans 8.28−30', *StEv* ii, *TU* 87 (1964), pp.576f.; G.Schille, *Frühchristliche Hymnen* (1965), pp.89f.; Luz, *Geschichtsverständnis*, pp.250ff.; P.v.d. Osten-Sacken, *Römer 8 als Beispiel paulinischer Soteriologie* (1975), pp.67ff.; Käsemann, *Römer*, p.233.

Eph 1.5, 11) indicates that they are not strange to him. So U. Luz is quite unwarranted in so lightly discarding the Pauline character of the language here by saying: 'Von den verwendeten Verben (i.e., 5 including εἶναι) ist nur καλέω und δικαιόω paulinisch'[1]. The argument from content is equally unconvincing. Schille's claim that, whereas for Paul the becoming like Christ of the baptized persons refers only to their dying with him, in 8.29f there is no mention of death, is completely wrong in view of 1Cor 15.49; 2Cor 3.18; Phil 3.20f. etc[2]. Luz's argument that while Paul expected συμμόρφωσις and glorification in the future, the tradition cited by Paul here perhaps with its aorist thought of them as a present event[3], is also untenable. For Paul not only thinks of συμμόρφωσις and glorification as the *present* process (2Cor 3.18), but also knows that 'if any man is in Christ he *is* a new creation' (2Cor 5.17)[4]. Even the argument from style, that it looks like a (liturgical) formula or hymn[5], is not decisive. For there is no reason why Paul himself could not have produced a liturgical formula.

The only argument that seems capable of indicating that Rom 8.29f. is traditional material, whether originally composed by Paul or not, is the consideration of the sorites in the context. First, it is clearly recognisable that v.29bc (συμμόρφους τῆς εἰκόνος τοῦ υἱοῦ αὐτοῦ, εἰς τὸ εἶναι αὐτὸν πρωτότοκον ἐν πολλοῖς ἀδελφοῖς) breaks into the sorites[6]. This leads one to think that the sorites was originally a separate self-contained tradition[7] and that Paul cites it here inserting v.29bc into it. For this view three more

---

[1]Luz, *op. cit.*, p.251.

[2]So Osten-Sacken, *op. cit.*, p.67 (n.29) against Schille, *op. cit.*, p.89(n.7).

[3]Luz, *op. cit.*, p.251.

[4]Cf. Osten-Sacken, *op. cit.*, p.67(n.29), 279ff. against Luz. It is strange that, having repudiated the arguments of Luz and Schille from content, Osten-Sacken adopts their conclusion.

[5]Schille, *op. cit.*, p.89(n.8); Luz, *op. cit.*, p.251., Kasemann, *Römer*, p. 233; Osten-Sacken, *op. cit.*, p.68.

[6]So Grayston, *op. cit.*, p.578; Luz, *op. cit.*, pp.251f.; Osten-Sacken, *op. cit.*, p.68.

[7]It probably runs:

ὅτι	οὕς	προέγνω,	
		(τούτους καὶ)	προώρισεν·
	οὕς δὲ	προώρισεν,	
		τούτους καὶ	ἐκάλεσεν·
καὶ	οὕς	ἐκάλεσεν,	
		τούτους καὶ	ἐδικαίωσεν·
	οὕς δὲ	ἐδικαίωσεν,	
		τούτους καὶ	ἐδόξασεν

observations have been made: the recitative ὅτι and anacoluthon character of the clause[1]; οἴδαμεν . . . in v.28[2]; and that vs. 29f. are spoken in the third person whereas before and after them in the first person[3]. In view of the clear Pauline elements (καλεῖν; δικαιοῦν), not to mention the rest of the sorites which are, to say the least, not incompatible with Paul's theology and vocabulary, as shown above, Paul may have composed the original sorites or at least contributed to the formation of it theologically and conceptually in the early Church[4]. However, our immediate concern is with the authorship of v.29bc. Luz and Osten-Sacken argue that the inserted phrase is also originally pre-Pauline traditional material, Luz pointing to Col 1.13—20 and Osten-Sacken to the 'bereits als traditionell erwiesenen Passus Phil 3,20f.'[5] The rationale behind Luz's pointing to Col 1.13—20 here is undoubtedly that in his view Col 1.13—20 is pre-Pauline. But is he prepared to regard the hymn as strictly pre-Pauline, i.e., as stemming from the period before Paul's conversion (32—34 A.D.)? If not, even if Col 1.13—20 were non-Pauline (which we have denied above), is it not possible that Paul introduced Εἰκών-Christology into the early Church and that the hymn reflects it?[6] This is not merely a theoretical possibility, since, as we have seen, Εἰκών-Christology and the idea of the Christian's transformation into the image of Christ occur

---

[1] Schille, *op. cit.*, p.90; Luz, *op. cit.*, p.251.

[2] Jervell, *Imago*, p.272; Grayston, *op. cit.*, pp.575ff.; Schille, *op. cit.*, p.90.

[3] Luz, *op. cit.*, p.251; Jervell, *Imago*, p.272.

[4] *Pace* Grayston, *op. cit.*, pp.576f. Cf. F.Hahn, 'Taufe und Rechtfertigung', *Rechtfertigung*, Käsemann FS, ed. J.Friedrich *et al.* (1976), pp.115f. Before one jumps to the conclusion that this or that formula is pre-Pauline one has to take heed of Hengel, who points out the most salient fact that Paul was there in the early Church right from the beginning (c. 32—34 A.D.), and ask with him: 'ob und wieweit der Paulus der dunklen 14—16 Jahre vor dem Apostelkonzil als schriftgelehrte theologische Autorität selbst an der Herausbildung derartiger Formeln aktiv mitwirkte bzw. wieweit er wirklich *fremdes* Gut übernahm' ('Christologie', p.46. Emphasis by H.).

[5] Luz, *op. cit.*, pp.251f.; Osten-Sacken, *op. cit.*, pp.73f. (quotation in p.73). The latter appeals to Güttgemanns and Becker, for whose view that Phil 3.20f. is a pre-Pauline hymn, however, we have found only fabricated evidence. In order to claim 2Cor 3.18 also as pre-Pauline, Osten-Sacken appeals further to S.Schulz, 'Die Decke des Moses', *ZNW* 49 (1958), 18ff., for whose thesis van Unnik has found 'not a shred of evidence' (' "With Unveiled Face" (2Cor. iii. 12—18)' *Sparsa Collecta*, p.197).

[6] Here again Hengel's sober remark must be taken seriously, especially by those who mean to identify pre-Pauline concepts and formulae just by pointing to their occurrences elsewhere: 'Der Aufweis, daß einzelne christologische und soteriologische Formulierungen auch in einem — stets späteren — außerpaulinischen Kontext erscheinen, reicht noch nicht aus, um sie eo ipso als "vorpaulinisch", d.h. dem Apostel ursprünglich fremdes Gut zu identifizieren' ('Christologie', p.46).

only in the Pauline corpus, and often at that. Even setting aside the passages which we have examined so far, there are passages like 1Cor 15.49; Gal 4.19; Phil 3.10 (cf. also Rom 6.5) which contain the idea and yet are not (or, shall we say more guardedly, not yet, at least in our knowledge) disputed of their Pauline authorship. Another idea implied in Rom 8.29bc, namely the relationship between Christ, the Son of God, and the Christians, the adopted sons of God, in terms of brothers, is also typically Pauline (Gal 3.26–4.7; Rom 8.14ff.)[1]. So it is evident that Rom 8.29bc, if not the rest of Rom 8.29–30, is Pauline[2].

With this we conclude that Εἰκών-Christology and the idea of the Christians' transformation into the image of Christ are distinctively Pauline.

2) Various Suggestions on the Origin of the Conception

The question now arises how Paul came to designate Christ as the εἰκών τοῦ θεοῦ and develop the soteriological conception of the redeemed being conformed to or transformed into the image of Christ. According to E. Larsson, the OT conception of the Messiah as the special bearer of the divine image and the later Jewish development of the conception in the speculations on the Son of Man and Wisdom form the background for Paul's Εἰκών-Christology[3]. If indeed the OT and Judaism did conceive of the Messiah as the special bearer of the divine image, it would, of course, be perfectly clear how Paul, having recognized Jesus of Nazareth as the Messiah, could have transferred the title εἰκών τοῦ θεοῦ to Jesus Christ. But unfortunately this was not the case[4]. In the absence of any reference in the OT to the Messiah or the messianic figure as the image of God, Larsson appeals to Ps 8.4ff.; 2.7; 110.1; 45.6f. and even to Ezek 28 in order to claim that the king or the Messianic King had ascribed to him a special divine image. It is true that Paul along with others in the early Church interprets Ps 8.4ff. and 110.1 Christologically to refer to Christ (e.g., 1Cor 15.25ff.)[5]. However, the question is: Does Ps 8.4ff. really speak of 'man' or 'son of man', who was later Christologically understood, as the image of God? Certainly it alludes to the Genesis account of the creation of Adam[6] and refers to the honour, glory and dominion given to him which

---

[1]So Hengel, *Sohn*, p.24. As we have seen, the same idea appears in Heb 2.10ff. But *traditionsgeschichtlich* Heb. may be reflecting the Pauline influence.

[2]So Grayston, *op. cit.*, p.578; cf. also H. Paulsen, *Überlieferung und Auslegung in Römer 8* (1974), pp.159f.

[3]E.Larsson, *Vorbild*, pp.138, 170ff.

[4]So Jervell, *Imago*, p.119.

[5]See C.H.Dodd, *According to the Scriptures* (1952), pp.32ff.

[6]H.J.Kraus, *Psalmen I* (1961), pp.67ff.; A.A.Anderson, *The Book of Psalms i* (1972),

are closely associated with the idea of the image of God[1]. But is it conceivable that Paul came to designate Jesus Christ as the εἰκὼν τοῦ θεοῦ on the basis of Ps 8.4–6? If Ps 8.4ff. is an insufficient ground for the presumption that in the OT there is a conception of the Messiah as the special bearer of the divine image, Ps 2.7; 45.6f. and 110.1 provide even less ground. An appeal to Ezek 28 for this view seems a last desperate recourse. Larsson argues that the conception of the King-Messiah as the bearer of the divine image continues in the idea of the Son of Man, which he considers to be 'a special form of the OT messianism'[2]. Quite apart from the disputed question whether there was indeed a messianic conception of *the* Son of Man in the OT and Judaism before Jesus[3], this view is untenable because there is no evidence that the Son of Man was ever designated as the image of God[4]. It is true that the personified Wisdom is designated as the image of God (Wis 7.25ff.), and Paul's conception of Christ as the pre-existent Wisdom forms, as we shall see later in detail, one of the two components of his Εἰκών-Christology, the other being his conception of Christ as the Last Adam. But Larsson's attempt to make a straight line of what he calls 'die messianische Gottebenbildlichkeit', beginning from the conception of King-Messiah in the OT and proceeding through the figure of Son of Man to the personified Wisdom by identifying them with one another[5], is too daring. We have already rejected the attempt to see in the pre-Christian Judaism, on the one hand, the figure of the Messiah and that of Wisdom merged, and, on the other, Son of Man and Wisdom *identified* with each other[6]. So Larsson's attempt to explain Paul's conception of Christ as the εἰκὼν τοῦ θεοῦ in terms of the alleged OT-Jewish conception of Messiah as the special bearer of the divine image is not successful[7].

---

pp.100ff.; F.H.Borsch, *The Son of Man in Myth and History* (1967), p.114.

[1]Cf. G.v.Rad, εἰκών, *TDNT* ii, p.391; Jervell, *Imago*, pp.100ff.

[2]Larsson, *Vorbild*, pp.121ff. (122), 128ff.

[3]*Infra* pp.248f.

[4]*Contra.* Larsson, *Vorbild*, p.122. For another way of looking at the association of the epiphanic term 'one like a son of man' with the concept of 'image of God' see below pp.205–223.

[5]*Ibid.*, pp.130ff.

[6]*Supra* pp.122f. *Infra* pp.239ff. for a more precise definition of their connection.

[7]Equally untenable is the bold assertion: 'Im spätjüdischen Material finden wir . . . – wie im AT – Vorstellungen von einer abgebildeten Gottebenbildlichkeit. Das Volk Gottes (die Frommen, die Weisen) erhält durch seine Verbindung mit dem Menschensohn resp. mit der Weisheit teil an der Gottebenbildlichkeit, deren Träger diese "Messiasgestalten" sind' (*Vorbild*, p.148).

Since the concept εἰκών τοῦ θεοῦ is reminiscent of the Genesis account of God's creation of Adam (Gen 1.26) and Paul designates Christ as the Last Adam (1Cor 15.45), it has often been suggested that his designation of Christ as the εἰκών τοῦ θεοῦ is part of his Adam-Christology and is based on Gen 1.26[1]. As will be seen in more detail below, the two conceptions are closely related to each other. The question is, however: which was prior in the sequence of Paul's thought? Was it, as assumed by many, the conception of Christ as the Last Adam that led Paul to designate Christ as the εἰκών τοῦ θεοῦ? Could it not have been the other way round? This question can be settled only by an examination of the still disputed question of the background of Paul's Adam-Christology.

Before going into that question, however, we must note that some scholars believe it is Paul's Wisdom-Christology that lies behind his conception of Christ as the image of God[2]. This belief is based on the fact that in Hellenistic Judaism Wisdom is designated as the image of God (Wis 7.26)[3] and that Paul conceives of Christ as the personified divine Wisdom. Indeed, we shall see that the conception of Christ as the Εἰκών of God is just as closely related to Wisdom-Christology as to Adam-Christology in Paul. In order to explain the elements of Adam-Christology in Paul's Εἰκών-Christology those who suggest the Wisdom speculation as the background for the latter appeal to Philo, who sometimes seems to identify the Logos with the heavenly Anthropos[4]. But Philo's heavenly, incorporeal Anthropos is not to be identified with the *Gnostic* Anthropos; and so it is not warranted to claim Philo as a witness to the merger of the figures of Wisdom and the Gnostic Anthropos in Hellenistic Judaism and then to derive Paul's Εἰκών-Christology from that background[5]. With his identification of the Logos with the heavenly Anthropos of Gen 1.26f., Philo rather illustrates the milieu in which Paul's

---

[1] A.E.J.Rawlinson, *The NT Doctrine of the Christ* (1926), p.132; G.Kittel, εἰκών, *TDNT* ii, pp.395f.; M.Black, 'The Pauline Doctrine of the Second Adam' *SJT* 7 (1954), pp.174ff.; Scroggs, *The Last Adam* (1966), p.97ff.; also Jervell, *Imago*, pp.174f., 200f. (but on p.217 he seems to contradict himself).

[2] Windisch, *2.Kor.*, p.237; Eltester, *Eikon*, pp.133f; Hengel, *Sohn*, p.118.

[3] See also Philo, *Leg. Alleg.*, i.43. See further *Op. Mund.* 24; *Leg. Alleg.* iii. 96; *Plant.* 18–20; *Conf. Ling.* 97, 147; *Fuga* 101, where the divine Logos is designated as the εἰκών of God. Against the usual view that in Philo the Logos and Sophia are identified (e.g., Jervell, *Imago*, p.69), A.J.M.Wedderburn maintains that 'although there is some overlap between the concepts and their backgrounds, they are by no means interchangeable' ('Philo's "Heavenly Man" ', *NovT* 15 (1973), pp.321f.).

[4] Eltester, *Eikon*, pp.139ff.; Hengel, *Sohn*, p.118; cf. also Dibelius-Greeven, *Kol.*, pp.8f., 10f.; E.Brandenburger, *Adam und Christus* (1962), p.118.

[5] *Infra* p.172, n.2.

conception of Christ as the divine Wisdom, the Εἰκών of God, could easily develop an association between Christ and Adam of Gen 1.26f.[1] If Paul derived his conception of Christ as the Εἰκών of God from his Wisdom-Christology, we can relate both that conception and Adam-Christology to the Damascus event. For, as we have already seen, Paul's Wisdom-Christology is rooted in the Damascus experience. However, we believe that there are strong grounds for linking the conception of Christ as the Εἰκών of God and as the Last Adam directly with the Damascus Christophany. When these grounds are set out, the evidence which Wisdom-Christology provides for the indirect link between them will serve merely as a confirmation.

3) Hypotheses on the Origin of Adam-Christology

However, before setting out these grounds we must take up the question of the background of Paul's Adam-Christology. First to be mentioned is the once influential suggestion that Paul's Adam-Christology is based on the Gnostic *Urmensch*-redeemer myth which spoke of the *Urmensch*, the divine ἄνθρωπος, his fall into matter and redemption from it. This view was pioneered by the *Religionsgeschichtliche Schule*, especially its most influential members, R. Reitzenstein and W. Bousset[2], and made an essential presupposition by R. Bultmann and his pupils[3] in their interpretation of the NT. But this hypothesis of the Gnostic *Urmensch*-redeemer myth or 'redeemed redeemer myth' has recently been subjected to searching criticisms[4]; and the myth has proved to be a modern construction produced from mosaics of various origins. C. Colpe has succinctly put the result of his examination of the 'myth':

> The formula 'redeemed redeemer' (this in various senses at that) and '*Urmensch*-redeemer' can be obtained only when the various processes of hypostatization are ignored through which a) the *Urmensch* is separated from the redeemer, b) the various redeemer figures are separated from one another and from the *Urmensch*, c)

---

[1] So Hengel, *Sohn*, p.118.

[2] E.g., R.Reitzenstein, *Die hellenistischen Mysterienreligionen* ([3]1927), pp.348f., 423; W.Bousset, *Kyrios Christos* ([2]192i), pp.140ff.

[3] E.g., Bultmann, *Theology* i, pp.174ff., 251, 289f.; E.Käsemann, *Leib und Leib Christi* (1933), pp.163ff.; G.Bornkamm, *Ges. Aufsätze* i, p.83; *Paulus*, p.135. For a historical account of the development of this hypothesis see Colpe, *Schule*, ch. 1 (pp. 9–68); also Schenke, *Gott "Mensch"*, ch. 2 (pp.16–33).

[4] A *full-scale* examination of the hypothesis is the subject of Colpe's book *Die religionsgeschichtliche Schule*, as its subtitle indicates: 'Darstellung und Kritik ihres Bildes vom gnostischen Erlösermythus'. See also Schenke, *Gott "Mensch"*, more generally also R.McL.Wilson, *The Gnostic Problem* (1958); E.M.Yamauchi, *Pre-Christian Gnosticism* (1973).

the redeeming light-substance above and that to be redeemed below are separated from each other, d) these two light-substances are separated from each other and the various redeemer figures. . . . If the hypostases are left separated, as the texts offer them, and are not identified, then the formulae '*Urmensch*-redeemer' and 'redeemed redeemer' can be seen only in a few cases.[1]

He exposes the hypothesis as falsely claiming:

The gnostic redeemer myth arose sometime in the distant past somewhere in the vast reaches of the Orient, which can only be imagined a little more precisely as 'Iran'; then wandered through space and time, in order to leave behind a few mosaic pieces now in this, now in that circle of tradition, e.g., in Wisdom poetry, Philo, Adam-speculation and apocalypticism, then grew together once again in a grand unity in Manichaeism and with the Mandeans finally disintegrated into its components.[2]

So Colpe does not think that the formula is a hermeneutically correct or suitable category in studies of Gnosticism[3]. While recognizing that the *Urmensch* (in the sense of 'heavenly', 'inner' man) in Gnosticism is an expression of speculation about self[4], and being open to the possibility that this *Urmensch* figure, like other hypostases of self or spirit, might have obtained the redeemer function independently of the figure of Jesus Christ[5], Colpe nevertheless denies that there is any evidence for a pre-Christian Gnostic conception of the *Urmensch* redeemer[6]. This confirms, though critically, the results of earlier scholars who insisted that there was no pre-Christian Gnostic Anthropos redeemer and that in fact the emergence of the figure of Jesus Christ acted as the catalyst for the precipitation of various previously suspended elements into the figure of the Gnostic Anthropos redeemer[7]. Colpe's conclusion is in turn confirmed by subsequent investigations[8]. So it

---

[1]Colpe, *Schule*, p.185.

[2]*Ibid.*, p.191.

[3]*Ibid.*, p.189.

[4]Cf. G.Quispel, 'Der gnostische Anthropos und die jüdische Tradition', *Gnostic Studies* I (1974), pp.173–195; Schenke, *Gott "Mensch"*, pp.69ff.

[5]Colpe, *Schule*, pp.205ff. (also p.202, n.1)

[6]Cf. *ibid.*, p.207; more definitely in his 'Gnosis', *RGG*[3] ii, 1652, and in 'NT and Gnostic Christology', *Religions in Antiquity*, Essays in Memory of E.R.Goodenough, ed. J.Neusner (1968), p.235.

[7]E.g., Quispel, *op. cit.*, p.195; Wilson, *Problem, passim* (esp. pp.218–28); E. Schweizer, *Lordship and Discipleship* (1960), pp.125ff. See also A.D.Nock, 'Gnosticism', *Arthur Darby Nock: Essays on Religion and the Ancient World* (1972), pp.956ff.; Schenke, *Gott "Mensch"*, pp.148, 155; Jervell, *Imago*, pp.145f. (n.91).

[8]In *Schule*, referring to the traditions of Simon Magus (p.202, n.2) and the Hymn of the Pearl in Acts of Thomas (p.207), Colpe keeps himself open to the possibility that independent of and, in the case of the former, prior to the NT figure of Jesus Christ, a

is not surprising, but nevertheless revealing, to find that E. Käsemann, once a champion of the Gnostic redeemer-myth, now recognizes that for the reconstruction of the myth 'reference was made almost throughout to post-Christian, contradictory material' and concedes:

> The debate is at the moment characterized *religionsgeschichtlich* through two negative results: the myth of the 'redeemed redeemer' does not form the centre of a pre- and non-Christian Gnosticism . . . However the fact thus envisaged but by no means exactly clarified may stand, secondly, Pauline and Deutero-Pauline Adam-Christ typology in its central problem is not comprehended from it, let alone solved. For Adam and Christ remain here as antipodes who are in no way related through original consubstantiality[1].

Nevertheless, appeal is continually made to the Gnostic background in order to explain Paul's Adam-Christ typology. This is typified by E. Brandenburger, who has provided what is to date the most extensive 'exegetical-*religionsgeschichtliche* investigation into Rom 5.12–21 (1Cor 15)'[2]. His fundamental thesis is that the Adam-Christ typology was no original construction of Paul, but his adoption and adaptation of the two Adam-Anthropoi doctrine which his opponents in Corinth held[3].

According to Brandenburger, the Corinthian heretics held a doctrine of resurrection similar to that of Hymenaeus and Philetus, namely that ἀνάστασιν ἤδη γεγονέναι (2Tim 2.18). This expressed their consciousness of present perfection or of 'possessing an indestructible spiritual nature or gnosis'[4]. That is why Paul, countering this enthusiasm, does not complete the antithetical correspondence in 1Cor 15.21f. with καὶ δι' ἀνθρώπου ζωή, but breaks it through the future ζωοποιηθήσονται in v.22b. From this Brandenburger presumes that Paul changes a given idea of correspondence against the Corinthian enthusiasts. 'The presumption becomes a certainty', writes Brandenburger, 'when one sees how the two πάντες, which correspond to the

---

Gnostic redeemer myth could have arisen. But recent critical investigations have shown that neither the Samaritan Simon of Acts 8 nor the third c. Manichaean Hymn of the Pearl is a witness to a pre-Christian Gnosticism: see Bergmeier, 'Quellen vorchristlicher Gnosis', *Tradition und Glaube*, K.G.Kuhn FS (1971), pp.200–21; K.Beyschlag, 'Zur Simon-Magus-Frage', *ZThK* 68 (1971), pp.395–426; also his *Simon Magus und die christliche Gnosis* (1974).

[1]Käsemann, *Römer*, pp.134f.

[2]E.Brandenburger, *Adam und Christus*.

[3]*Ibid.*, pp.68–157. This thesis is 'unwiderlegbar', according to U.Wilckens, 'Christus, der "letzte Adam", und der Menschensohn', *Jesus und der Menschensohn*, A.Vögtle FS (1975), p.389. Hamerton-Kelly, *Pre-Existence*, pp.132–143, also accepts it and follows Brandenburger's interpretation of 1Cor 15 closely.

[4]Brandenburger, *Adam*, pp.70f.

schema, are not only unnecessary in the context of Paul's foregoing argument, but the πάντες in v.22b in this form of statement stands actually opposed to Paul's preaching elsewhere'1.

In 1Cor 15.35–49, against the question of πῶς and ποίῳ σώματι, which was designed to ridicule Paul's teaching of bodily resurrection, Paul seeks to prove that a σῶμα πνευματικόν exists and that we the Christians will bear this spiritual body as we now bear the earthly physical body. He first of all proves the existence of 'a second or last heavenly spiritual Adam-Anthropos' from Gen 2.7[2]. But this Scriptural proof rests on two presuppositions: first, the decisive words πρῶτος and 'Αδάμ inserted into the text; and secondly, the presupposition vital to Paul's inference: ὁ ἔσχατος 'Αδάμ εἰς πνεῦμα ζωοποιοῦν (v.45b), namely the existence of two contrasting Adam-Anthropoi and the associated contrast of ψυχή and πνεῦμα[3]. This proof could be convincing only if the second presupposition was recognized also in Corinth. That it was is confirmed by the parenthetical statement in v.46, which is polemical. From this two points become clear: 1) for the τινες in Corinth the spiritual or the spiritual-heavenly Adam-Anthropos was the first – both in quality and in ontological order – while the physical-earthly-somatic was the deprecated second. 2) Paul shares the language and conception with the Corinthian heretics, so that they can serve as the basis of the argumentation. At the same time, however, he corrects the background of the conception and brings about in content a rupture of it[4].

So Brandenburger proposes to investigate the *religionsgeschichtliche* material first of all for the motifs in 1Cor 15.42ff. The witnesses he introduces are mostly post-Christian, from the second century and later, and there are very few from the first century. But this is of little consequence, for Brandenburger will argue mainly from those texts which somehow point to the Hellenistic Jewish milieu, then from those pagan sources not influenced by Christianity, and finally from the Christian witnesses which show the conception clearly as pre- or non-Christian[5]. Brandenburger then investigates 'the Jewish Gnosticising Prayers' in the magical papyri[6], the tradition of Zosimus, the Naassene Sermon, the Apocryphon of John, the Poimandres,

---

[1]*Ibid.*, p.72.

[2]*Ibid.*, p.73.

[3]*Ibid.*, pp.73f.

[4]*Ibid.*, pp.74f.

[5]*Ibid.*, pp.76f.

[6]K.Preisendanz ed. and tr., *Papyri Graecae Magicae I* ([2]1973), pp.12f. (I. 195–222), 112–115 (IV. 1167–1227).

two Christian Gnostic documents from Nag-Hammadi: the Hypostasis of the Archons and On the Origin of the World, and the Mandaean texts[1]. These texts, according to Brandenburger, have made visible a world of speculation which corresponds in essential lines to the background of 1Cor 15.45ff.[2] But this *Vorstellungswelt* is independent of 1Cor 15.45ff. and of any specifically Christian world of thought. So a common background is to be sought for both 1Cor 15.45ff. and the older traditions underlying those texts[3].

Then, under the heading 'Vor- und Frühformen im Spätjudentum', Brandenburger refers to some Jewish texts, most of which are pre-Christian. The Qumran writings (1QS 4.23; 1QH 17.15; CD 3.20) with a reference to כבוד אדם as a blessing for the elect, presuppose 'certain Adam-speculations'[4]. Behind Wis 10.1f. there stands an Adam-speculation similar to that in the Jewish Gnosticising Prayers[5]. In the idea of Adam's fall and return to the paradise in Vita Adae et Evae and the Apocalypse of Moses and in the idea of Enoch's ascension to be the Son of Man in 1En 71 (and 2En 21f.) Brandenburger traces an Adam speculation similar to those of the above mentioned Gnostic documents[6]. However, Brandenburger finds the most important pre-Christian witnesses to an Adam-Anthropos speculation in Philo. In *Op. Mund.* 134ff. he detects a Gnosticising background akin to that of Corp. Herm. I, XIII and the Mithras Liturgy[7]. Philo's conception of the heavenly Anthropos as a Platonic idea is a secondary interpretation of the Gnostic Adam-Anthropos, as *Leg. Alleg.* i.31f. shows[8]. Some mystery terms appearing in connection with the Adam-Anthropos speculation lead Brandenburger to conclude that there were milieux around Philo and the Hellenistic Judaism represented by him which were determined through mystery speculations and Gnostic thoughts and in which there were Gnostic Adam-Anthropos speculations[9]. Finally, in an excursus, Brandenburger discusses briefly the figure of 'Son of Man' in Dan 7, 4Ezra 13 and 1En (except chs. 70f.) and Jewish speculations on Adam, which tend to glorify Adam, and in both Brandenburger would like to see the influence of Gnostic Adam-Anthropos

---

[1]Brandenburger, *Adam*, pp.77–109.

[2]*Ibid.*, p.109.

[3]*Ibid.*, p.109.

[4]*Ibid.*, p.111.

[5]*Ibid.*, pp.112f.

[6]*Ibid.*, pp.113–117.

[7]*Ibid.*, pp.117–121.

[8]*Ibid.*, pp.122ff.

[9]*Ibid.*, pp.129ff.

specualtions[1].

Turning specifically to the question of the background of 1Cor 15.21f., 48f., Brandenburger points out three features: 1) the χοϊκοί and the ἐπου-ράνιοι are of the same substance as the ἄνθρωπος ἐκ γῆς and the ἄνθρω-πος ἐξ οὐρανοῦ respectively (v.48); 2) they bear their respective image (v.49); and 3) they exist in their respective Anthropos – ἐν τῷ Ἀδάμ or ἐν τῷ Χριστῷ (v.22)[2]. Dismissing the OT-Jewish idea of a *Stammvater* bringing fateful consequences upon his descendents, and the Rabbinic conception of Adam as גּוּף of souls, as irrelevant to 1Cor 15[3], Brandenburger finds the background for the three features in those texts where he earlier found the Gnostic Adam-Anthropos speculations. The texts (together with Od. Sol.) relate in various ways the following idea:

> To the ontological determination of man through the essential unity with the infer-ior Adam-Anthropos, through 'bearing' of the earthly phyiscal Adam-eikon or through being in the mortifying Adam-soma, there corresponds positively the essen-tial determination (of man) through identification with the heavenly-spiritual Adam-Anthropos. The ideas of the redemptive existence in the heavenly Anthropos or of bearing his eikon are in fact only variations of that fundamental idea[4].

Brandenburger's last step is to square the redemptive roles of the Anthro-pos in 1Cor 15 and Rom 5 with that of the Gnostic texts. The Anthropos of 1Cor 15.21 and Rom 5.12ff. has a definite earthly history. Ἄνθρωπος ἐξ οὐρανοῦ in 1Cor 15.47 indicates that the Corinthian Gnostics also thought of the heavenly Anthropos-redeemer's descent in the earthly-fleshly sphere. It is remarkable that in those Gnostic Anthropos speculations which are old-est and without Christian influence the redemptive function of the heavenly Adam-Anthropos is passive and limited to the heavenly world. After appar-ently reluctantly recognizing this fact, Brandenburger solves the problem by saying that in the Corinthian and other Christian forms of Gnosticism the figure of Christ was apparently drawn into the given schema of the pre-Christian Gnostic Adam-Anthropos – i.e., Christ 'was identified with the pre-existent first heavenly-spiritual Adam-Anthropos (1Cor 15.46!)'[5]. When this happened, the figure of Christ influenced the given soteriological speculation so that now it had to speak of the descent and ascent of the heavenly Anth-ropos-redeemer which inaugurated the redemptive event. Perhaps the early

---

[1] *Ibid.*, pp.131–139.

[2] *Ibid.*, pp.139f.

[3] *Ibid.*, pp.140–143.

[4] *Ibid.*, pp.143–151 (quotation p.147).

[5] *Ibid.*, p.155.

Christian understanding of Jesus as the 'Son of Man' also played a role in this. It is also possible that the Gnostic motif of the descent of messengers, 'helpers', and *sophia* played a role[1].

So, Brandenburger concludes that in 1Cor 15 and Rom 5 Paul adopted and adapted the Corinthian Christians' Gnostic Adam-Anthropos speculations which maintained:

> In the one fleshly-physical Anthropos the whole mankind is fatefully bound up to the mortal inferior sphere of existence, the sphere under the dominion of death and enslaving powers; but through the descent and ascent of the heavenly redeemer-Anthropos an event has been inaugurated, through which the totality of the men who are spiritual in origin and essence is redeemed into the heavenly-spiritual Anthropos[2].

Now, how convincing is this apparently impressive reconstruction? Very little. To begin with, on close scrutiny we find Brandenburger's attempt to infer from 1Cor 15.21ff. that Paul adopts and adapts the Corinthian Gnostic Christians' doctrine of two Adam-Anthropoi unconvincing. Brandenburger's assumption that when τινες in Corinth said 'ἀνάστασις οὐκ ἔστιν' (v.12) they meant something similar to 'ἀνάστασιν ἤδη γεγονέναι', is untenable. For, if so, why did Paul labour so hard in trying to prove the resurrection of Christ in 1Cor 15.20? The assumption stumbles, if nowhere else, at vs. 19 and 32[3]. So it is unwarranted to draw from this wrong assumption the far-reaching conclusion that, by substituting ζωοποιηθήσονται for ζωή in 1Cor 15.22, Paul corrects their own correspondence schema of two Adam-Anthropoi. Even if the assumption were right, we cannot allow Brandenburger's argument. For Paul does in fact neatly complete the antithetical parallelism in v.21:

ἐπειδὴ γὰρ δι' ἀνθρώπου θάνατος,
καὶ   δι' ἀνθρώπου ἀνάστασις νεκρῶν,

in which ἀνάστασις νεκρῶν surely means the same thing as ζωή or at least is as good an opposite concept to θάνατος as ζωή. Indeed it suits Paul's purpose better than ζωή, as he seeks to express that just as Adam, a man, has initiated death, so Christ, a man, has initiated the resurrection, i.e., the reversal of the fate which Adam has inflicted upon mankind. After all, is not ἀνάστασις νεκρῶν Paul's present subject? The future ζωοποιηθήσονται is

---

[1]*Ibid.*, pp.155f.

[2]*Ibid.*, p.157.

[3]So Conzelmann, *1.Kor.*, pp.309f. We need not discuss what we can only regard as a desperate resort, namely the suggestion that Paul 'misunderstood' the Corinthian Gnostics' position. See *ibid.*, p.310. Nor is it our concern here to discuss the whole thorny question of the heretics' position on resurrection. Conzelmann mentions all the major suggestions on this (pp.309ff.).

perfectly intelligible in terms of Paul's eschatology which sees the first-fruits (and therefore the guarantee) of the resurrection in the resurrection of Christ, but looks forward to the general resurrection of the Christians at the parousia (see 1Th 4.13ff.). There is here no question of Paul's correcting the Corinthians' realized eschatology expressed through the Gnostic Adam-Anthropos doctrine (see further the paragraph after the next).

While Brandenburger's judgement, that the two πάντες in v.22 are unnecessary in the context of Paul's argument, seems to reveal only his prejudice in holding that the schema of Adam-Christ correspondence was pre-Pauline, his view that the πάντες in v.22b is against Paul's usual teaching is hardly convincing. A proper understanding of the πάντες has already been supplied by C.K. Barrett in the context of Paul's universalistic and particularistic statements[1]. Rather than confirming Brandenburger's presumption that the Corinthian Gnostics held a schema of Adam-Christ correspondence, the two πάντες in v.22 seem, in fact, to repudiate it most effectively. For it is impossible to imagine that the Corinthian heretics, who according to Brandenburger were the same Gnostics throughout 1Cor.[2], could have said:

ὥσπερ ἐν τῷ Ἀδάμ   πάντες ἀποθνήσκουσιν

οὕτως καὶ ἐν τῷ Χριστῷ πάντες ζωοποιοῦνται (or ἔχουσιν ζωήν).

Does not the fact that the Corinthian heretics (Gnostics according to Brandenburger) apparently distinguished themselves as the πνευματικοί and τέλειοι from the others, the ψυχικοί, σάρκινοι or νήπιοι, who, be they non-Christians or 'weak' Christians, were thought to be without γνῶσις, σοφία and spiritual endowments (1Cor 2.6 – 3.4, 18; 8.1f.; etc.)[3], though not in the manner of the Valentinian Gnostics[4], militate against such a presumption? At any rate, it is inconceivable that the favourite phrase of Paul, ἐν τῷ Χριστῷ, attested from his earliest letter on, was something he took over from his Corinthian opponents and in c.54 A.D. at that![5]

Brandenburger's attempt, for the second time, to infer from 1Cor 15.35–49 that Paul adopts and adapts the Corinthian Gnostics' doctrine of two

---

[1]Barrett, *From First Adam to Last* (1962), pp.113f.; cf. also Wedderburn, 'The Theological Structure of Romans v.12', *NTS* 19(1972/73), pp.353f.

[2]Brandenburger, *Adam*, pp.70f. Our argument here is strictly on Brandenburger's own ground. If, as we believe (*supra* p.75.n.4), the Corinthian pneumatics were not Gnostics, the whole question does not arise in the first place.

[3]Wilckens, *Weisheit*, pp.81–91; σοφία, *TDNT* vii, pp.519ff.; Bornkamm, *Paulus* pp.88f.; B.A.Pearson, *The Pneumatikos-Psychikos Terminology in 1Corinthians* (1973), pp.27ff.; cf. also Bultmann, *Theology* i, pp.158, 180f.; Lietzmann-Kümmel, *Kor.*, p.171; Wendland, *Kor.*, pp.26, 28.

[4]See Pearson, *op. cit.*, pp.79ff.

[5]Cf. Scroggs, *Last Adam*, p.xx.

Adam-Anthropoi, stumbles likewise on his own presupposition. For, when he sees in v.45 Paul attempting to prove the existence of a σῶμα πνευματικόν by inferring from Gen 2.7 the sentence, ὁ ἔσχατος ᾿Αδὰμ εἰς πνεῦμα ζωοποιοῦν, or rather inserting it into the Genesis text, and says that Paul's proof could be convincing only if the Corinthians shared the presupposition that there were two contrasting Anthropoi, one the πνευματικός and the other the ψυχικός, Brandenburger is in effect trying to have his cake and eat it. For, while in vs. 21f. he infers the Corinthian doctrine of two Anthropoi from Paul's alleged correction of their correspondence schema by substituting ζωοποιηθήσονται for ζωή , in vs.45ff. he infers the same from the sentence ὁ ἔσχατος ᾿Αδὰμ (ἐγένετο) εἰς πνεῦμα ζωοποιοῦν. If the Corinthian Gnostics were in the swell of enthusiasm, as Brandenburger maintains, claiming to have obtained ζωή in Christ (i.e., saying something like: διὰ τοῦ ψυχικοῦ ἀνθρώπου θάνατος, ἀλλὰ διὰ τοῦ πνευματικοῦ ἀνθρώπου ζωή), surely the sentence ὁ (ἔσχατος) ᾿Αδὰμ (ἐγένετο) εἰς πνεῦμα ζωοποιοῦν would be the perfect expression of their view? Why then does Paul correct it in vs.21f. but use it himself in v.45 (with, of course, only the correction of order by the ἔσχατος) (cf. also 2Cor 3.6, 17f.)?

This consideration makes highly suspect the whole presumption that Paul adopts and adapts the Corinthian Gnostics' doctrine of two contrasting Adam-Anthropoi. Little significance is to be attached to Paul's insertion of the words πρῶτος and ᾿Αδάμ into the quotation from Gen 2.7. For Adam of Gen 2.7 was frequently called the first man by the Rabbis (אדם־הראשון or אדם־הקדמוני) as well as by Philo[1]. Nor does the contrast of ψυχή and πνεῦμα indicate that the Corinthian Gnostics held a doctrine of two Anthropoi. While Jas 3.15f. and Jude 10 seem to indicate that the distinction between the ψυχικός and the πνευματικός was a common Christian tradition, unless they are dependent on Paul (esp. 1Cor 1—3)[2], Paul's use of οἱ πνευματικοί in Gal 6.1 (N.B. the context: Gal 5.16 – 6.1) indicates that Paul himself introduced the distinction to the Corinthians and subsequently they abused it, rather than that Paul borrowed it from them[3]. Against the view

---

[1] See Str.-Bill. iii, p.478; in Philo, e.g., *Op. Mund.*, 140, 148; *Abr.* 56. So A.J.M. Wedderburn, *Adam and Christ: An Investigation into the Background of 1 Corinthians XV and Romans V 12–21*, unpublished Ph.D. thesis (Cambridge, 1970), p.138. In pp. 177ff. Wedderburn also gives an extensive alternative exegesis of 1Cor 15.35–49 against Brandenburger's.

[2] Cf. Wedderburn, *Adam*, pp.195f.; Pearson, *op. cit.*, p.13f.

[3] So Wedderburn, *Adam*, pp.187, 196. The failure to consider ψυχικός-πνευματικός terminology in this wider Christian context is the fatal weakness in R.Jewett's argument, which, following U.Wilckens and Brandenburger, affirms that the terminology was taken over by Paul from the Corinthian Gnostics (see his *Paul's Anthropological Terms*

that the distinction between πνεῦμα and ψυχή, the negative evaluation of ψυχή, and the πνευματικός – ψυχικός antithesis are Gnostic[1], we would at this stage simply refer to Wedderburn's fine treatment of the question[2].

Finally, 1Cor 15.46 does *not* confirm Brandenburger's presumption. While many think that at v.46 Paul is correcting the sort of doctrine which Philo occasionally advances[3], Brandenburger argues that Paul corrects the Corinthians' Gnostic doctrine which affirmed the heavenly-pneumatic and the earthly-psychic Anthropos as the first and the second respectively[4]. But both

---

(1971), pp.340–46, 352–56). He never mentions Jas 3.15f. or Jude 19; but even more difficult to comprehend is his failure to refer to Gal 6.1 in the context of discussing the ψυχικός-πνευματικός terminology. Precisely because he 'would insist that both the Gnostics and Paul use the term ψυχικός as if it were practically synonymous with σαρκικός' (p.353), should he not see the same (or, at least, a similar) ψυχικός-πνευματικός antithesis in Gal 5.16–6.1 as those in 1Cor 2 and 15? This failure is all the more curious because earlier, in another context, he did in fact bring Gal 6.1 and 1Cor 2.12–15 together under the rubric of 'the πνευματικός category' (p.189).

[1]E.g. Bultmann, *Theology* i, pp.165, 174, 181, 204; H.Jonas, *Gnosis und spätantiker Geist* ([2]1954), pp.210–214; Wilckens, *Weisheit*, pp.89ff. See 'The History of Research' in Jewett, *op. cit.*, pp.340ff. According to Pearson's survey of the πνευματικός-ψυχικός terminology (*op. cit.*, pp.51–81), only the Naassene Sermon, Justin's Book of Baruch, Hyp. Arch. and the Valentinian literature contain the antithesis, and Ap. John and Soph. Jes. Chr. contain ψυχή/ ψυχικός and view it negatively over against πνεῦμα (not πνευματικός, which does not occur in the latter two). But it is evident that at least the Naassene Sermon, Justin's Book of Baruch, Soph. Jes. Chr. and the Valentinian literature betray a Christian influence. It is difficult to understand why Pearson, pointing this out (pp.66f., 69, 71), should insist that the Gnostics obtained πνευματικός-ψυχικός terminology only from their exegesis of Gen 2.7 – something which he can hardly prove, his repeated claim to the contrary notwithstanding. Cf. E.Schweizer, πνεῦμα, *TDNT* vi, pp.395f.

[2]Wedderburn, *Adam*, pp.185–96 In conclusion, taking his key from the definition of ψυχικοί in Jude 19 as 'those who do not have the Spirit', Wedderburn says: 'This sort of terminology, we may surmise, was worked out by Jewish Christians in the tradition of the Jewish Wisdom speculation to do justice to the new phenomena of the Spirit present in their midst and to provide the necessary differentiation from the constitution of other men' (p.196). See also *supra* pp.75ff. (esp. n.4). L.Schottroff, *Der Glaubende und die feindliche Welt* (1970), p.142 (see also pp.13ff.) contends that ψυχή/ ψυχικός is not always negatively evaluated in Gnosticism. Wedderburn's explanation applies to all the Pauline passages except 1Cor 15.44ff., for which a more correct explanation will be proposed on pp. 228 (also n.3), 256, 263 below.

[3]*Op. Mund.*, 134; *Leg. Alleg.* i.31, 92–94; ii.4; *Quaest. Gen.* ii.56. See, e.g., Barrett, *1Cor.*, pp.429f.; Héring, *1Cor.*, p.178; Davies, *Paul*, pp.51f.; Cullmann, *Christology*, pp.167f. Cf. also Borsch, *The Son of Man*, p.242.

[4]Brandenburger, *Adam*, pp.74f. For him Philo's doctrine is but a variety of the same Gnostic two Anthropoi myth (pp.117f.). *Infra* p.172, n.2.

views stumble at the neuters of v.46: Paul is not talking about ὁ πνευμα-
τικὸς : ἄνθρωπος and ὁ ψυχικὸς ἄνθρωπος but τὸ πνευματικόν and τὸ
ψυχικόν![1] Even if this point is not pressed, the suppositions cannot be
maintained. Amidst at least four different (even contradictory) interpretations of the creation of the first man in Gen 1.26f. and 2.7 which are to be
found in Philo[2], we cannot isolate just those places where he indeed interprets Gen 1.26f. as referring to the heavenly man and Gen 2.7 as referring to
the earthly man and then claim that he held a clear doctrine of the two

---

[1] So Schmithals, *Gnosis*, p.133; Wedderburn, *Adam*, p.197. However, Schmithals
thinks that Paul here criticises the view that 'the spiritual substance of man is older than
the physical body'. But against this see Wedderburn, 'Philo's "Heavenly Man"', pp.301f.

[2] Out of the bewilderingly confusing material in Philo concerning the relationships
among the Logos, the heavenly man and the earthly man, the following points may be
brought out as salient features:
a) When Philo interprets Gen 1.27 as referring to the heavenly, incorporeal man, an
   idea, standing over against the earthly empirical man (of Gen 2.7), he seems to be
   concerned to explain the two accounts of the creation of man in Gen 1.27 and 2.7
   (*Op. Mund.* 134; *Leg. Alleg.* i.31, 92–4; ii.4; *Quaest. Gen.* ii.56). The heavenly
   man is designated as ὁ κατ᾽ εἰκόνα ἄνθρωπος and said to have been created κατ᾽
   εἰκόνα θεοῦ. But here the Logos is not mentioned (except in *Quaest. Gen.* i.4 –
   see point c) below).
b) When he interprets Gen 1.27 (sometimes in combination with Gen 2.7) as referring
   to the creation of the earthly man with a mind or soul, he says that the Logos is the
   εἰκών of God and the man (or his mind/soul) is created through the instrumentality
   of and after the image (or pattern) of the Logos (*Leg. Alleg.* iii. 96; *Quis. Rer. Div.*
   230f.; also *Op. Mund.* 25, 69, 139; *Plant.* 19f.; *Quis. Rer. Div.* 56; *Quaest. Gen.* ii.
   62). Here Philo does not say that the Logos is the heavenly (incorporeal) man.
c) When the Logos is considered in the context of explaining the two accounts of the
   creation of man, then the heavenly man is said to be a copy of the Logos, the archetypal idea, and a series of *Urbild-Abbild* relationships is envisaged: (God) – Logos –
   the heavenly man – the earthly man (*Quaest. Gen.* i.4).
d) Sometimes Philo identifies the Logos with the heavenly man (*Conf. Ling.* 41, 62f.,
   146f.). But this should not be understood as a sign of the influence of the Gnostic
   Anthropos. *Contra* Käsemann, 'Taufliturgie', pp.40f.; Eltester, *Eikon*, pp.139ff.
   (34ff.); Brandenburger, *Adam*, pp.117ff.; cf. also Jervell, *Imago*, pp.57ff., 64 (n.
   139). For *Quaest. Gen.* i.93 is clearly against the inference, where Philo says: 'Even
   ὁ οὐράνιος ἄνθρωπος is a mixture consisting of soul and body', obviously referring
   to Adam of Gen 2.7. Rather it should be understood as one of his ways of interpreting Gen 1.27 in the light of his Platonic and Stoic conception of the Logos and
   also of his conception of the Logos as the *Theophanieträger* (on this last point *infra*,
   pp.245f.). So Wedderburn, "Heavenly Man", pp. 301–26; Schenke, *Gott "Mensch"*,
   pp.123f.; further H.Hegermann, *Die Vorstellung vom Schöpfungsmittler im hellenistischen Judentum und Christentum* (1961), pp.85–87, 97f.; L.Schottroff, *Der Glaubende*, pp.127ff. Cf. also Colpe, *Schule*, p.202 (n.3); Hengel, *Sohn*, p.118. In the
   above mentioned article Wedderburn distinguishes more lines of Philo's exegesis.

Anthropoi — the first the heavenly spiritual man and the second the earthly empirical man. Indeed Wedderburn has demonstrated that Philo is little interested in chronology[1]. Nor did all Gnostics hold that the heavenly Anthropos was prior in time to the earthly[2]. But more fundamentally, as will be shown later, it is impossible to imagine that the Corinthian heretics (or, for that matter, Paul) could have identified Christ with the heavenly spiritual Anthropos of Gnosticism[3]. So it is impossible to see in v.46 Paul directing his polemic against their doctrine of the priority of the heavenly spiritual Anthropos[4]. So far[5] the view against which Paul directs his polemic

---

[1] Wedderburn, "Heavenly Man", pp.303–326.

[2] For example, in Apoc. Adam Seth, the heavenly man of Gnosis comes after Adam. See A.Böhlig and P.Labib, *Koptisch-gnostische Apokalypsen aus Codex V von Nag Hammadi* (1963), pp.86ff.; Schottroff, *Der Glaubende*, p.142.

[3] At this point we simply refer to Käsemann, *Römer*, pp.134f. However, his view that at v.46 Paul directs his polemic against Hellenistic Jewish speculations 'which follow an *Urmensch* -myth already reshaped by Philo' (p.134), is to be rejected.

[4] Cf. Schottroff, *Der Glaubende*, p.142, who denies that Paul is arguing against his opponents' affirmation of the *temporal* priority of the heavenly Anthropos or Gnostic nature. In fact, Brandenburger himself tries to understand the priority not just in terms of time but also 'quality and ontological rank' (*Adam*, p.75). But in view of the words ἔσχατος and δεύτερος in vs. 45 and 47, Schmithals rightly regards this qualification as a '*Verlegenheitsauskunft*' (*Gnosis*, p.138; similarly also Wedderburn, "Heavenly Man", p.304).

[5] We may mention three more suggestions:
a) According to Schweizer, πνεῦμα, *TDNT* vi, p.420, Paul refutes a Gnostic belief 'that regards the pneumatic σῶμα as original, as proper to man as such, as hidden under psychic body now, so that it survives after death and therefore does not have to be given for the first time in the resurrection.' But as Schweizer himself points out, 'v. 44b seems to presuppose that his (sc. Paul's) opponents knew nothing of this'.
b) Schottroff, *Der Glaubende*, pp.115–69, believes that in 1Cor 15 Paul confronts the Gnostic anthropology of dualism which affirmed both the negative ψυχή and the divine πνεῦμα in man and at v.46 Paul is contending 'daß das Heil zu dem total negativ Bestimmten kommt (and therefore not to him that is compounded of the negative ψυχή and the divine πνεῦμα). Seine (sc. Paulus) Polemik in V.46 trifft also tatsächlich dualistisches Denken, da der mindere Urmensch bzw. das negative ψυχικόν dort nicht das πρῶτον sein kann, das durch das Heil eine neue, zweite Bestimmtheit findet' (p.142). On the whole it is difficult to follow and consent to her exegesis of 1Cor 15; but this is one of the most difficult parts: we simply fail to see in v.46 Paul saying what she puts into his mouth (e.g., what is then the meaning of πρῶτον–ἔπειτα here?). 'But if that is what Paul is contending in 1Cor 15.46 he has chosen a strange way of saying so' (Wedderburn, "Heavenly Man", p.302, n.1). Finally,
c) Pearson, *op. cit.*, pp.24ff., thinks that the Corinthian opponents held 'a doctrine of asomatic immortality' on the 'basis of their exegesis of Gen 2.7 which, following the Hellenistic Jewish exegetical tradition, stressed the spiritual 'inbreathing' in man; and that Paul is here contradicting the doctrine with his own exegesis of Gen 2.7.

— if indeed there is a polemic here — does not seem to have been clearly identified[1]. What is to be affirmed here, however, is that there is no basis for the presumption that in 1Cor 15.21f., 45ff. Paul adopts and adapts the Corinthian doctrine of Adam-Christ correspondence[2].

Did then Paul himself create the Adam-Christ typology from material provided by the Gnostic Anthropos myth? It is greatly to our convenience that A.J.M. Wedderburn has made precisely this question the subject of his Ph.D. thesis at Cambridge with Brandenburger's contention especially in mind[3]. His answer is a firm 'no'. Analysing the three passages, 1 Cor 15.21f.,

---

But, his exaggerated claim notwithstanding, Pearson fails to produce a single Hellenistic-Jewish text which affirms the negative $\psi v\chi\acute{\eta}/\psi v\chi\iota\kappa\acute{o}\varsigma$ versus the divine $\pi v\epsilon\hat{v}\mu a/$ $\pi v\epsilon v\mu a\tau\iota\kappa\acute{o}\varsigma$ on the basis of Gen 2.7. Are the texts cited on pp.11f. valid? The Philonic texts Pearson introduces (pp.18ff.) prove, on the contrary, that in Philo $\pi v\epsilon\hat{v}\mu a$ and $\psi v\chi\acute{\eta}$ are more or less synonymous!

[1]So the cautious judgement of Conzelmann, *1.Kor.*, p.342. In this situation, Wedderburn's suggestion ("Heavenly Man", p.302) seems, though not completely satisfactory, at least worth consideration. So also is the suggestion by F.F.Bruce in 'Paul and Immortality', *SJT* 24 (1971), pp.464ff.

[2]So Schottroff, *Der Glaubende*, p.161. Borsch, *The Son of Man*, p.242, is right in saying that if the Corinthians had held such a Gnostic doctrine 'Paul would have attacked it more vigorously and directly'. Conzelmann, *1.Kor.*, pp.318ff., adopts, in the main, Brandenburger's view on 1Cor 15.21f., his only new argument being that, since Paul introduces the idea as self-evident, he must have taken it over from 'tradition'. But how long a preface is to be judged as adequate for the introduction of a new idea? Is not the Adam-Christ typology in 1Cor 15 (and Rom 5) readily understandable by anyone who knows Gen 1–3 and the Christian kerygma? Käsemann, *Römer*, p.134 (cf. also pp.136ff.) argues for its pre-Pauline character not just from Paul's apparent polemic at 1Cor 15.46 but also from the facts that there are variations between Rom 5.12–21 and 1Cor 15.21f., 45ff., that the Messianically interpreted passages (Ps 110.1; 8.7) are inserted in 1Cor 15.25, 27, and that it also appears in baptismal and liturgical contexts in Col 3.9f., Eph 4.24 and other texts containing the $\epsilon\grave{\iota}\kappa\acute{\omega}v$ motif. This sort of argument can be effective only for those who believe that Paul, if he was the author, should have written and left behind a systematic treatise on the typology. For us, however, it seems only to confirm our thesis that the Adam-Christ typology occupies a central place in Paul's theology and has vital relations with his other central doctrines — a thesis yet to be unfolded (*infra*, pp.263ff.). Both C.Colpe (in *TDNT* viii, p.471) and Wedderburn (*Adam*, p.55) argue that it is Paul who introduces the typology for the first time, in 1Cor 15.21. The latter also notes that in 1Cor 15 as elsewhere Paul presupposes that his readers know the OT and Judaism to some extent. However, we must also reckon with the possibility that in his first mission to Corinth Paul already expounded God's saving work in Christ in terms of the Adam-Christ typology. If we succeed in showing that the typology originated from Paul's Damascus experience, the suggestion would be made very plausible.

[3]We have already referred to it above: *Adam and Christ*. Some parts of the unpublished thesis appear as reworked articles in the following three journals: 'The Body

45ff.; Rom 5.12—21 under the headings: 'the two Men', 'in Adam and in Christ' 'the contrast of ψυχή and πνεῦμα', 'a question of order?', 'bearing the image of the two Men', 'the reign of sin and death', 'sin and the Law', and 'the one and the many' — all motifs which according to Brandenburger betray the basic Gnostic background — Wedderburn demonstrates that these thoughts and therefore Adam-Christ typology as a whole can be adequately explained in the light of the OT-Jewish background, the early Christian kerygma, and Paul's personal experience of Christ, especially that on the Damascus road. Thus Wedderburn joins R. Scroggs[1] in rejecting Brandenburger's thesis and improves on Scroggs' attempt to explain Adam-Christ typology against Paul's OT-Jewish and Christian background. While Scroggs has little confrontation with the Gnostic material that Brandenburger uses, and argues his case largely out of the Rabbinic sources, Wedderburn examines the Gnostic material critically and uses the OT and the earlier Jewish material rather than the Rabbinic. So Wedderburn can on the whole make out a better case for his thesis than Scroggs, and at the same time also show that to interpret the Adam-Christ typology against the Gnostic background is in fact to misunderstand not only Paul's thought but Gnosticism itself.

The first difficulty in an attempt to understand the Adam-Christ typology in terms of the Gnostic Anthropos-redeemer myth, as is well recognized, is the fact that there seems to be no clear pre-Christian evidence of the myth. So Brandenburger tries to make Philo's writings 'the most important pre-Christian witnesses' to the myth[2] and to see its 'Vor- und Frühformen' already in such Jewish writings as the DSS, Wis 10.1f., Vita Adae, Apoc. Mos., and 1En 71 (and 2En 21f.)[3]. But, as already noted above, the attempt to use Philo as a witness to a Gnostic Anthropos myth has been widely rejected[4]. Wedderburn shows clearly that the attempt is misguided and that in fact it is much more likely that Gnosticism later drew on the Philonic and other Jewish exegeses of the Genesis account of the creation of man in God's image for its Anthropos myth[5]. Thus he confirms the view which has been

---

of Christ and Related Concepts in 1Corinthians', *SJT* 24 (1971), pp 74—96; 'The Theological Structure of Romans v.12', *NTS* 19 (1972/73), pp.339—354; 'Philo's "Heavenly Man" ', *NovT* 15 (1973), pp.301—326.

[1] Scroggs, *The Last Adam* (1966).

[2] Brandenburger, *Adam*, pp.117ff.

[3] *Ibid.*, pp.109ff.; also pp.131ff.

[4] *Supra* p.172, n.2.

[5] Wedderburn, *Adam*, pp.115—164; also "Heavenly Man", pp.306—326; similarly Colpe, 'Leib-Christi-Vorstellung', p.182. Wedderburn thinks that 'in the tractate *Poimandres* we find a link in the chain of development that leads from Philo's more philo-

gaining support, namely that the Gnostics obtained their Anthropos myth by expressing their Hellenistic speculations on the self or soul in terms of the figure of Adam in Gen 1–3[1]. However, some authors do not rule out the possibility that there emerged such an Anthropos myth (as distinct from an Anthropos-redeemer or 'redeemed redeemer' myth) before or at the time of the beginning of Christianity[2]. If this was indeed so, Brandenburger would be entitled to look into the possibility of explaining the Adam-Christ typology against this background, although his material is throughout post-Christian, except, of course, the Philonic and some other Jewish material.

It is one of the major weaknesses of Wedderburn's otherwise fine study that he does not confront the last mentioned possibility in an adequate way and simply presumes that having shown 'that Hellenistic Jewish speculations on Genesis are responsible for the later traditions of Gnosticism on the heavenly man, and not *vice versa*'[3], he has pulled the rug from under Brandenburger's feet. Thus, in discussing the motifs in Paul's Adam-Christ typology he does not point out the weaknesses of Brandenburger's Gnostic hypothesis sharply enough, concentrating largely on a demonstration that since those motifs can be adequately, indeed better, understood against the background of Paul's Jewish heritage and Christian experience, it is unnecessary to introduce the hypothesis of the Gnostic background. So, on the whole consenting to his examination of the Gnostic material and his positive demonstration that Paul's OT-Jewish heritage and Christian experience are adequate for understanding the Adam-Christ typology, we would like to supplement his work by pointing out just a few fundamental flaws in Brandenburger's thesis.

Even if Brandenburger's reconstruction of the Gnostic Adam-Anthropos myth out of such diverse sources as those used by him is correct, which is doubtful at many points[4], it could hardly have provided a background for a Christian, whether a Corinthian pneumatic or Paul, in his understanding of Christ as the type or antitype of Adam. First of all, on Brandenburger's own

---

sophically orientated exegesis to the myth of the heavenly Man of Gnosticism' (*Adam*, pp.162ff.).

[1]So already C.H.Dodd, *The Bible and the Greeks*, (1935), pp.146ff. (esp. p.146, n.1); also Quispel, 'Der gnostische Anthropos und die jüdische Tradition', *Gnostic Studies* i, pp.173–195; Wilson, *Gnostic Problem*, esp. pp.208ff.; Schenke, *Gott "Mensch"*, esp. pp.69ff.

[2]Quispel, *op. cit.*, p.195; Schenke, *op. cit.*, p.71. But neither attempts to prove this point (Schenke's brief reasoning on p.71 hardly provides a satisfactory ground for his view).

[3]Wedderburn, *Adam*, p.164.

[4]Cf. *ibid.*, pp.115–164; Schottroff, *Der Glaubende*, pp.120ff.; above all Schenke, *Gott "Mensch"*.

assumption that in 1Cor 15.45ff. Paul reverses the Gnostic order of the two Anthropoi, how is Paul's conception of Christ as the pre-existent Son of God to be reconciled with this reversal? If Paul had known the Gnostic order, should he not rather have agreed with it? If he felt it necessary to correct it for some reason, should he not then at least have specified this in some such way as: Christ as the pre-existent Son of God is, of course, prior to the earthly Adam, but on his incarnation he *became* the last Adam, 'the second man' after 'the first man Adam' of Gen.? In point of fact, in 1Cor 15.45ff. Paul compares the temporal order of Adam and Christ exclusively on the historical plane — something that he could hardly have done if he had been conscious of the Gnostic two Anthropoi schema[1]. The fundamental problem for Brandenburger's thesis is, however, that it ignores the *essential* difference between the Gnostic Anthropos myth and the Pauline Adam-Christ typology: whereas the former (at any rate, as reconstructed by Brandenburger) tells mythologically of the self's (or soul's) heavenly origin, its fall into the earthly body, release from it and ascent back to heaven; the latter is concerned with two historical persons — the protological Adam and the eschatological Christ — who are not related to each other by original consubstantiality but rather set against each other antithetically[2].

From this essential difference there stem many problems for Brandenburger's thesis. Paul has no idea of the heavenly πνευματικός Adam imprisoned in matter and therefore neither any idea of redemption as a journey of this Adam to heaven in order to obtain or recover his self (μορφή and πνεῦμα). True, some Gnostic documents, especially the Mandaean, speak of the soul

---

[1]Cf. Käsemann, *Römer*, p.134; A.Vögtle, ' "Der Menschensohn" und die paulinische Christologie', *AnBib* 17 (1963), p.211.

[2]This problem is most succinctly stated by Käsemann. Though he states it as an objection to the application of the Gnostic 'redeemed redeemer' myth to Paul's Adam-Christ typology — a hypothesis he himself championed for so long! — it applies equally well to Brandenburger's thesis. Whether there was a pre-Christian Gnostic 'redeemed redeemer' myth or not, says Käsemann, 'wird die paulinisch-deuteropaulinische Adam-Christus-Typologie von da aus in ihrer zentralen Problematik nicht erfaßt, geschweige gelöst. Denn Adam und Christus bleiben hier Antipoden, die durch keinerlei ursprüngliche Konsubstantialität verbunden sind. Nicht Adam, der allein irdischer Protoplast, nicht gefallenes Himmelswesen ist, wird erlöst, sondern die von ihm in seinen Fall verstrickte Welt. Christus aber wird nicht als Adam redivivus betrachtet, sondern als der eschatologisch erscheinende Gottessohn. Kommensurabel sind beide nicht nach ihrem Wesen, sondern ausschließlich nach der Funktion, daß von beiden Welt verändert wurde. *Vom Mythos des Urmenschen her ist nur zu erklären, daß beide mit dem Titel des "Anthropos" bedacht wurden, und selbst das ist bloß auf dem Wege einer komplizierten Rekonstruktion möglich'*. (*Römer*, p.135. My emphasis). Cf. also Schottroff, *Der Glaubende*, pp.122f.; D.E.H.Whiteley, *The Theology of St. Paul* (1964), p.117.

(= the heavenly Adam) as 'putting off' the 'garment' or 'wall' of matter and as obtaining the original form or 'putting on' the 'garment' of light. But, Brandenburger's repeated assertion to the contrary notwithstanding, there is no actual reference in non-Christian Gnosticism to the *salvandus* as being ἐν τῷ (σαρκικῷ or ψυχικῷ) Ἀδάμ (or in his σῶμα) or to the *salvatus* as being ἐν τῷ (πνευματικῷ) Ἀδάμ (or in his σῶμα)[1]. Od. Sol. 8.22 (cf. 17.4f., 13ff.), where a parallel to the Pauline phrase, ἐν Χριστῷ is discernible, unmistakably exhibits the Johannine phraseology of 'abiding' in Christ and the Pauline conception of Christ as the head of the Church[2]. It is uncertain whether Brandenburger is right in ascribing to the heavenly Anthropos a soteriological function on the basis of the somewhat dubious texts of the Jewish Gnosticizing Prayers, the Naassene Sermon and the Mandaean texts[3]. Even if he is right, there is a fundamental difference between the conception of this heavenly Anthropos-redeemer and Paul's conception of Christ as the Last Adam, as Brandenburger himself acknowledges: For Paul, Christ, the Last Adam, has become the redeemer through his incarnation, life, death and resurrection, while 'the soteriological function of the heavenly Adam-Anthropos has almost throughout a *passive* character and remains confined to the sphere of the heavenly world'[4]. In view of these fundamental differences, how could it have occurred to the Corinthian Gnostics or Paul to draw the figure of Christ into the already given schema of the Gnostic Anthropos myth and identify him with the heavenly spiritual Anthropos? Brandenburger's attempt to solve this problem by referring to possible roles of the early Christian understanding of Jesus as the Son of Man, of Sophia and of the Gnostic conception of messengers, 'helpers', can only be regarded as an attempt born of desperation[5].

---

[1]So Jewett, *Anthropological Terms*; Schottroff, *Der Glaubende*, pp.122f.; Schenke, *Gott "Mensch"*, p.155: 'Die gnostische Lehre vom Gott "Mensch" (sc. what Brandenburger calls the 'Adam-Anthropos myth') . . . weist aber inhaltlich . . . keinerlei Berührungspunkte mit der Leib Christi-Vorstellung auf, so daß deren Ableitung von hier aus unmöglich ist'.

[2]So Wedderburn, *Adam*, p.167.

[3]Brandenburger, *Adam*, pp.77–79, 86 (n.10), 100f. In any case, the majority of scholars today deny the existence of an Anthropos-redeemer myth before the Christian beginning, as noted above pp.162ff.

[4]*Ibid.*, p.154 (emphasis by B.).

[5]Cf. F.H.Borsch, *The Christian and the Gnostic Son of Man* (1970), p.114, who, observing that the title 'Son of Man' was more popular among Christian (and non-Christian) Gnostics than with the orthodox Christians, says, however: 'in a significant number of instances (in Gnostic literature), there is no effort to indicate that the cosmic Son of Man who is mentioned (and rarely elaborated upon) is to be understood as the

With this question L. Schottroff's thesis is also shattered. Gnosticism's 'dualistic antithesis of two prototypes', the heavenly spiritual Anthropos and the earthly Anthropos compounded of (the positive) πνεῦμα and (the negative) ψυχή, does not provide an analogy to the Christological side of Paul's Adam-Christ typology. For Paul, Christ, the Last Adam, is Jesus of Nazareth who became the πνεῦμα ςωοποιοῦν through his resurrection and not just a spiritual being that remains in heaven. There is no question of Paul's 'reshaping' of the Gnostic '*Vermischungsanthropologie*' 'in that he assigns Adam as the prototype of the *salvandus*, the unredeemed man, to the negative pole of the dualism . . .'[1]. The Gnostic myth of the soul or the self that spoke of human existence in terms of the fall of the heavenly spiritual Anthropos into matter, could not have inspired Paul in any way[2].

If the background for Paul's Adam-Christ typology is not provided by the Gnostic 'redeemed redeemer' myth or by the Anthropos myth, is it perhaps to be found in the myth of the perfect first man, the king of paradise, who has often been confused and syncretised with the first two figures under the blanket designation '*Urmensch*' or '*Urmensch*-redeemer'[3]? The myth is supposed to have been widespread in the Near East. It is said to be represented not only by figures such as the Indian Yama-Yami and the Iranian Gayomart but also by the Adam of Genesis and by the 'Son of Man' of the later Jewish speculations[4]. Arguing that in correspondence to the parallelism between

---

heavenly Jesus. Even when this is done (as in the central sections of the *Sophia Jesu Christi* and in Irenaeus' *Against Heresies* I.12.4), it is often accomplished in a manner which might well indicate a later and not wholly satisfactory attempt to make an identification'. Against the attempt to understand the figure of Sophia in terms of the Gnostic redeemer, *supra* pp.75f., n.4.

[1]Schottroff, *Der Glaubende*, pp.133f.

[2]So the renewed attempt by U.Wilckens ('der "Letzte Adam" ', pp.388–403) to understand Paul's Adam-Christ typology on the basis of the myth is also to be rejected. Explicitly adopting Brandenburger's thesis and combining it, we suspect, with that of Schottroff, Wilckens suggests that Paul derived the typology by taking over 'the model of the *Urmenschlehre*': δι' ἀνθρώπου–δι' ἀνθρώπου and correcting, however, its content with his eschatological conception of Christ, which had materially the same structure as the Jewish and especially the early Christian conception of the Son of Man (see esp. pp.396ff.). But insofar as Wilckens builds his theory on that of Brandenburger some of the objections which we have raised above against the latter apply also to his. All that Wilckens has – though unwittingly – proved is the veracity of the last sentence in Käsemann's judgement on the matter, cited above on p.177, n.2.

[3]See Colpe, *Schule*, and Schenke, *Gott "Mensch"*, for the bewildering blendings of different mythical figures and hypostases by the representatives of the *religions-geschichtliche Schule* and its recent followers. But see also Borsch, *The Son of Man*, pp.68ff., who again emphasizes the close interrelationship of the various figures.

[4]Most recently again Borsch, *The Son of Man*, esp. pp.75ff., 132ff.

Urzeit and *Endzeit* there was in the *Urmensch* speculations also the parallelism between *Urmensch* and redeemer who represented the two ages respectively, B. Murmelstein once attempted to demonstrate the existence of such a parallelism also in Judaism: the parallelism between Adam and the Messiah, the latter as the second Adam who recovers the glory lost by the first Adam. Murmelstein conceded: 'For the perfect parallelism there lacks only the idea that Adam himself is the coming redeemer'; but he argued that this idea was suppressed in Judaism in response to the Christian doctrine of the second Adam and his identity with the first Adam[1]. But quite apart from the fact that Paul's Adam-Christ typology contrasts rather than identifies Adam and Christ, Murmelstein's arbitrary method of piecing a variety of totally unrelated material together for his argument makes his suggestion quite unacceptable[2].

In a similar way to Murmelstein, O. Cullmann also believes that in the non-Israelite religions of the Near East there was an identification of 'the ideal Heavenly Man' (or 'the divine *Urmensch*') with 'the first man' and that in connection with the conception of the eschatological return of the golden *Urzeit* this identification led to the expectation that precisely the first man would come at the end to redeem mankind[3]. Judaism could not however, according to Cullmann, make clear the connection between the first man and the eschatological 'Man' or 'Son of Man' because it knew that the first man is the source of sin. So in Judaism the idea of the *Urmensch* and that of the coming 'Son of Man' developed along two separate lines, so that their original identity is no longer apparent, although the fact that the eschatological redeemer is called 'man' (בר נשא) shows that the two concepts really belong together[4]. Wrestling with the problem of the connection between the ideal *Urmensch* and the first man ('the Adam problem'), the Jews found two ways of overcoming the problem: one was to place no emphasis on the identification of the two figures; and the other was to place no emphasis on the fall of Adam[5]. As a result the Heavenly Man of Oriental speculation appears in

---

[1]B.Murmelstein, 'Adam, ein Beitrag zur Messiaslehre', *Wiener Zeitschrift für die Kunde des Morgenlandes* 35 (1928), pp.242–275; 36 (1929), pp.51–86; esp. 35, pp.245ff., 253ff. (quotation from p.258). Apparently a similar suggestion was made by W.Staerk, *Die Erlösererwartung in den östlichen Religionen*: (*Soter* II) (1938), but this work is not available to me. Against Staerk, see Jervell, *Imago*, p.119 (n.174).

[2]See Scroggs, *Last Adam*, pp.x–xv; Wedderburn, *Adam*, p.8–11, for criticism of his method; see also Colpe, ὁ υἱὸς τοῦ ἀνθρώπου, *TDNT* viii, p.410 (n.67).

[3]Cullmann, *Christology*, p.143.

[4]*Ibid.*, pp.143f.

[5]*Ibid.*, p.145.

Judaism in two forms: 1) He is a heavenly being, now hidden, who will appear only at the end of time on the clouds of heaven to judge and to establish the 'nation of saints'. This exclusively eschatological figure is found in Dan., 1En. and 4Ezra. 2) He is the ideal Heavenly Man who is identified with the first man at the beginning of time. This form is developed by Philo, in the Pseudo-Clementine *Preaching of Peter* and in the Rabbinic Adam-speculations[1]. The fact that his Christology is so completely embedded in eschatology that he calls the second Adam the 'Last Adam' (1Cor 15.45) or the 'coming Adam' (Rom 5.14), and his reference in 1Th 4.17 to the Lord coming on the clouds of heaven, indicate that Paul does not ignore the eschatological 'Son of Man'. However, of the two Jewish conceptions stemming from the Oriental *Urmensch* idea, Paul's main interest lies in the one concerning Adam: in the idea of the incarnate Heavenly Man, the 'second Adam', and in the connection between the Incarnate and the 'last Man' who comes at the end[2]. Paul formulates the Christian solution to the Jewish problem of the relation between 'Son of Man' and Adam in agreement with Jesus' self-consciousness: he identifies the incarnate Heavenly Man, the 'second Adam', with the 'last Man', the 'Son of Man'. This he does in a polemic against Philo's attempt to identify the Heavenly Man with Adam of Gen 1.27, postulating two Adams at creation[3]. Rejecting the identification of Jesus, the Heavenly Man, with Adam, Paul relates the two figures in the following two-fold way: 1) positively, he shares with Adam the task of exhibiting the image of God; 2) negatively, he must atone for Adam's sin[4].

Before criticising Cullmann's view, a similar suggestion of F.H. Borsch must be examined. For he also starts from the assumption that the speculations on both Adam and 'Son of Man' stem from the myth of the *Urmensch* or the king of paradise. According to Borsch, Paul's use of terms like 'one man', 'the last Adam', 'the man' and 'the second man' indicates that he has refashioned for his own purpose the primitive teaching of the Son of Man (since the Semitic expression is best rendered by the Greek ὁ ἄνθρωπος), along with the Jewish speculations on Man[5]. Paul previously held a view on the Adam-Man question similar to Philo's, and probably also supposed that the first, Heavenly Man would return at the resurrection. Borsch finds Paul

---

[1] *Ibid.*, pp.150f.

[2] *Ibid.*, p.166.

[3] *Ibid.*, pp.166ff.

[4] *Ibid.*, pp.169f.

[5] Borsch, *The Son of Man*, pp.240ff. J.Jeremias, 'Αδάμ, *TDNT* i, pp.142f. holds a view similar to those of Cullmann and Borsch. Cf. also M.Black, 'The Pauline Doctrine of the Second Adam', *SJT* 7(1954), pp.173ff.

converting this previous view of his in 1Cor 15.46[1]. Paul's quotation of Ps 8.6 and 110.1 in 1Cor 15.24ff. indicates that he has the picture of the reigning King-Man in mind rather than specifically that of the Son of Man[2]. In Rom 5.12–21 'Paul is . . . virtually playing with the Man speculation and his Christian interpretation of it'[3]. However, in the light of the Christ-event Paul is forced to give up the idea of identity between the first Man and Christ, and instead to think in typological terms[4]. In a similar way to Cullmann, Borsch thinks that this enables Paul to reject the tendency to exonerate the first Man of his sin and to glorify him in some Jewish forms of the speculation, and to see the second Man as a type of Adam as much in terms of contrast as of comparison[5].

But the fundamental problem for the attempts of Cullmann and Borsch is that it is very uncertain whether the Adam-speculations in Judaism and especially the concept 'Son of Man' really stem from the *Urmensch* myth[6]. Even if the latter should be derived ultimately from the *Urmensch* myth, the figure 'like a son of man' in Dan., 1En. and 4Ezra no longer shares the distinctive characteristics of the *Urmensch*[7]. Moreover, as Cullmann himself recognizes[8], the figure 'Son of Man' is never brought into any connection either with the protoplast Adam of Genesis or the glorified Adam of the late Jewish speculations[9]. In this situation, is it conceivable that Paul was conscious of

---

[1] Borsch, *The Son of Man*, p.242f.

[2] *Ibid.*, pp.243f.

[3] *Ibid.*, p.245.

[4] *Ibid.*, p.245.

[5] *Ibid.*, pp.245ff.

[6] This is categorically denied by Colpe, *Schule*, pp.149f., 162ff., 194ff.; his ὁ υἱὸς τοῦ ἀνθρώπου, *TDNT* viii, pp.408ff. (esp. n.65 on p.410); J.A.Emerton, 'The Origin of the Son of Man Imagery', *JTS* 9 (1958), p.231; B.Lindars, 'Re-Enter the Apocalyptic Son of Man', *NTS* 22 (1976), p.60; cf. also Käsemann, *Römer*, p.135; Jervell, *Imago*, pp.41f. (n.73); Wedderburn, *Adam*, pp.87–93, 111, 114.

[7] Vögtle, "Der Menschensohn", pp.202ff.; see also Colpe, ὁ υἱὸς τοῦ ἀνθρώπου, *TDNT* viii, pp.408ff. This is also admitted by those who see the 'Son of Man' concept as derived from the *Urmensch* myths of the Orient – see e.g., E.Sjöberg, *Der Menschensohn im äthiopischen Henochbuch* (1946), pp.192ff.; S.Mowinckel, *He that Cometh* (1956), pp.434ff.; cf. also Borsch, *The Son of Man*, p.153.

[8] Cullmann, *Christology*, pp.143ff.

[9] Vögtle, "Der Menschensohn", pp.203f.; Sjöberg, *Menschensohn*, p.193; Käsemann, *Römer*, p.135; Lindars, 'Re-Enter', p.60, against M.D.Hooker, *The Son of Man in Mark* (1967), p.72. Mowinckel, *op. cit.*, p.431, believes that the difference between the Adam in Rabbinic legend and the Son of Man of 1En. is due to the fact that the Jews came to know the *Urmensch* myth in various forms from many quarters at different periods.

what Cullmann calls the 'Adam Problem', namely the problem of the relation between Adam and the *Urmensch* (later to come as the second 'Man' – i.e. the 'Son of Man' in Judaism), and gave the Christian solution to it?[1] As we shall see later, however, the heavenly figure 'like a son of man' whom the visionaries, Daniel (7.13), Enoch (1En. 46.1ff.) and Ezra (4Ezra 13.2ff.) see, is not characterized by humanness. The expression כבר אנש in Dan 7.13 and its equivalents in 1En. 46.1ff. and 4Ezra 13 should not mislead us into thinking that there we have a speculation on 'Man'. The phrase is a symbolical representation of a divine being appearing in human form and likeness. It is typical visionary or epiphanic language. In fact, the figure כבר אנש has as little to do with the *Urmensch* as does Yahweh-God who was seen by Ezekiel in his inaugural vision in דמות כמראה אדם (Ezek 1.26). So it is a mistake to try to see the heavenly figure appearing in a vision כבר אנש as part of the Oriental 'Man' speculation. Thus there is little basis for the view of Cullmann and Borsch that Paul obtained his Adam-Christ typology from or in response to the Jewish version of the *Urmensch* speculations[2].

Many scholars believe that Paul derived his Adam-Christ typology from Jesus' self-designation: 'the Son of Man'. Some of them would not exclude the influence, in the last analysis, of the *Urmensch* myth on Jewish apocalyptic symbolism concerning 'one like a son of man' and on some motifs in Paul's Adam-Christ typology. But regarding this influence as at most of secondary importance, they emphasize the direct origin of Paul's Adam-

---

With this sort of reasoning one can prove any thesis one wants!

[1]Cf. Scroggs, *Last Adam*, pp.xvif.

[2]There is some force in the argument used by W.Manson, *Jesus the Messiah* (1943), p.188, that Paul never connects the pre-existence and cosmological functions of Christ with the title 'Man' (= the Heavenly Man), though this is what we should expect if Reitzenstein (and therefore his recent followers on this point, like Cullmann & Borsch) are right in regarding the Iranian *Urmensch* myth as underlying Paul's Christology. Rather, he connects them mainly with the title 'Son of God' who exists prior to the world, not as Man but 'in the form of God' (Phil 2.6). Similarly also Vögtle, "Der Menschensohn", p.217: 'Paulus lehrt die wahre Menschwerdung des präexistenten Gottessohns. Er bezeichnet wohl den auferweckten und vom Himmel her sich offenbarenden Christus als den "himmlischen Menschen"; aber er kennt nicht die Vorstellung des HOMO homo factus est'. ὁ δεύτερος ἄνθρωπος ἐξ οὐρανοῦ refers not to the incarnation of the pre-existent Christ as the 'Heavenly Man' but to the parousia of the risen Christ – so Vögtle, "Der Menschensohn", p.209 (with literature in n.2); E.Schweizer, 'Menschensohn und eschatologischer Mensch im Frühjudentum', *Jesus und der Menschensohn*, Vögtle FS, p.113; J.D.G.Dunn, '1Cor 15.45 – Last Adam, Life-giving Spirit', *Christ and Spirit*, Moule FS, eds. B.Lindars and S.S.Smalley (1973), pp.140f. For further arguments against the sort of view which Cullmann represents, see Vögtle, "Der Menschensohn", pp.204–18. ·

Christology from the self-designation of Jesus[1]. For this view the following arguments are often advanced: 1) the inherent likelihood of Paul's acquaintance with Jesus' self-designation is enhanced by Paul's references to the parousia of Christ in which the ideas and imagery connected with the parousia of the Son of Man in the Gospels appear (e.g., 1Cor 4.5; 15.23; 2Cor 5.10; Phil 3.21; *passim* in 1Th., above all at 1.10, where some[2] think Paul has replaced the original 'the Son of Man' with 'his Son'[3]). 2) The Semitic idiom בר(א)־נשא, which stands behind ὁ υἱὸς τοῦ ἀνθρώπου in the Gospels, means 'man' and therefore can be rendered in Greek by ἄνθρωπος. So, when Paul designates Christ as ἄνθρωπος (Rom 5.15; 1Cor 15.21, 47) he renders בר־(א)נשא in idiomatic Greek, avoiding the literal ὁ υἱὸς τοῦ ἀνθρώπου, which would be incomprehensible and misleading to his Gentile audience. Since אדם also means 'man', Paul can reinterpret Jesus' self-designation 'the Son of Man' with אדם or ἄνθρωπος. In doing this, Paul brings out well Jesus' consciousness of his special representative humanity, which he expresses in the self-designation. Finally, 3) the application of a statement predicated of 'Son of Man' (Ps 8.6) to Christ in 1Cor 15.27 implies that Paul has Christ as the Son of Man in mind while unfolding his Adam-Christ typology in 1Cor 15.

However, these arguments are vigorously disputed by A. Vögtle[4]. He believes that Paul certainly knew Jesus' self-designation 'the Son of Man' and 'the Son of Man' logia, and that it is possible that the designation led to the Christological use of Ps 8 in the early Church[5]. But he firmly holds that Paul did not make use of the title at all. He points out, first of all, that Paul uses neither ὁ υἱὸς τοῦ ἀνθρώπου nor its alleged substitutes ὁ ἄνθρωπος, 'the second man', 'the heavenly man' or 'the new man', either in connection with his statements about the parousia of Christ or with those about the death and resurrection of Christ, in both of which, in view of the Synoptic tradition, the designation 'the Son of Man' would be expected[6]. Secondly, against the claim that Paul renders the Semitic idiom non-literally but still correctly by

---

[1]Rawlinson, *The NT Doctrine of Christ*, pp.122ff.;   T.W.Manson, *Teaching*, 232ff.; W.Manson, *Messiah*, pp.197ff.; A.M.Hunter, *Paul and His Predecessors* (²1961), pp.86f.;   Dodd, *Scriptures*, p.121;   Michel, *Römer*, p.137;   Wedderburn, *Adam*, pp.112ff.;   cf. also M.Black, 'The Second Adam', pp.173ff.; Colpe, *TDNT* viii, pp.470ff.

[2]*Infra* pp.251f.

[3]See more examples in K.Smyth, 'Heavenly Man and Son of Man in St. Paul', *AnBib* 17 (1963), pp.226f.

[4]Vögtle, "Der Menschensohn", pp.204–218.

[5]*Ibid.*, pp.204, 217.

[6]*Ibid.*, pp.204f.

the Greek ὁ ἄνθρωπος in order to avoid misunderstanding on the part of his Gentile audience, Vögtle points out that ὁ υἱὸς τοῦ ἀνθρώπου is exactly the form used without hesitation throughout the Gospels, even in Jn and Lk[1]. But against Vögtle it may be argued that whereas the Evangelists, knowing the uniqueness of Jesus' self-designation ('*the* Son of Man'), keep to its literal rendering in Jesus' logia Paul, not concerned in his letters with transmitting the logia, could use the idiomatic rendering. However, the real problem here is that Paul never seems to use the absolute ὁ ἄνθρωπος as a title for Christ. His contrast of the two Adams by means of the neutral ἄνθρωπος (the double ἑνὸς ἀνθρώπου in Rom 5.12, 15; the double δι' ἀνθρώπου in 1Cor 15.21; ὁ πρῶτος ἄνθρωπος – ὁ δεύτερος ἄνθρωπος in 1Cor 15.47) 'is meant to emphasize our common humanity with both Adam and Christ and to stress the link between the two'[2]. 'The ὁ εἷς ·ἄνθρωπος I.X. (Rom 5.15) does not refer back to the definite, absolutely used *bar-nasha* designation; the article is conditioned by εἷς; which is in turn conditioned by the contrast to "the many"'[3]. Similarly also in 1Cor 15.47 the article is conditioned by δεύτερος, and the contrast ὁ πρῶτος ἄνθρωπος – ὁ δεύτερος ἄνθρωπος is derived not from some two-Anthropoi myth but from Paul's contrast of 'the first man Adam' and Christ 'the last Adam' in v.45. If Paul had intended to render by ὁ ἄνθρωπος Jesus' self-designation and use it as a title equivalent to אדם, would he not have made the antithesis ὁ πρῶτος ἄνθρωπος 'Αδάμ – ὁ ἔσχατος correspond to the antithesis ὁ πρῶτος ἄνθρωπος – ὁ ἔσχατος ἄνθρωπος, indicating that the ἄνθρωπος in the latter pair renders 'Αδάμ in the former? Finally, concerning the argument from the quotation of Ps 8.6 in 1Cor 15.27, R.H. Fuller believes that 'in view of the atomistic exegesis current at the time it is a hazardous *argumentum e silentio* to infer that Ps 8.4 was in Paul's mind when he quoted Ps 8.6'[4]. Vögtle considers whether the idea of subjection of all things (πάντα) in Ps 8.6 rather than the phrase 'son of man' did not lead Paul to associate v.6 with the Messianic text Ps 110.1[5]. However, as Vögtle himself grants, in view of Heb 1.13 – 2.9 (cf. also Eph 1.20–22; 1 Pet 3.22) it is possible that the two Psalm passages were very early joined together to provide a Scriptural *testimonium* to the exaltation of

---

[1]*Ibid.*, p.205.

[2]E.Best, *One Body*, pp.38–41 (quotation from p.39); so also Vögtle, "Der Menschensohn", pp.208f., quoting Best.

[3]Vögtle, "Der Menschensohn", p.209.

[4]Fuller, *Foundation*, p.233.

[5]Vögtle, "Der Menschensohn", p.207.

'the Son of Man' as the *Kyrios* (cf. Mk 14. 62 par.)[1]. If the designation 'son
of man' in Ps 8.4 led Paul to quote Ps 8.6 in 1Cor 15.27 (cf. also Eph 1.20–22;
1Pet 3.22) it is possible that in the 'man' (אֱנוֹשׁ/ἄνθρωπος) or 'son of
man'(בֶּן-אָדָם/υἱὸς ἀνθρώπου) of Ps 8, which clearly alludes to the creation of
man (אָדָם)in Gen 1.26f.,Paul saw Christ as 'the last Adam' who has recovered
the glory and dominion that Adam lost[2]. Thus Paul may have obtained his
Adam-Christ typology from Jesus' self-designation *via* Ps 8, in which he
perhaps saw confirmed the claim implied in Jesus' self-designation, namely
the claim to be the representative of humanity ('the Man'). This is just possible but by no means certain[3]. To make it certain we need more solid evidence that Paul indeed rendered Jesus' self-designation 'the Son of Man' by
ὁ ἄνθρωπος, took it as his claim to be the Man representing the new humanity, and used Ps 8 to show Christ as such[4].

Of course, the theological truths that Paul expresses through his Adam-
Christ typology must be understood in the light of his conception of God's
saving event in Christ and against the background of the Jewish conceptions
of Adam and his fall, especially those which, on the one hand, held Adam
responsible for bringing sin into the world and death upon all his descendants
and which, on the other hand, held each individual responsible for his own sin
and death[5]. So it is proper for Wedderburn to sketch a wider Jewish back-

---

[1]Cf. Dodd, *Scriptures*, pp.117–22; A.Richardson, *An Introduction to the Theology
of the NT* (1969), p.139; Black, 'The Second Adam', p.173; Michel, *Hebräer*, pp.71,
138.

[2]Cf. Bruce, *Hebrews*, pp.34ff.; Michel, *Hebräer*, p.138; Ellis, *Paul's Use*, pp.95ff.;
Richardson, *Theology*, pp.138f.

[3]The attempt to explain Paul's Adam-Christology from Jesus' self-designation is also
rejected by Whiteley, *Theology*, p.117; Fuller, *Foundation*, pp.133f.; Kümmel,
Theologie, p.139; Käsemann, *Römer*, p.135. However, in view of what has been said
here in connection with Ps 8, it is inadequate to use the stereotype argument for the
rejection, namely that from Jesus' self-designation 'the Son of Man' the parallelization
and contrast of two men, the first and the last, cannot be derived (see, e.g., Vögtle, "Der
Menschensohn", p.207; Kümmel, *Theologie*, p.139).

[4]According to O.Moe, 'Der Menschensohn und der Urmensch', *StTh* 14 (1960),
pp.121–129, Jesus meant by his self-designation that he was 'the son of the first man'
(p.126) who as such had not only the glorious inheritance of Adam (Gen 1.27f.; Ps
8.6ff.) but also the responsibility to atone for the sin of mankind and restore the state of
man and the world originally intended by God (Gen 3.15). Paul's conception of Christ
as 'the last Adam' or 'the second Man' represents this self-consciousness of Jesus. But
then why does Paul not call Christ 'the Son of the first man' or represent him as the Son
of Adam, as Moe finds Luke does (Lk 3.38)?

[5]This is precisely what both Scroggs, *Last Adam*, and Wedderburn, *Adam*, demonstrate against Brandenburger's attempt to understand them against the Gnostic back-

ground for Paul's contrast of Adam and Christ rather than confining himself to Jesus' self-designation. His sketch of this background, what he calls 'the Jewish preparation', falls under three headings. Since this 'Jewish preparation', or at least part of it, will also be presupposed by our own thesis, we will here briefly summarize Wedderburn's presentation[1].

Under the first heading, 'the expectation of a restoration of the primal state', Wedderburn analyses various eschatological hopes of the OT and Judaism: for a restoration of the pre-fall state of man and the world, for a new creation in the Messianic age, and for a new Exodus under the Messiah as a new Moses, after the type of the first Exodus under Moses, which was often thought of as a new creation[2]. The Qumran expectation of the restoration of אדם כבוד to the community (1QS 4.23; CD 3.20; 1QH 17.15; cf. also 4QpPs37 3.1f; 1QH 8.4—14a) is also to be considered. In the Books of Adam and elsewhere the restoration of Adam in person, at the end, is expected, though not as a redeemer.

Then, secondly, Wedderburn surveys the tendency of Judaism to narrate its history in terms of the actions of a few representative individuals. It expressed its eschatological hope, sometimes expecting one of these figures, like Moses or Elijah, to return at the end, but more commonly expecting the Messiah or an eschatological figure to come at the end as a last link in the still unfinished chain of successive prophets or leaders. In Wis 10.11 Adam is regarded as the first of the line of wise heroes of Israel's history (cf. Wis 7.27); and the Book of Jubilees speaks of twenty-two heads of mankind from Adam to Jacob and implies that God's purpose in the creation of Adam is realized in Jacob as he inherits God's blessings upon Adam (2.20; 19.24—29; 22.13). Having shown all this, Wedderburn goes on to say: 'But by far the commoner view is that which sees Adam as a sinner and contrasts him with subsequent righteous men who must come to put right what Adam has vitiated or to be what Adam failed to be'[3]. In 4Ezra 3.4—36, Ezra recounts the fall of Adam and the history of mankind since then in terms of God's election and deliverance of the righteous Noah with his household, of the Patriarchs, and of David, contrasted with their evil generations. It is not quite clear, however,

---

ground. For the tension between 'determinism' and 'individual responsibility' in the Jewish conceptions of sin and death, see Scroggs, *Last Adam*, pp.17ff., 32ff.; Wedderburn, *Adam*, pp.57—66.

[1]Wedderburn, *Adam*, pp.66—112.

[2]For an elaborate delineation of different forms of the correlation between *Urzeit* and *Endzeit*, see N.A.Dahl, 'Christ, Creation and the Church', *The Background of the NT and Its Eschatology*, Dodd FS, ed. D.Daube and W.D.Davies (1956), pp.424—429.

[3]Wedderburn, *Adam*, pp.66—112.

whether it was the intention of the author of 4Ezra to contrast with Adam
Noah, Abraham, Isaac, Jacob, and David, as Wedderburn says. His concern
seems to be rather to show the universal sinfulness of mankind and Israel as
a whole, except some righteous individuals whom God chose[1]. In the books
of Enoch, Enoch is thought to have been brought into the paradise where he,
'saw the first fathers and the righteous who from the beginning dwell in that
place' (1En. 70); he is addressed as God's chosen 'redeemer of the sins of
man and helper of thy household' and asked to 'bless thy sons and all the
people' (2En. 64.3−5). However, it is going too far to infer from these that
Enoch is contrasted with Adam or regarded as a new *Stammvater* of a new
generation. Even in Philo's presentation of Noah we seem to have rather a
comparison than a contrast between Adam and Noah. True, Noah is, according to Philo, the τέλος of the condemned generation and the ἀρχή of the
innocent[2]. He is the 'ἀρχή of a second generation of mankind'[3]. That Philo
had in mind a comparison or parallelism rather than a contrast between Adam
and Noah, however, is clear in *Quaest. Gen.* ii.17, where, in explaining why
the flood occurred at the vernal equinox, the time of year when Adam, the
first earthborn man (γηγενής), had been formed, Philo says: 'since Noah
after the destruction (of mankind) by the flood becomes the first beginning
of the race, . . . he is made similar, so far as possible, to the first earthborn
man (γηγενῆ)'. After this, when Philo goes on to say in *Quaest. Gen.* ii.56
that Noah as the beginning of a second genesis of man is 'equal in honour not
with the moulded and earthy man (τῷ πλαστῷ καὶ γηΐνῳ) but with him
who was (made) in the form and likeness of the truly incorporeal Being', he
is, of course, showing his usual self-contradiction caused by his Platonic
presupposition which forces him occasionally to juxtapose the two accounts
of the creation of man (Gen 1.26f. and 2.7). Scarcely, so to speak, before the
ink on his sentence is dry, in *Quaest. Gen.* ii.66 he draws a parallel between
Adam's agricultural work after his expulsion from Eden and Noah's after his
coming out of the ark. Thus Philo seems to be interested in the parallelism
between Adam and Noah as the beginning of the first and the second race
respectively rather than in their contrast as the fallen and the righteous.
Wedderburn has a better ground, however, when he speaks of the contrast of
Adam with Abraham, Moses, Elijah, etc. in late Judaism. In Gen. R.14.6 R.

---

[1]The Jewish liturgy in the סדר עבודה for the Day of Atonement which narrates
stories about the figures in a way similar to 4Ezra 3 may just bear the interpretation that
Wedderburn puts on it. See *Service of the Synagogue. Day of Atonement*, Part II
(1904), pp.159f.

[2]*Praem.* 23; cf. *Abr.* 46; *Quaest. Gen.* i.96.

[3]*Vit. Mos.* ii.60; cf. 65; *Abr.* 46; 56; *Quaest. Gen.* ii.56.

Levi is represented as having said that Abraham was created after Adam, so that he might come to set things right after Adam's fall. In 2Bar. 17.18, Adam, who lived 930 years to no avail because of his sin, is contrasted with Moses, who lived only 120 years but brought the Law and light to Israel through his obedience[1]. According to Gen. R. 19.7, seven righteous men, Abraham, Isaac, Jacob, Levi, Korah, Amram and Moses brought the *shechina* down to earth again from the seventh heaven into which it had departed with the sins of the seven generations of mankind since Adam; and Moses, standing at the end of the chain of the seven righteous, brought it from the first heaven 'right down below'[2]. In Lev. R. 27.4, Adam, who sinned and forfeited life, is contrasted with Elijah, who did not sin and so lives for ever (see also Gen. R. 21.5; Eccl. R. 3.15). Then there is the contrast between Adam and the Messiah. The thought that the Messiah would remove sin and the curse which Adam brought upon mankind and restore the pre-fall state is most clearly expressed in Test. Levi 18.10f. But Wedderburn regards it as a Christian composition[3]. One strand of Rabbinic thought envisages that six things which Adam lost — his lustre, his immortality, his height, the fruit of the earth, the fruit of trees, and the luminaries — would be restored in the Messianic age[4]. Also noteworthy is the idea that the Messiah will not come until all the souls written in the book of Adam have been created[5]. This review of Wedderburn's material leads us to modify his conclusion to some extent: in Judaism Adam is sometimes co-ordinated with the righteous heroes of Israel's history; he serves as a parallel to Noah in Philo; and sometimes, especially in later Rabbinic traditions, he is contrasted with Abraham,

---

[1] For Philo the calling of Moses onto the mountain covered with a cloud on the seventh day 'is a second birth better than the first. For the latter is mixed with a body and had corruptible parents, while the former is an unmixed and simple soul of the sovereign . . . . he (sc. Moses) is called on the seventh day, in this (respect) differing from the earth-born first moulded man, for the latter came into being from the earth and with a body, while the former (came) from the ether and without a body' (*Quaest. Ex.* ii. 46). Is Philo contrasting Moses and Adam on account of the righteous obedience of one and the transgression of the other?

[2] See Scroggs, *Last Adam*, pp.53f., who points out the paucity of explicit comparisons between Adam and Moses in early Rabbinic traditions and rejects the attempts to see a typology between the two figures (*contra*, Murmelstein, *op. cit.*, pp.51ff. Jeremias, Μωυσῆς, *TDNT* iv, pp.856f.)

[3] With M.de Jonge, *The Testaments of the Twelve Patriarchs* (1953), p.90; O.Eissfeldt, *The OT: An Introduction* (1965), p.633.

[4] Gen. R.12.6; Num. R.13.12; cf. also Ex. R.30.3 — collected together in Str.-Bill. i, pp.19f.

[5] Gen. R.24.4. See Str.-Bill. ii, pp.173f.

Moses, Elijah and the Messiah.

Then Wedderburn considers the peculiar Jewish-Christian doctrine in the Pseudo-Clementine literature which traces a series of incarnations of 'the true prophet' in the persons of Adam, Enoch, Noah, Abraham, Isaac, Jacob, Moses and Christ, thus making Christ Adam *redivivus*. Since Wedderburn thinks with H.J. Schoeps[1] that the glorification of Adam in Pseud.-Clem. was an anti-Pauline polemic and its stress on the tradition of the true prophet an anti-Marcionite one, he finds it neither witnessing to Jewish beliefs in the NT age nor providing a help for understanding of Paul's Adam-Christ typology.

Perhaps here we must also introduce the Jewish idea of a *Stammvater* and of the solidarity of his descendants with him as conveniently summarized by E. Schweizer[2]. We have already seen how Philo's description of Noah as the beginning of a new innocent generation aligns him with Adam, the *Stammvater* of the old condemned generation. Owing to his love of hope, according to Philo, Enos received the name meaning 'man'. So he alone is 'a true man' and the founder of the pure and λογικόν generation in contrast to his predecessors who were the founders of the mixed race (*Abr.* 7–10; *Praem.* 14). Moses, whose prophetic call is a second birth into an incorporeal being in contrast to the earth-born Adam (*Quaest. Gen.* ii.46), is the path-finder (ἡγεμὼν τῆς ὁδοῦ) of the generation loved by God (τὸ θεοφιλὲς γένος) (*Conf. Ling.* 95). Jacob-Israel is one of the many names of the Logos (*Conf. Ling.* 146); he is the 'earliest offspring of the Uncreated One' (*Post.* 63); as the 'God-seer' he is the type of those who are able to see God directly (*Praem.* 43ff.); and he is of the pure, immortal and heavenly substance in contrast with Esau, who is of the mixed, corruptible and earthly substance (*Quaest. Gen.* iv. 164). Compare this last statement of Philo with 4Ezra 6.8f., according to which Esau represents the first age and Jacob the second[3]. The Book of Jubilees continues the OT tradition of referring to the nation Israel by the personal name 'Jacob', so that the solidarity of the *Stammvater*

---

[1] Schoeps, *Urgemeinde, Judenchristentum, Gnosis* (1956), pp.25, 65.

[2] Schweizer, 'Die Kirche als Leib Christi in den paulinischen Homologumena', *Neotestamentica*, pp.280–282. The idea is often included in the concept 'corporate personality'. See H.Wheeler Robinson's two essays, 'The Hebrew Conception of Corporate Personality' (1936) and 'The Group and the Individual' (1937), now collected together in *Corporate Personality in Ancient Israel*, ed. J.Reumann (1964). R.P.Shedd, *Man in Community* (1958), Part One. For the problems of the concept 'corporate personality' and a delineation of many different senses often included in it, see Wedderburn, 'The Body of Christ', pp.83f.

[3] Schweizer, 'eschatologischer Mensch', pp.106f., supposes in the interest of his new thesis (see n.1, next page) that here two aeons are thought of as lying 'nebeneinander' – no! *nacheinander*! (so G.H.Box, in Charles, *Apoc. & Pseud.* ii, p.573).

with his *Stamm* verges on identification, and the entire *Stamm* is regarded as one individual man with the *Stammvater* as his head (e.g., 2.24; 19.18, 29; 22.13; cf. also Test. Zeb. 9.4). As seen above, Jacob is regarded as the last of the 22 'heads of mankind' from Adam and therefore as a parallel (N.B. not a contrast!) to Adam and Noah (Jub. 2.23; 19.23ff.; 22.13). Jacob's seed will bring about a cosmic renewal (Jub. 19.25)[1].

As the third element in the 'Jewish preparation' for Paul's Adam-Christ typology, Wedderburn considers 'the expectation of the appearance of a heavenly Man or Son of Man'. He endeavours to show that both Adam and the eschatological redeemer could be depicted as heavenly men without being identified with each other. So here is considered the glorification of Adam in Judaism before his fall as the king of paradise, as a heavenly angelic being, as a giant body stretching from east to west or earth to heaven, composed of elements from all four corners of the earth, or as an androgynous figure. In the latter two conceptions Wedderburn recognises the influence of the Greek idea of cosmos as a macro-anthropos, the speculation on the four letters of Adam's name in Greek, and the Greek concept of androgynous man. These glorifications of Adam in his pre-fall state are the expressions of the authors' awareness of an ideal existence and their consciousness that their actual situation falls far short of that. They express their awareness of God's intent for man, once realized in the person of Adam in the primal golden

---

[1]In his recent essay 'eschatologischer Mensch', Schweizer wants to understand the Jewish apocalyptists' descriptions of the figures like Noah, Jacob and Moses, as well as Philo's, not only from the point of view of the *heilsgeschichtliche Stammvater–Stamm* idea, but also from the static-dualistic idea of two kinds of men (and so mankind): the true, heavenly man and the inferior, earthly man. In Philo's statements about Enos, Noah, Jacob and Moses, Schweizer is perhaps justified to see an amalgamation of the static-dualistic view that the true, heavenly Man lives in the group of 'wise men' and the *heilsgeschichtliche* view of the *Stammvater* who inaugurates a new race and a new world-period, although it should be remembered that Philo is more interested in the parallelism between Adam and Noah than in their contrast. But the same cannot be said of the Jewish apocalyptists' statements about Jacob or Moses. The Pseudo-Clementine *Kerygma of Peter* knows the dualism of the true prophets of the male principle and the prophets of the female principle, but embarrassingly identifies Adam with Christ under the rubric of the former. Schweizer's fanciful attempt to work out the same amalgamation of the two views in the Ethiopic redactor of the Dream Vision (1En. 85–90) (pp.107ff.) is shattered by the fact that not only the important *heilsgeschichtlichen* figures like Abraham, Jacob and David are represented as an animal and not a 'man', but also the Messiah himself is not designated as 'man' but as 'a white bull' (1En. 90.37ff.). This fact shows rather that the Ethiopic redactor's representation of Noah (a 'bull') and Moses (a 'sheep') turning into a 'man' (89.1 and 36) is motivated by his desire to explain how a 'bull' and a 'sheep' built the ark and the tabernacle respectively (So Charles, *Apoc. & Pseud.* ii, pp.151, 253).

age, thwarted in the present, but to be realized for all men or all the faithful in the age to come[1]. Perhaps a similar motive is behind the depiction of Adam as the type of the repentent sinner, restored to his original dignity and blessing.

Having dealt with the phenomenon of the glorification of Adam in Judaism, Wedderburn goes on to examine the Jewish expectations of the Messiah as 'man' and as 'son of man'. Following G. Vermes, he believes that the designation 'man' (איש/ זכר/גבר) in 1QH 3.9f. and the Biblical texts like 2Sam 23.1; Zech 13.7; Num 24.7, 17; Jer 31.21; Isa 66.7; 6.12 as understood in late Judaism (esp. in Targumim) has a Messianic significance[2], and that the texts express 'the usual Jewish expectation of a man of God's anointing who would rule his people'[3]. Noting that in the Messianic text Zech 6.12 איש in the MT is rendered by גברא (Targum), $d\nu\acute{\eta}\rho$ (LXX), and $\acute{a}\nu\theta\rho\omega\pi\sigma\varsigma$ (Philo, *Conf. Ling.* 62), he regards it as gratuitous to see in the expectation an influence of the *Urmensch* mythology. Indeed he believes it is against this background of the concept of the man of God's choice rather than that of a heavenly Man myth, that Philo's designation of the Logos as 'man' or 'man of God' should be understood. Wedderburn then carefully discusses the 'son of man' passages in Dan 7, the Similitudes of Enoch, and 4Ezra 13. We have already questioned the ways in which some scholars use the 'son of man' passages as a background for Paul's Adam-Christ typology. Wedderburn himself finds, as noted above, the immediate background for it in Jesus' self-designation.

As we said at the outset of this section, in order to understand the various motifs in Paul's Adam-Christ typology we need to take into account the Jewish conceptions of Adam and his fall and their expectations of a restoration of the pre-fall state of man and the world with the coming of the Messiah. Thus the 'Jewish preparation', as sketched by Wedderburn, forms a broad background for Paul's Adam-Christ typology. However it fails to provide a parallel or a direct background for Paul's contrasting of Adam and Christ, let alone his designation of Christ as 'the Last Adam'. For, as Wedderburn himself says, ' . . . we should resist any temptation to regard Paul as dependent on a tradition relating these eschatological "men" to Adam or as reacting

---

[1]So with emphasis Scroggs, *Last Adam*, pp.24ff, 52 *et passim*; cf. also Colpe, *TDNT* viii, pp.410f.

[2]G.Vermes, *Scripture and Tradition in Judaism* (1961), pp.56–66, believes that these nouns 'acquired the characteristics of a proper name in the same way as *zemah* (branch) in the Zechariah quotation, and *Mashiah* (an anointed) in many post biblical passages' (p.63).

[3]Wedderburn, *Adam*, p.94.

against one which identified the two'[1]. Neither does it materially increase the probability that Paul derived his Adam-Christ typology from Jesus' self-designation[2].

The result of all this discussion so far is that the origin of Paul's Adam-Christ typology has not yet been clarified[3].

4)   Christ the Εἰκών τοῦ θεοῦ

We propose, then, to reverse the priority between Paul's Adam-Christology and εἰκών-Christology and see whether in fact Paul could not have derived his conception of Christ as the Last Adam from his prior conception of Christ as the εἰκών τοῦ θεοῦ. For this view we submit here *the fundamental thesis* that the latter conception is rooted in the Damascus event: *Paul saw the exalted Christ in glory as the εἰκών τοῦ θεοῦ on the road to Damascus.*

In the course of research for this thesis, which had suggested itself to us from the early days of our research on the Damascus Christophany, we have been encouraged to discover the passing remarks made by a few scholars to the same effect.   P.Feine wrote, in the context of his discussion on 'the conversion of Paul as the fundamental experience of the Spirit': 'It was the heavenly Christ that revealed himself to him (sc. Paul) and flooded the fulness of his life upon him. This divine Christ Paul calls the image of God (2 Cor 4.4; Col 1.15), power of God (1Cor 1.24) and also "the Lord of glory"

---

[1]Wedderburn, 'The Body of Christ', p.92.

[2]The latest attempt by Schweizer, 'eschatologischer Mensch', esp. pp.112f., to relate the Adam-Christ typology to the concept 'Son of Man' does not alter this judgement.

[3]So Käsemann, *Römer*, p.136. Cf. also Conzelmann, *1.Kor.*, pp.338–341, who leaves the question undecided. Käsemann's hesitant 'hypothesis' is to connect the typology with the Jewish sophia myth. According to him, Judaism in the Hellenistic age adapted the motifs of the *Urmensch* myth into its sophia myth solely to obtain the idea of the mediatorship in creation. However, in the new situation provided by the early Church and still more by Gnosticism those motifs could again be expressed in their original conception. Now it is clear that the characteristics of the sophia are applied to Christ in the NT. So the Hellenistic Judaism must have mediated to the early Church together with the view of the mediator of creation his titles Logos and Anthropos (cf. Philo, *Conf. Ling.* 146). This complex was adapted in the early Church because with it the pre-existent Christ could be described as the inaugurator of a new humanity. 'Damit ist freilich erst der Weg aufgezeigt, auf dem es zur Bezeichnung des präexistenten Christus als des eschatologischen Urmenschen kommt, die dann im christlichen Gnostizismus weiter ausgebaut wird. Dagegen ist die Adam-Christus-Typologie als solche bisher noch nicht geklärt' (p.136). We have already rejected the attempt to link sophia in the Jewish wisdom literature and the Logos and Anthropos in Philo with the *Urmenschlehre*. But since neither the Philonic Logos and Anthropos nor the sophia in other Jewish literature is an eschatological Anthropos, Paul or the early Church could hardly have obtained from this the idea that the pre-existent Christ is the eschatological *Urmensch* (*supra*, 161f.).

($τὸν$ $κύριον$ $τῆς$ $δόξης$) (1Cor 2.8). Thus he designates the form of the appearance of the heavenly Christ[1]. In connection with J.Weiss' explanation that in Paul's designation of Christ as the $εἰκών$ of God there lies the idea that Christ is the reflection of the shining light of God's essence, i.e. God's $δόξα$[2], O. Michel says in his essay on the origin of Paul's Christology: 'Then we stand no more in the late Jewish thought of the Messiah but in Paul's Damascus experience itself'[3]. While discussing the phrase $ἐν$ $μορφῇ$ $θεοῦ$ $ὑπάρχων$ in Phil 2.6, R.P. Martin says: 'Christ, in the Corinthian passage (sc. 2Cor 4.4, 6), is portrayed as the risen and exalted heavenly being who appeared to Saul on the Damascus road . . . as to Stephen at an earlier point in the record ((Acts) 7.55)'[4]. A little later, expounding the view that ' "the form of God" is to be read against an OT background', Martin says:

> The $μορφὴ$ $θεοῦ$ may be the equivalent of $εἰκών$ = $δόξα$ of God; and thus describes the first man, Adam at his creation (Gen 1.26, 27). Adam reflected the glory of the eternal Son of God who, from eternity, is Himself the 'image' of the invisible and ineffable God. Both Adams are thought of as the possessors of celestial light. What Paul has learned at the feet of Gamaliel about the 'glory' of the first Adam . . . he transferred to the last Adam as He revealed Himself to him in a blaze of glory[5].

W.G. Kümmel and J. Dupont also think that 2Cor 4.4 alludes to the Damascus Christophany[6]. In this connection should also be noted H.A.A. Kennedy's suggestion that Paul's representation of Christ's resurrection body as the 'spiritual body' (1Cor 15.44ff.) and 'the body of glory' (Phil 3.21) was based on the Damascus Christophany[7]. However it is a pity that none of these scholars has attempted to substantiate his view in an adequate way and draw out its full consequences.

---

[1]P.Feine, *Theologie des NT* ([3]1919), p.320.

[2]Weiss, *Das Urchristentum* (1917), pp.367f.

[3]Michel, 'Entstehung', pp.329f.

[4]Martin, *Carmen Christi*, p.111.

[5]*Ibid.*, p.119.

[6]Kümmel, *Theologie*, p.145; Dupont, 'Conversion', p.192. Cf. also R.V.G.Tasker, *The Second Epistle of Paul to the Corinthians* (1958), pp.70f. See also F.F. Bruce, *Paul: Apostle of the Heart Set Free* (1977), pp.122f. Barrett, *2Cor.*, p.133, also connects Paul's designation of Christ as the image of God in 2Cor 4.4 with his conversion. This he does, however, not in view of the form of the appearance of Christ in $δόξα$, but less convincingly in view of the conception of Wisdom as God's agent in creation and in conversions (cf. Wis. 2.27).

[7]Kennedy, *St. Paul's Conceptions of the Last Things* (1904), pp.89–93; Dupont, 'Conversion', p.192, also sees 'the body of glory' in Phil 3.21 as alluding to the Damascus Christophany.

a) The Linguistic Data

The first step towards substantiating our thesis afore-stated is to define more closely the terms εἰκών and μορφή and their cognates and synonyms as they appear in Paul's letters. It is impossible to survey here the usages of these words by different authors at different periods[1]. From the various reference works[2] we observe that the most comprehensive definition of εἰκών is 'image' (*Bild*) which carries with it the senses of likeness, representation, appearance, form, etc. It is to be noted that the word in itself implies neither imperfection or inferior quality as of a copy over against its prototype[3], nor *perfect* representation[4]. It is primarily a functional term for manifestation, representation and revelation, although sometimes it carries an implication of substantial participation in the original or prototype[5]. It is widely supposed that just as in the Greek Bible and Gnosticism so also in Paul, μορφή and εἰκών are more or less synonymous[6]. The LXX usually renders the Hebrew צֶלֶם ('image')[7] and its Aramaic equivalent צְלֵם with εἰκών. But once, in Dan 3.19, the Aramaic צְלֵם is rendered with μορφή. Jervell has conveniently listed the Gnostic passages where εἰκών and μορφή appear synonymously[8]. The most interesting among them is *Corp. Herm.* I.12: ὁ δὲ πάντων πατὴρ ὁ νοῦς, ὢν ζωὴ καὶ φῶς, ἀπεκύησεν Ἄνθρωπον αὐτῷ ἴσον, οὗ ἠράσθη ὡς ἰδίου τόκου· περικαλλὴς γάρ, τὴν τοῦ πατρὸς εἰκόνα ἔχων· ὄντως γὰρ καὶ ὁ θεὸς ἠράσθη τῆς ἰδίας μορφῆς...[9]. Similarly *Oracula Sibyllina* also uses εἰκών and μορφή interchangeably in referring to Gen 1.26f. In VIII. 440, Gen 1.26f. is paraphrased: ποιήσωμεν ἰδοὺ πανομοίϊον ἀνέρα μορφῇ ἡμετέρῃ καὶ δῶμεν ἔχειν ζωαρκέα πνοιήν...[10]. In VIII. 265—8, however, the same Biblical passage is paraphrased at first with εἰκών but then with μορφή, thus demonstrating the interchangeability of the

---

[1] See Eltester, *Eikon*, esp. pp.1—25; J.Behm, μορφή, *TDNT* iv, pp.742ff.

[2] Liddell-Scott, *s.v.*; Bauer-Arndt-Gingrich, *s.v.*; H.Kleinknecht, εἰκών, *TDNT* ii, pp.388ff.; also Eltester, *Eikon*, pp.1—25.

[3] Kleinknecht and Kittel, *TDNT* ii, pp.389, 395.

[4] J.B. Lightfoot, *Saint Paul's Epistles to the Colossians and to Philemon* (1904), p.143.

[5] Cf. Kleinknecht, *TDNT* ii, p.389.

[6] So, e.g., J.Héring, *Le Royaume de Dieu et sa venue* (1959), p.161; A.M.Hunter *Predecessors*, p.43; Cullmann, *Christology*, p.176; Eltester, *Eikon*, p.133; Jervell, *Imago*, pp.204ff.; Feuillet, *Le Christ sagesse de Dieu*, pp.344ff.

[7] See BDB, *s.v.*

[8] Jervell, *Imago*, p.167.

[9] Cited from the edition of A.D.Nock and A.—J. Festugière (1945).

[10] Cited from *Die Oracula Sibyllina* ed. J.Geffcken (1902).

two terms as clearly as C.H.I.12 (cf. also Or. Sib. III. 8: ἄνθρωποι θεόπλαστον ἔχοντες ἐν εἰκόνι μορφήν ...). Many Church Fathers took the clause in Phil 2.6, ὃς ἐν μορφῇ θεοῦ ὑπάρχων, as parallel to that in 2Cor 4.4 and Col 1.15: ὅς ἐστιν εἰκὼν τοῦ θεοῦ[1]. The phrases of Rom 8.29 (... συμμόρφους τῆς εἰκόνος τοῦ υἱοῦ αὐτοῦ) and 2Cor 3.18 (... τὴν αὐτὴν εἰκόνα μεταμορφούμεθα ...) indicate that in Paul's usage εἰκών and μορφή are very closely related to each other, if not actually synonymous.

There are some scholars who would see some difference between the two terms, however. From the three Pauline passages, Rom 8.29; 2Cor 3.18; and Phil 2.6 (N.B. the presence of the preposition ἐν here in contrast to its absence in 2Cor 4.4 and Col 1.15), we may surmise that there is some fine difference in nuance between the two terms. But how the difference is to be defined is not so clear. When, rejecting the usual equation of the εἰκὼν τοῦ θεοῦ and the μορφὴ θεοῦ, J. Behm says, 'the image of God is Christ, while the μορφὴ θεοῦ is the garment by which his divine nature may be known'[2], he has not made clear how he understands the phrase εἰκὼν τοῦ θεοῦ. However, taking Behm's sentence here to imply that μορφή is an external form of appearance over against essence or substance[3], critics have protested by pointing out that in some Hellenistic, especially Gnostic, literature μορφή means not just the external form but the essence, substance or nature[4]. One should be careful, however, not to go to the other extreme and understand the concept μορφή exclusively in terms of the latter, as E. Käsemann seems to be doing when he, in a polemic against Behm, understands the μορφή in Phil 2.6f. exclusively in terms of substance and renders it 'Daseinsweise'[5]. R. Bultmann's judgement is probably the most satisfactory:

> Morphē is the shape, the form, in which a person or thing appears, and in the LXX it is used synonymously with εἶδος (shape, form), ὁμοίωμα (likeness), ὅρασις (appearance), and ὄψις (appearance), not however in contrast to its essence, but precisely

---

[1]For references see Jervell, *Imago*, pp.203f.

[2]Behm, *TDNT* iv, p.752.

[3]This is a valid inference in view of the summary statement Behm presents after his full examination of the Greek usage of the word: 'Aufs Ganze gesehen, kommt in der überwiegenden Mehrzahl der reichen Bedeutungsnuancen zum Ausdruck, daß μορφή eigentlich etwas Sinnenfälliges, sich der Wahrnehmung Darstellendes meint, eben als solches, ohne den Gedanken an Sein oder Schein auch nur zu berühren.' (*ThWb* iv, p.753).

[4]Käsemann, 'Kritische Analyse', pp.65ff.; Jervell, *Imago*, p.204 (n.122); Schweizer, *Erniedrigung*, pp.95f.

[5]Käsemann, 'Kritische Analyse', pp.66ff. For a critique of Käsemann's understanding here, see Schweizer, *Erniedrigung*, p.95 (n.382).

as the expression thereof. Hence, it is understandable that in Hellenistic usage *morphē* can be used to designate the divine nature[1].

Bultmann then goes on to show that Paul's use of the word μορφή (Phil 2.6) and its cognates συμμορφοῦσθαι (Rom 8.29), μεταμορφοῦσθαι (Rom 12.2; 2Cor 3.18), and of the word σχῆμα (Phil 2.8; 1Cor 7.31) and its cognates συσχηματίζεσθαι (Rom 12.2; 1Cor 11.13ff.) and μετασχηματίζειν (Phil 3.21; cf. also 1Cor 4.6) should be understood in terms of nature and change of nature[2]. But in this analysis of the meanings of the words in the Pauline usage Bultmann more or less ignores the primary sense of μορφή, namely 'form', thus being unfaithful to his own definition of the word: form as the expression of its essence[3]. With regard to the Pauline usage of συμμορφοῦσθαι, μεταμορφοῦσθαι and μορφοῦσθαι (Gal 4.19), E. Schweizer seems to be correct when he suggests that it indicates 'rather OT thought that does not distinguish form and matter (*Stoff*) as the Greek, but connects the essence of a thing with its appearance' than 'the classic Greek thinking, where essence is determined by form'[4].

As for the μορφή in Phil 2.6f., while emphasizing that it should be rendered in such a way that it retains its primary sense of 'form', we would here simply endorse what Spicq says on the matter: ' . . . it was the natural word to use when speaking of metamorphosis or incarnation, although we are unable to give it an exact theological meaning'[5]. So, to the extent that the phrase μορφή θεοῦ in Phil 2.6 retains the sense 'form of God' in some way, it is equivalent to the phrase εἰκὼν τοῦ θεοῦ, the image, likeness, form, representation of God. Spicq defines two fine points of difference between μορφή and εἰκών: 1) 'The *icon* . . . , since it resembles that of which it is an image, (is) unchangeable, whereas the *morphe* is essentially modifiable, . . . the variable aspect which something assumes without altering its nature'; and 2) 'the image, being "that which appears as the tangible manifestation of the invisible or

---

[1]Bultmann, *Theology* i, pp.192f.

[2]*Ibid.*

[3]The meaning of μορφή as 'form' is illustrated with many examples from the Hellenistic papyri and inscriptions by C.Spicq, 'Note sur ΜΟΡΦΗ dans les papyrus et quelques inscriptions', *RB* 80 (1973), pp.37–45.

[4]Schweizer, *Erniedrigung*, p.96 (n.383).

[5]Spicq, *op. cit.*, p.45. For various understandings and renderings of the word μορφή in Phil 2.6f., see Martin, *Carmen Christi*, pp.100–133. Cf. also Hofius, *Christus-hymnus,* pp.57f., who, claiming that the meaning of μορφή in Phil 2.6f. should be derived from the context of the hymn itself and not from the complex conceptual and *religionsgeschichtliche* considerations of the word, adopts Schweizer's rendering: 'Status', 'Position', 'Stellung' (*Erniedrigung*, pp.95f.).

the abstract", cannot correspond to *morphē theou*[1]. These differences are partly abnegated by the evidence on the one hand that εἰκών is also used for different 'forms' that an object assumes[2] and on the other that μορφή is also used for the visible appearance of the invisible God[3]. However, on the whole Spicq may be correct, and these differences may have led Paul to use the word εἰκών on the one hand and μορφή and its cognates on the other in the way he does. That is to say, these differences can be worked out from Paul's use of the words.

Now there is some evidence that the Greek word εἰκών was used in the context of theophany in order to describe the visible form of god therein appearing. This usage is clearly demonstrated by the following epigram on Pheidia's statue of Zeus at Olympia: Ἦ θεὸς ἦλθ' ἐπὶ γῆς ἐξ οὐρανοῦ, εἰκόνα δείξων, φειδία, ἢ σὺ γ'ἔβης τὸν θεὸν ὀψόμενος[4]. However, rather than stopping here to assemble more Greek-Hellenistic evidence for such a use[5], we will pass on to the evidence that דמות, a Hebraic equivalent of εἰκών, is frequently used in epiphany. For the latter is more relevant to the understanding of Paul's designation of Christ as the εἰκὼν τοῦ θεοῦ in 2Cor 4.4 and Col 1.15, since it must be seen against the OT-Jewish (including the Hellenistic Jewish) background rather than the Greek-Hellenistic.

There is no doubt that 2Cor 4.4ff. and Col 1.15ff. allude to Gen 1 and to the figure of the hypostatized Wisdom, while 2Cor 3.16ff. alludes to Ex 34. Having clearly acknowledged this[6], Jervell still attempts to see Paul's conception of Christ as the εἰκών of God against the background of the Gnostic conception of the divine Anthropos as the εἰκών of God[7].

Although the hymns, Col 1.15–20 and Phil 2.6–11, are primarily concerned not with the ontological relationship between God and Christ but with the salvation of man, asserts Jervell, the statements about Christ as the εἰκών of

---

[1]Spicq, *op. cit.*, pp.44f.

[2]References in Eltester, *Eikon*, p.11 (n.55).

[3]E.g., references cited from Preisendanz ed., *Papyri Graecae Magicae*, in Behm, *TDNT* iv, p.747.

[4]Cited from *Anthologia Palatina* XVI. 81 (ed. F.Dübner, II, p.542). Cf. the references from the magical papyri cited by Behm, *TDNT* iv, p.747: e.g., ἐπικαλοῦμαί σε, κύριε, ἵνα μοι φανῇ ἡ ἀληθωή σοῦ μορφή (Preisendanz ed., *PGM* XIII. 581f.).

[5]Does the same epiphany idea underlie the proclamation of Ptolemy Epiphanes as εἰκόνος ζώσης τοῦ Διός on the Rosetta Stone? (Cf. Kleinknecht, *TDNT* ii, p.390).

[6]Jervell, *Imago*, pp.173ff., 200f.

[7]*Ibid.*, pp.214ff.; so also Eltester, *Eikon*, pp.137ff., appealing to Käsemann, who used to champion the Gnostic mythological background for the εἰκών/μορφή concept in Paul.

God indicate indirectly something about his relationship with God[1]. This is correct. But Jervell cannot conceal a high degree of unreality when he goes on to assert that Paul's question in 2Cor 4.4 was concerning the relationship of Christ's δόξα with that of God and that 'precisely in answering this question Paul comes to speak of the *eikon* concept in reference to Christ'[2]. We will soon see how the phrases δόξα τοῦ Χριστοῦ in 2Cor 4.4 and δόξα τοῦ θεοῦ ἐν προσώπῳ Χριστοῦ describe the same δόξα that accompanied the Damascus Christophany. At this stage we would only point out the far-fetched character of Jervell's attempt to force the concept of εἰκών in 2Cor 4.4 to yield what he considers to be the Gnostic understanding: the presence or the indwelling of God in Christ. Indeed, Paul's conception of Christ as the εἰκών of God probably does imply God's presence in Christ or Christ's ontological relationship with God. We have already noted that the word εἰκών carries such an implication not just among Gnostics but also other ancient writers[3]. But such an ontological definition of εἰκών which Jervell tries to extract from 2Cor 4.4–6 by means of the Johannine motifs of δόξα and indwelling[4] is secondary to its functional definition as the agent of revelation and representation. With the assertion that Paul's distinction between Christ as the εἰκών and the Christians as the κατ' εἰκόνα (ἄνθρωποι) (Col 3.9f.; Eph 4.24) indicates 'the Philonic-Gnostic idea' of the divine Anthropos as the εἰκών and the earthly Adam as the κατ' εἰκόνα ἄνθρωπος[5], Jervell can hardly imagine that he has found the source of Paul's designation of Christ as the εἰκών of God. The distinction which Philo and some Gnostics sometimes make out of their different exegeses of the phrase κατ' εἰκόνα in Gen 1.26f.[6] hardly provides a parallel to that of Paul. When Paul speaks of Christians being 'conformed' (συμμορφοῦσθαι) or 'transformed' (μεταμορφοῦσθαι) to the εἰκών of Christ (Rom 8.29; 2Cor 3.18) and 'putting on the new (man) which is being renewed . . . κατ' εἰκόνα' of God (or Christ) (Col 3.9f.), he is not talking about the relationship between the heavenly Anthropos and the earthly Adam in (the first) creation but that between Christ the Last Adam

---

[1] Jervell, *Imago,* p.214.

[2] *Ibid.*

[3] See Kleinknecht, *TDNT* ii, pp.387f.

[4] Jervell, *Imago*, pp.216ff.

[5] *Ibid.*, p.217.

[6] One taking the whole phrase as expressing a relation, and the other taking εἰκών as an independent hypostasis between God and man and κατά as expressing the relation. See Wedderburn, *Adam*, pp.124ff.; Schenke, *Gott "Mensch"*, esp. pp.64ff. Note Philo's designation of the Logos as ὁ κατ' εἰκόνα ἄνθρωπος in *Conf. Ling.* 146, in contrast to his usual practice of calling it εἰκών.

and the Christians in redemption (the second creation), to which Jervell has brought no analogy from the 'Philonic-Gnostic' sources. At any rate, neither this far-fetched parallelism between Paul's language in Col 3.9f. (Eph 4.24) and the 'Philonic-Gnostic' distinction between the heavenly Man as the εἰκών and the earthly Adam as the κατ᾽ εἰκόνα ἄνθρωπος, nor the arguments from Col 1.15ff.[1] and Phil 2.6ff.[2] can surmount the problems that we have seen as lying in the way of trying to claim that Paul conceived of Christ in terms of the Gnostic Anthropos. However, having once conceived of Christ as the εἰκών of God on the basis of the OT-Jewish tradition, which we will presently set forth, Paul could well have included in that conception some of the implications and motifs which the Greek word εἰκών had in his Hellenistic milieu and which later became important in the Gnostic speculations; these could be what Jervell is so eager to show as Paul's borrowings from Gnosticism[3]. What these are specifically will, to some extent, become apparent in the course of our examination of the Pauline εἰκών/μορφή material in this chapter and the next. At this point, however, it is submitted that Paul's conception of Christ as the image of God should be seen primarily against the OT-Jewish background and therefore that in the designation one should see primarily the OT-Jewish mind 'that does not distinguish at all between form and matter like the Greek, but connects the essence of a thing with its appearance'[4] rather than the Greek-Hellenistic mind that is concerned to define Christ's being or essence as divine.

Let us return to דמות and other Semitic equivalents of εἰκών. In the LXX εἰκών normally renders the Hebrew צלם and the Aramaic צלם. צלם means 'image' both in the sense of a plastic copy, a representation of an object by a picture or statue, and in the sense of a non-physical picture of an object taking shape in the mind or in a dream[5]. However, once εἰκών renders דמות

---

[1]Jervell. *Imago*, pp.218ff., esp. 225f.; also Eltester, *Eikon*, pp.137ff.

[2]Jervell, *Imago*, pp.227ff.

[3]Jervell's undue emphasis on Gnostic elements in Paul's εἰκών/μορφή material is also criticized by Larsson, *Vorbild*, p.114. Schenke's acute criticism of Jervell's method of analysing the Gnostic material is also relevant here: 'Die Arbeit Jervells leidet an einer m.E. unvertretbaren Interpretationstechnik, bei der die Akzente verschoben und die Unterschiede verschleiert werden. Mit dieser Technik kann man alles beweisen, was man will. So kommt Jervell in allen Partien seines Buches nur zu halbwahren Ergebnissen' (*Gott "Mensch"*, p.121.n.2).

[4]Schweizer, *Erniedrigung*, p.96.

[5]Köhler-Baumgartner, *Lexicon in Veteris Testamenti Libros* (²1953): Nachbildung, Abbild, Bildnis, Zeichnung, Bild, (vergängliches) Bild. BDB: image, likeness, mere, empty image, semblance. See further H.Wildberger צלם, *ThHAT* ii, 555ff.; L.Koehler,

in the LXX. It is in Gen 5.1, where the account of God's creation of man in Gen 1.26f. is summarised in one sentence:

ביום ברא אלהים אדם בדמות אלהים עשה אתו ᾗ ἡμέρᾳ ἐποίησεν ὁ θεὸς τὸν 'Αδάμ, κατ' εἰκόνα θεοῦ ἐποίησεν αὐτόν. דמות, an abstract noun derived from the verb דמה ('be like, resemble'), has the basic meaning of 'likeness'[1]. In the LXX it is regularly rendered by ὁμοίωμα/ὁμοίωσις. Two of the only three places where it is rendered otherwise are Gen 5.1 and 3 where it is rendered by εἰκών and ἰδέα ('appearance')[2]. Some recent commentators argue that the two words צלם and דמות , which belong to the same semantic field, are often used interchangeably and synonymously[3]. This can be seen in a comparison between the description of God's creating Adam בצלמנו כדמותנו in Gen 1.26 and that of Adam's begetting Seth כצלמו בדמותו in Gen 5.3, which shows the interchangeable nature of both the ˙nouns and the prepositions used. Ezek 23 provides a further example, where for the picture of Babylonians צלם is used in v.14 and then דמות in v.15. In 2Chr 4.3 דמות is used for the moulded figures of gourds like צלם in 1Sam 6.5, 11. Also in Isa 40.18 דמות is used for a concrete 'image' like an image of an idol, for which צלם is often used. Finally, a summary reference to the account of the creation of man in Gen 1.26f. can be made with either one of the two words: with דמות in Gen 5.1 and with צלם in Gen 9.6. From these examples it is clear that דמות , originally an abstract noun for 'likeness', can take on a concrete meaning of 'image' and that in such a usage it is synonymous with צלם . In Gen 1.26 (and 5.3) the two words are joined, if not just for emphasis, for clarification of the similarity between God and man, but not for reference to two different aspects of it. K.L. Schmidt sees בצלם כדמות as a hendiadys, though within that hendiadys he sees a slight difference between the two parallel concepts, and the second concept (דמות) as explaining and supplementing the first con-

---

'Die Grundstelle der Imago-Dei-Lehre', *ThZ* 4 (1948), pp.16ff.; K.L.Schmidt, 'HOMO Imago Dei im Alten und Neuen Testament', *Eranos-Jahrbuch* 15 (1948), pp.169ff.; J.Barr, 'The Image of God in the Book of Genesis – A Study of Terminology', *BJRL* 51 (1968), pp.15ff.; D.J.A.Clines, 'The Image of God in Man', *TynB* 19 (1968), pp.70ff.; C.Westermann, *Genesis* (1974), pp.201ff.

[1]BDB: likeness, similitude; Baumgartner, *Hebräisches und Aramäisches Lexikon*, 1.Lief. (1967); Gleichheit, Gestalt, Nachbildung, Abbild. See further E.Jenni, צלם, *ThHAT* i, 451ff.; Preuss, דמות/דמה, *ThWAT* ii, 273ff.

[2]Isa 13.4 is the remaining place, but there it is rendered by ὅμοιος.

[3]This is emphasized by Westermann, *Genesis*, pp.201ff.; see further Jenni, *op. cit.*, 454; Preuss, *op. cit.*, 276; Schmidt, *op. cit.*, p.165ff.

cept (צלם)[1]. This view, now widely held[2], is well expressed by J. Barr
in a general way: '*D^emut* is added in order to define and limit (the) meaning
(of *selem*) by indicating that the sense intended for *selem* must lie within
that part of its range which overlaps with the range of *d^emut*'[3]. The more
specific question, in which way precisely דמות defines and limits צלם, is
not our present concern[4]. What is more important for us at the moment is.
that דמות can be used as a synonym of צלם for 'image'. The LXX seems
to understand this correctly when it not only renders the phrase בצלמנו
כדמותנו in Gen 1.26 by a hendiadys κατ᾽ εἰκόνα ἡμετέραν καὶ καθ.
ὁμοίωσιν[5] but also, as we have seen, renders once דמות actually by εἰκών
(Gen 5.1).

The synonymous character of the two Hebrew words corresponds to that
of their two Greek equivalents: εἰκών and ὁμοίωμα/ὁμοίωσις[6]. J. Schneider ascertains from the Greek usage that ὁμοίωμα ('what is made similar',
'copy') is a synonym of εἰκών. He goes on to say: 'εἰκών and ὁμοίωμα are
often used as equivalents, e.g., Plato, *Phaedr.* 250b: ὁμοιώματα and εἰκόνες
are in Plato the earthly copies of the heavenly prototypes. But there is often
a distinction between the two words. This may be formulated as follows:
εἰκών represents the object, whereas ὁμοίωμα emphasizes the similarity, but
with no need for an inner connection between the original and the copy'[7].
But to the Semitic mind that did not distinguish appearance and substance in
the Greek manner, such a distinction may not have been essential. So, if
Schneider is right, as he surely is, in observing that in the LXX ὁμοίωμα has
two senses: 'a) "copy" ("image" in the sense of "similitude" . . .) and b)

---

[1]Schmidt, *op. cit.*, pp.166–169.

[2]See the authors cited in n.3, p.201.

[3]Barr, *op. cit.*, p.24.

[4]See Clines, *op. cit.*, pp.91ff., who disputes the view that the two terms are completely synonymous, rejects both the view, that דמות 'strengthens' the meaning of צלם
and the view that it 'weakens' the physical sense of צלם , and says: 'דמות then speci-
fies what kind of image it is: it is a "likeness"–image, not simply an image; represen-
tational, not simply representative' (p.91).

[5]On the hendiadys character of this phrase see Schmidt, *op. cit.*, p.166; also Jervell,
Imago, p.22.

[6]See J.Schneider, ὁμοίωσις/ὁμοίωμα, *TDNT* v, pp.190f.; Jervell, *Imago*, pp.22,
117, 165f.

[7]Schneider, *op. cit.*, p.191. He affirms a similar distinction between ὁμοίωσις and
εἰκών (p.190). The distinction is perhaps more real for this abstract noun than the concrete noun ὁμοίωμα.

"form" '[1], then ὁμοίωμα is used at times as a synonym of εἰκών in the LXX just as דמות is of צלם in the Hebrew Bible[2].

This synonymous understanding of צלם and דמות is carried on in Judaism[3]. Jervell observes that in Rabbinic Judaism the two words are not distinguished: the phrase בצלם ובדמות is often used like a formula for the creation of man or only one of the two concepts is used[4]. It is significant to note with him that while the Greek speaking Gnostics mostly used the word εἰκών alone in connection with Gen 1.26f., making it a key concept in their systems, the Semitic (Aramaic and Syriac) speaking Gnostics used only the word דמות for the same purpose[5]. Again, Jervell shows that in the Mandaean literature דמות is used for both εἰκών and μορφή[6]. A most interesting phenomenon is the use of εἰκών as a loan-word in the form of דיוקן, איקונין, etc.[7] in late Judaism. Apparently in the Jerusalem Talmud and the earlier Midrashim only איקונין and its variants appear, while in the Babylonian Talmud, the later Midrashim and the Targum Pseudo-Jonathan both איקונין and דיוקן with their variants appear[8]. It was first introduced early in the Tannaitic period (if not earlier) probably in connection with the εἰκών,

---

[1]*Ibid.*, p.191.

[2]It is interesting to note that the LXX renders צלם twice in 1Sam 6.5 by ὁμοίωμα.

[3]See Jervell, *Imago*, pp.21f. (n.21), 90, 165. He notes, however, that in late sources the two words are sometimes differentiated (p.90, n.77). For the differentiation in the early Christian exegesis since Irenaeus, see A.Strucker, *Die Gottebenbildlichkeit des Menschen in der christlichen Literatur der ersten zwei Jahrhunderte* (1913), pp.87, 101ff.

[4]Jervell, *Imago*, p.90.

[5]*Ibid.*, pp.165ff. See K.Rudolph, *Die Mandäer, I Prolegomena* (1960), pp.127—161 for numerous references in the Mandaean literature; further Od.Sol.7.4; 17.4; 34.4; *Die Schatzhöhle, syrisch u. deutsch I—II*, ed. C.Bezold (1883—1889), 2.3ff.

[6]Jervell, *Imago*, pp.167f., 204.

[7]For variant forms see S.Krauss, *Griechische und lateinische Lehnwörter im Talmud, Midrasch, und Targum* ii (1964), pp.40, 202, 604. M.Jastrow, *A Dictionary of the Targumim, the Talmuds and the Midrashic Literature* i (1926), p.297, thinks that דיוקן is 'a reverential transformation of איקון'; J.Levy, *Neuhebräisches und chaldäisches Wörterbuch über die Talmudim und Midraschim* i (1876), pp.394f., explains it as a combination δύο — εἰκών. The latter is supported by Jervell, *Imago*, p.97 (n.101), who thinks that דיוקן indicates a *Bild* to be both *Urbild* and *Abbild*.

[8]For examples of the Rabbinic passages where איקונין or דיוקן appears, see Krauss, *Lehnwörter*, pp.40f., 202f.; Levy, *Wörterbuch*, i, pp.70, 394f. So also 4Ezra 8.44: '. . . but the son of man who . . . is made like thine image' (Syriac: *wlywqnk 'tdmy*; Latin: et tuae imagini (nominatus quoniam) similatus est; Greek probably: καὶ τῇ εἰκόνι σου ὡμοιώθη).

that is, the statue, of the Graeco-Roman rulers[1]. For both Lev.R.33.4 (a story about Hillel) and Mek. Ex 20.16, which are probably of the earliest references, use איקונין for the statue of the king and draw an analogy between the statue as the image of the king and man as the image of God. From this the use of the word איקונין for man as the divine image (i.e., for צלם or דמות) itself was a natural development[2]. In the Tg. Jon. דיוקן renders דמות at Gen 1.26 (כדיוקננא), צלם at 1.27 (בדיוקניה), דמות at 5.1 (בדיוקנא), and צלם at 9.6 (בדיוקנא) while איקונין renders צלם at 5.3 (לאיקוניה) and פנים at 4.5 (איקונין)[3]. Thus Pseudo-Jonathan incidentally confirms that in Judaism צלם and דמות are synonymous. However, of greater significance is the phrase דמות דיוקני, which occasionally appears in the Rabbinic literature. According to b.B.Bath.58a, when R. Bana'ch, after surveying the cave of Abraham, came to the cave of Adam, he was told by *bath qol:* 'You have seen דמות דיוקני, but דיוקני itself you may not see'. So Adam is God's image (דיוקן) and Abraham the image of Adam. B. Mo'ed Kat. 15b contains a sentence: 'I (sc. God) have set דמות דיוקני upon them'. In these two examples דיוקן appears as God's *Urbild* and דמות its *Abbild*. However, in b. Hul. 91b the story of Jacob in Gen 28.12 is told: 'They (sc. angels) ascend and see the דמות above; they descend and see דמות דיוקני'[4]. The formulation דמות דיוקן in the rather late Rabbinic Judaism may well reflect the Hellenistic distinction between *Urbild* and *Abbild* in the conception of εἰκών which is seen in Philo and Gnosticism[5]. In these examples דמות has throughout the concrete meaning of 'image' (*Abbild*).

There are a few Hebrew words which belong to the same semantic field as צלם and דמות. Among them מראה ('appearance'), תמונה ('shape', 'form') and תבנית ('shape', 'pattern') are relevant to our present study. They appear sometimes in association with דמות and sometimes as synonymous with דמות. The context of such a usage of these words is usually an

---

[1]Cf. M.Smith, 'The Image of God: Notes on the Hellenization of Judaism', *BJRL* 40 (1958), pp.475ff.

[2]For examples of such a use see the references in n.8, p.203.

[3]See C.C.Rowland, *The Influence of the First Chapter of Ezekiel on Jewish and Early Christian Literature*, an unpublished Cambridge Ph.D. Thesis (1974), pp.142f. From this survey and especially from a comparison between Gen 5.1 and 5.3 Rowland draws the conclusion that דיוקן is used for the divine image as the prototype for the creation of man while איקנין is used for Adam's begetting Seth in his image. However, he notes also that this distinction does not apply to other Jewish literature.

[4]See further examples in Levy, *Wörterbuch*, p.395.

[5]Cf. Jervell, *Imago*, pp.97ff.

epiphany vision[1], as we shall see presently. To these may be added כבוד (δόξα) and פנה (πρόσωπον), which also appear in association with or as synonymous with דמות or צלם especially in the context of an epiphany vision[2]. This also will be seen in the following.

b) Epiphany Visions

Now it is our task to establish that דמות and its related words are regularly used in the sense of 'likeness', 'form', and 'image' in descriptions of God and the heavenly objects revealed in an epiphany. This is, of course, the clearest in the call-vision of the prophet Ezekiel. In 'the fifth year of the exile of the king Jehoiachin' (Ezek 1.2), Ezekiel, the son of Buzi, received a call to be a prophet through a theophany by the river Chebar. The heavens were opened and he saw visions of God (מראות אלהים) (1.1). He saw 'a storm wind coming from the north, a vast cloud with flashes of fire and brilliant light about it' (1.4 NEB). In the midst of the fire there appeared something sparkling like the alloy of gold and silver, that is, something like a mirror[3]. In the disc of the mirror he saw the דמות of four living creatures, whose appearance (מראה) had the form (דמות) of man (1.5), that is, four living creatures each with four faces (פנים), whose form (דמות)was man-like in the front, lion-like on the right, ox-like on the left and eagle-like on the back (1.10). In between the creatures he saw something that had the appearance (ὅρασις) of burning coals, of torches (1.13 LXX). Then he saw four wheels upon the earth, one each beside the four creatures, whose appearance (מראה/εἶδος) was like the gleaming of a chrysolite[4] (1.16). Above the heads of the four creatures there was spread out something that appeared like (דמות) a firmament shining like a sheet of ice (or crystal)[5] (1.22). Above the firmament he saw something like a throne (דמות כסא) which had the appearance (מראה) of sapphire, and a figure like the appearance of a man (דמות כמראה אדם) seated upon the form of a throne (דמות הכסא) (LXX: ... καὶ ἐπὶ τοῦ ὁμοιώματος τοῦ θρόνου ὁμοίωμα ὡς εἶδος ἀνθρώπου ἄνωθεν) (1.26). The part above that which had the appearance (מראה)

----

[1]See Barr, *op. cit.*, pp.15ff. on these and three more words: מסכה ,פסל , and סמל. These three words are irrelevant to us because they, meaning 'cast idol', 'graven idol' and 'statue' respectively, are not related to an epiphanic vision.

[2]Cf. Jervell, *Imago*, pp.45, 100ff., 168.

[3]So O.Procksch, 'Die Berufungsvision Hesekiels', *Beiträge zur alttestamentlichen Wissenschaft*, K.Budde FS (1920), p.142 (n.1): ' עין kann hier nur "der Spiegel" sein'.

[4]*Ibid.*, p.142: 'wie ein durchsichtiger Spiegel aus Chrysolith'.

[5]*Ibid.*, p.142: 'klar wie ein Eisspiegel'.

of his loins Ezekiel saw as shining like the alloy of gold and silver, like the appearance (מראה) of fire, and the part below that as appearing (מראה) like fire. The figure was surrounded by brightness (1.27). The appearance (מראה) of the brightness was like a rainbow. With this Ezekiel concludes his description of the theophany: 'Such was the appearance of the likeness of the glory of the Lord' (1.28 RSV). However, it is probable that the מראה דמות כבוד יהוה in 1.28 refers not to the whole description of the theophany in Ezek 1, but rather to the climax of the vision, namely the description of the enthroned figure in human form in 1.26f., to which the rest of the description is introductory, concerning the attendant circumstances. For throughout the Book of Ezekiel (כבוד יהוה or אלהי ישראל) is described as sitting upon (or moving from) the throne above the cherubim (9.3; 10.4, 18f.; 11.22f.) or otherwise personified (3.12, 23; 8.4; 43.2–5; 44.4)[1]. כבוד יהוה in Ezek. is therefore the personal presence of Yahweh in brilliant light which often appears to the seer, Ezekiel, in human form[2]. In the course of his prophetic ministry Ezekiel repeatedly sees this כבוד יהוה or other objects which he saw in his inaugural vision. In 8.2f. he sees דמות כמראה־איש[3] in the same form as in ch. 1, putting forth the form (תבנית/ὁμοίωμα) of a hand to take him by his head. In 10.1 he sees upon the firmament over the cherubim something like sapphire כסא כמראה דמות; in 10.8 the cherubim appear to have ידי־אדם תבנית; in 10.9f. he sees four wheels beside the cherubim, whose appearances (מראה) are like shining chrysolite, having the same דמות; and in 10.20ff. he sees דמות ידי־אדם (ὁμοίωμα) underneath the wings of the cherubim, the דמות of whose faces is the same as that whose מראה he saw by the river Chebar. Again in 40.2f. Ezekiel sees in the visions of God (מראות אלהים) a man whose appearance (מראה) is that of bronze. Finally, in ch. 43 Ezekiel sees again a vision (מראה/ὅρασις) like that which he saw by the river Chebar and כבוד יהוה (vs. 1–5) in the heavenly temple whose ὅρασις he is commanded to describe to the house of

---

[1]Cf. Zimmerli, *Ezechiel*, p.58: A.Feuillet, 'Le Fils de l'homme de Daniel et la Tradition biblique', *RB* 60(1953), p.182; J.Maier, *Vom Kultus zur Gnosis* (1964) pp.119f.

[2]Also in later מרכבה mysticism and שעור קומה speculations which are rooted in Ezek 1 כבוד is often used as a *term. techn.* for God appearing in human form on the chariot throne. See G.Scholem, *Major Trends in Jewish Mysticism* (1941), pp.35f.(n.16); Maier, *Kultus*, pp.136ff., 144; Rowland, *Influence*, p.22 *et passim*; Quispel, 'Gnosticism and the NT', *Gnostic Studies* i, pp.210f.

[3]With the LXX (ὁμοίωμα ἀνδρός) and the majority of commentators איש should be read in the place of אש in the MT.

Israel (v.10 LXX)[1]. Thus in these descriptions of theophanies, Ezekiel constantly employs the words עין ,מראה, דמות and תבנית[2] in order to portray the appearance, likeness and forms (= shapes) of the heavenly objects in the visions with analogous objects on earth. The most interesting description for our present purpose is that reflected in the mirror of the alloy of gold and silver (מתוכה)כעין החשמל) 1.4), God, enthroned above the fiery wheels, appears in human form or in the likeness of man(דמות כמראה אדם) (1.26). From this two observations are to be made. Firstly, Ezekiel sees God not directly but as reflected in a mirror, that is, the (mirror) image of God[3]. This may well be in keeping with the OT belief that man cannot see God directly and live (e.g., Ex 33.20; Judg 13.22; Isa 6.5)[4]. However, neither this belief nor the descriptive words like דמות and מראה should lead us to think that Ezekiel is basically affirming the invisible nature of God or at best the impossibility of describing the form of God here. On the contrary he is affirming that he *saw* God, albeit in his mirror image, and that he saw him in the form of man[5]. This anthropomorphic theophany, that is, God appearing in human form to a seer, is not unique to Ezekiel in the OT, as we shall see below[6]. Secondly, when Ezekiel says he saw God in the form or likeness of man he is describing the reverse side of the great statement in Gen 1.26f. that man was made בצלם כדמות of God[7]. The implications of these observations for our present study will be seen later. For the present we must go on examining more descriptions of theophanies.

In Dan 7 Daniel sees in dream visions four beasts rising out of the sea

---

[1]Cf. Targum: לדמותה דביתא

[2]In the LXX εἶδος renders מראה and עין ; ὁμοίωμα דמות, מראה, עין, and תבנית; ὁμοίωσις דמות and תבנית; and ὅρασις מראה and עין.

[3]Procksch, 'Berufungsvision', p.144: 'Hesekiel sieht nicht die Urgestalt der göttlichen Herrlichkeit, sondern nur die εἰκὼν τοῦ θεοῦ.'

[4]J.Barr, 'Theophany and Anthropomorphism in the OT', *VT Supplement* vii (1960) p.34, makes the correct observation: it is 'not so much that the deity is invisible as that it is deadly for man to see him' in his holiness. On exceptional occasions and to special persons God makes himself visible.

[5]So Rowland, *Influence*, p.88; also Zimmerli, *Ezechiel*, p.81*.

[6]Cf. Barr, 'Theophany', pp.31ff.

[7]Procksch, 'Berufungsvision', p.148: 'Wenn Gottes Spiegelbild nun als eine דמות כמראה אדם beschrieben wird (V.26), so ist dies die Umkehrung zum Gedanken der Priesterschrift, daß der Mensch בצלם אלהים geschaffen ist (Gen. 1, 27)'. Similarly also v.Rad, *OT Theology* i, p.146. Cf. also Feuillet, 'Fils', p.190; Barr, 'Theophany', p.38.

which he describes by means of earthly analogies: like (כ/ὡσεί) a lion, like a bear, like a leopard, like a man, like the eyes of a man. Then he sees the fiery throne upon the wheels on which the divine figure, the Ancient of Days, is sitting. This figure is also described with earthly analogies: his raiment is white as (כ/ὡσεί) snow and his hair like pure wool. Then Daniel sees 'one like a son of man' (כבר אנש) coming with (or upon – LXX) the clouds of heaven to the Ancient of Days. This figure, having been presented to the Ancient of Days, receives dominion, glory and kingdom. Now it is clear that the phrase 'son of man' is no title here: Daniel does not see *'the Son of Man'* but 'one like a son of man'. It is rather a descriptive, pictorial phrase which expresses that the figure Daniel sees is like a man, has a human form or likeness[1]. The accompaniment of the clouds in his appearance clearly indicates that he is a divine figure. For in the OT clouds regularly accompany theophany[2]. So the figure Daniel sees, 'one like a son of man', is a deity appearing in human form or likeness. As the various Oriental – Iranian, Babylonian, Egyptian – myths and the Gnostic Anthropos-myth are now shown to be no source of the figure in Jewish apocalyptic literature[3], the Canaanite myth of the two deities – El and Baal – is appealed to as the possible source of the idea of two deities – the Ancient of Days and 'one like a son of man' – in Dan 7[4]. But even this hypothesis is not without difficulties, as the parallels between the Canaanite myth in the Ugaritic texts and the descriptions of Dan 7 are by no means unequivocal[5]. Moreover it is difficult to imagine how the author of Daniel came to know the myth[6]. For us, the

---

[1]Colpe, ὁ υἱὸς τοῦ ἀνθρώπου, *TDNT* viii, pp.419f.; Wedderburn, *Adam*, pp.95ff.; H.R.Balz, *Methodische Probleme der neutestamentlichen Christologie* (1967), pp.62f.; U.B.Müller, *Messias und Menschensohn in jüdischen Apokalypsen und in der Offenbarung des Johannes* (1972), pp.30, 32; cf. also Moule, 'Neglected Features in the Problem of "the Son of Man" ', *NT und Kirche*, Schnackenburg FS (1974), p.414.

[2]Among about 100 passages in which clouds are mentioned in the OT, Feuillet reckons that about 30 refer to a purely natural phenomenon and the rest to theophanies. He notes also that in angelophany clouds are absent. See Feuillet, 'Fils', pp.187f.; Emerton, 'the Son of Man Imagery', pp.231f.; Colpe, *TDNT* viii, pp.420f.

[3]See Colpe, *TDNT* viii, pp.408ff.; Müller, *Messias*, pp.30ff.

[4]Emerton, 'the Son of Man Imagery', pp.225–242; Colpe, *TDNT* viii, pp.415–419, regards this as 'a possible hypothesis'; cf. also Rowland, *Influence*, p.92.

[5]See Colpe, *TDNT* viii, pp.417ff.; cf. also Müller, *Messias*, p.34.

[6]Emerton has a considerable difficulty in making it plausible that the influence of the myth, having entered into the Jewish cultus after their settlement in Canaan or David's capture of Jerusalem, lived on in the Jewish cultus (*op. cit.*, pp.240ff.). If Emerton is right, it is surely strange that the myth of two deities, after a long time of hibernation, should suddenly surface in Daniel – precisely in the Book of Daniel, which

attempt to see the figure within the OT-Jewish tradition of theophanies seems to provide the best explanation of the figure. On this more will be said later. At this stage we are concerned only with the descriptions of God and other heavenly figures in epiphanies. So we must proceed to Dan 8.15, where Daniel sees Gabriel as 'one having the appearance of man' (כמראה־גבר/ὡς ὅρασις ἀνθρώπου). At his second appearance this Gabriel is then referred to by Daniel as '*the* man (האיש) Gabriel whom I had seen ın the vision at first' (9.21). Then in 10.5f. Daniel sees 'a man clothed in linen' (cf. Ezek 9.2) and describes him in a way that is reminiscent of Ezekiel's description of God in human form in Ezek 1.26f. (and 8.2), using many earthly analogies with the preposition 'like' (כ/ὡσεί) for different parts of his body. Again 10.16 Daniel sees a figure (an angel?) כדמות בני אדם(Th: ὡς ὁμοίωσις υἱοῦ ἀνθρώπου), and in 10.18 this figure is described as כמראה אדם(LXX & Th: ὡς ὅρασις ἀνθρώπου)[1]. These passages in Daniel in which a divine or angelic figure is described as having the form or likeness of man should be compared with Dan 4.25 where an angelic figure is seen by Nebuchadnezzar as being 'like a son of the gods'   (דמה לבר־אלהין/Th: ὁμοία υἱῷ θεοῦ /LXX: ὁμοίωμα ἀγγέλου θεοῦ)[2].

There are three documents — 1En 46; 4Ezra 13; and Rev 1 — which describe the heavenly figure appearing to the apocalyptic seer in a vision in the manner of Dan 7.13. It is generally recognized that these are under the influence of Daniel. In 1En 46.1 Enoch sees in a vision 'one who (has) a head of days' and with him 'another being whose countenance (has) the appearance of a man'. Enoch further describes the face of the latter as being full of graciousness, 'like one of the holy angels'. From 1En 46.2 onward right through the Similitudes except in 1En 62.7 this being in human form or appearance is referred to as '*that* (or *this*) son of man' or 'the son of man'[3]. As in Dan 7 'son of man' is no title here[4]. Being a shortened designation for 'one whose countenance has the appearance of a man', 'this (or that) son of man' (= 'the son of man') in the later passages of the Similitudes refers throughout back to the heavenly figure of human appearance in 46.1,

---

is so uncompromising with heathen cults! Cf. Wedderburn, *Adam,* p.97; Colpe, *TDNT* viii, p.418.

[1]This incidentally shows that דמות and מראה are synonymous in epiphanic language.

[2]Cf. Hengel, *Sohn*, p.36 (n.43).

[3]Ethiopic demonstratives ('this' and 'that') probably render the Greek article. See Charles, *The Book of Enoch* (²1912), pp.86f.

[4]See Colpe, *TDNT* viii, pp.423ff. for the various reasons for not taking it as a title in 1En. together with complicated linguistic data. *Contra* Charles, *op. cit.*, pp.86f.

just as in Dan 9.21 'the man' (האיש) is the shortened designation for Gabriel whom Daniel saw as 'one having the appearance of man' at the first vision (8.15)[1].

A similar description to this is found in 4Ezra 13. In a dream vision Ezra sees a being 'as the form of a man' (*'yk dmwṭ' dbrnš'*) coming out of the sea (v.3). Then this figure is referred to with the shortened designation 'this man', 'the man' or 'a man' throughout the rest of the ch. As in Dan 7 and the Similitudes of Enoch so also here 'man' or 'son of man' is no title, but a pictorial description for the supernatural figure seen in a vision: the figure who comes out of the sea and flies with the clouds of heaven is like a man or has the form of a man. This figure is then identified as God's son ('my son': the Latin text: *filius meus*; so also the Syriac text) in the divine interpretation of the vision given to the seer (vs. 32, 37, 52)[2].

The Apocalypse of John, concerning as it does many revelations of the heavenly realities, naturally abounds with the pictorial or symbolical phrases usually introduced by the preposition ὡς or its equivalent ὅμοιος. Such phrases, which we should perhaps call the 'epiphanic or apocalyptic language' provide earthly analogies to the heavenly objects which the seer sees in a vision. It is no intention of ours to examine here this imagery in Rev. which is drawn largely from Dan., Ezek., and other apocalyptic sections of the OT. We are mainly concerned with two passages in which the seer sees the exalted Christ as 'one like a son of man'. In his call vision (Rev 1.13ff.) John sees 'one like a son of man'. (ὅμοιον υἱὸν ἀνθρώπου) and describes him with the imagery which is used for the Ancient of Days in Dan 7.9 and for 'a man clothed in linen' in Dan 10.5f. (cf. also Ezek 1.24). It is striking that this exalted Christ who appears to John as 'one like a son of man' is later in 2.18 identified as 'the Son of God, who has eyes like a flame of fire, and whose feet are like burnished bronze' (cf. 1.14f.)[3]. In 14.14 John sees again the exalted Christ enthroned in the cloud with a golden crown as 'one like a son of man' (ὅμοιον υἱὸν ἀνθρώπου)[4]. These two passages in Rev. are striking because they are

---

[1]So Müller, *Messias*, p.41. 1En 62.7, where 'son of man' is not prefaced by a demonstrative, may well be a careless slip which Charles finds to be a characteristic of Ethiopic translation (Charles, *op. cit.*, p.86.).

[2]J.Jeremias, παῖς θεοῦ, *TDNT* v, pp.681f. (n.196), following B.Violet, says, however, that the Greek original underlying the versions of 4Ezra must have παῖς rather than υἱός in these verses. Cf. 4Ezra 7.28; 14.9.

[3]Rev 2.18 is the only place in Rev. where the title 'the Son of God' appears.

[4]For the various literary and exegetical problems of this passage see Müller, *Messias*, pp.190–199, with literature cited there; further E.Lohse, 'Der Menschensohn in der Johannesapokalypse', *Jesus und der Menschensohn*, Vögtle FS, pp.417f.

the only places in the NT where 'son of man' is not used as a title. Although in the letters Christ ('one like a son of man') sends to the seven churches there is one clear reference to a saying of the Son of Man in the Synoptic Gospels (Rev 3.5 = Lk 12.8 = Mt 10.32) as well as some reminiscences of the Synoptic *Herrenworte*, the title 'the Son of Man' does not appear[1]. John simply describes the appearance of the heavenly Lord with symbolical or epiphanic language, probably in dependence upon the Semitic text of Dan 7.13. This distinguishes these two passages also from another apocalyptic passage in the NT, namely Acts 7.56, where Stephen sees 'the heavens opened, and the Son of Man standing at the right hand of God'.

The Testament of Abraham[2] is also relevant to the present survey of epiphanic or visionary language. In the long recension Abraham is brought on the cherubim chariot to heaven and sees there two gates leading to two ways, one narrow and the other wide. Outside the two gates he sees 'a man sitting on a golden throne', whose appearance 'is fearsome, ὁμοία τοῦ δεσπότου'[3] (Rec.A. XI). Then he learns from Michael, his *angelus interpres*, that the glorious figure is Adam, ὁ πρωτόπλαστος. Inside the gates, between the two Abraham sees 'a fearsome throne which looks like fire' and upon it 'a wondrous man looking like the sun, like a son of God' (ἀνὴρ θαυμαστὸς ἡλιό-ρατος ὅμοιος υἱῷ θεοῦ), sitting (Rec.A. XII)[4]. The description of the fiery throne and of the figure sitting upon it are unmistakably reminiscent of those in Ezek 1; Dan 7; and 1En 14. Strikingly, however, Michael tells Abraham that the fearsome man sitting upon the throne and exercising judgement upon souls is Abel, the son of Adam. The description of the enthroned figure in

---

[1] See *ibid.*, pp.419f.

[2] A.M.Denis, *Introduction aux pseudepigraphes grecs d'Ancien Testament* (1970), pp.36f., dates the Hebrew original in the first c. A.D., while dating the two Greek recensions later.

[3] In view of Test.Abr.Rec.A.XIII; XVI, where God is repeatedly called δεσπότης, δεσπότης here must also refer to God. Rowland's attempt to make δεσπότης here refer to Abel (*Influence*, p.136), is quite incredible. If Abraham already here in Rec.A.XI knew Abel so as to describe Adam as being 'like Abel', he would hardly ask Michael in Rec.A.XIII about the identity of the enthroned figure in Rec.A.XII and learn from him that he is Abel! True, God is said to be ἀόρατος in Rec.A.XVI. Michael similarly is repeatedly called ἀσώματος (e.g., Rec.A.XI; XV), yet not only Abraham sees him as his escort but Sarah also embraces 'the feet of the incorporeal one' (Rec.A.XV)! We have here to do with the *seeing* in a vision of *invisible* heavenly realities. So Abraham can say on the one hand that God is invisible and on the other hand that Adam appears 'like God' the Lord (δεσπότης) – the latter meaning that Adam appears with shining light of glory, power and terror, etc., which are associated with God's appearance in human imagination.

[4] Cf. E.Stone, *The Testament of Abraham: the Greek Recensions* (1972), pp.26–33.

Rec.A. XII is the reverse of Ezek 1.26f.: whereas in the latter *God* appears
in the דמות כמראה אדם, in the former a *man* (ἀνήρ) appears ὅμοιος υἱῷ
θεοῦ . Finally in Rec.A. XVI we find the story of the personified Death
putting on at the command of God a very bright robe, making his appearance
like the sun (ἡλιόμορφος), thus taking upon himself the form of an archangel
(ἀρχαγγέλου μορφὴν περικείμενος). He comes to Abraham, and Abraham
at first mistakes him for Michael, the ἀρχιστράτηγος of God, and then greets
him: χαίροις ἡλιόρατε, ἡλιόμορφε, συλλήπτωρ ἐνδοξότατε, φωτοφόρε, ἀνὴρ
θαυμάσιε . . . καὶ τίς εἰ σύ, καὶ πόθεν ἐλήλυθας; Upon Death's disclosure of
his identity, Abraham, refusing to believe it, declares: . . . σὺ εἰ ἡ δόξα καὶ
τὸ κάλλος τῶν ἀγγέλων καὶ τῶν ἀνθρώπων, σὺ εἰ πάσης μορφῆς
εὐμορφότερος . . . This is, of course, fiction. Nevertheless, it is valuable in so
far as it also shows the basic idea which is there in all the material so far
examined: namely, that in epiphany-vision God or an angel is seen in a man-
like form, and the exalted man like Abel appears in such glorious form as to
be described as being 'sun-like' (ἡλιόμορφος) or 'like a son of God' (ὅμοιος
υἱῷ θεοῦ).

Very instructive at this point is Josephus' rendering of the story of the
divination by the medium of Endor. In the original version the medium
summoned the spirit of Samuel through divination. As Samuel appeared, she
cried to Saul: 'I see a god (אלהים/θεούς) coming out of the earth'. Saul
asked her: 'What is his appearance (תאר)?' She answered: 'An old man[1] is
coming up; and he is wrapped in a robe'. Upon this answer 'Saul knew that
it was Samuel, and bowed with his face to the ground and did obeisance'
(1Sam 28.13f.). Since only here in the OT the designation אלהים is used for
the spirit or ghost of the dead, already the original may well indicate that the
spirit of Samuel appeared in a visible form with some extraordinary, supernatural features which were usually associated with God in common human
imagination[2]. If this is so, Josephus understands it well and makes it more
explicit. For he says that when Samuel appeared the woman beheld 'a vener-
able and god-like man' (ἄνδρα σεμνὸν καὶ θεοπρεπῆ). Upon Saul's question
whence came her alarm, according to Josephus, 'she answered that she saw
someone in form like God arise' (βλέπειν εἶπεν ἀνελθόντα τῷ θεῷ τινὰ τὴν
μορφὴν ὅμοιον). 'At Saul's command (for her) to describe the image, the
shape and age of what was being seen, she represented him as old and glorious
and clad in a priestly robe' (τοῦ δὲ τὴν εἰκόνα φράζειν καὶ τὸ σχῆμα τοῦ
θεαθέντος καὶ τὴν ἡλικίαν κελεύσαντος, γέροντα μὲν ἤδη καὶ ἔνδοξον

---

[1]MT: איש זקן; cf. LXX: ἄνδρα ὄρθιον.
[2]Cf. H.J.Stoebe, *Das erste Buch Samuelis* (1973), pp.485f.

ἐσήμαινεν, ἱερατικὴν δὲ περικείμενον διπλοΐδα) (*Ant.*vi. 332f.). It is most interesting to find in this short passage of Josephus so many concepts clustered together which we have been looking for in various accounts of theophanic and apocalyptic visions: εἰκών, σχῆμα, δόξα, ἄνδρα θεοπρεπῆ, τινὰ τὴν μορφὴν ὅμοιον τῷ θεῷ. Although the vision of Samuel that the medium sees through divination is no apocalyptic vision of God and the heavenly world, it shares the common character with the latter as a vision of the supernatural. Hence the description of the vision has exactly the same character as that of the latter[1].

Finally we would briefly examine two more apocalyptic passages in this connection. In 4Ezra 5.37, to the complaint of Ezra concerning the fate of Israel and the apparent injustice of God, the angel Uriel answers:

> Open me the chambers that are closed
> and bring me forth the spirits shut up in them;
> Show me the image of faces thou hast never seen
> or show me the image of a voice;
> and I will then display to thee the
> objective thou askest to see[2].

This is the translation of the Syriac version, in which 'image' renders *dmwt*'[3]. The third line is omitted by the Latin, one Arabic and the Armenian versions, while it appears in the Syriac, Ethiopic and the other Arabic versions[4]. However, the Latin version renders 'the image of a voice' in the fourth line by *vocis imaginem*[5]. Here it should be remembered that in the Syriac-speaking Gnosticism the word *dmwt*' is exclusively used in connection with Gen 1.26f. and it stands for both εἰκών and μορφή of Greek-speaking Gnosticism[3]. In view of this fact and of the Latin rendering '*vocis imaginem*' A. Hilgenfeld must be correct in his reconstruction of the lost Greek text

---

[1]Cf. b.Sot.36b: when the wife of Potiphar caught Joseph by his garment, 'his father's image came and appeared to him through the window ... (באתה דיוקנו של)'; further b. Yom. 69a: דיוקנו של זה מנצחת לפני (אביו נראתה לו ·בחלון בבית מלחמתי דמות .

[2]Translation by G.H.Box, *The Ezra-Apocalypse* (1912), p.57.

[3]See the Syriac text edited by A.M.Ceriani, *Monumenta sacra et profana*, Tom V, p.55. This word occurs also in 4Ezra 13.3: '*yk dmwt*' *dbrnš*.

[4]See the synopsis of different versions in B.Violet, *Die Ezra-Apokalypse,* 1. Teil (1910), pp.74f.

[5]See the Latin text edited by R.L.Bensley, *The Fourth Book of Ezra: the Latin Versions,* Texts and Studies III. 2 (1889). Box, *op. cit.*, p.57 (n.1), cites the phrase 'imago vocis' from Vergil, *Georgic* iv.50.

[6]*Supra* p.203.

underlying the different versions: . . . καὶ δεῖξόν μοι εἰκόνα ὧν οὐδέποτε εἶδες ἀνθρώπων ἢ δεῖξόν μοι φωνῆς εἰκόνα[1]. Now these words Uriel speaks to Ezra in order to show him that just as he cannot do these things, the latter, being a mortal, cannot comprehend the mystery of God's judgement and 'goal of love' for his people (v.40). However, the idea underlying these words interests us here, and it has been brought out well by H. Gunkel: 'The ancient world is convinced that sound too, like all things existing, has form (*Gestalt*) and could be seen, although the coarse organs of men cannot see many forms of existence which are visible to the eye of God. The ancient world thinks of God and the divine in the same way: all this is invisible not in itself but only to ordinary men'[2]. Thus in 4Ezra 5.37 'image' is used to mean the visible form or representative of a usually invisible object. In Test. Benj. 10.1 Benjamin says: ὅτι δὲ Ἰωσὴφ ἦν ἐν Αἰγύπτῳ , ἐπεθύμουν ἰδεῖν τὴν εἰδέαν αὐτοῦ καὶ τὴν μορφὴν τῆς ὄψεως αὐτοῦ ⸱ καὶ δι' εὐχῶν Ἰακὼβ τοῦ πατρός μου εἶδον αὐτόν, εν ἡμέρᾳ γρηγορῶν, καθ' ὃ ἦν πᾶσα ἡ εἰδέα αὐτοῦ [3]. Here is the idea of seeing in a vision someone's μορφή and εἰδέα, both of which in this context surely are synonymous with εἰκών. Thus these last two passages, Test. Benj. 10.1 and 4Ezra 5.37, confirm what we have so far ascertained from the various descriptions of visions.

We may now *summarize some of the salient points* which we have ascertained from descriptions of apocalyptic visions so far. 1) In vision the seer sees the מראה or דמות, that is, the εἰκών, εἰδέα or μορφή of the otherwise invisible God, heavenly beings or other invisible beings. 2) The heavenly, supernatural realities are regularly described by means of earthly analogies, and therefore in the descriptions of visions such pictorial or symbolical words as כ, מראה , דמות, תבנית, עין, and their Greek equivalents ὡς, εἶδος, ὅρασις, ὅμοιος, ὁμοίωμα, ὁμοίωσις, μορφή, εἰκών are regularly used, in order to express the basic idea that the heavenly objects seen in vision are 'like' such and such earthly objects, that is, have the 'form', 'likeness', or 'appearance' of such and such earthly objects. These words should perhaps be called the 'apocalyptic' or 'visionary' language[4]. 3) A divine figure appearing in a vision is regularly described as being 'like' a man: In Ezek. God appears דמות כמראה אדם   (1.26 – cf. also 1.28: (מראה דמות כבוד־יהוה

----

[1]A.Hilgenfeld, *Messias Judaeorum* (1869), p.51.

[2]H.Gunkel in Kautzsch ed.*Apok. u. Pseud.* ii, p.362; so also Box, *op. cit.*, p.57 (n.1).

[3]From the text edited by M.de Jonge, *Testamenta XII Patriarcharum* (1964), p.84. Cf. R.H.Charles ed., *The Greek Versions of the Testament of the Twelve Patriarchs* (³1966), p.228, for some insignificant variants.

[4]Cf. Balz, *Probleme*, p.86 (n.5); Müller, *Messias*, p.32. On the symbolism employed in the apocalyptic literature in general see Russell, *Method*, pp.122ff.

and again as כמראה־איש דמות (8.2f.); in three places a divine figure is
seen כבר־אנש (Dan 7.13), as 'a being whose countenance (has) the appearance of man' (1En 46.1) and 'like the form (or image – *dmwt'*) of a son of
man' (4Ezra 13.3); in Rev 1.13f.; 14.14 the enthroned Christ appears ὅμοιον
υἱὸν ἀνθρώπου; and in Dan 8.15; 10.16ff. an angel like Gabriel is seen
כמראה־גבר ((8.15) or כדמות בני־אדם (10.16) and כמראה אדם (10.18). All
these passages describe the heavenly, divine figure – God or angel – as having
the 'appearance', 'form' or 'likeness' of a man. 4) Man exalted in heaven or
existing in the supernatural realm (*Jenseits*) is seen in a vision 'like' God or
a son of God: in Test. Abr. Abel appears ἡ λιόρατος and ὅμοιος υἱῷ θεοῦ
(Rec.A. XII); in 1Sam 18.13f. the spirit of Samuel is seen θεοπρεπῆ, as τῷ
θεῷ τὴν μορφὴν ὅμοιον. Dan 3.25 is also relevant here: the angelic figure
beside the three Jewish youths in the furnace was seen at first as a man (N.B.:
'four men') by Nebuchadnezzar. This was so not only because the figure was
with the three *men* and Nebuchadnezzar naturally expected to see only men
in the furnace, but also because the figure had the form or likeness of a man.
But he had at the same time a more exalted appearance than Daniel and his
two friends. Hence Nebuchadnezzar exclaimed later that the figure was
דמה לבר־אלהין. Note also that in Test. Abr. Rec.A. XVI the personified
Death appears ἡ λιόμορφος, in the μορφὴ ἀρχαγγέλου. The difference between the last two points would seem to bear a simple rational explanation.
Both have to do with the appearance of a glorious, exalted, supernatural
figure in vision. When the figure is known to the seer to be God or a divine
being, his appearance can hardly be described as being 'like God'. For that
would be a tautology and no description. For the same reason, if the figure
is known to the seer to be a man, his exalted appearance cannot be described as being 'like a man'. In the light of this our final point is to be
seen: 5) twice the heavenly figure appearing 'like a son of man' is subsequently identified as the Son of God (υἱὸς τοῦ θεοῦ in Rev 2.18; and
presumably παῖς τοῦ θεοῦ in 4Ezra 13.32, 37, 52). This identification is
especially significant in Rev 2.18 for two reasons: first, the title, υἱὸς τοῦ
θεοῦ occurs only once here in Rev.; and, secondly, by describing the Son of
God as one 'who has eyes like a flame of fire, and whose feet are like
burnished bronze', that is, with the words used to describe the appearance of
the figure 'like a son of man' in 1.14f., the seer in Rev 2.18 indicates not only
that the figure appearing 'like a son of man' is in fact the Son of God, that is,
the Messiah Jesus exalted to God's right hand (cf. Rom 1.3f.), but probably
also that the figure he sees in vision *appears* also 'like a son of God' (cf. other
descriptions of the 'one like a son of man' at the heads of the other six letters
in Rev 2.1, 8, 12; 3.1, 7, 14). At any rate it is a reasonable inference from
the above data that the glorious, supernatural figure appearing in a vision can
in himself be described either as being 'like a son of man' (= 'like a man') or

'like a son of God' (= 'like God'), and that what determines the seer's choice of one expression or the other depends on whether the figure is already known (or later turns out) to be a divine being or an exalted man.

> While some of the accounts examined here are undoubtedly fictitious, some others must have a genuine basis in the experience of epiphanic visions by the apocalyptic seers. In view of the strong traditions of theophanies and the apocalyptic visionary experiences of the prophets and the apocalyptists stretching from the earliest strata of the OT right through to the later Jewish texts of the מרכבה and קומה שעזר mysticism[1], the genuineness of the experiences can hardly be doubted. The fictitious accounts, insofar as they are literary imitations of the genuine accounts, serve only to confirm the general features of the genuine apocalyptic visions. The problems such as whether what a seer, Ezekiel, for example, saw in vision were conditioned by his prior imaginations of God and the heavenly beings and by the Temple furnitures and the like, or whether later apocalyptists and mystics were conditioned in their seeing by their familiarity with the accounts of their predecessors, cannot be discussed here[2]. Whatever the correct explanation of the psychological mechanism at work in a visionary experience may be, here we must be content with ascertaining that there are genuine experiences of epiphanic visions, and the above five points are among the general features in the descriptions of such visions.

In this context of examining the visions of some prophets and apocalyptists we should also include a survey of the abundant accounts of theophanies, angelophanies and apocalyptic visions seen by other prophets in the OT. Since many of them report God's appearance in the form of a man, this fact undoubtedly strengthens the conlusions that we have just reached, and therefor our thesis concerning Paul's conception of Christ as the image of God. It is very helpful that James Barr has already examined the evidence under the suggestive title 'Theophany and Anthropomorphism in the OT'[3]. Hence a brief summary of Barr's essay will be of value to our study.

From the outset Barr makes it clear that the word 'anthropomorphism' should properly suggest the *form* in which God is known, rather than such ways of speech which refer to God's hands, ears or nose, his speaking, walking, rejoicing, etc. In the OT, according to Barr, 'it is in the theophanies where God lets himself be seen that there is a real attempt to grapple with the form of his appearance'[4]. 'For Hebrew thought "form" and "appearance" may be taken as correlative', says Barr, so that 'where there is no "appearance" a

---

[1] For the Jewish mysticism see G. Scholem, *Major Trends*; also his *Jewish Gnosticism, Merkabah Mysticism and Talmudic Tradition* (1960).

[2] On the question of the genuineness of some apocalyptic visionary experiences and of the psychological mechanism involved therein see Russell, *Method*, esp. pp.158–202.

[3] In *VT Supplement* 7 (1960), pp.31–38.

[4] *Ibid.*, pp.31f.

passage is of only secondary importance for the idea of form'[1]. Theophanies are introduced often with some form of the Hebrew word 'to see', commonly *way-yēra'*, 'and Yahweh let himself be seen, showed himself'. But there are some theophanic statements where no attempt is made to describe the form of the appearance and the words spoken form the main part. Even in such cases, however, there remain traces of theophanic description: e.g., in the theophany to Samuel in 1Sam 3, *way-yityaṣṣah* (v.10) is probably a trace of the common picture of theophany in erect human form; cf. *niṣṣa* in Gen 18.2; 28.13; Amos 7.7; 9.1. Thus, 'there is adequate evidence for a strong tradition in early Israel that Yahweh let himself be seen at times in the form of man'[2]. In Gen 19.1f. it is said that Yahweh appeared to Abraham and Abraham saw 'three men' standing in front of him. In Gen 32.23–33 Elohim appears to Jacob as a man and wrestles with him. So Jacob saw 'Elohim face to face' (v.30). The question arising out of such descriptions of theophanies, according to Barr, is not, 'Is God conceived of as essentially in human form?' but rather, 'When he does appear in a form at all, is it thought that the human form is the natural or characteristic one for him to assume?', and the answer to it is affirmative[3]. Barr rejects the common supposition that from an early period anthropomorphism was felt to be an embarrassment so that mitigating devices such as dreams and angelic mediations were introduced: 'It would be argued that on the contrary the dream increases the directness (of an anthropomorphic appearance) and gives a stronger vision'[4]. Neither are the stories of a *mal'ak* a device for the mitigation of anthropomorphism: 'If anything, the *mal'ak* might be better understood as the accompaniment of the anthropomorphic appearance rather than as a dilution of it' (e.g., Gen 18.1–19.1)[5]. The OT asserts not so much that God is invisible as that it is deadly for man to see him on account of his holiness and awfulness. So only on exceptional occasions and to special persons God makes himself visible. Barr then examines the accounts of theophany in Ex 33; Isa 6; and Ezek 1. From the latter two he finds the prophetic tradition preserving the two old themes of theophany: 'the appearing to the special person and the discernible human form of the appearing'[6]. Barr notes that the *mal'ak*, the being, perhaps an angelic being, who accompanies or represents the appearance of Yahweh is called

[1]*Ibid.*, p.32.
[2]*Ibid.*, p.32.
[3]*Ibid.*, p.33.
[4]*Ibid.*, p.33.
[5]*Ibid.*, pp.33f.
[6]*Ibid.*, p.37.

more often a man than a *mal'ak*: e.g., Dan 8.15; 9.21; 10.5f., 16ff. The being who is *ke-bar 'enash* in Dan 7.13, according to Barr, is also 'an angelic anthropomorphic appearance of the same kind'[1]. Then, most significantly for our present study, Barr asks whether any direct line can be drawn from the tradition of anthropomorphic theophanies to the idea of man having been created in the image of God. His judgement is:

> Thoughts of God appearing in human shape are by no means naturally reversible into thoughts of man sharing the shape of God. But the naturalness, or propriety, of the human likeness for divine appearances when they occasionally do occur, coupled. with their comparative rarity, may have been one element in the thinking of those who developed the thought of the *selem 'elohim*.

Barr goes on:

> Certainly the word *selem* should lead us towards a kind of manifestation or presentation, such as a statue would perform in an iconic religion, and it might be reasonable to say that the interpretation of the Image among modern theologians, as apart from OT scholars, have tended to make the Image too much a relatedness, a capacity, an adaptability, and too little a likeness, a manifestation[2].

The first part of Barr's judgement[3] is important for our present study. However, the latter part gives us an opportunity to state clearly, in agreement with Barr, that the basic idea of likeness and manifestation cannot be removed completely from the conception of *Imago Dei*, whether in Gen 1.26f. or in 2Cor 4.4 and Col 1.15. It is not just modern theologians who debate where the *Imago Dei* lies in man. Jewish theologians, both pre-Rabbinic and Rabbinic, early Christian theologians, and Gnostics all saw it as an important theological or anthropological topic and produced many different views. These have been surveyed by a number of recent authors[4]. It is quite possible

---

[1]*Ibid.*, p.37.

[2]*Ibid.*, p.38.

[3]With it should be compared the more positive statement by v.Rad: 'Israel conceived even Jahweh himself as having human form. . . . according to the ideas of Jahwism, it cannot be said that Israel regarded God anthropomorphically, but the reverse, that she considered man as theomorphic. As well as many passages in the prophets or in the poets . . . the very carefully formulated statement in Ezek 1.26 is of particular importance. The light phenomenon of the "glory of God" clearly displays human contours. It has been rightly said that Ezek 1.26 is the theological prelude to the *locus classicus* for the *imago* doctrine in Gen 1.26' (*OT Theology* i, pp.145f.). Cf. also the authors cited in n.2, p.206.

[4]The most comprehensive survey of the Jewish and Gnostic conceptions of *Imago Dei* has been made by Jervell in his book *Imago Dei*, which, however, should be read

that the conception of man as *Imago Dei* implies his relatedness to God, his being the counterpart to God in an I-Thou relationship, his being vice-regent or representative of God, and many more qualities of human existence. Can the words צלם and דמות, however, ever be understood without a connotation (if not indeed denotation) of physical representation and external likeness of form? Certainly they could not be for many Rabbis. Hence the anthropomorphic understanding of *Imago Dei* was far more frequent among them than among the Church Fathers – and modern Christian theologians[1]. In 1Cor 15.49 'bearing' the εἰκὼν of the earthly or the heavenly is spoken of, and εἰκὼν τοῦ χοϊκοῦ and εἰκὼν τοῦ ἐπουρανίου are paralleled by σῶμα ψυχικόν and (σῶμα) πνευματικόν of v.44. Here the word εἰκὼν seems to have a 'material' connotation – as 'material' as σῶμα (πνευματικόν!) – and also the sense of 'likeness'. In any case, the conception of Christ as the εἰκὼν τοῦ θεοῦ both in 2Cor 4.4 and Col 1.15 clearly conveys the sense that Christ is the (visible, therefore material) manifestation of (the invisible) God, and therefore his likeness to God is strongly implied in it. This likeness of Christ to God may consist in all those qualities, in their perfection, which we have listed above as possible implications of the conception of man as *Imago Dei*. However, here again the basic connotation of the word εἰκὼν, visible, material, plastic or physical likeness and representation, cannot be removed completely[2].

In this connection it should also be remembered that when Wisdom is said to be the εἰκὼν of God in Wis 7.26, and the Logos in Philo, it is the personified and hypostatized Wisdom and Logos that are thus spoken of. In fact, the designation of Wisdom and the Logos as the εἰκὼν of God is closely related to the idea that the figures are the bearers of theophany, if indeed it does not originate from the latter. Here H. Hegermann's fine

---

with some caution throughout. His section on Rabbinic conceptions has been extensively corrected by M.Smith, 'On the shape of God and the Humanity of Gentiles', *Religions in Antiquity*, Goodenough memorial volume, pp.315–326, who, emphasizing the importance of the understanding of *Imago Dei* in terms of man's bodily likeness with God, i.e., the anthropomorphic understanding of the concept, among many Rabbis, argues that for the Rabbis all men, not just the Israelites as Jervell claims (*op. cit.*, pp. 86ff.), are or bear *Imago Dei*. On Jewish, early Christian and Gnostic understandings of Gen 1.26f., see further Schenke, *Gott "Mensch"*, pp.120–143. On the history of Christian exegesis of Gen 1.26f., see conveniently the excursus in Westermann, *Genesis*, pp.203–214, with abundant literature.

[1]See Smith, *loc. cit.*; Schenke, *loc. cit.*; Westermann, *loc. cit.*

[2]Larsson, *Vorbild*, p.187, conjectures that the reason why both the OT-Jewish tradition and Paul never actually affirmed that mankind completely *lost* the image of God at the fall of Adam was because they thought of it in anthropomorphic terms (cf. also pp.123ff., 152, 163f., etc.).

exposition of Wisdom and the Logos as the *Theophanieträger* in the Wisdom literature and Philo is valuable[1], although he does not pay any special attention to the concept εἰκών, which is strange in view of his concern to expound the Colossian hymn. In their interpretation of the theophany passages in the OT both the Book of Wisdom and Philo let Wisdom or the Logos appear in the place of God rather than God himself directly. So, in Wis 10.1f. the Genesis account of God's appearance to and protection of Adam before and after his fall is reproduced as: 'Wisdom it was who kept guard over the first father of the human race, when he alone had yet been made; she saved him after his fall, and gave him the strength to master all things' (NEB). In Wis 10.6f. the appearance of Yahweh with his angelic companions to destroy Sodom and to save Lot (Gen 18f.) is interpreted as that of Wisdom. Again in Wis 10.10 Wisdom is said to have appeared to Jacob at Bethel and 'showed him God's kingdom and gave him knowledge of holy things (or holy angels)' (Gen 28). It was Wisdom who led the Israelites at the Exodus as 'a covering for them by day and a blaze of stars by night' (Wis 10.17)[2]. That the designation of Wisdom as 'the εἰκών of his (sc. God's) goodness' in Wis 7.26 is related to (if it does not actually originate from) the idea of the personified Wisdom as the bearer of theophany, is confirmed by Philo's calling Wisdom εἰκόνα καὶ ὅρασω θεοῦ (*Leg. Alleg.* i.43). What is seen in theophany is Wisdom 'the image and vision of God'. Here the two words εἰκών and ὅρασις may be interpreted as standing *vis-à-vis* each other in both the following combinations: Because Wisdom is the εἰκών of God she is the ὅρασις of God and conversely because she is the ὅρασις of God she is the εἰκών of God.

However, the most important evidence for our whole thesis is provided by Philo's interpretation of the theophany to Jacob in Gen 31.13. It is found in *Somn.* i.227–241[3]. There Philo introduces the LXX version of Gen 31.13: ἐγώ εἰμι ὁ θεὸς ὁ ὀφθείς σοι ἐν τόπῳ θεοῦ as having been addressed to 'the man who relies on the hope of the divine comradeship' (227). Then he asks whether the quoted sentence implies that there are two Gods: 'For we read "I am the God who appeared to thee", not "in my place" but "in the place of God", as though it were another's' (228). To this Philo answers: 'He that is truly God is One, but those that are improperly so called are more than one. Accordingly the holy word in the present instance has indicated him who is truly God by the article saying, "I am the God", while it omits the article when mentioning him who is improperly so called, saying "who

---

[1] Hegermann, *Schöpfungsmittler*, pp.67–87; also pp.37ff.

[2] On Wis 10 see *ibid.*, pp.39, 77.

[3] Cf. *ibid.*, pp.71ff.

appeared to thee in the place not "of the God", but simply "of God". Here
it gives the title of "God" to his chief Word . . .' (229). Then Philo distinguishes two kinds of men: one, the intelligent who have 'the souls . . . which
are incorporeal and are occupied in his (sc. God's) worship, and the other, the
dull who have 'the souls which are still in a body'. To the former, Philo says,
God reveals himself as he is; but to the latter he reveals himself 'assuming
the likeness of angels (ἀγγέλοις εἰκαζόμενον), not altering his own nature
for he is unchangeable, but conveying to those which receive the impression
of his presence a semblance in a different form, such that they take the image
to be not a copy, but that original form itself' (ἀλλὰ δόξαν ἐντιθέντα ταῖς
φαντασιουμέναις ἑτερόμορφον, ὡς τὴν εἰκόνα οὐ μίμημα, ἀλλ' αὐτὸ
τὸ ἀρχέτυπον ἐκεῖνο εἶδος ὑπολαμβάνειν εἶναι) (232). Philo quotes an
old saying that 'the deity goes the round the cities, in the likeness now of
this man now of that man (τὸ θεῖον ἀνθρώποις εἰκαζόμενον ἄλλοτε ἄλλοις
περιωστεῖ τὰς πόλεις ἐν κύκλῳ), taking note of wrongs and transgressions',
and says that though it may not be true it is still profitable (233). For Scrip-
true, which entertains holier and nobler conceptions of Him that Is (τοῦ ὄντος,
i.e., God), 'likened God to man' (ἀνθρώπῳ μὲν εἴκασεν) in order to provide
teaching to those who are without wisdom (234). Philo illustrates this point
with the anthropomorphic language in Scripture, God's face, hands, voice,
wrath, movements up and down etc. Such language 'is concerned not with
truth but with the profit for its pupils' (235). 'For some there are altogether
dull in their natures, incapable of forming any conception whatever of God
without a body . . . ' (236). Philo restates the two approaches in Scripture:
'one, that which keeps truth in view and so provides the thought "God is not
as man" (Num 23.9), the other, that which keeps in view the ways of thinking
of the duller folk, of whom it is said "the Lord will chasten thee, as if a man
should chasten his son" ' (Dt 8.5) (237). With this explanation Philo returns
to the statement of Gen 31.13:

> Why, then, do we wonder any longer at his (sc. God's) assuming the likeness of
> angels, seeing that for the succour of those that are in need he assumes that of men
> (. . . εἰ ἀγγέλοις, ὁπότε καὶ ἀνθρώποις ἕνεκα τῆς τῶν δεομένων ἐπικουρίας
> ἀπεικάζεται;). Accordingly, when he says 'I am the God who was seen of thee in the
> place of God', understand that he occupied the place of an angel only so far as ap-
> peared, without changing, with a view to the profit of him who was not yet capable
> of seeing the true God. For just as those who are unable to see the sun itself see
> the gleam of the parhelion and take it for the sun, and take the halo round the moon
> for that luminary itself, so some regard the image of God, his angel the Word, as his
> very self (. . . οὕτως καὶ τὴν τοῦ θεοῦ εἰκόνα, τὸν ἄγγελον αὐτοῦ λόγον,
> ὡς αὐτὸν κατανοοῦσιν) (238f.)

Philo then illustrates this point with Hagar's word to the angel: 'Thou art
the God who looked upon me' (Gen 16.13). Being an Egyptian she was not

qualified to see the supreme Cause, so that seeing the angel she took him as God himself[1]. The same was true of Jacob on the occasion of the Bethel theophany (Gen 28.10–22). 'But in the passage upon which we are occupied (i.e., Gen 31. 13)., the mind (sc. Jacob's) is beginning, as the result of improvement, to form a mental image ($\phi\alpha\nu\tau\alpha\sigma\iota o\hat{\upsilon}\sigma\theta\alpha\iota$) of the sovereign Ruler of all such potencies. Hence it is that he himself says, "I am the God", whose image thou didst aforetime (i.e., at Bethel) behold deeming it to be I myself ("$\acute{\epsilon}\gamma\acute{\omega}$ $\epsilon\grave{\iota}\mu\iota$ $\acute{o}$ $\theta\epsilon\acute{o}\varsigma$", $o\hat{\upsilon}$ $\tau\grave{\eta}\nu$ $\epsilon\grave{\iota}\kappa\acute{o}\nu\alpha$ $\acute{\omega}\varsigma$ $\acute{\epsilon}\mu\grave{\epsilon}$ $\pi\rho\acute{o}\tau\epsilon\rho o\nu$ $\acute{\epsilon}\theta\epsilon\acute{a}\sigma\omega$), and didst dedicate a pillar engraved with a most holy inscription'. The purport of the inscription was that God alone is the creator who 'sustained the universe to rest firm and sure upon the mighty Word, who is my (sc. God's) viceroy' (240f.).

There seem to be at least two incongruities in this exposition of Philo. Firstly, at one moment he says that God reveals himself to the dull 'assuming the form of angels', but then he calls the image of God 'his angel the Word' (232, 238f.). Secondly, in the end Philo turns the sentence, 'I am the God who appeared to thee in the *place* of God' into 'I am the God who appeared to thee in the *form* ($\epsilon\grave{\iota}\kappa\acute{\omega}\nu$) of God', or, I am the God whose image appeared to thee'. The first is probably only a seeming incongruity which can be intelligibly explained in the light of Philo's conception of theophany. In a theophany the seer sees the image ($\epsilon\grave{\iota}\kappa\acute{\omega}\nu$) of God. Insofar as God is a pure being ($\acute{o}$ $\mathring{\omega}\nu$), incorporeal and so invisible, the image of God can only be the angel (= the Logos) whose form ($\epsilon\grave{\iota}\kappa\acute{\omega}\nu$) God assumes to reveal himself to the dull or who represents (or manifests) God — Philo is forced to use such seemingly incongruous language by his subject matter![2] The second incongruity may also be explained along this line[3]. At any rate, it is most important for our thesis to ascertain here the clear idea of Philo: *In theophany God appears 'assuming the $\epsilon\grave{\iota}\kappa\acute{\omega}\nu$ of angel' (which must also be the $\epsilon\grave{\iota}\kappa\acute{\omega}\nu$ of man — see esp. 233, 238)[4]; that is to say, in theophany not God himself*

---

[1] The same thought is expanded in *Quaest. Gen.* iii.34.

[2] It goes without saying that the difficulty is created by two conflicting desires: on the one hand Philo wants to protect the invisible, ideal nature of God as $\acute{o}$ $\mathring{\omega}\nu$; but on the other hand he must square it with the Biblical accounts of theophanies. He tries to solve this problem by means of the concepts $\epsilon\iota\kappa\acute{\omega}\nu$ of God and the Logos as the medium. Hegermann shows that the conception of Wisdom/Logos as the divine medium in Wisdom literature and Philo is grounded upon the idea of the divine $\delta\acute{\upsilon}\nu\alpha\mu\iota\varsigma$ (= spirit) that formed, ordered and sustains the universe: Wisdom/Logos is the personified divine spirit-$\delta\acute{\upsilon}\nu\alpha\mu\iota\varsigma$ (*op. cit.*, pp.26, 27ff., 71, *et passim*).

[3] This line of approach seems to be more promising than Hegermann's unconvincing attempt to see Philo correcting a given tradition here (*op. cit.*, pp.71–73).

[4] Sometimes angels appear in human form: *Quaest. Gen.* i.92.

directly but his εἰ κ ών *is seen. So at Bethel Jacob saw not God himself directly but his* εἰκών. *And this* εἰκών *of God seen in theophany is the Logos, the angel of God*[1]. It is highly probable that the passages like *Conf. Ling.* 62; 146f., where Philo calls the Logos 'the εἰκών of God' or ' ὁ κατ᾿ εἰκόνα ἄνθρωπος', also witness Philo's conception of the Logos as *Theophanieträger* (i.e., his conception of theophany as the appearance of the εἰκών of God, which is the Logos); and they probably also witness the process of thought initiated by the concept εἰκών which led him to identify the Logos with Adam or rather the ideal archetype of Adam in Gen 1.26f.[2].

c) The Damascus Christophany as the Source of the Conception of Christ as the εἰκών τοῦ θεοῦ

Now the evidence we have adduced so far from the OT and the Jewish literature provides strong grounds for us to see Paul's designation of Christ as the εἰκών τοῦ θεοῦ in the light of a similar apocalyptic or epiphanic vision. So we submit that *Paul obtained his conception of Christ as the* εἰκών τοῦ θεοῦ *at the Damascus Christophany.*

Earlier we ascertained that on the Damascus road Paul saw the exalted Christ appearing in the bright light of glory from heaven and that his vision was analogous to those of the open court of heaven granted to prophets and apocalyptic seers[3]. In view of the descriptions by the apocalyptic seers of

---

[1]See also *Quaest. Ex.* ii.13, for the same idea of the Logos, the angel, as the bearer of theophany to the dull.

[2]Cf. Hegermann, *op. cit.*, pp.73ff., 84ff.: 'Die Vorstellung vom Logos als dem urbildlichen Menschen läßt sich also aus der Tradition der Epiphanieexegese, in deren Zusammenhang sie begegnet, ohne jeden Rückgriff auf den Anthroposmythos ableiten' (p.85). Bearing in mind what we have discovered from the apocalyptic literature and Josephus above, we can easily understand Philo's designation of the Logos as the (arch-) angel, the Son of God (*Conf. Ling.* 62f.) and the δεύτερος θεός (*Quaest. Gen.* ii.62) likewise from his conception of the Logos as the *Theophanieträger*, which is most clearly demonstrated in *Somn.* i.227–241, but also visible in passages like *Conf. Ling.* 134–148: in theophany God appears 'assuming the image of an angel', so that in it the image of God is seen. The image of God is the Logos, who appears 'like a son of God' or 'like God', whom the seer takes as God himself. Hence the Logos can be called the Son of God and the second God as well as the image of God, the archangel and the viceroy of God (*Somn.* i.241). It is most interesting to find that the conception of Wisdom/Logos as *Theophanieträger* is carried on in Justin Martyr and other Church Fathers. In *Dial.* 56–63 Justin proves that the God who appeared to Abraham, Jacob and Moses was another God ministering to God the Creator, the Father, that in the Scriptures he is called 'the glory of the Lord', 'the Son', 'Wisdom', 'Angel', 'God', 'Logos', etc. (61), and that this figure was then incarnate in the person of Jesus Christ. See Hegermann, *op. cit.*, pp.76f.

[3]*Supra* esp. pp.5ff., 91ff.

God or of a heavenly figure seen in epiphanic vision which we have just examined, we can infer that Paul must have seen the exalted figure surrounded by a bright light as 'one like a son of man' (= 'one like a man'), 'one like a son of God' or 'one like God'. In so far as the figure had human contours, he was 'one like a son of man' or דמות כמראה אדם[1]. At the same time, in so far as he was surrounded by a bright light and appeared altogether exalted in heaven, he was 'one like (a son of) God' or had the εἰκόνα τοῦ θεοῦ[2]. So Paul was compelled to ask: τίς εἶ, κύριε; (Acts 9.5; 22.8; 26.15)[3]. On learning that it was Jesus of Nazareth, whom he thought to have been accursed by God on the cross but whom the Christians proclaimed to have been raised and exalted by God, he could describe the awe-inspiringly shining face of Jesus Christ only by saying that he was 'like a son of God' and had the

---

[1]On Ezek 1.26 v.Rad says: 'The light-phenomenon of the "glory of God" clearly displays human contours' (*OT Theology* i, p.146). The same thing must have happened at the Damascus Christophany.

[2]Paul regularly joins the concept εἰκών with the light of δόξα (Rom 8.29f.; 1Cor 11.7; 2Cor 3.18; 4.4, 6; cf. also Rom 1.23). Cf. Michel, 'Entstehung', pp.329f. M.R. James, *The Lost Apocrypha of the OT* (1920), p.9, quotes an apocryphal fragment: 'He (sc. Seth) was also called god because of the shining of his face . . . Moses also had this grace, and so veiled himself when he spoke with the Jews, for forty days'. Again in the same fragment Seth is called 'son of God' because of the shining of his face. In Lev. R.1.1 Phinehas is called an angel because 'the face of Phinehas, when the holy spirit rested upon him, flamed like a torch'.   Similarly also Acts 6.8—15. See further Str.-Bill. ii, pp.665f.

[3]An interesting attempt has been made by J.W.Bowker, ' "Merkabah" Visions and the Visions of Paul', *JSS* 16 (1971), pp.157—173, to draw parallels between the accounts of the Damascus event in Acts and those of the מרכבה visions of Johanan b.Zakkai. On the basis of the supposed parallels (as well as 2Cor 12) Bowker presumes that being acquainted with מרכבה mysticism Paul must have been meditating upon Ezek 1 and 2 on the road to Damascus when the Christophany took place. However, the 'parallels' are 'only very superficial' (Rowland, *Influence*, p.xxii, n.59) and Bowker's attempt to explain Paul's sense of call from Ezek 2.1—7 is far-fetched. His essay shows *only* that Paul's Damascus vision could have been in the general pattern of the מרכבה visions and that Paul could have interpreted it in the light of Ezek 1 and 2 as well as Isa 6; 49; and Jer 1. The thesis that we are here unfolding, of course, brings the Damascus vision into a close connection with Ezek 1—2 — though not in terms of direct dependence of Paul on Ezek 1—2 but rather in terms of the *Gattungs- und Formgeschichte* (and probably also *Traditionsgeschichte* — *infra* pp.239ff.) of the prophetic and apocalyptic theophany visions and also in terms of Paul's interpretation of his call-vision in the light of Ezek 1—2 as well as Isa 6; 49; and Jer 1. In so far as מרכבה mysticism also stands in this tradition, it is possible to draw parallels between it and the Damascus vision. However, there is no basis for Bowker's presumption that Paul was meditating on Ezek 1 and 2 while on the Damascus road or that the Damascus Christophany was the result of his acquaintance with מרכבה mysticism.

εἰκόνα τοῦ θεοῦ. Having known the Christian proclamation of Jesus of Nazareth as the Son of God, the Davidic Messiah exalted by God to his right hand through his raising him from the dead (Rom 1.3f.; 8.34; Acts 2.32ff.; etc.), Paul now became convinced that Jesus of Nazareth was indeed the Son of God. For he saw him enthroned in heaven[1] and really appearing 'like a son of God'. This is made clear when he tells of the Damascus Christophany as God's ἀποκάλυψις of the Son to him (Gal 1.16; Acts 9.20). It is possible that Paul was acquainted with the conception of the king as the 'son of God' and, as such, also as the 'image of God' — a claim often made by monarchs in Egypt and Mesopotamia[2]. Perhaps he was also acquainted with the conception of Wisdom and the Logos as the daughter and the son of God respectively and, as such, (especially as the *Theophanieträger*) also as the 'image of God'. If this was so, we can see how easily Paul could recognize not just that Jesus of Nazareth was 'like God' or had the εἰκόνα τοῦ θεοῦ but that as the Son of God he *is* the εἰκών τοῦ θεοῦ[3]. Even if Paul did not know either of the two conceptions, in the light of the thought pattern we have ascertained from Philo and the Wisdom of Solomon which affirms the *Theophanieträger*, the Wisdom/Logos, to be God's εἰκών itself, we can understand how easily Paul could affirm that Jesus of Nazareth, the Son of God, who appeared 'like God', that is, in 'the image of God', is the εἰκών τοῦ θεοῦ. Just as Wisdom or the Logos who is seen in epiphany as having the εἰκόνα of God *is* the εἰκών of God, so also Christ who is seen by Paul as having the εἰκόνα of God *is* the εἰκών of God.

That this understanding of Jesus Christ really took place at the Damascus Christophany (or shortly thereafter, but, in any case, in the light of it), can

---

[1]Hahn, *Hoheitstitel*, pp.128ff., suggests that the old Palestinian idea of Jesus' sitting at the right hand of God only as a future eschatological event was later turned into the idea of his exaltation and enthronement because of the delay of the parousia. If this were true, the process must have been completed by the time of the Damascus Christophany (i.e., 32–34 A.D.). However, it is our opinion that following the suggestion of Jesus himself (Mk 14.61f. and par.) the early Palestinian Church already (i.e., before the Damascus event) interpreted Jesus' resurrection as his exaltation at God's right hand in the light of 2Sam 7.12ff.; Ps 2; 8; 110 which they very early combined to provide the Scriptural proofs for the messiahship of Jesus (cf. Hengel, 'Christologie', p.66). The confession of the exaltation and enthronement of Jesus Christ as the Son of God is found already in Rom 1.3f., a pre-Pauline formula in its true sense (see Betz, *What Do We Know about Jesus?*, p.97; Hengel, *Sohn*, pp.93ff.).

[2]See H.Wildberger, 'Das Abbild Gottes', *ThZ* 21 (1965), pp.483–491; Clines, *op. cit.*, pp.83ff. Whether the Near Eastern king-ideology formed the background of Gen 1.26 and continued to influence OT thought (e.g., Ps 8), cannot be discussed here. See Westermann, *Genesis*, pp.209–213.

[3]Cf. Hengel, *Sohn*, p.36.

be gathered from a number of Pauline passages apart from Gal 1.16 already mentioned. We cite, first of all, Paul's statement in 1Cor 15.49: καὶ καθὼς ἐφορέσαμεν τὴν εἰκόνα τοῦ χοϊκοῦ, φορέσομεν καὶ τὴν εἰκόνα τοῦ ἐπουρανίου. The phrases (ὁ δεύτερος ἄνθρωπος) ἐξ οὐρανοῦ, ὁ ἐπουράνιος and (τὴν εἰκόνα) τοῦ ἐπουρανίου in 1Cor 15.47–49 are best understood in the light of the Damascus Christophany, for they are reminiscent of the epiphanic scenes which, as we have observed, are usually located in the heavenly court. Just as Ezekiel saw the heavens opened and God appearing from heaven in the form or image of man (Ezek 1) and just as Daniel saw 'one like a son of man' coming with the clouds of heaven (Dan 7.13), so on the Damascus road Paul also saw the glorious Christ appearing ἐξ οὐρανοῦ as ὁ ἐπουράνιος, as the Son of God[1]. So the εἰκὼν τοῦ ἐπουρανίου refers to the image of Christ (which is the image of God) which he saw at the Damascus Christophany. A similar allusion to the Damascus Christophany is found in 1Th 1.10, where Paul says: 'We are waiting for his (sc. God's) Son ἐκ τῶν οὐρανῶν'. The Damascus vision of the enthroned Christ as the Son of God was a proleptic parousia. So Paul waits with confidence for the coming of the Son of God from heaven (cf. also 1Th 4.16: ὅτι αὐτὸς ὁ κύριος . . . καταβήσεται ἀπ' οὐρανοῦ. . .).

C.C. Rowland correctly sees the force of τοῦ ἀοράτου in Col 1.15 when he is led by it to interpret the phrase εἰκὼν τοῦ θεου τοῦ ἀοράτου in the light of Ezek 1.26: 'Christ is then the image – even the features – of a God who cannot be seen. The stress on invisibility lends credence to the supposition that Christ is not simply to be regarded *in general terms* as the *locus* of re-velation but the form or the features of God. He is the physical embodiment of divinity, who, unlike God himself, was visible'[2]. Although Rowland fails to recognize the fact[3], it was precisely on the Damascus road that Christ was visible as the image of the invisible God. Rowland is again correct in trying to see the difficult statement in Col 2.9: ὅτι ἐν αὐτῷ (sc. Χριστῷ) κατοικεῖ πᾶν τὸ πλήρωμα τῆς θεότητος σωματικῶς in the light of an apocalyptic vision of the מרכבה or שעור קומה kind. Noting the stress on corporeality in the

---

[1]Cf. Manson, *Teaching*, pp.233ff.; Larsson, *Vorbild*, pp.319f.; Barrett, *Adam*, pp.75f.; Wedderburn, *Adam*, p.186. The opening of heaven is a prelude to an epiphanic vision: e.g., 3 Macc. 3.18; 2Bar. 22.1; Test.Lev. 2.6; 5.1; 18.6; Mt 3.16 and par.; Acts 7.56; 10.11; Rev 10.1.

[2]Rowland, *Influence*, pp.291f. (My emphasis). Christ is the *locus* or medium of revelation precisely because he is the visible embodiment of divinity.

[3]This is a pity, especially because he seems very near to this recognition when he continues: 'In other words he (sc. Christ) is none other than the *kabod* of God which could be seen (cf. 2Cor 4.4)' (*ibid.*, p.292).

two other uses of the word in the NT (Lk 3.22; 1Tim 4.8), he says that the word σωματικῶς should be translated 'in bodily form' and that it refers to the glorified body of Christ[1]. Jervell is also correct in observing that the statement in Col 2.9 is a parallel to the idea of εἰκών in Col 1.15f.[2] We would agree with him again that the σῶμα in Col 2.17 is synonymous with εἰκών (cf. Heb 10.1) and that the word σωματικῶς in Col 2.9 could therefore be translated εἰκονικῶς[3]. But his conclusion from these observations that σωματικῶς means not Christ *qua* body but as 'the highest degree of reality'[4], is not quite correct, insofar as he sets up this unnecessary dichotomy. Precisely because the statement in Col 2.9 is parallel to that in 1.15f. we should try to understand it in the light of a vision of Christ, i.e., the Damascus Christophany. The best support for this is provided by Lk 3.22, where it is said that on the occasion of Jesus' baptism καὶ καταβῆναι τὸ Πνεῦμα τὸ Ἅγιον σωματικῷ εἴδει ὡ ς περιστερὰν ἐπ' αὐτόν. Just as the Holy Spirit descended upon Jesus in a visible bodily form, the exalted Christ appeared to Paul 'in a bodily form' — in the senses both of concrete corporeality (or reality) and of the shape of the human body, although only the former appears in Lk 3.22. Therefore, just as Paul recognized Christ as the εἰκών of God, so also he saw him as the *em-bodi-ment* of the divine כבוד , the deity (θεότης). To be sure, just as the designation of Christ as the εἰκών τοῦ θεοῦ implies much more than the mere divine *appearance* or *form* of Christ, so also the statement in Col 2.9 has much more profound implications than the mere bodily appearance of the divine glory in Christ. However, we suggest that the conceptions of Christ as the εἰκών of God and as the embodiment of the deity *originated* in Paul's mind because he saw the exalted Christ on the Damascus road as such, and that the more profound implications are only the results of theological contemplations on the inaugural vision. In other words, Paul *developed* the conception of Christ as the εἰκών of God in a progressively more profound way, but its starting-point lay in the Damascus Christophany[5].

---

[1]*Ibid.*, pp.266f. Similarly L.Cerfaux, *Christ in the Theology of St. Paul* (1959), p.427. For various interpretations of the word σωματικῶς see Moule, *Col.*, pp.92f.

[2]Jervell, *Imago*, p.223.

[3]*Ibid.*, p.224.

[4]*Ibid.*, pp.223f.

[5]This process of development can also be illustrated with its parallels in the conception of Wisdom/Logos as the image of God in Wis. and Philo. It is impossible for us to tarry here in order to demonstrate this. We would simply refer to Hegermann, *Schöpfungsmittler*, since the book as a whole clearly suggests this possibility. It should be remembered, of course, that in the Pauline development of the conception of Christ as

Phil 3.20f. also provides good support for this thesis. We have already seen that Paul's waiting for the parousia of the exalted Christ as the Son of God or the Lord ἐξ οὐρανοῦ is based on his experience of the proleptic parousia on the Damascus road. The Philippian passage confirms this view when it refers to 'the body of his (sc. Christ's) glory' (cf. also 1Cor 15.43), which is materially the same as the εἰκών of Christ in 1Cor 15.49; Rom 8.29; and 2Cor 3.18. Paul saw the body of Christ's glory when the exalted Christ appeared to him in the bright light of glory on the Damascus road[1]. He saw him as the κύριος τῆς δόξης (1Cor 2.8)[2]. If our exposition so far is correct, then there is little difficulty in seeing how Paul could have designated the glorious body of Christ as the σῶμα πνευματικόν (1Cor 15.43ff.), which is also materially the same as the εἰκών of Christ in 1Cor 15.49; Rom 8.29; and 2Cor 3.18. The body of Christ which Paul saw on the Damascus road was the real body of Christ, but at the same time it was shining with the light of glory. It was no ordinary mortal, physical body. It was a *spiritual* body[3]. Thus Paul knows that the Christian's resurrection body will be like that of Christ: the σῶμα πνευματικόν. From this it is but a small step to the conception of Christ as the πνεῦμα (1Cor 15.45; 2Cor 3.17f.)[4]. On the Damascus

---

the image of God other elements of his understanding of Christ which he obtained from his predecessors as well as from his experience on the Damascus road and thereafter, are also involved.

[1] According to Rowland, *Influence*, p.xxii(n.57), Scholem has suggested that the phrase σῶμα τῆς δόξης in Phil 3.21 shows the influence of the שעור קומה speculation (*Von der mystischen Gestalt der Gottheit* (1962), p.276, n.19 – unavailable to me). To this we would say only that it bears witness not to the influence of such speculation, but to the Damascus Christophany – a real vision!

[2] *Supra* pp.79ff.;. cf. also Feine, *Theologie*, p.321.

[3] As noted above, p.194, n.7, Kennedy already saw both 'the body of glory' in Phil 3.21 and 'the spiritual body' in 1Cor 15.44ff. as alluding to the Damascus Christophany, while Dupont saw the former in the same way. Here it should be remembered not only that epiphanic visions are often mediated by the Spirit (e.g., Ezek 1–3; 8.3; 11.24; 1En 37.4; Rev 1.10) but also that the shining of a face with light like the face of an angel or God is supposed to indicate the effect of the Holy Spirit upon it (e.g., Lev. R.1.1; Num.R.10.5; cf. also Acts 6.8–15; further Sjöberg, πνεῦμα, *TDNT* vi, pp.381f.). Thus the πνευματικός–ψυχικός antithesis in 1Cor 15.44ff. is derived from the Damascus Christophany and not from the Gnostic or any other source (*supra* pp.170f.).

[4] In Wisdom of Solomon, Wisdom is identified with πνεῦμα: 1.6; 7.7, 22 (See Bieder, πνεῦμα, *TDNT* vi, pp.371f.). This identification (esp. 7.22) may not be unconnected with the idea of Wisdom being the εἰκών of God's goodness (7.26). Schweizer, πνεῦμα, *TDNT* vi, p.422, also suggests that Paul's identification of the κύριος with τὸ πνεῦμα in 2Cor 3.17f. is derived from 'the view of the spiritual body of the exalted Lord'.

road Paul saw the glorious Christ as being spiritual, as a spiritual being, indeed as the Spirit[1].

This brings us to what we consider to be *the most convincing evidence* for the thesis that Paul derived the conception of Christ as the εἰκὼν τοῦ θεοῦ from the Damascus Christophany, namely, 2Cor 3.1–4.6. We have already seen how clearly the passage alludes to the Damascus Christophany[2]. We noted also that R.P, Martin, J. Dupont and W.G. Kümmel saw Paul's designation of Christ as the εἰκὼν τοῦ θεοῦ in 4.4 as alluding to the Damascus Christophany[3]. As before we must start our demonstration from the most evident part of the passage, namely 4.6. There, as we argued in Chapter I with the support of the majority of commentators, Paul is referring to the bright light of the divine glory that shone in the face of the exalted Christ as he appeared to him on the Damascus road. Two expressions in the verse are especially important in our present context. Firstly, the πρόσωπον of Christ. In the light of what we have seen from the descriptions of epiphanic visions, we can easily understand why precisely the face of man should be supposed to bear the image of God in the apocalyptic and Gnostic literature[4]. If the heart stands for the entire being of man, the face represents his external form. It is natural, therefore, that in an epiphanic vision the face of the figure appearing should receive the special attention of the seer. Secondly, the δόξα τοῦ θεοῦ. Glory regularly accompanies theophany. It refers to the light that shines round about God or the divine figure in epiphany. Often in descrip-

---

[1]If πνεύματος in 2Cor 3.18 is *gen. qualitatis* (so Plummer, *2Cor.*, pp.108f.; Hughes, *2Cor.*, p.120; Lietzmann-Kümmel, *Kor.*, pp.114f.; cf. also Windisch, *2.Kor.*, pp.129f.), it would be easier tò understand the process of thinking by which the identification of him with τὸ πνεῦμα was derived from the experience of Christ as a spiritual being (= 'spirit'). Cf. Schweizer, *op. cit.*, p.419: 'It is thus maintained that the exalted Christ is the πνεῦμα . . . If κύριος and πνεῦμα are distinguished in v.17b, this simply makes it plain that v.17a is not asserting the identity of two personal entities. πνεῦμα is defined as the mode of existence of the κύριος. Where there is reference to the πνεῦμα κυρίου, his mode of existence is depicted, and this means the power in which he encounters his community'. Also Hermann, *Kyrios*, 1.Abschnitt, esp. pp.38–57: 'Dieses Pneuma ist der Kyrios Christos, insofern er – in dieser Weise seit der Erhöhung – sich dem Menschen gewährt und von ihm erfahren werden kann' (p.57). Our explanation of the language of 2Cor 3.17f. in the light of the Damascus Christophany provides this understanding with a concrete basis in the actual experience of Paul.

[2]*Supra* pp.5ff.

[3]*Supra* pp.193f.

[4]E.g., Vita Adae 13.2; 2En.44.1; *Schatzhöhle*, 2.12ff.; Od.Sol.17.2. See Jervell, *Imago*, pp.45, 168, 175. For the same idea in the Samaritan literature, see J.Macdonald, *The Theology of the Samaritans* (1964), p.178.

tions of epiphanic visions the light of glory is taken not just as an accompanying phenomenon, but as in fact being the appearance or the form of God. This understanding of the glory of God may have its root in the fact that in an epiphanic vision the seer sees the light of the glory of God forming or displaying the human contours, as v. Rad says[1]. In any case, as we have seen, כבוד יהוה is already in Ezek. (1.28; 9.3; 10.4, 18f.; 11.22f.; etc.) virtually a *term. techn.* for God appearing in human form or likeness, sitting upon the throne, in a vision. This symbolism continues through the apocalyptic literature to מרכבה mysticism of the Rabbinic sources[2]. It is possible, then, that when Paul says that God shone his divine light into the depth of his being 'so that (he=Paul) may illuminate (others) with the knowledge of the glory of God in the face of Christ'[3], he is suggesting that he saw God's form ($\epsilon i\kappa\dot\omega\nu$) in the face of Christ. Even if the $\delta\acute o\xi a$ $\tau o\hat v$ $\theta\epsilon o\hat v$ is not used in 2Cor 4.6 in the technical sense, this interpretation is still possible. For, in any case, the language of the verse suggests that Paul saw the divine light displaying the contours of the face of a God-like figure who turned out to be the exalted Christ. Paul regularly joins $\delta\acute o\xi a$ and $\epsilon i\kappa\dot\omega\nu$, and this suggests that they are virtually synonymous (Rom 1.23; 8.29f.; 1Cor 11.7; 2Cor 3.18; 4.4)[4]. Such a synonymous use of $\delta\acute o\xi a$ and $\epsilon i\kappa\dot\omega\nu$ (צלם or דמות) is well attested also in the Jewish literature[5]. Here 2Cor 3.18 is particularly interesting: 'We all, beholding $\tau\dot\eta\nu$ $\delta\acute o\xi a\nu$ $\kappa\nu\rho i o\nu$ as in a mirror, are transformed into $\tau\dot\eta\nu$ $a\dot v\tau\dot\eta\nu$ $\epsilon i\kappa\acute o\nu a$ ...'. The pronoun phrase $\tau\dot\eta\nu$ $a\dot v\tau\dot\eta\nu$ in this verse clearly refers to the $\delta\acute o\xi a$ $\kappa\nu\rho i o\nu$. So the phrase $\tau\dot\eta\nu$ $a\dot v\tau\dot\eta\nu$ $\epsilon i\kappa\acute o\nu a$ indicates that $\delta\acute o\xi a$ and $\epsilon i\kappa\dot\omega\nu$ are synonymous here[6]: to see the $\delta\acute o\xi a$ $\kappa\nu\rho i o\nu$ is to see his $\epsilon i\kappa\dot\omega\nu$. It is clear therefore that the phrase $\delta\acute o\xi a$ $\tau o\hat v$ $\theta\epsilon o\hat v$ $\dot\epsilon\nu$ $\pi\rho o\sigma\dot\omega\pi\omega$ $X\rho\iota\sigma\tau o\hat v$ in 2Cor 4.6 is only another expression of the phrase $\delta\acute o\xi a$ $\tau o\hat v$ $X\rho\iota\sigma\tau o\hat v$, $\acute o\varsigma$ $\dot\epsilon\sigma\tau\iota\nu$ $\epsilon i\kappa\dot\omega\nu$ $\tau o\hat v$ $\theta\epsilon o\hat v$ in 2Cor 4.4[7]. The $\delta\acute o\xi a$ of God which Paul saw on the Damascus road was also the $\delta\acute o\xi a$ of Christ because it shone in the face of Christ. When that $\delta\acute o\xi a$ of God shone in the face of Christ, Christ appeared to Paul as the $\epsilon i\kappa\dot\omega\nu$ of God. Thus, just as in Gal 1.16 Paul says that the exalted Christ who was revealed to him as the Son of God on the Damascus road is the content of his $\epsilon\dot v a\gamma\gamma\acute\epsilon\lambda\iota o\nu$, so here also he says that the glory of Christ who was

---

[1]v.Rad, *OT Theology* i, p.146; Windisch, *2.Kor.*, pp.115, 137; cf. also Michel, 'Entstehung', p.330.

[2]*Supra* p.206, n.2.

[3]For the reason for this rendering, *supra* pp.9f.

[4]So Jervell, *Imago*, pp.180ff., 194f., 2o0f., 299f., 325f.; also Conzelmann, *1.Kor.*, p.219; cf. also Larsson, *Vorbild*, p.185.

[5]See Jervell, *Imago*, pp.100ff.

[6]Cf. Larsson, *Vorbild*, p.281.

[7]So Bruce, *Paul*, p.123.

revealed to him as the image of God is the content of the εὐαγγέλιον which he
was then commissioned to preach (2Cor 4.6). Proclaiming Jesus Christ as the
Son of God (Gal 1.16) is the same as proclaiming him as the image of God
(2Cor 4.4). In this proclamation of the gospel the glory of Christ or the glory
of God in Christ is manifested (4.4). All this is perfectly intelligible in the
light of what we have gathered from the descriptions of epiphanic visions.
Thus Martin, Kümmel and Dupont are correct in perceiving that v.4 as well as
v.6 alludes to the Damascus Christophany.

The same conclusion is reached from an examination of 2Cor 3.16—18.
We have already argued in Chapter I and suggested again in the preceding
paragraph that these verses allude to the Damascus Christophany. In fact,
3.18 is a close parallel to 4.4 and 6 as far as the concepts δόξα and εἰκών
are concerned.

Both v.16 and v.18 are meant to apply to all Christians. But we suggested that in
these verses Paul applies his own experience, as typical, to them[1]. By the word 'typical'
we do not mean that Paul supposed that every Christian should have such a dramatic
visionary experience at conversion as he had. We suggest only that what all Christians
experience in conversion at the proclamation of the gospel is essentially the same as his
Damascus experience, namely turning to the Lord and seeing the perfect revelation of
God in Christ. Outwardly Paul's seeing God's glory and image in the face of Christ is,
of course, different from that of his converts, as the latter experience is purely spiritual
apprehension while the former involved 'physical' seeing as well. However, *in-essence*
they are the same. That is why Paul can use his Damascus experience with its 'physical'
as well as spiritual aspect as a paradigm for every Christian's experience of conversion;
that is to say, Paul uses in 3.16—18 (also 4.4) his Damascus experience in order to describe symbolically or graphically a typical Christian conversion experience, just as he
does in 4.6 for the typical experience of the apostolic commission.

In v.16 Paul alludes to his seeing and turning to the exalted Christ on the
Damascus road in language taken from Ex 34.34 where Moses' going into
God's presence on Mt. Sinai is described. Just as Moses removed the veil upon
his face then, so at his seeing the exalted Lord the veil that lay on Paul's
heart and prevented him from understanding the true revelation of God's will
was removed. This removal was effected by the Lord whom he experienced
as a spiritual being, as the Spirit (v.17f.)[2]. While both the Mosaic covenant
and the hearts of its adherents remain veiled, so that the Jews cannot appre-
hend God's true revelation, all Christians, 'beholding the glory of the Lord as
in a mirror with an unveiled face, are being transformed into the same image
from glory to glory' (v.18). It was in blind obedience to the Mosaic law that

---

[1]*Supra* pp.5ff.

[2]*Supra* p.228, n.4; p.229, n.1.

Paul was on his way to Damascus to persecute the followers of Jesus of
Nazareth. Then the exalted Christ appeared to him in the radiance of the
divine glory. He saw the δόξα κυρίου, the כבוד יהוה, and the εἰκών of
God in the face of Christ. Like many commentators, we felt it difficult
to decide between the two possible ways of rendering the participle κατοπτριζόμενοι: to 'reflect' or to 'behold as in a mirror', and allowed both meanings[1]. Now, in the light of the descriptions of epiphanic visions that we have
examined, especially Ezek 1, we know that its primary sense is to 'behold as
in a mirror'. In epiphanic visions God appears on a throne surrounded by a
shining firmament and floor which are like the alloy of gold and silver, crystal,
or ice[2]. To see God in such a surrounding is like seeing him reflected in a
mirror, that is seeing his mirror image[3]. In Ezek 1.5 we are given a picture of
a mirror in the midst of fire, in which God's throne and the דמות כמראה אדם
(or מראה דמות כבוד יהוה) appear. So Ezekiel saw God 'as in a mirror'[4].
In 2Cor 3.18 with the word κατοπτριζόμενοι Paul is conveying exactly the
same impression, which he obtained as Christ appeared to him on the Damascus road. He saw the exalted Christ as if he was reflected in a mirror. It was
not like two human beings seeing each other face to face. It was indirect and
somewhat blurred. Nevertheless, the contours of Christ, displayed by the
sparkling light, that looked as though they were reflected from a mirror of
the alloy or crystal, were clear enough for Paul to recognize them as being of
a human form with glory, and that form he perceived as the εἰκών τοῦ θεοῦ.
Elsewhere Paul says: 'Now we see (Christ or God) in a mirror dimly, but then
face to face' (1Cor 13.12). This symbolism well reflects the Damascus
Christophany and the hope that it engendered in Paul: at the parousia he will
see Christ more clearly, i.e., 'face to face'. In our present passage, the δόξα
κυρίου in v.18, which echoes the כבוד יהוה in Ex 24.17, is the glory of
God. But since the glory of God appeared in the face of Christ (4.6) it is
also the glory of Christ (4.4). Likewise, τὴν αὐτὴν εἰκόνα in v.18 refers to
the image of God. However, since that image of God appeared in the face of
Christ and it was Christ who appeared to Paul, it refers also to the image of
Christ which Paul saw. Here we are not to think in terms of the Gnostic
gradual emanation of some such schema as: God — the image of God (=

---

[1] *Supra* p.13, n.2; *infra* p.237.

[2] See Rowland, *Influence*, p.13 *et passim*.

[3] It seems that the combination of the (sometimes synonymous) εἰκών and mirror
in Wis 7.26 and other Jewish Hellenistic literature and Jewish Gnostic literature should
be seen in the light of this phenomenon. Cf. Jervell, *Imago*, p.185; also Windisch,
2.Kor., p.128, who cites Philo, *Leg. Alleg.* iii.101.

[4] So Procksch, 'Berufungsvision', pp.142, 144.

Christ) – the image of Christ – the image of the believer that conforms to the image of Christ. Rather, in the light of the epiphanic phenomenon, we must understand that the image of God which Paul saw as in a mirror *is* also the image of Christ. Only in the light of the epiphanic phenomenon can we understand how Paul can speak of Christ as the 'image of God' on the one hand and speak at the same time of the 'image of Christ' (cf. Rom 8.29; 1Cor 15.49) on the other[1]. In a vision the seer sees an image. So in the Damascus Christophany Paul saw an image. It was the image of God, and it turned out to be the exalted Christ. Thus Paul can refer to that image also as the image of Christ. We have seen an exact parallel to this in Philo[2]. Hence the δόξα κυρίου and the ἡ αὐτὴ εἰκών in v.18 refer to the glory and image of Christ that Paul saw on the Damascus road as the glory and image of God. Here as elsewhere (Rom 8.29; 1Cor 15.49; Phil 3.21) Paul speaks also about the Christians' transformation into the image of Christ. However, this side of the question, namely the soteriological significance of the εἰκών-Christology, will be examined in the next chapter.

Excursus: The Antithetical Typology between the Sinai Theophany and the Damascus Christophany (2Cor 3.1 – 4.6)

The observations that we have made in Chapter I and again in this chapter make it abundantly clear that in 2Cor 3.1 – 4.6 Paul refers to the Damascus Christophany. Clearly he refers to it in defence of his apostleship and gospel against the accusations of his opponents[3]. They charged that Paul was not properly commissioned to be an apostle: he was a self-made apostle recognized by nobody, as his inability to produce letters of recommendation proved (3.1–5). They also accused Paul of distorting the gospel by not requiring the Gentile converts to observe the law of Moses (4.2)[4]. They said that such a gospel was 'veiled' (4.3), meaning that it was unintelligible because it cut itself loose from God's revelation given to Moses on Sinai. They may have chosen the word κεκαλυμμένον in order to ridicule Paul's claim that he received his gospel

---

[1]This question is usually ignored or inadequately grasped by commentators.

[2]*Supra* p.222: the image of God (= the Logos) = the image of the Logos in theophany.

[3]It is impossible to inquire here into the thorny problem of identifying the opponents of Paul in Corinth. See the latest survey of the problem by E.E.Ellis, 'Paul and his Opponents', *Prophecy and Hermeneutic* (1977), pp.78–113. Further, G.Friedrich, 'Gegner des Paulus im 2.Korintherbrief', *Abraham unser Vater*, O.Michel FS, ed. O.Betz *et al.* (1963), pp.181–215; C.K.Barrett, 'Paul's Opponents in II Corinthians', *NTS* 17 (1970/71), pp.233–254; D.Georgi, *Die Gegner des Paulus im 2.Korintherbrief* (1964); E.Käsemann, 'Die Legitimität des Apostels', *ZNW* 41 (1942), pp.33–71.

[4]Barrett, *2Cor.*, pp.128ff.; cf. also Plummer, *2Cor.*, p.112; Windisch, *2.Kor.*, p.133; Strachan, *2Cor.*, p.91; Hughes, *2Cor.*, p.123.

directly from the Lord by ἀποκάλυψις (Gal 1.12)[1]. They charged further that in order to cover the deficiencies of his gospel and apostleship Paul aggrandized himself (3.1; 4.5; 5.12) and employed underhand methods (4.2)[2]: tampering with the gospel and practising cunning, Paul preached himself rather than Christ (4.2–5)[3].

Paul counters these charges first by appealing to the fruits of his ministry, namely the Corinthian church, and then by referring to the Damascus Christophany in which he received his gospel and apostleship. In fact, he does not just counter the charges but counter-attacks his opponents by turning their charges upon them. First, the appeal to the letters of recommendation by his opponents who accuse Paul on the basis of the Mosaic law for neglecting it, leads him to contrast the old covenant engraved on the tablets of stone with the new covenant written with the Spirit of God on human hearts. For it is in line with the characteristic of the Mosaic covenant as a written code (γράμμα). In this contrast it is clearly suggested that the prophecy of the new covenant by Jeremiah (31.33; cf. also Ezek 11.19; 36.26) has been fulfilled. God has qualified Paul to be a minister of his new covenant. Therefore he administered it to the Corinthians and as they have become Christians they bear the new covenant written on their hearts. Thus they are a visible sign of Paul's true, effective apostleship – his letter of recommendation. This new covenant is not a written code (γράμματος), like the old, that kills, but it is spiritual (πνεύματος), i.e., of the Spirit that gives life. This launches Paul into a full comparison between the ministry of the old covenant and that of the new (3.7–11) and between Moses the minister of the old covenant and Paul the minister of the new with the effects of their ministries upon Israel and the Church respectively (3.12–4.6). This he makes by comparing and contrasting the theophany to Moses on Sinai and his own Christophany on the Damascus road.

It is plain that in 2Cor 3.1–4.6, especially 3.7–18, Paul refers to the Sinai theophany recorded in Ex 33–34, in which Yahweh concluded a covenant with Israel and gave Moses the tables of the law for the second time[4]. The first giving of the law took place in

---

[1] A.Fridrichsen, 'The Apostle and His Message', *Uppsala Universitets Arsskrift* (1947), pp.14f. But Kümmel rejects this conjecture – Lietzmann-Kümmel, *Kor.*, p.201, though without a good reason.

[2] τὰ κρυπτὰ τῆς αἰσχύνης refers to the underhand methods which dishonourable religious propagandists employ to press their (false) message. Cf. Plummer, *2Cor.*, p.111; Windisch, *2.Kor.*, pp.132f.; Bruce, *Cor.*, p.195; Lietzmann-Kümmel, *Kor.*, p.115.

[3] Cf. 2Cor 3.1; 5.12; Fridrichsen, *op. cit.*, p.15; Hughes, *2Cor.*, p.130; Strachan, *2Cor., p.92.*

[4] S.Schulz, 'Die Decke des Moses: Untersuchungen zu einer vorpaulinischen Überlieferung in II. Cor. 3, 7–18', *ZNW* 49(1958), pp.1–30, attempts to show that the midrash was a pre-Pauline tradition. He thinks that Paul's opponents first used it against Paul but then Paul took it over and reworked it to speak against his opponents. This thesis is accepted by G.Friedrich, *op. cit.*, pp.184f. See also Georgi, *Gegner*, esp. pp.274–282, But van Unnik, ' "With Unveiled Face", An Exegesis of 2 Corinthians iii 12–18', *Sparsa Collecta*, part one (1973), p.197, rejects it: 'There is not a shred of evidence that the apostle (Paul) is commenting upon a previously existing document or teaching, nor is it clear why Paul himself should have been unable to make this application of the Exodus-story'. Cf. also Ellis, *op. cit.*, p.103   Jervell's view that in 3.7–17 Paul unfolds a Rabbinic interpretation of the image of God and then in 3.18–4.6 formulates his own

a theophany on Mt. Sinai (Ex 19.16ff.). In the course of that giving, it is related, Moses, Aaron and their companions went up and 'saw the God of Israel; and there was under his feet as it were a **pavement of sapphire stone,** like the very heaven for clearness' (24.9f.) — a theophanic scene reminiscent of some of those which we examined above (esp. Ezek 1). Then Moses went up Mt. Sinai which was covered with the cloud, and יהוה כבוד settled there (24.15ff.). After forty days he came down from the mountain with the two stone tables of the law (31.18). However, on discovering the apostasy of his people in making the golden calf, he threw the tables down and broke them (32.19). In the course of making atonement for the sin of his people and entreating Yahweh to accompany their journey, Moses prayed to him: 'Show me thy glory'. Since men cannot see Yahweh and live, however, Yahweh let him see only his back, and not his face, while his glory passed by (33.18ff.). Then, on the command of Yahweh, Moses went up Mt. Sinai again with two tables of stone like the first (34.1ff.) and there Yahweh made a covenant with the people of Israel (34.10, 27). After forty days Moses came down with the tables on which the words of the covenant, the ten commandments, were written (34.27f.). When Moses came down with the tables of the testimony, 'the skin of his face shone because he had been talking with God' (34.29). After giving the people the commandments that he had heard from Yahweh on Mt. Sinai Moses covered his face with a veil since the people were afraid of its shining (34.30ff.). 'But whenever Moses went in before Yahweh to speak with him he took off the veil until he came out' (34.34).

This is the story that Paul has in mind in our passage. Underlying Paul's contrasts between the ministry of the old covenant and that of the new in 2Cor 3.1—4.6 are two fundamental parallels between their respective minister's receiving them: 1) as Moses saw God appearing *in glory* on Mt. Sinai (3.7ff.), so Paul saw Christ appearing *in glory* on the Damascus road (3.16—18; 4.4—6); and 2) as it was then that Moses received the ministry of the old covenant (3.7ff.), so it was then that Paul received the ministry of the new covenant (3.6; 4.1, 4—6). Thus, just as the ministry of the old covenant came to Moses in glory, so the ministry of the new came to Paul in glory (3.7—12). Whereas Moses was the only minister of the old covenant, Paul is, of course, only one of the many ministers of the new covenant, and Paul must have been aware that other ministers did not receive their ministry of the new covenant in a theophany or Christophany which could be compared with the Sinai theophany to Moses. But here Paul does not think of them at all. Insofar as it is his gospel and apostleship which are attacked by the Judaizers who appealed to Moses and the Mosaic law, he thinks only of himself and his ministry of the new covenant as opposed to Moses and the Mosaic ministry of the old. The 'we' in our passage (except ἡμεῖς πάντες in 3.18) is a stylistic plural referring to Paul himself alone, although here as often elsewhere Paul may involve his co-workers in assertions which are basically about himself[1]. J. Munck has correctly observed that in our passage Moses is compared not with Christ but with Paul, and his statement that in our passage 'Judaism and Christianity appear personified in the figures of Moses and Paul respectively. It comes without surprise that as far as the Gentiles are concerned the apostle to the Gentiles embodies Christianity — that is as obvious as Moses' embodiment of Juda-

---

interpretation against it, making use of the concepts and ideas of the Hellenistic church (*Imago*, pp.173f.), is also untenable. *Supra* **pp.141ff.**

[1] *Supra* p.5, n.7.

ism'[1], is only an exaggeration of a valid point. So, in our passage, Paul establishes an antithetical typology between Moses the minister of the old covenant and Paul himself *the* minister of the new[2]. If Paul is aware of other ministers of the new covenant, he is treating his commission as the paradigm of all apostolic commissions. The typology is suggested to Paul by the two parallels outlined above.

It is interesting to note that in Ex.R.23.15 the words of the Palestinian R. Berekia (c.340) which are reported suggest that he took Ex 33.18ff. as meaning that Moses saw the דמות of Yahweh. In Num 12.8 Yahweh says that Moses is privileged to see the תמונת יהוה (LXX: δόξα κυρίου; Tg. Onk. דמות יקראירי) whereas a mere prophet is only able to see him in a vision or dream. In Lev.R.20.10 R. Joshua of Sikinin (c.330) transmits the words of the Palestinian R. Levi (c.300) which cite Num 12.8 in the context of discussing the theophany of Ex 33–34. These Rabbinic discussions seem to suggest that from Ex 33–34 Paul could have thought that Moses saw God or his image at the Sinai theophany. Even if he is not aware of such Rabbinic discussions, he himself could easily have inferred this in view of Ex 24.9f. and Num 12.8. Here we should also remember the Jewish conception of the Exodus and the Sinai revelation of the law as a second creation: in *Quaest. Ex.* ii.46, commenting on Ex 24.16, Philo draws a parallel between God's creation of the world and the election of the 'beholding nation' (ἡ τοῦ ὁρατικοῦ γένους ἐκλογή), i.e., Israel, and also between the natural law that God set in the universe and the law revealed on Mt. Sinai[3]. Numerous Rabbinic passages also draw a parallel between the creation and the Sinai revelation, in that the כבוד of God which accompanied the Sinai revelation of the law is compared with the glory which Adam originally possessed and then lost through his fall: at the Sinai revelation of the law the primeval glory was restored[4]. This Jewish conception of the Sinai revelation as a second creation, as the restoration of the primeval glory, provides a good parallel to Paul's conception of the Damascus revelation of the gospel as a new creation, as the restoration of the primeval light of glory, in 2Cor 4.6. The Philonic passage cited above goes on to speak of the change wrought in Moses through God's call at Sinai. It was from a being mixed with a body to 'an unmixed and simple soul'. Philo calls the divine call δευτέρα γένεσις and contrasts the Moses of the δευτέρα γένεσις with Adam, the earth-born. There is also evidence that some Rabbis thought that with the revelation of the law the image of God (or some aspects of it) which had been lost or reduced in mankind through Adam's fall was restored to Israel, though she later lost it again through sin (e.g., Num.R.16.24; Ex.R.32.1; Mek.Ex 20.19)[5]. This idea is to be compared with Paul's idea of the believer's transformation into the image of Christ in 2Cor 3.18. Furthermore the LXX renders Ex 34.29 as: . . . ὅτι δεδόξασται ἡ ὄψις τοῦ χρώματος τοῦ προσώπου αὐτοῦ ἐν τῷ λαλεῖν αὐτὸν αὐτῷ. Similarly all the Targum versions of Ex 34.29 elaborate that the shining of Moses' face was due to the 'light of glory', that is, the light of God's glory reflected from it. Tg.Jon. is the most

---

[1]Munck, *Paul*, pp.58–61 (quotation f. p.58); cf. also Jeremias, Μωυσῆς, *TDNT* iv, p.869.

[2]Cf. *ibid.*

[3]Cf. Hegermann, *Schöpfungsmittler*, p.34.

[4]See Jervell, *Imago*, pp.100ff., 113ff. Some of the abundant evidence cited by Jervell should be treated with reservation.

[5]See *ibid.*, pp.113ff.; and *infra* pp.260ff.

interesting: 'And Moses did not know that the splendour of his features (**איקונין ויו**) was made glorious, which (happened) to him from the splendour of the glory of the Shekinah of the Lord at the time of his converse with him'[1]. Suggesting that the primary sense of the participle κατοπτριζόμενοι in 2Cor 3.18 is 'to see as in a mirror', we have left open the possibility that Paul deliberately retains the other sense of the word, to 'reflect', secondarily[2]. This is probably suggested by the phrase ἀπὸ δόξης εἰς δόξαν[3].   From beholding the glory of God as in a mirror the beholder has that glory reflected on his face. If this is so, the LXX and the Targum versions of Ex 34.29 provide an interesting parallel to 2Cor 3.18. All these observations suggest that in formulating 2Cor 3.18; 4.4, 6 on the basis of the Damascus Christophany Paul has also the Sinai theophany in mind. That is to say, Paul is drawing a typology between the Sinai theophany to Moses and the Damascus Christophany to himself.

However, the typology is an antithetical one. For Paul draws out not only parallels but also contrasts between them, and the latter are more important because he is aiming at proving the superiority of the ministry of the new covenant to that of the old, indeed the supersession of the latter by the former. The contrasts can be tabulated as follows:

The Ministry of the Old Covenant	*The Ministry of the New Covenant*
I It is of a written code (3.6f.) of death (3.6) of condemnation (3.9) in the process of abolition (3.11) of less glory	It is of the Spirit (3.6, 8) of life (3.6) of righteousness (3.9) permanent (3.11) of greater glory (3.7−11)
II − Moses, its minister, veiled himself in order to prevent the Israelites from seeing the end of the covenant which was being abolished (3.13)	− Paul, its minister, acts with confidence, hope, freedom and frankness (3.4, 12; 4.1ff.)
− In consequence the old covenant remains veiled (3.14)	− The new covenant reveals the glory of God (3.16−18; 4.4, 6)
− Its adherents, the Israelites, are also veiled in their hearts, so that they cannot understand the revelation of God (3.14f.; 4.3f.)	− Its adherents, the Christians, have their veil removed in Christ, and see the glory of the Lord,
− Implied: (the glory and image of God were restored to Israel on Sinai; but they lost them through sin. The observance of the law does not restore them).	− and are transformed into the image of Christ who operates as the Spirit (3.16−18; 4.4−6).

---

[1]Translation by M.McNamara, *The NT and the Palestinian Targum to the Pentateuch* (1966), pp.172f. His suggestion that the mention of εἰκών in 2Cor 3.18 may have been occasioned by a tradition such as Tg.Jon.Ex 34.29 (pp.172f., n.62), is far-fetched. For whereas the Targum speaks of the **איקונין** of Moses, Paul has the εἰκών of Christ (= God) in view in 2Cor 3.18.

*Footnotes 2 & 3 on the next page.

The parallels between the Sinai theophany and the Damascus Christophany enable Paul to see a typology between the old covenant and the new, between Moses and himself. But the particular circumstances and content of the Damascus revelation lead him to make it an antithetical one. The particular circumstances are that Paul was on the way to Damascus in obedience to the old covenant and in opposition to the new represented by the followers of the crucified Jesus of Nazareth. The content consists in the appearance of the crucified Jesus exalted in glory, revealing the supersession of the old covenant by the new and commissioning him to be a minister of the new.

This antithetical typology is used by Paul in order to counter-attack his Judaizing opponents who, appealing to Moses and the Mosaic law, question the legitimacy of Paul's apostleship, accuse him of distorting the gospel and of employing underhand methods. First of all, in 3.6−11 Paul demonstrates the superiority of the ministry of the new covenant to that of the old, indeed the supersession of the old by the new (3.15). In 3.12 he draws out the consequences of his argument in 3.6−11: since, therefore, Paul has such a hope that the glory of the new covenant ministry will continue, he is very frank, concealing nothing[1]. In 3.13 this openness of Paul is contrasted with Moses' taking a veil upon his face[2], so that the Israelites might not see the end of the old covenant that was being abolished. 'Furthermore[3] the minds of the Israelites are dulled' (3.14). This state of Moses (so of the Mosaic covenant) and the Israelites has not changed, 'for[4] to this day the same veil remains whenever the old covenant is read in the Synagogue' (3.14), i.e., whenever Moses' work is repeated in the reading of the law[5], and whenever Moses (= the law) is read a veil lies also upon the hearts of the Israelites (3.15). But when a man turns to the Lord, the veil is taken away, and he receives freedom[6] which the Lord operating as the **Spirit**[7] gives. All Christians have had this experience and therefore they are 'with unveiled face', i.e., they have frankness, openness and freedom[8]. With such freedom they behold the glory of the Lord and are transformed into

---

[2]Similarly also Jervell, *Imago*, pp.184f. *Supra* p.232.

[3]van Unnik, *op. cit.*, p.208.

[1]For this meaning of παρρησία, see Bauer-Arndt-Gingrich, s.v.1.

[2]van Unnik, *op. cit.*, pp.202ff., shows convincingly that to 'uncover the face or head' is an Aramaic expression equivalent to the Greek παρρησία. So Moses' covering of his face is to be understood as concealing in contrast to Paul's παρρησία.

[3]For this sense of ἀλλά, see B–D, §448.6; van Unnik, *op. cit.*, p.203.

[4]For this sense of γάρ, see van Unnik, *op. cit.*, p.265, who appeals to Bauer-Arndt-Gingrich.

[5]van Unnik, *op. cit.*, p.205.

[6]ἐλευθερία is the opposite of 'covering with a veil', which means bondage (and in the context is synonymous with παρρησία of 3.12) − cf. van Unnik, *op. cit.*, pp.206ff.; Bruce, *Cor.*, p.193; Barrett, *2Cor.*, p.124.

[7]Cf. Hermann, *Kyrios*, pp.38ff.

[8]Besides this idiomatic sense (see n.2 above) a literal meaning may also be intended in the phrase 'with unveiled face'. Christians have had the experience of a veil removed from their face, so that they can now see God's revelation and glory, whereas the Jews with a veil on their heart cannot see it.

the image of Christ the Lord. Paul knows both the state of the old covenant and its adherents and the state of the new covenant and its adherents, because on the Damascus road he turned from a blind obedience to the old covenant to the Lord and his new covenant.

Therefore, being confident of his ministry of the new covenant, Paul is in effect saying that it is not he but Moses who has something to hide because of the defective nature of his ministry, and that it is not his gospel but the Mosaic law that is veiled. Paul draws this contrast between the ministry of the old covenant and that of the new, and between Moses and himself because it is the most effective way of countering his opponents. For they, appealing to Moses and his law, specifically accuse Paul of neglecting them. 4.1–6 is then a restatement in plainer terms of the argument in 3.12–18: it is not Paul but the followers of Moses who practise the underhand methods; it is not Paul but they who distort the Word of God; it is not Paul's gospel but their minds that are veiled[1]. Having received the ministry of the new covenant that has superseded the old through the revelation of the glorious Jesus Christ, Paul has absolutely no reason why he should still be bound by the old covenant ministered by Moses. His opponents, however, insofar as they are still adherents of the Mosaic covenant, are veiled in their hearts (3.14f.) and blind (4.4)[2], and insofar as they nevertheless claim to be apostles of Christ, they distort the Word of God and employ underhand methods (4.2).

d) Tradition-Historical Consideration of the Throne-Theophany Visions and the Figure כבר־אנש

To return to the main theme of our discussion, we have so far attempted to demonstrate that Paul obtained his conception of Christ as the εἰκὼν τοῦ θεοῦ from the Damascus Christophany. This we have done first by drawing out the *formgeschichtlichen* links between the Damascus Christophany and the epiphanic visions which we examined, and then by verifying from the Pauline texts that indeed he saw the exalted Christ on the Damascus road as the image of God. Now the question is whether there is still another link between some of the epiphanic visions and the Damascus Christophany, namely a *traditionsgeschichtliche* link. Here we would like to make it clear that our thesis already set forth above is in no way dependent on this new consideration. In the following we consider the possible tradition-historical link only because, if proved, it might illuminate some other, related elements in Paul's theology as well as consolidate what we have just ascertained.

---

[1]Lietzmann-Kümmel, *Kor.*, pp.115, 201, suggest that the accusation of Paul's opponents that Paul's gospel is 'veiled' may have caused Paul's imagery of 'veil' in 3.13ff. It is possible that the accusation is responsible for Paul's understanding in 2Cor 3.13ff. of Moses' veiling himself in Ex 34.30ff. in terms of concealing the deficient covenant.

[2]οἱ ἀπολλύμενοι in 4.3 and οἱ ἄπιστοι in 4.4 are general references to unbelievers. However, in view of the polemical context, it is probable that among these Paul includes his Judaizing opponents (so Lietzmann-Kümmel, *Kor.*, p.115, but Kümmel (p.201) regards this assumption as uncertain).

Already in 1920 O. Procksch had hinted at such a link. We have already mentioned that he saw the description of the mirror-image of God as דמות כמראה אדם in Ezek 1.26 as the reverse side of the idea of the creation of man in the image of God (Gen 1.26f.). At the same time he saw the figure in Dan 7.13 as the hypostatization of the mirror-image of God in Ezek 1: 'He is the hypostatized εἰκών τοῦ θεοῦ grown out of the frame of the mirror: in him is embodied the universal sovereignity of God. The hypostatization of the εἰκών τοῦ θεοῦ corresponds to the מימרא in the Targum. In Jesus Christ the εἰκών τοῦ θεοῦ (Col 1.15; 2Cor 4.4) and the λόγος τοῦ θεοῦ (Rev 19.13; Jn 1.1ff.) have become embodied reality'[1]. Independently of Procksch, other scholars have also noted many similarities between Ezek 1 and Dan 7, without, however, inferring from them that the vision of the heavenly figure כבר אנש in Dan 7 originated from the vision of God appearing in human form in Ezek 1.26ff.; 8.2f.; etc.[2] However, A. Feuillet was the first to accept Procksch's suggestion of the connection between Ezek 1 and Gen 1.26f.[3] and to develop his suggestion of the connection between Ezek 1 and Dan 7 by drawing out the literary and theological links between Ezekiel and Daniel, especially between these two chapters[4]. His conclusion is that the כבר אנש in Dan 7 is 'a kind of manifestation of the invisible God'[5] and that 'the Son of Man in Daniel clearly belongs to the category of the divine and is like a kind of incarnation of the divine glory, with the same title as the human form seen by Ezekiel (1.26)'[6]. In two recent articles M. Black has also seen Dan 7.9–13 as standing within the theophanic throne-vision tradition of 1Kings 22.19–22; Isa 6; Ezek 1; 8; 10, and has come to concur with Feuillet in understanding the 'Son of Man' figure in the light of Ezek 1.26ff.[7] In the second of the two articles Black goes on to trace the

---

[1]Procksch, 'Berufungsvision', pp.149f. He often repeated this view. See, e.g., his 'Der Menschensohn als Gottessohn', *Christentum und Wissenschaft* 3 (1927), pp.432f.; *Theologie des AT* (1950), pp.416f.

[2]E.g. J.Bowman, 'The Background of the Term "Son of Man" ', *ExpT* 59 (1948), p.285;. R.B.Y.Scott, "Behold, He Cometh with Clouds", *NTS* 5 (1958/59), p.129. The former (pp.285f.) notes also the influence of Ezek 1 and Dan 7 upon the Similitudes of Enoch and on *merkabah* mysticism.

[3]Feuillet, 'Fils', p.190.

[4]*Ibid.*, pp.180–202.

[5]*Ibid.*, p.187.

[6]*Ibid.*, pp.188f.

[7]Black, 'Die Apotheose Israels: eine neue Interpretation des danielischen "Menschensohns"', *Jesus und der Menschensohn*, Vögtle FS, pp.95–99; 'The Throne-Theophany Prophetic Commission and the "Son of Man": A Study in Tradition-History', *Jews, Greeks and Christians*, W.D.Davies FS (1976), pp.56–73.

development of the 'Son of Man' tradition in the throne-visions throughout 1Enoch. For convenience, we mention the work of H.R. Balz[1] here, although it appeared before the essays of Black. It seems to have been unknown to Black, and Balz, in turn, seems to have been unaware of the essay by Feuillet. Having dismissed the *Urmensch* hypothesis concerning the origin of the idea of the eschatological Man, Balz takes up, more explicitly than Feuillet, the suggestion of Procksch, which he sees as 'einen entscheidenden, bisher wenig beachteten Neuansatz'[2]. Through a) an analysis of the theophany visions in Ezek 1; 8–11; 40; 43; Dan 7; 4 Ezra 13; and b) an observation of the tendency in the OT-Judaism to hypostatize God's functions and attributes (like Wisdom, Word, Glory), split them off from God and then personify and deify them; and c) an observation of the Jewish speculations about a heavenly mediator figure like the Metatron, Balz comes to the conclusion: The figure אנש כבר in Dan 7 is a 'splitting-off' (*Abspaltung*) of the glory of God in the theophany of Ezek 1. The vision-tradition of Ezek 1 provided the decisive material for this development, and Ezek 8–11; 43 provided an independent, Messianic, priestly figure. The author of Dan 7.1–14 took a further decisive step by forming from the glory of God appearing in human form and his agent, the priestly representative, two glorious heavenly beings in visionary language: the Ancient of Days and a man-like figure[3]. Balz then also goes on to trace the further development of the 'Son of Man' tradition in 1En., 3En. and Slavonic En. (= 2En.)[4].

However, the most exhaustive study on the tradition of the throne-vision of Ezek 1 has been made by C.C. Rowland in his Cambridge thesis under the title *The Influence of the First Chapter of Ezekiel on Jewish and Early Christian Literature* (1974). As it is obviously impossible to enter into a discussion on details of this study, we can here only summarize the bare outline of its course. After a long introduction, in the first chapter Rowland examines the descriptions of theophanies on the heavenly chariot-throne (מרכבה) in 1En 14; Dan 7; Apoc.Abr.17f.; 4QS1; Rev 4; and Gnostic literature, in order to establish the widespread influence of the throne-vision of Ezek 1. In the second chapter Rowland concentrates on 'the use of the human figure of Ezek 1.26f. in Jewish and Christian literature'. First of all, he establishes that the דמות כמראה איש in Ezek 8.2 refers to God appearing in דמות כמראה אדם in 1.26. From the fact that no throne is mentioned

---

[1] Balz, *Probleme*, pp.80–106.

[2] *Ibid.*, p.80.

[3] *Ibid.*, p.94.

[4] *Ibid.*, pp.96ff.

in 8.2, however, Rowland infers 'the splitting of the form of God from the throne to act as an angelic mediator of God's purpose'[1]. He thinks that Ezek 1 provided a quarry for the material of Dan 7, though some features in the latter, including the presence of two divine beings, cannot be explained from the former[2]. There are some similarities between Ezek 8.2 and Dan 7.13, and both should be seen in the light of the OT conception of מלאך־יהוה, the angelic representative of God who in epiphany communicates the presence of God himself. Dan 7.9 and 13 show not the hypostatization of God's glory or function in Ezek 1.26ff. as Balz maintains, but rather a development of this OT idea of the close connection between God and his representative by presenting it in images derived from the Canaanite myth of El and Baal[3]. Here Dan 7 can be thought of as presenting a binitarianism as some later *merkabah* mysticism does. There is a connection between the figure who appears in Dan 10.6 and God who appears in human form in Ezek 1.26f. 'via the figure . . . in Ezek 8.2'[4]. The figures appearing in Ezek 8.2; Dan 7.13; 10.6 'are to be regarded as aspects of his self-revelation. Nevertheless in addition to the trappings of divinity there is a very strong sense – especially in Dan 7.13 and Dan 10.6 – that these figures are in some sense independent of the deity. What we seem to have in Dan. and Ez. is the beginning of a hypostatic development similar to that connected with Wisdom'[5]. Having ascertained this, Rowland goes on to examine the appearance of 'this exalted divine angelic figure' in Rev 1.13ff., Apoc.Abr., Similitudes of Enoch, and Test.Abr.[6] Noting the interesting use of the loan words איקונין and דיוקנא, especially in Tg.Jon., Rowland examines the Targumic tradition on Gen 28.12, which often appears in the Rabbinic literature[7], that the איקונין of Jacob is engraved on the throne. This tradition suggests that as it is forbidden for them to gaze upon the image on the throne itself (cf. 1En 14.21) the angels descend and look at Jacob and thus come to know the

---

[1] Rowland, *Influence*, p.92.

[2] *Ibid.*, p.92.

[3] *Ibid.*, pp.92–94. This attempt to see the Canaanite myth behind Dan 7 we have already rejected – *supra* p.208.

[4] *Ibid.*, p.100.

[5] *Ibid.*, p.101. Thus, after all the polemic against Balz's view (pp.91f., 94), Rowland himself comes to speak of the 'man-like' figure in Ezek 8 and Dan 7 as 'a hypostatic development' of God's 'self-revelation'! See also pp.156ff. His charge that Balz 'concentrates all his attention on the angelic scribe who appears in 9.2ff.' (p.91), is surely unjust.

[6] *Ibid.*, pp.102–140.

[7] For references see Maier, *Kultus*, p.129, n.131.

image engraved on the throne. Rowland sees 'identity between the אִיקוֹנִין engraved on the throne of glory and the human form mentioned in Ez.1.26f.'[1] and also a connection between Ezek 1.26f. and Gen 1.26f.[2] Then he briefly observes the development of the tradition of the heavenly 'man-like' figure in the later speculations on the body of God (שִׁעוּר קוֹמֹה) and its influence on the angel-Christology of the NT (esp. Heb 1–2), which shows a binitar-ianism[3]. Rowland devotes his third chapter to the *merkabah* mysticism reported in the Tannaitic sources concerning R. Johanan b. Zakkai and his pupils, and R. Akiba and his contemporaries in order to trace the important influence on Rabbinism of the tradition originating from Ezek 1[4]. Most interesting for our purpose here is the well known tradition that R. Elisha b. Abuyah (*alias* Acher), who entered the heavenly paradise along with three other Rabbis, Akiba, Ben Azzai and Ben Zoma, seeing the enthroned Meta-tron, exclaimed that there were two powers in heaven[5].

In the fourth and final chapter Rowland then seeks to understand both the false teaching and Paul's response to it in Col. in the light of this Jewish *merkabah* mysticism[6]. He characterizes the Colossian false teaching as involving on the one hand a strict (Jewish) ritual and ethical observance and on the other hand a keen interest in the heavenly realm and especially the angelic powers. These characteristics are in line with those of *merkabah* mysticism, for the Jewish mystics also practised ritual observance and rigorous asceticism as part of the preparation for the mystical, visionary experience of the heavenly realm. He also brings out some interesting paral-lels in terms and motifs between Col. and *merkabah* mysticism: e.g., θρόνοι in 1.16; the difficult verse, 2.18. Then he goes on to establish connections with the *merkabah* from Paul's reply. Behind 2.8ff. and the idea of putting off 'the body of the flesh' (2.11), τὰς ἀρχὰς καὶ τὰς ἐξουσίας (2.15) and τὸν παλαιὸν ἄνθρωπον (3.9) Rowland sees a belief in Christ's glorious body, which is the basis of Paul's reply to the false teaching: 'First of all, . . . at his death Christ laid aside the body of flesh and with it subservience to the

---

[1]Rowland, *Influence*, p.148.

[2]*Ibid.*, p.150.

[3]*Ibid.*, pp.152ff.

[4]*Ibid.*, pp.159–238.

[5]*Ibid.*, pp.224–238.

[6]*Ibid.*, pp.239–298. Here it should be noted that there have been other scholars who have expounded the *merkabah*-vision tradition originating from Ezek 1: e.g., Scholem, *Major Trends*, esp. pp.40–79; *Jewish Gnosticism*; Maier, *Kultus*, 3. Teil. However, they do not pay special attention to the development of the tradition of God appearing in human form in Ezek 1.26ff., which is our concern here.

powers and their ordinances. These are benefits also for those who participate in Christ's death . . . Secondly, in the body of the risen Christ all the
fullness of deity dwells . . . (So) there is no reason for the false teachers to
look for deity in any other place than in the risen and glorified Christ'[1].
However, the hymn in 1.15—20 is the real test as to whether there is in Col.
influence of the tradition deriving from Ezek 1. The θρόνοι, κυριότητες,
ἀρχαί and ἐξουσίαι in 1.16 refer primarily to the heavenly powers, although
their earthly representatives are not excluded. Mistakenly disputing the
usual view that the Hellenistic Jewish conception of Wisdom and the Philonic
conception of the Logos provide the best background for the hymn, Rowland
establishes close parallels between the description of Christ in the hymn and
that of the exalted Christ in the opening chapters of Rev. and tries to explain
the former as well as the latter in the light of the throne-vision tradition of
Ezek 1, as though the conception of Wisdom/Logos as the *Theophanieträger*
did not itself stand in that tradition. As is often observed, the two documents connected with the same geographical area, namely Asia Minor, show
many common features. Just as in Col 2.9 Paul asserts that the fullness of
deity dwells in Christ's glorious body, so in Rev 1.13ff. the heavenly Christ
is described as glorious and divine in the language of Ezek 1 and Dan 7; 10.
Both documents affirm Christ as the πρωτότοκος (ἐκ) τῶν νεκρῶν (Col
1.18; Rev 1.5) and the priority of Christ to the creation (πρωτότοκος πάσης
κτίσεως in Col 1.15; ἡ ἀρχὴ τῆς κτίσεως τοῦ θεοῦ in Rev 3.14). The
heavenly host's praise of God in Rev 4.11 (σὺ ἔκτισας τὰ πάντα, καὶ διὰ
τὸ θέλημά σου ἦσαν καὶ ἐκτίσθησαν) is reminiscent of Col 1.16 (ἐν αὐτῷ
ἐκτίσθη τὰ πάντα · · · τὰ πάντα δι' αὐτοῦ καὶ εἰς αὐτὸν ἔκτισται), and
both, in turn, of the frequent praise of God as creator in the *merkabah*
texts. On the conception of Christ as the εἰκὼν τοῦ θεοῦ in Col 1.15
Rowland would turn rather to the Targumic tradition of Gen 28.12 and the
tradition of Ezek 1 than to Wis 7.26 or Philo's conception of the Logos:

> In the Sim (ilitudes of Enoch), AA (= Apoc.Abr.) and Rev.4 we noticed a reluctance
> either to speak of God sitting on the throne of glory or a complete absence of anthro-
> pomorphism in describing God. At the same time there arises a glorious angelic figure
> who has the attributes of God and who seems to be a development of Ez. 1.26. We
> can understand the phrase εἰ κὼν τοῦ θεοῦ τοῦ ἀοράτου just as well if we see it in the
> light of this angelic man-figure. Christ is then the image — even the features — of a
> God who cannot be seen[2].

With the last sentences of Rowland's we are only too glad to agree. How-

---

[1] Rowland, *Influence*, p.272.
[2] *Ibid.*, p.291.

ever, one of the major weaknesses of Rowland's otherwise valuable study is that, as suggested above, he fails to trace the development of the theophany-vision tradition in the conception of the hypostatized and personified Wisdom and Logos as the *Theophanieträger* in the Wisdom literature and Philo. For such a tradition-historical study Hegermann has provided many useful suggestions[1], as we have observed briefly above. From a detailed study of the tradition-history of the conception of Wisdom/Logos as the *Theophanieträger* we might well be able to obtain a clear picture as to how the OT theophany-vision tradition developed along two apparently different lines: the apocalyptic line which involves the appearance of God in human form and the gradual hypostatization of that form or glory of God into a heavenly figure 'like a man' (כבר אנש) on the one hand, and the line of the Wisdom literature and Philo which presents Wisdom/Logos as the bearer of theophany, i.e., as the agent that shows the image of God in theophany, on the other hand. Philonic passages like *Conf. Ling.* 146, where the Logos is called, among other things, ἀρχάγγελος, ὄνομα θεοῦ, ὁ κατ᾽ εἰκόνα ἄνθρωπος, ὁ ὁρῶν and Ἰσραήλ, seem to invite such a study, as these names may well have tradition-historical links with מלאך־יהוה as the *Theophanieträger*, the Metatron (cf. 3En 12.4f.), Adam or rather his prototype in Gen 1.26f., and Jacob, *alias* Israel, who saw God at Bethel (Gen 28.12ff.) and Jabbok (Gen 32.34ff.), respectively. The two lines of development of the same theophany-vision tradition seem to be well merged in the figure of the Metatron in 3En.[2], while the same cannot be said for 1En[3]. A similar confluence of the two lines seems to be present in the presentation of the exalted Christ in Col. and Rev. Failing to recognise this Rowland disputes in vain the real parallels between the Christologies of Col. and Rev. on the one hand and the conceptions of Wisdom/Logos in the Wisdom literature and Philo on the other[4]. Since he has difficulty in explaining away the real Wisdom-Christological motifs like πρωτότοκος πάσης κτίσεως, ἀρχὴ τῆς κτίσεως, Christ's mediatorship in creation, the title of Christ 'Word of God' in Rev 19.13,

---

[1]Hegermann, *Schöpfungsmittler,* part A. Apparently A.Feuillet traces the *Traditionsgeschichte* of the theophany-vision through the Wisdom literature in the second part of his article cited above, 'Le Fils de l'homme et la tradition biblique', *RB* 60 (1953), pp.321–346, which unfortunately we are not able to read. Philo and Wisdom of Solomon have not only the conception of Wisdom/Logos as the *Theophanieträger* but also the idea of Wisdom (e.g., Wis 9.10; cf. also Prov 8.22ff. LXX) or the Logos (e.g., Wis 18.15; Philo, *Somn.* i.157) sitting on the heavenly throne.

[2]Cf. Hegermann, *Schöpfungsmittler*, pp.82f.

[3]*Supra* pp.122f.

[4]Rowland, *Influence*, pp.275ff.

etc., he is forced to postulate in a rather confusing manner the 'combination' of 'the two strands of Wisdom and the heavenly man'[1] behind the Christologies of Col. and Rev. and to appeal to E. Käsemann for this. However, Käsemann understood 'the heavenly man' rather differently from Rowland himself, deriving it from sources entirely different from the OT-theophany tradition. Nevertheless, Rowland has made a valuable contribution to explaining certain aspects of the Christologies of Col. and Rev. in the light of the theophany-vision tradition of Ezek 1.

Inevitable disagreements over details notwithstanding, we are inclined to think that the above mentioned authors are essentially right in trying to see a tradition-historical link between the descriptions of theophanies in Ezek 1; 8 (or even still earlier ones in the OT) and those of the heavenly figure 'like a son of man' in Dan 7 and the later apocalyptic literature. Despite some criticisms[2], their supposition that the heavenly figure אנש כבר in Dan 7;1En 37—71; 4Ezra 13 is a product of the hypostatization of the כבוד יהוה appearing in דמות כמראה אדם in Ezek 1.26ff.; 8.2ff., seems to be the best explanation available for the rise of the figure in the apocalyptic literature[3]. This development culminates in the conception of the Metatron in 3En., in which the other line of development of the same theophany-vision tradition, namely the conception of Wisdom/Logos as the *Theophanieträger*, is fully conflated with the apocalyptic line of the heavenly figure כבר אנש.

The experiential or psychological basis behind this development we can hardly discuss here. However, we need to state our view regarding the identity and role of the heavenly figure כבר אנש in Dan 7; 1En 37—71; and 4Ezra 13. To do this in an adequate way would take us too far afield. Thus we can only state what seems to us to be the best among the various explanations proposed by scholars. Contrary to the view held in some quarters that the figure כבר אנש in Dan 7.13 is a man symbolizing the faithful of Israel[4], his coming with the clouds of heaven clearly indicates, as we have seen, that he is a heavenly, divine figure. In the interpretation of the vision he seems to be identified with the 'saints of the Most High' (v.18). However, just as in

---

[1]*Ibid.*, p.287.

[2]See, e.g., Müller, *Messias*, pp.34f. Müller's three points of criticism are not so weighty as the positive evidence for the supposition.

[3]Taking note also of J.Barr's suggestion concerning the link between the figure מלאך in OT theophany accounts and the Danielic figure כבר אנש (*Supra* p.218) one could undertake valuable research on this question.

[4]E.g., Moule, 'Neglected Features', pp.414ff.

the interpretation of the four beasts there is an oscillation between the individual understanding as kings[1] (v.17) and the collective understanding as kingdoms (vs. 23ff.), so there may well also be such an oscillation in the interpretation of the figure אנש כבר. If so, just as the four beasts are both the symbols and representatives of four empires, so the figure כבר אנש is both the symbol and representative (or leader) of the 'saints of the Most High'. Since C.H.W. Brekelmans has demonstrated against M. Noth[2] and his followers that in the apocryphal and pseudepigraphical literature and in the Qumran literature קדשים is used both for angels and for the people of God (cf. also Ps 34.10; Dt 33.3)[3], the 'saints of the Most High' in Dan 7, as the context demands, seems to refer to the faithful portion of Israel[4]. M. Black, who takes the divine figure כבר אנש to be the symbol for the 'saints of the Most High', therefore goes so far as to say that 'what Daniel was contemplating was nothing less than the *apotheosis* of Israel in the End-time'[5].

Then, arguing against J.T. Milik[6], Black goes on to establish that the Similitudes of Enoch or the Second Vision of Enoch (1En 37–71), 'is essentially a Jewish work . . . from the same period and vintage as the 2Esdras Apocalypse, i.e., 1–2 c. A.D.'; further that it has taken over motifs and ideas from the First Vision and has also preserved old and lost material from it[7]. Thus having established the usefulness of the Second Vision of Enoch for the present discussion, he compares the various throne-visions in 1En. (14.18–22; 46.1–3; 60.1ff.; 71.5–14; 90.20–23, 31–33, 37f.) with one another, and notes with R.H. Charles that they show influences of Isa 6; Ezek 1; and Dan 7[8]. We cannot enter into a discussion of these matters. The best we

---

[1]The LXX and Theodotion give βασιλεῖαι. It represents probably not the original rendering but an alteration occasioned by the desire to give a consistent interpretation of the beasts in view of vs. 23ff.

[2]M.Noth, "Die Heiligen des Höchsten", *Gesammelte Studien zum AT* (1957), pp. 274–290.

[3]Brekelmans, 'The Saints of the Most High and Their Kingdom' *Oudtestamentische Studien* 14 (1965), pp.305–326.

[4]*Ibid.*, pp.326–329; most recently also A.Deissler, 'Der "Menschensohn" und "das Volk der Heiligen des Höchsten" in Dan 7', *Jesus und der Menschensohn*, Vögtle FS, pp.81–91, following Brekelmans.

[5]Black, 'Throne-Theophany', p.62; also 'Apotheose', p.99.

[6]J.T.Milik, 'Problèmes de la Littérature Hénochique à la Lumière des Fragments Araméens de Qumrân', *HTR* 64 (1971) – I have not read this article.

[7]Black, 'Throne-Theophany', p.66.

[8]*Ibid.*, pp.67ff.

can do is to quote the conclusion of Black's tradition-historical study and, partly agreeing with it, suggest an alternative to it. It is:

> While the actual evidence of the parables of Enoch for a pre-NT period is now suspect and late, we cannot rule out altogether a tradition of interpretation of Dan 7.13 *individually* – whether of Enoch or a so-called Messiah – in the pre-Christian period. Side by side therefore with the concept of the apotheosis of Israel at the End-time, an expectation may also have existed in the first c. B.C. of *Enoch redivivus* or of a Messianic Deliverer, *both of whom were also considered as divine-human figures.* But even as individuals they are also 'corporate personalities', the Heads and inclusive representatives of the apotheosized Israel. The origin and growth of this Son of Man messianism is traceable within the developing tradition of the throne-vision prophetic commissions of Israel[1] .

To this we would only say that, in view of the oscillation between the individual and the collective understanding of the figure אנש כבר in Dan 7 itself, Jesus and the NT writers themselves could have started to take him individually and messianically directly from Dan 7, even if there had been no such understanding before them. Recently it has been made clear that before the NT there was no such messianic *title* as '*the* Son of Man'[2]. However, this does not exclude the possibility that before the NT the heavenly figure אנש כבר in Dan 7 was already conceived of as the heavenly Messiah and identified by different Jewish apocalyptic groups with personalities like Enoch (cf.Abel in Test.Abr.Rec.A. XIff.; Melchizedek in 11Q Melch.10ff.) who were believed to have been exalted to heaven and to be coming again to earth as judge and saviour at the end[3]. However, since the undisputed examples of this sort of conception, namely the Similitudes and 4Ezra 13, are, at least in their present version, later than the NT Gospels, we find it more probable that Jesus himself started the messianic interpretation of the figure אנש כבר in Dan 7[4]. By this we do not mean that the Similitudes and 4Ezra 13 developed their messianic conception of the figure in dependence upon the NT.

---

[1]*Ibid.*, p.73 (emphasis by Black); cf. O.Michel, υἱὸς τοῦ ἀνθρώπου, *Begriffslexikon* II/2, pp.1154f.; Lindars, 'Re-Enter', esp. pp.54–60.

[2]Leivestad, 'Exit the Apocalyptic Son of Man', *NTS* 18 (1971/72), pp.243–267; Moule, 'Neglected Features', pp.413ff.; Vermes, *Jesus the Jew* (1973), pp.160ff.; also Lindars, 'Re-Enter', p.58.

[3]So Black, 'Throne-Theophany', esp. p.73; Lindars, 'Re-Enter, p.58; Michel, *op. cit.*, pp.1154f.

[4]It is noteworthy that in spite of the fact that Dan. was a favourite book in the Qumran sect no reference to the vision of Dan 7 is found among the texts so far published, let alone one to the identification of the figure אנש כבר with Melchizedek. Cf. Lindars, 'Re-Enter', p.56.

They could have developed it independently and yet parallel to the NT[1]. All that we wish to assert is the possibility that the heavenly figure כבר אנש in Dan 7, though in itself no messianic title, could have been taken individually and messianically as a description of the heavenly Messiah at the time of Jesus and that Jesus himself started this conception independently of any prior tradition. If the anonymous apocalyptists behind the Similitudes and 4Ezra could do it, why could not Jesus do the same?

'It is no "sound historical method" to deny Jesus the use of the expression "Son of Man" '[2]. For in the Gospels it is exclusively Jesus' self-designation and it is not used by others as an address or a Christological confession. Now, observing that the expression 'Son of Man' with the definite article is virtually unknown prior to the NT, C.F.D. Moule emphasizes that when Jesus designates himself as '*the* Son of Man' he is doing so in reference to the Danielic phrase כבר אנש[3]. The Similitudes of Enoch provides a parallel to this: when from 1En 46.2 onward it prefaces the expression 'Son of man' with a demonstrative, which is generally understood to be the Ethiopic rendering of the Greek article, it refers to 'another being whose countenance had the appearance of man' in 46.1, which in turn refers to the figure כבר אנש in Dan 7.13. So, with the self-designation '*the* Son of Man' Jesus is in effect saying: 'I am *the* Son of Man whom Daniel saw in a vision'[4].

At this point we find instructive the almost completely ignored article by O. Procksch, 'Der Menschensohn als Gottessohn'[5]. Procksch examines many sayings of 'the Son of Man' taken from all three usual categories — relating to the present circumstances, to future suffering, and to the apocalyptic glory — and attempts to show that they can be correctly understood only if 'the Son of Man' is replaced by 'the Son of God', i.e., that by the puzzling self-designation 'the Son of Man' Jesus lets his audience draw (if they have ears to hear!) the conclusion that he claims to be. 'the Son of God'[6]. 'The

---

[1]Cf. Moule, 'Neglected Features', p.416.

[2]Michel, *op. cit.*, p.1158.

[3]Moule, 'Neglected Features', pp.419ff.

[4]From this point our interpretation is different from Moule's. Moule takes the figure כבר אנש in Dan 7 to be a human symbol for the true people of God, so that he understands Jesus' self-reference as being 'to his authority whenever it was exercised in his capacity as the focus of God's dedicated people, both on earth and through his sufferings and beyond them in his ultimate vindication' (*ibid.*, p.422).

[5]*Supra* p.240, n.1.

[6]Cf.M.D.Hooker, *The Son of Man in Mark* (1967), who emphasizes the claim to authority involved in Jesus' self-designation as the Son of Man and has a summarizing sentence which is rather similar to ours: 'Jesus, like Israel, can be termed "Son of Man"

Son of Man' sayings in passages like Mk 2.1–12 and par.; Lk 6.1–5 and par.; Mk 8.38 and par.; and Jn 1.51, among others, seem to bear out this surprising thesis. But because of the exceedingly complicated nature of 'the Son of Man' problem in the Gospels we have to give up any attempt to demonstrate this here. We would therefore only suggest that this is quite intelligible in the light of the character of the descriptions, 'one like a son of man' and 'one like a son of God' which we have seen in epiphanic visions[1]. The heavenly figure in Dan 7.13 is described as being כבר אנש because he is seen as a heavenly divine being. If he were seen as an exalted and yet *human* figure, as the angelic being in Dan 3.25 at first was, he would be described as being כבר אלהין. So it is possible that Jesus understands the heavenly figure כבר אנש in Dan 7 to be in reality the Son of God who *appeared* כבר אנש. When he designates himself as 'the Son of Man' in reference to Dan 7.13, he is then both disclosing and hiding his true being as the Son of God. He is the Son of God now revealed who then proleptically appeared to Daniel כבר אנש in a vision. But on earth his true identity as the Son of God is still concealed in the self-designation 'the Son of Man' until through the resurrection he is revealed and declared as the Son of God clearly. How such a self-understanding is possible may also be explained by means of analogies from the tradition-history of the theophany-vision as developed, for example, in the Enoch tradition in the Similitudes and 3 En., in the Wisdom tradition, or in the Targumic and Rabbinic tradition on Gen 28.12 that the איקונין of Jacob-Israel is (engraved) upon the throne of glory[2].

Jesus' teaching of his unique filial relationship to God and his ingathering of his disciples to participate in that relationship[3] also support the view that he designated himself as 'the Son of Man' in full consciousness that he was the

---

only because his relationship with God is such that he can also be described as "Son of God" ' (p.192). However, her interpretation of the self-designation is on the whole very different from the one suggested here. Our interpretation is also against Leivestad's view that Jesus' self-designation as the Son of Man 'is irrelevant to "the messianic secret" ' (*op. cit.*, p.255) and that the sayings relating to the earthly lowliness, to the suffering and to the death of the Son of Man are devoid of any emphasis on paradox like that of the crucified Messiah (e.g., 1Cor 1.23) (pp.263f.). On the latter point see Procksch, 'Menschensohn', pp.437ff.

[1] *Supra* pp.205–216.

[2] Some hints for this may be perceived in Rowland, *Influence*, pp.120–132, 141–151; also Balz, *Probleme*, pp.96ff. Cf. Justin, *Dial.* 126.1–2. The angel-Christology of the early (esp. Jewish) Church would also be a valuable help in providing the explanation. On this see Werner, *Entstehung*, pp.302ff.; J.Daniélou, *Theology of Jewish Christianity* (1964), pp.117ff.; R.N.Longenecker, *The Christology of Early Jewish Christianity*, pp.26ff.; Rowland, *Influence*, pp.152ff.

[3] See Jeremias, *Abba*, pp.15–67; *NT Theology I*, pp.61ff., 178ff.

Son of God, the inclusive representative of the faithful or ideal Israel[1], whom Daniel saw appearing as one 'like a son of man' in a vision[2]. But, as said above, it is impossible to pursue this line of study here[3].

However, if what has just been said about Jesus' self-designation is correct, Paul understood him well on this point. We have already suggested that when the exalted Jesus Christ appeared in glory to him on the Damascus road Paul at first saw him as a heavenly, divine being דמות כמראה אדם or כבר אנש and then, on learning that he was Jesus of Nazareth, he perceived him as having the εἰκόνα τοῦ θεοῦ and being 'like a son of God'. This is, as we have seen, precisely what is suggested by Paul's testimony in Gal 1.16 that on the Damascus road God revealed 'his Son' (ἀποκαλύψαι τὸν υἱὸν αὐτοῦ) to him. U. Wilckens has drawn a parallel between the revelation of the Son of God to Paul in this verse and that of the Son of Man to Stephen in Acts 7.56[4]. Stephen also could have designated the exalted Jesus seen in vision standing at the right hand of God, as 'the Son of God'. The reason why he designates him instead as 'the Son of Man' seems to be the desire to echo Jesus' word to the Sanhedrin in his trial (Lk 22.69 and par.). On the basis of the parallelism between the two visions, E. Schweizer has suggested: 'Perhaps there is an echo of apocalyptic Son of Man ideas in Gal 1.16'[5]. Now we can see that Schweizer has made a correct observation, although he has not adequately grasped the rationale behind the phenomenon he has observed. Paul's Damascus experience must have led him immediately to Dan 7.13 because he saw a heavenly figure 'like a son of man' just as Daniel did. It must also have led him to understand that with the self-designation 'the Son of Man', which he in all likelihood had already known, Jesus referred to himself as the Son of God who had appeared to Daniel כבר אנש. Now the cumbersome ὁ υἱὸς τοῦ ἀνθρώπου would be, as a title, not only meaningless but positively misleading to Paul's Gentile hearers and would not so easily be understood in the sense of the Son of God even by his Jewish hearers. Moreover, since the exalted Christ who appeared to him is none other than the man Jesus of Nazareth, according to the regular pattern of epiphanic descriptions, Paul would naturally have found the title 'the Son of God' more

---

[1]*Infra* pp. 254–256. See G.Fohrer & E.Lohse, υἱός, *TDNT* viii, pp.351–353, 359ff. for the OT/Jewish tradition that designates Israel or the righteous and wise Israelites (= the ideal Israel) as the son(s) of God. See also Hengel, *Sohn*, pp.68ff.

[2]*Infra*, pp.318f.

[3]We hope to take this up in a future research.

[4]Wilckens, 'Ursprung', pp.83f. (n.67).

[5]Schweizer, ὁ υἱὸς τοῦ θεοῦ, *TDNT* viii, p.383.

congenial than 'the Son of Man'. For these reasons, avoiding ὁ υἱὸς τοῦ ἀνθρώπου, Paul uses only the title, 'the Son of God' not only in connection with the Damascus Christophany (Gal 1.16; Acts 9.20) but also in the apocalyptic context where, in view of Dan 7.13ff. and Jesus' apocalyptic sayings about the coming of the Son of Man, the title 'the Son of Man' would fit in well: 1Th 1.10 (cf. 1Cor 15.28). We have already suggested that 1Th 1.10 also alludes to the Damascus Christophany: the proleptic parousia of the exalted Christ to Paul is the basis of his hope and waiting for his coming from heaven. But here again as in Gal 1.16 Paul recalls the vision of the exalted Christ only as that of 'the Son of God' and so says that we are waiting for 'the Son of God' from heaven[1]. Nevertheless, with the title 'the Son of God' Paul correctly brings out the true intention of Jesus in his self-designation as 'the Son of Man'[2].

e) The Throne-Theophany Tradition and the Conception of the Church as the Body of Christ and as the True Israel

We have already suggested that Paul's conception of the risen body of Christ as the σῶμα πνευματικόν (1Cor 15.43ff.) and τὸ σῶμα τῆς δόξης (Phil 3.21) and his statement in Col 2.9 about Christ as the embodiment of all the fullness of the deity also allude to the Damascus Christophany. That was quite intelligible simply in the light of a form-historical analysis of epiphanic visions among which we reckon the Damascus Christophany. If, however, Paul was familiar with the theophany-vision or *merkabah*-vision tradition, which Rowland and others have outlined as an important part of Jewish theology, and saw his Damascus Christophany in connection with it, then the Damascus vision could have contributed to his conception of the Church as the Body of Christ. That Paul was probably acquainted with מרכבה-mysticism, has already been suggested by G. Scholem on the basis of Paul's reference to his journey into the paradise in 2Cor 12.2–4[3]. Scholem sees also

---

[1]Thus, although we cannot accept G.Friedrich's view that in 1Th 1.10 Paul is reinterpreting a baptismal hymn about the Son of Man with the title 'the Son of God' ('Ein Tauflied hellenistischer Judenchristen', *ThZ* 21 (1965), pp.502ff.; so also Schweizer, *op. cit.*, p.370), we can grant that he is right in his observation that 1Th 1.10 would also have made good sense with 'the Son of Man' instead of 'the Son of God'.

[2]Cf. also Rev 2.18; the Gregorian translation of Didache 16.8: 'Then will the world see our Lord Jesus Christ, the Son of Man who (at the same time) is Son of God, coming on the clouds with power and great glory . . . ' (cited from Hennecke-Schneemelcher, *NT Apocrypha* ii, p.628).

[3]Scholem, *Jewish Gnosticism*, pp.17f.; also Rowland, *Influence*, p.199. The ὀπτασίαι καὶ ἀποκαλύψεις κυρίου of 2Cor 12.1 or at least some of them may well have been of the same kind as the Damascus vision. Thus they could have *confirmed*

the phrase τὸ σῶμα τῆς δόξης in Phil 3.21 as pointing to the influence from the שׁעוּר קוֹמה, which as the speculation on the body of God was part of the mysticism[1].

In a recent article A.J.M. Wedderburn points out that the imagery of the Church as the Body of Christ is the result of a creative interplay of various elements: the understanding of the representative nature of Christ's person and work, especially his death (ὑπὲρ ὑμῶν); the belief that all Christians share in the one person of Christ, which is tangibly expressed in the common union with him in baptism and in the common sharing of his body in the eucharist; the Jewish idea of representation and solidarity; the Hellenistic metaphor of the body and its limbs, etc.[2] To these he adds Paul's realization of the unity of Christ and his people on the Damascus road[3]. Of course, others have already suggested that the conversation of the risen Christ with Paul on the Damascus road, as reported in Acts (9.4f.; 22.7f.; 26.14f.), contributed to the conception of the Church as the Body of Christ[4]. For the remarkable conversation: 'Saul, Saul, Why do you persecute *me*? . . . Who are you, Lord? . . . *I am Jesus whom you persecute*', must have led Paul to recognize the unity of Christ with his people: to persecute the followers of Jesus is to persecute him[5].

---

and deepened the conception of Christ which Paul had derived from the Damascus vision. It is doubtful, however, whether they could have provided anything new which was fundamental to his theology. For in Gal 1.12–16 Paul says that he received his gospel δι' ἀποκαλύψεως (singular!) Ἰησοῦ Χριστοῦ, namely God's revelation of his Son on the Damascus road. Jesus Christ revealed as the Son of God at that time was *the gospel* which he was commissioned to preach to the Gentiles and therefore he began to preach Christ immediately. Cf. Lührmann, *Offenbarungsverständnis*, pp.57f.; Stuhlmacher, *Evangelium*, pp.77ff. (n.1).

[1] Schoiem, *Von der mystischen Gestalt der Gottheit* (1962), p.276 (n.19) cited from Rowland, *Influence*, p.xxii (n.57). Though this may well be the case, it is unnecessary, as we have seen, to presuppose Paul's acquaintance specifically with the שׁעוּר קוֹמה speculation in order to understand the phrase as originating from the Damascus vision. Scholem's comparison of Paul's exhortation in Rom 13.14 ('Put on the Lord Jesus Christ') with the *merkabah*-mystic's practice of putting on clothing on which the name of God was written in order to obtain a revelation (*Major Trends*, pp.77, 368 (n.131)), is far-fetched.

[2] Wedderburn, 'The Body of Christ and Related Concepts in 1Corinthians', *SJT* 24 (1971), pp.74–96.

[3] *Ibid.*, p.86.

[4] E.g., J.A.T.Robinson, *The Body* (1952), p.58; Jeremias, *Schlüssel*, p.27.

[5] Such an identification of Christ with his people as this is unique in the NT, to which 1Cor 8.12 is the closest parallel. This is probably evidence for the historical authenticity of the conversation – i.e., it was Paul's authentic testimony. It is beyond our comprehension how C.Burchard, who fails to cite 1Cor 8.12 and denies its authen-

If the Damascus Christophany is seen in connection with the *merkabah*-vision tradition, we can consider two more elements in it which could have contributed to Paul's conception of the Church as the Body of Christ. First is the שעור קומה . Literally meaning 'the measurement of the body', it was a speculation on the glorious body of God who appears to the *merkabah*-mystic in דמות כמראה אדם (Ezek 1.26). It describes the limbs of God in the figures of the human body, measures them and assigns secret names to each limb, sometimes using the description of the figure of the lover in the Song of Songs. In the Hekhaloth writings it is attributed to Tannaitic authorities like R. Akiba and R. Ishmael. G. Scholem traces the rise of this speculation into the late first or the early second c. A.D. and suggests that it was later adopted by the Christian and pagan Gnostics[1]. If Paul was acquainted with such a speculation, then it is possible that he obtained the conception and the imagery of the Church as the Body of Christ and individual Christians as members or limbs of that Body (1Cor 12.12–27) from his meditation upon the Damascus vision of the glorious body of Christ along the lines of the שעור קומה , as well as upon the Christian tradition of the crucified body of Christ given 'ὑπὲρ ὑμῶν' which is symbolized by the eucharistic bread.

The second element worthy of consideration is what is generally known as the 'corporate personality'[2] of some figures connected with some *merkabah*-visions. We have already seen how the heavenly figure כבר אנש in Dan 7 appears at once as an individual representative and as the symbol of the ideal Israel. With this should be compared the wide-spread Targumic and Rabbinic Tradition which in connection with Gen 28.12 speaks of Jacob's איקון (or איקונין) as sitting on, or being engraved on, the throne of glory (e.g., Tg. Jon.; Tg.Neof.; the Fragment Tg.; Gen.R.68.12; b.Hul.91b; Hekhaloth R.9). The Targumic versions are almost identical and most interesting. According to them, the angels who accompanied Jacob from his father's house ascended to inform their colleagues in heaven that it was Jacob's image which was (engraved) upon the throne of glory and invite them to come and see Jacob in order to know what sort of image was (engraved) upon the throne. For although they desired, they were forbidden to see it directly.

---

ticity, can explain that Paul is here reproached not for the 'moral' sin of persecuting Christians (and therefore Christ) but for the 'existential' sin, 'the hubris', of rejecting Christ (*Zeuge*, p.94). As if Burchard were a Humpty-Dumpty who could force the verb διώκεω to yield such a fine, fashionable meaning!

[1]For all these see Scholem, *Jewish Gnosticism*, pp.36–42.

[2]Wedderburn, 'The Body of Christ', pp.83ff., criticises the imprecise use of the term 'corporate personality' and prefers to speak of representation and solidarity in connection with the concept 'the Body of Christ'. But he does not say which is the best term to describe phenomena such as the two we are considering here.

So the angels of the Lord ascended and descended, and gazed upon Jacob. Now Rowland has suggested that the איקונין of Jacob (engraved) on the throne is a development of the דמות כמראה אדם in Ezek 1.26ff. If this is so, this Targumic and Rabbinic tradition is part of the *merkabah*-vision tradition which developed the figure כבר אנש in Dan 7; 1En 46ff.; 4Ezra 13 from Ezek 1.26ff[1]. Although b.Hul.91b attributes this tradition to a Tanna, it is impossible to date its rise precisely. However, if those who see this tradition behind Jn 1.51[2] are right, it is not impossible that Paul also knew it. To this tradition belongs also the Rabbinic discussion whether בו of Gen 28.12 refers to the ladder or Jacob (Gen.R.68.12). The saying in Jn 1.51 seems to know and accept the interpretation which took Gen 28.12 as meaning that the angels ascended and descended upon Jacob. For Jacob, however, it substitutes 'the Son of Man'. If the Targumic-Rabbinic tradition on Jacob as well as the tradition on the heavenly figure כבר אנש is part of the same *merkabah*-vision tradition, this is, of course, only natural. In Jewish literature, owing to his God-given name Israel, Jacob is often conceived of as the inclusive representative of the nation Israel, as the *Stammvater* who incorporates, as it were, the entire *Stamm* Israel in himself[3]. It is possible that the Targumic and Rabbinic tradition on Gen 28.12 also conceived Jacob-Israel in this way. At any rate, that this conception is one of the elements in Jn 1.51, is suggested by the conversation in which Jesus calls Nathanael 'a true Israelite' and Nathanael in turn confesses Jesus as 'the King of Israel' (Jn 1.47–49). In replacing Jacob-Israel here, Jesus the Son of Man appears then as the inclusive representative of the new Israel. This is quite in line with Dan 7.13ff. where the heavenly figure כבר אנש is the inclusive representative of the ideal Israel. Quoting C.F. Burney, C.H. Dodd puts the matter well:

'Jacob, as the ancestor of the nation of Israel, summarizes in his person the ideal Israel *in posse*, just as our Lord, at the other end of the line, summarizes it *in esse* as the Son of Man'[4]. For John, of course, 'Israel' is not the Jewish nation, but the new humanity, reborn in Christ, the community, of those who are 'of the truth', and of

---

[1] Rowland, *Influence*, pp.141–151; also Jervell, *Imago*, pp.116f.

[2] E.g., H.Odeberg, *The Fourth Gospel* (1968), pp.35ff.; Bultmann, *Johannes*, p.74 (n.4); Schweizer, 'Die Kirche als Leib Christi in den paulinischen Homologumena', *Neotestamentica*, p.284. Cf. also Philo, *Conf. Ling.* 146, where Jacob-Israel is conceived of as the archangel ὁ κατ᾽ εἰκόνα ἄνθρωπος, God's πρωτόγονος, λόγος, etc.; similarly also The Prayer of Joseph (on the latter see J.Z.Smith, 'The Prayer of Joseph', *Religions in Antiquity*, pp.254–294).

[3] See Schweizer, *Neotestamentica*, pp.281f.

[4] Burney, *The Aramaic Origin of the Fourth Gospel* (1922), p.115.

whom Christ is king. In a deeper sense He is not only their king, He is their inclusive representative: they are in Him and He in them[1].

Now it is possible that Paul knew this tradition of seeing the figure appearing in throne-visions in human likeness in terms of the inclusive representative of the ideal Israel. If so, the risen Christ's identification of himself with his people in his conversation with Paul on the Damascus road must have confirmed to him the truth of the tradition. Thus the Damascus vision of the exalted Christ could have contributed both to his conception of Christ as incorporating his people in himself and to his understanding of the Christians as the new, true Israel (Gal 6.16; Phil 3.3). The heavenly figure כבר אנש whom Daniel proleptically saw in vision as the inclusive representative of the ideal Israel has now become reality in Christ. So Christ is the inclusive representative of the ideal Israel. However, the ideal Israel is not the Jewish nation which has rejected its Messiah but the community of those who belong to Christ as his people by faith in him, those who are recreated in him (2Cor 5.17) or transformed into his image (2Cor 3.18; Rom 8.29; 1Cor 15.49). As the inclusive representative of this new humanity, Christ incorporates it in himself; to say it in reverse: the new humanity, the Church, is the Body of Christ.

Thus, the two elements of the *merkabah*-vision tradition, namely שעור קומה speculation and the conception of the heavenly figure in a vision in terms of the inclusive representative of the ideal Israel, could, along with others, have contributed to Paul's conception and imagery of the Church as the Body of Christ. It is perhaps the sublime quality of that conception and imagery, which are so apt and profound for the relationship between Christ and his people, that has been partly responsible for preventing interpreters from seeing them in connection with the Damascus Christophany and in particular with the often fantastic and bizarre שעור קומה speculation. There is much more to explore along this line, but we cannot pursue it further here.

f) The Son of God and the εἰκών of God

The conception of Christ as the Son of God is closely connected with that of him as the image of God. We have already suggested that Paul's definition of his gospel in terms of 'the Son of God' in Gal 1.16 is a parallel to that in terms of the εἰκὼν τοῦ θεοῦ in 2Cor 4.4–6. The parallelism between the two conceptions is again clearly shown in Col 1.13–15: . . . εἰς τὴν βασι-

---

[1]Dodd, *The Interpretation of the Fourth Gospel* (1970), p.246; cf. also Schweizer, *Neotestamentica*, p.284.

λείαν τοῦ υἱοῦ τῆς ἀγάπης αὐτοῦ ... ὅς ἐστιν εἰκὼν τοῦ θεοῦ τοῦ
ἀοράτου ... Their close connection appears also in Rom 8.29, where the
believer's divine sonship is conceived of in terms of conforming to the εἰκών
of the Son of God. We are waiting for the Son of God from heaven (1Th
1.10), so that we may bear his image, τὴν εἰκόνα τοῦ ἐπουρανίου (1Cor
15.49), and our lowly body may be transformed into the likeness of his
σῶμα τῆς δόξης (Phil 3.21). This soteriological aspect of the relationship
between the divine sonship and the divine image will be seen in more detail
in the next chapter. However, it has already become quite clear that for
Paul Jesus is the εἰκών of God because he is the Son of God, and *vice versa*.
Whether this suggests that Paul was acquainted with the Oriental conception
of the king as the son and image of God and with the conception of Wisdom/
Logos as the son (or daughter) and image of God is uncertain. Be that as it
may, we have suggested that the parallelism between the conceptions of
Christ as the Son of God and as the image of God can adequately be explained
in the light of the Damascus Christophany alone, if seen against the background of the descriptions of epiphanic visions[1]. To see the risen Christ as
appearing 'like a son of God' is the same as to see him as having the εἰκόνα
of God, and the risen Christ who appeared to Paul as one 'like a son of God'
and having the εἰκόνα of God *is* the Son of God and the εἰκών of God. Paul
saw the risen Christ as the Son of God and as the Image of God at the same
time, namely at the Damascus Christophany. Hence the parallelism between
Gal 1.16 and 2Cor 4.4—6.

g) Two Lines of Development of the εἰκών-Christology

There is no doubt that Paul developed both conceptions more profoundly
as he contemplated the person and work of Christ, starting from these fundamental data obtained from his inaugural vision. An essential contribution to
this development was, of course, the early Christian kerygma that Jesus of
Nazareth is the Messiah, the Son of God. If Paul had been extremely provoked by this kerygma before the Christophany on the Damascus road, he
came to see at that Christophany the truth of the proclamation in a much
deeper way than the original preachers had implied. The exalted Christ who
appeared to him 'like a son of God' *is* indeed the Son of God as the Christians
proclaimed. He is the Son of God, however, not just in the sense of the
Davidic Messiah. He is rather the transcendent, metaphysical Son of God
(Rom 1.3f.; cf. 2Cor 5.16). Two lines of development are discernible in the
conceptions of Christ as the Son and Image of God: Wisdom-Christology and
Adam-Christology.

---

[1] *Supra* pp. 207ff.

h) Wisdom-Christology

In the foregoing chapter we attempted to show that, building upon Jesus' self-disclosure as the final representative of the personified, hypostatized Wisdom of God, Paul developed for the first time in the early Church a full Wisdom-Christology, ascribing to Christ pre-existence and mediatorship in creation. The decisive factor for this development, we submitted, was Paul's realization at the Damascus Christophany that Christ superseded the Torah as the revelation of God and as the means of salvation. Now that Christ has superseded the Torah, Wisdom, the revelation of God, is found in him, and not in the Torah as the Jews thought. It is not the Torah but Christ who embodies Wisdom. So Paul began to ascribe all the attributes and functions of the divine Wisdom to Christ: pre-existence and mediatorship in creation, revelation and salvation. Paul expressed these attributes and functions especially clearly through the formula of God's sending his Son into the world to save mankind (Rom 8.3; Gal 4.4) and the hymn in Col 1.15–20.

When arguing for this thesis in the last chapter, we referred to the present chapter for further support. Now that we have ascertained that Paul obtained his conception of Christ as the εἰκών of God at the Damascus Christophany, we can see how both conceptions of Christ – as the end of the Torah and as the image of God – must have led Paul to conceive of Christ as the divine Wisdom. For Wisdom/Logos as the *Theophanieträger* in the Wisdom literature and Philo not only stands in the same theophany-vision tradition as the Damascus Christophany, as we have seen, but Wis 7.26 specifically declares: Wisdom is 'the brightness that streams from everlasting light, the flawless mirror of the active power of God and the εἰκών of his goodness'[1]. Hence Wisdom-Christology, which thus partly originated from the εἰκών-Christology, is naturally present in both 2Cor 3.16–4.6 and Col 1.15ff. where Christ is called the εἰκών of God. In both places Christ is the agent both of revelation and (new) creation – i.e., the functions of the divine Wisdom. The Damascus Christophany opened Paul's blind eyes and dark heart to see the light of the glory of God in the face of Christ, to see Christ as the embodiment of the divine glory or deity (Col 2.9), as the εἰκών of God. The light that shone from the face of Christ into Paul's heart was the same divine light that shone in the first creation. So a new creation took place in respect of Paul himself. But that was not all: he was commissioned to illuminate others with the knowledge of this divine glory in Christ. That Christ is the embodiment of the divine glory or deity, the εἰκών of God, i.e., the revelation of God – that is the gospel which Paul received on the Damascus road. In his faithful administration of that gospel according to his apostolic commission there

---

[1] For the Logos and Wisdom as the εἰκών of God in Philo, *supra* p.161, n.3.

takes place illumination and new creation in respect of those who believe it (cf. 2Cor 5.17ff.). A much fuller and more systematic statement about Christ as the divine Wisdom is made in the hymn in Col 1.15–20, especially in the first half: Christ, the Son of God, is the Image of the invisible God, that is, the visible manifestation of the invisible God; he is the agent of the divine revelation. He is the first-born of all creation, so that he is pre-existent. The universe was created in, through and for him, so that he is the agent, sustainer and goal of creation. He is also the beginning and agent of the new creation marked by the resurrection and the universal reconciliation.

In the foregoing chapter we ascertained that the title 'Son of God' is the best vehicle for Wisdom-Christology, with its connotation of the intimate relationship between Christ and God from eternity, as shown by the sending- and giving-up-formulae and the definition of the gospel with that title. There we saw how Wisdom-Christology, developed partly from Paul's realization on the Damascus road that on the cross Christ superseded the Torah, logically led him to the conception of Christ as the transcendent Son of God and therefore as a divine being. In this chapter we see the Damascus vision of the risen Christ directly leading Paul to perceive Christ as a divine being: Christ is the transcendent Son of God beyond the Davidic Messiah; and he is the εἰκὼν τοῦ θεοῦ, not as a man who may be said to be the image of God (Gen 1.26f.; 1Cor 11.7), but as the Son of God. Himself being divine, Christ is the perfect revelation of God. The word εἰκὼν here has no negative sense of a pale image or mere shadowy copy of reality. Rather it implies that Christ, being the embodiment of the fullness of deity (Col 2.9), is the perfect manifestation of the invisible God. These conceptions of Christ as the transcendent Son of God and the perfect revelation of God are, of course, deepened by means of the 'identification' of Christ with the divine Wisdom. We can hardly understand such conceptions only in terms of a functional Christology. Rather, in them both functional and ontological categories of understanding are combined[1]. '... ἐν Χριστῷ Ἰησοῦ, ὃς ἐν μορφῇ θεοῦ ὑπάρχων οὐχ ἁρπαγμὸν ἡγήσατο τὸ εἶναι ἴσα θεῷ ...' (Phil 2.6). When his appointed time had arrived, God sent forth his own pre-existent Son into the world to be born of woman, in the likeness of sinful flesh, and under the law, so that through his sin-offering God might condemn sin in the flesh, redeem us from under the law, and adopt us as his sons (Rom 8.3 and Gal 4.4). Thus the eternal Son of God has become flesh to be our Saviour, and in

---

[1]Cf. A.Schlatter, *Die Theologie der Apostel* (1922), p.338: 'Vielleicht besaß er (sc. Paul) im Begriff "Bild Gottes" eine Denkform, mit der er sich das ewige Verhältnis des Vaters zum Sohn verdeutlicht hat'; also Ridderbos, *Paulus*, pp.52–60; Hengel, *Sohn*, p. 119.

him, especially in his death on the cross, God's will to save lost mankind, i.e., his love, is perfectly manifested. He who was 'in the form of God' from eternity is the perfect revelation of God. All this profound Christology is, we submit, developed out of the Damascus Christophany in which Paul saw Christ as the Son and Image of God and as the supersession of the Torah.

i) Adam-Christology

The other line along which the εἰκών-Christology developed is Adam-Christology. The perception of Christ as the εἰκών of God on the Damascus road quite naturally led Paul to the great passage in Gen. (1.26f.), where the creation of Adam בצלם כדמות (LXX: κατ᾽ εἰκόνα καὶ καθ᾽ ὁμοίωσιν) of God is narrated as the culmination of creation, just as the conception of the Logos as the εἰκών of God led Philo to the same passage.

Neither in the OT nor in post-biblical Judaism is there a definite statement that through his fall Adam lost the image of God. However, as we have seen, there is a strand of Rabbinic thought which held that through Adam's fall six things were lost to mankind — the lustre on the face of man (זיו), his eternal life, his upright stature or height (קומה), the fruit of the earth, the fruit of trees, and the luminaries (מאורות) — and envisaged their restoration in the messianic age (e.g., Gen.R.12.6). This idea was, of course, part of the broad stream of Jewish thought which sometimes compared Adam with the new *Stammväter* like Noah, the Patriarchs, Moses, David, etc. To the latter, the righteous heroes, was ascribed the function of restoring what Adam lost or putting right what Adam vitiated. The restoration through them, however, was only partial and temporary. Hence it was natural to hope that the Messiah would restore the pre-fall state completely, according to the correspondence schema *Urzeit = Endzeit*[1]. Among the six things that Adam was supposed to have lost through his fall, the first three are among the components which for the Rabbis constituted the divine image in Adam[2]. The lustre (זיו) upon his face which Adam lost was nothing other than the divine כבוד , which, as we have seen, is virtually synonymous with the divine image (צלם or דמות) (e.g., Gen.R.11.2). The Dead Sea Scrolls witness to a fervent expectation of the Qumran community for the restoration of כבוד אדם to it (1QS 4.23; CD 3.20; 1QH 17.15; etc.). Then there are some Rabbinic pronouncements which *imply* that the divine image was lost through Adam's fall (e.g., Gen.R.8.12[3]; Dt.R.11.3; Num.R.16.24). Alongside this view,

---

[1] *Supra* pp.186ff.

[2] See Jervell, *Imago*, pp.113f. (also pp.96ff.); Schenke, *Gott "Mensch"*, pp.127–130.

[3] On this passage cf. M.Smith, 'Shape of God', p.324, with Kittel, εἰκών, *TDNT* ii, p.394.

however, there is also the view that even after the fall Adam and mankind retained or remained as the divine image. The latter is, in fact, more pre-valent and, assumed as a matter of fact, it often serves as the sign of the dig-nity of man and as the foundation for moral conduct among men (e.g., b.B. Bat.58a; Lev.R.34.3; Gen.R.24.7; Mek.Ex20.16). Yet a third view is that which connects the divine image with an individual's moral conduct and fulfilment of the law: if a man keeps the law he retains or is the image of God; but if he sins, he loses it (e.g., b.Moʻed Kat.15b; Ex.R.32.1; Gen.R.8. 12[1]). These divergent views do not necessarily contradict one another. M. Smith probably judges the matter correctly: 'Likeness of God seems often to have been thought of as a complex relationship, of which some elements could be lost and others retained'[2]. In other words, on the whole the Rabbis believed that through Adam's fall and then through individual's sin the divine image was diminished[3].

For our present purpose it is important to ascertain, however, that in certain contexts some Rabbis could say, at least implicitly, that Adam (and mankind in him) lost the divine image through his fall[4]. The best examples of this are found in their reflections on the Exodus and the revelation of the law on Mt. Sinai. We have already seen how late Judaism conceived of the Exodus and the Sinai revelation as a second creation and as the restoration of the primeval glory and how it contrasted Moses with Adam[5]. In Sinai the divine glory, the lustre of man's face, and immortality were restored to Israel. Most interesting here is the debate between Adam and Moses in Dt.R.11.3 as to who is greater: Adam argues for his greatness on the basis that he was created in the image of God. Moses retorts that whereas Adam did not re-main in that honour he retains the lustre of his face which God gave him. Here then is the idea that at Sinai the glory and image of God were restored. But the Rabbis held that through Israel's sin in making the golden calf they lost them again and eternal life as well. So they looked forward to the messianic age for the ultimate restoration of all that Adam lost[6].

Like the Jewish theologians, Paul also assumed that man remained as the

---

[1]See the preceding note.

[2]Smith, *op. cit.*, p.324.

[3]So Larsson, *Vorbild*, pp.183ff., who also suggests that the absence of a definite statement both in Judaism and Paul that the divine image was lost is due to the anthro-pomorphic conception of the 'image'(p.187).

[4]So L.Ginzberg, *Legends of the Jews* v (1925), p.113; Jervell, *Imago*, pp.112ff.; Schenke, *Gott "Mensch"*, p.129; Smith, *op. cit.*, p.324; against Moore i, p.479; Kittel, *op. cit.*, p.393.

[5]*Supra* pp.189, 236.

[6]For all these see Str.-Bill. iv, pp.886ff.; also Jervell, *Imago*, pp.114ff.

image and glory of God even after Adam's fall (1Cor 11.7). However, like
them, he must have thought at the same time that the divine image was
reduced through the fall and hoped that it would be restored in the messianic
age. It is probably true to say that the greater the significance they saw in the
Sinai revelation or in the messianic age, the more negatively the Jewish
theologians judged Adam's fall. Likewise, the greater the significance Paul
saw in Jesus Christ, the more negatively he judged Adam's fall. So, having
seen the divine image in Christ on the Damascus road, Paul could have
thought, just as the Jewish theologians did under certain circumstances, that
it had been *lost* through Adam's fall. As far as the divine glory, which in the
contemporary thought was sometimes virtually synonymous with the divine
image, is concerned, Paul, like the Rabbis, unequivocally declares in Rom 3.
23: 'All have sinned and (so) lack the glory of God'. 'Though he does not
explicitly relate this loss to Adam's disobedience', observes R. Scroggs correctly, 'such a thought cannot be far from his mind'[1]. For all men sin in their
own persons as a result of their solidarity with Adam, the initiator of sin (cf.
Rom 5.12).

However, when the glory of God shone in the face of Christ and Christ
appeared as the image of God on the Damascus road, Paul knew that the hope
for their restoration in the messianic age had become reality in Christ. In the
face of Christ (2Cor 4.6) Paul saw shining the original divine כבוד, the lustre
on the face of Adam, which was supposed to have outshone the sun but had
been lost through his fall[2]. Since Christ in whom the divine glory was restored was none other than the crucified and risen Jesus of Nazareth, Paul also
knew that the life (חיים, i.e., the eternal life or immortality) which had been
lost through Adam's sin, was now restored in Christ. Likewise Paul found the
divine image which had been lost or diminished through Adam's fall, perfectly restored in Christ. If there was a restoration of these in Sinai, it was
only partial and temporary; only in Christ had their ultimate restoration
become reality (2Cor 3.7–4.6). On account of this temporary restoration the
Sinai revelation of the law was regarded as a new creation. How much more
then should God's saving act in Christ, which was made known to Paul on the
Damascus road, be regarded as such (2Cor 4.6; 5.17; Gal 6.15)?! Thus
Paul's perception of the divine image and glory in Christ on the Damascus
road naturally led him to contrast Christ with Adam.

In the section in which we attempted to demonstrate that Paul obtained
his conception of Christ as the image of God from the Damascus Christo-

---

[1] Scroggs, *Last Adam*, p.73.

[2] Cf. Black, 'The Second Adam', p.174; Scroggs, *Last Adam*, p.96.

phany, we found ourselves already examining 1Cor 15.42–49, a passage in which the Adam-Christ antithesis occurs[1]. There we found that Paul's descriptions of Christ as the Last Adam all point to his Damascus vision of the exalted Christ: Christ is a man ἐξ οὐρανοῦ and so ὁ ἐπουράνιος; he has the glorious σῶμα πνευματικόν and is indeed the πνεῦμα ζωοποιοῦν (cf. 2Cor 3.16ff.). Over against Christ, Adam, the first man, is ἐκ γῆς χοϊκός and so ὁ χοϊκός, he has the ignoble σῶμα ψυχικόν and is a mere ψυχή ζῶσα. After making these contrasts between Adam and Christ, Paul echoes the Jewish idea of the solidarity between the *Stammvater* and the *Stamm*, and contrasts the old and the new humanity in accordance with their respective *Stammväter*: just as Adam is ὁ χοϊκός, so the old humanity represented by him is οἱ χοϊκοί; but just as Christ is ὁ ἐπουράνιος, so the new humanity represented by him is οἱ ἐπουράνιοι. Along with all mankind, believers have been participating in the former, but at the general resurrection they will be finally and perfectly redeemed from the former into the latter: 'Just as we have borne the image of the man of dust, we shall also bear the image of the man of heaven'. The same thought appears in Phil 3.20f.: the body we have· at present is the weak, ignoble body of the fallen Adam; but Christ, coming from heaven, will transform it to conform to his glorious body. The complete transformation is an eschatological hope. However, it has already begun in the present. For as we behold the glory of Christ as in a mirror we are already being transformed into his image, from one degree of glory to another, through Christ who operates as the Spirit (2Cor 3.18). This process can be described also in terms of 'putting off the old man with its practices and putting on the new which is being renewed in knowledge after the image of its creator' (Col 3.9f.; cf. Eph 4.24), i.e., a new creation (2Cor 5.17). This renewal or new creation is not confined to mankind alone; it encompasses the entire creation. For the creation was subjected to futility not of its own will but by God, who on account of the transgression of Adam, its ruler, condemned it along with him (so mankind) – but in hope that it will be liberated from the bondage to decay when the glory of the children of God is revealed, i.e., at the parousia (cf. Col 3.4). The entire creation, then, is anxiously waiting for the revelation of the children of God, so that it may be redeemed together with them as its rulers from the bondage to decay (Rom 8.19ff.). This side of the question we shall discuss in more detail in the next chapter. However, it has already become clear that Paul describes redemption in Christ in terms of a new creation, a restoration of the image and glory of God and of life which have been lost to mankind through the fall of Adam. While Adam, the first man, is the *Stammvater* of the old, fallen humanity,

---

[1] *Supra* p.226.

responsible also for the subjection of the creation to futility, Christ is the
πρωτότοκος, the *Stammvater* of the new, redeemed humanity (Rom 8.29;
Col 1.18), responsible also for the redemption of the entire creation (1Cor
15.21f., 42–49)[1].

In most of the passages referred to in the previous paragraph the Adam-
Christ antithesis is used, explicitly or implicitly, mainly to describe the old
and the new humanity represented by Adam and Christ respectively. There
the risen, glorious, heavenly Christ whom Paul saw on the Damascus road is
in view, rather than his earthly career. In Rom 5.12–21, however, the typological antithesis between Adam and Christ is more fully stated soteriologically and *heilsgeschichtlich* in terms of transgression and obedience, sin and
grace, the law and grace, condemnation and justification, and death and life.
Here the contrast is essentially between Adam's act of transgression that
brought sin and death into the world and Christ's act of obedience supremely
on the cross that has brought about justification and life to sinners. Since
one of the central thoughts in Rom 5.12–21 already appears in 1Cor 15.21f.,
rather than seeing a *development* in the Adam-Christ typology between 1Cor
15 and Rom 5, one should understand that the Adam-Christ typology is one
of the fundamental theological motifs in Paul and is used in association with
various motifs for various purposes[2]. In Rom 5.12–21 it appears in conjunction with Paul's fundamental doctrine of justification by grace, which was
itself developed out of his Damascus experience. We can hardly attempt to
expound this complex and profound passage here. Since our present concern

---

[1]It is true that in 1Cor 15.44–49 there is no reference to a fall of Adam. The reference to Gen 2.7 seems to indicate that Paul is contrasting Christ with Adam as he was
created rather than with the fallen Adam (so Bultmann, *Theology* i, p.174; also Barrett,
1Cor., p.374). However, the idea of Adam's fall and of the fallen humanity is implicitly
there as Paul has already spoken of our present existence as mortal, ignoble and weak
in contrast to our new resurrected existence as immortal, glorious and strong (1Cor
15.42f.). For it is clear to Paul that it is Adam who brought sin and death into the world
and that it is on account of this solidarity with Adam that all men have sinned, lost
eternal life and lack the glory of God (Rom 5.12; 3.23; 1Cor 15.22; Phil 3.20f.).
The reason why Paul contrasts Christ and Adam nevertheless without making an explicit
reference to the latter's fall in 1Cor 15.44–49, is because for Paul Adam is always a
sinner. For him Adam means simply the fallen first man. He knows no glorious Adam
before his fall as some Rabbis fantastically depicted. What Adam was before his fall
does not interest him. In contrast to Christ in whom Paul saw the image and glory of
God and the eternal life restored, Adam is from the beginning the fallen *Stammvater*
of fallen humanity. That is why even in Gen 2.7 Paul can see only the ignoble, weak and
mortal Adam.

[2]Cf. Black, 'The Second Adam', p.173: '. . . the Second Adam doctrine provided
Paul with the scaffolding, if not the basic structure, for his redemption and resurrection
Christology'.

is to demonstrate that Paul's Adam-Christ typology originated from the Damascus Christophany, however, we note Wedderburn's suggestion that Paul's Damascus experience is reflected in two specific elements in our passage: firstly, Paul's conviction of universal sinfulness is not just a reproduction of the Jewish view as expressed in, e.g., 4Ezra or the Qumran Thanksgiving Hymns, but also the result of the devastating discovery on the Damascus road that his zeal for righteousness by the law had led him to sin against the Messiah and God and that salvation is by grace alone[1]. Secondly, his experience of Christ's justifying grace at that time 'supplies the rationale behind the form of the Rabbinic וחומר קל argument of Rom 5.15−17 and the "(ὑπερ) ἐπερίσσευσεν" of vv.15 and 20'[2].

Despite many doubts, it is highly probable that the Adam-Christ antithesis also lies behind the Philippian hymn (Phil 2.6−11). Behind the depiction of the *heilsgeschichtliche* drama of the pre-existent divine Christ's incarnation, obedience unto death on the cross, and exaltation to the universal lordship there is the antithetical picture of Adam, who, being not content with his status as God's image and vice-regent over creation, sought to 'be equal with God' and as a result of the disobedience was condemned to death (Gen 1−3)[3]. Earlier we saw that μορφή and εἰκών are closely related to each other and sometimes even synonymous. Thus even if the phrase ἐν μορφῇ θεοῦ in v.6 is not quite synonymous with the εἰκὼν θεοῦ, it clearly must be very closely related to it. The affirmation that the pre-existent Christ was ἐν μορφῇ θεοῦ is a result of Paul's extension of his conception of Christ as the image of God backward into his pre-existent state which is witnessed to also in Col 1.15.

Now all these Adam-Christ antitheses could be expressed without Christ being called 'the Last Adam'. After all, the Jewish theologians compared and contrasted Adam with the righteous heroes or *Stammväter* of mankind or Israel without calling any of them, even Moses, by the name. Although they expected in the messianic age the restoration of what was lost in Adam, they did not call the Messiah 'the Last Adam'. What then caused Paul to call Christ 'the Last Adam'? The answer once again lies in his perception of Christ as the image of God on the Damascus road. This perception of Christ as the image of God naturally led him to Gen 1.26f. According to the great Genesis passage it is Adam who was created in the image of God. But he was unfaithful to his vocation and so lost the divine image. Seeing that Christ is

---

[1] Wedderburn, *Adam*, pp.227f.

[2] *Ibid.*, p.274.

[3] See Martin, *Carmen Christi, passim* (esp. pp.161ff.).

the image of God, Paul could therefore think of Christ as the Adam of the new humanity in contrast to the Adam of the old. Adam and Christ stand to each other in an antithetical typology as the Adam of *Urzeit* and the Adam of *Endzeit* respectively. Thus Paul came to conceive of Christ in terms of 'Adam'[1]. Therefore he not only calls Christ 'the Last Adam' over against 'the first man Adam' (1Cor 15.45) but also works out the contrast between Adam and Christ in terms of two 'men': 'the first man' — 'the second man' (1Cor 15.47); 'through man' — 'through man' (1Cor 15.21); and 'through one man' — 'through one man' (Rom 5.21–21)[2]. Adam was 'the first man' who initiated the old humanity; and Christ is the 'second man' who has initiated the new eschatological humanity.

Thus Adam-Christology basically affirms the humanity of Christ, while Wisdom-Christology affirms the divinity of Christ. Thus from the former anthropology and soteriology are developed, while from the latter the functions of Christ as the agent of creation, revelation and salvation are developed. Christ as the εἰκὼν τοῦ θεοῦ is both the Son of God who perfectly reveals God and 'the Last Adam', the new Man, who perfectly embodies God's original intent in creating man which was frustrated in the first Adam. Moreover, he is the active mediator of the true, perfect humanity, which he has restored, to those who believe in him, both Jews and Gentiles, so that God creates in and through him a new race[3]. This anthropological and

---

[1] The conception of the Logos as the image of God similarly leads Philo to Gen 1.26f. But as, unlike Paul, Philo does not think in terms of the *Urzeit = Endzeit* schema but rather in terms of the Platonic dualism, he often distinguishes the Logos and Adam as the heavenly, ideal man and the earthly, corporeal man respectively rather than as 'the Last Adam' and '(the first) Adam'.

[2] Cf. Best, *One Body*, p.39, who correctly sees that Paul builds an Adam-Christ contrast into this schema in order 'to emphasize our common humanity with Adam and Christ and to stress the link between the two'.

[3] Cf. Scroggs, *Last Adam*, pp.100ff., who emphasizes that Paul uses Adam-Christology in order to portray Christ as 'the perfect realization of God's intent for man', 'the realization of true humanity' (p.100) and as 'the mediator of true humanity' (p.102). Following K.Barth (*Rudolf Bultmann, ein Versuch ihn zu verstehen/Christus und Adam nach Röm. 5* (1964), esp. p.75), Scroggs contends that for Paul the anthropological understanding of Christ is prior to that of Adam. Our thesis that Paul came to think of Christ in terms of Adam because he saw him as the image of God on the Damascus road and not because he had some speculations on the first man in a Gnostic, Rabbinic or any other form confirms the correctness of this insight. Of course, neither Barth nor Scroggs obtains it from this understanding of the origin of Paul's Adam-Christology. Thus to match this insight Scroggs suggests a hypothesis as to the origin of Paul's Adam-Christ typology by speculatively postulating 'a pressing need' Paul felt 'to know God's design for man' (p.100). Did Paul think so abstractly? It goes without saying that we cannot follow Barth on many points of exegesis of Rom 5, either.

soteriological application of the Adam-Christ typology will be examined in more detail in the next chapter.

But here it should be noted that both the elements derived from Wisdom-Christology and those from Adam-Christology are often found together in the passages where Paul speaks of Christ as the εἰκών of God and of our transformation into that image. For example, in 2Cor 3.18–4.6, Christ as the εἰκών τοῦ θεοῦ is the revelation of God (2Cor 4.4–6), i.e., the embodiment of Wisdom, but as such he is also the Last Adam who has recovered the divine image so that we may be transformed into his image (2Cor 3.18) and become a new creature (2Cor 4.6). Col 1.15–20 and Rom 8.29f. are further examples where the elements of Adam-Christology and those of Wisdom-Christology appear combined. The reason why the elements of Wisdom-Christology and Adam-Christology are found together is because both Christologies are derived from the same conception of Christ as the image of God. The two lines of development of the εἰκών-Christology in Paul neatly correspond to the two lines of development of the theophany-vision tradition in the OT-Judaism: the anthropomorphism of God and theomorphism of man on the one hand, and the conception of Wisdom/Logos as the *Theophanieträger*, as the revelation, on the other. Thus the two lines are very closely related to each other[1].

j) Conclusion

In conclusion we would summarize our main thesis in this chapter briefly:

Paul saw the exalted Christ as the εἰκών τοῦ θεοῦ and as the Son of God on the Damascus road. This perception led him to conceive of Christ in terms of the personified, hypostatized Wisdom of God (together with his realization at that time that Christ had superseded the Torah) on the one hand, and in terms of Adam, on the other. Thus, both Paul's Wisdom-Christology and Adam-Christology are grounded in the Damascus Christophany. Along with this main thesis we have submitted two further points: firstly, Paul's desig-

---

[1]While Jervell, *Imago*, pp.214ff., reveals his total failure to understand this when he insists on seeing only the divinity of Christ in the εἰκών-Christology, Scroggs, *Last Adam*, p.98, shows his inadequate grasp of it when he formulates: 'Christ is the true revelation of God *precisely because* he is true man' (emphasis by Scroggs). A.Schlatter comes much nearer the truth when he says: 'Der Gedanke "Bild Gottes" ließe sich leicht als Grundgedanke benützen, der alle christologischen Sätze des Paulus umfaßt'. When he goes on to say: 'Man darf aber bei der Darstellung der paulinischen Gedanken nicht konstruieren' (*Theologie der Apostel*, p.338 (n.1)), he seems to be warning against a metaphysical or 'Gnostic' speculation. However, Jervell's recognition of this warning (p.214, n.162), does not prevent him from constructing the εἰκών-Christology along the Gnostic, speculative line himself (*supra* pp.198ff.).

nation of Christ as the Son of God based on the Damascus Christophany exactly corresponds to Jesus' intention in his self-designation as the Son of Man. Secondly, the Damascus Christophany contributed also to Paul's conception and imagery of the Church as the Body of Christ and the true Israel.

The main thesis and its corollaries in Paul's theology may be shown in a diagram as follows:

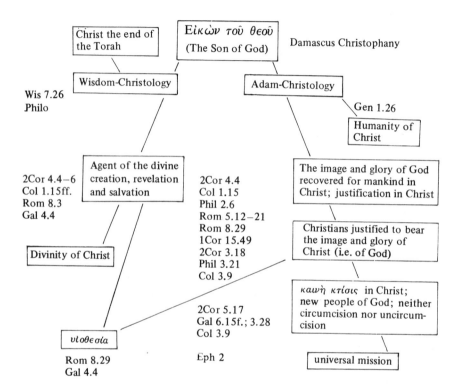

Chapter VII   Paul's Gospel: C. Soteriology

To expound Paul's gospel from the soteriological perspective is an enormous task which we can scarcely presume to undertake in an adequate way here. However, since our whole thesis is concerned with the origin of Paul's gospel in the Damascus experience, we propose to examine only some elements in Paul's soteriology which we see as direct consequences of this experience. They can be characterized by the following three keywords: justification, reconciliation and transformation. Limiting ourselves to an examination of the process by which Paul derives these elements of his soteriology from the Damascus experience, however, brings another problem: how to present it within a short space in a form which is more than just a repetition of what has already been said. For already in the preceding chapters we have dealt with it to some extent. Especially in the two chapters concerning Paul's Christology we have constantly found ourselves discussing his soteriology. This was only natural because soteriology is but the expression of the anthropological (and cosmological) reference of Christology. In the following we shall attempt to summarize in a more systematic way our discussions about the three elements scattered in various contexts above, and further reflect upon them to some extent.

1   Justification

It is now widely recognised that the distinctive Pauline doctrine of justification *sola gratia* and *sola fide* without works of the law was derived from Paul's Damascus experience[1]. However, this view is called into question by G. Strecker, who, following W. Wrede and A. Schweitzer[2], argues for the view

---

[1] See, e.g., Dibelius-Kümmel, *Paulus*, pp.45ff.; W.Grundmann, 'Paulus, aus dem Volk Israel, Apostel der Völker', *NovT* 4 (1960), pp.267ff.; Bruce, *NT History,* pp.228f.; Blank, *Paulus*, pp.184–248; Dupont, 'The Conversion of Paul', pp.176–194; Jeremias, *Schlüssel*, pp.20ff.; Stuhlmacher, "Ende", pp.19ff.; Haacker, 'Berufung', pp.10ff.

[2] W.Wrede, *Paulus* (1904), reprinted in *Das Paulusbild in der neueren deutschen Forschung*, ed. K.H.Rengstorf, p.67; A.Schweitzer, *The Mysticism of Paul the Apostle* ([2]1956), pp.220f.

that the doctrine originated later from Paul's struggles with Jewish Christians in Galatia[1]. Strecker starts from the observation that in 1Th., which he regards as the earliest letter of Paul, the doctrine is not present. Before Gal. was written, according to Strecker, the problem of the law had not been thought through and Paul treated the Torah as an 'adiaphoron'[2]. But as the Jewish Christians demanded circumcision from the Gentile Christians in Galatia, says Strecker, Paul began to 'draw consequences from his understanding of the Christian faith and from his commission as they had been grounded in his "Damascus experience" but at the time of his conversion had not yet been articulated'[3]. For the reason of the limited space here we abandon an attempt to summarize Strecker's ensuing interpretation of the Damascus event[4], which is questionable at every point. But can it be imagined that the realization about God's saving work in the crucified and risen Messiah Jesus of Nazareth[5] did not lead Paul to think through the question of the law so long? A Pharisee zealous for Judaism understood God, the world and himself first and foremost in terms of the Torah (cf. Phil 3.5: κατὰ νόμον Φαρισαῖος)[6]. Is it possible to imagine that Paul the zealous Pharisee failed to see the problem of the law when he learned that God had raised and exalted Jesus of Nazareth who had been crucified, that is, pronounced by the law as accursed by God (Dt 21.23; Gal 3.13)? How is one to believe that Paul the Pharisee whose whole life had been oriented to achieving his salvation by keeping the law could perceive God's saving work in the crucified and risen Jesus Christ and yet fail to consider how this saving work of God in Christ was related to the law? On what ground could Paul the Pharisee treat the law as an 'adiaphoron'? If a former Pharisee began to treat the law as an 'adiaphoron', does this not already presuppose that he had thought through the problem of the law? Could a Jew start preaching God's saving act to the Gentiles without having thought through the problem of the law *vis-à-vis* the Gentiles?

---

[1] Strecker, 'Befreiung und Rechtfertigung. Zur Stellung der Rechtfertigungslehre in der Theologie des Paulus', *Rechtfertigung*, E.Käsemann FS, eds. J.Friedrich *et al.* (1976), pp.479ff.

[2] *Ibid.*, pp.480f.

[3] *Ibid.*, p.481.

[4] *Ibid.*, pp.481ff.

[5] According to Strecker (*ibid.*, pp.484ff.) this was what Paul learned at the Damascus event.

[6] See Haacker, *op. cit.*, p.8; O.Betz, 'Paulus als Pharisäer nach dem Gesetz. Phil. 3, 5–6 als Beitrag zur Frage des frühen Pharisäismus', *Treue zur Thora*, G.Harder FS, ed. P.v.d. Osten-Sacken (1977), p.57: 'der Pharisäer lebt in, mit und unter dem Gesetz'.

When critics argue for the late origin of Paul's doctrine of justification on the basis of the superficial observation that it seems to appear for the first time in Gal. among the letters of Paul[1] and in the polemical context[2] at that, they forget the fundamental fact that the gospel — the law-free gospel — which Paul defends in Gal. is precisely the gospel which he already preached in his initial mission to Galatia (Gal 1.11: τὸ εὐαγγέλιον τὸ εὐαγγελισθὲν ὑπ᾽ ἐμοῦ). Precisely the gospel which Paul preached in Galatia is under attack, and the ground of the attack was precisely that it neglected the observance of the law and especially circumcision. For this reason the Judaizing Jewish Christians and the Galatian Christians under their influence alleged that Paul perverted the original gospel which he had received from the Jerusalem apostles[3]. This allegation provokes his spirited defence in Gal 1–2: the gospel, that is, the law-free gospel, which he preached in Galatia he neither received from man, either by way of tradition or instruction, nor tampered with to turn it into a merely 'human' thing; rather, he received it 'through the revelation of Jesus Christ' (Gal 1.11f.). This basic fact he proves through a report of his life — his successful Pharisaic past; his zeal for 'the traditions of (his) fathers', i.e., both the Torah and the traditions of the elders, which was so great as to persecute the Church of God; God's revelation of Jesus of Nazareth as his Son, and his call of Paul to proclaim him as God's saving act among the Gentiles; and his immediate response to the call in Arabia, Damascus, and Syria and Cilicia. These biographical data already make it abundantly clear that Paul perceived the revelation of the Son of God on the Damascus road as the revelation of God's righteousness apart from the law (Rom 3.21) immediately. For not only does he say explicitly that he had received through the revelation of Jesus Christ as the Son of God the law-free gospel which he preached in Galatia and which is now under attack; in addition his immediate response to God's call to the Gentile mission and his preaching the gospel in Galatia without demanding that the Gentiles keep the law and circumcision clearly indicate that from the beginning, certainly long

---

[1] If Gal. is the earliest surviving letter of Paul, of course, the argument for the late origin of Paul's doctrine of justification is even harder to advance. See F.F.Bruce, 'Galatian Problems: 4. The Date of the Epistle', *BJRL* 54(1972), pp.250–267; J.W.Drane, *Paul Libertine or Legalist*? (1975), pp.140ff.

[2] Now even U.Wilckens joins the critics ('Christologie und Anthropologie im Zusammenhang der paulinischen Rechtfertigungslehre', *ZNW* 67(1976), p.68). The *theologiegeschichtliche Problem* of Wilckens' 'Bekehrung' on this question we cannot elucidate. However, we believe that the best reply to this new view of Wilckens is his earlier argumet in his 'Die Bekehrung des Paulus als religionsgeschichtliches Problem', pp.14f.

[3] *Supra* pp.67ff.

before the Judaizing trouble began in Galatia, he had a gospel which proclaimed God's saving act in Christ apart from works of law. Only because he
and his colleagues had proclaimed the law-free gospel among the Gentiles did
the need for a consultation such as that depicted in Gal 2.1–10 arise. In the
consultation with the leaders of the Jerusalem church, which could be the
Apostolic Council described in Acts 15 (c.49 A.D.) or the one on the occasion of the famine relief visit described in Acts 11 (c.46 A.D.)[1], he laid before
'the reputed' τὸ εὐαγγέλιον ὃ κηρύσσω ἐν τοῖς ἔθνεσιν (Gal 2.2), i.e., the
law-free gospel which is under attack in Galatia at the moment. Beating off
the challenge from 'false brethren' upon his law-free gospel and maintaining
the ἀλήθεια τοῦ εὐαγγελίου which guaranteed freedom in Christ for the
Gentiles, Paul successfully demonstrated the right of the εὐαγγέλιον τῆς ι
ἀκροβυστίας and of the law-free Gentile mission. So the conference ended
with a mutual recognition of the εὐαγγέλιον τῆς ἀκροβυστίας and the
apostleship of Paul for the Gentiles on the one hand and the εὐαγγέλιον
τῆς περιτομῆς and the apostleship of Peter for the Jews on the other, and
accordingly with an agreement on the division of mission-field between Paul
and Barnabas on the one hand and the Jerusalemites, James, Peter and
John, on the other[2].

This historical data shows that, contrary to the view of Strecker and
Wilckens, long before his mission to Galatia Paul thought through the
problem of the law and obtained the law-free gospel. In fact, for Paul's
defence of his law-free gospel in Gal 1–2 it is essential that he maintained
basically the same gospel throughout from the beginning. Had he ever
preached a gospel with the Torah and circumcision among the Gentiles in
Arabia, Damascus, Syria and Cilicia, or elsewhere, his argument in Gal 1–2
would fall to the ground completely. For, then, his opponents could easily
expose the falsehood of Paul's claim in Gal 1 that the gospel which he
preached in Galatia, i.e., the law-free gospel, he received through the revelation of Jesus Christ at his apostolic call. What does it mean then that a
former Pharisee of great zeal for the Torah and the ancestral tradition in
Judaism began to proclaim God's saving act in Jesus Christ among the
Gentiles without requiring them to observe the Torah and circumcision?
It means that he turned against his former belief, the Pharisaic (i.e., Jewish)
doctrine, that salvation was available only to those who were incorporated
into Israel, the chosen covenant-people of God, by circumcision and who

---

[1]For the latter see F.F.Bruce, 'Galatian Problems: 1. Autobiographical Data',
BJRL 51(1969), pp.305ff.

[2]For the details and significance of Gal 1–2 concerning Paul's gospel, see Stuhlmacher, *Evangelium*, pp.63–108.

observed the Torah, and that he turned against the Jewish practice of imposing circumcision upon proselytes (cf. Gal 5.11). Now, is it possible to imagine that Paul, the zealous and successful Pharisee, could have made this turning without thinking through the problem of the law? These considerations make the conclusion inescapable that, perceiving the revelation of the crucified Jesus as the exalted Son of God to be the revelation of God's saving act in him apart from the law, Paul preached from the beginning a law-free gospel among the Gentiles. The absence of the doctrine of justification without works of the law in 1Th. is not an indication that it developed late and only in the context of a struggle with the Judaizers but that the problems in the Thessalonian church did not concern the doctrine, so that Paul had no need to expound it again[1]. Our summary exposition of Paul's autobiographical statements in connection with the Damascus event will further make it clear that his doctrine of justification *sola gratia* and *sola fide* without works of the law was integral to his gospel from the beginning of his Christian and apostolic career.

From Gal 1.11ff.; Phil 3.4ff.; 1Cor 15.8ff. and other passages referring to the Damascus event, some of which we assembled in Ch. I. supplemented by the account of Paul in Acts, we obtain the following picture of Paul about the time of the Damascus event[2]. He was born of 'Hebrew' parents in Tarsus but moved to Jerusalem at an early age to study at the feet of the Rabbi Gamaliel the elder. He joined the fellowship of the Pharisees and probably belonged to its strictest wing represented by the school of Shammai. As such a Pharisee he had an extremely zealous devotion to the Torah and the tradition of the elders. He was so successful in learning and observing them that he not only surpassed many of his peers in Judaism but he could actually say that 'according to the criterion of the righteousness which rests on the law' he was 'blameless' (Phil 3.6). His zeal for Judaism was such that he was prepared to persecute violently any apostate who threatened the Torah and the ancestral tradition. So, when the Church, especially its 'Hellenist' wing (i.e., the Greek-speaking Jewish Christians), proclaimed Jesus of Nazareth as the Messiah and criticized the Temple-cult and the law in his name, Paul was

---

[1] *Supra* pp.133ff. n.2. Some would argue that the doctrine also does not appear in 1 and 2 Cor. But against this, see not only pregnant sentences like 1Cor 1.30; 6.11; 2Cor 5.21, but also passages like 1Cor 1–2; 2Cor 3–4. The reason why the doctrine is not *unfolded* in the Corinthian letters as in Gal. and Rom. is, as in the Thessalonian letters, because of the different concerns in the Corinthian church at the time of writing.

[2] For details *supra* Chs.II–III. With the following few paragraphs cf. the authors cited in n.1 on p.269, especially Stuhlmacher's treatment of the Damascus event as the origin of Paul's law-free gospel in his "Ende", pp.19ff.

provoked to persecute it violently. For Paul the law had clearly pronounced God's curse upon Jesus of Nazareth for his blasphemy against God since he was crucified on a tree (Dt 21.23; Gal 3.13). So the Christian proclamation of the crucified Messiah was an equally unbearable blasphemy to God and attack upon the upholders of the law and the ancestral tradition. Thus, presented with the alternative: either the law or the crucified Messiah, Paul, the Pharisee zealous for the law, violently persecuted the Christians.

While Paul was pursuing the fugitive Hellenistic Jewish Christians towards Damascus, God revealed to him Jesus of Nazareth as his exalted Son (Gal 1.16), that is, the crucified Jesus appeared to him as the risen Christ (1Cor 15.8), so that Paul saw him as the Lord (1Cor 9.1) and as the image of God (2Cor 4.4–6). This encounter with the risen and exalted Jesus Christ brought about a revolution in Paul – both in his thought (i.e., theology) and life: he received his gospel and apostolic call to preach it among the Gentiles. The encounter convinced Paul, first of all, of the correctness of the Christian proclamation: the crucified Jesus of Nazareth was raised from the dead by God and he is the Messiah. Since both the revelation of the Messiah and the resurrection from the dead were expected in Judaism to be God's eschatological acts of salvation signalling the end of this aeon and the beginning of the new, Paul realized that the *eschaton* or the Messianic age of salvation had broken in with God's saving act in Jesus Christ. So Paul says: 'When the fullness of time came, God sent forth his Son . . . ' (Gal 4.4), and also: 'Behold, now is the acceptable time; behold, now is the day of salvation' (2Cor 6.2).

Then, secondly, Paul realized that the crucified Jesus of Nazareth was not accursed by God as the law had pronounced (Dt 21.23), but, on the contrary, exalted by him as his own Son (cf. Rom 1.3f.). This means that God reversed or annulled the verdict of the law upon Jesus. Paul was thus compelled to recognize that it is no longer the Torah but Christ who truly represents the will of God, that Christ has superseded the Torah as the revelation of God. This is implied when Paul says in Rom 10.4: 'Christ is the end of the law'[1]. To this significant verse we shall return.

However, that was not the only line of thinking concerning the law and the crucifixion of Jesus which Paul derived from the Damascus Christophany. There is another line, a line which recognizes the reality of the power of the law to curse its trespassers. Insofar as Jesus is the Messiah, the Son of God,

---

[1]Cf. esp., Stuhlmacher, "Ende", p.30; also his 'Achtzehn Thesen zur paulinischen Kreuzestheologie', *Rechtfertigung*, Käsemann FS, pp.511ff.; J.Blank, 'Warum sagt Paulus: "Aus Werken des Gesetzes wird niemand gerecht"?', *Evangelisch-Katholischer Kommentar Vorarbeiten*, Heft 1(1969), p.94.

who is both by definition and in reality sinless (2Cor 5.21; Rom 8.3), the law cursed him wrongly, thus demonstrating that it no longer represented God's will. On the other hand, however, insofar as the sinless Jesus actually fell under the cursing power of the law and was crucified on a tree, he bore the curse for us, the trespassers of the law, in our place and for our advantage. Thus by giving up his life as a ransom Christ has redeemed us from the curse of the law which falls upon us who cannot keep the whole law (Gal 3.10–13; cf. 1Pet 2.24)[1]. In this way the Damascus encounter with the crucified and risen Christ led Paul to accept the Christian interpretation of the death of Christ as God's saving event, as the atoning sacrifice for our salvation (1Cor 11.24ff.; 15.3; cf. also Rom 3.25f.), and develop it further so as to make it an essential ingredient of his theology[2].

He often expresses this saving significance of Christ's death in epigrammatic sentences: Gal 3.13; Rom 8.3; 2Cor 5.21; Gal 4.4f.; Rom 4.25; 5.6–10; Gal 1.4; etc. In Rom 8.3 Paul interprets Christ's crucifixion in terms of God's condemnation of sin. The law was incapable of condemning sin and liberating us from sin and death as it was weak because of the flesh. But having sent his Son in the likeness of sinful flesh, God condemned sin in his flesh. Paul's thought in this difficult verse is well brought out by C.E.B. Cranfield: 'Paul had in mind Christ's death as the event in which the full weight of God's wrath against sin was, in the flesh of Christ, that is, in His human nature, so effectively brought to bear upon all the sin of all mankind, as to rule out its ever having to be brought to bear upon it in any other flesh . . .'[3]. So, for those who are incorporated in Christ and are under the domin-

---

[1]Cf. Duncan, *Gal.*, pp.231ff.; Oepke, *Gal.*, pp.74f.; Mussner, *Gal.*, pp.231ff.; Schlier, *Gal.*, pp.136ff. There is a certain degree of incongruity between the two lines of his thinking concerning the law and the crucifixion of Jesus. Even in his latest essay, 'Achtzehn Thesen', Stuhlmacher has not grasped this clearly. This incongruity may, however, be closely related to Paul's dialectic of the law. *Infra*, pp.281ff. Cf. A.van Dülmen, *Die Theologie des Gesetzes bei Paulus* (1968), pp.210ff. Whether Paul's use of Dt 21.23 also involves the idea of the *Akedah* of Gen 22 is not certain (cf. M.Wilcox, "Upon the Tree", *JBL* 96(1977), pp.94ff.).

[2]See Stuhlmacher, 'Achtzehn Thesen', pp.512f. *Contra* E.Käsemann, 'Die Heilsbedeutung des Todes Jesu bei Paulus', *Paulinische Perspektiven*, p.79.

[3]Cranfield, *Romans*, p.383. This interpretation would be clearer if περὶ ἁμαρτίας is used here as a *term. techn.* for sin-offering (חטאת) or guilt-offering (אשם) as in the LXX (e.g., Lev 5.6; *et passim*; Isa 53.10; cf. also Heb 13.11). If the phrase means just 'for sin' or 'to deal with sin', as many commentators think (e.g., Michel, *Römer*, p.190; Cranfield,*Romans*, p.382), it would be a pleonasm in the context: so Käsemann, *Römer*, p.206. See also RV; NEB; Bruce, *Romans*, p.161 (also p.37); Schweizer, υἱός, *TDNT* viii, p.383; 'Die "Mystik" des Sterbens und Auferstehens mit Christus bei Paulus', *EvTh* 26(1966), p.256; cf. also Stuhlmacher, 'Achtzehn Thesen', p.512.

ion of the life-giving Spirit there is no condemnation. God's purpose in comdemning sin was that his law's requirement might be fulfilled in us who, liberated from the dominion of the law of sin and death, walk according to the Spirit and not according to the flesh.

Similar to Gal 3.13 and Rom 8.3 is 2Cor 5.21, where Paul says: 'Him who knew not sin he (sc. God) made sin for us, so that we might become God's righteousness in him'. The phrase 'him who knew not sin' clearly refers to the sinlessness of Christ. The phrase δικαιοσύνη θεοῦ probably refers to the righteousness given by God, the genitive being *gen. auctoris*, and the ἴνα-clause means: 'we might be justified by God in him' or better 'we might become the justified of God in him'[1]. What is meant by the striking expression that God made the sinless Christ 'sin'? According to Barrett, it means: Christ 'came to stand in that relation with God which normally is the result of sin, estranged from God and the object of his wrath (*sic*!)'[2]. What does it mean then that the sinless Christ became the object of God's wrath for us? It can only mean that the sinless Christ bore our sin and suffered God's wrath upon it 'for us', i.e., in our place and on our behalf as well as for our advantage. This may not be the conclusion that Barrett himself would like to draw from his interpretation of 2Cor 5.21a. It seems nevertheless to be the correct conclusion. As in Gal 3.13 and Rom 8.3, so also here Paul is saying that Christ suffered on the cross the penalty of our sin as our substitute and representative[3], so that we might be acquitted in God's court as

---

[1] So Bultmann, *Der zweite Brief an die Korinther* (1976), p.167; Windisch, *2.Kor.*, pp.198f.; Barrett, *2Cor.*, p.180f.; Bauer-Arndt-Gingrich, s.v. 3; and most commentators. Differently Stuhlmacher, *Gerechtigkeit*, pp.74ff.

[2] Barrett, *2Cor.*, p.180.

[3] Cf. Windisch, *2.Kor.*, pp.196ff.; Hughes, *2Cor.*, pp.211ff.; Bultmann, *2.Kor.*, pp.166f.; *Theology* i, pp.286f.; Morris, *Preaching*, pp.56ff., 281; W.Pannenberg, *Jesus – God and Man* (1968), pp.258–280 (esp. p.265); H.Riesenfeld, ὑπέρ, *TDNT* viii, pp.509f. In the second ἁμαρτία of the verse Paul may have included the meaning 'sin-offering' or 'guilt-offering' as the LXX often does and may have had especially Isa 53 in mind (So Burce, *Cor.*, p.210; Cullmann, *Christology*, p.76; also Lohse, *Märtyrer*, p. 154 (n.2); cf. also Pannenberg, *op. cit.*, p.265).

It should be clear how our exegesis here parts company with that of M.D. Hooker, 'Interchange in Christ', *JTS* 22(1971), pp.349–361. It is characteristic of her approach that the cross is overshadowed by the incarnation, being regarded only as 'the completion of the obedience which characterizes the whole of Christ's life' (p.358). For this reason she can hardly explain correctly Paul's language in the statements: Christ 'became a *curse* for us' (Gal 3.13); God '*condemned* sin in the flesh' (of Christ) (Rom 8.3); God 'made him *sin*' (2Cor 5.21). On the centrality of the cross in Paul's theology see Stuhl-macher, 'Achtzehn Thesen'. True, 'Christ became what we are, in order that (in him) we might become what he is' (Hooker, *op. cit.*, p.354, similar expressions throughout), but

by faith and baptism we are incorporated in Christ.

In this context Gal 4.4f. should also be discussed. There Paul says that when the time at which God had determined to fulfil his promise fully came he sent his pre-existent Son to be born of woman and under the law. γενό-μενον ἐκ γυναικός means that the pre-existent Son became a man, a real man like any other man. γενόμενον ὑπὸ νόμον probably means in the first instance that the pre-existent Son was born a Jew — a man under the yoke or the slavery of the law. This had the purpose of redeeming 'those who were under the law'. But why or how did the Son's becoming a man under the law

---

this schema is incomplete so long as it ignores the vital question *why* Christ's becoming what we are results in our becoming what he is (see e.g., her embarrassment in pp.350f.) — something clearly implied in Paul's statements. Therefore we can hardly take it as 'the real clue to Paul's understanding of the atonement' (p.358). We reject also her statement: 'It is as man's *representative* rather than as his substitute, that Christ suffers' (p.358, emphasis by H.). If a sinner suffers for other sinners, so that the latter may be acquitted, of course, his suffering is more of representative than of substitutionary character. But if a *sinless* one suffers for sinners, so that the latter may be acquitted, his suffering is surely as much substitutionary or vicarious as representative? We find her following statement extraordinary: 'The work of reconciliation between God and man is not achieved by the work of an outside Saviour (though, of course, it originates in the purpose of God), but is the working-out of utter love and obedience in human nature' (p.358). Is this what Paul says in 2Cor 5.14–21, not to mention other passages? For similar reasons we cannot accept Whiteley's attempt to interpret the passages under discussion exclusively in terms of his 'participation' theory of the atonement, which is similar to Hooker's (*Theology*, pp.130ff.). In these passages we simply fail to see the 'presupposition of the firstfruits' as the background against which Paul understood salvation in Christ. J.D.G.Dunn, 'Paul's Understanding of the Death of Jesus', *Reconciliation and Hope*, Morris FS, pp.123–141, also tries to interpret Paul's view of Jesus' death in terms of representation rather than substitution. Improving, in our opinion, upon the attempts of Hooker and Whiteley, he explains Paul's view of Jesus' death in terms of the OT/Jewish ideas of sacrifice — sin-offering and scapegoat. But that explanation surely leads us to see both representative *and* substitutionary characters in Jesus' death? Dunn acknowledges this (p.140; cf. also p.136), but he attempts to weaken the substitutionary character by unjustifiably playing it off against the representative character (pp.140f.). Similarly Dunn also attempts to weaken the punishment character of Jesus' death by by-passing the offensive penal language of Paul ('condemned' in Rom 8.3; 'curse' in Gal 3.13; and 'sin' in 2Cor 5.21) and by substituting for it a purely immanentalistic process: 'The wrath of God destroys the sin by letting the full destructive consequences of sin work themselves out and exhaust themselves in Jesus', — for which Dunn finds a bizarre 'parallel' in 'vaccination' (p.139). What is all this but an attempt to remove the offence of Paul's thought, which Dunn himself condemns (pp. 131, 141)? Cf. Stuhlmacher, 'Achtzehn Thesen', pp.512f.; H.Ridderbos, 'The Earliest Confession of the Atonement in Paul', *Reconciliation and Hope*, Morris FS, pp.79ff. See Pannenberg, *Jesus – God and Man*, pp.258ff., especially pp.264ff. against modern ethical individualism that rejects the idea of substitution.

result in the redemption of those who were under the law? The answer lies in the deeper meaning of γενόμενον ὑπὸ νόμον which the context discloses. For already in Gal 3.13 Paul explained what was meant by Jesus Christ's subjection to the law: it was to bear the curse of the law that fell upon all those who were under the law but who could not keep it completely. By bearing the curse vicariously and representatively, Jesus Christ, the Son of God, redeemed them from the curse of the law so that the law has no more claim upon them[1]. 'Those who were under the law' refers not only to the Jews but to all men, both Jews and Gentiles, who were ὑπὸ τὰ στοιχεῖα τοῦ κόσμου (Gal 4.3) to which the Torah also belonged. Redemption from the law means positively our adoption as sons of God[2].

In Rom 3.21–26, setting out his fundamental thesis of justification solely by grace and through faith apart from the law, Paul presents the redemption in Christ's death as the ground of our justification: all are justified through the redemption that is in Christ Jesus (v.24). In vs.25–26 he explains how God has wrought redemption in order to justify those who believe in Jesus. This concise, stylistically striking explanation is as difficult as it is crucial for understanding Paul's doctrine of the atonement and justification. Accordingly there are many widely divergent interpretations of the verses. Having carefully examined some of them, we have found it impossible to reach a definite conclusion as to the correct interpretation ourselves. In order to obtain an understanding which is certain at least to one's own mind, one would have to devote an entire monograph to the passage. This obviously we cannot do here. So, we present two types of interpretation represented by two recent commentators on Romans, supposing that one or the other must broadly represent Paul's meaning in the passage. The one is C.E.B. Cranfield's, and is basically traditional[3]. The other is E.Käsemann's, and represents an interpretation now dominant in Germany[4]. First we reproduce

---

[1]Parallel to Gal 3.13; 4.4f. is Col 2.13f.: 'And you, who were dead in trespasses and the uncircumcision of your flesh, God made alive together with him, having forgiven us all our trespasses, having cancelled the bond which stood against us with its legal demands; this he set aside, nailing it to the cross' (RSV) (cf. also Eph 2.14f.).

[2]This interpretation of Gal 4.4 is shared by Schlier, *Gal.*, pp.194ff.; Mussner, *Gal.*, pp.268ff.; Bultmann, *Theology* i, p.297; Blank, *Paulus*, pp.269f.; Schweizer, υἱός, *TDNT* viii, pp.383f. For the significance of the use of the title 'Son of God' in Gal 4.4 and Rom 8.3 *supra* pp.119f.

[3]Cranfield, *Romans*, pp.208–218. A similar line of interpretation is given by, e.g., Barrett, *Romans*, pp.72–80; Kuss, *Römer*, pp.155–161; Murray, *Romans*, pp.116–121; Ridderbos, *Paulus*, pp.123ff.; cf. also Bultmann, *Theology* i, p.295.

[4]Käsemann, *Römer*, pp.89–94. To this type belong the interpretations by, e.g., W.G.Kümmel, 'πάρεσις und ἔνδειξις', *Heilsgeschehen und Geschichte*, pp.260–270;

their translations of vs.25f., which indicate their different interpretations.

Cranfield: ' . . . 23 for all have sinned and lack the glory of God, 24being justified
               freely by his grace through the redemption *accomplished* in Christ Jesus;
               25whom God purposed to be by the shedding of his blood a propitiatory
               sacrifice, *the benefit to be appropriated* by faith, in order to prove his
               righteousness (*this was necessary* on account of the overlooking of past
               sins 26in God's forbearance), in order, *I say*, to prove his righteousness in
               the present time, so that he might be righteous even in justifying the man
               who believes in Jesus'[1].

Käsemann: 23' . . . Alle sündigten und sind der Herrlichkeit Gottes verlustig. 24(So)
               werden sie umsonst in seiner Gnade gerechtfertigt durch die Erlösung in
               Christus Jesus. 25Den hat Gott öffentlich als Sühne herausgestellt, (die
               ergriffen wird) durch Glauben kraft seines Blutes. (Das geschah) zum
               Erweis seiner Gerechtigkeit so, daß die in göttlicher Geduld früher gesche-
               henen Sündenschulden erlassen wurden; 26zum Erweis seiner Gerechtig-
               keit in der gegenwärtigen Schicksalsstunde, auf daß er gerecht sei und
               gerecht mache den, der aus Glauben an Jesus lebt'[2].

The former interpretation takes God's $\delta\iota\kappa\alpha\iota\sigma\sigma\acute{\nu}\eta$ in vs.25f. as referring to
his nature of being righteous or his judicial righteousness. According to this
interpretation, the main concern in these verses is to show how the righteous
and merciful God could justify sinners without compromising his righteousness. In the past, in his forbearance, hoping for the repentance of sinners,
God passed over ($\pi\acute{\alpha}\rho\epsilon\sigma\iota\varsigma$) sins, holding back his wrath upon them (cf. Rom
2.4; Acts 17.30). For God to pass over sins unpunished indefinitely, how-
ever, would bring his righteous nature into question. But, being truly merciful, he willed to forgive sinners. Being truly righteous, however, he could
forgive them only righteously, i.e., without compromising his righteousness.
So he made Christ a propitiatory sacrifice, so that he might vicariously bear
the full weight of God's wrath which they deserved. This redemptive act of
God had the purpose of proving ($\check{\epsilon}\nu\delta\epsilon\iota\xi\iota\varsigma$) his righteousness as it was called
in question because of his passing over sins committed until then. Further-

---

Lohse, *Märtyrer*, pp.149–153; K.Kertelge, *"Rechtfertigung" bei Paulus* (21971), pp.
48–62, 81–84; Bornkamm, *Paulus*, p.149; Stuhlmacher, 'Zur neueren Exegese von
Röm 3, 24–26', *Jesus und Paulus*, Kümmel FS, pp.315–333. It goes without saying that
on details (esp. on $\iota\lambda\alpha\sigma\tau\acute{\eta}\rho\iota\sigma\nu$) there are differences of opinion among the authors within each of these two groups.

[1]Cranfield, *Romans*, p.201. The words in italics are, of course, what the author has
inserted into the text in order to produce an idiomatic and intelligent translation of the
Greek original into English.

[2]Käsemann, *Römer*, p.84.

more, it had the purpose of showing forth his righteousness in the present (in which the coming aeon of salvation had already broken in with Christ), so that he might be righteous even in justifying the sinner who has faith in Jesus, i.e., so that he might justify him righteously, without compromising his own righteousness.

According to the latter interpretation, however, vs.25–26a (except the phrase διὰ πίστεως) is part of a Jewish Christian liturgical tradition which Paul has adopted, giving it a somewhat different interpretation by adding v.26bc. Ἔνδειξις in both verses does not mean to 'prove' but to 'show'. Πάρεσις means 'pardon' like ἄφεσις rather than 'passing over', and the phrase διὰ τὴν πάρεσιν means 'through pardoning'. God's δικαιοσύνη means, not his nature of being judicially righteous, but his faithfulness. So, the original tradition spoke of God's setting forth Christ as an atoning sacrifice in order to show his faithfulness to his covenant with Israel through pardoning their past sins (on the basis of the atonement in Christ). With v.26bc Paul extends the meaning of the atonement in Christ's death from the idea of the eschatological restitution of the covenant with Israel and forgiveness of their past sins to the idea of God's faithfulness to his entire creation and his justification of anyone who has faith in Jesus.

However we may interpret this most difficult passage of Rom 3.25f., it is clear that Paul understands Christ's death on the cross as God's own provision of the means whereby, or the ground on which, our sins may be forgiven and we may be justified (cf. Rom 5.5–11). God's offer of Christ as a propitiatory or atoning sacrifice was his redemptive act for fallen mankind.

With this understanding of the death of Christ as God's saving act there came to Paul also the realization that 'no man is justified by (works of) the law' (Gal 2.16; 3.11; Rom 3.20). This realization, which must have been absolutely revolutionary to a zealous Pharisee, had several components. First of all, as we have seen, Paul came to understand that on the cross of Jesus Christ God annulled the verdict of the law against Jesus, so that Jesus has superseded the law as the true revelation of God's will[1]. Secondly, Paul realized that his zeal for the law had led him only to the sin of opposing God's will in the crucified and risen Christ and of attacking his witnesses[2]. Guided by the law (Dt 21.23; Num 25.1–18; Ps 106.28–31; etc.)[3], Paul, the zealous Pharisee, had persecuted Christians who then appeared to his eyes

---

[1] So Stuhlmacher, "Ende", p.30; Blank, 'Warum sagt . . . ', p.94.

[2] So Grundmann, 'Paulus', pp.270f.; Stuhlmacher, "Ende", pp.50f.; F.F.Bruce, 'Paul and the Law of Moses', *BJRL* 57(1975), p.262.

[3] *Supra* pp.41ff.

to be apostates from the law. Thus he found out that the law paradoxically leads only to sin and condemnation and not to righteousness and life (cf. Gal 2.19ff.; 3.19ff.; Rom 5.20; 7.5; 8.3) — a revolutionary insight indeed! So, thirdly, the righteousness (ἰδία δικαιοσύνη) which he had hoped to achieve and in fact boasted of having achieved by keeping the law — even the *blameless* righteousness ἐν νόμῳ —turned out to be no righteousness. In the face of the righteousness from God it was but 'loss' (ζημία) and 'refuse' (σκύβαλα) (Phil 3.6—9).

Fourthly, Paul discovered that no man can actually keep the law perfectly. In the grand indictment in Rom 1.18—3.20 he demonstrates that all men, both the Gentiles and the Jews, are sinners because they do not keep the law or do not do good according to God's will (Rom 3.9, 23). In Rom 3.20 this factual sin of all men is made the ground for the assertion that no man will be justified before God by works of the law[1]. Their works of the law show only that they are sinners and not righteous. This argument presupposes that at least theoretically by a *perfect* observance of the law man can be justified. It is because man — Jew or Gentile — does not keep the law perfectly that he cannot be justified by works of the law. This presupposition — a thoroughly Jewish doctrine of justification — finds its echo occasionally in Paul (Rom 2.7—13; 10.5; Gal 3.12). It in turn presupposes that the law is still the true revelation of God's will and a means of obtaining righteousness and life. Indeed Paul says that the law is holy, just, good and spiritual, given for life (Rom 7.10ff.). But then this view of the law and justification appears incongruous with the first three reasons above why justification is not by works of the law. There is no doubt that here we are faced with the dialectic of Paul's doctrine of the law. Much ink has been spilt on this most intricate problem[2], but even now as ever it is far from being transparent. In this situation we find P.Stuhlmacher's explanation the least problematic — though by no means completely satisfactory[3].

Stuhlmacher starts by distinguishing the will of God and the Mosaic Torah. God's good will which was meant εἰς ζωήν (Rom 7.10), i.e., for the preservation of life

---

[1]Cf. U.Wilckens, 'Was heißt bei Paulus: "Aus Werken des Gesetzes wird kein Mensch gerecht"?' *Rechtfertigung als Freiheit*, pp.77—109.

[2]See, besides the essays cited in pp.280f., Bultmann, *Theology* i, pp.259—269; C.E.B.Cranfield, 'St. Paul and the Law', *SJT* 17(1964), pp.43—68; O.Kuss, 'Nomos bei Paulus', *MThZ* 17(1966), pp.173—227; A.van Dülmen, *Die Theologie des Gesetzes bei Paulus*; F.Hahn, 'Das Gesetzesverständnis im Römer- und Galaterbrief', *ZNW* 67(1976), pp.29—63.

[3]Stuhlmacher, *Gerechtigkeit*, pp.94—97; also "Ende", pp.35f. For a criticism of this view, see Hahn, 'Gesetzesverständnis', pp.61f.

which he gave, was already transgressed by Adam (Rom 5.12–14). With this transgression sin and with it death fatefully broke into the world, and thus God's original good will for life became a judicial sentence of death. So, from the beginning God's will alone could not protect life (Gal 3.21) as it was seized by man's self-assertive will and fell under the lordship of sin (Rom 7.7ff.). The codex of the will of God which was distorted by sin was the Torah given to Moses (Rom 5.13f.; cf. Gal 3.19f.). In it the good will of God was still effective, even if in a broken and concealed way, so that it had the salvation-historical function of a 'pedagogue' who shut up all mankind under sin in order thus to lead them to Christ. The eschatological situation arose with the sending of the Son of God. He vicariously took upon himself the curse of the Torah. The cross meant the end of the Torah which was only a distorted picture of the good will of God and the liberation of the good will of God from the shackles of sin. Christ with his commandment is now the representative of this good will of God which is thus freed. In Christ the good will of God has become the helper for life again. Christ is a new Adam in whom and to whom the situation of the pre-fall paradise is repeated. However, as yet the νόμος Χριστοῦ is the manifestation of the good will of God only in the body of Christ. This νόμος Χριστοῦ has the function of preserving the righteousness and life given to the Christian in baptism against σάρξ, but not the power to give life itself. In the light of Christ one can see also in the Mosaic Torah the commandment of love, which has been enslaved to sin. Because of this continuity of God's will Paul sees in the law of Christ the true intention of the Mosaic Torah preserved (Rom 13.9f.; Gal 5.6) and in Christian obedience its demands fulfilled in the way in which God wants (Rom 8.4).

If Stuhlmacher correctly represents the mind of Paul in seeing the Mosaic law as that in which the good and true will of God is concealed and distorted by the flesh and sin, Paul must mean that by keeping the Mosaic law — even by a perfect keeping of it — no man can be justified. When he contemplates the possibility of justification by a perfect observance of the law, then, he must be thinking of the good will of God in the Mosaic law. However, since the good will of God is found in the Mosaic law only distorted by sin and is constantly seized by the flesh as the vehicle to establish man's own righteousness and καύχησις before God, no man can actually keep the good will of God perfectly (i.e., in the way in which God wants)[1]. The factual sin of all men is only the symptom of this impossibility, which derives from the deeper

---

[1]One-sidedly emphasizing the factual sin of all men as the sole ground for Paul's statement: 'No man is justified by works of the law', Wilckens ('Was heißt . . . ') fails to see the dialectic in Paul's understanding of the law itself. For this criticism, see Stuhlmacher, "Ende", p.36 (n.46); Hahn, 'Gesetzesverständnis', p.61; also Blank, 'Warum sagt . . . ', p.89. Emphasizing that the saving event in Christ has brought the law itself into a crisis, on the other hand, Blank (*ibid.*, pp.88ff.) tends unduly to tone down the positive observation of Wilckens and so in the end to dissolve the dialectic of Paul's understanding of the law into an anthropological dialectic, a dialectic in human existence, in the manner of Bultmann, *Theology* i, pp.259–269.

problems of the law itself and of human existence[1]. So no man can actually be saved by *works of the law* (Gal 2.16; Rom 3.20) — and this means that no man can actually be saved *by the law* (Gal 3.11). We would be the last to imagine that we have here satisfactorily explained the problem of the law in Paul. However, one thing is beyond doubt: namely that at the Damascus revelation Paul came to understand that 'no man is justified by (works of) the law' and so to see the fundamental problem of the law itself[2].

From the realization, on the one hand, that 'no man is justified by (works of) the law' and, on the other, that Christ's death and resurrection[3] was God's saving act for us, it logically follows: 'But now the righteousness of God has been manifested χωρὶς νόμου' (Rom 3.21). God's righteousness has been manifested apart from the law not only in the sense that it is obtained χωρὶς ἔργων νόμου (Rom 3.28)[4] but more fundamentally in the sense that it is what the law, being weak through the flesh, could not work, but which God has wrought by sending his Son and condemning sin in his flesh (Rom 8.3). Δικαιοσύνη θεοῦ in Paul is usually a forensic concept referring to the righteousness or the righteous status which God confers upon man as a gift[5]. It has been manifested through or as a result of the redemption which

---

[1]Cf. Blank, 'Warum sagt . . . ', p.89.

[2]Cf. *ibid.*, pp.91, 94; Stuhlmacher, "Ende". Thus the law became problematic to Paul and he radicalizes the antithesis between God's grace (and man's faith) and the works of the law not because he had had a defective 'diaspora' understanding of the Torah (*contra* Schoeps, *Paul*, pp.213ff.) but because his Damascus experience led him to see the real meaning of the cross of Christ and to know that his genuine zeal for the law had only resulted in sin against God. So Bruce, 'The Law of Moses', p.262.

[3]For Paul as well as for the NT as a whole the cross and the resurrection belong together and together they constitute one saving event of God. For but for the resurrection (which was in Paul's case experienced on the Damascus road) the cross would have been meaningless. The significance of the cross as the atoning sacrifice ὑπὲρ ἡμῶν and as the triumph over the evil powers of sin, the flesh, the law, Satan and death is visible only in the light of the resurrection. For Paul as for the NT as a whole the cross is the centre of theology, but what makes the cross the centre of theology is the resurrection. Cf. W.Künneth, *Theologie der Auferstehung* ([5]1968), pp.154ff.; Käsemann, 'Heilsbedeutung', pp.98f.; Stuhlmacher, "Ende", p.33.

[4]Cranfield, *Romans*, p.201, takes the phrase χωρὶς νόμου in Rom 3.21 as equivalent in significance to χωρὶς ἔργων νόμου of v.28. But he does not seem to pay adequate attention to the tense of the verb πεφανέρωται in the verse. With the perfect Paul is speaking of God's saving work in Christ in the past as the revelation of his righteousness (vs.24ff.), which is, as a result, available in the present. So, χωρὶς νόμου must be related in the first instance to that historic work of God in Christ.

[5]That is, the genitive θεοῦ is usually a *gen.auctoris*. As is widely recognized, however, at least in two passages, namely Rom 3.5 and 3.28f., the genitive is a *gen.subjectivus*,

signifying righteousness as God's attribute. In Rom 3.5 θεοῦ δικαιοσύνη probably refers to God's character or activity in which he remains faithful to his covenant and shows his saving mercy to his people, as it often does in the OT and Judaism, rather than to his judicial righteousness that judges sinners. In Rom 3.25f., as we noted above, opinions are divided whether it refers likewise to God's faithfulness to his covenant and to his creation or to his judicial righteousness. Some commentators would see also in other passages δικαιοσύνη θεοῦ as a subj. gen. and as referring to God's saving activity (e.g., G.Schrenk, δικαιοσύνη, *TDNT* ii, pp.203f.; Dodd, *Romans*, pp.38ff.; Barrett, *Romans*, pp.29f.). But this view neglects Paul's coordination of δικαιοσύνη θεοῦ with faith. Paul usually speaks about δικαιοσύνη θεοῦ conferred upon or appropriated by faith, so that he stresses its character as a gift.   However, it is a gift of God as a result of his saving work, so that the latter meaning may be present at least in the background sometimes (e.g., Rom 3.21; 10.3). Discussion on δικαιοσύνη θεοῦ has taken a new turn since, against the view that it refers to God's gift, Käsemann argued that it refers primarily to his power. Taking the phrase δικαιοσύνη θεοῦ as an apocalyptic *term. techn.* rather than explaining it from the concept δικαιοσύνη, Käsemann and, following him, P.Stuhlmacher have described it variously as God's power, his sovereignty, his *Recht*, his saving activity, his faithfulness to his covenant and to his creation, his grace, etc. See Käsemann, 'Gottesgerechtigkeit bei Paulus', *EVB* ii, pp.181–193; *Römer*, pp.21–27; Stuhlmacher, *Gerechtigkeit*. According to Käsemann, the phrase 'spricht von dem Gott, der gefallene Welt in den Bereich seines Rechtes zurückholt, sei es im Zuspruch oder im Anspruch, in Neuschöpfung oder Vergebung oder in der Ermöglichung unseres Dienstes und . . . in den Stand gewisser; Hoffnung, uns also nach Phil 3, 12 in den ständigen irdischen Aufbruch stellt' (*Römer*, p.26). Paul holds fast to the aspect of righteousness as power, according to Käsemann ('Gottesgerechtigkeit', p.186): 'Zur Gabe wird die Macht, wenn sie von uns Besitz ergreift und dabei gleichsam in uns eingeht, so daß wie in Gal 2, 20 gilt: "Nicht mehr ich lebe, sondern Christus lebt in mir". Von da aus wird die doppelte Ausrichtung der Genetivkonstruktion begriffen: Die hier mitgeteilte Gabe ist nicht und nie von ihrem Geber ablösbar. Sie partizipiert am Charakter der Macht, sofern in ihr Gott selber auf den Plan tritt, und mit ihr auf dem Plane bleibt. So ist mit ihr unablösbar auch Anspruch, Verpflichtung und Dienst verbunden. Wenn Gott auf den Plan tritt, erfahren wir selbst in seinen Gaben noch seine Herrschaft, sind gerade seine Gaben die Mittel, welche uns seiner Herrschaft einordnen und damit in Verantwortung stellen' (*ibid.*, p.186). But this understanding of δικαιοσύνη θεοῦ has been widely criticised: see. e.g., Bultmann, 'Δικαιοσύνη θεοῦ', *Exegetica*, pp.470–475; G.Klein, 'Gottes Gerechtigkeit als Thema der neuesten Paulus-Forschung', *VF* 12(1967), pp.1–11; Conzelmann, *Outline*, pp.214–220; E.Lohse, 'Die Gerechtigkeit Gottes in der paulinischen Theologie', *Die Einheit des NT* (1973), pp.210–227, who all argue that θεοῦ is a *gen. auctoris* and the phrase refers to God's gift (so also Cranfield, *Romans*, pp.92–99). It is impossible to enter into a critical discussion on this matter here as the complex subject matter would require a much greater space for an adequate discussion and lead us too far afield.   Besides, now Stuhlmacher explicitly says that he accepts Lohse's criticism of his thesis (Stuhlmacher, 'Zur neueren Exegese', p.331 (n.62)), and Käsemann seems to have modified his understanding in some respects: e.g., whereas in his earlier essay he repeatedly stressed that θεοῦ is a subjective gen. and δικαιοσύνη θεοῦ refers in Paul as in the OT/Judaism to God's saving activity, now he rejects this view (*Römer*, p.24). At any rate, while arguing for the primary sense of δικαιοσύνη θεοῦ to be power, Käsemann himself says that its dominant sense in Paul is that of gift ('Gottesgerechtigkeit', p.181 (n.*)).   For 'if righteousness through faith and righteousness through works are to be sharply contrasted, obviously the whole emphasis will fall on

God has wrought by offering Christ as a propitiatory or atoning sacrifice. So Christ, the crucified one, is our righteousness and redemption from God (1Cor 1.30). The righteousness of God is now being revealed in the gospel, as in the proclamation of God's act in Christ it is granted to those who respond to the message by faith. Thus the righteousness which is valid before God, the condition for our salvation[1], is granted by God in the gospel. Therefore, the gospel is God's saving power for any believer (Rom 1.16f.). Here we have a neat antithesis between the gospel and the law: δικαιοσύνη θεοῦ is revealed χωρὶς νόμου – but ἐν εὐαγγελίῳ.

The fact that the righteousness of God has been manifested χωρὶς νόμου, through God's own saving act in Christ, and so is obtained χωρὶς ἔργων νόμου, is the basis of three further distinctive features of Paul's doctrine of justification, in all of which we can again see his Damascus experience clearly reflected. The first of these is that God justifies the ungodly (ἀσεβής) (Rom 4.5). Like δικαιοσύνη θεοῦ, to 'justify' (δικαιοῦν) or to 'be justified' (δικαιοῦσθαι) is in Paul a forensic concept equivalent to the Hiphil or the Qal of צדק respectively in the OT and Judaism. It has to do with the verdict in God's court. Δικαιοῦν means to ' "put someone in the right" by giving judgement in his favour'[2], or to 'acquit'. The passive δικαιοῦσθαι means accordingly to 'be in the right', to 'be pronounced righteous', or to 'be acquitted'. So justification is the divine act of imputing a righteous status (δικαιοσύνη) to man, so that he may be acknowledged as righteous. R.Bultmann thinks that the old dispute as to whether the justified is made really righteous or only regarded 'as if' he were righteous arose from the misunderstanding of δικαιοσύνη as ethical perfection[3]. Δικαιοσύνη is not an ethical concept but rather a forensic and relational concept meaning a favourable standing before God, the Judge. So justification means neither to 'make someone righteous' in an ethical sense nor to 'regard him "as if" he were righteous' while he is in

---

the gift' (*ibid.*, p.185). So, for example, commenting on Rom 3.21, Käsemann says, 'whatever else the eschatological righteousness of God may be, it is at any rate a gift which comes to man διὰ πίστεως' (*Römer*, p.87). On the meaning of righteousness in Paul, see, besides the works cited above, D.Hill, *Greek Words and Hebrew Meanings* (1967), pp.82–162.; K.Kertelge, "*Rechtfertigung*," pp.6–109; J.A.Ziesler, *The Meaning of Righteousness in Paul* (1972).

[1]Cf. Bultmann, *Theology* i, pp.270f.: 'Strictly speaking, righteousness is the condition for receiving salvation or "life" . . . But since this connection between righteousness and salvation is so tight and inevitable, righteousness itself can become the essence of salvation'.

[2]Hill, *Greek Words*, p.160.

[3]Bultmann, *Theology* i., pp.276f.

reality a sinner. It means to 'make someone righteous' in the sense that God absolves his sin by his verdict, so that he is really righteous[1].

Δικαιοσύνη is not only a forensic but also an eschatological concept, and justification or God's verdict of acquittal is what the Jews hoped to obtain at the last judgement. But Paul proclaims that God's righteousness has already been manifested (πεφανέρωται) through his redemption in Christ (Rom 3.21) and therefore it is now being revealed (ἀποκαλύπτεται) in the gospel (Rom 1.17). With the apocalyptic language (ἀποκαλύπτεω/ἀποκάλυψις)[2] Paul means that the eschatological revelation of God's righteousness has taken place in Christ's death and resurrection and is taking place in the proclamation of the saving event. The eschaton has broken in, and, so, now is the time of salvation (Gal 4.4; 2Cor 6.2). God's judgement is taking place now. Already in the present he declares the believer righteous. So, to the Corinthian Christians Paul says: 'You were justified (ἐδικαιώθητε) . . .' (1Cor 6.11). To the Roman Christians he says: 'Justified (δικαιωθέντες) therefore by faith we have peace with God . . . ' (Rom 5.1; so also v.9). The Gentile Christians 'have attained righteousness' (κατέλαβεν δικαιοσύνην) (Rom 9.30). At the same time, however, Paul says to the Galatian Christians, i.e., those who have already been justified: ' . . . through the Spirit, by faith, we are waiting for the hope of righteousness' (Gal 5.5). We wait for God's Son from heaven, 'Jesus who will deliver us from the wrath to come' (1 Th 1.10; cf. also Rom 5.9). In Rom 2.13 Paul echoes the Jewish hope of justification at the last judgement. We, the Christians, also 'must appear before the judgement seat of Christ, so that each one may receive good or evil according to what he has done in the body' (2Cor 5.10; cf. also Rom 2.16; 14.10; 1Cor 3.13ff.; 4.4ff.). Thus we see here the characteristic tension between 'already' and 'not yet' in Paul's eschatology and soteriology. God passes his eschatological judgement already in the present and believers are already declared righteous. Yet there will be the last judgement at the parousia of Christ and believers

---

[1]*Ibid.*, pp.276f.; similarly Barrett, *Romans*, pp.75f.; cf. also Kertelge, "*Rechtfertigung*," pp.112–129. Kertelge emphasizes that justification is effective as well as forensic because God's verdict, his word of declaring righteous, has an effective power (p.115 *et passim*). But happily he defines the 'effective' justification in the following terms: Justification 'erschöpft sich aber nicht in einem nur äußerlich bleibenden Dekret, sondern sie bedeutet die wirksame Schaffung einer neuen Realität durch Gott. Die von Gott geschaffene neue Wirklichkeit des Gerechtfertigten ist jedoch nicht als eine statische Verfaßtheit des Menschen zu denken, sondern als eine *Beziehungsrealität*, d.h., eine Wirklichkeit, die in nichts anderem besteht als in dem von Gott geschaffenen neuen Verhältnis des Menschen zu Gott, das von Gott her Herrschaft und vom Menschen aus Gehorsam beinhaltet' (p.127. Emphasis by K.).

[2]*Supra* pp.71ff. See further Lührmann, *Offenbarungsverständnis*, pp.145–153; Bultmann, *Theology* i, pp.275f.; Käsemann, *Römer*, p.27.

hope to obtain righteousness, that is, acquittal, and to be delivered from con-
demantion at it. Here we can only note that Paul solves this tension by taking the present situation of justification, which is sealed by the Spirit, as the
first-fruits (ἀπαρχή: Rom 8.23) and pledge (ἀρραβών: 2Cor 1.22; 5.5;
Eph 1.⁫ †)[1] which awaits consummation at the parousia[2]. So 'we were saved
in the sphere of hope' (Rom 8.24). But 'hope does not disappoint us'
(Rom 5.5). 'Since, then, we have now been justified by his (sc. Christ's)
blood, much more shall we be saved through him from the wrath' (Rom 5.9)[3].

'God justifies the ungodly'. This is a paradox. In the OT God not only
forbids the practice among men of justifying the ungodly (רשע / ἀσεβής)
(Prov 17.15; Isa 5.23) but also explicitly says: 'I will not justify the ungodly'
(Ex 23.7: לא / c.. LXX: καὶ οὐ δικαιώσεις τὸν ἀσεβῆ . . .)[4].
Judaism also maintains that it is godless or wicked to justify the ungodly
(CD 1.19). Furthermore, in some quarters shedding the blood of the ungodly
was supposed to be a sacrifice to God (Num.R.21.3), and in Ps 106.30f.
Phinehas' slaying an apostate is said to have been 'reckoned to him as righteousness'[5]. Earlier we suggested that motivated by these ideas Paul persecuted Christians[6]: persecuting Christians who were the ungodly apostates
in his eyes then was, he thought, to bring a sacrifice to God (cf. Jn 16.2)
and so to earn merit or righteousness. But at the Damascus Christophany he
came to know that he had been opposing God and therefore that it was he
who was ungodly, not the Christians. This terrible knowledge was, however,
accompanied by the experience of God's justification as God forgave him and
called him to be an apostle of Christ (Phil 3.9). Thus, from the Damascus
experience Paul obtained the knowledge that God justifies the ungodly.
Only in the light of Paul's own experience of justification on the Damascus
road can we fully appreciate the striking formulation[7]. If his own exper-

---

[1]τοῦ πνεύματος in Rom 8.23; 2Cor 1.12; 5.5 is an appositional gen. rather than a
possessive or partitive gen. (as Eph 1.14 clearly indicates), so that it is the Spirit who is
the ἀπαρχή and the ἀρραβών. However, since the Spirit represents God's saving work in
us, we may regard justification itself as part of the ἀπαρχή and the ἀρραβών. Cf.
Cranfield, *Romans*, p.418.

[2]Here we cannot go into the questions concerning Paul's view of the last judgement.

[3]On this question of the relationship between the present and the future justification,
cf. Kertelge, *"Rechtfertigung"*, pp.128–158.

[4]Cf. Barrett, *Romans*, pp.88f.; Stuhlmacher, *Gerechtigkeit*, pp.226f.; also Cranfield,
Romans, p.232 (n.1).

[5]Cf. Haacker, 'Berufung', pp.8–10, 13ff.

[6]*Supra* pp.41ff., 49f.

[7]Cf. Stuhlmacher, "Ende", pp.30f.

ience thus provides the experiential basis for the doctrine, however, it is the fact that God's righteousness has been manifested χωρὶς νόμου, through his own saving act in Christ, which provides the theological basis for it. No man can be justified by works of the law. Justification is through God's saving act in Christ. So it is not those who achieve righteousness by keeping the law but the ungodly that God justifies. Justification of the ungodly is a 'Kampf-formel' directed against the Jewish (and Judaizing Christian) doctrine that God justifies those who are godly (εὐσεβής) and righteous (δίκαιος) by works of the law[1], that is, against Paul's own former understanding of justification. It is, as E. Käsemann sees, 'die schärfste Angriffsspitze' of Paul's theology and 'the indispensable key' of his doctrine of justification[2].

That no man is justified by works of the law but through God's saving act in Christ, and that he is therefore justified as ungodly, means that justi-fication is by the grace of God. This is the second distinctive feature of Paul's doctrine of justification. It also reflects his Damascus experience. God's justification and apostolic call of Paul, the ungodly, who had opposed his will, was by sheer grace, the free, undeserved favour[3] of God. That is why in giving an account of the Damascus event Paul repeatedly emphasizes the grace of God: 'For I am the least of the apostles, unfit to be called an apostle, because I persecuted the Church of God. But by the grace of God I am what I am, and his grace toward me was not in vain. On the contrary, I worked harder than any of them, though it was not I, but the grace of God which is with me' (1Cor 15.9f.). It was through his grace that God called Paul to preach his Son (Gal 1.15).

Excursus: Paul and the Grace of His Apostleship

Earlier we observed how Paul designates his apostolic call as χάρις of God (Rom 1.5) and constantly refers to it as the χάρις ἡ δοθεῖσα μοι (Rom 12.3; 15.15; 1Cor 3.10; Gal 2.9; Eph 3.2, 7, 8)[4]. In Phil 1.7 Paul speaks of the Philippian Christians as being partakers of his 'grace', namely his apostolic ministry[5]. Thus he regards his apostolic call as God's χάρις for him. Otherwise he uses the word χάρις only in

---

[1] Michel, *Römer*, p.117; Stuhlmacher, *Gerechtigkeit*, pp.226f.

[2] Käsemann, 'Der Glaube Abrahams in Röm 4', *Paulinische Perspektiven*, pp.148f.

[3] On grace see H. Conzelmann and W. Zimmerli, χάρις', κτλ, *TDNT* ix, pp.372–402.

[4] *Supra*, pp.25ff. There we also observed how Paul repeatedly refers to God's ἔλεος in connection with his Damascus call (1Cor 7.25; 2Cor 4.1; 1Tim 1.12f., 16).

[5] So A. Satake, 'Apostolat und Gnade bei Paulus', *NTS* 15(1968/69), p.99; cf. Gnilka, *Phil.*, p.49.

connection with salvation through faith (e.g., Rom 3.24; 5.2; 6.14). Other offices and services than his own apostolic ministry, however, he does not call χάρις but χάρισμα. A.Satake observes that this use of the word χάρις is paralleled by Paul's use of the word καλεῖν/κλητός[1]. Paul usually uses καλεῖν for God's call of man to faith and salvation, i.e., to be a Christian (e.g., Rom 8.30; 1Cor 1.9; Gal 1.6), and κλητός for him who has been called to faith, i.e., a Christian (Rom 1.6f.; 8.28; 1Cor 1.2, 24). While never using the word καλεῖν/ κλητός for the call of others to any office, Paul does use it for his own apostolic call (Gal 1.15; Rom 1.1; 1Cor 1.1). From these two observations Satake concludes not only that for Paul the call to faith and the call to apostleship coincided, but also that his 'Apostelsein' is grounded in exactly the same way as the 'Christsein' of other Christians[2]. Then Satake attempts to see the full significance of this in the light of a few Pauline passages. According to him, in Phil 1.19 the τοῦτο refers to the progress of the gospel due to Paul's imprisonment (vs. 12–18), so that Paul is saying that the success of the gospel will lead to his salvation. In 1Cor 9.27; Phil 2.15; and 1Th 2.19f., according to Satake, Paul sees his own salvation in a close connection with his missionary work, indeed as dependent upon the latter. 'Er wird gerettet, indem er andere zum Heil bringt'[3]. The same idea is found still more clearly in 1Cor 9.23 : Paul has made himself a slave to all in order to save some. This he does for the sake of the gospel, so that he may share in the blessings of the gospel. For him his missionary work is 'an absolute presupposition for his own salvation'[4]. In the light of this last observation the significance of the first two observations becomes clear : that he is called to be an apostle, means for him that he is given the promise of salvation in this sense, namely that he will be saved as he brings others to salvation. That is why he describes his apostolic call with the word καλεῖν/ κλητός, with which he otherwise describes the coming of others to faith and salvation. For him the call to faith and the call to apostleship coincide not only chronologically but more fundamentally: 'Paul sees precisely in his call to be an apostle his call to the promise of salvation'[5]. This does not mean, however, that for him his apostolic ministry is the means of salvation. For then his apostleship would no longer be grace. Rather, he understands his apostleship as pure grace which was freely given by God. That is why he attributes not only his call to apostleship but also his apostolic activity itself to the grace of God (1Cor 15.10; 2Cor 1.12). 'Paul understands his apostleship as the grace of God which calls him and entrusts him with the task of proclamation, so that he may not only bring salvation to others but come to salvation himself'[6].

This stimulating study by Satake may be supported further by a couple more Pauline passages which he does not consider. One of these is 1Cor 9.16, where Paul says : 'For ἀνάγκη is laid upon me. For woe befalls me if I do not preach the gospel'.

---

[1]Satake, 'Apostolat', pp.96–103.

[2]*Ibid.*, pp.97, 102.

[3]*Ibid.*, p.105.

[4]*Ibid.*, p.105. Cf. Barrett, *1 Cor.*, p.216: 'It is in fulfilling his own vocation as an evangelist that he (sc. Paul) appropriates the gospel himself'.

[5]Satake, 'Apostolat', p.107.

[6]*Ibid.*, p.106.

This striking word Paul says in the context of explaining why he does not make use of the right which the Lord has given the preachers of the gospel to be materially supported by their converts. Paul has abandoned this right lest he should be deprived of his boasting and reward. For his reward consists precisely in his preaching the gospel without charge. His preaching free of charge is itself the reward, because, as he has been enlisted by God to the office of preaching and therefore has not chosen it of his own will, for him merely to preach would not bring him any reward or ground of boasting. It is his duty, indeed ἀνάγκη, to preach the gospel. The meaning of the word ἀνάγκη here is determined by the word οὐαί. Οὐαί μοι is reminiscent of the recurring formula אוֹי לִי (לָנוּ) which is in the OT a cry of dread in the face of threatening disaster or a cry of lamentation over the disaster in which one finds oneself. The formula ל + אוֹי + second or third person suffix usually issues a threat[1]. So, in our verse Paul is expressing his fear that disaster will befall him if he does not preach the gospel[2]. Then, ἀνάγκη here must mean nothing less than 'fateful necessity'[3]. For Paul it is 'fateful necessity' to preach the gospel because if he fails to do it disaster will befall him[4]. Earlier we suggested that in the present verse Paul is reflecting upon his apostolic call on the Damascus road[5]. Thus 1Cor 9.16 as well as 1Cor 9.23 seems to suggest that Paul's own salvation is bound up with his apostolic ministry[6]. The same thought is expressed in a negative form in the former and in a positive form in the latter.

Rom 1.14 may also be relevant here. Paul declares that he is ὀφειλέτης to the entire Gentile humanity. The word ὀφειλέτης, which originated as a commercial and legal term for 'debtor', is also well attested in a transferred sense for one who is obliged, one who is under obligation[7]. Paul clearly uses the word in the transferred sense in Rom 8.12; Gal 5.3. But in Rom 15.27 the original sense of the word is, to say the least, not completely dissolved in the transferred sense[8]. Most commentators take the word in Rom 1.14 in the transferred sense and see Paul as saying that as he

---

[1] See G.Wanke, ' אוֹי und הוֹי ', *ZAW* 78(1966), pp.215−218; Zobel, הוי, *ThWAT* ii, 382−388; E.Jenni, הוֹי, *ThHAT* i, 474ff.

[2] Cf. Käsemann, 'Eine paulinische Variation des "amor fati" ', *EVB* ii, p.234.

[3] Cf. *ibid.*, pp.233f.; Conzelmann, *1.Kor.*, p.186. However, both differentiate Paul's ἀνάγκη from the Graeco-Roman concept of '*fatum*'. Conzelmann: 'Aber dieses (sc. the former) ist nicht ein Fatum, das mit kausaler Notwendigkeit wirkt. Sonst könnte nicht der Fall gedacht werden, daß sich Paulus dem Zwang verweigerte'.

[4] This is to be more definite than Käsemann, "amor fati", pp.234ff., is prepared to be. Besides, he thinks that it is the gospel itself which is for Paul the ἀνάγκη, 'jene Gottesmacht, welche den Menschen derart schicksalhaft überfällt, wie Paulus es tatsächlich bei Damaskus erfahren hat, und ihn so in ihren Dienst zwingt . . . ' (p.235). But it is more likely that by ἀνάγκη here Paul is referring to his apostolic *commission* (οἰκονομία) to preach the gospel rather than to the gospel itself.

[5] *Supra* pp.4f.

[6] Cf. V.C.Pfitzner, *Paul and the Agon Motif* (1967), p.85.

[7] See F.Hauck, ὀφείλω, κτλ, *TDNT* v, pp.559−566.

[8] Cf. A.Schlatter, *Gottes Gerechtigkeit* (⁴1965), p.390; Michel, *Römer*, p.371; Cranfield, *Romans*, p.85.

was called by God to be the Gentiles' apostle he is obliged to preach the gospel to them: he has a duty towards them[1]. According to A.Schlatter, Paul here reflects Jesus' teaching that he gave a gift to his disciples, so that they might give it to others. Paul is the debtor of all because he has what all need[2]. Developing this understanding, P.S.Minear says: 'Obligation to him who died produces obligation to those for whom he died. This very "law". applies with special force to the particularity of Paul's call as an apostle. God's intention in bringing Paul to faith in Christ had been to send him as a "minister of Christ Jesus to the Gentiles" (15.16). To the extent that Paul was indebted to God for this call, to that very extent he was indebted to those Gentiles for whose sake God had called him'[3]. But could it be that the original sense of ὀφειλέτης is more definitely retained in our verse than Minear would allow? Paul's sense of indebtedness to the Gentiles is probably not because of the 'law' which Minear talks about[4]. It may rather be straightforward. Paul is perhaps saying here that he owes his apostolic call to the Gentiles because for their sake and with a view to their salvation God called him in his grace. Negatively put: but for the Gentiles Paul would not have been called by God to be an apostle. So he is indebted to them for his apostolic call. If the debt was just the apostolic call, however, his sense of indebtedness to the Gentiles might not have been so great as the strong expression[5] ὀφειλέτης εἰμί seems to convey here. Can we in our verse overhear Paul saying that he owes to the Gentiles his own salvation as well as his apostolic call as it came together with or in the form of the latter? Does Paul imply that he was saved and called to be an apostle for the sake of the Gentiles, so that he owes to them his salvation and apostolic call? Indebted to them for both, then, Paul is under obligation to preach the gospel to them. This line of interpretation may be just a fancy. If it is correct, however, Rom 1.14 would suggest that Paul's salvation is bound up with his apostolic call.

Thus 1Cor 9.16 and Rom 1.14 may support Satake's conclusion. On the whole his observations are rather striking. However, they are not without difficulties. 1) The phenomenon that while Paul uses the καλεῖν terminology for his apostolic call he never uses it for other Christians' appointments to an office is probably not so significant as Satake thinks. It is, after all, already well established in the OT (e.g., Ex 31.2; 35.30; Isa 41.9; 42.6; 49.1) for God's election and call of his servant for a task. In the Gospels also we have the account of Jesus' calling his disciples (Mk 1.20 = Mt 4. 21). In Gal 1.15f. Paul uses the word καλεῖν for his Damascus call in dependence upon Isa 49.1. Thus it is clear that Paul uses the word for God's call to a task as well as for his call to salvation. The absence of evidence for his use of the word in the former sense with regard to other Christians may be quite accidental; it may be due to the fact that Paul had no occasion to speak *concretely* of the *call* of others. In

---

[1]E.g., Barrett, *Romans*, p.26; A.Nygren, *Commentary on Romans* (1952), pp.62f.; F.J.Leenhardt, *The Epistle to the Romans* (1961), p.45; Cranfield, *Romans*, p.85.

[2]Schlatter, *Gerechtigkeit*, p.31.

[3]P.S.Minear, *The Obedience of Faith* (1971), p.104.

[4]Minear's attempt to see more applications of the 'law' elsewhere in Rom. and other letters of Paul and with regard to every Christian (*op.cit.*, pp.104ff.), is not successful – so Käsemann, *Römer*, p.17.

[5]Cf. Michel, *Römer*, p.50.

1Cor 12.28, as he generally speaks about the offices of apostles, prophets, teachers, miracle workers, etc., and not about a specific appointment of an individual apostle, prophet or teacher, he may say: God ἔθετο them rather than God ἐκάλεσεν them. Since the word, to 'call', is well established for God's call of his servant for a task, it would be rather strange if Paul deliberately avoided the word with regard to commissioning other Christians to a task.

   2) Satake's insistence that Paul never uses χάρις for the office of other Christians is probably not correct. It is true that Paul never connects χάρις so directly with the office of another Christian as with his own apostolic office. Nevertheless, Gal 2.7−9 seems to suggest that he saw Peter's apostleship as God's χάρις. Certainly τὴν χάρω τὴν δοθεῖσάν μοι in v.9 refers to his own Damascus call. However, since in vs.7−8 he draws an exact parallel between God's work in his apostolic commission and that in Peter's, it may not be improper to see that Paul thinks also of Peter's apostolic commission in terms of χάρις. Satake tries to avoid this inference by taking the view that vs.7f. are part of the minute of the Jerusalem accord between James, Peter and John on the one hand and Paul and Barnabas on the other. Satake argues that since in vs.7f. Paul cites the minute without comment and then resumes in v.9 to write in his own words he is not himself drawing the parallel between himself and Peter[1]. But recently the view that in vs.7f. Paul cites the minute has rightly been rejected[2]. It is Paul who formulates vs.7−9 throughout and draws the parallel between God's commissioning of him and Peter. The idea of χάρις for both Paul's apostleship and Peter's apostleship is clearly implied in v.8[3]. In Rom 12.6 Paul says: ἔχοντες δὲ χαρίσματα κατὰ τὴν χάρω τὴν δοθεῖσαν ἡμῖν διάφορα... Satake's dispute as to whether Paul includes himself in ἡμῖν[4] is quite unjustified. As the aorist participle δοθεῖσαν indicates, by χάρις here Paul refers to the saving grace which led all believers − the Roman Christians and Paul − to salvation. Most commentators explain that χάρισμα is the concretization and individualization of χάρις[5]. Then, from Rom 12.6 we can gather two points relevant to our present discussion. One is that every Christian has a χάρισμα (or χαρίσματα) as a concrete and individualized expression of χάρις. The other is that Paul also has a χάρισμα (or χαρίσματα). From 1Cor 12.28 we may gather that he regarded his apostleship also as a χάρισμα. For there he numbers apostleship along with the offices of prophets, teachers, etc. among χαρίσματα[6]. These two points then weaken Satake's conclusion considerably, as

---

[1]Satake, 'Apostolat', pp.98, 102. There is some confusion in his statements on p.102.

[2]See Stuhlmacher, *Evangelium*, pp.93−96 and the literature cited there. Further, see Mussner, *Gal.*, pp.117f. 9n.93).

[3]For an exegesis of this verse in the context, *supra* p.27.

[4]Satake, 'Apostolat', p.101.

[5]So, e.g., Bultmann, *Theology* i, p.325; Barrett, *Romans*, p.237; Käsemann, *Römer*, p.318; already in his 'Amt und Gemeinde im NT', *EVB* i, p.117; Michel, *Römer*, p.298; Ridderbos, *Paulus*, p.325; Conzelmann, χάρισμα, *TDNT* ix, pp.403, 405. Satake himself agrees with this ('Apostolat', p.103, n.1).

[6]This seems to be clear in the context, although admittedly apostleship is not directly called a χάρισμα. So Schütz, *Paul and the Anatomy of Apostolic Authority*, pp.251− 259 (esp. 251, 258); Käsemann, 'Amt', p.124.

they together seem to dismantle the wall of separation that he erects between Paul's apostleship only as χάρις and the offices of other Christians only as χαρίσματα.

3) Phil 1.19 is problematic. Many commentators take the τοῦτο in the verse to refer to Paul's present **situation of suffering**[1]. But Satake argues that it refers to the progress of the gospel which in vs.12–18 Paul says has taken place in spite of or rather because of his imprisonment. This is possible especially because in v.18 Paul has already used τοῦτο to refer to the progress of the gospel. But this interpretation is attended with problems. First of all, it is possible that with ἀλλὰ καὶ χαρήσομαι in v.18 Paul starts a new thought[2]. Then, having said that he rejoices in the progress of the gospel in v.18a (... καὶ ἐν τούτῳ χαίρω), now in v.18b he looks to the future: 'But I will rejoice also (in the future). For I know that ...'. If so, the τοῦτο in v.19 may be different from the τοῦτο in v.18. Secondly, since τοῦτο in v.19 appears as part of the quotation from Job 13.16 it is more probable that it refers to Paul's present situation of suffering than to the progress of the gospel. Just as Job was certain of his eventual vindication, so Paul is confident that his present situation will turn out to his salvation. This confidence is the ground of the statement: ἀλλὰ καὶ χαρήσομαι. Thirdly, it is much more natural to think that the phrase διὰ τῆς ὑμῶν δεήσεως καὶ ἐπιχορηγίας τοῦ πνεύματος is directly connected with Paul's salvation than to contemplate an indirect link between them as though Paul were saying that the progress of the gospel, fostered through the Philippians' prayers and the help of the Spirit, would lead to his Salvation[3]. Fourthly, if Paul thought that his salvation was dependent upon the progress of the gospel, why does he desire to be with Christ through death now (v.23) before his task of proclaiming the gospel to the Gentiles has been completed (cf. Rom 15.24)? For these reasons it is probably incorrect to take Phil 1.19 as implying that Paul's own salvation is bound up with the progress of the gospel.

1Cor 9.27 cannot be used for Satkes's view, either. For there Paul does *not* say: 'I pommel my body and subdue it, so that I may preach the gospel to others effectively and thus come to salvation myself'. On the contrary, he separates his salvation from his preaching to others! It is also unwarranted to draw such a far-reaching conclusion from Phil 2.15f. and 1Th 2.19f., as Satake does, namely that Paul views his converts as the ground of his own salvation at the judgement seat of Christ. For, if Paul says that the Philippian and the Thessalonian Christians are his ground of boasting, hope and joy before Christ at his parousia, he can say the reverse to the Corinthian Christians: '... we are your ground of boasting as you are ours in the day of our Lord Jesus' (2Cor 1.14; cf. Phil 1.26). Here surely Paul does not mean that the salvation of the Corinthians is dependent upon his salvation!

4) Satake's claim that Paul never speaks of the grace of God given to him without reference to his apostleship is not correct. It is possible that Gal 2.19–21 is based upon Paul's own Damascus experience[4]. Even if the ἐγώ is merely stylistic for every

---

[1]E.g., Lightfoot, *Phil.*, p.91; Lohmeyer, *Phil.*, p.51; W.Michaelis, *Der Brief des Paulus an die Philipper* (1935), p.22; K.Barth, *The Epistle to the Philippians* (1962), p.33; Gnilka, *Phil.*, p.66.

[2]So RSV; NEB; Michealis, *Phil.*, p.22; Barth, *Phil.*, p.33; Gnilka, *Phil.*, p.65.

[3]*Contra* Satake, 'Apostolat', p.104 (n.1).

[4]So, e.g., Burton, *Gal.*, pp.132f.; Schnackenburg, *Baptism in the Thought of St.*

true Christian, for that very reason it represents Paul also. Here, arguing against the doctrine of justification by works of the law, Paul says that he died to the law with Christ through the law and that now he lives by faith in the Son of God who loved him and gave up his life for him. This self-offer of Christ for him is the χάρις. That grace, through which he like every other Christian is justified, Paul says, he does not nullify. In Rom 5.2 he says that through Jesus Christ 'we have obtained access to this grace in which we stand . . . '. So Paul like all other Christians has obtained (perf. ἐσχήκαμεν!)   access to grace and is standing in it now. This is another way of saying that 'we', all believers, therefore including Paul himself, were justified (aorist δικαιωθέντες!) by faith and as a result 'we' have peace with God now through our Lord Jesus Christ (Rom 5.1). Similarly Paul uses the word καλεῖν for God's saving call of all Christians in which he is included: e.g., Rom 9.24; 1Th 4.7.

Thus Satake's argument that Paul sees his own salvation as dependent upon his apostolic ministry is not so persuasive as it appears at first sight. Paul's constant use of χάρις for his apostolic call may merely underline his perception that as he was a persecutor of the Church and an enemy of God his apostolic call was the sheer grace of God − something which χάρισμα could not quite convey. Furthermore, the reason why he speaks of his own salvation only a few times by using καλεῖν and χάρις and then only in general statements affecting all Christians, while using the two words more frequently and directly in connection with his apostleship, may well be that he in fact has very few occasions in his letters to speak specifically about his own salvation. When he uses καλεῖν or χάρις in connection with his apostleship, we can recognize most of the time that he wants to establish the authenticity and authority of his apostleship. This is necessary because they are often challenged and he needs to impart teaching authoritatively. But he seldom has reason to speak about his own salvation, as it is taken for granted and not challenged. It is no accident that he narrates the Damascus event usually in connection with his apostleship and gospel rather than in connection with his own salvation. But this does not mean that he does not see it also as the moment of his personal salvation, i.e., of God's call for him to receive his saving grace. Otherwise he would hardly speak as he does in Gal 2.19−

Paul (1964), p.63; Jeremias, *Schlüssel*, p.22; Bruce, 'The law of Moses', p.262. First of all, the fact that the passage falls at the concluding climax of Paul's autobiographical argument for the authenticity of the gospel he received on the Damascus road, speaks for the view. The emphatic ἐγώ seems to be, in any case, more than just stylistic. The fact that Paul was driven by the law to persecute the Church and, having received God's judgement and forgiveness on the Damascus road, did away with the claims of the law, makes the sentence easily understandable: ἐγὼ γὰρ διὰ νόμου νόμῳ ἀπέθανον ἵνα θεῷ ζήσω. To be sure, the following sentence, Χριστῷ συνεσταύρωμαι provides the basis for the statement, so that Paul is here primarily thinking of his participation by faith and in baptism in Christ's crucifixion under the curse of the law which has brought about the redemption from the law (Gal 3.12f.; Rom 7.4). But an allusion to his rebellion against God out of zeal for the law may well be included as well. In the foregoing two chapters we have seen that the title   'Son of God' is particularly closely linked with Paul's Damascus experience. If in Phil 3.8 he calls Christ who appeared to him on the Damascus road very personally 'my Lord', here he speaks equally personally of Christ's love 'for me'. 'The grace of God' also may well have a double reference to God's grace in sending and giving up his Son 'for me' and to his salvation and call of Paul on the Damascus road.

21; Rom 5.2; 9.24; 1Th 4.7. Furthermore, Phil 3.4–14 makes it clear that he sees the Damascus event also as the event in which he came to know Christ, surrendered his law-righteousness and received God's righteousness, although this salvation is yet to be consummated at the end. See further 2Cor 4.6.[1]

Nevertheless, two verses, namely 1Cor 9.16, 23, and possibly also Rom 1.14, remain striking with the implication that Paul's own salvation is bound up with his apostolic ministry. Phil 2.16 also deserves another look. The blameless Philippian Christians will be Paul's ground of boasting before the judgement seat of Christ, as they are the proof that he did not run or labour in vain. The idea behind this language is expounded in 1Cor 3.10–15; 4.1–5: each servant of God must give an account of his commission at the last judgement. If he is found to have been faithful to his commission, he will receive a reward from God, but, if he is not, he will lose his reward although he himself will be saved. Paul would like to present the Philippian and Thessalonian Christians as part of the account of his stewardship before the Judge. So they are his ground of boasting and his hope, joy and crown before Christ (Phil 2.16; 4.1; 1Th 2.19; also 2Cor 1.14). 1Cor 3.15 precludes Satake's inference from this idea that Paul's salvation is dependent upon the salvation of his converts or his apostolic ministry. However, is there a grain of truth in A.v. Harnack's view that Paul's voluntary abstention from getting his living by the gospel (1Cor 9.15ff.), his extraordinary toil, his concern for reward at the last judgement, and his fear that he might labour in vain, i.e., fail in his commission, reflect his consciousness that as a former persecutor of the Church he must make an extraordinary achievement[2]? Do the passages discussed in this paragraph betray Paul's consciousness that as a former persecutor of the Church he must compensate for the sin with his apostolic toil[3]? If Paul entertained such an idea, it may not only explain his extraordinary toil, his fear that he might labour in vain, and his view of his converts as his καύχησις at the last judgement, but also go a long way towards explaining his expressions in Rom 1.14; 1Cor 9.16, 23[4]. Paul's salvation itself is not in question. It is not by his works of the law nor by his apostolic ministry. It is by God's grace alone. Nevertheless, he would like to be saved at the last judgement not simply ὡς διὰ πυρός, not losing the reward of God's commendation (1Cor 3.15; 4.5)[5]. For this it is imperative (ἀνάγκη) for the former persecutor that he preach the gospel to the Gentiles for whose sake he has been called. At any rate, H. Conzelmann is correct in saying on 1Cor 9.23 '. . . the statement must not be separated from the totality of his (sc. Paul's) understanding of salvation and the saving-event,

---

[1] For an exegesis of this verse *supra* pp.5–11.

[2] A.v.Harnack, 'κόπος (κοπιᾶν, οἱ κοπιῶντες) im frühchristlichen Sprachgebrauch', *ZNW* 27(1928), p.5. On the passages that we are discussing, see, besides commentaries, Pfitzner, *Agon*, pp.82–109.

[3] In a seminar in the Summer Semester 1975 M.Hengel suggested such a 'Wiedergutmachungs' hypothesis. Before that, however, I had drawn his attention to the possibility of taking ὀφειλέτης in Rom 1.14 in favour of such a hypothesis.

[4] The difficult idea in Col 1.24 may also belong to this context.

[5] We cannot enter into a discussion of the difficult passage in 1Cor 3.10–15. See commentaries.

election and call. The appeal to strive for salvation which here he directs to himself and in the next verse to his readers presupposes the election *sola gratia*. Cf. Phil 2.12ff.; 3.12ff.'[1].

This long excursus has made it clear how firmly the concept of grace is rooted in Paul's Damascus experience. From his own experience of the grace of God in his justification and apostolic call, Paul came to see that justification is solely by God's grace. J. Jeremias and K. Haacker go so far as to think that the Pauline use of the word χάρις, having no real *Vorgeschichte*, is his own innovation out of his Damascus experience[2]. God's grace[3] means not just his favour by which he justifies the unmeriting sinner (Gal 1.6), but it is more fundamentally God's saving act in the vicarious death of Christ for us (Rom 3.24ff.; Gal 2.20f.; 2Cor 6.1). We are justified by this grace (Rom 3.24; 5.16ff.). When we respond to the proclamation of the gospel by faith, we appropriate this grace and are justified by it. So, although grace is basically God's saving work in Christ's death, Paul can speak of grace as a free gift (δωρεά : Rom 3.24; 5.15ff.), and of our standing in grace (Rom 5.2), being under grace (Rom 6.14f.) and even falling away from grace (Gal 5.4). Grace is the same as the love of God (Rom 5.5ff.) or of Christ (Gal 2.20f.) and the mercy of God (Rom 11.32; 1Cor 7.25; 2Cor 4.1). In Rom 5.5−11, which is a close parallel to Rom 3.21−26, Paul says that while we were yet sinners, helpless to save ourselves, Christ died for us, the ungodly, at God's appointed time. Dying vicariously for the sake of[4] *the ungodly* − this is something unheard of. For scarcely will anyone die even for a righteous man, although some might perhaps dare to die for their benefactor[5]. This unique event is the proof of God's love: 'God demonstrates his love for us by the fact that Christ died for us while we were still sinners' (v.8). This death of Christ as the atoning sacrifice is the ground on which or the means by which we are justified (v.9). So justification is by grace alone. This principle of justification *sola gratia* is the antithesis of the attempt to obtain justification by the law. In Rom 3.21−24 the righteousness of God χωρὶς νόμου is

---

[1]Conzelmann, *1.Kor.*, p.191. See also Käsemann, "amor fati", p.237 on 1Cor 9.16 for the question: 'Wie kann der vom Evangelium geradezu schicksalhaft zum Dienst gezwungene zugleich der Liebende sein und bleiben?'

[2]Jeremias, *Schlüssel*, pp.22f.; Haacker, 'Berufung', p.12. Cf. also Stuhlmacher, "Ende", pp.30f.

[3]Cf. Bultmann, *Theology* i, pp.288−292.

[4]ὑπέρ in this passage means both 'for the advantage of' and 'vicariously' − so Käsemann, *Römer*, p.128.

[5]See Cranfield, *Romans*, pp.264f. for this rendering of τοῦ ἀγαθοῦ in Rom 5.7.

positively defined not only as the righteousness of God $\delta\iota\grave{\alpha}$ $\pi\iota\sigma\tau\epsilon\omega\varsigma$ but also as that by the grace of God. In Gal 2.21 Paul says that to attempt to obtain righteousness through the law is to nullify the grace of God. It is in fact to fall away from grace (Gal 5.4). Believers are not under the law but under grace (Rom 6.14f.; cf. further Rom 4.4; 11.5f.).

That no man is justified by works of the law but only by God's grace in Christ means that justification is through faith. This is the third distinctive feature of Paul's doctrine of justification. This is made crystal clear in Rom 3.21–31. The righteousness of God that has been revealed $\chi\omega\rho\grave{\iota}\varsigma$ $\nu\acute{o}\mu\omega\upsilon$ is the righteousness of God that is to be appropriated $\delta\iota\grave{\alpha}$ $\pi\iota\sigma\tau\epsilon\omega\varsigma$. That the righteousness of God is appropriated through faith is emphasized again and again in the passage. It is him who has faith in Jesus that God justifies (v.26). Since man is justified through faith apart from works of the law, all men, not just Jews but also Gentiles, are justified, and they are all justified by faith alone (vs. 22, 28ff.). In fact, Paul declares this doctrine of justification *sola fide* as the content of the gospel in Rom 1.16f., where he defines the gospel in thesis form in order to expound it throughout the rest of the letter: the gospel is God's saving power for every one who has faith, for the Jew first and also for the Greek. For in it as it is proclaimed God's righteousness is being revealed, offering itself to men so that they may appropriate it by faith alone. Then Paul cites Hab 2.4 in order to prove that justification is through faith. Having reaffirmed in Rom 3.21–31 that justification is solely by God's grace and solely through man's faith apart from works of the law, similarly in Rom 4 he goes on to prove this thesis Scripturally by means of an extensive exegesis of Gen 15.6, where Abraham's faith is said to have been reckoned to him for righteousness. Having proved this thesis, Paul joyously declares in Rom 5.1: 'Having been justified then on the basis of faith, we have peace with God through our Lord Jesus Christ . . .'.

In Gal. also we have similar declarations and Scriptural demonstrations. So, in Gal 2.15f. Paul reports his declaration in front of Cephas, Barnabas and other Jewish Christians in Antioch who wavered on the principle of justification *sola fide*: 'We ourselves, who are Jews by birth and not Gentile sinners, yet knowing that a man is not justified by works of the law but through faith in Christ Jesus, believed in Christ Jesus, in order to be justified by faith in Christ and not by works of the law, because by works of the law no flesh will be justified'. Then in Gal 3–4 he proceeds to argue for the thesis of justification *sola fide* Scripturally and *heilsgeschichtlich*.

In Phil 3.4–14 he argues for the doctrine autobiographically. Warning the Philippian Christians of the danger of infiltration by Judaizers, Paul contrasts the $\delta\iota\kappa\alpha\iota\sigma\sigma\acute{\upsilon}\nu\eta$ $\mathring{\eta}$ $\grave{\epsilon}\kappa$ $\nu\acute{o}\mu\omega\upsilon$ and the $\delta\iota\kappa\alpha\iota\sigma\sigma\acute{\upsilon}\nu\eta$ $\mathring{\eta}$ $\delta\iota\grave{\alpha}$ $\pi\iota\sigma\tau\epsilon\omega\varsigma$ $X\rho\iota\sigma\tau\omicron\mathring{\upsilon}$. The former is what the Judaizers are trying to establish for themselves. He tells the Philippians that it was also what he had tried to establish for himself and in fact succeeded in establishing through his Pharisaic observation of the law and zealous persecution of the Church but that when he met the risen Christ on the Damascus road he decided to count it as but loss. He considers his own blameless righteousness based on the law along with all other gains which he inherited or achieved, as but loss because knowing Christ Jesus, who is the δικαιοσύνη ἀπὸ θεοῦ (1Cor 1.30), far surpasses it. Indeed, he counts it as refuse in order that he may gain Christ and be found in him. His decision on the Damascus road, which still abides[1], was, in other words, to throw away like refuse his own righteousness that comes from or is based on the law and to receive the righteousness that is through faith in Christ, namely the righteousness which God gives on the basis of faith. For only the latter can secure Paul's being found in Christ now and at the last judgement[2]. Thus the Philippian passage illuminates the experiential basis of his doctrine of justification[3] and of his contrast between the righteousness on the basis of the law and the righteousness on the basis of faith.

In the light of his own conversion experience he sees the tragedy of Israel's unbelief in Rom 9.30–10.4[4]. Just as he had before the Damascus Christophany, Israel have a zeal for God and seek to establish their own righteousness, the righteousness based on the law, by their works of the law. Stupendous efforts for this aim notwithstanding, they have failed to keep the law perfectly and obtain righteousness, whereas the Gentiles who did not pursue righteousness have attained it. This paradox has taken place because, having a zeal for God which is unenlightened and being mistaken regarding the righteousness which God wrought in Christ and now grants as a gift on the basis óf faith, they do not submit to this righteousness of God, seeking instead to establish their own based on the law. They do not know that Christ has brought an end to the law, so that every one who has faith may be justified, whereas Paul learned this on the Damascus road. Now the Gentiles

---

[1]Note the intermingling of tenses in this passage: Paul's recognition that in the face of the surpassing worth of knowing Christ his own righteousness, namely the law-righteousness, and all the other gains in Judaism were but loss and refuse and his decision thereupon to count them as such in order to gain Christ and be found in him, took place once on the Damascus road (perf. ἥγημαι in v.7; aor. ἐʒημιώθην· in v.8). But this value-judgement and resolution are still what Paul holds in the present (pres. ἡγοῦμαι in v.8). He holds on to them to the End with a view to the consummation of that knowing and gaining Christ and being found in him which began on the Damascus road (ἵνα-clause in vs.8ff.).

[2]On the connection of v.9b: μὴ ἔχων ἐμὴν δικαιοσύνην . . . with the foregoing, cf. Michael, *The Epistle of Paul to the Philippians* (1939), p.149; Barth, *Phil.*, pp.99f.

[3]Cf. Blank, *Paulus*, pp.211–237; Stuhlmacher, "Ende", pp.31f.

[4]*Supra* pp.3f. for a parallelism between Phil 3.4ff. and Rom 10.2–4.

have attained righteousness through faith, but Israel have stumbled over the scandal of the crucified Christ in whom God wrought his righteousness for every one who has faith. In vs.5–13 Paul goes on to contrast the impossible, therefore futile attempt to obtain the righteousness based on the law – the law-righteousness – by keeping the law perfectly, which he has elsewhere already shown to lead only to a curse (Gal 3.10–12), with the easy way of obtaining the righteousness based on faith – the faith-righteousness.

This contrast leads Paul to expound in Rom 10.6–13 the way of obtaining the faith-righteousness. To obtain the faith-righteousness, we do not have to ascend into heaven or descend into the abyss in order to bring Christ, the embodiment of God's righteousness[1], down or up. For the word of faith, namely the gospel, in which the risen and exalted Christ, the embodiment of God's righteousness, is manifested, is near us as it is proclaimed by Paul and other preachers. We need only to respond to the preached word by faith. If we believe with our heart that God raised Christ from the dead and confess with our lips Jesus as Lord, we shall be justified and saved. The present passage makes it clear that faith is essentially a response to the preached word. It is acceptance of the message of salvation. Faith comes from hearing the word of Christ preached (Rom 10.14–17). So the object of faith, the message of salvation, is sometimes summarized in a ὅτι-clause or its equivalent as in Rom 10.9; 1Th 4.14; also 1Cor 15.3–5(2, 11). It is God's saving work in Christ, namely Christ's death and resurrection. The ὅτι-clause expressing the content of faith is often abbreviated to a phrase πιστεύειν εἰς Χριστὸν Ἰησοῦν (Gal 2.16b; also Rom 10.14; Phil 1.29; Col 2.5) or to an objective genitive phrase πίστις Χριστοῦ Ἰησοῦ (Gal 2.16, 20; 3.22; Rom 3.22, 26; Eph 3.12; Phil 3.9). So the saving faith is basically faith in Christ as the one in whom God has wrought salvation for us. This acceptance of the message of salvation means that the believer holds the message to be true and decides to accept what it demands as well as what it offers. It is a surrender of one's attempt to achieve one's own salvation and submission to God's provision of salvation in Christ (Rom 10.3, 16; 11.30–32). It establishes a personal relationship between Christ and the believer which is expressed in his public confession of Jesus as Lord (Rom 10.9f.) and accordingly in his obedience to the Lord (Rom 1.8; 15.18; 2Cor 9.13). We can scarcely go on here discussing these and other elements like trust, hope. fear, knowledge, etc. in the structure of the Pauline conception of faith[2]. We may say in summary,

---

[1] For the argument that in this passage Christ, as the one who superseded the Torah, is thought of as the true divine Wisdom and therefore as the true embodiment of the divine righteousness, *supra* pp.129ff.

[2] See Bultmann, πιστεύω, *TDNT* vi, pp.203–222; *Theology* i, pp.314–324; Kuss,

however, that when Paul speaks of 'faith' by which we are justified he means essentially acceptance of the gospel which offers God's salvation in Christ and presents Christ as our Lord demanding our obedience to him, and that this acceptance of the gospel includes in itself all the elements mentioned above.

If we are justified through faith and through faith alone, is faith then the condition of our justification? This is a further question to be clarified here. When Paul says that we appropriate God's righteousness or are justified διά πίστεως or ἐκ πίστεως (e.g., Rom 1.17; 3.22ff.; 5.1; Gal 2.16; Phil 3.9), it is clear that faith is conceived of as the means through which we appropriate God's righteousness which God grants us as a gift of his grace. Insofar as faith is the absolutely necessary means of justification, it is also the condition of justification. This sense of condition seems to appear especially clearly when Paul contrasts justification ἐκ πίστεως with justification ἐξ ἔργων νόμου (e.g., Rom 3.27ff.; Gal 2.16). For ἐκ πίστεως is clearly a parallel formulation to ἐξ ἔργων νόμου, which expresses the Jewish idea of works of the law as the condition for justification. At the same time, however, precisely this contrast rules out an understanding of faith as a work which earns merit that obliges God to justify the believer. Faith is the condition of justification not because it is a meritorious work but because it is the only means whereby man can receive God's free gift of righteousness[1].

Now it is to be observed that sometimes in connection with justification Paul refers to baptismal ideas as well as to faith. The clearest example is 1Cor 6.11, which some scholars think reflects the pre-Pauline doctrine of justification: 'But you were washed, you were sanctified, you were justified, in the name of the Lord Jesus Christ in the Spirit of our God'. In Gal 3.23–25 Paul says: Before faith came along with Christ we were confined under the law, so that the law was only our custodian until Christ came. This was so that we might be justified on the basis of faith and not on the basis of works of the law. But now that faith has come, we are no longer under the custodian: 'For you are all sons of God, through faith, in Christ Jesus'. So the divine sonship, which refers to the same reality of the right relationship with God as that defined by justification, was mediated to us through faith. Through faith we obtained our divine sonship ἐν Χριστῷ Ἰησοῦ, who is

---

Römer, pp.131–154; Käsemann, *Römer*, pp.100–103.

[1]Cf. Kertelge, *"Rechtfertigung"*, pp.182ff.; Käsemann, *Römer*, p.101. The latter puts the matter well: 'Wenn man überhaupt so formulieren will, ist für ihn (sc. Paul) der Glaube nicht eine, sondern die Bedingung des Heils schlechthin. Das muß so sein, weil das Heil im Evangelium zu uns kommt und darin ergriffen werden muß, nur darin ergriffen werden kann. Sachlich wird das zur "Bedingung" eben nur in seiner Ausschließlichkeit, also im Gegesatz zu anderen angebotenen oder geforderten Heilsmöglichkeiten'.

Abraham's seed and the bearer of the divine promise to Abraham (3.8, 14, 16). In v.27 Paul explains how we came to be ἐν Χριστῷ Ἰησοῦ, i.e., incorporated in Christ: 'For as many of you as were baptised εἰς Χριστόν, have put on Christ'. Here then both faith and baptism are mentioned as the media for the appropriation of the divine sonship or justification (compare also Gal 3.7 with 3.29).

In Rom 6.1–11, countering the wrong inference from the doctrine of justification *sola gratia*, Paul refers to baptism in which the believer shared the death and resurrection of Christ. Behind this conception of baptism as the event in which we participate in the death and resurrection of Christ, there stand the idea of Christ as the Last Adam and the vicarious and representative conception of Christ's death[1]. The latter is clearly indicated in 2Cor 5.14: ' . . . One died for all; therefore all died'. The sinless Christ bore our sin and curse and died as our substitute and representative, so that in his death on the cross we all died. Christ as the Last Adam is the *Stammvater* of the new humanity in whom the new humanity is incorporated. So, in his death and resurrection the new humanity died and rose again. Our death and resurrection in Christ's substitutionary and representative death and resurrection is, however, only a matter of God's decision to see us as having died and risen in Christ's death and resurrection until through baptism we are united with Christ and accept the divine decision as it really and personally concerns us[2]. In baptism we die and rise with Christ, not in the sense that Christ again dies and rises with us in our baptism, but chiefly in the following two senses. The first sense is that we are drawn into the death and resurrection of Christ. To put it in the words of R. Schnackenburg:

> Because Christ died and rose as Representative and Substitute of redeemed mankind, we also are 'buried with Him and raised with Him' in baptism (Col ii.12). So soon as we establish through faith and baptism the union with Him as our spiritual founder of the (new) race, we participate in that which happened to Him: his death becomes our death, his resurrection becomes our resurrection[3].

The second sense is that corresponding to the first sense we actually suffer in baptism a death and resurrection like Christ's, so that in our lives 'an end is put to (our) old God-estranged life and a new one begins in Christ and His

---

[1] So Schnackenburg, *Baptism*, pp.112–121; G.R.Beasley-Murray, *Baptism in the NT* (1962), pp.135–138; Grundmann, 'Paulus', p.272; Kertelge, "*Rechtfertigung*", pp. 234f.; cf. also Käsemann, *Römer*, pp.154, 156; Cranfield, *Romans*, p.299.

[2] Cf. Cranfield, *Romans*, p.299.

[3] Schnackenburg, *Baptism*, p.115.

Kingdom and His Spirit[1]. Our death with Christ in baptism means our death to sin (Rom 6.2) because Christ died to sin once for all (v.10). In baptism 'our "old man" was crucified with Christ, so that we might no longer be enslaved to sin. For he who died is freed (δεδικαίωται) from sin' (vs.6f.). This dying to sin with Christ in baptism had the purpose that 'as Christ was raised from the dead through the glory of the Father so we also might walk in newness of life' (v.4)[2]. The death Christ, our *Stammvater* and representative, died, he died to sin once for all, but the life he lives, he lives to God. So we must consider ourselves dead to sin and alive to God in Christ Jesus, that is, in our *Stammvater* and representative with whom we are united in baptism (vs.10f.)[3]. With this Paul moves from the indicative of the *Heilsgeschehen* to the imperative of ethics which is grounded upon the indicative: 'Let not sin therefore reign in your mortal bodies . . . ' (vs.12f.).

Similar thoughts to those in Rom 6.1–11 are found in Gal 2.19f. Here again Paul alludes to the baptismal ideas in the context of his argument for the doctrine of *sola fide*. As in Rom 6.6, so here also he speaks of his having been crucified with Christ, and as in Rom 6.3, 10f., he speaks here of his having died to the law. Having been crucified with Christ and having died to the law, he no longer lives; rather Christ lives in him. The old Adamitic man died with Christ in baptism, and the new life that he obtained in baptism is the life of the risen Christ, the life that Paul lives in the flesh by faith in the Son of God who loved him and gave himself for him. A similar idea of having died with Christ recurs: 'You died to the law through the body of Christ, so that you might belong to another, to him that was raised from the dead . . . ' (Rom 7.4); see further Gal 5.24; 6.14; Eph 2.5f.; Col 2.12ff., etc.[4] In the last reference cited both baptism and faith are mentioned in connection with our dying and rising with Christ.

---

[1]Beasley-Murray, *Baptism*, p.132. He mentions one more sense: Baptism 'demands a corresponding "crucifixion" of the flesh and a new life in the power of the Spirit that accords with the grace received, which "dying" and "rising" begins in the baptismal event'. Cf. also Cranfield, *Romans*, pp.299f.

[2]Beasley-Murray, *Baptism*, pp.138f., correctly observes that although in Rom 6.5, 8 our resurrection with Christ is spoken of as a future eschatological event while our death with Christ as a past event in baptism the present verse (v.4) and vs.10f. presuppose our participation in Christ's resurrection as well as in his death in baptism (cf. Col 2.12). So also Kuss, *Römer*, p.299. The future tense in vs.5 and 8 warns, however, against an enthusiastic evaluation of baptism and indicates that what has been proleptically realized in baptism is yet to be fully realized at the resurrection.

[3]Cf. Cranfield, *Romans*, pp.315f.

[4]On these and other passages with the idea of dying and rising with Christ, cf. the monograph by R.C.Tannehill, *Dying and Rising with Christ*.

Although in the above passages Paul does not say so clearly that we are justified in baptism as he says elsewhere that we are justified through faith, there he indicates clearly enough that baptism is also related to justification. The question is then how to define precisely the relationship between them and that between faith and baptism. Is A. Schweitzer correct in insisting that the doctrine of justification by faith is only a fragment which for polemical purposes Paul broke off and developed apart from the central doctrine, the doctrine of redemption through dying and rising with Christ or being in Christ[1]? He can scarcely be correct if there is a grain of truth in our attempt to derive Paul's doctrine of justification by faith from his Damascus experience.

According to F. Hahn[2], the pre-Pauline Christianity held a doctrine of justification through baptism and Paul resorts to it in Rom 3.24–26a; 4.25; 6.7; 1Cor 1.30b; 6.11, which are all, Hahn believes, pre-Pauline formulations of the doctrine of justification through baptism. Paul takes over this doctrine and corrects it. Whereas the pre-Pauline tradition connects justification with the single event of baptism and therefore with the single event of becoming a believer, so that after that event faith is no longer important,   Paul understands God's justifying activity as a continuous reality for the existence of the believer, so that only with the never ceasing faith, that is, with the continually renewed response of trust to the proclaimed word, does the believer participate in God's justification[3]. According to Hahn, 'für Paulus ist irgend-ein Rückbezug auf die Bekehrung hinsichtlich Rechtfertigung und Taufe nicht mehr konstitutiv. So bewußt er die Rechtfertigungsbotschaft den Taufaussagen voranstellt, es geht ihm dabei nicht um das Gläubigwerden oder einen bestimmten Glaubensakt als Voraussetzung für die Taufe. Die Voranstellung hat vielmehr den Sinn, daß christliche Existenz als solche grundsätzlich nur mit πιστεύειν sachgerecht beschrieben werden kann'[4]. So, according to Hahn, whereas baptism is spoken of in the aorist, Paul speaks of πιστεύειν in the present[5]. But this view of Hahn's is scarcely plausible. We name only three objections to it. Firstly, if Paul has such a fundamental disagreement with the tradition, why does he cite it so often as Hahn alleges? If Hahn is right in his conclusion, he can hardly speak at the same time of Paul's 'taking account of' the given connection between baptism and justification and 'joining' his doctrine of justification to it[6]. Secondly, what does Hahn make of the aorist and perfect statements in Rom 5.1f.: δικαιωθέντες οὖν ἐκ πίστεως εἰρήνην ἔχομεν πρὸς τὸν θεὸν διὰ τοῦ κυρίου ἡμῶν Ἰησοῦ Χριστοῦ, δι' οὗ καὶ τὴν προσαγωγὴν ἐσχήκαμεν (τῇ πίστει) εἰς τὴν χάριν ταύτην ἐν ᾗ ἐστήκαμεν ...

---

[1] Schweitzer, *Mysticism*, pp.219–226.

[2] F.Hahn, 'Taufe und Rechtfertigung', *Rechtfertigung*, Käsemann FS, pp.95–124.

[3] *Ibid.*, p.117.

[4] *Ibid.*, p.120.

[5] *Ibid.*, p.121.

[6] *Ibid.*, p.117. His explanation as to how Paul takes the tradition into account in pp.122ff. is hardly plausible.

and again in v.9? What about the aorist statements in Gal 2.16ff.; Rom 9.30? Are they all only 'a few exceptions conditioned by their respective context'[1]? We have already seen that Paul speaks of the justifictation of the believer as having already occurred although he at the same time looks forward to its consummation at the last judgement[2]. The reason why in many places Paul uses the present tense of δικαιοῦν and πιστεύειν is because in those places he enunciates the principle of justification through faith. Thirdly, it is revealing that Hahn passes over without discussing Rom 10.9f. where many think[3] Paul is speaking of the confession of faith at baptism for justification and salvation. Even if the verses reflect a pre-Pauline formulation, its importance for Paul's view of the connection between justification and faith (and baptism) can hardly be exaggerated. Thus, our second and third observations make it clear that Paul definitely connects justification with the faith with which a man comes to believe in Christ, i.e., with his *Gläubigwerden* and therefore with his conversion and baptism. Certainly, for Paul the believer needs to have faith constantly in order to continue to participate in justification, that is, to remain in the right relationship with God, which will be consummated at the last judgement. Both aspects of justification – as a single event that takes place through the initial act of faith at conversion and as the right relationship with God in which the believer stands through his continued faith – seem to be intertwined in Phil 3.2–14, where Paul speaks of his Damascus experience, his present resolution and his hope for the future, the latter two being grounded upon the first.

In fact, it is generally agreed that in Paul faith and baptism belong together with regard to justification and salvation, each referring to the other[4]. There is also a general agreement on the definition of this belonging together on the level of missionary practice: baptism is a public demonstration of faith, for in it the believer publicly confesses Jesus Christ as the Lord (Rom 10.9f.) and thus enters into the sphere under the lordship of Christ and becomes incorporated into the Body of Christ, the Church[5]. So, genuine faith leads to baptism and at baptism becoming a Christian is consummated. By the same token, baptism without faith is unthinkable. So, faith is chronologically prior to baptism; it is publicly confessed in baptism; and it is always required even after the single act of public demonstration in baptism for the believer to stand continually in the right relationship with God. Therefore baptism can be regarded as a moment of faith[6].

---

[1]*Ibid.*, p.121.

[2]*Supra* pp.286f.

[3]E.g., Dodd, *Romans*, p.178; Michel, *Römer*, pp.258f.; Käsemann, *Römer*, p.279; also Bultmann, *Theology* i, p.312.

[4]E.g., Schnackenburg, *Baptism*, pp.121–127; Beasley-Murray, *Baptism*, pp.266–275; E.Lohse, 'Taufe und Rechtfertigung bei Paulus', *Die Einheit des NT*, esp. pp.240–244; Kertelge, *"Rechtfertigung"*, pp.228–249, and the authors cited by Kertelge on p.229.

[5]As in the immediately preceding note.

[6]So Kertelge, *"Rechtfertigung"*, p.230, citing W.Mundle, *Der Glaubensbegriff bei*

Opinions differ, however, as to a deeper understanding of the relationship between faith and baptism beyond the level of missionary practice. Some think it impossible to ascertain a complete synthesis or systematic connection between Paul's statements about faith and those about baptism with regard to justification[1]. However, is it enough to say that Paul thinks of 'salvation mediated' not one-sidedly through word and faith, but also through baptism'[2]? It seems rather significant that in Rom 1.16–5.21, where Paul systematically unfolds his doctrine of justification, baptism is not referred to and it 'first emerges in the description of the outworking and obligations of justification by faith'[3], or, as we would like to put it, in the exposition of the implications of justification *by faith*. Corresponding to this fact, he never says that we are justified or saved διά (or ἐκ) βαπτίσματος whereas he constantly says that we are justified διά (or ἐκ) πίστεως. So, apparently he does not think of baptism as a means of justification *parallel* to faith. K. Kertelge puts the matter well:

> Since in Paul faith is predominantly related to the event of justification, and as man's organ of acceptance corresponding to the event of justification at that, the question could be raised whether baptism also is related to justification in the same sense as faith. This question is to be denied, in so far as Paul nowhere grounds the event of justification directly in baptism. It is, however, to be affirmed, in so far as Paul knows no faith without baptism and the sacramentally grounded fellowship with Christ is nothing else than that which is presupposed for justification through faith. The sacramental grounding of fellowship with Christ in baptism which is presupposed by the event of justification must not, however, be designated . . . simply as 'sacramentally making righteous'[4].

Does faith then as conceived by Paul include in itself the idea of dying and rising with Christ which is publicly dramatized in baptism?[5] Does faith already implicitly unite us with Christ in his substitutionary and representative death and baptism demonstrate it explicitly? That this is the case may be confirmed from an analysis of the essential character of faith as the acceptance of the message of salvation, namely the kerygma that Jesus Christ died

---

Paulus (1932), p.124.

[1] Lohse, 'Taufe', p.241; Kertelge, *"Rechtfertigung"*, p.247.

[2] Kertege, *"Rechtfertigung"*, p.247. Similarly also Schnackenburg, *Baptism*, pp.121–127 under the heading: 'Baptism as a means along with faith of appropriating salvation'.

[3] Schnackenburg, *Baptism*, p.125.

[4] Kertelge, *"Rechtfertigung"*, p.247.

[5] So Hill, *Greek Words*, p.144. But his conclusion from this that the doctrine of justification by faith is secondary to that of 'union with Christ' is to be rejected. Cf. V.Taylor, *Atonement*, pp.92–97.

'for us' — as our substitute and representative. The substitutionary character of Christ's death affirms that the sinless Christ bore the penalty of our sins, the death we incurred, in our place: so, Christ died our death. The representative character of Christ's death affirms that he represented us in his death, so that in God's decision our death was included in his death: 'One has died for all; therefore all have died' (2Cor 5.14). These two characters of Christ's death may be combined in the concept of inclusive substitution[1]: Christ's death included ours in itself. Christ's death is substitutionary because the sinless Christ died in our place; but it is inclusive because it included our death in itself by being a representative death for us. So, we can say that in God's decision all died in Christ and with Christ. This is God's objective saving-event for us. Faith is the acceptance of this message, that Jesus Christ died 'for us' — as our substitute and representative, that is, that our death was substituted for by and included in Christ's death. Thus, being the acceptance of this message, faith identifies or unites us with Christ, our substitute and representative, in his death on the cross. And, thus, faith incorporates us in Christ, the Last Adam, the *Stammvater* of the new humanity; it makes us be ἐν Χριστῷ (Gal 3.26)[2].

If faith thus brings about our union with Christ[3], we can understand better why faith is the means of justification. It is that means, not simply because it is our acceptance of the message of the death and resurrection of Christ as God's saving act for us and our surrender to God, but because precisely as the acceptance of that message it is the act in which we are united with Christ in such a way that his obedience becomes our obedience, his bearing sin, God's condemnation upon it and the curse of the law (Rom 8.3f.; 2Cor 5.21; Gal 3.13) in his substitutionary and representative death becomes our bearing them, and his freedom from those powers of destruction in his resurrection becomes our freedom (cf. Rom 4.25). Baptism demonstrates this faith with the public confession of God's saving work in Christ and of Christ's lordship and dramatizes it by immersion — a striking symbol of dying (being buried) and rising with Christ (Rom 6.4)[4]. Since faith brings about

---

[1]Cf. Pannenberg, *Jesus*, pp.263f.

[2]According to F.Neugebauer, being ἐν Χριστῷ means 'ein Bestimmtsein vom Christusgeschehen und ein Einbezogensein in dieses' ('Das paulinische "In Christus" ', *NTS* 4 (1957/58), p.132), and what ἐν Χριστῷ defines is expressed in πίστις, so that ἐκ (or διά) πίστεως and ἐν Χριστῷ are interchangeable (*In Christus*, pp.171ff.). This contention seems to support our view here. But we cannot unfold this in detail here; nor can we examine Neugebauer's sometimes problematic thesis here.

[3]This is denied by Käsemann, *Römer*, p.100.

[4]Beasley-Murray, *Baptism*, p.133; Dodd, *Romans*, p.107; Barrett, *Romans*, p.123;

our union with Christ in his death and resurrection, in Gal 2.16–21 Paul can refer to our dying with Christ in his argument for justification *sola fide*, without, however, explicitly mentioning baptism. In Rom 6.1ff., on the other hand, since his doctrine of justification *sola gratia* and *sola fide* is misconstrued as an antinomian doctrine for more sinning, he explicitly refers to baptism as it documentarily, and therefore most effectively, brings out the implication of the justifying faith which is dramatized in it — namely dying with Christ to sin and rising with him to a new life of obedience to God. In Gal 3.26ff. faith and baptism appear side by side as the media for our being ἐν Χριστῷ, and baptism appears both as the dramatization of faith and as the consummation of *Gläubigwerden*.

In short, baptism is a moment of faith not only in the chronological sense but in the more fundamental sense that it is already implicit in it. This shows how wrong it is to construct two separate lines — one 'juridical' and the other 'mystical' — in Paul's soteriology. They belong together and are in fact one[1].

Our exposition so far of Paul's doctrine of justification in the light of his Damascus experience seems to make the conclusion inescapable that the word τέλος in Rom 10.4 means termination rather than goal or fulfilment. Paul knows that Christ is the fulfilment of God's promise to Abraham (Gal 3.14; cf. also 2Cor 1.20), that the gospel was promised in advance by God through his prophets in the Holy Scriptures (Rom 1.2), and that God's righteousness eschatologically manifested in Christ is witnessed by 'the law and the prophets', namely the (OT) Scriptures (Rom 3.21). In Rom 3.31 he even speaks of establishing rather than abolishing the law through faith (cf. Gal 2.18, however). But at the same time he knows that by raising the crucified Jesus from the dead God annulled the verdict of the law against him, so that Jesus has superseded the law as the true revelation of God's will (Gal 3.13). Christ (and we with him) died to the law (Rom 7.4; Gal 2.19). In 2Cor 3.4–4.6 Paul conceives of the *'old* covenant' mediated through Moses with the Torah as its content as having been superseded by the *'new* covenant' through

---

Kuss, *Römer*, p.298; Schnackenburg, *Baptism*, p.127; J.D.G.Dunn, *Baptism in the Holy Spirit* (1970), p.141. Käsemann, *Römer*, pp.154f., has a harsh word against this interpretation of Rom 6.4. But his objection that the expression 'to be crucified with Christ' cannot be harmonized with it does not carry much weight. For it is perfectly possible that having once developed the symbolism of the baptismal immersion and rising above the water to represent dying (being buried) and rising with Christ, Paul could refer to the specific mode of our dying with Christ, i.e., being crucified with him, in order to bring out more sharply the significance of our baptismal participation in Christ's death.

[1] Cf. E.Schweizer, 'Die "Mystik" des Sterbens und Auferstehens mit Christus bei Paulus', *EvTh* 26 (1966), pp.239–257.

Christ[1]. In Gal 3.6–4.31 Paul distinguishes, indeed contrasts, God's promise
to Abraham which is fulfilled in Christ on the one hand and the law on the
other, and reckons the latter among the enslaving powers of the world from
which Christ has redeemed us. We have already abandoned the attempt to
work out this dialectic in Paul's conception of the law[2]. At the same time,
however, we have seen how emphatically he affirms that God's righteousness
has been manifested χωρὶς νόμου (Rom 3.21) – in Christ (Rom 3.24ff.) or
ἐν εὐαγγελίῳ (Rom 1.17), so that it is to be obtained χωρὶς ἔργων νόμου
(Rom 3.28), through faith[3]. Since in the context of Rom 10.4 Paul is talking
about Israel's zeal to establish their own law-righteousness in ignorance of this
divine righteousness which has been manifested in Christ χωρὶς νόμου,
the word τέλος in the verse seems to mean termination (cf. Eph 2.15; Col
2.14) rather than goal or fulfilment, and the verse as a whole seems to mean:
Christ is the end of the law in the sense that he has superseded it as the will
of God and has therefore terminated it as the means of salvation, so that
righteousness may be granted to every one who has faith[4]. Surely the contrast in the following verses between Moses the law-giver and the personified
faith-righteousness supports this view.

'Christ is the end of the law, so that righteousness may be granted to
every one who has faith' (Rom 10.4). 'To every one who has faith, to the
Jew first and also to the Greek' (Rom 1.16). Since God justifies man apart
from works of the law, by his grace in Christ and on the basis of his faith, the
Gentiles as well as the Jews can be justified through faith alone. This is what
Paul argues for whenever he comes to unfold his doctrine of justification. In
Gal 3–4, against the Judaizers' doctrine of justification which maintains that
the Gentiles must be circumcised and keep the law in order to be incor-
porated into Israel, the covenant people, and be sons of Abraham, Paul denies
Abraham's sonship to the unbelieving Jews and claims it instead for those –

---

[1]*Supra* pp.129ff. for the parallelism between 2Cor 3.4–4.6 and Rom 10.1–13.

[2]*Supra* pp.280ff.

[3]*Supra* pp.285ff.

[4]So, e.g., Sanday-Headlam, *Romans*, pp.283ff.; Schlatter, *Gerechtigkeit*, p.311;
Michel, *Römer*, p.255; Murray, *Romans*, ii, pp.49ff.; Käsemann, *Römer*, p.270; Luz,
Geschichtsverständnis, pp.139ff.; Stuhlmacher, "Ende", p.30. For the view that τέλος
here means 'goal' or 'fulfilment', see e.g., K.Barth, *A Shorter Commentary on the
Romans* (1959), p.126; Cranfield, 'The law', pp.48ff.; R.Bring, 'The Message to the
Gentiles', *StTh* 19(1965), pp.35ff. Some commentators see both meanings: e.g.,
Barrett, *Romans*, pp.197f.; Bruce, 'The Law of Moses', p.264; M.Black, *Romans*
(1973), p.138. C.F.D.Moule's view that Paul here means: 'Christ put an end to legalism'
('Obligation in the Ethic of Paul', *Christian History and Interpretation*, J.Knox FS, eds.
W.R.Farmer *et al.* (1967), p.402) is unlikely.

both Jews and Gentiles – who have faith like that of Abraham. God's promise to Abraham in Gen 12.3; 18.18: 'In you shall all the nations be blessed' had in view his plan to justify the Gentiles on the basis of faith. 'So those who are men of faith are blessed with Abraham who had faith' (3.8f.). In 3.13f. Paul says that the purpose of Christ's redeeming us[1] from the curse of the law by bearing himself the curse for us on the cross was 'that in Christ Jesus the blessing of Abraham might come upon the Gentiles that we might receive the promise of the Spirit through faith'. God promised the blessing of righteousness and life to Abraham and to his offspring. The law, which came 430 years later, neither has the power to annul God's covenant to make the promise void nor is it the means by which the promised blessing may be obtained. Rather, it had the *heilsgeschichtliche* function of keeping us under its custodianship until Christ came. In fulfilment of his promise, God sent his Son, Jesus Christ, to redeem us from the law, so that through faith, the means of justification which has now been provided in Christ, we might be adopted as sons of God. In Christ we are all sons of God through faith because faith unites us with Christ the Son of God – the union which is demonstrated in baptism: 'There is neither Jew nor Greek . . . ; for you are all one in Christ Jesus. And if you are Christ's, then you are Abraham's offspring, heirs according to promise' (3.28f.). The same thought of Abraham being the father of those who have faith – both the Jewish and the Gentile believers – but not of the unbelieving Jews, is expressed in Rom 4. Thus Paul's doctrine that justification is on the basis of God's redemption in Christ and is for those who have faith necessarily breaks down the barrier between the Jews and the Gentiles and makes the latter as well as the former the recipients of justification and the divine sonship by faith.

That this consequence of his doctrine of justification is very important to Paul is suggested by the fact that he explicitly sets it forth as part of the definition of his gospel in the 'text' of Rom (1.16). Here the *heilsgeschichtliche* priority[2] of the Jews to the Gentiles is maintained. But the really

---

[1] $\dot{\eta}\mu\hat{a}\varsigma$ in v.13 refers to all, both Jews and Gentiles, not just to the Jews, as Schlier, *Gal.*, pp.136f., clearly shows. To the reasons he brings together for the view, we would add one more: Gal 4.5f. conclusively demonstrates that in 'we/us' Paul includes 'you', namely the Galatian Christians; similarly also 3.23–27; 4.21–31. $\dot{\upsilon}\mu\epsilon\hat{\iota}\varsigma$ in 3.28d, on the other hand, includes the Jewish Christians as well as the Gentile Christians. *Contra* K.Stendahl, *Paul among Jews and Gentiles* (1977), pp.22f.

[2] Self-evidently Paul does not mean that the Jews must first be saved before the Gentiles could receive the gospel. Rather, he means that salvation is *available* first and foremost to the Jews as the chosen people of God, although he knows that actually and chronologically they as a whole will be saved after the Gentiles have been saved (Rom 11.25f.). Cf. **Munck**, *Paul*, **pp.247ff.**

striking thing is that unlike the Jewish doctrine of salvation which did not hold out much hope for the Gentiles, sometimes not even for the proselytes who became Jews by taking upon themselves circumcision and the yoke of the law, Paul declares that the gospel is the power of God for salvation both for the Jews and the Gentiles on the same ground, that is, faith. The thought is then unfolded in Rom 3.21–31. Before that, however, in Rom 1.18–3.20 he has demonstrated that all, the Jews as much as the Gentiles, have sinned and fall short of the glory of God (3.23). So there is no distinction between them. God justifies them both by his grace in Christ and they both receive justification through faith. In 3.29f. monotheism and therefore God's being the God of the Gentiles as well as of the Jews is employed to support Paul's doctrine of justification through faith without works of the law: the one God of all mankind justifies the circumcision (= the Jews) and the un-circumcision (= the Gentiles) on exactly the same ground – faith. Here it is implied that the particularistic *Heilsgeschichte* of circumcision and the law has given way to the universalistic *Heilsgeschichte* of the gospel of grace and faith. This is explicitly declared in Rom 10.4, and then its consequence is drawn out in v.12 as in Rom 3.29f.: 'For there is no distinction between Jew and Greek; the same Lord is Lord of all and bestows his riches upon all who call upon him'. These words occur in the midst of Paul's explanation of the *heilsgeschichtliche* problem raised by Israel's failure to obtain God's righteousness through their unbelief in the Messiah while ironically the Gentiles receive it through faith. Having concerned himself with this problem in Rom 9–11, in Rom 14–15 Paul exhorts the 'weak' Jewish Christians and the 'strong' Gentile Christians to accept one another as Christ welcomed them both: 'For I tell you that Christ became a servant to the circumcision to show God's truthfulness, in order to confirm the promises given to the patriarchs, and in order that the Gentiles might glorify God for his mercy' (15.8f.).

In Rom 10.12 Paul appeals to Jesus' universal lordship in order to affirm that he grants his salvation to the Gentiles as well as to the Jews. But Paul also knows that Jesus is the universal Lord to whom all the nations together with all the spiritual powers must be brought into subjection (Rom 1.5; 15.16, 18; 1Cor 15.24; Eph 1.20f.; Phil 2.9–11; Col 1.15ff.; etc). As nations submit themselves to Christ by calling upon his name, they are saved. Paul saw Christ as the exalted Lord of the universe on the Damascus road and was commissioned there by God to proclaim the gospel to the Gentiles. Now we can see the inner unity of Paul's gospel and his apostleship to the Gentiles, both of which he received on the Damascus road. On the one hand, the gospel that proclaims God's institution of Jesus Christ as the Son of God in power, the universal Lord, *spells an imperative* for Paul to go to the Gentiles, proclaim him to them, and bring about the 'obedience of faith' among them

(Rom 1.5; 15.16—18). On the other hand, the gospel which is at the same time 'God's power for salvation to every one who has faith, to the Jew first and also to the Greek' *justifies* Paul's mission to the Gentiles now. Only because Paul saw Christ's death and resurrection as God's redemptive act for our justification *sola gratia* and *sola fide*, could he so freely go to the Gentiles and proclaim the gospel of God's grace to them, while the Jewish Christians, failing to see the principle of *sola fide* so clearly as he, hesitated to do the same but rather criticized him for his law-free Gentile mission. The Letter to the Galatians is an eloquent testimony to this contrast as well as to the unity of Paul's gospel and apostleship[1].

2 *Reconciliation*

The understanding of Christ's death as the atoning sacrifice for our sins is pre-Pauline (1Cor 11.25ff.; 15.3; possibly also Rom 3.25f.). Nevertheless, in view of Paul's unique use of the theologumenon καταλλάσσειν/καταλλαγή we suggested in Ch.I, 5) that it could well have been Paul who first introduced it in the *Religionsgeschichte* for God's reconciliation of rebellious mankind to himself rather than man's reconciliation of the angry God to himself. When pre-Pauline Christianity understood that it was God who provided Christ as the atoning sacrifice for our sins, it clearly understood the reconciliation between God and man that had been brought about by the atoning death of Christ, in the sense of the Pauline doctrine of reconciliation[2]. However, in view of the fact that a positive unfolding of this doctrine is lacking in the New Testament outside the Pauline corpus[3], we may be justified in thinking that 'reconciliation' is a distinctive Pauline theologumenon to des-

---

[1]On this last paragraph cf. Bornkamm, *Paulus*, pp.74ff.; Grundmann, 'Paulus', pp. 274, 277; Hengel, 'Ursprünge', pp.22f. Our study so far contradicts Stendahl's 'guess that the doctrine of justification originates in Paul's theological mind from his grappling with the problem of how to defend the place of the Gentiles in the Kingdom — the task with which he was charged in his call' (*op. cit.*, p.27).

[2]It goes without saying that the Pauline as well as the pre-Pauline doctrine of the atonement presupposes that the atoning sacrifice of Christ involves the idea of propitiation of God's wrath against our sins as well as that of expiation of our sins and that therefore a change on God's part is also included in Paul's doctrine of reconciliation. Cf. Morris, *Preaching*, pp.214—250 But the originator of this reconciliation is God and not man, so that all the emphasis in Paul's doctrine of reconciliation is put on God's initiative.

[3]Pre-Pauline Christianity probably saw the atonement of Christ primarily in terms of God's forgiveness of past sins and institution of the new covenant with the Church, the new people of God (cf. Heb 9). Cf. Stuhlmacher, 'Zur neueren Exegese', pp.330ff.

cribe the purpose of the atonement God has wrought in Christ[1]. We suggested
further that Paul developed it out of his Damascus experience, for it appears
most prominently in 2Cor 5.16—21, where we saw Paul alluding to his
Damascus call. When God revealed Jesus of Nazareth to him as his Messiah
and exalted Son on the Damascus road, Paul came to know that in persecuting
Christians he had been acting as an enemy against God as well as against
them. But God accepted him and called him to be an apostle, so that he
might preach his Son among the Gentiles. This grace of God Paul experienced
as his forgiveness, justification and reconciliation. This intensely personal
experience led him to see the purpose of God's atonement in Christ not just
in terms of forgiveness of past sins (which is in Paul replaced by the more
significant theologumenon 'justification') and institution of the new covenant
but also of reconciliation.

Only when this is presupposed, we believe, can we have a coherent understanding of 2Cor 5.16—21. Earlier[2] we saw that in this passage Paul conducts
an apologetic polemic against his Jewish opponents who, probably proclaiming Jesus exclusively in terms of the Jewish nationalistic Messiah and boasting
of their relation with him, insinuated that Paul had hated him and persecuted
his followers. At first Paul concedes that, like his opponents, he judged
Christ according to the Jewish conceptions of the Messiah, and became,
unlike them, a persecutor of the adherents of Christ, because he thought their
proclamation of the crucified Jesus of Nazareth as the Messiah was a blasphemy against God. But now that Paul came to perceive the significance of
Jesus' death, he no longer entertains such a fleshly judgement of Christ.
Through God's saving work in Christ and through his call of Paul to be in
Christ he became a new creature. The exact reason why Paul's being in Christ
meant a new creation by God in respect of him is because it involved not only
his participation in Christ's representative death and resurrection (vs.14f.)
through faith and baptism but also God's reconciliation of Paul to himself.
While Paul was persecuting Christians and thus acting as an enemy of Christ
and of God, God by his grace revealed Christ to him and reconciled him to
himself. Since Paul knew as a Jewish theologian that atonement and forgive-

---

[1]*Supra* pp.19f. So L.Goppelt, 'Versöhnung durch Christus', *Christologie und Ethik*
(1969), pp.148—153. At the same time he rightly emphasizes the *'sachliche Ansatz'* of
the Pauline doctrine in Jesus' acceptance of sinners on God's behalf and in his teaching
expressed, e.g., in the parable of the prodigal son, as well as in the early Christian tradition of Jesus' atoning death. See also the section under the heading 'Rechtfertigung und
Versöhnung als spezifisch paulinische Begriffe' in his *Theologie des NT* (1976), pp.467—
470: 'Daß man in der Urkirche schon vor Paulus von der Versöhnung durch Christus
redete, ist unwahrscheinlich' (p.469).

[2]For the exegetical details of 2Cor 5.16—21, *supra* Ch.I. 5) (pp.13—20).

ness of sin was like a new creation, he could describe his experience of reconciliation with God, which was like the atonement Isaiah experienced at his call (Isa 6.6f.), only as a new creation. From this personal experience of reconciliation with God, Paul developed the insight that the purpose of Christ's atoning death on the cross was God's reconciliation of rebellious mankind to himself. So Paul says, 'In Christ God was (or, God was in Christ) reconciling the world to himself, not counting their transgressions against them'. Just as God so reconciled the world to himself (or, rather, on the basis of that work of reconciliation in Christ), he reconciled Paul to himself through Christ, and gave him the ministry of reconciliation and committed to him the message of reconciliation. So Paul acts as an ambassador on Christ's behalf, and God makes his appeal through him. So Paul's appeal on Christ's behalf, which is in fact God's appeal through Paul, is: 'Be reconciled to God'. In this passive form of appeal the distinctive characteristic of the Pauline doctrine of reconciliation comes out most clearly. God has already wrought the objective work of reconciliation by offering Christ as the atoning sacrifice on Golgotha, that is, by making the sinless Christ bear our sins and God's wrath upon them in our place and for our advantage, so that we might be the justified of God in him. Man has nothing to contribute to his reconciliation to God. He can only *receive* the reconciliation that God offers. Yet he must *do* that if reconciliation is to be truly effected. It is Paul's ministry to proclaim God's work of reconciliation in Christ and to appeal to men and women to accept it. So in this Corinthian passage Paul not only adequately answers his opponents' insinuation of his former hostility to Christ but also takes the opportunity positively to describe God's atonement in Christ in terms of his reconciliation of rebellious mankind to himself, and to present his apostolic ministry as the ministry of reconciliation, issuing a call to the Corinthians.

In Rom 5.1–11 Paul explicitly connects reconciliation with justification whereas in 2Cor 5.16–21 he just hints at their connection. Some think that justification and reconciliation are only different metaphors describing the same reality[1] or that reconciliation is a consequence of justification[2]. But trying to be more precise, Cranfield maintains that God's justification involves reconciliation:

> Where it is God's justification that is concerned, justification and reconciliation, though distinguishable, are inseparable. Whereas between a human judge and the person who appears before him there may be no really personal meeting at all, no personal hostility if the accused be found guilty, no establishment of friendship if the

---

[1] E.g., Barrett, *Romans*, p.108; Kuss, *Römer*, p.211; Käsemann, *Römer*, p.129.

[2] Cf. Bultmann, *Theology* i, p.286.

accused is acquitted, between God and the sinner there is a personal relationship, and God's justification involves a real self-engagement to the sinner on His part. He does not confer the status of righteousness upon us without at the same time giving Himself to us . . .[1]

So, when Paul says: 'Having been justified then on the basis of faith, we have peace with God through our Lord Jesus Christ . . . ' (Rom 5.1), he does not collocate two metaphors describing the same reality but rather indicates that 'the fact that we have been justified means that we have also been reconciled and have peace with God'[2]. 'Peace' here means primarily the objective state of being at peace with God instead of being in enmity against him, i.e., the fulness of salvation which the Jew calls שלום, although the subjective feeling of peace which results from this is probably included here secondarily. This peace has resulted from God's reconciliation of us to Himself. Before that divine act we were God's 'enemies', rebels against him and as such the objects of his wrath[3]. Yet God reconciled us to himself through the atoning death of Christ (v.10f.). This is the manifestation of his sheer grace, his incomparable love for us. So, having already been reconciled, we can be confident that we shall receive the consummation of salvation at the end through the risen Christ.

If in 2Cor 5.18 Paul speaks about God's reconciliation of the κόσμος, meaning the whole of mankind, to himself in Christ, in Col 1.20 he expands its scope to include all things including the cosmic powers: through Christ God reconciled (ἀποκαταλλάξαι) to himself 'all things, whether on earth or in heaven, making peace by the blood of his cross'. Among these are included the Colossian Christians, 'who once were estranged and hostile (ἐχθρούς) in mind, doing evil deeds' (v.21). Them Christ 'has now reconciled (ἀποκατ-ήλλαξεν) in his body of flesh by his death' (v.22), and so they are to preserve the state by continuing in faith (v.23). In Eph 2.13–18 reconciliation is conceived of as having taken place not only between God and men but also between the Jews and the Gentiles. This thought Paul presents by means of an exegesis of Isa 9.5f.; 52.7; 57.19, as recently P. Stuhlmacher has clearly

---

[1]Cranfield, *Romans*, p.258.

[2]*Ibid.*

[3]Here the word ἐχθροί has primarily an active sense as ἔχθρα in Rom 8.7: we were rebels hostile to God. At the same time, however, it involves a passive sense as well: in view of our rebellion against God, he sees us as enemies (cf. Rom 11.28, where the passive sense is dominant). So Taylor, *Forgiveness and Reconciliation* (1941) pp.88f.; Morris, *Preaching*, p.226 (see also pp.220–225); Cranfield, *Romans*, p.267; Bultmann, *Theology* i, p.286.

shown[1]. In Eph 2.11f. Paul reminds the Gentile Christians that once they were excluded from the commonwealth of Israel, being strangers to the divine covenant of promises. But now, according to his promise (Isa 57.19), God has wrought the atonement through Christ's bloody death and thus in Christ brought near to himself them who were once 'far off', i.e., the Gentiles. For Christ is, as promised in Isa 9.5f., our 'peace'. He is our 'peace' because he abolished the law, so that he might reconcile and unite the Gentiles and the Jews and reconcile both to God. The law was regarded by the Jews as a wall that surrounded Israel and separated and protected them from the Gentiles[2]. The law is also a wall that hinders fellowship between God and men as it forces men to the establishment of their own righteousness and to self-assertion before God. Now, by his death on the cross Christ has abolished the law and so has broken down 'the dividing wall of hostility' between the Jews and the Gentiles and between God and mankind. This he did in order that he might unite the two groups of mankind and create out of the two 'one new man' in himself (cf. 2Cor 5.17; Gal 3.28) and that he might reconcile them both to God. Thus, in fulfilment of the promise in Isa 57.19, the Messiah came and preached 'peace' to the Gentiles who were 'far off' and to the Jews who were 'near'. And, thus, the Gentile Christians are no longer strangers but fellow citizens with the Jewish Christians and members of the household of God.

At the end of the last section we saw how the Pauline doctrine of justification *sola fide* theologically justified his universal mission. Here in Eph 2.11–22 Paul presents a meditation upon the wonderful result of the Gentile mission, for which he is *the* apostle, in terms of reconciliation between the Jews and the Gentiles and of creation of the new, eschatological people of God[3].

3 *Sonship, Transformation, and New Creation*

Before Christ came, we were 'minors' kept under the custodianship of the law and enslaved to the elemental powers of the world. But when the time came at which God had planned to fulfil his promises, he sent forth his pre-existent Son to be born of woman, to bear the curse of the law on our behalf, and so to redeem us from the law. Our redemption from the law means positively our adoption as sons of God. So, God's purpose in sending his Son

---

[1] Stuhlmacher, ' "Er ist unser Friede" (Eph 2, 14)', *NT und Kirche*, Schnackenburg FS, pp.347–357.

[2] The Letter of Aristeas, 139–142.

[3] One remaining reference to reconciliation is Rom 11.15, where the Gentile mission or its result is described as God's 'reconciliation of the world' to himself.

into the world was to grant us his sonship (υἰοθεσία) or to adopt us as his sons. We experience this divine sonship that God grants on the basis of his redemptive work in Christ as God sends the Spirit of his Son into our hearts (cf. Gal 2.20), crying 'Abba! Father!'[1]. So we are no longer a slave but a son, and as a son of God we are an heir (Gal 4.1–7). This is a re-statement of what Paul has already said in Gal 3.23–29. If the former explains how God has wrought our redemption to grant us his sonship and how the reality of our experience of the adoption is expressed, the latter explains how we actually appropriate the divine redemption and sonship. We become sons of God as by faith and baptism we put on Christ and are incorporated into Christ. It is Christ who is properly the Son of God. But Christ is the *Stammvater*, a 'corporate personality', in whom the *Stamm*, the redeemed humanity, is incorporated. So, as we are by faith and baptism united with him and incorporated in him, we participate in his divine sonship[2]. We the Christians were called by God into the κοινωνία of his Son, Jesus Christ, that is, to share in Christ's filial relationship with God the Father (1Cor 1.9)[3]. Among us who thus by faith and baptism have become sons of God in Christ Jesus, the old human and *heilsgeschichtlichen* distinctions between Jew and Gentile, between slave and free man, and between male and female, have ceased to matter. For now we are all one kind of human being, namely the Christian, in Christ Jesus (Gal 3.28)[4]. In Gal 3.29 Paul says: 'And if you are Christ's, then you are Abraham's seed, heirs according to promise'. Again, it is Christ who is properly the seed of Abraham (Gal 3.16). But, as by confessing Jesus as the Lord in baptism we become his possession we participate in his status as the seed of Abraham, and become with him heirs to Abraham to inherit God's blessings upon Abraham.

In view of the parallelism between Gal 3.26f., 29; 4.4–7, 21–31 it appears that being Abraham's seed is the same as being God's son. This is confirmed by the fact that Paul sees God's call of the Gentiles to faith and

---

[1]Cf. Blank, *Paulus*, p.276: 'Während Gal 4, 5 von Empfang der Sohnschaft aufgrund der Heilstat Christi die Rede ist, geht es in V.6f. *um die pneumatische Erfahrung der Sohnschaft*. Oder anders ausgedrückt: Während V.4f. das Zustandekommen der Sohnschaft von "außen", von der objektiven Seite des Handelns Gottes am Menschen her und deshalb auch in vorwiegend juristischer Terminologie beschrieben wird, wird sie in V.6f. in dem, was ihre innere Wirklichkeit, ihren lebendigen Vollzug ausmacht, gesehen' (Emphasis by B.).

[2]Cf. W.Thüsing, *Per Christum in Deum* (1965), pp.116f.; Mussner, *Gal.*, p.262.

[3]Cf. Barrett, *1 Cor.*, p.40.

[4]For this understanding of Gal 3.28b: πάντες γὰρ ὑμεῖς εἷς ἐστε, see Mussner, *Gal.*, pp.264ff.

salvation as the fulfilment of Hosea's prophecy (Hos 2.23; 2.1; 1.10):
'Those who were "not-my-people" I will call "my people", and her who was
"not-beloved" I will call "my beloved"; and in the place where it was said to
them "you are not-my-people", they will be called "sons of the living God" '
(Rom 9.25f.). The divine sonship belongs to Israel, the descendants of Abraham, Isaac and Jacob (Rom 9.4f.). But by unbelief the Jews prove themselves to be not the true descendants of Abraham from Sarah according to the
divine promise, but rather the descendants of the slave woman Hagar according to flesh, whereas the Gentiles, who were no part of God's people, are
now by faith in Christ adopted as sons of God and as the true descendants of
Abraham according to promise, together with the believing Jews (Rom 9.6ff.,
24ff.; Gal 4.21–31). So, in the mission fields Paul sees Hosea's prophecy
being fulfilled: the believing Gentiles are called to be God's sons and his
people[1]. This line of thought reflects both the OT/Jewish conception of
Israel as the son (collectively) or sons of God and the Wisdom-tradition that
especially designates the wise and righteous among the Jews as sons of God[2].
For Paul those who are justified by faith in Christ are sons of God and the
new, eschatological people of God (cf. also 2Cor 6.18). Drawn from both the
Jews and the Gentiles, the believers are the people of the new covenant, 'the
Israel of God' (Gal 6.16; cf. Phil 3.3).

As in Gal 4.1–7, so also in Rom 8.14–23 Paul connects our adoption as
sons of God with the Spirit and with the theme of freedom. Just as in Gal
3.26–29; 4.6 Paul says that we experience God's adoption as his sons when
by faith-baptism we are incorporated into Christ and God sends the Spirit
of his Son into our hearts, so also here in Rom 8 he bases our sonship on our
union with Christ and on the dwelling of the Spirit of Christ in us or our
dwelling in the Spirit (Rom 8.9–11). The Spirit of Christ, who is also the
Spirit of God, is the Spirit of υἱοθεσία because he makes us participants in
Christ's Sonship. As in Gal 4.6 Paul speaks of the Spirit of his Son in us crying 'Abba! Father!', so here in Rom 8.15 he says that it is in the Spirit that
we cry 'Abba! Father!'. Gal 4.6 and Rom 8.15 describe the same reality
because the Spirit's dwelling in us and our dwelling in the Spirit describe the
same reality as shown by Rom 8.9–11. The dwelling of the Spirit of Christ
in us makes us participants in Christ's Sonship because it means the dwelling
of Christ himself, the Son of God, in us, the Spirit being the mode of Christ's
dwelling in us (Gal 4.6; Rom 8.9–11). So, 'all who are led by the Spirit of
God are sons of God' (Rom 8.14), and 'the Spirit himself assures our spirit

[1]Cf. Bruce, *Romans,* pp.195f.; Blank, *Paulus,* pp.259f.

[2]See G.Fohrer, E.Schweizer and E.Lohse, υἱός, *TDNT* viii, pp.351ff., 354ff., 359f.;
Hengel, *Sohn,* pp.68ff.

that we are children of God' (Rom 8.16)[1]. That we participate in Christ's Sonship means that we participate in his status as the heir of God. Thus, as children of God we are heirs of God, fellow-heirs with Christ (Rom 8.17). Just as in Gal 4.1–7 Paul saw a consequence of our sonship in our freedom from the law and the elemental powers of the world, so also here in Rom 8.12–17 he speaks of a consequence of our sonship in terms of our freedom from the flesh. But our sonship and freedom are not yet complete; they are only the first-fruits of the Spirit. They will be consummated with the resurrection of our bodies at the parousia when we will be glorified with Christ. Until then we groan inwardly and have to suffer with Christ, in order that we may be glorified with him. The destiny of the whole creation is also bound up with this destiny of the children of God (Rom 8.17–25).

In Rom 8.29 Paul conceives of Christ, the Son of God, as the 'first-born' (πρωτότοκος) and of the believers as the brothers of Christ whom God predestined to be conformed to the image of his Son (cf. Heb 2.10ff). This is another expression of the idea that the believers participate in the Sonship of Christ and are therefore fellow-heirs with him. We are sons of God as we are conformed to the *Urbild* of the Son of God. In these ideas of the believers' participation in Christ's Sonship, of their being conformed to the *Urbild* of the Son of God, and of their crying 'Abba! Father!', we may see reflected three ideas. The first one is Jesus' own expression of his unique filial relationship, as the cry 'Abba! Father!' shows[2]. The second is the conception of Christ as the Last Adam who is the *Urbild* or *Vorbild* of the new humanity. The third is the conception of Christ as the Son of God/ the Son of Man who is the inclusive representative of the ideal Israel. In Ch.VI we suggested that on the Damascus road Paul saw the exalted Christ appearing from heaven not only as the Son and image of God but probably also as the inclusive representative of the ideal Israel according to the Jewish tradition which understood the man-like-figure seen in epiphany visions as the inclusive representative of the ideal Israel, identifying him with Jacob-Israel[3]. This conception of Christ seems to be reflected in Paul's idea that through incorporation in Christ, the believers participate in his Sonship and become the 'Israel of God', the sons of God[4]. If so, it is remarkable that Jesus' own teaching of his unique filial

---

[1]For this rendering see Cranfield, *Romans*, p.403.

[2]See Jeremias, *Abba*, esp. pp.58–67.

[3]*Supra* p.256.

[4]Philo's conception of the Logos as the son of God who mediates sonship to wise Israelites or incorporates them as sons of God in himself (e.g., *Conf. Ling.* 62f., 145–148) may well belong to this same theophany-vision tradition (*supra* p.245, also pp.110f.).

relationship to God and his invitation of his disciples to participate in that relationship completely agrees with Paul's conception of Christ as the Son of God who is the inclusive representative of the ideal Israel, the sons of God — the conception which he obtained from seeing Christ as one 'like a son of God'/'like a son of man' at the Damascus Christophany. This seems to be another piece of evidence for our earlier suggestion that Jesus designated himself as '*the* Son of Man' in full consciousness that he was the Son of God, the inclusive representative of the ideal Israel, whom Daniel saw as one 'like a son of man' in a vision; and that with the title 'the Son of God' Paul correctly represents Jesus' true intention in his self-designation as 'the Son of Man'[1].

When Paul says that God predestined us to be conformed to the εἰκών of his Son (Rom 8.29), he remembers the image of the Son of God which he saw on the Damascus road. In accordance with the Jewish tradition, Paul sees human existence since Adam's fall as lacking the image and glory of God (Rom 3.23) as well as lacking righteousness[2]. In fact, just as the image of God and the glory of God are closely related to each other almost to the point of being synonymous[3], the glory of God is likewise closely related to righteousness. In Apoc. Mos. 20.1f. Eve says that as soon as she ate the fruit she 'knew that I was bare of the righteousness with which I was clothed (upon), and I wept and said to him (sc. Satan): "Why hast thou done this to me in that thou hast deprived me of the glory with which I was clothed?" ' This lament of Eve is followed by that of Adam: 'O wicked woman! What have I done to thee that thou hast deprived me of the glory of God?' (21.6). Here righteousness and the glory of God are taken synonymously and both are thought to have been lost as a result of the transgressions of Eve and Adam. This thought finds a close parallel in Rom 3.23, where, after demonstrating that all men — both Jews and Gentiles — have sinned and are therefore without righteousness (Rom 1.18—3.20), Paul declares: 'All have sinned and (so) lack the glory of God', so that all need to be given righteousness by God through his free grace. The close inter-relationship of the three concepts of righteousness, the glory of God and the image of God is clearly shown in Rom 8.29f. When Paul breaks the sorites of vs.29f. by inserting into it v.29bc: (καὶ προώρισεν) συμμόρφους τῆς εἰκόνος τοῦ υἱοῦ αὐτοῦ, εἰς τὸ εἶναι αὐτὸν πρωτότοκον ἐν πολλοῖς ἀδελφοῖς, he wants to indicate with the sentence in v.29bc the consummated state of salvation that God

---

[1] *Supra* pp.249ff.

[2] *Supra* pp.260ff.

[3] *Supra* pp.230f.

predestined for us in his divine counsel. Then, resuming the sorites in v.30, Paul indicates in v.30b–f the historical process of God's saving acts towards that state, the process of actualization of that predestination of God mentioned in v.29bc[1]. The process begins in time with God's effectual call to faith of those whom he predestined, proceeds with his justification of them as they respond to his call by faith, and is consummated at the *eschaton* with glorification of them.

> Although once Paul speaks of glorification as the believer's present experience (2Cor 3.18), he usually looks forward to it as an eschatological consummation of our salvation (Rom 5.2; 8.17ff.; 1Cor 15.43; Phil 3.21). Even in 2Cor 3.18 he does not think of the believer's glorification as having already been completed but as being still in progression towards consummation. But why then does he use the aorist ἐδόξασεν in Rom 8.30 as though our glorification had already been completed? Most commentators see the aorist as 'the "prophetic past", by which a predicted event is marked out as so certain of fulfilment that it is described as though it had already taken place'[2]. But some think that Paul is there citing an enthusiastic baptismal tradition which holds that in baptism the believer's transformation into a heavenly being already takes place[3]. But this is highly unlikely in view of the fact that in the context Paul is at pains to emphasize that our glorification is in the future, at the parousia of Christ, and that therefore we should endure the present suffering in the hope for that consummation of salvation. The former view, on the other hand, agrees with the context very well as in it Paul tries to assure believers that the hope for the consummation of salvation, i.e. glorification, is a sure one because it has been decreed by God.

From Rom 8.29f. it is clear that the believer's glorification is the same as his being conformed to the image of the Son of God. The same idea is found also in 1Cor 15.43–49 and Phil 3.21. It is also clear from Rom 8.30 that glorification is the consummation of salvation, i.e., of justification[4]. So, being conformed to the glorious image of the Son of God or bearing that image is the consummated state of justification.

Human existence since Adam's fall lacks the image and glory of God as well as righteousness (Rom 3.23). As a result of our unavoidable solidarity with Adam, our *Stammvater*, we bear instead his fallen image, his earthly shameful image, and his weak, mortal and ignoble σῶμα ψυχικόν (1Cor 15.42–49; Phil 3.21). This is the plight from which we need to be saved.

---

[1]Cf. Sanday-Headlam, *Romans*, p.218; Dodd, *Romans*, p.156; Barrett, *Romans*, pp.169f.; Michel, *Römer*, p.212; Murray, *Romans*, p.320.

[2]Bruce, *Romans*, p.178; so, similarly, e.g., Sanday-Headlam, *Romans*, p.218; Barrett, *Romans*, p.170; Michel, *Römer*, p.212; Murray, *Romans*, p.312.

[3]Käsemann, *Römer*, p.234; Jervell, *Imago*, p.273; Hahn, 'Taufe', p.176.

[4]Cf. Thüsing, *Per Christum*, p.132; also Jervell, *Imago*, pp.182f.

When Paul saw on the Damascus road the exalted Christ in glory as the image of God, he knew that the hope for the restoration of the divine image and glory in the messianic age had become reality in Christ. This experience led Paul, as we saw earlier[1], to see Christ as the Last Adam who has restored what the first Adam lost. So, he began to envisage also the restoration to us of the divine image and glory as we are transferred from the solidarity with the first Adam, the *Stammvater* of the old fallen humanity, to that with the Last Adam, the *Stammvater* of the new humanity. The risen Christ, as the *Stammvater* of the new humanity, is also the *Vorbild* for that new humanity. So, to describe the consummated state of the believer's salvation Paul applies the expressions with which he describes the risen Christ whom he saw on the Damascus road[2]. Just as Adam was ὁ χοϊκός, so are we οἱ χοϊκοί in solidarity with him; but just as Christ is ὁ ἐπουράνιος, so shall we be οἱ ἐπουράνιοι in solidarity with him. Just as Adam has a mortal and ignoble σῶμα ψυχικόν, so have we that body in solidarity with him; but just as Christ has the immortal and glorious σῶμα πνευματικόν, so shall we have that body in solidarity with him. That is to say, 'just as we have borne the image of the man of dust, we shall also bear the image of the man of heaven' (1Cor 15.42–49). This will take place at the *eschaton* when Christ returns as Saviour 'who will transform our lowly body to be conformed to his body of glory' (Phil 3.21; cf. also 1Cor 15.52; Col 3.4). Then our adoption as sons of God will be consummated because we shall bear the image of the Son of God (Rom 8.29; cf. 1Jn 3.2). But this change is what God predestined for us in his eternal counsel and has already begun to actualize by calling us and justifying us (Rom 8.29f.). Since Paul can see the first-fruits of our eschatological glorification and transformation already in our call and justification[3], he can actually speak of our glorification and transformation as a present process progressing towards the eschatological consummation: 'But we all, with unveiled face, beholding the glory of the Lord as in a mirror, are transformed into the same image from one degree of glory to another' (2Cor 3.18).

Indeed, while firmly holding to the futurity of our glorification (Col 3.4), Paul can say at the same time that we have already 'put off (ἀπεκδυσάμενοι) the παλαιὸς ἄνθρωπος with its practices and put on (ἐνδυσάμενοι) the νέος (ἄνθρωπος) which is being renewed for knowledge according to the image of

---

[1] *Supra* pp.258ff.

[2] *Supra* pp.223ff.

[3] Cf. Jervell, *Imago*, p.281; Thüsing, *Per Christum*, p.130.

its creator' (Col 3.9f.)[1]. The 'old man' refers to the Adamitic humanity which bears the ignoble image of the man of dust, and the 'new man' refers to the new humanity which has the image of God restored to it, i.e., which is conformed to the glorious image of Christ, the Last Adam[2]. But when in the next verse (Col 3.11) Paul goes on to say that in new humanity the racial and social distinctions do not matter because πάντα καὶ ἐν πᾶσιν Χριστός, i.e., because 'Christ is everything and is in all' members of the Church[3], he also indicates that the 'new man', the new humanity, is that in which Christ dwells as the Spirit[4]. For this reason Paul can speak of 'putting-on' Christ instead of the 'new man': ' . . . as many of you as were baptized into Christ have put on Christ' (Gal 3.27). The Galatian passage also shows that the 'putting-off' of the 'old man' and the 'putting-on' of the 'new man' took place when we came to faith and experienced in baptism the symbolic drama-tization of our dying to the 'old man' and rising to the 'new man' in union with Christ, i.e., of our participation in Christ's destiny, which faith in Christ involves (Rom 6.1–11; Eph 2.5f.; Col 2.12ff.; 3.1–3). The same idea of the surrender of the old Adamitic ego for the new ego, which is the indwell-ing Christ, is expressed in yet another way in Gal 2.19: 'I have been crucified with Christ; it is no longer I who live, but Christ who lives in me'. It appears then that being conformed to the image of Christ or bearing his image is the same as having Christ dwelling in us. These two synonymous expressions seem to be combined in the striking statement that Paul suffers birth-pangs again for the sake of the back-sliding Galatian Christians μέχρις οὗ μορφωθῇ Χριστὸς ἐν ὑμῖν (Gal 4.19).

While affirming that we already put off the 'old man' and put on the 'new man' when we came to faith, Col 3.9f. also makes it clear that that 'new man' is in the process of constantly being renewed. Whereas in 2Cor 3.18 Paul says that our glorification and transformation into the image of Christ is

---

[1] κατ' εἰκόνα τοῦ κτίσαντος αὐτόν refers to the image of God (so the majority of commentators: e.g., Moule, *Col.*, p.120; Lohse, *Kol.*, p.206; Jervell, *Imago*, pp.249f.; cf. Eph 4.24). But, as we have seen earlier, for Paul the image of God is the same as the image of Christ (*supra* pp.232f.). So, although Paul usually speaks of the Christian's transformation into the *image of Christ* (Rom 8.29; 1Cor 15.49; 2Cor 3.18; Phil 3.21), he can also speak of the Christian's putting on the 'new man' created according to the image of God (*contra* Jervell, *Imago*, p.250). While the latter makes it clear that the redeemed become the 'new man' or καινὴ κτίσις to whom the image of God which Adam lost is restored, the former indicates that this restoration of the divine image to the redeemed is nothing other than their transformation into the image of Christ.

[2] Cf. Jervell, *Imago*, pp.240–250.

[3] Cf. Moule, *Col.*, pp.121f.

[4] Cf. Jervell, *Imago*, pp.246ff.

progressing towards the eschatological consummation, in Col 3.10 he implies that the 'new man' created according to the image of God is an already existing reality given to us, the believers. However, as yet we do not have it as a firm and perfect possession; it must constantly be renewed or actualized in our lives until it becomes a perfect reality at the *eschaton*. So the thought in Col 3.9f. is essentially the same as that in 2Cor 3.18. Because the 'new man' is something that has to be constantly renewed or actualized, Paul calls those who have already put on the 'new man' or Christ: 'Put off the old man which belongs to your former manner of life and is being destroyed through deceitful lusts, be renewed in the spirit of your minds, and put on the new man which has been created after the likeness of God in true righteousness and holiness' (Eph 4.22–24); or, 'Put on the Lord Jesus Christ, and make no provision for the flesh, to gratify its desires' (Rom 13.14). When the Galatian Christians desert the truth of the gospel, Paul must suffer birth-pangs for them again, so that the 'new man', the new humanity in which Christ dwells as its Lord, conforming it to his own image, may be renewed in them (Gal 4.19). These passages suggest that to hold firm to the truth of the gospel and to live a life worthy of the gospel (cf. Phil 1.27), i.e., a life that has been transferred from this evil age to the new age, from the dominion of darkness to the Kingdom of Christ, the Son of God (Col 1.13), is to have the 'new man' renewed in us. God has wrought our redemption in Christ, and he has called us and justified us with a view to glorifying us at the *eschaton*. This is the ground on which Paul appeals to us: 'Offer your bodies as a living sacrifice, holy and well-pleasing to God; this is the spiritual worship you owe him. And do not be conformed (συσχηματίζεσθε) to this age, but be transformed (μεταμορφοῦσθε) by the renewing of your mind, that you may try and approve what is the will of God, what (that is) is holy and acceptable and perfect' (Rom 12.1f.)[1].

Since Paul conceives of the 'new man' as the new humanity in us in which Christ dwells, conforming it to his image, and since he thinks of the renewal of this 'new man' first and foremost in terms of the renewal of our mind (Rom 12.2; Eph 4.23), he can also speak of the 'new man' as the 'inner man' (ὁ ἔσω ἄνθρωπος, 2Cor 4.16; cf. also Rom 7.22; Eph 3.16)[2]. That the 'inner man' refers to the 'new man' and the 'outer man' (ὁ ἔξω ἄνθρωπος) refers to the 'old man' is clearly suggested by the parallelism between 2Cor 4.16 on the one hand and Eph 4.22 and Col 3.10 on the other: just as in Eph 4.22 the 'old man' is said to be in the process of decaying (φθειρόμενον), so in 2Cor 4.16 the 'outer man' is said to be in the process of decaying (δια-

---

[1] This translation is by Barrett, *Romans*, p.230.

[2] Cf. Windisch, *2.Kor.*, p.152.

φθείρεται); and just as in Col 3.10 the 'new man' is said to be constantly renewed (ἀνακαινούμενον), so in 2Cor 4.16 the 'inner man' is said to be daily renewed (ἀνακαινοῦται)[1]. Perhaps Paul conceives of the 'new man' as residing in the ψυχικὸν σῶμα which is dominated by the power of this age, i.e., in the 'body of sin' (Rom 6.6).

2Cor 4.17 suggests that the decaying of the 'outer man' or the 'old man' is taking place in suffering, which, however, 'is producing for us out of all proportion an eternal weight of glory'. The present suffering is wearing out our 'outer man' or 'old man' and is producing the renewal of our 'inner man' or 'new man' which has glory[2]. The consummation of our transformation into the 'new man' and of our glorification will take place at the *eschaton*; but the 'new man', which is already inside of us, is being renewed, and the eschatological glory has begun to be imparted to us as we suffer and our 'old man', which resides in the flesh, is being destroyed in suffering. 2Cor 4.16f. is, then, a restatement of what Paul has already said in 2Cor 4.10f.: in the course of the apostolic ministry Paul suffers all sorts of deadly afflictions (vs. 8f.; 1Cor 4.9–13; 2Cor 6.3–10; 11.23–33). For him this means carrying the νέκρωσις of Jesus in the body, i.e., to experience the dying of Jesus (cf. 2Cor 1.5). As Paul participates through his sufferings in the dying of Jesus, the life of Jesus is being manifested in his body. This life of Jesus, the resurrection life, will be manifested in our bodies at the *eschaton* when our perishable natural bodies are transformed into immortal spiritual bodies like that of the risen Jesus. But as we share in the dying of Jesus through our sufferings for his sake, the resurrection life of Jesus has already begun to be manifested even in our mortal flesh. This life of Jesus which has already begun to be manifested in our bodies is nothing other than the life of the 'new man' in us, the 'inner man', which is constantly being renewed. A similar thought to that in 2Cor 4.10–17 is found in Phil 3.10f.[3] In the latter Paul speaks of his decision on the Damascus road to abandon all his privileges as a Jew and all his achievements as a zealous Pharisee in order to orient his whole life towards knowing Christ. To know Christ is to know the power of his resurrection. But Paul can know Christ and the power of his resurrection only if he enters into the fellowship of his sufferings, that is, only if he shares Christ's sufferings, being conformed (συμμορφιζόμενος) to his death, i.e., dying as Jesus died. By sharing Christ's sufferings to the point of the death on the

---

[1]Cf. Barrett, *2Cor.*, pp.146f.; Jervell, *Imago*, pp.240–248; Bruce, *Cor.*, p.189.

[2]Cf. Windisch, *2.Kor.*, p.153.

[3]Cf. Beare, *Phil.*, p.124; Gnilka, *Phil.*, p.196.

cross Paul hopes to attain resurrection from the dead. Our[1] being conformed at present to the death of Christ in fellowship of his sufferings will finally give way to the transformation of our lowly body so that it may be conformed to the glorious body of Christ at the parousia (Phil 3.20f.). Whereas in 2Cor 4.10–17 Paul speaks of the life of the risen Jesus, the life of the 'new man' in us, as having already begun to be manifested in our bodies through our sharing Christ's sufferings, in Phil 3.10f. he seems to speak of the present as the time of our sharing Christ's sufferings, and to look forward to the parousia for the glorious resurrection life. But this difference is not essential, for Paul also implies in the former passage that the full manifestation of the life of Jesus in our bodies will take place at the parousia, while implying in the latter that the new life has already begun for the believer through God's call and justification. Finally, Rom 8.17 also indicates that the believers, who have already received divine sonship as the first-fruits of the Spirit, must share Christ's sufferings in order to share his glory.

Our participation in Christ's sufferings is the actualization in life of our dying with Christ in faith, which was dramatized in baptism[2]. In faith-baptism we 'became assimilated to the form of his death' (Rom 6.5: σύμφυτοι γεγόναμεν τῷ ὁμοιώματι τοῦ θανάτου αὐτοῦ), i.e. we were conformed to Christ's death[3]. The perfect γεγόναμεν in Rom 6.5 indicates that this past event has continuing effect in the present, and Phil 3.10 indicates how that continuing effect is manifested: the believer, who was conformed to the death of Christ in faith-baptism, is continually being conformed to the death of Christ (συμμορφιζόμενος τῷ θανάτῳ αὐτοῦ)[4] as he shares in Christ's sufferings. In faith-baptism our 'old man was crucified with (Christ)' (Rom 6.6) and we were raised with Christ to a new life (Rom 6.4, 11; Eph 2.5f.; Col 2.12ff.). In faith-baptism we already 'put off' the 'old man' and 'put on' Christ or the 'new man' (Gal 3.27; Col 3.9f.). But what happened in faith-baptism is only the first-fruits of what will happen at the *eschaton*. Only at the *eschaton* will the dying of our 'old man' and our attainment of the 'new man' be complete. Until then we must actualize in our lives our dying and rising with Christ in faith-baptism: we must continually 'put off' our 'old man' and 'put on' the 'new man' (Eph 4.22–24; Col 3.12ff.; Rom 12.1f.).

---

[1]Although both in 2Cor 4.10–17 and Phil 3.10f. Paul speaks primarily about himself, what he says in both places applies to all believers, in so far as Paul portrays his life as a paradigm for the Christian existence.

[2]For this paragraph cf. Schweizer, "Mystik", pp.246–250; Tannehill, *Dying*, pp.80–129; *contra* P.Siber, *Mit Christus leben* (1971), pp.182–188.

[3]Cf. Cranfield, *Romans*, p.308.

[4]Cf. *ibid.*; Thüsing, *Per Christum*, p.139; Beare, *Phil.*, p.124; Gnilka, *Phil.*, p.196.

We must continually have the 'new man' or the 'inner man' renewed. This actualization takes place in the life of Christian discipleship and especially in its sufferings. Thus the life of discipleship, which involves our participation in Christ's sufferings and our being conformed to his death, is paradoxically the process in which we are being transformed into the image of Christ from one degree of glory to another (2Cor 3.18) and in which the resurrection life of Jesus is being manifested in our mortal bodies (2Cor 4.10f.; Phil 3.10). At the *eschaton* this process will be complete, and we shall be completely conformed to the resurrection of Christ (Rom 6.5) and completely transformed into the glorious image of Christ, the Son of God and the Last Adam.

Nevertheless, the fact that in faith-baptism we have put on the 'new man' which has been created in the image of God and is continually being renewed according to that image (Col 3.10; Eph 4.24) means that we are καινὴ κτίσις. Jewish theologians conceived of the Sinai revelation of the law as a new creation because they saw in it a restoration of the divine image and glory. But they held that the divine image and glory were lost or diminished again through Israel's sin in making the golden calf, and looked forward to the messianic age for their complete restoration[1]. So, when Paul saw on the Damascus road that the hope for their perfect restoration as well as the hope for resurrection had become reality in Christ, he knew that God had wrought a new creation in Christ (2Cor 4.6) and that Christ is the Adam of the *Endzeit*, the 'Last Adam' (1Cor 15.45ff.). As the 'Last Adam', who has restored the divine image and glory which the first Adam lost, Christ is the πρωτότοκος and *Stammvater* of the new humanity (Rom 8.29; Col 1.18). As we are transferred from the solidarity with the first Adam to that with the Last Adam, we become new creatures to whom the divine image and glory are restored. Paul describes this transfer in various ways as we have seen: it is to die and rise again with Christ, to 'put off' the 'old man' and to 'put on' the 'new man', or to have Christ dwell in us as the Spirit. In 2Cor 5.16–21 Paul designates as καινὴ κτίσις those who like himself have been justified and reconciled to God through the atonement in Christ[2]. Since Adam's fall, all men have sinned so that the old humanity is characterized by the lack of righteousness and of the divine image and glory (Rom 3.23). So God's granting us his righteousness and reconciling us to himself is his act of new creation. Thus, to be justified and reconciled is to be καινὴ κτίσις, that is, to 'put on' the 'new man' to which the image of God is restored. God's act of new creation takes place, as we have seen, when we come to be united with Christ in

---

[1] *Supra* pp.235f.

[2] *Supra* pp.312f.

faith-baptism. It took place in respect of Paul on the Damascus road when God shone his creation light into Paul's heart, and it takes place in respect of others when through Paul's apostolic preaching they are illuminated with the knowledge of the divine glory in Christ and are justified and reconciled to God by faith (2Cor 4.6; 5.17–21)[1].

Since we have become καινὴ κτίσις through our union with Christ, the *Stammvater* of the new humanity, in faith-baptism, the old values and the old human divisions between the Jew and the Gentile, between male and female, between slave and free man have ceased to matter: we are all one kind of human being, namely the 'new man', the new humanity, in Christ[2] (Gal 3.28; 6.15; Col 3.11; 2Cor 5.16f.; 1Cor 12.13). Through his death on the cross Christ has abolished the law and thus broken down the 'dividing wall of hostility' between the Jews and the Gentiles and between God and both groups of mankind so that he might reconcile the Jews and the Gentiles to God and unite the two groups of mankind, creating out of the two 'one new man' in himself (Eph 2.14f.). If this new. humanity, which comprises the believing Jews and Gentiles who have been reconciled to God and incorporated into the Last Adam, the *Stammvater* of the new humanity, is to be designated with a *heilsgeschichtliche* term, it is 'the Israel of God' (Gal 6.16), the designation for the eschatological people of God (cf. Phil 3.3)[3]. Since

---

[1] *Supra* pp.9f., 15ff.

[2] *Supra* p.316, n.4.

[3] *Supra* pp.256f. The designation ὁ 'Ισραὴλ τοῦ θεοῦ in Gal 6.16 refers to the Christians as a whole, the Church: so J.B.Lightfoot, *Saint Paul's Epistle to the Galatians* (1900), p.225; Oepke, *Gal.*, p.163; Schlier, *Gal.*, p.283; N.A.Dahl, *Das Volk Gottes* (1941), pp.209–217; 'Zur Auslegung von Gal. 6, 16', *Judaica* 6 (1950), pp.161–170; Stuhlmacher, 'καινὴ κτίσις', pp.6f. καί before ἐπὶ τὸν 'Ισραὴλ τοῦ θεοῦ is either epexegetic (so Lightfoot) or, more probably, copulative, indicating that with 'the Israel of God' Paul has the whole Church of Christ in mind while with αὐτούς he has in mind *those in Galatia* 'who will walk according to this canon' — the canon of the gospel of Paul which announces the dawn of the new age (so Oepke; Schlier; Dahl, 'Auslegung', p.165. On κανών see Stuhlmacher, *op. cit.*, p.6f.). The view that ὁ 'Ισραὴλ τοῦ θεοῦ refers to the Jewish Christians is untenable (so Dahl, 'Auslegung', pp.161–170; Oepke, *Gal.*, p.163; Mussner, *Gal.*, pp.416f.; against G.Schrenk, 'Was bedeutet "Israel Gottes"?' *Judaica* 5 (1949), pp.81–94; 'Der Segenswunsch nach der Kampfepistel', *Judaica* 6 (1950), pp.170–190). Mussner's view that the designation refers to the Jewish nation (*Gal.*, p.417), is implausible. For it is difficult to imagine that having fought hard in Gal 3–4 to reject the Jewish nationalistic claims and having demonstrated that the believers in Christ and not the Jews are the children of God, the children of Abraham and the heirs of Abraham's promise, Paul would pray for God's mercy upon the Jewish nation in the same breath as he prays for God's peace upon the Church, thereby acknowledging the special status of the Jews as the chosen nation (cf. Dahl, 'Auslegung', pp. 167f.; Oepke, *Gal.*, p.163). For the same reason P.Richardson's attempt to see the

Christ is the *Stammvater* of the new humanity and both Jews and Gentiles are made καινὴ κτίσις through their incorporation into Christ, the old particularistic *Heilsgeschichte* of Israel κατὰ σάρκα (1Cor 10.18) has given way to the universalistic *Heilsgeschichte* of 'the Israel of God', the new humanity. Paul's apostleship has a vital role to play in this new *Heilsgeschichte* as he was commissioned on the Damascus road to proclaim to the Gentiles the message of reconciliation and to illuminate them with the knowledge of the glory of God in Christ so that they might be made καινὴ κτίσις in Christ (2Cor 4.6; 5.17–21)[1].

However, our existence as καινὴ κτίσις is also subject to the eschatological tension between 'already' and 'not yet', and therefore we must have the 'new man' that we have put on in faith-baptism, constantly renewed until the *eschaton*, as we have seen. When we are completely made καινὴ κτίσις, the whole creation, including inanimate objects, will also be recreated. For God's act of new creation is not concerned only with mankind but with the whole creation, the whole cosmos. The destiny of the whole creation is bound up with that of mankind. On account of the transgression of Adam, the vice-regent of the creation, God condemned it along with Adam and subjected it to futility and decay. But God has not left it without a hope for the eventual renewal and recreation in which it will be set free from bondage to decay. This recreation of the whole creation will take place when the glory of the children of God is revealed. And at the parousia when our adoption as God's sons and our transformation into the glorious image of Christ, that is,

---

designation as referring to those of the Jewish nation who will eventually accept the gospel and receive salvation (*Israel in the Apostolic Church* (1969), pp.74–84), is not convincing, either. There is nothing in Gal. that leads us to think that in Gal 6.16 Paul has in mind, as he does in Rom 9–11, those of the Jewish nation who will eventually come to faith and salvation, nor is there anything in the entire Pauline corpus (not even in Rom 9–11) that suggests that Paul would designate that part of the Jewish nation as 'the Israel *of God*'. Richardson's claim that 'strong confirmation of (his) position comes from the total absence of an identification of the Church with Israel' (p.83, n.2), is not correct. For Paul does wrench the designation ἡ περιτομή (the designation for the covenant people of God) from the Jews and apply it to the Church (Phil 3.3; cf. Rom 2.28f.), just as he wrenches Abraham's sonship and God's sonship from the Jews and applies them to the Church in Gal 3–4. The Jewish trouble-makers who demand that Christians be circumcised in order to participate in the people of God are 'dogs' and ἡ κατατομή and the Christians are ἡ περιτομή, i.e., the covenant people of God (cf., e.g., Beare, *Phil.*, p.104; Gnilka, *Phil.*, pp.187f.). Richardson (pp.111–117) is forced to recognize in Phil 3.3 'the beginning of the transpositions' between the Church and the Jewish nation as the people of God, but he suppresses the significance of Phil 3.3 in the interest of his thesis, which is unfolded in a questionable manner at many points.

[1] *Supra* 9f., 15ff.

our new creation, is consummated, the whole creation will be redeemed and renewed together with us (Rom 8.19–22).

To *sum up* briefly the results of our discussion in this chapter: Paul's soteriology is strongly stamped by his experience at the Damascus Christophany. The characteristics of his doctrine of justification *sola gratia* and *sola fide* are due to the insights into the questions of the law, human existence and man's relation to God which he developed out of his Damascus experience. It was out of his personal experience of God's forgiveness and God's reconciliation on the Damascus road that Paul developed the imagery of 'reconciliation' to interpret God's saving work in Christ. And, finally, it was by seeing the risen and exalted Christ as the Son and image of God who has restored the divine image and glory lost by Adam that Paul developed his soteriological conception of the believers' being adopted as sons of God, their being transformed into the glorious image of Christ and their being made the 'new man' or καινὴ κτίσις through their incorporation into Christ, the *Stammvater* of the new humanity.

Conclusion

Now it remains to gather up the main results of this investigation and to briefly indicate their significance.

1. Paul was born in Tarsus but was raised and educated in Jerusalem. He excelled in the Rabbinic scholarship and belonged to the fellowship of the Pharisees, probably to its strictest wing, the school of Shammai. Being extremely zealous for the law and the ancestral traditions of Israel, Paul persecuted the Church violently for two chief reasons: one, because the Christians proclaimed Jesus of Nazareth, who had been crucified under God's curse pronounced by the law, as the Messiah raised and exalted by God; the other, because they, especially the Hellenistic Jewish Christians, attacked the law and the Temple cult in the name of Jesus of Nazareth. Since he saw this proclamation of the crucified Jesus as the Messiah and their criticism of the law and the Temple cult as an apostasy from and a threat to the law and the ancestral traditions, he persecuted them violently after the example of Phinehas, Matthathias and other 'zealots' for God, the law, and the purity of Israel.

2. While Paul was pursuing Christians on the road to Damascus, the risen Christ appeared to him, and so Paul saw him. In that encounter Paul received the gospel and Christ's commission for him to go to the Gentiles and proclaim the gospel, that is, to be his apostle to the Gentiles. Paul responded to this call immediately and went to Arabia, the Nabataean Kingdom, to proclaim the gospel there.

3. At the Christophany, which was of the same kind as the visions granted to OT prophets at their call and also to some apocalyptists, Paul received the revelation (ἀποκάλυψις) of the gospel, the good news concerning the salvation in Christ which has been realized in the death and resurrection of Jesus Christ and awaits its consummation at his parousia, and, together with it or as part of it, the revelation of the 'mystery' (μυστήριον), namely God's plan of salvation embodied in Christ for both the Jews and the Gentiles.

4. As the appearance of Jesus of Nazareth raised from the dead and exalted by God confirmed the primitive Church's proclamation of him, Paul accepted not only the Christian confession of the crucified Jesus as the Messiah, the Lord and the Son of God, but also the ideas contained in the

confessions. This meant Paul's abandoning his Jewish conception of the Messiah and taking what Jesus of Nazareth was and did as the true characteristics of the Messiah. Paul saw Jesus as the Lord exalted by God and enthroned at his right hand in fulfilment of Ps.110.1, being ready to return to earth for judgement and redemption, so that he came to know that now salvation depends on entering into the sphere of Jesus' Lordship by confessing 'Jesus is Lord'. Paul also saw confirmed at the Christophany the primitive Church's confession of Jesus as the Son of God. But at the same time he realized that Jesus was the Son of God not just in the sense of the Davidic Messiah who was confessed by the Christians as having been installed as God's Son through his resurrection, but more profoundly in the sense of the being who stood in an intimate relationship with God from the beginning, acted as his agent in creation and was sent forth by God into the world to redeem us from sin and the law. For the revelation of the crucified Jesus of Nazareth as enthroned at God's right hand proved to Paul that through the cross Jesus Christ has superseded the Torah as the medium of divine revelation and salvation, and therefore that he is the one who had formerly been described as Wisdom. Thus on the basis of his Damascus experience Paul initiated, probably building upon Jesus' Wisdom sayings, this explicit 'identification' of Jesus with Wisdom in the early Church. Because the title 'Son of God' means Jesus' being the perfect agent of the divine revelation and salvation, in supersession of the Torah, Paul defines or abbreviates his gospel with that title.

5. Paul also saw the exalted Jesus Christ as the εἰκών τοῦ θεοῦ and as the Son of God. This perception led Paul to conceive of Christ in terms of the personified, hypostatized Wisdom of God (together with his realization at that time that Christ had superseded the Torah) on the one hand, and in terms of Adam, on the other. Thus, both Paul's Wisdom-Christology and Adam-Christology are grounded in the Damascus Christophany. Furthermore, seen in the *Traditionsgeschichte* as well as in the *Formgeschichte*, the Damascus Christophany leads us to think that Paul's designation of Jesus as the Son of God, based on that Christophany, exactly corresponds to Jesus' intention in his self-designation as the Son of Man, and also that that vision of Christ contributed to Paul's conception and imagery of the Church as the Body of Christ and the true Israel.

6. Having seen Jesus of Nazareth crucified under the pronouncement of God's curse by the law, as exalted and enthroned by God, Paul came to think that Christ has brought the law to an end as the medium of God's revelation and salvation and that the sinless Christ died not for his sin but 'for us', 'for our sins'. At the same time, having seen that his zeal for the law, for the righteousness based on the law, had led him only to the gravest sin of opposing God and his Messiah, Paul realized that man cannot be justified by works of the law. But when God nevertheless justified Paul, the 'ungodly', the

enemy of God, by his sheer grace, Paul came to know that justification is by God's grace alone. Thus the characteristics of Paul's doctrine of justification *sola gratia* and *sola fide* are due to the insights into the questions of the law, human existence and man's relation to God which he developed out of his Damascus experience. It was also out of his personal experience of God's forgiveness and reconciliation on the Damascus road that Paul developed the imagery of 'reconciliation' to interpret God's saving work in Christ. Finally, it was by seeing the risen and exalted Christ as the Son and image of God who has restored the divine image and glory lost by Adam that Paul developed his soteriological conception of the believers' being adopted as sons of God, their being transformed into the glorious image of Christ and their being made the 'new man' or καινὴ κτίσις through their incorporation into Christ, the Last Adam, the *Stammvater* of the new humanity.

7. Corresponding to the fundamental importance and the constitutive character of Paul's Damascus experience for his theology is the fact that Paul repeatedly refers or alludes to the experience. From this fact and from the nature of his references to the experience, we can safely surmise that in his missionary proclamation Paul narrated the Damascus Christophany and his biographical data surrounding the event as an integral part of his gospel.

Thus it is clear that Paul's gospel and apostleship are grounded solely in the Christophany on the Damascus road. The Damascus event is the basis of both his theology and his existence as an apostle. This is what he means when he insists that he is an 'apostle, not from man nor through man but through Jesus Christ and God the Father, who raised him from the dead' (Gal 1.1) and that the gospel which he preached is not a 'human' gospel, 'for I did not receive it from man, nor was I taught it; but it came δι' ἀποκαλύψεως Ἰησοῦ Χριστοῦ', that is, through God's 'revelation of his Son, so that I might proclaim him as the content of the gospel among the Gentiles' (Gal 1.11f., 16). So Paul's gospel is nothing but God's *revelation* on the Damascus road.

Ignoring this fundamental testimony of Paul himself, for far too long his modern interpreters have attempted to explain his gospel only by analysing it in the light of literary and *religionsgeschichtliche* parallels. They assign some elements of his theology to Palestinian Judaism, some to Hellenistic Judaism, some to mystery-cults, some to Gnosticism, and others to 'any exegetical semi-divinity of the ancient world'[1] that they can resurrect from

---

[1] K.Barth, *Romans*, p.8.

the ruins of history. Some exegetes content themselves with drawing out alleged parallels between Paul's theology and some Jewish and pagan literary sources under the illusion that thereby they have *explained* Paul's gospel. Others, being theologically more alert, take another step and advance an opinion as to *why* and *how* Paul borrowed these elements from the 'exegetical semi-divinities of the ancient world'. But, ignoring Paul's own loud testimony, the latter invariably suggest Paul's speculative thinking and his controversies with the representatives of rival religions and with his erring converts and other opponents as the driving force behind his turning Jesus of Nazareth into a divine figure and into the agent of God's salvation. This sort of interpretation results only in giving the impression that Paul's theology is a hotchpotch syncretism of various mosaic pieces derived from many diverse sources which are all very precariously pieced together to form a 'Jesus Christ' the Lord and the Son of God miles away from the historical Jesus[1]. If only modern interpreters of Paul would take Paul's own testimony and his unshakable conviction of the crucified Jesus of Nazareth as the Messiah, the Lord and the Son of God just as seriously as the alleged *religionsgeschichtlichen* parallels, they would not suffer the illusion that by merely drawing out parallels between Paul's theology and the thoughts of others they have *explained* Paul's theology. For then they would be confronted with the *riddle* as to *how* and *why* the zealous Pharisee who had been so fiercely opposed to the crucified Jesus of Nazareth came to the unshakable conviction that precisely that Jesus who was crucified under the authoritative pronouncement of God's curse by the Torah only a couple of years before and whose brother he knew personally (Gal 1.19; 2.9; cf. 1Cor 9.5) is not only the Messiah but the pre-existent Son of God through whose incarnation, death and resurrection God has wrought the eschatological salvation of the whole world[2]. How did the fanatic opponent of Jesus become his bond-slave, an apostle of his, who went about the *oecumene*, proclaiming him as the embodiment of God's saving act, in such terrible sufferings? How can we imagine a Paul traversing land and sea in untold sufferings for the sake of a phantom 'Jesus Christ' which he pieced together with mosaic pieces borrowed from this or that background?

He who does not think Paul was insane, must take Paul's own testimony seriously, namely that he received his gospel 'through the revelation of Jesus Christ' on the Damascus road. As we have already seen[3], Paul's insistence

---

[1] Hengel, *Sohn*, p.17, also finds this problem with many theologians.

[2] Cf. *ibid.*, pp.30f., also 9ff.

[3] *Supra* pp.103f.

that he received his gospel through God's revelation of his Son on the Damascus road does not mean that up to that moment his mind was theologically a *tabula rasa*. Paul certainly had known the messianic beliefs, the conceptions of the law and Wisdom, and other ideas and concepts in Judaism and the primitive Christian kerygma, and perhaps also became acquainted with some Hellenistic ideas and concepts later in his mission field. But these *religionsgeschichtlichen* materials neither made Paul a Christian nor produced his theology. They were suspended, needing a catalyst for solution into Paul's theology. Only when there was the catalyst of the living experience of seeing the crucified Jesus as the exalted Messiah, the Lord, and the Son and image of God on the Damascus road, were these materials precipitated into Paul's Christian theology[1]. To put it another way, the real experience of the Damascus revelation led Paul to use all those *religionsgeschichtlichen* materials as interpretative categories and concepts for his Christian theology. That is to say, those materials provided Paul only with certain categories and concepts with which he could interpret the Damascus experience and produce his theology. But without the real experience of the Damascus revelation Paul could not have had his gospel at all, not to mention his unshakable and lively conviction in it.

As we saw earlier[2], Paul's insistence that he received his gospel 'through the revelation of Jesus Christ' on the road to Damascus does not also mean that there and then he explicitly obtained his whole theology as seen in his letters. Rather, it means that the essential elements and main lines of his theology have their origin in the fundamental revelation. This we hope to have demonstrated in this book. Further reflections on the revelation in the light of the OT Scriptures, his experience in the mission field and his con-

---

[1]Dunn, *Jesus*, p.4, puts our present concern well: 'Where in the earliest decades of this century study after study of Paul's life and faith focussed to greater or lesser degree on his conversion experience as the great explanatory key to unlock the whole, today the great quest is for literary parallels, the "older elements", which can be adjudged to explain his language and theology – to such an extent indeed that one might be tempted to conclude that Paul's theology is simply the end product of a process of literary natural selection. Such a conclusion is patently absurd . . . I readily acknowledge Paul's debt to both Jew and Greek for the great bulk of his language and concepts. But his own writings bear eloquent and passionate testimony to the creative power of his own religious experience – a furnace which melted many concepts in its fires and poured forth new moulds . . . Nothing should be allowed to obscure that fact. As Hermann Gunkel asserted by way of protest against similar emphases in the research of his own day, "The theology of the great apostle is an expression of his experience, not of his reading . . . Paul believes in the divine Spirit, because he has experienced it/him" '.

[2]*Supra* pp.102f.

troversies with his opponents led him to deepen and sharpen his understanding of the gospel revealed on the Damascus road. We should also mention Paul's continual experience of God's revelations through the Spirit (e.g., 2Cor 12.1ff.) which constantly deepened his understanding of the gospel. Thus his theology developed. But in view of the nature of the elements of his theology which we delineated as having originated from the Damascus Christophany, it is probably better to think that Paul saw the full implications of the Damascus revelation and more or less completely formulated the main lines of his theology soon after the Damascus revelation — certainly, at latest by the time of the Apostolic Council or on the eve of his world-wide missionary journey — than to posit a long period of slow development.

At any rate, it is most important to ascertain that *Paul received his gospel from the Damascus revelation of Jesus Christ.* We submit that *only when this insistence of Paul is taken seriously can we really understand Paul and his theology.*

Two tasks remain. One is to draw more systematic theological consequences from the results of our exegetical investigation into Paul's theology. The other is to complete the expositions of the correlation between Paul's gospel and his universal mission, and of his understanding of the *Heilsgeschichte*, his apostleship and the place of his universal mission in the *Heilsgeschichte*, which we have been able only to begin in this study. Only when these are done, will the exposition of the Damascus revelation be complete. But for the moment we must rest content with the completion of this exegetical groundwork.

Select Bibliography

I. Sources

i. The Bible

H KAINH ΔIAΘHKH, ed. E.Nestle & G.D.Kilpatrick (London, [2]1965)
Biblia Hebraica, ed. R.Kittel *et al.* (Stuttgart, [3]1973)
Septuaginta, ed. A.Rahlfs, 2 vols. (Stuttgart, 1935)
The Holy Bible, Revised Version (Oxford and Cambridge, 1885) (RV)
The Holy Bible, Revised Standard Version: OT (New York, 1952); NT (New York, 1946) (RSV)
The New English Bible with the Apocrypha (Oxford and Cambridge, 1970) (NEB)

ii. Jewish Sources

The Apocrypha and Pseudepigrapha of the Old Testament, ed. R.H.Charles, 2 vols. (Oxford, 1913)   (*Apoc. & Pseud.*)
Die Apokryphen und Pseudepigraphen des Alten Testaments, ed. E.Kautzsch, 2 Vols. (Tübingen, 1900)   (*Apok. u. Pseud.*)
Altjüdisches Schrifttum außerhalb der Bibel, ed. P.Riessler (Heidelberg, [2]1966)
The Apocalypse of Abraham, ed. G.H.Box & J.I.Landsman, TED I, Palestinian Jewish Texts (Pre-Rabbinic) (London, 1919)
The Testament of Abraham: the Greek Recensions, ed. M.E.Stone, SBLTT 2 **Pseudepigrapha Series 2 (Missoula,** 1972)
The Book of Enoch, ed. R.H.Charles (Oxford, [2]1912)
3 Enoch, or the Hebrew Book of Enoch, ed. H.Odeberg (Cambridge, 1928)
Die Esra-Apokalypse, ed. B.Violet, 2 vols. GCS18, 32 (Leipzig, 1910, 1924)
The Ezra-Apocalypse, ed. G.H.Box (London, 1912)
The Fourth Book of Ezra: the Latin Version, ed. R.L.Bensly, Texts S III.2 (Cambridge, 1895)
Die Oracula Sibyllina, ed. J.Geffcken, GCS 8 (Leipzig, 1902)
The Greek Versions of the Testaments of the Twelve Patriarchs, ed. R.H.Charles (Oxford, 1908)
Testament XII Patriarcharum, ed. M.de Jonge, PVTG 1 (Leiden, 1964)
The Lost Apocrypha of the Old Testament, ed. M.R.James, TED I, Palestinian Jewish Texts (Pre-Rabbinic) (London, 1920)
Messias Judaeorum, ed. A.Hilgenfeld (Leipzig, 1869)
Die Texte aus Qumran, Hebräisch und Deutsch, ed. E.Lohse (München, 1964)
11Q Melchizedek in: M.de Jonge & A.S.v.d.Woude, '11Q Melchizedek and the New Testament', *NTS* 12 (1965/66), pp.302f.
Das Fragmententhargum (Thargum jeruschalami zum Pentateuch), ed. M.Ginsburger (Berlin, 1899)
Pseudo-Jonathan (Thargum Jonathan ben Usiël zum Pentateuch), ed. M.Ginsburger (Berlin, 1903)

The Targums of Onkelos and Jonathan ben Uzziel on the Pentateuch with the Fragments of the Jerusalem Targum from the Chaldee, tr. J.W.Etheridge (New York, 1968)
Targum Neophyti, ed. A.D.Macho, E.T.McNamara & M.Maher, 4 vols. (Madrid, 1968–1974)
The Targum of Isaiah, ed. & tr. J.F.Stenning (Oxford, 1953)
A Rabbinic Anthology, ed. C.G.Montefiore & H.Loewe (London, 1938)
Mekilta de Rabbi Ishmael, ed. & tr. J.Z.Lauterbach, 3 vols. (Philadelphia, 1933, 1976)
Midrash on Psalms, tr. W.G.Braude, 2 vols., Yale Judaica Series 13 (New Haven, 1959)
Midrash Rabbah, tr. H.Freedman & M.Simon, 10 vols (London, 1939)
The Mishnah, tr. H.Danby (Oxford, 1933)
Pesikta Rabbati, tr. W.G.Braude, 2 vols., Yale Judaica Series 18 (New Haven, 1968)
The Babylonian Talmud, ed. I.Epstein, 18 vols. (London, 1935–1952)
Le Talmud Jerusalem, tr. M.Schwab, 6 vols. (Paris, 1960)
Josephus, *Works*, ed. H.St.Thackeray, R.Marcus, A.Wikgren, & L.H.Feldman, 9 vols., Loeb (London, 1926–1965)
Philo, *Works*, ed. L.Colson & G.H.Whitaker, 10 vols., Loeb (London, 1929–1962), with Supplementary vols. I & II, ed. R.Marcus (London, 1953)
Service of the Synagogue: Day of Atonement, Part II (London, [10]1904)

iii. Early Christian Sources

New Testament Apocrypha, ed. E.Hennecke & W.Schneemelcher, English edition by R.McL.Wilson, 2 vols. (London, 1965)
Die ältesten Apologeten, ed. E.J.Goodspeed (Göttingen, 1914)
The Writings of Justin Martyr and Athenagoras, ed. & tr. A.Roberts & J.Donaldson, Ante-Nicene Christian Library II (Edinburgh, 1967)
Hippolytus, *Refutatio Omnium Haeresium*, ed. P.Wendland, GCS 26 (Leipzig, 1916)
Jerome, *Liber Viris illustribus*, in: *Opera* II, ed. J.P.Migne, *PL* 23 (Paris, 1845)
The Odes of Solomon, ed. & tr. J.H.Charlesworth (Oxford, 1973)
Die Schatzhöhle, syrisch und deutsch, ed. Bezold, 2 vols. (Leipzig, 1883–1889)

iv. Greek & Hellenistic Sources

Corpus Hermeticum, ed. A.D.Nock, tr. A. –J.Festugière, 4 vols. (Paris, 1945–1954)
Epigrammatum Anthologia Palatina II, ed. F.Dübner (Paris, 1872)
Papyri Graecae Magicae I, ed. K.Preisendanz (Stuttgart, [2]1973)
Plato, *Phaedrus*, in: *Platonis Opera* II, ed. J.Burnet (Oxford, 1901)
The Geography of Strabo VI, ed. H.L.Jones, Loeb (London, 1960)

v. Gnostic Sources

Koptisch-gnostische Apokalypse aus Codex V von Nag-Hammadi im koptischen Museum zu Alt-Kairo, ed. A.Böhlig & P.Labib (Halle-Wittenberg, 1963)
Die gnostischen Schriften des koptischen Papyrus Berolinensis 8502, ed. W.C.Till, TU 60 (Berlin, 1955)
Ginza: der Schatz oder das große Buch der Mandäer, ed. M.Lidzbarski (Göttingen, 1925)
The Canonical Prayerbook of the Mandaeans, ed. E.S.Drower (Leiden, 1959)
'Vom Ursprung der Welt: eine titellose gnostische Abhandlung aus dem Funde von Nag-Hammadi', ed. & tr. H. –M.Schenke, *ThLZ* 84 (1959), cols. 243–256.
The Hypostasis of the Archons, ed. & tr. R.A.Bullard (Berlin, 1970)

II. *Reference Works used but not cited in this book*

E.Hatch & H.A.Redpath,	*A Concordance to the Septuagint and the Other Greek Versions of the Old Testament,* 3 vols. (reprint: Graz, 1954)
G.Lisowsky,	*Konkordanz zum Hebräischen Alten Testament* (Stuttgart,. ²1958)
G.Mayer,	*Index Philoneus* (Berlin, 1974)
W.F.Moulton & A.S.Geden,	*A Concordance to the Greek Testament*, 4th ed. revised by H.K.Moulton (Edinburgh, 1974)

III. *Secondary Literature*

The following volumes of collected essays are abbreviated in this section of Bibliography as:

Apostolic History	*Apostolic History and the Gospel*, F.F.Bruce FS, ed. W.W. Gasque & R.P.Martin (Exeter, 1970)
Geschichte	*Neues Testament und Geschichte*, O.Cullmann FS, ed. H. Baltensweiler & B.Reicke (Zürich, 1972)
Kirche	*Neues Testament und Kirche*, R.Schnackenburg FS, ed. J. Gnilka (Freiburg, 1974)
Menschensohn	*Jesus und der Menschensohn*, A.Vögtle FS, ed. R.Pesch & R.Schnackenburg (Freiburg, 1975)
Paul and Qumran	*Paul and Qumran*, ed. J.Murphy–O'Connor (London, 1968)
Reconciliation	*Reconciliation and Hope*, L.L.Morris FS, ed. R.Banks (Exeter, 1974)
Rechtfertigung	*Rechtfertigung*, E.Käsemann FS, ed. J.Friedrich, W.Pöhlmann & P.Stuhlmacher (Tübingen, 1976)
Religions	*Religions in Antiquity*, Essays in Memory of E.R.Goodenough, ed. J.Neusner (Leiden, 1968)
T.K.Abbott,	*The Epistles to the Ephesians and to the Colossians*, ICC (Edinburgh, 1897)
P.Althaus,	*Paulus und Luther über den Menschen* (Gütersloh, ⁴1963)
A.A.Anderson,	*The Book of Psalms I*, NCB (London, 1972)
L.Baeck,	'The Faith of Paul', *JJS* 3 (1952), pp.93–110
W.Baird,	'What is the Kerygma?', *JBL* 76 (1957), pp.181–191
H.R.Balz,	*Methodische Probleme der neutestamentlichen Christologie*, WMANT 25 (Neukirchen, 1967)
E.Bammel,	'Judenverfolgung und Naherwartung', *ZThK* 56 (1959) pp.294–315
	'Versuch zu Col. 1.15–20', *ZNW* 52 (1961), pp.88–95
R.Banks,	*Jesus and the Law in the Synoptic Gospels*, SNTSMS 28 (Cambridge, 1975)

E.Barnikol,	*Die vorchristliche und frühchristliche Zeit des Paulus* (Kiel, 1929)
J.Barr,	'Theophany and Anthropomorphism in the Old Testament', *VT Supplement* 7 (1960), pp.31–38 'The Image of God in the Book of Genesis – A Study of Terminology', *BJRL* 51 (1968/69), pp.11–26
C.K.Barrett,	*A Commentary on the Epistle to the Romans*, BNTC (London, 1957) *A Commentary on the First Epistle to the Corinthians* BNTC (London, 1968) *A Commentary on the Second Epistle to the Corinthians*, BNTC (London, 1973) *From First Adam to Last* (London, 1962) 'Paul's Opponents in II Corinthians', *NTS* 17 (1970/71) pp. 233–254
K.Barth,	*The Epistle to the Romans*, E.T. from the 6th edition of *Der Römerbrief* (1928) (London, 1968) *A Shorter Commentary on Romans* (E.T.London, 1959) *The Epistle to the Philippians* (E.T.London, 1962) *Rudolf Bultmann, ein Versuch, ihn zu verstehen/Christus und Adam nach Röm 5*, zwei theologische Studien (Zürich, 1964)
M.Barth,	*Ephesians*, AB, 2 vols. (Garden City, N.Y., 1974)
F.Baumgärtel,	καρδία, *TDNT* iii, pp.606–607 πνεῦμα, *TDNT* vi, pp.359–368
F.W.Beare,	*A Commentary on the Epistle to the Philippians*, BNTC (London, 1958)
G.R.Beasley-Murray,	*A Commentary on Mark Thirteen* (London, 1957) *Baptism in the New Testament* (London, 1962)
J.Becker,	'Erwägungen zu Phil.3, 20–21', *ThZ* 27 (1971), pp.16–29
J.Behm,	καρδία, *TDNT* iii, pp.608–613 μορφή, κτλ, *TDNT* iv, pp.742–759 νοῦς, *TDNT* iv, pp.951–960
H.Bellen,	'Συναγωγὴ τῶν 'Ιουδαίων καὶ θεοσεβῶν: Die Aussage einer bosporanischen Freilassungsinschrift (CIRB 71) zum Problem der "Gottesfürchtigen" ', *Jahrbuch für Antike und Christentum* 8/9 (Münster, 1965/66), pp.171–176
P.Benoit,	'Qumran and the New Testament', *Paul and Qumran*, pp. 1–30
K.Berger,	'Zum Problem der Messianität Jesu', *ZThK* 71 (1974) pp. 1–30
R.Bergmeier,	'Quellen vorchristlicher Gnosis', *Tradition und Glaube*, K.G.Kuhn FS, ed. G.Jeremias, H.–W.Kuhn & H.Stegemann (Göttingen, 1971), pp.200–220

| G.Bertram, | ἐπιστρέφω, *TDNT* vii, pp.722–729 |

G.Bertram,   ἐπιστρέφω, *TDNT* vii, pp.722–729

E.Best,   *One Body in Christ* (London, 1955)
                    A Commentary on the First and Second Epistles to the Thessalonians, BNTC (London, 1972)

H.D.Betz,   'Das Verständnis der Apokalyptik in der Theologie der Pannenberg-Gruppe', *ZThK* 65 (1968), pp.257–270

O.Betz,   *Offenbarung und Schriftforschung in der Qumransekte*, WUNT 6 (Tübingen, 1960)
                    What Do We Know about Jesus? (E.T.London, 1968)
                    'Die Vision des Paulus im Tempel. Apg.22, 17–21 als Beitrag zur Deutung des Damaskuserlebnisses', *Verborum Veritas*, G.Stählin FS, ed. O.Böcher & K.Haacker (Wuppertal, 1970)
                    'Paulus als Pharisäer nach dem Gesetz: Phil.3, 5–6 als Beitrag zur Frage des frühen Pharisäismus', *Treue zur Thora*, G. Harder FS, ed. P.v.d.Osten-Sacken (Berlin, 1977), pp.54–64

K.Beyschlag,   'Zur Simon-Magus-Frage', *ZThK* 68 (1971), pp.395–426

W.Bieder,   πνεῦμα, *TDNT* vi, pp.359–375

M.Black,   *Romans,* NCB (London, 1973)
                    'The Pauline Doctrine of the Second Adam', *SJT* 7 (1954), pp.170–179
                    'The Christological Use of the Old Testament in the New Testament', *NTS* 18 (1971/72), pp.1–14
                    'Die Apotheose Israels: eine neue Interpretation des danielischen "Menschensohns" ', *Menschensohn*, pp.92–99
                    'The Throne-Theophany Prophetic Commission and the "Son of Man": A Study in Tradition-History', *Jews, Greeks and Christians,* W.D.Davies FS, ed. R.Hamerton-Kelly & R.Scroggs (Leiden, 1976), pp.56–73

E.P.Blair,   'Paul's call to the Gentile Mission', *Biblical Research* 10 (1965), pp.19–33

J.Blank,   *Paulus und Jesus*, SANT 18 (München, 1968)
                    'Warum sagt Paulus: "Aus Werken des Gesetzes wird niemand gerecht"?', *Evangelisch-Katholischer Kommentar Vorarbeiten* Heft 1 (Neukirchen, 1969), pp.79–95

H.Boers,   'The Form Critical Study of Paul's Letters, 1 Thessalonians as a Case Study', *NTS* 22 (1976), pp.140–158

P.Borgen,   'From Paul to Luke', *CBQ* 31 (1969), pp.168–182

G.Bornkamm,   *Paulus* (Stuttgart, ²1969)
                    μυστήριον, *TDNT* iv, pp.802–827
                    'Paulus', *RGG*³ v, cols. 166–190
                    'Taufe und neues Leben bei Paulus', *Das Ende des Gesetzes,* Gesammelte Aufsätze i, BEvT 16 (München, ⁵1966), pp. 34–50
                    'Sünde, Gesetz und Tod', *ibid.*, pp.51–69
                    'Paulinische Anakoluthe im Römerbrief', *ibid.*, pp.76–92

'Glaube und Vernunft bei Paulus', *Studien zu Antike und Urchristentum*, Ges. Aufsätze ii, BEvT 28 (München, 1970), pp.119–137
'Das Bekenntnis im Hebräerbrief', *ibid.*, pp.188–203
'The Missionary Stance of Paul in 1Corinthians 9 and in Acts', *Studies in Luke-Acts*, P.Schubert FS, ed. L.E.Keck & J.L.Martyn (London, 1968), pp.194–207
'Revelation of Christ to Paul on the Damascus Road and Paul's Doctrine of Justification and Reconciliation. A Study in Galatians 1', *Reconciliation*, pp.90–103

F.H.Borsch, *The Son of Man in Myth and History* (London, 1967)
The Christian and Gnostic Son of Man, SBT 14 (London, 1970)

W.Bousset, *Kyrios Christos* (Göttingen, [2]1921)

W.Bousset and H. Greßmann, *Die Religion des Judentums im späthellenistischen Zeitalter*, HNT 21 (Tübingen, [4]1966)

J.W.Bowker, ' "Merkabah" Visions and the Visions of Paul', *JSS* 16 (1971), pp.157–173

J.Bowman, 'The Background of the Term "Son of Man" ', *ExpT* 59 (1948), pp.283–288

G.H.Box, '4 Ezra', *Apoc. & Pseud.* ii, ed. Charles, pp.542–624

E.Brandenburger, *Adam und Christus*, WMANT 7 (Neukirchen, 1962).

C.H.W.Brekelmans, 'The Saints of the Most High and Their Kingdom', *Oudtestamentische Studien* 14 (1965), pp.305–329

R.Bring, *Commentary on Galatians* (Philadelphia, 1961)
'The Message to the Gentiles', *StTh* 19 (1965), pp.30–46

L.H.Brockington, 'The Septuagintal Background to the New Testament Use of Δόξα', *Studies in the Gospels*, Essays in Memory of R.H. Lightfoot, ed. D.E.Nineham (Oxford, 1955), pp.1–8

R.E.Brown, 'The Semitic Background of the New Testament *Mysterion*', *Biblica* 39 (1958), pp.426–448; 40 (1959), pp.70–87

F.F.Bruce, *The Acts of the Apostles* (London, [2]1970)
The Book of Acts, NLC (London, 1970)
The Epistle to the Colossians, NLC (London, 1957)
The Epistle to the Hebrews, NLC (London, [3]1971)
Romans, Tyndale New Testament Commentaries (London, 1969)
1 and 2 Corinthians, NCB (London, 1971)
This is That (Exeter, 1968)
New Testament History (London, [2]1971)
Paul and Jesus (Grand Rapids, 1974)
Paul: Apostle of the Heart Set Free (Exeter. 1977)
"Jesus is Lord", *Soli Deo Gloria*, W.C.Robinson FS, ed. J.M.Richards (Richmond, 1968), pp.23–36
'Galatian Problems: 1. Autobiographical Data', *BJRL* 51 (1968/69), pp.292–309

F.F.Bruce (*con'd*)   'Galatian Problems: 4. The Date of the Epistle', *BJRL* 54
                             (1971/72), pp.250–267
                             'Paul and the Law of Moses', *BJRL* 57 (1974/75), pp.259–
                             279
                             'Christ and Spirit in Paul', *BJRL* 59 (1976/77), pp.259–
                             285
                             'Paul and Immortality', *SJT* 24 (1971), pp.457–472
F.Büchsel,   καταλλάσσω,κτλ, *TDNT* i, pp.254–259
R.Bultmann,   *Das Evangelium des Johannes*, MeyerK 6 (Göttingen,
                             19̄1968)
                             Theology of the New Testament, 2 vols. (E.T.London, 1968)
                             Der zweite Brief an die Korinther, MeyerK 2 (Göttingen,
                             1976)
                             'Paulus', *RGG²* iv, cols. 1020–1045
                             πιστεύω, *TDNT* vi, pp.197–228
                             'Die Christologie des Neuen Testaments', *Glauben und
                             Verstehen* i (Tübingen, 7̄1972), pp.245–267
                             'Das christologische Bekenntnis des ökumenischen Rates',
                             Glauben und Verstehen ii (Tübingen, 1952), pp.246–261
                             'Römer 7 und die Anthropologie des Paulus', *Exegetica*
                             (Tübingen, 1967), pp.198–209
                             'Jesus und Paulus', *ibid.*, pp.210–229
                             'Exegetische Probleme des zweiten Korintherbriefes', *ibid.*,
                             pp.298–322
                             'Ursprung und Sinn der Typologie als hermeneutischer
                             Methode', *ibid.*, pp.369–380
                             'ΔΙΚΑΙΟΣΥΝΗ ΘΕΟΥ', *ibid.*, pp.470–475
C.Burchard,   *Der dreizehnte Zeuge*, FRLANT 103 (Göttingen, 1970)
F.C.Burney,   *The Aramaic Origin of the Fourth Gospel* (Oxford, 1922)
                             'Christ as the APXH of Creation', *JTS* 27 (1926), pp.160–
                             177
E.de Witt Burton   *The Epistle to the Galatians*, ICC (Edinburgh, 1921)
H.J.Cadbury,   'The Hellenists', *Beginnings* v, pp.59–74
H.Frh.von Campenhausen,   'Der urchristliche Apostelbegriff', *StTh* 1 (1948), pp.96–
                             130
                             'Das Bekenntnis im Urchristentum', *ZNW* 63 (1972), pp.210
                             –253
L.Cerfaux,   *Christ in the Theology of St.Paul* (E.T.London, 1959)
                             The Church in the Theology of St.Paul (E.T.London, 1959)
                             'La vocation de S.Paul', *Euntes Docete* (Rome, 1961)
F.Christ,   *Jesus Sophia*, ATANT 57 (Zürich, 1970)
D.J.A.Clines,   'The Image of God in Man', *TynB* 19 (1968), pp.53–103
C.Colpe,   *Die religionsgeschichtliche Schule*, FRLANT 87 (Göttingen,
                             1961)
                             ὁ υἱὸς τοῦ ἀνθρώπου, *TDNT* viii, pp.400–477
                             'Gnosis', *RGG³* ii, cols. 1648–1652
                             'Zur Leib-Christi-Vorstellung im Epheserbrief', *Judentum* –

Urchristentum – Kirche, J.Jeremias FS, BZNW 26 (Berlin, ²1964), pp.172–187
'New Testament and Gnostic Christology', *Religions*, pp.227 –243

H.Conzelmann, *An Outline of the Theology of the New Testament* (E.T. London, 1969)
Der erste Brief an die Korinther, MeyerK 5 (Göttingen, ¹¹1969)
Die Apostelgeschichte, HNT 7 (Tübingen, ²1972)
Geschichte des Urchristentums, NTD Ergänzungsreihe 5 (Göttingen, ²1971)
φῶς, *TDNT* ix, pp.310–358
χάρις, κτλ., *TDNT* ix, pp.372–376, 387–402
χάρισμα, *TDNT* ix, pp.402–406
'Paulus und die Weisheit', *NTS* 12 (1965/66), pp.231–244

J.Coppens, ' "Mystery" in the Theology of Saint Paul and its Parallels at Qumran', *Paul and Qumran*, pp.132–158

C.E.B.Cranfield, *The Epistle to the Romans* I, ICC (Edinburgh, ⁶1975)
'St. Paul and the Law', *SJT* 17 (1964), pp.43–68

O.Cullmann, *The Christology of the New Testament* (E.T.London, 1959)
Die Tradition als exegetisches, historisches, und theologisches Problem (Zürich, 1966)
Petrus:Jünger-Apostel-Märtyrer (Zürich, ²1960)
The Johannine Circle (E.T.London, 1976)
Πέτρος, *TDNT* vi, pp.100–112
'Der eschatologische Charakter des Missionsauftrags und des apostolischen Selbstbewußtseins bei Paulus', *Vorträge und Aufsätze 1925–1962* (Tübingen, 1966), pp.305–336

N.A.Dahl, *Das Volk Gottes* (Oslo, 1941)
'Zur Auslegung von Gal. 6, 16', *Judaica* 6 (1950), pp.101– 170
'Die Messianität Jesu bei Paulus', *Studia Paulina*, J.de Zwaan FS, ed. J.N.Sevenster & W.van Unnik (Haarlem, 1953), pp. 83–95
'Formgeschichtliche Beobachtungen zur Christusverkündigung in der Gemeindepredigt', *Neutestamentliche Studien für R.Bultmann*, BZNW 21 (Berlin, ²1957), pp.1–9
'Christ, Creation and the Church', *The Background of the New Testament and Its Eschatology*, C.H.Dodd FS, ed. D.Daube & W.D.Davies (Cambridge, 1956), pp.422–443
'The Atonement – an Adequate Reward for the Akedah? (Ro 8:32)', *Neotestamentica et Semitica*, M.Black FS, ed. E.E.Ellis & M.Wilcox (Edinburgh, 1969), pp.15–29

J.Daniélou, *Theology of Jewish Christianity* (E.T.London, 1964)

W.D.Davies, *Paul and Rabbinic Judaism* (London, ³1970)
Christian Origins and Judaism (London, 1972)
'The Apostolic Age and the Life of Paul'. *Peake's Commen-*

W.D.Davies (*con'd.*)   *tary on the Bible,* ed. H.H.Rowley & M.Black (London, 1967), pp.870–881

R.Deichgräber,   *Gotteshymnus und Christushymnus in der frühen Christenheit,* SUNT 5 (Göttingen, 1967)

A.Deissler,   'Der "Menschensohn" und "das Volk der Heiligen des Höchsten" in Dan 7', *Menschensohn,* pp.81–91

G.Delling,   ἀνεξερεύνητος, *TDNT* i, p.357

A.M.Denis,   *Introduction aux pseudépigraphes grecs d'Ancien Testament* (Leiden, 1970)

J.D.M.Derrett,   'Cursing Jesus (1Cor XII.3): the Jews as Religious "Persecutors" ', *NTS* 21 (1975), pp.244–254

M.Dibelius,   *An die Thessalonicher I/II. An die Philipper,* HNT 11 (Tübingen, ³1937)

M.Dibelius and H. Greeven,   *An die Kolosser, Epheser, An Philemon,* HNT 12 (Tübingen, ³1953)

M.Dibelius and W.G.Kümmel,   *Paulus* (Berlin, ³1964)

K.Dick,   *Der schriftstellerische Plural bei Paulus* (Halle, 1900)

E.Dinkler,   'Tradition im Urchristentum', *RGG*³ vi, cols. 970–974

C.H.Dodd,   *The Parables of the Kingdom,* Fontana ed. (London, 1969)
The Bible and the Greeks (London, 1935)
The Epistle of Paul to the Romans, NMNTC, Fontana ed. (London, 1970)
According to the Scriptures (London, 1952)
The Interpretation of the Fourth Gospel (Cambridge, 1970)

J.W.Doeve,   *Jewish Hermeneutics in the Synoptic Gospels and Acts* (Assen, 1954)

J.W.Drane,   *Paul: Libertine or Legalist?* (London, 1975)

D.C.Duling,   'The Promises to David and Their Entrance into Christianity – Nailing Down a Likely Hypothesis', *NTS* 19 (1974), pp. 55–77

A.v.Dülmen,   *Die Theologie des Gesetzes bei Paulus,* SBM5 (Stuttgart, 1968)

G.S.Duncan,   *The Epistle of Paul to the Galatians,* MNTC (London, 1934)

J.D.G.Dunn,   *Baptism in the Holy Spirit,* SBT 15 (London, 1970)
Jesus and the Spirit (London, 1975)
'2 Corinthians III. 17 – "The Lord is the Spirit" ', *JTS* 21 (1970), pp.309–320
'1Cor. 15:45 – Last Adam, Life-giving Spirit', *Christ and the Spirit,* C.F.D.Moule FS, ed. B.Lindars and S.S.Smalley (Cambridge, 1973), pp.127–141
'Rom.7, 14–25 in the Theology of Paul', *ThZ* 31 (1975), pp. 257–273

'Paul's Understanding of the Death of Jesus', *Reconciliation*, pp.123–141

J.Dupont, 'The Conversion of Paul and Its Influence on His Understanding of Salvation by Faith', *Apostolic History*, pp.176–194

G.Eichholz, *Tradition und Interpretation*, TBü 29 (München, 1965)
Die Theologie des Paulus im Umriß (Neukirchen, 1972)

O.Eissfeldt, *The Old Testament: An Introduction* (E.T.Oxford, 1965)

E.E.Ellis, *Paul's Use of the Old Testament* (Edinburgh, 1957)
"Christ Crucified", *Reconciliation*, pp.69–75
' "Wisdom" and "Knowledge" in 1Corinthians', *TynB* 25 (1974), pp.82–98
'The Role of the Christian Prophets in Acts', *Apostolic History*, pp.50–67
'Paul and his Opponents', *Prophecy and Hermeneutic* (Tübingen, 1977), pp.78–113

F.-W.Eltester, *Eikon im Neuen Testament*, BZNW 23 (Berlin, 1958)

J.A.Emerton, 'The Origin of the Son of Man Imagery', *JTS* 9 (1958), pp.225–242

W.R.Farmer, *Maccabees, Zealots and Josephus* (New York, 1956)

E.Fascher, *Jesaja 53 in christlicher und jüdischer Sicht* (Berlin, 1958)

P.Feine, *Das gesetzesfreie Evangelium des Paulus* (Leipzig, 1899)
Theologie des Neuen Testaments (Leipzig, [3]1919)

F.Feuillet, *Le Christ Sagesse de Dieu* (Paris, 1966)
'Le Fils de l'homme de Daniel et la Tradition biblique', *RB* 60 (1953), pp.170–202, 321–346

K.M.Fischer, *Tendenz und Absicht des Epheserbriefes*, FRLANT 111 (Göttingen, 1973)

A.Flanagan, 'A Note on Philippians iii. 20–21', *CBQ* 18 (1956), pp.8–9

G.Fohrer, υἱός, *TDNT* viii, pp.340–354

A.Fridrichsen, 'The Apostle and his Message', *Uppsala Universitets Arsskrift* 3 (1947), pp.3–23

G.Friedrich, *Der Brief an die Philipper*, NTD 8 (Göttingen, 1962)
εὐαγγελίζομαι, *TDNT* ii, pp.707–721
κηρύσσω, *TDNT* iii, pp.697–714
προφήτης, κτλ, *TDNT* vi, pp.828–856

'Die Gegner des Paulus im 2.Korintherbrief', *Abraham unser Vater*, O.Michel FS, ed. O.Betz, M.Hengel, & P.Schmidt, AGSU5 (Leiden, 1963), pp.181–215
'Ein Tauflied hellenistischer Judenchristen', *ThZ* 21 (1965), pp.502–516

R.H.Fuller, *The Foundations of New Testament Christology*, Fontana ed. (London, [3]1974)

H.J.Gabathuler,   *Jesus Christus, Haupt der Kirche – Haupt der Welt*, ATANT
                       45 (Zürich, 1965)

P.Gaechter,   *Petrus und seine Zeit* (Innsbruck, 1958)

D.Georgi,   *Die Gegner des Paulus im 2.Korintherbrief,*WMANT 11 (Neu-
                       kirchen, 1964)
                       Die Geschichte der Kollekte des Paulus für Jerusalem (Ham-
                       burg-Bergstedt, 1965)

B.Gerhardsson,   *Memory and Manuscript*, ASNU 22 (Uppsala, 1961)

H.Gese,   'Natus ex virgine', *Probleme biblischer Theologie*, G.von Rad
                       FS, ed. H,W.Wolff (München, 1971), pp.73–89

L.Ginzberg,   *Legends of the Jews* v (E.T.Philadelphia, 1925)

J.Gnilka,   *Der Philipperbrief*, HTKNT x.3 (Freiburg, 1968)
                       Der Epheserbrief, HTKNT x.2 (Freiburg, 1971)

D.Goldsmith,   'Acts 13.33–37: A *Pesher* on II Samuel 7' *JBL* 87 (1968),
                       pp.321–324

L.Goppelt,   *Christologie und Ethik* (Göttingen, 1969)
                       Theologie des NT (Göttingen, 1976)

E.Grafe,   'Das Verhältnis der paulinischen Schriften zur Sapientia
                       Salomonis', *Theologische Abhandlungen*, C.v.Weizsäcker FS
                       (Freiburg, 1892), pp.251–286

H.Grass,   *Ostergeschehen und Osterberichte* (Göttingen, [2]1962)

K.Grayston,   'The Doctrine of Election in Romans 8, 28–30', *StEv* ii,
                       TU 87 (1964), pp.574–583

F.W.Grosheide,   *Commentary on the First Epistle to the Corinthians*, NLC
                       (London, [2]1954)

W.Grundmann,   *Das Evangelium nach Matthäus*, THKNT 1 (Berlin, 1972)
                       ἀνάγκη, *TDNT* i, pp.344–347
                       δύναμις, *TDNT* ii, pp.284–317
                       'Paulus, aus dem Volke Israel, Apostel der Völker', *NovT* 4
                       (1960), pp.267–291

G.Gutbrod,   Ἐβραῖος, κτλ, *TDNT* iii, pp.369–391

E.Güttgemanns,   *Der leidende Apostel und sein Herr*, FRLANT 90 (Göttingen,
                       1966)

K.Haacker,   'War Paulus Hillelit?', *Das Institutum Judaicum der Univer-
                       sität Tübingen 1971–72*, pp.106–120
                       'Die Bekehrung des Verfolgers und die Rechtfertigung des
                       Gottlosen', *Theologische Beiträge* 6 (1975), pp.1–19

O.Haas,   *Paulus der Missionar* (Münsterschwarzach, 1971)

E.Haenchen,   *Die Apostelgeschichte*, MeyerK 3 (Göttingen, [15]1968)

F.Hahn,   *Christologische Hoheitstitel*, FRLANT 83 (Göttingen, [3]1974)
                       Das Verständnis der Mission im Neuen Testament, WMANT
                       13 (Neukirchen, 1963)

Der urchristliche Gottesdienst, SBS 41 (Stuttgart, 1970)
'Das Gesetzesverständnis im Römer- und Galaterbrief',
G.Bornkamm FS, *ZNW* 67 (1976), pp.29–63
'Taufe und Rechtfertigung. Ein Beitrag zur paulinischen
Theologie in ihrer Vor- und Nachgeschichte', *Rechtfertigung*,
pp.95–124

R.G.Hamerton-Kelly,   *Pre-existence, Wisdom and the Son of Man*, SNTSMS 21
(Cambridge, 1973)

A.v.Harnack,   'κόπος (κοπιᾶν, οἱ κοπιῶ ντες) im frühchristlichen Sprachgebrauch', *ZNW* 27 (1928), pp.1–10

F.Hauck,   ὀφείλω, κτλ., *TDNT* v, pp.559–566

H.Hegermann,   *Die Vorstellung vom Schöpfungsmittler im hellenistischen
Judentum und Christentum*, TU 82 (Berlin, 1961)

H.W.Heidland,   λογίζομαι, *TDNT* iv, pp.284–292

M.Hengel,   *Die Zeloten*, AGSU 1 (Leiden, 1961)
Judentum und Hellenismus, WUNT 10 (Tübingen, [2]1973)
Der Sohn Gottes (Tübingen, 1975)
'Die Synagogeninschrift von Stobi', *ZNW* 57 (1966), pp.145–
183
'Die Ursprünge der christlichen Mission', *NTS* 18 (1971/
72), pp.15–38
'Christologie und neutestamentliche Chronologie', *Ge-
schichte*, pp.43–67
'Zwischen Jesus und Paulus. Die "Hellenisten", die "Sieben"
und Stephanus (Apg 6, 1–15; 7, 54–8, 3)', *ZThK* 72 (1975),
pp.151–206
'Mors turpissima crucis', *Rechtfertigung*, pp.125–184

J.Héring,   *The First Epistle of Saint Paul to the Corinthians* (E.T.
London, 1966)
Le Royaume de Dieu et sa venue (Paris, 1959)

I.Hermann,   *Kyrios und Pneuma*, SANT 2 (München, 1961)

D.Hill,   *Greek Words and Hebrew Meanings*, SNTSMS 5 (Cambridge,
1967)
'Prophecy and Prophets in the Revelation of St. John',
NTS 18 (1971/72), pp.401–418
'On the Evidence for the Creative Role of Christian Prophets',
NTS 20 (1974), pp.262–274

E.Hirsch,   'Die drei Berichte der Apostelgeschichte über die Bekehrung
des Paulus', *ZNW* 28 (1929), pp.205–312

O.Hofius,   *Der Christushymnus Phil 2, 6–11*, WUNT 17 (Tübingen, 1976)

T.Holtz,   'Zum Selbstverständnis des Apostels Paulus', *ThLZ* 91
(1966), cols. 321–330

M.D.Hooker,   *The Son of Man in Mark* (London, 1967)
'Interchange in Christ', *JTS* 22 (1971), pp.349–361

H.Hübner,   'Gal 3, 10 und die Herkunft des Paulus', *KD* 19 (1973), pp.215–231

P.E.Hughes,   *Paul's Second Epistle to the Corinthians*, NLC (London, 1961)

A.M.Hunter,   *Paul and His Predecessors* (London, [2]1961)

E.Jenni,   דמה, *ThHAT* i, cols. 451–456
                הוי, *ThHAT* i, cols. 474–477
                מתי, *ThHAT* i, cols. 933–936

G.Jeremias,   *Der Lehrer der Gerechtigkeit*, SUNT 2 (Göttingen, 1963)

J.Jeremias,   *Jerusalem in the Time of Jesus* (E.T.London, [3]1976)
                Jesus' Promise to the Nations (E.T.London, 1958)
                The Parables of Jesus (E.T.London, [3]1976)
                Der Opfertod Jesu Christi, Calwer Hefte 62 (Stuttgart, 1963)
                Der Schlüssel zur Theologie des Apostels Paulus, Calwer Hefte 115 (Stuttgart, 1971)

                'Ἀδάμ, *TDNT* i, pp.141–143
                Μωυσῆς, *TDNT* iv, pp.848–873
                παῖς θεοῦ, *TDNT* v, pp.677–717
                'Abba', *Abba* (Göttingen, 1966), pp.15–80
                'Chiasmus in den Paulusbriefen', *Abba*, pp.276–290
                'Paulus als Hillelit', *Neotestamentica et Semitica*, M.Black FS, ed. E.E.Ellis & M.Wilcox, (Edinburgh, 1969), pp.88–94

J.Jervell,   *Imago Dei*, FRLANT 76 (Göttingen, 1960)
                Luke and the People of God (Minneapolis, 1972)

R.Jewett,   *Paul's Anthropological Terms*, AGJU 10 (Leiden, 1971)

H.Jonas,   *Gnosis und spätantiker Geist I*, FRLANT 33 (Göttingen, [2]1954)

M.de Jonge,   *The Testaments of the Twelve Patriarchs* (Assen, 1953)

E.Käsemann,   *Leib und Leib Christi*, BHT 9 (Tübingen, 1933)
                Das wandernde Gottesvolk, FRLANT 37 (Göttingen, [4]1961)
                An die Römer, HNT 8a(Tübingen, [2]1974)
                'Eine urchristliche Taufliturgie', *EVB* i, pp.34–51
                'Kritische Analyse von Phil. 2, 5–11', *ibid.*, pp.51–95
                'Zum Verständnis von Röm. 3, 24–26', *ibid.*, pp.96–100
                'Amt und Gemeinde im Neuen Testament', *ibid.*, pp.109–134
                'Zum Thema der urchristlichen Apokalyptik', EVB ii, pp.105–131
                'Gottesgerechtigkeit bei Paulus', *ibid.*, pp.181–193
                'Paulus und Israel', *ibid.*, pp.194–197
                Eine paulinische Variation des "amor fati" ', *ibid.*, pp.223–239
                'Paulus und der Frühkatholizismus', *ibid.*, pp.239–252
                'Zur paulinischen Anthropologie', *Paulinische Perspektiven* (Tübingen), pp.9–60

'Die Heilsbedeutung des Todes Jesu bei Paulus', *ibid.*, pp.
61–107
'Der Glaube Abrahams in Röm.4', *ibid.*, pp.140–177
'Die Legitimität des Apostels. Eine Untersuchung zu II.
Korinther 10–13', *ZNW* 41 (1942), pp.33–71
'Erwägungen zum Stichwort "Versöhnungslehre im Neuen
Testament" ', *Zeit und Geschichte*, R.Bultmann FS, ed.
E.Dinkler (Tübingen, 1964), pp.47–59

H.Kasting,   *Die Anfänge der urchristlichen Mission*, BEvT 55 (München,
                            1969)

N.Kehl,   *Der Christushymnus im Kolosserbrief*, SBM 1 (Stuttgart,
                            1967)

H.A.A.Kennedy,   *St. Paul's Conceptions of the Last Things* (London, 1904)

K.Kertelge,   *"Rechtfertigung" bei Paulus*, NT Abh 3 (Münster, [2]1971)
                            'Apokalypsis Jesou Christou (Gal. 1, 12)', *Kirche*, pp.266–
                            281

G.Kittel,   ἀκούω, *TDNT* i, pp.216–225
                            ἀπαύγασμα, *TDNT* i, p.508
                            δόξα, *TDNT* ii, pp.233–237, 242–253
                            εἰκών, *TDNT* ii, pp.392–397

J.Klausner,   *From Jesus to Paul* (London, 1946)

G.Klein,   *Die Zwölf Apostel*, FRLANT 77 (Göttingen, 1961)
                            'Gottes Gerechtigkeit als Thema der neuesten Paulus-For-
                            schung', *Verkündigung und Forschung* 12/2 (1967), pp.1–11

H.Kleinknecht,   εἰκών, *TDNT* ii, pp.388–390

W.L.Knox,   *St. Paul and the Church of the Gentiles* (Cambridge, 1939)

L.Koehler,   'Die Grundstelle der Imago-Dei-Lehre', *ThZ* 4 (1948) pp.
                            16–22

H.Köster,   Review of U.Wilckens, *Weisheit und Torheit*, in *Gnomon*
                            33 (1961), pp.590–595
                            'The Structure and Criteria of Early Christian Beliefs', *Tra-
                            jectories through Early Christianity* by J.M.Robinson & H.
                            Köster (Philadelphia, 1971), pp.205–231

W.Kramer,   *Christ, Lord, Son of God*, SBT50 (E.T.London, 1966)

H.J.Kraus,   *Psalmen I*, BKAT IX/1 (Neukirchen, 1961)

K.G.Kuhn,   'Εβραῖος, κτλ., *TDNT* iii, pp.359–369
                            προσήλυτος, *TDNT* vi, pp.727–744
                            'Der Epheserbrief im Lichte der Qumrantexte', *NTS* 7 (1960/
                            61), pp.334–346

W.G.Kümmel,   *Römer 7 und das Bild des Menschen im Neuen Testament*,
                            TBü53 (München, 1974)
                            Introduction to the New Testament (E.T.London, [2]1977)
                            Die Theologie des Neuen Testaments, NTD Ergänzungsreihe
                            3 (Göttingen, [2]1972)

W.G.Kümmel, (*con'd.*)   *Promise and Fulfilment*, SBT 23 (E.T.London, [2]1966)
'Jesus und Paulus', *Heilsgeschehen und Geschichte* (Marburg, 1965)

W.Künneth,   *Die Theologie der Auferstehung* (München, [5]1968)

O.Kuss,   *Der Römerbrief*, 1. & 2. Lieferungen (Regensburg, [2]1963)
Paulus/Die Rolle des Apostels in der theologischen Entwicklung der Urkirche, Auslegung und Verkündigung III (Regensburg, 1971)
'Nomos bei Paulus', *Münchener Theologische Zeitschrift* 17 (1966), pp.173–227

G.E.Ladd,   *Jesus and the Kingdom* (London, 1966)

K.Lake,   'Proselytes and God-fearers', *Beginnings* v, pp.74–96
'The Conversion of Paul and the Events immediately following it', *ibid.*, pp.188–191

W.R.Lane,   'A New Commentary Structure in 4Q Florilegium', *JBL* 78 (1959), pp.343–346

E.Larsson,   *Christus als Vorbild*, ASNU 23 (Uppsala, 1962)

F.-J.Leenhardt,   *The Epistle to the Romans* (E.T.London, 1961)

R.Leivestad,   'Exit the Apocalyptic Son of Man', *NTS* 18 (1971/72), pp.243–267

H.J.Leon,   *The Jews of Ancient Rome* (Philadelphia, 1960)

R.Liechtenhan,   *Die urchristliche Mission* (Zürich, 1946)

H.Lietzmann & W.G.Kümmel,   *An die Korinther I/II*, HNT 9 (Tübingen, [5]1969)

J.B.Lightfoot,   *Saint Paul's Epistle to the Galatians* (London, 1900)
Saint Paul's Epistle to the Philippians (London, 1927)
Saint Paul's Epistle to the Colossians and to Philemon (London, 1904)

B.Lindars,   *New Testament Apologetic* (London, 1961)
'Re-Enter the Apocalyptic Son of Man', *NTS* 22 (1976), pp.52–72

J.Lindblom,   *Gesichte und Offenbarungen* (Lund, 1968)

G.Lohfink,   *Paulus vor Damaskus*, SBS 4 (Stuttgart, 1966)

E.Lohmeyer,   *Kyrios Jesus* (Heidelberg, [2]1961)
Die Briefe an die Philipper, an die Kolosser und an Philemon, MeyerK 9 (Göttingen, [8]1930, [13]1964)
Der Brief an die Philipper, MeyerK 9 (Göttingen, [13]1964)

E.Lohse,   *Märtyrer und Gottesknecht*, FRLANT 64 (Göttingen, [2]1963)
Die Briefe an die Kolosser und an Philemon, MeyerK 9 (Göttingen, [14]1968)
υἱός, *TDNT* viii, pp.357–362
'Die Gerechtigkeit Gottes in der paulinischen Theologie', *Die Einheit des Neuen Testaments* (Göttingen, 1973), pp.210

−227

'Taufe und Rechtfertigung bei Paulus', *ibid.*, pp.228−244
'Der Menschensohn in der Johannesapocalypse', *Menschensohn*, pp.415−420

R.N.Longenecker,   *The Christology of Early Jewish Christianity*, SBT 17 (London, 1970)

D.Lührmann,   *Das Offenbarungsverständnis bei Paulus und in paulinischen Gemeinden*, WMANT 16 (Neukirchen, 1965)

U.Luz,   *Das Geschichtsverständnis des Paulus*, BEvT 49 (München, 1968)

S.Lyonnet,   *Les étapes du mystère du salut selon l'épître aux Romains* (Paris, 1969)

J.Macdonald,   *The Theology of the Samaritans* (London, 1964)

J.Maier,   *Vom Kultus zur Gnosis*, Kairos 1 (Salzburg, 1964)

T.W.Manson,   *The Sayings of Jesus (*London, 1949)
The Teaching of Jesus (Cambridge, ²1963)
Studies in the Gospels and Epistles (Manchester, 1962)
On Paul and John, SBT 38 (London, ²1967)
'The Problem of the Epistle to the Hebrews', *BJRL* 32 (1949), pp.1−17

W.Manson,   *Jesus the Messiah* (London, 1943)
The Epistle to the Hebrews (London, 1951)

I.H.Marshall,   *Luke: Historian and Theologian* (Exeter, 1970)
The Origins of New Testament Christology (Downers Grove, Ill., 1976)
'The Divine Sonship of Jesus', *Interpretation* 21 (1967), pp.87−103
'The Christ-Hymn in Philippians 2:5−11. A Review Article', *TynB* 19 (1968), pp.104−127
'Palestinian and Hellenistic. Christianity: Some Critical Comments', *NTS* 19 (1972/73), pp.271−287

R.P.Martin,   *Carmen Christi: Phil.ii.5−11*, SNTSMS 4 (Cambridge, 1967)

W.Marxsen,   *The Resurrection of Jesus of Nazareth* (E.T.London, 1970)

C.Masson,   *L'épître de Saint Paul aux Collossiens*, CNT 10 (Neuchatel, 1950)

C.Maurer,   'Die Begründung der Herrschaft Christi über die Mächte nach Col. 1, 15−20', *Wissenschaft und Dienst* NF 4 (1955), pp. 79−93

M.McNamara,   *The New Testament and the Palestinian Targum to the Pentateuch*, AnBib 27 (Rome, 1966)

P.H.Menoud,   'Revelation and Tradition', *Interpretation* 7 (1953), pp.131−141

H.Merklein,   *Das krichliche Amt nach dem Epheserbrief*, SANT 33 (München, 1973)

B.M.Metzger,	*A Textual Commentary on the Greek New Testament* (London, 1971)
J.H.Michael,	*The Epistle of Paul to the Philippians*, MNTC (London, 1939)
W.Michaelis,	*Der Brief des Paulus an die Philipper*, THKNT (Leipzig, 1935) ὁράω, *TDNT* v, pp.315−367 πρωτότοκος, *TDNT* vi, pp.871−881
O.Michel,	*Der Brief an die Hebräer*, MeyerK 13 (Göttingen, [12]1966) *Der Brief an die Römer*, MeyerK 4 (Göttingen, [13]1966) ὁ υἱὸς τοῦ ἀνθρώπου, *Begriffslexikon* II/2, pp.1153−1166 'Die Entstehung der paulinischen Christologie', *ZNW* 28 (1929), pp.324−333 ' "Erkennen dem Fleisch nach" (2.Kor. 5, 16)', *EvTh* 14 (1954), pp.22−29 'Fragen zu 1Thessalonicher 2, 14−16: Antijüdische Polemik bei Paulus', *Antijudaismus im Neuen Testament?*, ed. W Eckert, N.P.Levinson & M.Stöhr (München, 1969), pp.50−59
P.S.Minear,	*The Obedience of Faith*, SBT 19 (London, 1971)
L.Mitton,	*The Epistle to the Ephesians* (Oxford, 1951)
O.Moe,	'Der Menschensohn und der Urmensch', *StTh* 14 (1960), pp.121−129
C.G.Montefiore,	*Judaism and St.Paul* (London, 1914)
H.W.Montefiore,	*The Epistle to the Hebrews*, BNTC (London, 1964)
L.Morris,	*The Apostolic Preaching of the Cross* (London, [3]1965) 'The Meaning of ΊΛΑΣΤΗΡΙΟΝ in Romans III.25', *NTS* 2 (1955/56), pp.33−43
C.F.D.Moule,	*The Epistles of Paul the Apostle to the Colossians and to Philemon* (Cambridge, 1957) *Origin of Christology* (Cambridge, 1977) 'Once More, Who Were the Hellenists?', *ExpT* 70 (1958/59), pp.100−102 'Obligation in the Ethic of Paul', *Christian History and Interpretation*, J.Knox FS, ed. W.R.Farmer, C.F.D.Moule & R.R.Niebuhr (Cambridge, 1967), pp.389−406 'Jesus in New Testament Kerygma', *Verborum Veritas*, G.Stählin FS, ed. O.Böcher & K.Haacker (Wuppertal, 1970), pp.15−26 '2 Cor 3.18b, καθάπερ ἀπὸ κυρίου πνεύματος', *Geschichte*, pp.413−428 'Neglected Features in the Problem of the "Son of Man" ', *Kirche*, pp.413−428
S.Mowinckel,	*He That Cometh* (E.T.Oxford, 1956)
J.Muilenburg,	'The Son of Man in Daniel and the Ethiopic Apocalypse of Enoch', *JBL* 79 (1960), pp.197−209

C.Müller,	*Gottes Gerechtigkeit und Gottes Volk*, FRLANT 86 (Göttingen, 1964)
U.B.Müller,	*Messias und Menschensohn in jüdischen Apokalypsen und in der Offenbarung des Johannes*, SNT 6 (Gütersloh, 1972)
J.Munck,	*Paul and the Salvation of Mankind* (E.T.London, 1959) *Christ and Israel* (Philadelphia, 1967)
W.Mundle,	*Der Glaubensbegriff bei Paulus* (Leipzig, 1932)
B.Murmelstein,	'Adam, ein Beitrag zur Messiaslehre', *WZKM* 35 (1928), pp. 242–275; 36 (1929), pp.51–86
J.Murray,	*The Epistle to the Romans*, 2 vols., NLC (London, 21970)
F.Mussner,	*Der Galaterbrief*, HTKNT 4 (Freiburg, 1974) 'Contributions made by Qumran to the Understanding of the Epistle to the Ephesians', *Paul and Qumran*, pp.159–178
F.Neugebauer,	*In Christus* (Göttingen, 1961) 'Das paulinische "In Christus" ', *NTS* 4 (1957/58), pp.124–138
J.Neusner,	*The Rabbinic Traditions about the Pharisees before 70, Part I The Masters* (Leiden, 1971)
K.Niederwimmer,	'Erkennen und Lieben', *KD* 11 (1965), pp.75–102
A.Nissen,	'Tora und Geschichte im Spätjudentum', *NovT* 9 (1967), pp.241–277
A.D.Nock,	*Arthur Darby Nock: Essays on Religions and the Ancient World* ii, ed. Z.Stewart (Oxford, 1972)
M.Noth,	"Die Heiligen des Höchsten", *Gesammelte Studien zum Alten Testament*, TBü 6 (München, 1957), pp.274–290
F.Nygren,	*Commentary on Romans* (E.T.London, 1952)
H.Odeberg,	*The Fourth Gospel* (Amsterdam, 1968)
A.Oepke,	*Der Brief des Paulus an die Galater*, THKNT 9 (Berlin, 21957) καλύπτω, κτλ., *TDNT* iii, pp.556–592 'Probleme der vorchristlichen Zeit des Paulus', *Das Paulusbild in der neueren deutschen Forschung*, ed. K.H.Rengstorf (Darmstadt, 1964), pp.410–446
P.v.d.Osten-Sacken,	*Römer 8 als Beispiel paulinischer Soteriologie*, FRLANT 112 (Göttingen, 1975)
A.Pallis,	*To the Romans* (Liverpool, 1920)
W.Pannenberg,	*Jesus – God and Man* (E.T.London, 1968) 'Dogmatische Thesen zur Lehre von der Offenbarung', *Offenbarung als Geschichte*, ed. W.Pannenberg (Göttingen, 21963)
H.Paulsen,	*Überlieferung und Auslegung in Römer 8*, WMANT 43 (Neukirchen, 1974)
B.A.Pearson,	*The Pneumatikos – Psychikos Terminology in 1 Corinthians,*

B.A.Pearson (*con'd.*)   SBLDS 12 (Missoula, 1973)
'1 Thessalonians 2:13–16: a Deutero-Pauline Interpolation', *HTR* 64 (1971), pp.79–94

E.Percy,   'Zu den Problemen des Kolosser- und Epheserbriefes', *ZNW* 43 (1950/51), pp.178–194

E.Pfaff,   *Die Bekehrung des H.Paulus in der Exegese des 20. Jahrhunderts* (Rome, 1942)

V.C.Pfitzner,   *Paul and the Agon Motif*, NovTSup 16 (Leiden, 1967)

C.Plag,   *Israels Wege zum Heil* (Stuttgart, 1969)

A.Plummer,   *The Second Epistle of St.Paul to the Corinthians*, ICC (Edinburgh, [2]1925)

Preuss,   דמות/דמה, *ThWAT* ii, cols. 266–277

O.Procksch,   *Theologie des Alten Testaments* (Gütersloh, 1950)
'Die Berufungsvision Hesekiels', *BZAW* 34, K.Budde FS (1920), pp.141–149
'Der Menschensohn als Gottessohn', *Christentum und Wissenschaft* 3 (1927), pp.425–443, 473–481.

G.Quispel,   'Der gnostische Anthropos und die jüdische Tradition', *Gnostic Studies* I (Istanbul, 1974), pp.173–195
'Gnosticism and the New Testament', *ibid.*, pp.196–212

G.von Rad,   *Old Testament Theology*, 2 vols. (E.T.London, 1975)
δόξα, *TDNT* ii, pp.238–242
εἰκών, *TDNT* ii, pp.390–392

A.E.J.Rawlinson,   *The New Testament Doctrine of the Christ* (London, 1926)

B.Reicke,   'Chronologie der Pastoralbriefe', *ThLZ* 101 (1976), cols. 81–94

K.H.Rengstorf,   *Die Auferstehung Jesu* (Witten/Ruhr, [4]1960)
ἀπόστολος, *TDNT* i, pp.398–447

, ed.,   *Das Paulusbild in der neueren deutschen Forschung* (Darmstadt, 1964)

J.Reumann,   'οἰκονομία-Terms in Paul in Comparison with Lucan *Heilsgeschichte*', *NTS* 13 (1966/67), pp.147–167

A.Richardson,   *Introduction to the Theology of the New Testament* (London, [4]1969)

P.Richardson,   *Israel in the Apostolic Church*, SNTSMS 10 (Cambridge, 1969)

H.Ridderbos,   *Paulus: ein Entwurf seiner Theologie* (German tr. Wuppertal, 1970)
'The Earliest Confession of the Atonement in Paul', *Reconciliation*, pp.76–89

B.Rigaux,   *The Letters of St.Paul* (Chicago, 1968)

A.Robertson & A.Plummer,   *The First Epistle of St.Paul to the Corinthians*, ICC (Edinburgh, [2]1925)

H.Wheeler Robinson,	'The Hebrew Conception of Corporate Personality', *Corporate Personality*, ed. J.Reumann (Philadelphia, 1964), pp.1–20
	'The Group and the Individual in Israel', *ibid.*, pp.21–35
J.M.Robinson,	'A Formal Analysis of Colossians 1.15–20', *JBL* 76 (1957), pp.270–287
	'Kerygma as Hermeneutic Language Event', *Trajectories through Early Christianity* by J.M.Robinson & H.Köster (Philadelphia, 1971), pp.20–70
	'LOGOI SOPHŌN: on the Gattung of Q', *ibid.*, pp.71–113
J.A.T.Robinson,	*The Body*, SBT 5 (London, 1952)
	Redating the New Testament (London, 1976)
J.Roloff,	*Apostolat-Verkündigung-Kirche* (Gütersloh, 1965)
K.Romaniuk,	'Die "Gottesfürchtigen" im Neuen Testament', *Aegyptus* 44 (Milan, 1964), pp.66–91
	'Le Livre de la Sagesse dans le Nouveau Testament', *NTS* 14 (1967/68), pp.503–513
J.H.Ropes,	*The Singular Problem of the Epistle to the Galatians*, HTS 14 (Cambridge, Mass., 1929)
D.Rössler,	*Gesetz und Geschichte*, WMANT 3 (Neukirchen, [2]1962)
C.C.Rowland,	*The Influence of the First Chapter of Ezekiel on Jewish and Early Christian Literature*, unpublished Ph.D.Thesis (Cambridge, 1974)
K.Rudolph,	*Die Mandäer, I. Prolegomena*, FRLANT 56 (Göttingen, 1960)
D.S.Russell,	*The Method and Message of Jewish Apocalyptic* (London, 1964)
W.Sanday & A.C.Headlam,	*The Epistle to the Romans*, ICC (Edinburgh, [5]1905)
J.T.Sanders,	'Hymnic Elements in Eph.1–3', *ZNW* 56 (1965), pp.214–232
	'Paul's Autobiographical Statements in Galatians 1–2', *JBL* 85 (1966), pp.335–343
A.Satake,	'Apostolat und Gnade bei Paulus', *NTS* 15 (1968/69), pp.96–107
H.-M.Schenke,	*Der Gott "Mensch" in der Gnosis* (Göttingen, 1962)
G.Schille,	*Frühchristliche Hymnen* (Berlin, 1965)
A.Schlatter,	*Die Theologie der Apostel* (Stuttgart, 1922)
	Gottes Gerechtigkeit (Stuttgart, [4]1965)
	Paulus der Bote Jesu (Stuttgart, [3]1962)
H.Schlier,	*Der Brief an die Galater*, MeyerK 7 (Göttingen, [14]1971)
	Der Brief an die Epheser (Düsseldorf, [7]1971)
	ἀνατολή, *TDNT* i, pp.351–353
	'Kerygma und Sophia', *Die Zeit der Kirche* (Freiburg, [5]1972)
	'Zu Röm 1, 3f.', *Geschichte*, pp.207–218

K.L.Schmidt,   κλητός, *TDNT* iii, pp.494–496
                    'HOMO Imago Dei im Alten und Neuen Testament', *Eranos-Jahrbuch* 15 (1948), pp.149–195

W.Schmithals,   *Die Gnosis in Korinth*, FRLANT 66 (Göttingen, [3]1969)
                    Paulus und Jakobus, FRLANT 85 (Göttingen, 1963)
                    Paulus und die Gnostiker (Hamburg-Bergstedt, 1965)

R.Schnackenburg,   *Baptism in the Thought of St.Paul* (E.T.Oxford, 1964)
                    'Römer 7 im Zusammenhang des Römerbriefes', *Jesus und Paulus*, W.G.Kümmel FS, ed. E.E.Ellis & E.Grässer, (Göttingen, 1975), pp.283–300

J.Schneider,   ὁμοίωσις/ὁμοίωμα, *TDNT* v, pp.190–198

H.-J.Schoeps,   *Urgemeinde, Judenchristentum, Gnosis* (Tübingen, 1956)
                    Paul: the Theology of the Apostle in the Light of Jewish Religious History (E.T.London, 1961)

G.Scholem,   *Major Trends in Jewish Mysticism* (New York, 1941, [3]1954)
                    Jewish Gnosticism, Merkabah Mysticism and Talmudic Tradition (New York, 1960)

L.Schottroff,   *Der Glaubende und die feindliche Welt*, WMANT 37 (Neukirchen, 1970)

W.Schrage,   συναγωγή, *TDNT* vii, pp.798–841
                    ' "Ekklesía" und "Synagoge" ', *ZThK* 60 (1963), pp.178–202

G.Schrenk,   δικαιοσύνη, *TDNT* ii, pp.192–210

S.Schulz,   'Die Decke des Moses: Untersuchungen zu einer vorpaulinischen Überlieferung in II.Cor. 3, 7–18', *ZNW* 49 (1958), pp.1–30

E.Schürer,   *Geschichte des jüdischen Volkes im Zeitalter Jesu Christi*, 3 vols., (Leipzig, [3]1901–09, reprinted: Hildesheim, 1964)

J.H.Schütz,   *Paul and the Anatomy of Apostolic Authority*, SNTSMS 26 (Cambridge, 1975)

P.Schwanz,   *Imago Dei* (Halle, 1970)

A.Schweitzer,   *The Mysticism of Paul the Apostle* (E.T.London, [2]1956)

E.Schweizer,   *Erniedrigung und Erhöhung*, ATANT 28 (Zürich, 1955)
                    = *Lordship and Discipleship*, SBT 28 (E.T.London, 1960)
                    πνεῦμα, *TDNT* vi, pp.389–451
                    υἱός, *TDNT* viii, pp.354–357, 363–392
                    'Zur Herkunft der Präexistenzvorstellung bei Paulus', *Neotestamentica* (Zürich, 1963), pp.105–109
                    'Aufnahme und Korrektur jüdischer Sophiatheologie im Neuen Testament', *ibid.*, pp.110–121
                    'Röm. 1, 3f. und der Gegensatz von Fleisch und Geist vor und bei Paulus', *ibid.*, pp.180–189
                    'Kirche als Leib Christi in den paulinischen Homolegomena', *ibid.*, pp.272–292
                    'Kirche als Leib Christi in den paulinischen Antilegomena',

ibid., pp.292–316
'The Church as the Missionary Body of Christ', *ibid.*, pp. 317-329
'Die "Mystik" des Sterbens und Auferstehens mit Christus bei Paulus', *EvTh* 26 (1966), pp.239–257
'Zum religionsgeschichtlichen Hintergrund der "Sendungsformel" Gal.4, 4f., Rö.8, 3f., Jn3, 16f., 1Jn4, 9', *ZNW* 57 (1966), pp.199–210
'Menschensohn und eschatologischer Mensch im Frühjudentum', *Menschensohn*, pp.100–116

E.F.Scott,	*The Epistles of Paul to the Colossians, to Philemon and to the Ephesians*, MNTC (London, 91958)
R.B.Y.Scott,	"Behold, He Cometh with Clouds", *NTS* 5 (1958/59), pp. 127–132
R.Scroggs,	*The Last Adam* (Oxford, 1966) 'Paul: ΣΟΦΟΣ and ΠΝΕΥΜΑΤΙΚΟΣ', *NTS* 14 (1967/68), pp.33–55
J.N.Sevenster,	*Do You Know Greek?*, NovTSup 19 (Leiden, 1968)
R.P.Shedd,	*Man in Community* (London, 1958)
P.Siber,	*Mit Christus leben*, ATANT 61 (Zürich, 1971)
M.Simon,	*St.Stephen and the Hellenists* (London, 1958)
E.Sjöberg,	*Der Menschensohn im äthiopischen Henochbuch* (Lund, 1946) 'Wiedergeburt und Neuschöpfung im palästinischen Judentum', *StTh* 3 (1950/51), pp.44–85 'Neuschöpfung in den Toten-Meer-Rollen', *StTh* 9 (1956), pp.131–136
J.Z.Smith,	'The Prayer of Joseph', *Religions*, pp.254–294
M.Smith,	'The Image of God: Notes on the Hellenization of Judaism', *BJRL* 40 (1958), pp.473–512 'On the Shape of God and the Humanity of the Gentiles', *Religions*, pp.315–326
K.Smyth,	'Heavenly Man and Son of Man in St.Paul', *AnBib* 17 (1963), pp.219–230
C.Spicq,	Note sur ΜΟΡΦΗ dans les papyrus et quelques inscriptions', *RB* 80 (1973), pp.37–45
G.Stählin,	*Die Apostelgeschichte*, NTD 5 (Göttingen, 101962)
O.H.Steck,	'Formgeschichtliche Bemerkungen zur Darstellung des Damaskusgeschehens in der Apostelgeschichte', *ZNW* 67, Bornkamm FS (1976), pp.20–28
K.Stendahl,	*Paul among Jews and Gentiles* (London, 1973)
H.J.Stoebe,	*Das erste Buch Samuelis*, KAT VIII/1 (Gütersloh, 1973)
R.H.Strachan,	*The Second Epistle to the Corinthians*, MNTC (London, 51948)

G.Strecker,   'Redaktion und Tradition im Christushymnus Phil.2, 6–11',
                              ZNW 55 (1964), pp.63–78
                              'Befreiung und Rechtfertigung. Zur Stellung der Recht-
                              fertigungslehre in der Theologie des Paulus', *Rechtfertigung*,
                              pp.479–508

A.Strucker,   *Die Gottebenbildlichkeit des Menschen in der christlichen
                              Literatur der ersten zwei Jahrhunderte* (München, 1913)

P.Stuhlmacher,   *Gerechtigkeit Gottes bei Paulus*, FRLANT 87 (Göttingen,
                              1966)
                              Das Paulinische Evangelium: I. Vorgeschichte, FRLANT
                              95 (Göttingen, 1968)
                              'Erwägungen zum ontologischen Charakter der καινὴ κτίσις
                              bei Paulus', *EvTh* 27 (1967), pp.1–35
                              'Erwägungen zum Problem von Gegenwart und Zukunft
                              in der paulinischen Eschatologie', *ZThK* 64 (1967), pp.
                              423–450
                              'Theologische Probleme des Römerbriefpräskripts', *EvTh* 27
                              (1967), pp.374–389
                              'Christliche Verantwortung bei Paulus und seinen Schülern',
                              EvTh 28 (1968), pp.165–186
                              ' "Das Ende des Gesetzes", über Ursprung und Ansatz der
                              paulinischen Theologie', *ZThK* 67 (1970), pp.14–39

                              'Zur Interpretation von Römer 11, 25–32', *Probleme bibli-
                              scher Theologie*, G.von Rad FS, ed. H.W.Wolff (München,
                              1971), pp.555–570

                              ' "Er ist unser Friede" (Eph 2, 14)', *Kirche*, pp.337–357
                              'Zur neueren Exegese von Röm 3, 24–26', *Jesus und Paulus*,
                              W.G.Kümmel FS, ed. E.E. Ellis & E.Grässer (Göttingen, 1975)
                              'Achtzehn Thesen zur paulinischen Kreuzestheologie', *Recht-
                              fertigung*, pp.509–525

M.J.Suggs,   *Wisdom, Christology and Law in Matthew's Gospel* (Cam-
                              bridge, Mass., 1970)

C.H.Talbert,   'The Myth of a Descending-Ascending Redeemer in Mediter-
                              ranean Antiquity', *NTS* 22 (1976), pp.418–440

R.C.Tannehill,   *Dying and Rising with Christ*, BZNW 32 (Berlin, 1967)

R.V.G.Tasker,   *The Second Epistle of Paul to the Corinthians*, Tyndale NT
                              Comm. (London, 1958)

V.Taylor,   *Forgiveness and Reconciliation* (London, 1941)
                              The Names of Jesus (London, 1953)
                              The Person of Christ (London, 1958)
                              The Atonement in New Testament Teaching (London, [3]1963)

M.E.Thrall,   'The Origin of Pauline Christology', *Apostolic History*,
                              pp.304–316

W.Thüsing,   *Per Christum in Deum*, NTAbh 1 (Münster, 1965)
                              Erhöhungsvorstellung und Parusieerwartung in der ältesten

nachösterlichen Christologie, SBS 42 (Stuttgart, 1969)

W.C.van Unnik,   'Aramaisms in Paul', *Sparsa Collecta*, Part One, NovTSup 29 (Leiden, 1973), pp.129–143
'Reisepläne und Amen-Sagen, Zusammenhang und Gedankenfolge in 2.Korinther i,15–24', *ibid*., pp.144–159
' "With Unveiled Face" (2Cor iv. 12–18)', *ibid*., pp.194–210
'Tarsus or Jerusalem. The City of Paul's Youth', *ibid*., pp. 259–320

G.Vermes,   *Jesus the Jew* (London, 1973)
Scripture and Tradition in Judaism, SPB 4 (Leiden, 1961)

A.Vögtle,   ' "Der Menschensohn" und die paulinische Christologie', *AnBib* 17 (1963), pp.199–218

H.Vorländer,   'Versöhnung', *Begriffslexikon* II/2, pp.1307–1309

G.Wanke,   ' אוֹי und הוֹי', *ZAW* 78 (1966), pp.215–218

A.J.M.Wedderburn,   *Adam and Christ: An Investigation into the Background of 1 Corinthians XV and Romans V 12–21*, unpublished Ph.D. Thesis (Cambridge, 1970)
'The Body of Christ and Related Concepts in 1Corinthians', *SJT* 24 (1971), pp.74–96
'Theological Structure of Romans v.12', *NTS* 19 (1972/73), pp.339–354
'Philo's "Heavenly Man" ', *NovT* 15 (1973), pp.301–326

K.Wegenast,   *Das Verständnis der Tradition bei Paulus und in den Deuteropaulinen*, WMANT 8 (Neukirchen, 1962)

J.Weiss,   *Das Urchristentum* (Göttingen, 1917)
Der erste Korintherbrief, MeyerK 5 (Göttingen, 9 1970)

H.D.Wendland,   *Die Briefe an die Korinther*, NTD 7 (Göttingen, 12 1968)

K.Wengst,   *Christologische Formeln und Lieder des Urchristentums* (Gütersloh, 1972)

M.Werner,   *Die Entstehung des christlichen Dogmas* (Bern, 2 1954)

C.Westermann,   *Genesis* 1, BKAT I/i (Neukirchen, 1974)

D.E.H.Whiteley,   *The Theology of St.Paul* (Oxford, 1963)

R.N.Whybray,   *The Heavenly Counsellor in Isaiah xl 13–14*, SOTSMS 1 (Cambridge, 1971)

U.Wilckens,   *Weisheit und Torheit*, BHT 26 (Tübingen, 1959)
Die Missionsreden der Apostelgeschichte, WMANT 5 (Neukirchen, 3 1974)
σοφία, *TDNT* vii, pp.496–526
χαρακτήρ, *TDNT* ix, pp.418–423
'Die Bekehrung des Paulus als religionsgeschichtliches Problem', *Rechtfertigung als Freiheit* (Neukirchen, 1974), pp. 11–32
'Was heißt bei Paulus: "Aus Werken des Gesetzes wird kein

U.Wilckens (con'd.)   Mensch gerecht"?', ibid., pp.77–109
'Der Ursprung der Überlieferung der Erscheinung des Aufer-standenen', Dogma und Denkstrukturen, E.Schlink FS, ed. W.Joest & W.Pannenberg (Göttingen, 1963), pp.56–95
'Christus, der "letzte Adam", und der Menschensohn', Menschensohn, pp.387–403
'Christologie und Anthropologie im Zusammenhang der paulinischen Rechtfertigungslehre', ZNW 67, G.Bornkamm FS (1976), pp.64–82

M.Wilcox,   ' "Upon the Tree" – Deut. 21:22–23', JBL 96 (1977), pp.85–99

H.Wildberger,   Jesaja 1, BKAT X/1 (Neukirchen, 1972)
צלם, ThHAT ii, cols. 556–563
'Das Abbild Gottes', ThZ 21 (1965), pp.245–259, 481–501

R.McL.Wilson,   The Gnostic Problem (London, 1958)
'Gnostics – in Galatia?', StEv 4 (1968), pp.358–367
'How Gnostic Were the Corinthians?', NTS 19 (1972/73), pp.65/74

S.G.Wilson,   The Gentiles and the Gentile Mission in Luke-Acts, SNTSMS 23 (Cambridge, 1973)

H.Windisch,   Der zweite Korintherbrief, MeyerK 6 (Göttingen, [9]1970)
Paulus und Christus (Leipzig, 1934)
Ἑλληνιστής, TDNT ii, pp.504–516
'Die göttliche Weisheit der Juden und die paulinische Christo-logie', Neutestamentliche Studien, G.Heinrici FS, ed. H. Windisch (Leipzig, 1914), pp.220–234
'Die Sprüche von Eingehen in das Reich Gottes', ZNW 27 (1928), pp.163–192

H.G.Wood,   'The Conversion of St.Paul: Its Nature, Antecedents. and Consequences', NTS 1 (1954/55), pp.276–282

W.Wrede,   Paulus (1904), reprinted in: Das Paulusbild der neueren deutschen Forschung, ed. K.H.Rengstorf (Darmstadt, 1964), pp.1–97

Y.Yadin,   'Pesher Nahum (4Q pNahum) Reconsidered', IEJ 21 (1971), pp.1–12

E.Yamauchi,   Pre-Christian Gnosticism (London, 1973)

T.Zahn,   Der Brief des Paulus an die Römer (Leipzig, [3]1925)

D.Zeller,   Juden und Heiden in der Mission des Paulus (Stuttgart, 1973)

J.A.Ziesler,   The Meaning of Righteousness in Paul, SNTSMS 20 (Cam-bridge, 1972)

W.Zimmerli,   Ezechiel 1, BKAT XIII/1 (Neukirchen, 1969)

Zobel H.-J.,   הוי, ThWAT ii, cols. 382–387

Indexes

II. THE NEW TESTAMENT

III. JEWISH APOCRYPHA AND PSEUDEPIGRAPHA

Tobit

14.4–7	96

Wisdom of Solomon

1.3	139
6	228
2.27	194
7	228
10	128
21	116
22	228
25f.	117
26	228
25ff.	160
25–30	128
26	129, 137f., 161, 219f., 232, 244, 258
27	187
8.3	120
9.-	118
1f.	116
2ff.	242
4	121
9	116
10	118, 121, 245
10–17	118
17	118
10.-	220
1f.	166, 175, 220
6f.	220
10	220
11	187
17	220
17f.	116
11.4	116
18.4	128
15	245

Ecclesiasticus

1.4ff.	116
24.-	118
3	121
3ff.	115
3–12	116
8–12	121
9	121
23	127
34.-	122

42.21	116
45.23	42
48.12f.	79
24	79

Baruch

3.9	130
12	130
23	130
29ff.	117, 130
37f.	127
4.1	130

1 Maccabees

2.23ff.	42
26	42
54	42

3 Maccabees

3.18	226

4 Maccabees

1.17	127
7.21–23	127
8.7	127
18.12	42

Jubilees

2.20	187
23f.	191
19.18	191
23ff.	191
24–29	187
29	191
22.13	187, 191

Testaments of the Twelve Patriarchs

Levi

2.3	79
6	226
5.1	226
16.5	96
18.6	226
10f.	189

Judah

22.5	96
23.5	96

Zebulun

9.-	87

VII. EARLY CHRISTIAN LITERATURE

VIII. GREEK, LATIN AND GNOSTIC LITERATURE

IX. Modern Authors